The Theory and Practice of Item Response Theory

Methodology in the Social Sciences
David A. Kenny, Founding Editor
Todd D. Little, Series Editor

This series provides applied researchers and students with analysis and research design books that emphasize the use of methods to answer research questions. Rather than emphasizing statistical theory, each volume in the series illustrates when a technique should (and should not) be used and how the output from available software programs should (and should not) be interpreted. Common pitfalls as well as areas of further development are clearly articulated.

THE
THEORY AND
PRACTICE OF
ITEM RESPONSE
THEORY

R. J. de Ayala

Series Editor's Note by David A. Kenny

THE GUILFORD PRESS
New York London

Library of Congress Cataloging-in-Publication Data

de Ayala, R. J. (Rafael Jaime), 1957–
   The theory and practice of item response theory / R.J. de Ayala.
       p. cm. — (Methodology in the social sciences)
   Includes bibliographical references and index.
   ISBN 978-1-59385-869-8 (hardcover)
   1. Item response theory. 2. Social sciences—Mathematical models.
   3. Social sciences—Statistical methods. 4. Psychometrics. I. Title.
   H61.25.D4 2009
   150.28′7—dc22

                                                    2008043393

A mi esposa, Stephanie, y mi hija, Isabel

Series Editor's Note

One could make a case that item response theory (IRT) is the most important statistical method about which most of us know little or nothing. The seeds of IRT lie in the psychometric tradition of classical test theory (CTT). In that theory an observed score is presumed to be a function of true score plus a random error. Frederic Lord and others realized in the 1950s that CTT did not work in the testing of ability, because it presumes a linear model in which there is a single factor. However, when items for standardized tests were factor analyzed, "difficulty" factors emerged in which the easy and hard items formed separate factors. Also, in CTT an item's mean and error variance were independent, whereas with standardized tests very easy and very difficult items have less variance than do moderately difficult items. After some attempt to rescue CTT, Lord and others realized that a completely new perspective on measurement was required; the method that emerged from these efforts was IRT.

IRT was rapidly embraced by test manufacturers as a much more realistic model than CTT. Additionally, worries began to emerge that standardized tests were unfair to certain groups, and IRT provided a principled way to determine if items were "fair."

However, IRT was not embraced by everyday researchers. There were several different reasons for this. First, IRT requires sample sizes too large for most research projects. Second, IRT is much more complicated than CTT, and researchers have been intimidated by the mathematics. Third, readily accessible software has not enabled the estimating of the parameters of the IRT model.

There have also been social reasons why most of us know so little about IRT. IRT experts have seemed more interested in communicating with each other than with the general research community. In this book, we have an expert in the field of IRT who is reaching out to explain IRT to us. IRT requires radically rethinking measurement in a model that is not linear. The familiar concepts of "error" and "reliability" do not appear in standard IRT models. Therefore, the reader of this book needs to work hard to learn not only a new language but also a new way of thinking about measurement. We need to realize, as Lord did in the 1950s, that for many problems of measurement, IRT, not CTT, is the way to approach the problem. This book can aid us with that rethinking.

DAVID A. KENNY

Preface

Item response theory (IRT) methodology forms the foundation of many psychometric applications. For instance, IRT is used for equating alternate examination forms, for instrument design and development, for item banking, for computerized adaptive testing, for certification testing, and in various other psychological assessment domains. Well-trained psychometricians are increasingly expected to understand and be able to use IRT.

In this book we address the "how to" of applying IRT models while at the same time providing enough technical substance to answer the "why" questions. We make extensive use of endnotes and appendices to address some technical issues, and the reader is referred to appropriate sources for even greater technical depth than is provided here. To facilitate understanding the application of the models, we use common data sets across the chapters. In addition, the exemplary model applications employ several common software packages. Some of these are free (BIGSTEPS, NOHARM), while others are commercially available (BILOG-MG, MULTILOG, PARSCALE). The terminology used in this book is more general than is typically seen in IRT textbooks and is not specific to educational measurement. The reader is assumed to be familiar with common psychometric concepts such as reliability, validity, scaling, levels of measurement, factor analysis, as well as regression analysis.

Chapter 1 "begins at the beginning" by presenting the basic concept of why we are interested in performing measurement. There is a short philosophical treatment of measurement, pointing out the desirable characteristics that we would like measurement to have. The traditional psychometric concepts of levels of measurement, reliability, validity, and various approaches to measurement, such as IRT, latent class analysis, and classical test theory, are woven into this introduction.

Chapter 2 introduces the simplest IRT model, the Rasch or one-parameter logistic (1PL) model. This model establishes the principles that underlie the more complex models discussed in subsequent chapters. The chapter also introduces the empirical data set that is used in the next four chapters and discusses philosophical differences between Rasch and non-Rasch models. Chapters 3 and 4 conceptually present two different parameter estimation techniques, applied to the data set introduced in Chapter 2. Chapter 3's application begins by examining the unidimensionality assumption through nonlinear factor analysis and proceeds to item parameter estimation and interpretation. In Chapter 4 we reanalyze our data using a different estimation technique and a different program. In addition, we present alternative item- and model-level fit analyses by using statistical and graphical methods.

Chapter 5 presents the two-parameter logistic (2PL) model. Building on the 1PL model presentation, the chapter is concerned only with the features that are unique to this model. Additional fit analysis methods are introduced in this chapter in our reanalysis of the data used with the 1PL model. Similarly, Chapter 6 introduces the characteristics specific to the three-parameter logistic model and reanalyzes the data used in the 1PL and 2PL model examples. By the end of Chapter 6 our fit analysis has evolved to include both item- and model-level fit analyses, model comparison statistics, and person fit analysis. The chapter also examines IRT's assumptions regarding functional form and conditional independence. As such, through these chapters we demonstrate the steps of model and data fit that would normally be used in practice.

Because data are not always dichotomous, we next discuss models that are appropriate for polytomous data (e.g., data from Likert response scales) in Chapters 7–9. The models are divided between those for ordered and those for unordered polytomous data. Chapters 7 and 8 address ordered polytomous data from both Rasch and non-Rasch perspectives (i.e., Rasch: partial credit and rating scale models; non-Rasch: generalized partial credit and graded response models). As in other parts of the book, common data sets are used across these chapters. Modeling unordered polytomous data as well as simultaneously using multiple IRT models are addressed in Chapter 9.

All of the models presented to this point assume that an individual's responses are a function of a single-person latent variable. In Chapter 10 we generalize the models presented in Chapters 5 and 6 to multiple latent variables.

As mentioned, IRT is used for equating multiple forms and in the creation of item banks. Techniques for accomplishing both of these purposes are presented in Chapter 11. Our final addition to our model–data fit toolbox is provided in Chapter 12, where we are concerned with whether an item functions differently for different groups of people. Stated another way, do factors (e.g., the respondents' gender) that are tangential to the construct an item is supposed to be measuring affect how people respond to the item? If so, then the item may be biased against those individuals. Techniques for identifying items with such discrepancies are presented in this, the last chapter.

I would like to acknowledge that this book has been influenced by my interactions with various individuals over the past two decades. Barbara Dodd, Bill Koch, Earl Jennings, Chan Dayton, Bill Hays, Frank Baker, Mark Reckase, Dave Weiss, and Seock-Ho Kim are some of them. My apologies to anyone whom I have omitted. I would also like to acknowledge the graduate students in psychometrics I have had the pleasure of teaching. Thanks also to Bruno Zumbo, Department of Education, University of British Columbia, who reviewed the book. I am appreciative of the support and patience of C. Deborah Laughton and David A. Kenny, whose unenviable task was to edit earlier drafts of the manuscript. Finally, I would like to thank Dorothy Hochreich for her sage advice many years ago. Additional output and the data sets are available at the author's website: *http://cehs.unl.edu/EdPsych/RJSite/home*

Contents

10 • Models for Multidimensional Data   275

11 • Linking and Equating   306

12 • Differential Item Functioning   323

APPENDIX A. Maximum Likelihood Estimation of Person Locations   347

APPENDIX B. Maximum Likelihood Estimation of Item Locations   356

APPENDIX C. The Normal Ogive Models   360

Symbols and Acronyms

INDICES

F	number of factors	f = 1, ... , F
L	number of items	j = 1, ... , L
N	number of persons	i = 1, ... , N
m	number of response categories	k = 1, ... , m
m	number of operations, thresholds, boundaries	k = 1, ... , m or k = 0, ... , m
R	number of quadrature points	r = 1, ... , R
S	number of cognitive operations	s = 1 , ... , S
$\underline{x}$	response vector	
x_j	dichotomous response or category score on item j	
x_{jk}	polytomous response on item j's k*th* category	
v	index for latent classes (nu)	v = 1, ... , G
π_v	latent class v proportion	

SYMBOLS

$\underline{w}$	eigenvector	λ	eigenvalue (lambda)
$\underline{\Sigma}$	variance/covariance matrix	p	probability
h^2	communality	a	item loading
$\underline{\upsilon}$	population parameters vector; MMLE (upsilon)	$\underline{\vartheta}$	item parameter matrix (capital alternative form of phi)
X_i	observed score person i	P_j	item traditional difficulty, proportion correction
q_j	item j score		
Γ	DIF, group variable (capital gamma)	Λ	DIF, person location (e.g., θ or X_i) (capital lambda)

L	likelihood function	T	true or "trait" score (capital tau)
$\ln L$	log likelihood function	$\mathcal{E}$T	expected proportion (of 1s) trait score
$\mathcal{E}$	expectation	E_i	error score (capital epsilon)
$I(\theta)$	total information	$I_j(\theta)$	item information
$I_\omega(\boldsymbol{\theta})$	multidimensional total information	$I_{j\omega}(\boldsymbol{\theta})$	multidimensional item information
$\mathbf{W}$	information matrix, nominal response model	Φ	cumulative normal distribution (capital phi)
$\prod$	product operator or symbol	D	scaling constant
Ξ	convergence criterion (capital xi)		

PARAMETERS

θ person location (theta)

α item discrimination (alpha) τ threshold (tau)

δ_j item j location (delta) δ_{jh} or δ_{jk} item j transition location

δ_{xj} category boundary location

χ pseudo-guessing (lower asymptote) (chi) ε upper asymptote (epsilon)

γ intercept (gamma) $\delta_{k|jv}$ conditional probability (LCA)

ϕ "don't know" category (phi)

Δ_j multidimensional item location (capital delta)
A^j multidimensional item discrimination (capital alpha)
A_ω^j multidimensional directional discrimination (capital alpha)
ω angle or direction in the multidimensional space (omega)

η_s elementary component s
$\sigma_e(\hat{\theta})$ standard error of person location $s_e(\hat{\theta})$ sample standard error
$\sigma_e(\hat{\theta})$ standard error item location $s_e(\hat{\theta})$ sample standard error
σ_{meas} standard error of measurement

The estimate of a parameter is represented with a circumflex. For example, the estimate of the parameter θ is symbolized as $\hat{\theta}$, the estimate of the parameter α is represented as $\hat{\alpha}$, etc.

TRANSFORMATION EQUATIONS

$$\xi^* = \xi(\zeta) + \kappa \qquad \gamma^* = \gamma - \frac{\alpha(\mu)}{\sigma} \qquad \alpha^* = \frac{\alpha}{\sigma}$$

$$\underline{\theta}_i^* = \underline{Z}\underline{\theta}_i + \underline{\kappa} \qquad \gamma_j^* = \gamma_j - \underline{\alpha}_j' \underline{Z}^{-1} \underline{\kappa} \qquad \underline{\alpha}_j^* = (\underline{Z}^{-1})' \underline{\alpha}_j$$

κ and ζ, metric transformation coefficients or equating coefficients; ξ is either δ_j or θ (κ: kappa; ζ: zeta; ξ: lowercase xi, pronounced "kas-eye").

ACRONYMS

CTT	classical test theory
df	degrees of freedom
DIF	differential item functioning
EAP	expected a posteriori
GUI	graphical user interface
IRF	item response function
IRS	item response surface
IRT	item response theory (latent trait theory)
JMLE	joint maximum likelihood estimate (*also called* unconditional maximum likelihood estimation)
LCA	latent class analysis
LSA	latent structure analysis
MAP	maximum a posteriori
MINF	multidimensional information
MIRT	multidimensional item response theory
MMLE	marginal maximum likelihood estimation
SD	standard deviation
SEE	standard error of estimate
TCC	test characteristic curve *or* total characteristic curve
TCF	total characteristic function

IRT MODELS (NONEXHAUSTIVE)

1PL	one-parameter logistic model
2PL	two-parameter logistic model
3PL	three-parameter logistic model
GPC	generalized partial credit model
GR	graded response model
LLTM	linear logistic test model
M2PL	multidimensional compensatory two-parameter logistic model
M3PL	multidimensional compensatory three-parameter logistic model
MC	multiple-choice model
NR	nominal response model
PC	partial credit model

1

Introduction to Measurement

> I often say that when you can measure what you are speaking about and express it in numbers you know something about it; but when you cannot measure it, when you cannot express it in numbers, your knowledge is of a meagre and unsatisfactory kind: it may be the beginning of knowledge, but you have scarcely, in your thoughts, advanced to the state of *science*, whatever the matter may be.
>
> —SIR WILLIAM THOMSON (Lord Kelvin) (1891, p. 80)

This book is about a particular measurement perspective called *item response theory* (IRT), *latent trait theory*, or *item characteristic curve theory*. To understand this measurement perspective, we need to address what we mean by the concept of measurement. Measurement can be defined in many different ways. A classic definition is that measurement is "the assignment of numerals to objects or events according to rules. The fact that numerals can be assigned under different rules leads to different kinds of scales and different kinds of measurement" (Stevens, 1946, p. 677). Although commonly used in introductory measurement and statistics texts, this definition reflects a rather limited view. Measurement is more than just the assignment of numbers according to rules (i.e., labeling); it is a process by which an attempt is made to understand the nature of a variable (cf. Bridgman, 1928). Moreover, whether the process results in numeric values with inherent properties or the identification of different classes depends on whether we conceptualize the variable of interest as continuous or categorical. IRT provides one particular mathematical technique for performing measurement in which the variable is considered to be continuous in nature.

MEASUREMENT

For a simple example of measurement as a process, imagine that a researcher is interested in measuring generalized anxiety. Anxiety may be loosely defined as feelings that may range from general uneasiness to incapacitating attacks of terror. Because the very nature of anxiety involves feelings, it is not possible to directly observe anxiety. As such, anxiety is an unobservable or *latent* variable or construct.

The measurement process involves deciding whether our latent variable, anxiety, should be conceptualized as categorical, continuous, or both. In the categorical case we would classify individuals into qualitatively different latent groups so that, for example, one group may be interpreted as representing individuals with incapacitating anxiety and another group representing individuals without anxiety. In this conceptualization the persons differ from one another in *kind* on the latent variable. Typically, these latent categories are referred to as *latent classes*. Alternatively, anxiety could be conceptualized as continuous. From this perspective, individuals differ from one another in their *quantity* of the latent variable. Thus, we might label the ends of the *latent continuum* as, say, "high anxiety" and "low anxiety." When the latent variable is conceptualized as having categorical *and* continuous facets, then we have a combination of one or more latent classes and one or more latent continua. In this case, the latent classes are subpopulations that are homogeneous with respect to the variable of interest, but differ from one another in kind. Within each of these classes there is a latent continuum on which the individuals within the class may be located. For example, assume that our sample of respondents consists of two classes. One class could consist of individuals whose anxiety is so severe that they suffer from incapacitating attacks of terror. As such, these individuals are so qualitatively different from other persons that they need to be addressed separately from those whose anxiety is not so severe. Therefore, the second class contains individuals who do not suffer from incapacitating attacks of terror. Within each of these classes we have a latent continuum on which we locate the class's respondents.

Although we cannot observe our latent variable, its existence may be inferred from behavioral manifestations or *manifest* variables (e.g., restlessness, sleeping difficulties, headaches, trembling, muscle tension, item responses, self-reports). These manifestations allow for several different approaches to measuring generalized anxiety. For example, one approach may involve physiological assessment via an electromyogram of the degree of muscle tension. Other approaches might involve recording the number of hours spent sleeping or the frequency and duration of headaches, using a galvanic skin response (GSR) feedback device to assess sweat gland activity, or more psychological approaches, such as asking a series of questions. These approaches, either individually or collectively, provide our *operational definition* of generalized anxiety (Bridgman, 1928). That is, our operational definition specifies how we go about collecting our observations (i.e., the latent variable's manifestations). Stated concisely, our interest is in our latent variable and its operational definition is a means to that end.

The measurement process, so far, has involved our conceptualization of the latent variable's nature and its operational definition. We also need to decide on the correspondence between our observations of the individuals' anxiety levels and their locations on the continuum and/or in a class. In general, *scaling* is the process of establishing the correspondence between the observation data and the persons' locations on the latent variable. Once we have our individuals located on the latent variable, we can then compare them to one another. IRT is one approach to establishing this correspondence between the observation data and the persons' locations on the latent variable. Examples of other relevant scaling processes are Guttman Scalogram analysis (Guttman, 1950), Coombs Unfolding (Coombs,

1950), and the various Thurstone approaches (Thurstone, 1925, 1928, 1938). Alternative scaling approaches may be found in Dunn-Rankin, Knezek, Wallace, and Zhang (2004), Gulliksen (1987), Maranell (1974), and Nunnally and Bernstein (1994).

SOME MEASUREMENT ISSUES

Before proceeding to discuss various latent variable methods for scaling our observations, we need to discuss four issues. The first issue involves the *consistency of the measures*. By way of analogy, assume that we are measuring the length of a box. If our repeated measurements of the length of the box were constant, then these measurements would be considered to be highly consistent or to have high *reliability*. However, if these repeated measurements varied wildly from one another, then they would be considered to have low consistency or to have low reliability. In the former case, our measurements would have a small amount of error, whereas in the latter they would have a comparatively larger amount of error. The consistency (or lack thereof) would affect our confidence in the measurements. That is, in the first scenario we would have greater confidence in our measurements than in the second scenario.

The second issue concerns the *validity* of the measures. Although there are various types of validity, we define validity as the degree to which our measures are actually manifestations of the latent variable. As a contrarian example, assume we use the "frequency and duration of headaches" approach for measuring anxiety. Although some persons may recognize that there might be a relationship between "frequency and duration of headaches" and anxiety level, they may not consider this approach, in and of itself, to be an accurate "representation" of anxiety. In short, simply because we make a measure does not mean that the measure necessarily results in an accurate reflection of the variable of theoretical interest (i.e., our measurements may or may not have validity). A necessary, but not sufficient condition for our measurements to have validity is that they possess a high degree of reliability. Therefore, it is necessary to be concerned not only with the consistency of our measurements, but also with their validity. Obtaining validity evidence is part of the measurement process.

The third issue concerns a desirable property we would like our measurements to possess. Thurstone (1928) noted that a measuring instrument must not be seriously affected in its measuring function by the object of measurement. In other words, we would like our measurement instrument to be independent of what it is we are measuring. If this is true, then the instrument possesses the property of *invariance*. For instance, if we measure the size of a shoe box by using a meter stick, then the measurement instrument (i.e., the meter stick) is not affected by and is independent of which box is measured. Contrast this with the situation in which measuring a shoe box's size is done not by using a meter stick, but by stretching a string along the shortest dimension of the box and cutting the string so that its length equals the shortest dimension. This string would serve as our measurement instrument and we would use it to measure the other two dimensions of the box. In short, the measurements would be multiples of the shortest dimension. Then suppose we use this approach to measure a cereal box. That is, for the cereal box its shortest dimension is used to define the measurement instrument. Obviously, the box we are measuring affects our measurement instrument and our measurements would not possess the invariance property. Without invariance our comparisons across different boxes would have limited utility.

The final issue we present brings us back to the classic definition of measurement mentioned above. Depending on which approach we use to measure anxiety (i.e., GSR, duration of headache, item responses, etc.), the measurements have certain inherent properties that affect how we interpret their information. For instance, the "duration of headaches" approach produces measurements that cannot be negative and that allow us to make comparative statements among people as well as to determine whether a person has a headache. These properties are a reflection of the fact that the measurements have not only a constant unit, but also a (absolute) zero point that reflects the absence of what is being measured. Invoking Stevens's (1946) levels of measurement taxonomy or Coombs's (1974) taxonomy these numbers would reflect a *ratio* scale.

In contrast, if we use a GSR device for measuring anxiety we would need to establish a baseline or a zero point by canceling out an individual's normal skin resistance static level before we measure the person's GSR. As a result, and unlike that of the ratio scale, this zero point is not an absolute zero, but rather a relative one. However, all of our measurements would still have a constant unit and would be considered to be on an *interval* scale. Another approach to measuring anxiety is to ask an individual to rate his or her anxiety in terms of severity. This ratings approach would produce numbers that are on an *ordinal* scale. These approaches allow us to make comparative statements, such as "This person's anxiety level is greater than (or less than) that of another," or in the case of the interval scale, "This person's anxiety level is half as severe as that person's anxiety level." Alternatively, if our question simply requires the respondent to reply "yes," he or she is experiencing a symptom, or "no," he or she is not, then the "yes/no" responses would reflect a *nominal* scale. These various scenarios show that how we interpret and use our data needs to take into account the different types of information that the observations carry.

In the following discussion we present three approaches for establishing a correspondence between our observations and our latent variable. We begin by briefly introducing IRT, followed by classical test theory (CTT). Both of these approaches assume that the latent variable is continuous. The last approach discussed, latent class analysis (LCA), is appropriate for categorical latent variables. Appendix E, "Mixture Models," addresses the situation when a latent variable is conceptualized as having categorical and continuous facets.

ITEM RESPONSE THEORY

"Theory" is used here in the sense that it is a paradigm that attempts to explain all the facts with which it can be confronted (Kuhn, 1970, p. 18). IRT is, in effect, a system of models that defines one way of establishing the correspondence between latent variables and their manifestations. It is not a theory in the traditional sense because it does not explain why a person provides a particular response to an item or how the person decides what to answer (cf. Falmagne, 1989). Instead, IRT is like the theory of statistical estimation. IRT uses latent characterizations of individuals and items as predictors of observed responses. Although some researchers (e.g., Embretson, 1984; Fischer & Formann, 1982) have attempted to use item characteristics to explain why an item is located at a particular point, for the most part, IRT like other scaling methods (e.g., Guttman Scalogram, Coombs Unfolding) treats the individual as a black box. (See Appendix E, "Linear Logistic Test Model [LLTM]," for a brief presentation of one of these explanatory approaches, as well as De Boeck & Wilson [2004] for alternative approaches.) The cognitive processes used by an individual to respond to an item are not modeled in the commonly used IRT models. In short, this approach is analogous to measuring the speed of an automobile without understanding how an automobile moves.[1]

In IRT persons and items are located on the same continuum. Most IRT models assume that the latent variable is represented by a unidimensional continuum. In addition, for an item to have any utility it must be able to differentiate among persons located at different points along a continuum. An item's capacity to differentiate among persons reduces our uncertainty about their locations. This capacity to differentiate among people with different locations may be held constant or allowed to vary across an instrument's items. Therefore, individuals are characterized in terms of their locations on the latent variable and, at a minimum, items are characterized with respect to their locations and capacity to discriminate among persons. The gist of IRT is the (logistic or multinomial) regression of observed item responses on the persons' locations on the latent variable and the item's latent characterizations.

CLASSICAL TEST THEORY

Like IRT, *classical test theory* (CTT) or *true score theory* also assumes that the latent variable is continuous. CTT is the approach that most readers have been exposed to throughout their education. In contrast to IRT in which the item is the unit of focus, in CTT the respondent's observed score on a whole instrument is the unit of focus. The individual's observed score, X, is (typically) the unweighted sum of the person's responses to an instrument's items. In ability or achievement assessment this sum reflects the number of correct responses.

CTT is based on the true score model. This model relates the individual's observed score to his or her location on the latent variable. To understand this model, assume that an individual is administered an instrument an infinite independent number of times. On each of these administrations we calculate the individual's observed score. The mean of the infinite number of observed scores is the expectation of the observed scores (i.e., $\mu_i = \mathcal{E}(X_i)$). On any given administration of the instrument the person's observed score will not exactly agree with the mean, μ, of the observed scores. This difference between the observed score and the mean is considered to be error. Symbolically, we may write the relationship between person i's observed score, the expectation, and error as

$$X_i = \mu_i + E_i \tag{1.1}$$

where E_i is the error score or the *error of measurement* (i.e., $E_i = X_i - \mu_i$); E is the capital Greek letter epsilon. Equation 1.1 is known as the *true score model*. In words, this model states that person i's observed performance on an instrument is a function of his or her expected performance on the instrument plus error. Given that the error scores are considered to be random and that $\mu_i = \mathcal{E}(X_i)$, then it follows that the mean error for an individual across the infinite number of independent administrations of the instrument is zero.

By convention μ_i is typically represented by the Latin or Roman letter T. However, to be consistent with our use of Greek letters to symbolize parameters, we use the capital Greek letter tau, T. The symbol T represents the person's *true score* (i.e., $T_i = \mathcal{E}(X_i)$). The term *true score* should not be interpreted as indicating truth in any way. As such, *true score* is a misnomer. To avoid this possible misinterpretation, we refer to T_i (or μ_i) as individual i's *trait score*.[2] A person's trait score represents his or her location on the latent variable of interest and is fixed for an individual and instrument. The common representation of the model in Equation 1.1 is

$$X_i = T_i + E_i \tag{1.2}$$

Although Equation 1.1 may be considered more informative than Equation 1.2, we follow the convention of using T for the trait score.

There is a functional relationship between the IRT person latent trait (θ) and the CTT person trait characterization. This relationship is based on the assumption of parallel forms for an instrument. That is, each item has the same response function on all the forms. Following Lord and Novick (1968), assume that we administer an infinite number of independent parallel forms of an instrument to an individual. Then the *expected proportion* of 1s or *expected trait score*, $\mathcal{E}T$, across these parallel forms is equal to the average probability of a response of 1 on the instrument, given the person's latent trait and an IRT model. As a consequence, the IRT θ is the same as the expected proportion $\mathcal{E}T$ except for the difference in their scales of measurement. That is, θ has a range of $-\infty$ to ∞, whereas for $\mathcal{E}T$ the range is 0 to 1. The expected trait score $\mathcal{E}T$ is related to the IRT latent trait by a monotonic increasing transformation. This transformation is discussed in Chapters 4 and 10.

In addition to the true score model, CTT is based on a set of assumptions. These assumptions are that, in the population, (1) the errors are uncorrelated with the trait scores for an instrument, (2) the errors on one instrument are uncorrelated with the trait scores on a different instrument, and (3) the errors on one instrument are uncorrelated with the error scores on a different instrument. These assumptions are considered to be "weak" assumptions because they are likely to be met by the data. In contrast, IRT is based on "strong" assumptions.[3] These IRT assumptions are discussed in the following chapter.

These CTT assumptions and the model given in Equation 1.1 (or Equation 1.2) form the basis of the psychometric concept of reliability and the validity coefficient. For example, the correlation of the observed scores on an instrument and the corresponding trait scores is the index of reliability for the instrument. Moreover, using the variances of the trait scores (σ_T^2) and observed scores (σ_X^2) we can obtain the population reliability of an instrument's scores:

$$\rho_{XX'} = \frac{\sigma_T^2}{\sigma_X^2} \tag{1.3}$$

Because trait score variance is unknown, we can only estimate $\rho_{XX'}$. Some of the traditional approaches for estimating reliability are KR-20, KR-21, and coefficient alpha. An assessment of the variance of the errors of measurement in any set of observed scores may be obtained by substituting $\sigma_T^2 = \sigma_X^2 - \sigma_E^2$ into Equation 1.3 to get

$$\sigma_E^2 = \sigma_X^2(1-\rho_{XX'}) \qquad (1.4)$$

The square root of σ_E^2 (i.e., σ_E) is referred to as the *standard error of measurement*. The standard error of measurement is the standard deviation of the errors of measurement associated with the observed scores for a particular group of respondents.

From the foregoing it should be clear that because an individual's trait score is latent and unknown, then the error associated with an observed score is also unknown. Therefore, Equations 1.1 and 1.2 have two unknown quantities, an individual's trait score and error score. Lord (1980) points out that the model given in Equations 1.1 or 1.2 cannot be disproved by any set of data. As a result, one difference between IRT and CTT is that with IRT we can engage in model–data fit analysis, whereas in CTT we do not examine model–data fit and simply assume the model to be true.

As may be obvious, the observed score X is influenced by the instrument's characteristics. For example, assume a proficiency testing situation. An easy test administered an infinite number of independent times to an individual will yield a different value of T_i than a difficult test administered an infinite number of independent times to the same individual. This is analogous to the example of measuring the shoe and cereal boxes by using the shortest dimension of each box. In short, as is the case with the box example, in CTT person measurement is dependent on the instrument's characteristics. Moreover, because the variance of the sample's observed scores appears in both Equations 1.3 and 1.4, one may deduce that the heterogeneity (or lack thereof) of the observed scores affects both reliability and the standard error of measurement. Moreover, Equations 1.3 and 1.4 cannot be considered to solely be properties of the instrument, but rather also reflect the sample's characteristics. In short, the instrument's characteristics affect the person scores and sample characteristics affect the quantitative indices of the instrument (e.g., item difficulty and discrimination, reliability, etc.). Thus, Thurstone's (1928) idea of invariance does not exist in CTT. In contrast, with IRT it is possible to have invariance of both person and item characterizations. See Appendix E, "Dependency in Traditional Analysis Statistics and Observed Scores," for a demonstration of this lack of invariance with CTT. In addition, Gulliksen (1987) contains detailed information on CTT and Engelhard (1994, 2008) presents a historical view of invariance.

LATENT CLASS ANALYSIS

Unlike IRT's premise of a continuous latent variable, in *latent class analysis* (LCA) the latent variable is assumed to be categorical. That is, the latent variable consists of a set of mutually exclusive and exhaustive *latent classes*.[4] To be more specific, "there exists a set of latent classes, such that the manifest relationship between any two or more items on a test can be accounted for by the existence of these basic classes and by these alone" (Stouffer, 1950, p. 6). In LCA the comparison of individuals involves comparing their latent class memberships rather than comparing their locations on a continuous latent variable.

For an understanding of the nature of a categorical latent variable, we turn to two empirical studies. The first is a study of the nosologic structure of psychotic illness by Kendler, Karkowski, and Walsh (1998). In their study, these authors conceptualized this latent variable as categorical. Their LCA showed that their participants belonged to one of six classes: (1) classic schizophrenia, (2) major depression, (3) schizophreniform disorder, (4) bipolar-schizomania, (5) schizodepression, and (6) hebephrenia. The second example involves cheating on academic examinations (Dayton & Scheers, 1997); the latent variable is cheating. The LCA of the investigators' data revealed a structure with two latent classes. One class consisted of persons who were "persistent cheaters," whereas the second class consisted of individuals who would either exhibit "opportunistic" cheating or might not cheat at all.

In both of these examples, we can see that respondents differ from one another on the latent variable in terms of their class membership rather than in terms of their locations on a continuum. In Appendix E, "Mixture Models," we discuss an approach in which we combine LCA and IRT. That is, we can conceptualize academic performance as involving both latent classes and continua. For example, we can have one class of persistent cheaters and another class of noncheaters. Within each class there is a proficiency variable continuum. Therefore, the cheater class has its own continuum on which we can compare individual performances. Similarly, the noncheater class has a separate continuum that we use to compare the noncheaters' performances with one another. These latter comparisons are not contaminated by the cheaters' performances and the noncheaters are not disadvantaged by the presence of the cheaters.

In general, LCA determines the number of latent classes that best explains the data (i.e., determining the latent class structure). This process involves comparing models that vary in their respective number of classes (e.g., a one-class model, a two-class model, and so on). Determining the latent class structure involves not only statistical tests of fit, but also the interpretability of the solution. With each class structure one has estimates of the items' characteristics. Based on these item characteristics and the individuals' responses, the respondents are assigned to one of the latent classes. Subsequent to this assignment, we obtain estimates of the relative size of each class. These relative sizes are known as the *latent class proportions* (π_vs, where v is the latent class index). The sum of the latent class proportions across the latent classes is constrained to 1.0. For example, if the latent variable, say algebra proficiency, has a two-class structure, then π_1 might equal 0.65 and $\pi_2 = 1 - 0.65 = 0.35$. Moreover, our latent classes' interpretation may reveal that the larger class (i.e., $\pi_1 = 0.65$) consists of persons who have mastered algebraic problems, whereas the other class consists of individuals who have not mastered the problems. In short, the data's latent structure consists of masters and nonmasters.

One may conceive of a situation in which if one had a large number of latent classes and if they were ordered, then there would be little difference between conceptualizing the latent variable as continuous or as categorical. In point of fact, a latent class model with a sufficient number of latent classes is equivalent to an IRT model. For example, for a data set with four items, then a latent class model with at least three latent classes would provide "equivalent" item characterizations as an IRT model that uses only item location parameters. Appendix E, "Mixture Models," contains additional information about LCA.

SUMMARY

Typically, measurement is viewed as analogous to using a ruler to measure the length of an object. In effect, this is analogous to Stevens's (1946) definition of measurement in that the ruler provides the "rules" and the numeric values associated with the ruler's tick marks provide the numeric labels. However, Stevens's definition invites misinterpretation. Although one can infer from his definition that he is describing an act or a process, this aspect of the definition is not made salient. Moreover, by focusing only on the assignment of numbers, one is left with the impression that measurement results in only a set of numeric labels. We consider measurement to be a process by which one attempts to understand the nature of a variable by applying mathematical techniques. The result may or may not be numeric labels and may or may not involve a continuous variable. For example, LCA is a measurement paradigm that allows one to understand the nature of a latent variable, such as ethnocentrism or test anxiety, without resulting in numeric labels. The use of LCAs involves the application of mathematical techniques that results in individuals being classified into latent classes and an assessment of how well the class structure describes the manifest data.

The term *manifest data* refers to the information obtained by direct observation, whereas the term *latent* refers to the information obtained on the basis of additional assumptions and/or by making inferences from the original (manifest) data (Lazarsfeld, 1950). Presumably, one or more latent variables can account for the patterns or relationships that are evident in the manifest data. Therefore, a *manifest variable* is an observed manifestation of one or more *latent* (i.e., unobservable) *variables*. We outlined different paradigms that allow the tools of mathematics to be applied to explaining manifest observations from a latent variable perspective.

A latent variable may be conceptualized as continuous, categorical, or some combination of the two. When the variable is conceptualized as continuous, then the use of CTT or IRT may be the appropriate mathematical technique. However, if the variable is conceptualized as categorical, then LCA may be the most appropriate psychometric method to use. It is possible to conceptualize the latent space as a set of latent classes, within each of which there is a continuum, or as a combination of latent classes and a latent continuum. In this situation a mixture of IRT and LCA may be considered an appropriate representation of the latent space.

As part of measurement it is necessary to operationalize the variable(s) of interest (i.e., provide operational definitions). The measurement process also involves assessing how much information the measures yield about the participants (e.g., reliability) as well as how well the measures reflect the latent variable(s) (i.e., validity).

When IRT is appropriate and when there is model–data fit, then IRT offers advantages over CTT. For instance, with IRT our person location estimates are invariant with respect to the instrument, the precision of these estimates is known at the individual level and not just at the group level (as is the case with Equation 1.4), and the item parameter estimates transcend the particular sample used in their estimation. Moreover, unlike CTT, with IRT we are able to make predictive statements about respondents' performance as well as examine the tenability of the model vis-à-vis the data. In the next chapter the simplest of the IRT models is presented. This model, the Rasch or one-parameter logistic model, contains a single parameter that characterizes the item's location on the latent variable continuum. We show how this single-item parameter can be used to estimate a respondent's location on a latent variable.

NOTES

1. Although understanding how the automobile moves is not necessary in order to measure the speed with which it moves, nonetheless fully understanding how the automobile moves can lead to an improved measurement process.

2. A trait is exemplified primarily in the things that a person can do (Thurstone, 1947) and is any "distinguishable, relatively enduring way in which one individual varies from another" (Guilford, 1959, p. 6). However, we do not consider traits to be rigidly fixed or predetermined (see Anastasi, 1983).

3. There is an implicit unidimensionality assumption in CTT. That is, for observed scores to have any meaning they need to represent the sum of responses to items that measure the same thing. For instance, assume that an examination consists of five spelling questions and five single-digit addition problems. Presumably our examination data would consist of two dimensions representing spelling and addition proficiencies. If a person had an observed score of 5, it would not be possible to determine whether he or she is perfect in spelling, perfect in addition, or in some combination of spelling and addition proficiencies. In this case, the observed score has no intrinsic meaning. In contrast, if the examination consists of only spelling questions, then the score would indicate how well a person could spell the questions on the test and would have intrinsic meaning.

4. Both IRT and LCA can be considered to be special instances of the general theoretical framework for modeling categorical variables, known as latent structure analysis (LSA; Lazarsfeld, 1950). Moreover, both linear and nonlinear factor analysis may be regarded as special cases of LSA (McDonald, 1967).

2

The One-Parameter Model

There are many possible construct domains to which IRT may be applied. These involve psychological constructs, such as neuroticism, motivation, social anxiety, cognitive development, consumer preferences, proficiency, and so on. Although each of these constructs could be conceptualized as being categorical (e.g., consisting of only latent classes), in the current context we would conceptualize each of these latent variables as a continuum. Whatever the construct of interest may be, we assume that it is manifested through an individual's responses to a series of items. The simplest IRT model that could be used in this situation is one that characterizes each item in terms of a single parameter. This parameter is the item's location on the latent continuum that represents the construct. The concept that an item has a location is not new and may be traced back to Thurstone (1925, 1928); also see Andrich (1978a), Lumsden (1978), and Yen (1986). In this chapter a one-item parameter IRT model is conceptually developed. In the context of this model the general principles and assumptions underlying IRT, as well as a parameter estimation approach, are presented. In subsequent chapters more sophisticated estimation approaches and more complicated models are discussed.

CONCEPTUAL DEVELOPMENT OF THE RASCH MODEL

Assume that we are interested in measuring the mathematics proficiencies of a group of individuals. Although we cannot directly observe mathematics proficiency, we can infer its existence through behavioral observations. As such, mathematics proficiency is considered to be a latent variable and, in the current context, this means that it is conceptualized as a latent continuum. To assess the individuals' mathematics proficiencies, they are administered an instrument containing five questions. Their responses to this instrument constitute our behavioral observations. The instrument's items are located at various points along the continuum representing mathematics proficiency. For instance, Figure 2.1 depicts the locations of the items on the continuum, as well as one person's location on the same

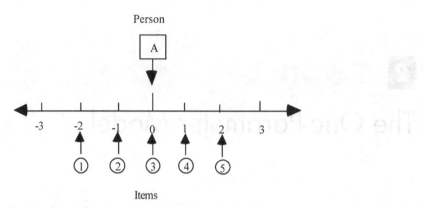

FIGURE 2.1. Graphical representation of latent variable continuum with five items (circles).

continuum. Typically, we use standard scorelike values (i.e., z-scores) to mark off the continuum and represent the metric in IRT.

For this continuum assume that the upper end of the continuum indicates greater mathematics proficiency than does the lower end. This means that items located toward the right side require an individual to have greater proficiency to correctly answer the items than items located toward the left side. As can be seen, our instrument's items are located throughout the continuum with some above 0 and others below 0. For instance, the first item is located at −2, the second item at −1, and so on. We use the Greek letter δ (delta) to represent an item's location, and δ_j represents the *jth item location* on this continuum. Using this notation, the first item's location is represented as $\delta_1 = -2$ and the fifth's as $\delta_5 = 2$. Moreover, the Greek letter θ (theta) is used to represent the *person location* on this continuum. In the context of this example, a person's location reflects his or her mathematics proficiency. According to the figure, person A is located at 0.0 (i.e., $\theta_A = 0.0$). As should be clear from Figure 2.1, both items and persons are located on the same continuum.

One implication of having both persons and items located on the same continuum is that it is possible to make comparative statements about how a typical person might respond to an item. For example, because the lower end of the continuum represents less mathematics proficiency than the upper end, items that are located in the lower end require less proficiency to be correctly answered than those in the upper end. As a result, chances are that a person located at 0 will correctly respond to items located in the lower end of the continuum (e.g., item 1 with a $\delta_1 = -2$). However, if we administer an item located closer to 0, say item 2 with $\delta_2 = -1$, then chances are that the person will respond correctly, but we recognize that there is an increased possibility that he or she may incorrectly respond. This incorrect response may be due to a lapse in being able to recall relevant information, the tip-of-tongue phenomenon, or another such cause. Similarly, administering an item, such as item 4 ($\delta_4 = 1$), to a person located at 0 will likely result in an incorrect response, but there is still a sizeable chance that he or she may correctly answer the item because of the closeness in the proficiency required by the item and that which the person possesses. In other words, the greater the distance between the person and item locations, the greater the certainty we have in how the person is expected to respond to the item. However, as this distance approaches zero, then the more likely we are to say that there is a 50:50 chance that the person will correctly respond to the item. These expectations about how a person will respond are expressed probabilistically (i.e., "chances of a correct response are . . .").

Although the foregoing may make intuitive sense, one might ask, "Are there data that support a pattern of an increasing probability of a correct response as person location increases?" In Figure 2.2 we see that the answer is yes. This figure shows that the proportion of individuals correctly responding to an item is an S-shape (sigmoidal) function of their standard scores on a test. In this case, the participants were administered an examination to assess their latent mathematics proficiency. The complete data from this administration are presented in Table 2.1.

From the graph we see that as the z-scores increase, there is an increase in the proportion of examinees correctly responding to the item; however, this increase is not constant across the continuum. Moreover, we see that as one progresses beyond a z of 1 the points begin to form a plateau. Conversely, as one progresses below a z of –1 the proportions also start to level off. However, there is a range on the z-score metric around –0.5 where the proportion of individuals with a correct response is around 0.50. That is, this is the point at which we would say that there is a 50:50 chance that the person will correctly respond to the item.

We can trace the nonlinear pattern of the empirical proportions in Figure 2.2 and obtain an empirical *trace line* (Lazarsfeld, 1950). This trace line would clearly be a sigmoid or S-shaped curve (i.e., an ogive). However, rather than being satisfied to simply describe the pattern, we can develop a model that incorporates our ideas about how an observed response is governed by a person's location in order to be able to predict response behavior. The nonlinearity shown in Figure 2.2 eliminates using the linear regression of proportions on the person locations to predict response behavior. Because this ogival pattern is evident

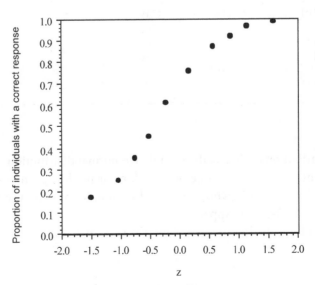

FIGURE 2.2. Empirical proportions of individuals with a correct response on one item as a function of standardized number correct scores.

TABLE 2.1. Response Patterns and Their Frequency on a Mathematics Test

Pattern	Frequency	X
00000	691	0
10000	2280	1
01000	242	1
00100	235	1
00010	158	1
00001	184	1
11000	1685	2
10100	1053	2
01100	134	2
10010	462	2
01010	92	2
00110	65	2
10001	571	2
01001	79	2
00101	87	2
00011	41	2
11100	1682	3
11010	702	3
10110	370	3
01110	63	3
11001	626	3
10101	412	3
10011	166	3
01101	52	3
01011	28	3
00111	15	3
11110	2095	4
11101	1219	4
11011	500	4
10111	187	4
01111	40	4
11111	3385	5

Note. N = 19,601.

in cumulative distributions, such as the cumulative normal distribution or the logistic distribution, we might consider using one of these for our modeling. In point of fact, we use the logistic function in the following because of its simplicity. (The use of the cumulative normal function is discussed in Appendix C.)

In its simplest form the logistic model may be presented as

$$p(x) = \frac{e^z}{1+e^z} \tag{2.1}$$

where p(x) is the probability of values of 1 when the predictor takes on the value of x, e is a constant equal to 2.7183 . . . , and z is some linear combination of, for example, predictor variable(s) and a constant. By appropriately specifying z, we can arrive at a model for predicting response behavior on an item j.

To specify z, we return to the idea above that the distance between the person and the item locations (i.e., $(\theta - \delta_j)$) is an important determinant of the probability of his or her response (cf. Rasch, 1980; Wright & Stone, 1979). Therefore, letting $z = (\theta - \delta_j)$ results in a model that would allow one to predict the probability of a response of 1 as a function of both the item and person locations.[1] By substitution of this z into the logistic model we have

$$p(x_j = 1|\theta, \delta_j) = \frac{e^{(\theta-\delta_j)}}{1+e^{(\theta-\delta_j)}} \tag{2.2}$$

where $p(x_j = 1|\theta, \delta_j)$ is the probability of the response of 1 (i.e., $x_j = 1$), θ is the person location, and δ_j is item j's location. This model is called the *Rasch* model (Rasch, 1980). Expressed in words, Equation 2.2 says that the probability of a response of 1 on item j is a function of the distance between a person located at θ and the item located at δ. (Technically, we are talking about the probability of a randomly selected individual from those located at θ.) The right side maps the (potentially infinite) distance between the person's location and the item's location onto the [0, 1] probability scale. A response of 1 simply indicates that an event occurred or we observed a success. (We use the phrase "response of 1" instead of "correct response" because the instrument may not be an examination; given a proficiency context, we may refer to the response as correct or incorrect.) For convenience, p_j is used for $p(x_j = 1|\theta, \delta_j)$ in the following.

The theoretical range of the item locations δs, as well as the person locations θs, is from $-\infty$ to ∞. However, typical item and person locations fall within -3 to 3. In proficiency testing the item locations are referred to as *item difficulties*.[2] In general, items located somewhat below 0.0 are said to be "easy" items (e.g., below -2.0) and items somewhat above 0.0 are "hard" items (e.g., above 2.0). In general, the items that are considered to be "easy" are the ones that persons with low proficiencies have a tendency to answer correctly. Conversely, the "harder" items are the items that persons with high proficiencies tend to get correct. Items around 0.0 are considered to be of "average difficulty."

As an example of using the Rasch model to predict response behavior, assume that we administer a mathematics item located at 1 (i.e., $\delta = 1$) to individuals located at 0 (i.e., $\theta = 0$). According to the model in Equation 2.2 the probability of a correct response for a randomly selected individual from this group would be

$$p_j = \frac{e^{(0-1)}}{1+e^{(0-1)}} = 0.2689$$

That is, the probability that a randomly selected person located at 0 will correctly respond to this item is only 0.2689. The magnitude of this probability should not be surprising, given that this item is located above (or to the right of) the individual's location and so the item requires more mathematical proficiency to be correctly answered than the person possesses. Actually, chances are that a person located at 0 will *incorrectly* respond to this item rather than respond correctly because the probability of an incorrect response to this item by someone located at 0 is $1 - 0.2689 = 0.7311$.

Another way of interpreting our probabilities is to convert them to the *odds* of a correct response on the item. For example, converting these probabilities to odds we find that the odds of a response of 1 are approximately 1 to 2.7, or that it's almost three times more likely that the person will *incorrectly* respond to the item than correctly respond. Appendix E, "Odds, Odds Ratios, and Logits," contains more information on odds.

For a given item location, the substitution of different values of θ into Equation 2.2 produces a series of probabilities that when graphed show a pattern similar to that shown in Figure 2.2. The trace line produced by the model given in Equation 2.2 is referred to as an *item characteristic curve* (Lord, 1952), an *item curve* (Tucker, 1946), or an *item response function* (IRF). Example IRFs are shown in Figure 2.3 and are discussed below. For the Rasch model the item's location, δ, is defined as the point of inflexion or the "middle" point of the IRF; an inflexion point is where the slope of a function changes direction. Because the Rasch model IRF has a lower asymptote of 0 and an upper asymptote of 1, this midpoint has a value of 0.50. Therefore, for the Rasch model the item's location corresponds to the point on the continuum where the probability of a response of 1 is 0.50.

THE ONE-PARAMETER MODEL

In the IRT literature one sometimes sees reference to a one-parameter model. In this section we present the one-parameter model, and in the subsequent section we discuss whether the Rasch model and the one-parameter model should be considered distinct models.

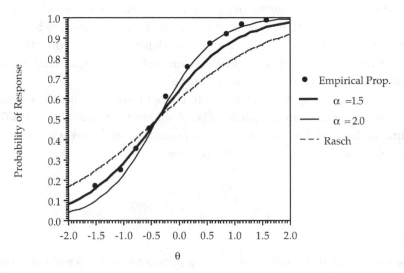

FIGURE 2.3. Empirical proportions and IRFs corresponding to different discrimination values.

Figure 2.3 shows a series of IRFs overlaid on the item data shown in Figure 2.2. Each of these IRFs uses an estimated item location of –0.37 (i.e., $\hat{\delta}_j$ = –0.37).[3] The dashed IRF (labeled Rasch) is based on the Rasch model and is created by substituting $\hat{\delta}$ = –0.37 for δ in Equation 2.2 and using values of θ from –2.0 to 2.0.

As we see, the predicted Rasch IRF is not as steep as the observed response function (i.e., the empirical trace line suggested by the proportions). To better match the empirical trace line we need to increase the slope of the IRF. To do this we revisit the exponent in Equation 2.2. This exponent, $(\theta - \delta)$, can be considered to have a multiplier whose value is 1. That is, if we symbolize this multiplier by α, then the exponent becomes $\alpha(\theta - \delta)$. Distributing α across $(\theta - \delta)$ and letting

$$\gamma = -\alpha\delta \qquad (2.3)$$

our exponent becomes

$$\alpha(\theta - \delta) = \alpha\theta - \alpha\delta = \alpha\theta + \gamma \qquad (2.4)$$

Equation 2.4 is the slope–intercept parameterization of the exponent. In this form we have the equation for a straight line, where α represents the slope and γ symbolizes the intercept; "$\alpha\theta + \gamma$" is sometimes referred to as being in linear form. Although the intercept is related to the item location, it is not the item's location. To obtain the item's location we would use

$$\delta = -\frac{\gamma}{\alpha} \qquad (2.5)$$

To better understand the slope–intercept form, examine Figure 2.4. (We refer to the line in the graph as a *logit regression line*.) This figure shows $\alpha\theta + \gamma$ as a function of θ for an item located at –0.37. As can be seen, the line's intercept (γ) equals 0.37 and the slope (α) is 1. From these values we can obtain the item's location on the θ continuum using Equation 2.5:

$$\delta = -\frac{\gamma}{\alpha} = -\frac{0.37}{1.0} = -0.37 \qquad (2.6)$$

Because α is directly related to the logit regression line's slope, a change in α leads to a change in the line's slope. The effect of changing α "passes through" the reparameterization of the slope–intercept form into the $\alpha(\theta - \delta)$ deviate form. That is, the slope of the IRF may be modified by changing the value of α.[4] For example, by increasing α we arrive at the other two IRFs shown in Figure 2.3. The solid bold and nonbold IRFs are the IRFs when α = 1.5 or α = 2.0, respectively. As we see, using an α = 2.0 results in a predicted IRF that almost perfectly matches the empirical trace line. Stated another way, in this case the net effect of increasing the value of α is to improve the fit of the model to the data.

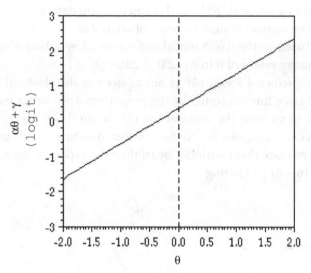

FIGURE 2.4. Logit space plot for item located at –0.37.

We can rewrite Equation 2.2 to explicitly incorporate α. Doing this produces the *one-parameter logistic* (1PL) model:

$$p(x_j = 1|\theta, \alpha, \delta_j) = \frac{e^{\alpha(\theta - \delta_j)}}{1 + e^{\alpha(\theta - \delta_j)}} \tag{2.7}$$

For computational efficiency Equation 2.7 is sometimes written as

$$p(x_j = 1|\theta, \alpha, \delta_j) = \frac{1}{1 + e^{-\alpha(\theta - \delta_j)}} \tag{2.8}$$

The lack of a subscript on α means that α does not vary across items. As such, the corresponding IRFs do not cross one another.[5] Sometimes "$\alpha(\theta - \delta)$" (or "$\gamma + \alpha\theta$") is referred to as a *logistic deviate*. For simplicity of presentation p_j is used in lieu of $p(x_j = 1|\theta, \alpha, \delta_j)$ in the following.

Because α is related to the IRF's slope, it reflects how well an item discriminates among individuals located at different points along the continuum. As a consequence, α is known as the *item discrimination* parameter. To understand this, assume we have three items with different αs, but located at 0.0 (i.e., $\delta_1 = \delta_2 = \delta_3 = 0$). Our three discrimination parameters are 0, 1, and 2. In addition, we have a respondent A located at –1 ($\theta_A = -1$) and another respondent B located at 1 (i.e., $\theta_B = 1$).

For the item with $\alpha = 0.0$ our IRF, as well as logit regression line, is horizontal. As a result, the predicted probabilities of a response of 1 for the two respondents is 0.5. In this case, the item does not provide any information for differentiating between the two respondents. This lack of discriminatory power is a direct function of $\alpha = 0.0$. In contrast, with the second item ($\alpha = 1$) we have different predictions for our respondents; for respondent A the $p_2 = 0.2689$ and for person B the $p_2 = 0.7311$. Therefore, this item's α allows us to distinguish between the two respondents.

Developing this idea further, the third item ($\alpha = 2.0$) would have the steepest IRF (and logit regression line) of the three items. This steepness is reflected in a greater difference in the predicted probabilities for our respondents than seen with the previous two items. That is, for this item respondent A has a $p_3 = 0.1192$ and for person B we have $p_3 = 0.8808$. In short, the magnitude of the difference in these predicted probabilities is a direct function of the item's α. Therefore, items with larger αs (i.e., steeper logit regression lines and IRFs) do a better job of discriminating among respondents located at different points on the continuum than do items with smaller αs.

THE ONE-PARAMETER LOGISTIC MODEL AND THE RASCH MODEL

To summarize, both the 1PL and Rasch models require that items have a constant value for α, but allow the items to differ in their locations. For the Rasch model this constant is 1.0, whereas for the 1PL model the constant α does not have to be equal to 1.0. Mathematically, the 1PL and the Rasch models are equivalent. The values from one model can be transformed into the other by appropriate rescaling. The use of the Rasch model sets α to 1.0, and this constant value is absorbed into the metric used in defining the continuum; this is demonstrated in Chapter 4.

However, to some the Rasch model represents a different *philosophical* perspective than that embodied in the 1PL model. The 1PL model is focused on fitting the data as well as possible, given the model's constraints. In contrast, the Rasch model is a model used to *construct* the variable of interest (cf. Andrich, 1988; Wilson, 2005; Wright, 1984; Wright & Masters, 1982; Wright & Stone, 1979). In short, this perspective says that the Rasch model is the standard by which one can create an instrument for measuring a variable. This perspective is similar to that seen in Guttman Scaling and Coombs Unfolding (Coombs, 1950), and is analogous to what is done in the physical sciences.[6] For example, consider the measurement of time. The measurement of time involves a repetitive process that marks off equal increments (i.e., units) of the (latent) variable time. In order to measure time we need to define our unit (e.g., a standard period of oscillation). With the Rasch model the unit is defined as the logit. That is, the unit is the distance on our continuum that leads to an increase in the odds of success by a factor equal to the transcendental constant e. Therefore, analogous to time measurement, our measurements with a one-parameter model are based on the (repetitive) use of a unit that remains constant across our metric.

For simplicity in the following discussion we use the general term 1PL model to refer to both $\alpha = 1.0$ (i.e., the Rasch model) and to the situation where α is equal to some other constant. However, when we use the term Rasch model, we are referring to the situation when $\alpha = 1.0$ and a measurement philosophy that states that the Rasch model is the basis for constructing the variable of interest.

ASSUMPTIONS UNDERLYING THE MODEL

IRT models assume that the response data are a manifestation of one or more person-oriented latent dimensions or factors. This is typically referred to as the *dimensionality assumption* and is reflected both in the models and in their graphical representations. For instance, in the 1PL model we use a single person location variable, θ, to reflect that one latent variable accounts for a person's response behavior. Moreover, in the 1PL model's conceptual development, as well as in its IRF, this assumption is reflected in a single continuum to represent the latent variable (see Figures 2.1 and 2.3). All the models presented in Chapters 2–9 assume a single latent person variable. Therefore, for these models the dimensionality assumption is referred to as the *unidimensionality assumption*. Specifically, the unidimensionality assumption states that the observations on the manifest variables (e.g., the items) are solely a function of a single continuous latent person variable. If one has a unidimensional latent space, then the persons may be located and compared on this latent variable. In terms of our example, this assumption states that there is a single latent mathematics proficiency variable that underlies the respondents' performance on our instrument. In contrast, if we needed to also know the respondents' locations on an obsessiveness latent variable to account for their performance on our instrument, then the response data would be best modeled using a two-dimensional, not a unidimensional, model.

We view the unidimensionality assumption as representing an ideal situation analogous to the homogeneity of variance assumption in analysis of variance (ANOVA). In practice, there will most likely be some degree of violation of the unidimensionality assumption. This degree of violation may or may not be problematic. That is, although the data may in truth be a manifestation of, for example, two latent variables, a unidimensional model may provide a sufficiently accurate representation to still be useful. (This is similar to an ANOVA in which the homogeneity of variance assumption is violated, but the *F* test is still useful under certain conditions.) Of course, in some situations the degree of violation may be so large that a unidimensional model is not useful. In these situations one might consider the use of a multidimensional model (Chapter 10) or some other approach to modeling the data. However, regardless of whether one uses a unidimensional model or not, it should be noted that whether the *estimated* θs are meaningful and useful is a validity issue. In short, the estimated θs, in and of themselves, do not guarantee that the latent variable that is intended to be measured (e.g., mathematics proficiency) is, in fact, measured.

A second assumption is that the responses to an item are independent of the responses to any other item conditional on the person's location. This assumption is referred to as *conditional independence* or *local independence*. We use the term conditional independence in the following because we consider it to be more descriptive than the term *local independence*.

In the unidimensional case, the conditional independence assumption says that how a person responds to a question is determined solely by his or her location on the latent continuum and not by how he or she responds to any other question on the examination. If this were not true, then more than the person's, say, mathematics ability, would be affecting his or her responses and one would have a nonunidimensional situation. Given this interpretation, it is not surprising that sometimes the unidimensionality assumption and the conditional independence assumption are discussed as being one and the same. However, they may not be one and the same in all cases; also see Goldstein (1980). For instance, certain instrument formats lead to a dependency among item responses that does not appear to invoke additional *latent* variables to define the latent space. For example, we might have a series of questions that all relate to the same passage or a set of hierarchically related items in which answering later items is based, in part, on answer(s) to earlier item(s). With these formats item responses will most likely violate the conditional independence assumption.

In contrast, there are cases of item interdependency that are due to additional latent variables. For example, consider the case of *speededness* in which an individual has insufficient time to respond to all the items on an instrument. In this situation, unless we use an additional latent variable, such as an individual's rapidity, in defining the latent space, then conditional independence is violated for the speeded items. That is, the unidimensionality assumption is violated because we have two latent person variables, rapidity and the target latent variable (e.g., mathematics proficiency). Furthermore, to the extent that the latent variable rapidity is associated with gender or ethnic group differences, then one may also observe that the speeded items exhibit differential item functioning (Chapter 12). Verhelst, Verstralen, and Jansen (1997) and Roskam (1997) both present models for time-limited measurement.

Strictly speaking, the conditional independence assumption states that for "any group of examinees all characterized by the same values $\theta_1, \theta_2, \ldots, \theta_k$, the (conditional) distributions of the item scores are all independent of each other" (Lord & Novick, 1968, p. 361).[7] That is, when all the latent variables that define the complete latent space are known and taken into account, then the item responses are independent of one another. Therefore, the conditional independence assumption applies not only to unidimensional, but also to the multidimensional IRT models.

A third assumption is the *functional form* assumption. This assumption states that the data follow the function specified by the model. For instance, for Equations 2.2 and 2.7 the functional form is that of an "S"-shaped curve. This ogival form matches the empirical data for the item shown in Figure 2.2. (Although these data were modeled using a logistic function, an alternative approach would be to use a probit strategy; see Appendix C.)

In the context of the 1PL model, the functional form assumption also embodies that all items on an instrument have IRFs with a common lower asymptote of 0 and a common slope. This common slope (i.e., constant α) across items is reflected in parallel IRFs. As is the case with the unidimensionality assumption, this assumption is rarely exactly met in practice. However, if the IRFs are parallel within sampling error, then this is interpreted as indicating model–data fit. Several different ways of determining model–data fit are addressed in the following chapters.

AN EMPIRICAL DATA SET: THE MATHEMATICS DATA SET

To demonstrate the principles underlying person and item parameter estimation, we use response data from the administration of a five-item mathematics examination. Consistent with the measurement issues discussed in Chapter 1, we assume that we have content validity evidence for our instrument. Although there is some controversy concerning the concept of content validity, in this book we assume that it is a useful concept. See Sireci (1998) for a discussion of the concept of content validity. We conceptualize mathematics proficiency as a continuous latent variable.

Although our example data come from proficiency assessment, we could have just as easily used data from a personality, attitude, or interest inventory. Moreover, our IRT model does not make an assumption about the item response format used on our instrument. Whether the questions, for example, use a multiple-choice, open-ended, true-false, forced-choice, or fill-in-the-blank response format is irrelevant. All that matters is that the data analyzed are dichotomous and that the assumptions are tenable. The appropriateness of the model to the data is a fit issue.

For our example, the dichotomous data were determined by classifying the examinees' responses into one of two categories, correct or incorrect. If the examinee correctly performed the mathematical operation(s) on an item, then his or her response was categorized in the "correct" category and assigned a value of 1. Otherwise, his or her response was categorized as incorrect and received a value of 0. Table 2.1 contains the response patterns and their frequency of occurrence.

With binary data and five items there are $2^L = 2^5 = 32$ possible unique response patterns, where L is the number of items. As can be seen from Table 2.1, each of these possible patterns is observed in the data set. There are 691 persons who did not correctly respond to any of the items (i.e., the response pattern 00000 with an X = 0 or a "zero score"), and there are 3385 persons who obtained a perfect score of 5 (i.e., X = 5, for the response pattern 11111). For pedagogical purposes the items are presented in ascending order of item location. Therefore, one would expect that if a person had item 2 correct, then that person should have also had item 1 correct.[8]

CONCEPTUALLY ESTIMATING AN INDIVIDUAL'S LOCATION

In practice, we know neither the item parameters (e.g., the δs) nor the person parameters (θs). Because, in general, our interest is in estimating person locations, we begin with estimating respondent locations on the latent continuum. For estimating a respondent's location ($\hat{\theta}$), we assume that we know the items' locations on the latent continuum. Although we conceptually present the estimation process here, in Appendix A we furnish a mathematical treatment and address obtaining the item location estimates in Appendix B.

Figure 2.5 shows the locations of our mathematics items. Item 1 has a location at −1.9 (i.e., $\delta_1 = -1.9$) , item 2 is located at $\delta_2 = -0.6$, and the remaining items are located at $\delta_3 = -0.25$, $\delta_4 = 0.30$, and $\delta_5 = 0.45$; these values correspond to their locations in Figure 2.5. Stated in words, item 1 is almost two units below the zero point and item 5 is almost a half unit above the zero point. The units defining the metric are called *logits*; see Appendix E, "Odds, Odds Ratios, and Logits," for information on logits. In general, and given that we are assessing mathematics proficiency, item 1 would tend to be considered an "easy" item and is comparatively easier than the remaining items on the instrument. Items 2 through 5 are generally considered to be of "average" difficulty.

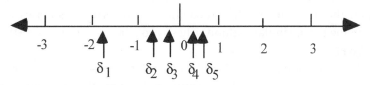

FIGURE 2.5. Graphical representation of the item locations for the mathematics test.

To demonstrate person location estimation, we arbitrarily select the response pattern of 11000 (i.e., two correct responses followed by three incorrect responses, X = 2). In this case, the estimation of a person's location is conceptually equivalent to asking the question, "Which θ has the highest likelihood of producing the pattern 11000?" To answer this question we need to perform a series of steps. The first step is to calculate the probability of each response in the pattern according to Equation 2.2. The second step is determining the probability of the response pattern. Step 2 is accomplished by capitalizing on the conditional independence assumption (i.e., for a given θ the responses are independent of one another). This assumption allows us to apply the multiplication rule for independent events to the item probabilities to obtain the probability for the pattern, given a particular θ. The third "step" is to reperform steps 1 and 2 for a range of θ values. For our example the range of θ will be from –3 to 3. The final step is to determine which of the various values of θ from step 3 has the highest likelihood of producing the pattern 11000.

Equation 2.2 specifies the probability of a response of 1, and its complement indicates the probability of a response of 0 (i.e., $p(x_j = 0) = 1.0 - p(x_j = 1)$). For the pattern in question (11000) items 1 and 2 are correctly answered and items 3–5 are incorrectly answered. Therefore, given our range of interest, the probability of a correct response to item 1 by someone located at –3.0 is

$$p(x_1 = 1|\theta = -3.0, \delta_1 = -1.9) = 0.2497$$

For our second item, and using δ_2 in lieu of δ_1, the probability of a correct response to item 2 for someone located at –3.0 is

$$p(x_1 = 1|\theta = -3.0, \delta_2 = -0.6) = 0.0832$$

These probabilities reflect what one would expect—namely, that a randomly selected person located at –3.0 has a higher probability of correctly answering the easiest item on the instrument than of correctly answering a harder item.

The responses to items 3 through 5 are incorrect. Therefore, to determine the probability of an incorrect response, we use the complement of Equation 2.2 for items 3 through 5. Item 5 is used to demonstrate obtaining the probability of an incorrect response. For item 5 the probability of an incorrect response for someone located at –3.0 is

$$p(x_5 = 0|\theta = -3.0, \delta_5 = 0.45) = 1.0 - p(x_5 = 1|\theta = -3.0, \delta_5 = 0.45) =$$
$$1.0 - 0.0308 = 0.9692$$

That is, a person located at −3.0 has a very high probability of *incorrectly* answering the hardest item on the instrument. The probabilities of incorrect responses to items 3 and 4 would be obtained in a similar fashion. These probabilities are $p(x_3 = 0) = 0.9399$ and $p(x_4 = 0) = 0.9644$.

So far we have the individual item probabilities for a $\theta = -3.0$. To obtain the likelihood of the observed response pattern 11000 requires multiplying the individual item probabilities (step 2). For individuals located at $\theta = -3.0$ the likelihood of observing the response pattern 11000 is given by

$$p(x_1 = 1) * p(x_2 = 1) * p(x_3 = 0) * p(x_4 = 0) * p(x_5 = 0)$$
$$= 0.2497 * 0.0832 * 0.9399 * 0.9644 * 0.9692 = 0.0182$$

As stated in words, the likelihood of individuals located at −3.0 providing the response pattern 11000 is about 0.02.

These two steps, calculating the individual item probabilities and then the joint probability of the pattern, would be repeated for the θs in the range −3.0 to 3.0 (step 3). Conceptually, the resulting series of probabilities from −3.0 to 3.0 collectively form the *likelihood function* (L). In step 4 the L is examined to determine the *location* of the maximum of the likelihood function. This location is the estimate of the person location ($\hat{\theta}$) that would most likely produce the response pattern 11000 on this mathematics examination, using our model and item parameters.

We may symbolically represent the above steps for calculating a likelihood. Letting $\underline{x}$ represent a response pattern (e.g., $\underline{x} = 11000$), then the likelihood of person i's response vector, $\underline{x}_i$, is

$$L(\underline{x}_i | \theta, \alpha, \underline{\delta}) = \prod_{j=1}^{L} p_j^{x_{ij}} (1 - p_j)^{(1 - x_{ij})} \qquad (2.9)$$

where p_j is short for $p(x_{ij} = 1 | \theta_i, \alpha, \delta_j)$, x_{ij} is person i's response to item j, $\underline{\delta}$ is a vector containing item location parameters, L is the number of items on the instrument (i.e., its length), and " $\prod$ " is the product symbol. From Equation 2.9 one sees that as the number of items increases, the product of these probabilities will potentially become so small that it will become difficult to represent on any calculational device. Therefore, rather than working directly with the probability, the natural logarithmic transformation of the probability (i.e., $\log_e(p_j)$ or $\ln(p_j)$) is typically used. This transformation results in a summation rather than a multiplication. The utilization of logs results in a likelihood that is called the *log likelihood function*, $\ln L(\underline{x}_i)$, where

$$\ln L(\underline{x}_i | \theta, \alpha, \underline{\delta}) = \sum_{j=1}^{L} (x_{ij} \ln(p_j) + (1 - x_{ij}) \ln(1 - p_j)) \qquad (2.10)$$

A graphical representation of the log likelihood for the pattern 11000 is presented in Figure 2.6. The vertical line in the body of the graph shows that the location of the maximum of the log likelihood occurs at approximately at –0.85 (i.e., this is the value that is most likely to result in the response pattern 11000 on this instrument). This value would be the estimated person location for this response pattern (i.e., $\hat{\theta}$ = –0.85).

What would the lnLs look like for the other response patterns that have the same observed score of 2 (e.g., 10100, 01100, etc.)? All of these lnLs exhibit the same form as seen with the pattern 11000 and with their maxima located at the same θ, but each likelihood is less in magnitude throughout the entire θ continuum than that shown for 11000. Figure 2.7 contains these lnLs for all 10 patterns with an X = 2. This pattern of lnLs is intuitively appealing because incorrectly answering the easiest three items and correctly answering the hardest two items (i.e., 00011) is not as likely to occur as the reverse pattern 11000. In short, none of the other patterns for X = 2 are as likely to occur as 11000. Moreover, although different patterns of responses may produce the same X and have varying degrees of likelihood, for the 1PL model a given X yields the same $\hat{\theta}$ regardless of the pattern of responses that produced X. Stated another way, Figure 2.7 shows that for the 1PL model the person's observed score (i.e., $X_i = \alpha \sum x_{ij}$) contains all the information necessary for estimating θ_i or, statistically speaking, X_i is a sufficient statistic for estimating θ_i (cf. Rasch, 1980).[9] In effect, the data shown in Table 2.1 may be collapsed into six observed scores of 0, 1, 2, 3, 4, and 5. As such, and in the context of the 1PL model, the actual pattern of responses that make up each observed score is ignored in our estimate of θ when we use the maximum likelihood approach.[10] We can proceed to obtain the $\hat{\theta}$s for the remaining patterns in Table 2.1 by determining their lnLs in a fashion similar to that used with 11000.

Although we located the maximum of the lnL by visual inspection, there are alternative, more sophisticated approaches that can be used to find the maximum's location. One of these

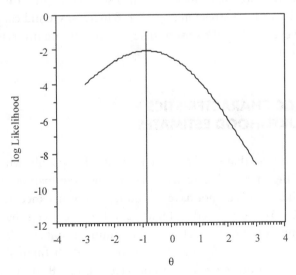

FIGURE 2.6. Log likelihood function for the pattern 11000.

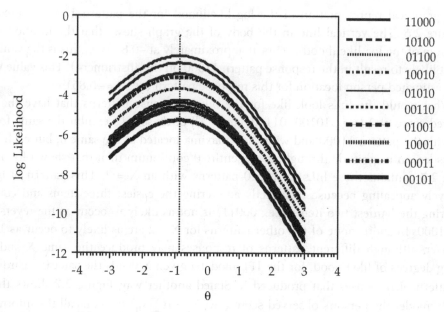

FIGURE 2.7. Log likelihood functions for the all patterns that result in an X = 2.

approaches is Newton's method for *maximum likelihood estimation* (MLE); this approach is discussed in Appendix A. Assume that we use Newton's method to find the MLE $\hat{\theta}$s for the remaining observed scores. For the individuals who obtained only one correct answer (X = 1), their $\hat{\theta}$ = –1.9876. That is, these 3099 individuals (i.e., 2280 + 242 + . . . + 184) are located approximately two logits below the zero point on the mathematics proficiency continuum metric. For the observed scores of 2, 3, and 4, the obtained $\hat{\theta}$s are –0.8378, 0.1008, and 1.1796, respectively. Comparing the MLE $\hat{\theta}$ for X = 2 with our visual inspection estimate ($\hat{\theta}$ = –0.85; X = 2) shows close agreement. We also see that as an individual answers more questions correctly, his or her corresponding MLE $\hat{\theta}$ increases to indicate greater mathematics proficiency. However, unlike the observed scores, our $\hat{\theta}$s are invariant of this particular mathematics examination.

SOME PRAGMATIC CHARACTERISTICS
OF MAXIMUM LIKELIHOOD ESTIMATES

It may have been noticed that $\hat{\theta}$s were not provided for people who obtained either a zero score (X = 0) or a perfect score (X = 5) on the examination. This is because the corresponding log likelihoods do not have a maximum. For instance, the log likelihood for the perfect score (X = 5) is presented in Figure 2.8. It can be seen that this log likelihood conforms to what one would expect. There are an infinite number of θs above 4 that could produce the observed score of 5. Because there is no way of distinguishing which θ among them is most likely, given our data, we do not have a finite $\hat{\theta}$ for a perfect score. In this case, our log likelihood is asymptotic with 0.0 and the estimate of θ would be ∞. For a zero score the log likelihood would be the mirror image of the one shown in Figure 2.8 and our $\hat{\theta}$ would be $-\infty$.

When zero and perfect scores are encountered in practice, the various computer estimation programs have different kludges for handling these scores. For example, in the next chapter the perfect and zero scores are modified so that they are no longer perfect and zero, respectively. Alternatively, an estimation approach that incorporates ancillary population information can be used to provide $\hat{\theta}$s for zero and perfect scores. This approach falls within Bayesian estimation and is discussed in Chapter 4.

THE STANDARD ERROR OF ESTIMATE AND INFORMATION

In general, we can obtain a measure of the amount of error in a statistic's estimate of a parameter. This measure, known as a standard error, is an index of the variability (i.e., the standard deviation) of an estimator with respect to the parameter it is estimating. The larger the value of a standard error, the greater the error and the less certain we are about the parameter's value. Similarly, in IRT our uncertainty about a person's location can be quantified through the estimate's *standard error of estimate* (SEE), $\sigma_e(\hat{\theta})$; we use $\sigma_e(\theta)$ as shorthand for $\sigma(\hat{\theta}|\theta)$.[11] The SEE specifies the accuracy of $\hat{\theta}$ with respect to the person location parameter, θ. When there is a small degree of uncertainty about a person's location, then its SEE is comparatively smaller than when there is a greater degree of uncertainty. The SEE should not be confused with the standard error of measurement used in classical test theory (CTT).[12]

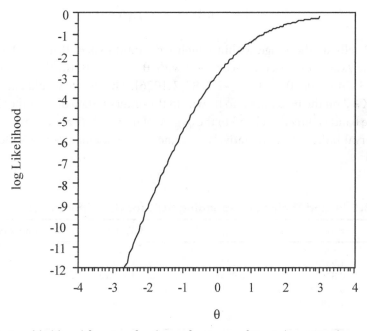

FIGURE 2.8. Log likelihood function for the perfect score of X = 5 (x = 11111).

The asymptotic variance error of estimate for $\hat{\theta}$ is

$$\sigma_e^2(\hat{\theta}\,|\,\theta) = \frac{1}{-\mathcal{E}\left[\dfrac{\partial^2}{\partial\theta^2}\ln L\right]} = \frac{1}{\displaystyle\sum_{j=1}^{L}\dfrac{[p_j']^2}{p_j(1-p_j)}} \qquad (2.11)$$

where p_j is given by the IRT model, p_j' is the model's first derivative, and $\mathcal{E}$ is the symbol for expectation (Lord, 1980). Given that the first derivative of the 1PL model is $p_j' = \alpha[p_j(1-p_j)]$, then Equation 2.11 simplifies to

$$\sigma_e^2(\hat{\theta}\,|\,\theta) = \frac{1}{\displaystyle\sum^{L}\alpha^2[p_j(1-p_j)]} \qquad (2.11)$$

In practice, $\hat{\theta}$ is substituted for θ in the IRT model. For example, for the person location estimate of -0.8378 our SEE is 0.9900 (i.e., roughly a full logit).

Table 2.2 contains the MLE $\hat{\theta}$s and their corresponding SEEs. The magnitude of the SEE is influenced not only by the quality of the items on the instrument, but also by the instrument's length. The addition of items similar to those on the instrument will lead to a decrease in the standard errors of $\hat{\theta}$. For example, if we lengthen our example mathematics test to 20 items by quadrupling the five-item set (i.e., four items at -1.9, four items at -0.6, etc.), then our SEE for $\hat{\theta} = -0.8378$ decreases to 0.4950.

We can use our SEEs to create a maximum likelihood confidence limit estimator (Birnbaum, 1968) by

$$(1-\alpha)\% \text{ CB: } \hat{\theta} \pm z_{(1-\alpha)}\sigma_e(\hat{\theta}) \qquad (2.13)$$

Equation 2.13 tells us the range within which we would expect θ to lie $(1-\alpha)\%$ of the time.[13] For the example's observed score of 2 with $\hat{\theta} = -0.8378$, the 95% confidence band would be $[-0.8378 \pm 1.96*0.9900] = [-2.7783, 1.1026]$. That is, we would expect the θ that produced an $X = 2$ on the instrument to lie within this interval 95% of the time. The width of the confidence band is directly related to the degree of uncertainty about a person's location. A narrow interval indicates comparatively less uncertainty about a person's location than a wider interval.

TABLE 2.2. MLE $\hat{\theta}$s and Their Corresponding SEEs for the Different Xs

X	$\hat{\theta}$	$s_e(\hat{\theta})$	95% CB	Number of Iterations
0	$-\infty$	∞	∞	∞
1	1.9876	1.2002	$-4.3401, 0.3648$	4
2	0.8378	0.9900	$-2.7783, 1.1026$	3
3	0.1008	0.9717	$-1.8037, 2.0053$	3
4	1.1796	1.1562	$-1.0864, 3.4457$	3
5	∞	∞	∞	∞

Note. ∞ and $-\infty$ symbolize infinity and negative infinity, respectively. CB, confidence band.

So far we have viewed the estimation of a person's location from the perspective of how uncertain we are about the person's location. We can also take the opposing perspective. That is, how certain are we about a person's location or, similarly, how much *information* do we have about a person's location? From this perspective, the confidence band's width is indirectly related to the information we have for estimating a person's location with an instrument. A narrow interval indicates comparatively more information for estimating a person's location than does a wider interval. If we take the reciprocal of Equation 2.11, we obtain an expression that directly specifies the "amount of information to be expected in respect of any unknown parameters, from a given number of observations of independent objects or events, the frequencies of which depend on that parameter" (Fisher, 1935, p. 18).

Because the instrument's items are our "observations," and given the conditional independence assumption, Fisher's idea about information may be applied to quantify the amount of information that the items as well as the instrument provide for estimating the person location parameters. Following Fisher's use of "I" to represent the concept information, then an estimator's information equals the reciprocal of Equation 2.11:

$$I(\theta) = \mathcal{E}\left[\frac{\partial}{\partial\theta}\ln L\right]^2 = -\mathcal{E}\left[\frac{\partial^2}{\partial\theta^2}\ln L\right] = \frac{1}{\sigma_e^2(\theta)} \qquad (2.14)$$

By substitution of Equation 2.11 into Equation 2.14 we obtain the *total information* ($I(\theta)$) provided by the instrument for estimating θ:

$$I(\theta) = \frac{1}{\sigma_e^2(\theta)} = \sum_{j=1}^{L} \frac{[p_j']^2}{p_j(1-p_j)} \qquad (2.15)$$

where all terms have been defined above. Equation 2.15 is also referred to as *test information* or *total test information*. Unlike the concept of reliability that depends on both instrument and sample characteristics, an instrument's total information is a property of the instrument itself (cf. Samejima, 1990). In this book the term *total information* is used in lieu of *test information* or *total test information* to reflect the fact that the instrument may not necessarily be a test.

Equation 2.15 specifies how much information an instrument provides for separating two distinct θs, θ_1 and θ_2, that are in proximity to one another. By analogy, in simple linear regression the steeper the slope of the regression line, the greater the difference between the predicted values for two different predictor values than when the slope is less steep. (For example, imagine the slope is 0 in one case and 0.9 in another case. In the former situation one would predict the same value for two different predictor values, whereas in the latter one would predict two different values for two different predictor values.) The numerator of Equation 2.15 is the (squared) slope, whereas the denominator is a reflection of the variability at the point at which the slope is calculated. Therefore, less variability (i.e., greater certainty) at the point at which one calculates the slope combined with a steep slope provides more information for distinguishing between θ_1 and θ_2 than if one had more variability and/or a less steep slope. Moreover, Equation 2.15 shows, all things being equal, that lengthening an instrument leads to a concomitant increase in precision for estimating person locations.

An instrument's total information reflects that each of the items potentially contributes some information to reduce the uncertainty about a person's location *independent* of the other items on the instrument. It is because of this independence that we can sum the individual item contributions to obtain the total information (Equation 2.15). This individual item contribution is known as *item information*, $I_j(\theta)$ (Birnbaum, 1968):

$$I_j(\theta) = \frac{[p'_j]^2}{p_j(1-p_j)} \qquad (2.16)$$

(The subscript j on I signifies item information, whereas the lack of a subscript indicates total information.) Therefore, total information equals the sum of the item information, $I(\theta) = \Sigma\, I_j(\theta)$.

For the 1PL model Equation 2.16 simplifies to

$$I_j(\theta) = \alpha^2\, p_j(1 - p_j) \qquad (2.17)$$

Because the product $p_j(1 - p_j)$ reaches its maximum value when $p_j = (1 - p_j)$, the maximum item information for the 1PL model is $\alpha^2 0.25$. Figure 2.9 shows an example item information function for an item located at 0.35 based on the Rasch model (i.e., $\alpha = 1.0$). As can be seen, the item information function is unimodal and symmetric about the item's location with a maximum value of 0.25.

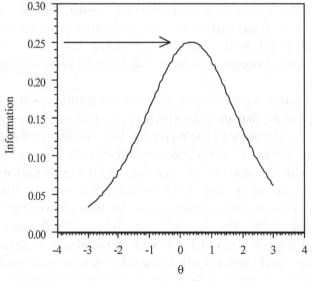

FIGURE 2.9. Item information for item ($\delta = 0.35$, $\alpha = 1.0$).

With the 1PL model all the items exhibit the same pattern seen in Figure 2.9. Namely, (1) an item provides its maximum information at its location, (2) the item information function is unimodal and symmetric about δ, and (3) all items on an instrument provide the same maximum amount of information of $\alpha^2 0.25$ at their respective locations. We now apply these concepts to our instrument.

AN INSTRUMENT'S ESTIMATION CAPACITY

The likelihood principles outlined above for person estimation can also be applied to the estimation of item locations. The MLE of item locations is presented in Appendix B. Using MLE we estimated the five item locations. These estimates, $\hat{\delta}$s, are presented in Table 2.3 along with their corresponding standard errors. As we see, item 1 is located at $(\hat{\delta}_1 =) -2.5118$, item 2 is located at $\hat{\delta}_2 = -0.1592$, and so on; $\alpha = 1$. In general, item 1 would be considered to be an easy item. The most difficult item on the mathematics instrument is item 5 with a location of 1.6414.

Figure 2.10 contains the items' corresponding IRFs. Because the items have a common α and α is related to an IRF's slope, it is not surprising that the IRFs are parallel to one another. One also sees that the probability of a correct response is 0.5 at the items' estimated locations (i.e., an item's location corresponds to the IRF's point of inflexion).

To obtain an idea of how well an item and the entire instrument can estimate person locations, we examine the item and total information. Figure 2.11 shows the information provided by each item ($I_j(\theta)$) and by the instrument ($I(\theta)$) as a function of θ. As can be seen, item 1 (nonbold solid line) provides its maximum information for estimating θ at its location of -2.5118. As we move away from this point, in either direction, the item provides progressively less information about θ. In fact, above 2.0 this item provides virtually no information for estimating persons located at and above 2.0. Therefore, using this item and others like it to estimate individuals with $\theta > 2.0$ would not yield precise estimates and the corresponding standard errors would be comparatively large.

The total information function (labeled "Total") shows that the instrument provides its maximum information for estimating θ in a neighborhood around 0.70. As we progress away from this neighborhood the instrument provides less information for estimating θ so that, for example, at $\theta = 3.0$ the instrument provides one half less information for estimating θ than at 0.70.[14] Recalling the inverse relationship between information and SEE, this

TABLE 2.3. MLE $\hat{\delta}$s and Their Corresponding SEEs for the Five-Item Instrument

Item	$\hat{\delta}$	$s_e(\hat{\delta})$
1	−2.5118	0.0246
2	−0.1592	0.0183
3	0.3518	0.0183
4	1.3203	0.0198
5	1.6414	0.0209

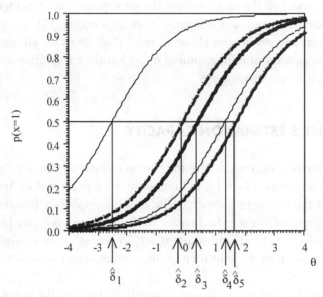

FIGURE 2.10. IRFs for all five items on the mathematics instrument.

observed decrease in information is commensurate with an increase in the standard errors for the $\hat{\theta}$s located away from 0.70.

This knowledge of how an instrument will behave in estimating person locations permits the design of an instrument with specific estimation properties. For example, if we are interested in providing better estimation below 0.7, then we need to improve the operational range of the test. We can do this by the addition of one or more items at the lower

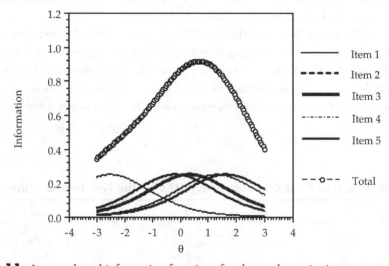

FIGURE 2.11. Item and total information functions for the mathematics instrument.

end of the continuum to increase the information about individuals located at the lower end of the continuum. If it were necessary to restrict our instrument to five items, then we might remove one or more items from the instrument that provide redundant information. For example, we might consider removing item 4 ($\delta_4 = 1.3203$) because it and item 5 ($\delta_5 = 1.6414$) are providing somewhat redundant information about examinee location. In contrast, if we desired to provide better estimation above 0.7, then items located around 0.7 and greater would be included in the instrument. In this fashion we can design an instrument to measure along a wide range of the continuum or, conversely, very precisely in a narrow range by adding items located within the range of interest.

To facilitate designing an instrument with specific estimation properties, we can specify a *target total information function* for the instrument. This target total information function would provide a blueprint for the area(s) on the continuum for which we wish to provide a high degree of precision for estimating person locations. For instance, consider a certification or licensure situation that involves a (decision) cutpoint above which a person would be, for example, certified and below which the person would not be certified. In this case it would be desirable to have an instrument with a total information function that is peaked at the cutpoint. This instrument would have enhanced capacity for distinguishing between individuals who were located near the cutpoint. To achieve this goal we would add items whose information maxima were at or near the cutpoint. Moreover, this greater information would reduce our SEEs at the cutpoint and thereby reduce the confidence band width (Equation 2.13) used to decide whether someone is above or below the cutpoint. (That is, we could use the interval estimate from Equation 2.13, not the point estimate $\hat{\theta}$, for deciding whether an individual is above or below the cutpoint.)

Alternatively, we may wish to have equiprecise estimation across a range of θ (i.e., "constant" SEE). In this case, the corresponding target total information function would resemble a rectangular (i.e., uniform) distribution across the θ range. To achieve this objective we would add items whose information maxima are located at different points along the θ range of interest.

In summary, information functions may be used to design an instrument with specific characteristics. This capability takes advantage of the fact that items and persons are located on the same continuum, as well as our capacity to assess the amount of information for estimating person locations based solely on the item parameter estimates. Success in developing an instrument whose observed total information function is similar to the target information function depends on having an adequate pool of items to work with and imposing constraints on the item selection to ensure that the resulting instrument has validity with respect to the construct of interest. Theunissen (1985), van der Linden and Boekkooi-Timminga (1989), and van der Linden (1998) contain detailed information for automating instrument development using a target instrument information function and taking into consideration content representation; also see Baker, Cohen, and Baarmish (1988) as well as Luecht (1998). In general, it is not possible to use CTT to design an instrument in this fashion. Of course, after developing the instrument it would still be necessary to perform a validation study for the instrument.

SUMMARY

Although for some individuals the Rasch and 1PL models reflect different perspectives for performing measurement, the models are mathematically equivalent. For some the Rasch model is seen as the standard by which to create a measurement device. From this perspective, for the data to be useful for measurement they must follow the model. Data that do not exhibit fit with the model are seen as suspect and may need to be discarded. In contrast, the 1PL model may be viewed as representing a statistical approach of trying to model response data. In this case, if one has model–data misfit, it is the model that is seen as suspect. For both models and for IRT in general, the graphical representation of the predicted probabilities of a response of 1 on an item are referred to as an item response function.

Because the 1PL model states that items have a common discrimination parameter (α), the corresponding IRFs are parallel to one another. The item's location (δ) on the latent continuum is defined by the location of the IRF's point of inflexion. In addition, we assume that the construct of interest is unidimensional, that the data are consistent with the model's function form, and that the responses are conditionally independent. The unidimensionality assumption states that the observations may be explained solely on the basis of a single latent person trait, θ. The functional form assumption states that the response data for an item follow an ogival pattern. In the context of the 1PL model the conditional independence assumption states that the responses to an item are independent of the responses to another item, conditional on person location. The tenability of these assumptions for a data set needs to be examined.

In contrast to CTT, in IRT both persons and items are located on the same continuum. Although items are allowed to vary in their locations, an item's capacity to differentiate among individuals is held constant across items. This capacity is captured by the item discrimination parameter. For the Rasch model $\alpha = 1.0$ and for the 1PL model α may be equal to some constant other than 1.0.

With the 1PL model the sum of person i's responses (observed score) is a sufficient statistic for estimating his or her location, and the sum of the responses to an item j (item score) is a sufficient statistic for estimating the item's location. All individuals who receive the same observed score will obtain the same estimated person location ($\hat{\theta}$), and all items that have the same item score will receive the same estimated location ($\hat{\delta}$). The accuracy of the $\hat{\theta}$ and $\hat{\delta}$ is indexed by their respective standard errors. Smaller standard errors of estimate reflect greater accuracy than do larger standard errors. Moreover, one's uncertainty of each parameter is reflected in the concept of information. In general, each item provides information for estimating a person's location. The sum of the item information functions is the instrument's total information function. The concept of total information can be used to design instruments with specific psychometric properties.

In this chapter we conceptually presented maximum likelihood estimation; Appendices A and B contain a more formal treatment for estimating the person and item parameters, respectively. In the next chapter the estimation of person and item parameters is further developed, using the likelihood principle presented above. Further, we demonstrate a process that can be used in practice for obtaining IRT parameter estimates. As part of this process we assess some of IRT's assumptions and examine model–data fit.

NOTES

1. There are other ways of conceptualizing the relationship between the person and item locations that do not involve taking their difference. For instance, Ramsay (1989) examined the ratio of the person and item locations (i.e., θ/δ). Although Ramsay's model is slightly more complicated than the standard approach of examining the difference between θ and δ, it does have the benefits of allowing different estimates of θ for different response patterns that yield the same observed score, as well as a way of accounting for examinee guessing.

2. Some treatments of the Rasch model (e.g., Rasch, 1961; Wright, 1968) use the concept of an item's "easiness" (E_j) to represent an item's location. In these cases, easiness may be transformed to item difficulty, δ, by $\delta_j = -\ln(E_j)$ (i.e., $E_j = e^{(-\delta_j)}$).

3. To obtain this δ_j, we use an approximation strategy based on the item's *traditional item difficulty*, P_j; this approach is discussed in Chapter 5 and Appendix C. Specifically, δ_j is equal to the z-score that delimits an area above it that equals P_j. The P_j for the item in Figure 2.2 is 0.644. From a standard unit normal curve table we find that a z = –0.37 corresponds to the point above which lies 0.644 of the area under the normal curve. Therefore, the estimate of the item's location is –0.37. A more sophisticated approach for estimating an item's location is presented in Appendix B.

4. The first derivative, p_j', of Equation 2.7 is

$$p_j' = \alpha[p_j(1-p_j)] = \alpha\left[\frac{e^{\alpha(\theta-\delta_j)}}{(1+e^{\alpha(\theta-\delta_j)})^2}\right] \qquad (2.18)$$

and because by definition α is defined at $\theta = \delta_j$, p' simplifies to

$$p_j' = \alpha\left[\frac{e^{\alpha(0)}}{(1+e^{\alpha(0)})^2}\right] = \alpha\left[\frac{e^0}{(1+e^0)^2}\right] = 0.25\alpha \qquad (2.19)$$

Therefore, strictly speaking, α in Equation 2.7 is proportional to the slope of the *tangent* line to the IRF at δ_j. Note that, by convention, we define the IRF's slope to be the one calculated at the item's location (i.e., an IRF has different slopes at different points along the function).

5. Strictly speaking, the IRFs are parallel when α is constant across items with different locations *and* when the lower asymptote of the corresponding IRFs is constant (e.g., the IRF lower asymptotes equal 0.0). Moreover, it is the tangent lines to the IRF at δ_j for the items that are parallel.

6. This philosophy is similar to the Guttman Scalogram (Guttman, 1950) technique for measuring, for example, attitudes. In scalogram analysis *if* one can successfully apply the technique, then the resulting scale is unidimensional and has certain known properties. However, there is no guarantee that one will be able to successfully apply scalogram analysis to a particular data set. In short, simply because one would like to measure a particular construct does not necessarily mean one will be successful. This standard is greater than simply asking a series of questions—the data must fit a scalogram in order for the creation of an instrument to be considered successful. (Strictly speaking,

there is some latitude.) Similarly, using the Rasch model as the standard for being able to measure a construct means that the data must fit the Rasch model. Whether the unidimensional scale produced by the Rasch model is meaningful or useful is a validity question. The Rasch model differs from the Guttman Scalogram model most notably in that the Rasch model is a probabilistic model, whereas the scalogram model is deterministic.

7. McDonald (McDonald, 1979, 1981; McDonald & Mok, 1995) has asserted that there are two principles of conditional independence. The first is the *strong principle of conditional (local) independence* and the second is the *weak principle of conditional (local) independence*. The strong principle is the one defined by Lord and Novick (1968); that is, after taking into account (conditioning on) all the relevant latent variables, the item responses for *all* subsets of items are mutually statistically independent. The weak principle states that the covariability between *two* item vectors is zero after conditioning on all the relevant latent variables (i.e., pairwise conditional independence). McDonald refers to these two forms as *principles* rather than assumptions because "the (strong or weak) principle of local independence is not an assumption, but serves to provide the mathematical definition of latent traits" (McDonald & Mok, 1995, p. 25). The existence of weak conditional independence is a necessary, but not sufficient, condition for the existence of strong conditional independence.

The weak principle of conditional independence is the basic assumption that underlies common factor analysis (McDonald, 1979). This connection with factor analysis and the capability of factor analysis to distinguish between major and minor factors provides another way of looking at the dimensionality assumption. *Essential dimensionality* (d_E; Stout, 1990) is the minimal number of major factors necessary for a weakly monotone latent model to achieve *essential independence* (EI). Stout (1990) states that EI exists when the conditional covariances between items, on average, approach zero as test length becomes infinite. When d_E equals 1, then one has *essentially unidimensionality*. Stout (1987) developed a statistical test, T, to detect departure from (essential) unidimensionality in a data set. This approach is implemented in DIMTEST; DIMTEST is available from the Assessment Systems Corporation (*assess.com/xcart/home.php*). Nandakumar (1991) and Hattie, Krokowski, Rogers, and Swaminathan (1996) contain readable presentations of the DIMTEST approach to assessing dimensionality.

8. This idea of logically consistent response patterns or *ideal response patterns* is seen in a perfect Guttman scale (Guttman, 1950) or in Walker's (1931) *unig test*. A unig test consists of observed scores, X, composed of the correct answers to the X easiest items. Moreover, the observed score X + 1 contains the correct answers of score X plus one more. In the context of the 1PL model, the condition for an ideal response pattern for person i is $x_{ij} \geq x_{iv}$ when $p_{ij} \geq p_{iv}$, where j and v are two items. For example, assuming three items are ordered from easy to hard, then the logically consistent patterns are 000 (all items incorrect), 100 (easiest item correct, harder items incorrect), 110 (hardest item incorrect, easier items correct), and 111 (all items correct). These ideal response patterns are also known as *Guttman patterns* or *conformal patterns*. Although our instrument does not conform to a unig test (or a perfect Guttman scale), the ideal response patterns (i.e., 00000, 10000, 11000, 11100, 11110, 11111) do have the largest frequency for a given observed score, X. For instance, for X = 1 (i.e., the patterns 10000, 01000, 00100, 00010, 00001), the 10000 pattern has the largest frequency. There are $C_X^L = \frac{L!}{X!(L-X)!}$ different pattern combinations for a given X score.

9. According to Fisher (1971b), "if θ [is] the parameter to be estimated, θ_1 a statistic which contains the whole of the information as to the value of θ, which the sample supplies, and θ_2 any other statistic, then . . . when θ_1 is known, knowledge of the value of θ_2 throws no further light upon the value of θ" (pp. 316–317). By definition, a statistic or estimator (y) for a parameter is *sufficient* if it contains all of the information regarding the parameter that can be obtained from the sample (i.e., no further information about the parameter can be obtained from any other sample statistic (e.g., y') that

is functionally independent of y. In short, a sufficient statistic represents a form of data reduction that preserves the information contained in the data. To demonstrate the existence of sufficient statistics for the Rasch model, we follow Wright and Stone (1979). Starting with an $N \times L$ data matrix $\underline{X}$ whose entries x_{ij} represent the binary response on the jth item by the ith person, then the marginal totals (i.e., row and column sums) for $\underline{X}$ are

person i's observed score (i.e., row i in $\underline{X}$): $\quad X_i = \sum_{j=1}^{L} w_j x_{ij}$

and item j's item score (i.e., column j in $\underline{X}$): $\quad q_j = \sum_{i=1}^{N} v_i x_{ij}$

where $w_j = 1.0$ and $v_i = 1.0$.

The probability of the entire data matrix $\underline{X}$ is given by taking the products across the N persons and the L items:

$$ p_j = \prod_{i=1}^{N} \prod_{j=1}^{L} \frac{e^{x_{ij}(\theta_i - \delta_j)}}{1 + (e^{(\theta_i - \delta_j)})} $$

Converting these products to sums and then factoring the numerator, we have

$$ p_j = \frac{\exp\left[\sum_i X_i \theta_i\right] \exp\left[-\sum_j q_j \delta_j\right]}{\prod_{i=1}^{N} \prod_{j=1}^{L} (1 + \exp[\theta_i - \delta_j])} $$

where we use "exp[z]" instead of "e^z" to simplify presentation. This numerator has the form of sufficient statistics: one for estimating θ_i and the other for estimating δ_j. (See Fisher (1971b) for the condition that must be satisfied for the existence of a sufficient statistic.) Specifically, the observed score X_i (= $\sum x_{ij}$) is a *sufficient statistic* for estimating θ_i and the item score q_j (= $\sum x_{ij}$) is a sufficient statistic for estimating δ_j (also see Rasch, 1980).

The sufficient statistic X_i is the sum of person i's responses to the items and does not involve item characteristics (e.g., item locations or discriminations). This is why the 10 patterns with an $X_i = 2$ (Figure 2.7) all have the same $\hat{\theta}$. Similarly, the sufficient statistic q_j is the sum of the responses on item j and involves only item responses and not person characteristics.

10. This does not mean that an alternative estimation procedure that does not involve the criterion of maximizing the likelihood function will also yield the same $\hat{\theta}$ for all response patterns that produce a given observed score, X. For example, the minimum X^2 estimation method seeks to estimate the parameters that minimize a X^2 criterion (i.e., maximize data–model fit). (See Linacre (2004) or Baker and Kim (2004) for more information on this estimation method.) Utilizing this procedure, "persons with different response patterns, but with the same raw <observe> score, obtain different measures <$\hat{\theta}$s> characterized by different standard errors, and similarly for items" (Linacre, 2004, p. 6).

11. Strictly speaking, one has only the sample standard error of estimate ($s_e(\hat{\theta})$); that is, an estimate of $\sigma_e(\hat{\theta})$.

12. The standard error of measurement is a *global* measure of error across the manifest variable score metric for a given sample. It may (and most likely will) over- or underestimate the degree of error at different points along the score metric (Feldt & Brennan, 1989; Livingston, 1982). In our example, there are six possible X_is, but there is only one standard error of measurement. One could calculate a *conditional standard error of measurement* at each X_i between the zero and perfect scores that would provide a more accurate reflection of the error at that particular score than would the standard error of measurement. See Livingston (1982), Kolen, Hanson, and Brennan (1992), and Kolen, Zeng, and Hanson (1996) for approaches to calculating a conditional standard error of measurement. These conditional standard errors would be the same for everyone who obtained the same X_i score.

13. The use of z in this formula is based on the fact "that a maximum likelihood estimator has approximately (asymptotically) the normal distribution with mean θ, the true ability value, and variance $1/I(\theta)$, under conditions satisfied by most of the models" (Cramér, 1946, p. 500; cited in Birnbaum, 1968, p. 457).

14. As Lord (1980) points out, "information is not a pure number; the units in terms of which information is measured depend on the units used to measure ability" (p. 87). Therefore, the foregoing description of the locations of item and total information maxima as well as the shape of the information function is tied to the particular θ metric used and should not be considered absolute.

Joint Maximum Likelihood Parameter Estimation

In Chapter 2 we introduced the Rasch model. As part of its presentation we discussed using the likelihood of the observed responses as a mechanism for estimating the model's parameters; also see Appendices A and B. There are, in fact, multiple approaches that use a likelihood function for estimating item and person parameters. In this chapter one approach is presented and in Chapter 4 a second procedure, marginal maximum likelihood estimation, is discussed.

Chapter 2's (as well as Appendix A's) presentation of estimating person locations assumes that the item parameters are known. Similarly, in Appendix B the estimation of item locations assumes that the person locations are known. However, in practice, neither the person nor the item locations are known. In this chapter we conceptually introduce a procedure for the simultaneous estimation of both item and person parameters. We then present an example of applying this estimation procedure and some of the steps involved in assessing model–data fit, such as dimensionality and invariance assessment.

JOINT MAXIMUM LIKELIHOOD ESTIMATION

Various strategies have been developed to solve the problem of estimating one set of parameters (e.g., the person set) without knowledge of another set of parameters (e.g., the item set). One of these approaches maximizes the joint likelihood function of both persons and items in order to simultaneously estimate both person and item parameters. This strategy is referred to as *joint maximum likelihood estimation* (JMLE). To arrive at the joint likelihood function for persons and items, we begin with the likelihood function for persons. Assuming conditional independence and (without loss of generalizability) dichotomous responses, the probability of a person's responses is simply the product of the probability of the responses across an instrument's items. Symbolically, this can be represented for an L-item long instrument by

$$p(\underline{x}|\theta, \alpha, \underline{\delta}) = \prod_{j=1}^{L} p_j^{x_j}(1 - p_j)^{1-x_j} \qquad (3.1)$$

The term $p(\underline{x}|\theta, \alpha, \underline{\delta})$ is the probability of the response vector, $\underline{x}$, conditional on the person's location, θ, item discrimination α, and on a vector of item location parameters, $\underline{\delta}$ (i.e., $\underline{\delta} = (\delta_1, \ldots, \delta_L)$). The probability for item j, p_j, is calculated according to a particular model (e.g., the 1PL model).

To obtain the joint likelihood function, L, across both persons and items, one multiplies Equation 3.1 across the N persons:

$$L = \prod_{i=1}^{N} \prod_{j=1}^{L} p_j(\theta_i)^{x_{ij}}(1 - p_j(\theta_i))^{1-x_{ij}} \qquad (3.2)$$

Recall from Chapter 2 that to avoid numerical accuracy issues, the likelihood function is typically transformed by using the natural log (ln). Therefore, by applying the natural log transformation to Equation 3.2 we obtain the joint log likelihood function:

$$\ln L = \sum_{i=1}^{N} \sum_{j=1}^{L} [x_{ij}\ln(p_j(\theta_i)) + (1 - x_{ij})\ln(1 - p_j(\theta_i))] \qquad (3.3)$$

The values of the θs and δs that maximize Equation 3.3 are taken as the person and item parameter estimates, respectively. These estimates are determined by setting the first derivatives of $\ln L$ to zero in a fashion similar to what is presented in Appendices A and B.

This strategy of maximizing the joint likelihood function proceeds in a series of steps and stages. (For simplicity we assume the Rasch model in describing these steps.) In step 1 the item locations are estimated using provisional estimates of person locations. These provisional person location estimates are treated as "known" for purposes of estimating the item locations. The estimation of item locations is done first because, typically, one has substantially more persons than items and thereby there is more information for estimating the item locations. Because the estimation of one item's parameter does not depend on the parameters of other items, the items are estimated one at a time. In step 2 these estimates are treated as "known" and are used for estimating person locations. Each person's location is estimated independently of those of the other individuals.

In step 1 the estimation of the item locations used provisional estimates of person locations. However, after step 2 these provisional person estimates have been improved and these improved estimates should lead to more accurate item location estimates. Therefore, in our second stage, step 1 is repeated using the improved estimates of person locations from step 2 to obtain better estimates of the item locations. With these improved item location estimates, step 2 is repeated using the improved item location estimates to improve the person location estimates. This "ping-pong" stage process continues until successive improvements in the person and item location estimates are considered "indistinguishable" from one another (i.e., these improvements are less than the *convergence criterion*; see Appendix A). See Baker and Kim (2004) and Lord (1980) for further details and the relevant equations.

On occasion one encounters the term *unconditional maximum likelihood estimation* (UCON). UCON is a synonymous term for JMLE. The term UCON has been used by Ben Wright (e.g., Wright & Stone, 1979) to distinguish this approach from another estimation approach used with the Rasch model called *conditional maximum likelihood estimation*, or CMLE (Andersen, 1972). (CMLE takes advantage of the separability of the person and item parameters in the Rasch model to condition the likelihood function on the Rasch model's sufficient statistics. The result provides consistent maximum likelihood estimators of δ [Andersen, 1972]. CMLE can only be used with the Rasch model and its various extensions.)

JMLE (UCON) is used in estimation programs such as WINSTEPS (Linacre, 2001a), BIGSTEPS (Linacre & Wright, 2001), FACETS (Linacre, 2001b), and Quest (Adams & Khoo, 1996), as well as in LOGIST (Wingersky, Barton, & Lord, 1982). CMLE is one of two estimation techniques available in OPLM (Verhelst, Glas, & Verstralen, 1995). More technical information about JMLE and CMLE estimation may be found in Baker and Kim (2004).

INDETERMINACY OF PARAMETER ESTIMATES

Although with CTT the trait score's metric is specified by the expectation of the observed scores, in IRT this is not the case. To understand why this is so, consider our development of the Rasch model. In developing the model our concern is only with the distance between the person and an item's locations, $(\theta - \delta)$. If $\theta = 2$ and $\delta = 1$, then this distance is 1.0 and the probability of a response of 1 with the Rasch model would equal 0.7311. However, for any θ and δ whose difference equals 1.0 the Rasch model would result in exactly the same probability of a successful response (e.g., if $\theta' = 50$ and $\delta' = 49$, then $p_j = 0.7311$). This raises the question, "Should the person be located at 2 and the item located at 1, or should the person be located at 50 and the item located at 49?" In other words, because multiple values of θ and δ lead to the same probability, the continuum's metric is *not absolute*, but rather it is *relative* and *nonunique*. In IRT we have an indeterminacy in the origin and unit of measurement of the metric. In short, our metric is determined or is unique *only* up to a linear transformation. For our example the linear transformation for the θs is $\theta^* = \theta(1) + 48$ and for the δs it is $\delta^* = \delta(1) + 48$. This property is referred to as the *indeterminacy of scale*, *indeterminacy of metric*, or the model *identification problem*.

An implication of this indeterminacy is the need to fix or anchor the metric to a particular origin to estimate the model's parameters (i.e., the item or the person parameters); with the Rasch model the unit of measurement is fixed at 1.0. Because people and items are located on the same continuum, we only need to fix either the person or the item locations. One method for fixing the metric, *person centering*, sets the mean of the $\hat{\theta}$s to 0.0 after each step of person location estimation. A second approach, *item centering*, sets the mean of the $\hat{\delta}$s to 0.0 after each step of item estimation.[1] Although these two approaches will most likely result in different estimates, the relative nature of the metric means that model–data fit will not be adversely affected by the centering approach used.

To see the effect of this indeterminacy with the JMLE algorithm, recall that initially the item locations are estimated, given provisional estimates of the person locations. In the next step the person locations are estimated *relative* to the item location estimates. Subsequently, the item locations are reestimated *relative* to the new estimates of person locations, and so on across the stages. Because with each step the estimation proceeds relative to the improved estimates from the previous step, the metric's mean begins to drift across the steps. Therefore, for the JMLE algorithm the metric of either the person or item locations needs to be fixed after each step. For instance, and to exemplify item centering, we would first estimate the item locations, calculate the mean $\hat{\delta}$, and then subtract it from each $\hat{\delta}$. This would produce a metric centered at 0.0, and we would perform this centering after the relevant estimation step. Centering is really an example of the application of a linear transformation.

Of the various commonly available IRT programs, WINSTEPS (Linacre, 2001a), BIG-STEPS (Linacre & Wright, 2001), and FACETS (Linacre, 2001b) all use item centering. An older program, LOGIST, uses person centering. Newer programs such as BILOG-MG (Zimowski, Muraki, Mislevy, & Bock, 2003), BILOG 3 (Mislevy & Bock, 1997), PARSCALE (Muraki & Bock, 2003), and MULTILOG (Thissen, Chen, & Bock, 2003) use a variant of person centering based on the posterior latent variable (person) distribution (Baker, 1990); this approach is discussed in Chapter 4.

HOW LARGE A CALIBRATION SAMPLE?

The process of obtaining estimates of person and item parameters is known as *calibration*. Wright (1977a) stated "that calibration sample sizes of 500 are more than adequate in practice and that useful information can be obtained from samples as small as 100" (p. 224). However, in this latter situation one has less calibration precision than with larger sample sizes (Wright, 1977a) as well as a loss of power for detecting model–data misfit (Whitely, 1977).[2] That is, the degree of model–data misfit that one is willing to tolerate should be taken into consideration when discussing calibration sample sizes. We feel that another consideration in determining calibration sample sizes should include the sample size requirement(s) of ancillary technique(s), such as methods to be used for dimensionality assessment (e.g., factor analysis). For example, there are various rules of thumb for factor analysis sample sizes, such as the number of persons should be from 3 to 10 times the number of items; these ratios interact with the magnitude of the factor loadings. The 10:1 ratio is a very common suggestion, whereas the smaller ratios are applicable only when the communalities are large (cf. MacCallum, Widaman, Zhang, & Hong, 1999). As such, our calibration sample size is affected by the requirements for performing the factor analysis.

It cannot be stressed enough that sample size guidelines should not be interpreted as hard-and-fast rules. Specific situations may require more or fewer persons than other situations, given the (mis)match between the instrument's range of item locations and the sample's range of person locations, the desired degree of estimation accuracy of both items and persons, and pragmatic issues concerning model–data fit, ancillary technique sample size requirements, estimation technique, the amount of missing data, and generalizability. For instance, if one is interested in establishing norms for a particular population, then the representativeness of the sample would be paramount. This may require obtaining a large sample in order to formulate a convincing argument to support the utility of the norms. As such, it may be tempting to simply adopt the philosophy that one should have as large a sample size as one can obtain. However, the increased cost of collecting a large sample may not always be justified. For example, if one is performing a survey, then approximately 1200 randomly sampled individuals may be sufficient, provided that the size of the population is large (Dillman, 2000). Another consideration is that the smaller the sample size, the higher the probability, all other things being equal, that everyone will provide the same response (e.g., a response of 0) to one or more items. As a result, the item location is unestimatable. The same problem may occur with "short" instruments. That is, with short instruments there is an increased chance of a person's providing a response of, for example, 1 for all items. This individual's location could not be estimated using MLE. Given the foregoing caveats and considerations, a rough sample size guideline is that a calibration should have a few hundred respondents. This should not be interpreted as a minimum, but rather as a desirable target. Certain applications may require more respondents, whereas in others a smaller sample may suffice.

EXAMPLE: APPLICATION OF THE RASCH MODEL TO THE MATHEMATICS DATA, JMLE

To demonstrate the application of the Rasch model for measurement we use the mathematics data introduced in Chapter 2 (Table 2.1). We use JMLE for estimating our item and person parameters. In Chapter 4 we reanalyze these data using a different program, BILOG-MG, to demonstrate a second estimation technique.

For this example, we use the BIGSTEPS software program. This calibration program implements JMLE for the Rasch model and certain extensions of it. In this chapter we use some of the program's features and introduce additional features in Chapter 7 when it is used with polytomous data. One distinguishing feature of BIGSTEPS is its lack of a GUI, or graphical user interface (i.e., menus and dialogs). We recognize that many readers are more comfortable using a program with a GUI. An alternative program, WINSTEPS, uses a GUI and can accomplish everything that BIGSTEPS can and more. However, our decision to use BIGSTEPS is based on the fact that it is free (WINSTEPS is not) and that its output is similar enough to WINSTEPS' that the reader can easily make the transition to WINSTEPS. A third program, MINISTEPS, is a free "student version" of WINSTEPS that cannot be used with our data, owing to the program's limitations on the number of items and cases, but that can suffice for classroom examples.

The application of IRT for measuring a variable requires three categories of activities. The first category consists of calibration-related activities. A second category involves model–data fit assessment, and the third category requires obtaining validity evidence. To varying degrees, all three categories inform one another. We use the term *category* rather than, say, *stages*, to emphasize that the corresponding activities are not necessarily done in sequence (i.e., category 1 activities precede category 2 activities, etc.). In the following discussion the primary emphasis is on the first two categories. These two categories are discussed first and then followed by an example.

Category 1 involves the calibration-related activities. Obviously, the entire process begins with the construction of an instrument. The instrument is pilot tested, refined (if necessary), and then administered to the individuals of interest. After this administration the data are inspected for anomalous responses (e.g., miscoded responses, multiple responses to an item, etc.) and, if necessary, appropriately corrected. After this "cleaning" of the data, we perform some of the category 2 activities, and these, in turn, lead to our calibration (category 1).

Category 2 consists of model–data fit activities. Some of these activities are performed prior to the calibration, whereas others occur after the calibration. Although there are some model–data fit activities that transcend individual programs, some approaches for assessing model–data fit are easier to perform with some calibration programs than with others. For example, the assessment of the data's dimensionality and the examination of invariance of parameter estimates (discussed below) are examples of activities that transcend individual calibration programs. In contrast, specific fit statistics/indices and graphical assessment of fit tend to be particular to a specific program because individual programs provide different fit information.

The following example begins with an assessment of the tenability of the IRT unidimensionality assumption. In short, and in the context of the Rasch model, the question being asked is, "Do our data conform to the unidimensional Rasch model?" After we perform our dimensionality assessment we proceed to the data's calibration. As part of this calibration various fit statistics are produced at both the model and item/person levels. The model-level fit statistics are examined first, followed by the item-level fit statistics. In some cases, model-level *misfit* may be diagnosed by examining the item-level fit statistics. The final step in our fit examination for this example involves assessing the invariance of the item parameter estimates. This is followed by a brief discussion of obtaining validity evidence for the instrument (i.e., category 3 activities).

Dimensionality Assessment

In assessing dimensionality our interest is in the number of *content-oriented* factors. The traditional approach for assessing dimensionality involves the factor analysis of a correlation matrix. Whenever one factor analyzes a correlation matrix derived from binary data, there is a possibility of obtaining artifactual factor(s) that are related to the nonlinearity between the items and the common factors. These "factors of curvilinearity" have sometimes been referred to as "difficulty" factors and are not considered to be content-oriented factors (Ferguson, 1941; McDonald, 1967; McDonald & Ahlawat, 1974; Thurstone, 1938). To avoid extracting these difficulty factors, McDonald (1967) suggests the use of nonlinear factor analysis. Because our data are dichotomous, we use this nonlinear approach for our dimensionality analysis. This nonlinear strategy is implemented in the program NOHARM (Fraser, 1988; Fraser & McDonald, 2003).

An alternative to using NOHARM is to use TESTFACT (Wood et al., 2003) and perform full-information factor analysis (Muraki & Engelhard, 1985; Wood et al., 2003). We selected NOHARM over TESTFACT on the basis of research showing that NOHARM performs well in dimensionality recovery studies (e.g., De Champlain & Gessaroli, 1998; Finch & Habing, 2005; Knol & Berger, 1991) and because it is available at no cost. For additional information on approaches for assessing unidimensionality, see Hattie (1985) and Panter, Swygert, Dahlstrom, and Tanaka (1997).

NOHARM (Normal *Ogive Harmonic Analysis Robust* Method) is a general program that takes advantage of the relationship between nonlinear factor analysis and the normal ogive model in order to fit unidimensional and multidimensional normal ogive models (see Appendix C). In the current context, we fit one- and two-dimensional two-parameter (2P) models to the data. To determine which dimensional solution is "best," the differences in fit among the models are examined. Because the models we are fitting do not address guessing, we are assuming that the response data are not influenced by guessing. Moreover, we are also assuming that the latent trait is normally distributed or is multivariate normal (McDonald, 1981). Rather than calculate the raw product–moment matrix on more than 19,600 individuals for each of the NOHARM analyses, we calculate the raw product–moment matrix once and then use it as input to the NOHARM analyses; Chapter 10 shows how to perform the analysis with individual case data.[3]

The raw product–moment matrix, $\underline{P}$, is obtained by $\underline{X}'\underline{X}(1/N)$, where N is the number of cases and $\underline{X}$ is the data matrix. If we let $\underline{X}$ consist of binary responses, then $\underline{P}$ contains the item means or traditional item difficulties, P_js, along its main diagonal and the sums of product terms divided by N as its off-diagonal elements. For example, for a three-item instrument the raw product–moment matrix is

$$\underline{P} = \begin{bmatrix} P_1 & (\Sigma X_1 X_2)/N & (\Sigma X_1 X_3)/N \\ (\Sigma X_2 X_1)/N & P_2 & (\Sigma X_2 X_3)/N \\ (\Sigma X_3 X_1)/N & (\Sigma X_3 X_2)/N & P_3 \end{bmatrix} \qquad (3.4)$$

where $P_1 = \Sigma X_1/N$, $P_2 = \Sigma X_2/N$, $P_3 = \Sigma X_3/N$, and all subscripts refer to items.

The input file for performing the one-dimensional analysis is shown in Table 3.1. The first command line in the input file contains a title for the analysis, with the remaining lines specifying the analysis setup. For instance, the line "5 1 19601 1 1 0 0 0" specifies that there are five items, to perform a one-dimensional analysis, that there are 19,601 cases, that the input is the product–moment matrix, that an exploratory analysis (rather than confirmatory analysis) is requested, that NOHARM should generate its starting values, and that the correlation, covariance, and residual matrices be printed, respectively. The subsequent line allows the user to provide the IRF's lower asymptote value for each of the five items. In this case, the lower asymptote for each item is set to 0 because we are assuming that the response data are not influenced by guessing. Following these lines is the lower triangle of the product–moment matrix; because $\underline{P}$ is symmetric, only $\underline{P}$'s lower triangle is provided as input.

Table 3.2 contains the corresponding output. The beginning of the output contains echoes of the input specifications. Beginning with "Residual Matrix (lower off-diagonals)" is where we find NOHARM's fit information. NOHARM produces a residual

TABLE 3.1. One-Dimensional Input Command File

```
5 Items/ one dimension / product-moment input
5 1 19601 1 1 0 0 0
0 0 0 0 0
0.566
0.275   0.387
0.317   0.223   0.427
0.531   0.360   0.401   0.887
0.442   0.302   0.352   0.607   0.644
```

Note. Name = math1D.dat.

matrix to facilitate model–data fit analysis. The residual matrix is the discrepancy between the observed covariances and those of the items after the model has been fitted to the data. Therefore, the ideal situation is where the discrepancies are zero. In general, our unidimensional solution's residuals are comparatively small relative to the item covariances. Moreover, examination of the residual matrix does not reveal any large residuals. To summarize the residual matrix, NOHARM provides its root mean square (RMS). The RMS is the square root of the average squared difference between the observed and predicted covariances. Therefore, small values of RMS indicate good fit. This overall measure of model–data misfit may be evaluated by comparing it to four times the reciprocal of the square root of the sample size (i.e., the "typical" standard error of the residuals; McDonald, 1997). For these data this criterion is 0.0286. A second measure is Tanaka's (1993) goodness-of-fit index (GFI); Chapter 10 contains a description of the GFI. McDonald (1999) suggests that a GFI of 0.90 indicates an acceptable level of fit and a value of 0.95 indicates "good" fit; GFI = 1 indicates perfect fit. Therefore, according to these indices and in light of the residuals, there does not appear to be sufficient evidence to reject a unidimensional solution.

The subsequent NOHARM analysis for obtaining the two-dimensional solution is performed by modifying the second line in the input command file to be "5 2 19601 1 1 0 0 0".[4] As is the case with the one-dimensional solution, the solution's residuals are comparatively small relative to the item covariances and the matrix does not reveal any large residuals. The solution's RMS of 0.00102 is substantially less than the criterion of 0.0286. Not surprisingly, as the dimensionality of the models increased, the corresponding residuals decreased and, therefore, so did the RMS. With respect to Tanaka's index, the two-dimensional solution's value is 0.9999. Although the two-dimensional 2P model has the lower RMS and larger Tanaka index, the application of Occam's razor leads us to *not* reject the unidimensional model of the data. Therefore, we conclude that our unidimensional model is a sufficiently accurate representation of the data to proceed with the IRT calibration.[5] Appendix E contains an approximate chi-square statistic that can be used to supplement NOHARM's fit information.

Calibration Result, BIGSTEPS

With BIGSTEPS a text (i.e., an ASCII) input file is created that contains control information for the calibration. The first few lines of this file are presented below; the text

TABLE 3.2. Abridged One-Dimensional Analysis Output

```
                              NOHARM
               Fitting a (multidimensional) Normal Ogive
                   by Harmonic Analysis - Robust Method

      Input File : math1D.dat

      Title :  5 Items/ one dimension / product-moment input

      Number of items         =  5
      Number of dimensions     =  1
      Number of subjects       =  19601

      An exploratory solution has been requested.

Sample Product-Moment Matrix
            1       2       3       4       5
      1    0.566
      2    0.275   0.387
      3    0.317   0.223   0.427
      4    0.531   0.360   0.401   0.887
      5    0.442   0.302   0.352   0.607   0.644

Item Covariance Matrix
            1       2       3       4       5
      1    0.246
      2    0.056   0.237
      3    0.076   0.057   0.245
      4    0.028   0.017   0.022   0.100
      5    0.078   0.053   0.077   0.035   0.229


Fixed Guesses
       1       2       3       4       5
      0.0     0.0     0.0     0.0     0.0

Initial Constants
            1       2       3       4       5
      1    0.186  -0.320  -0.206   1.356   0.413

                          =======
                          Results
                          =======
Success. The job converged to the specified criterion.

:


Residual Matrix (lower off-diagonals)
            1       2       3       4
      2   -0.002
      3    1.5e-4  -0.001
      4    7.9e-5   0.003   0.004
      5    0.001    0.002  -5.0e-4  -0.005


   Sum of squares of residuals (lower off-diagonals)     = 0.0000543
   Root mean square of residuals (lower off-diagonals) =  0.0023298    ⇐ The RMS
   Tanaka index of goodness of fit                      =  0.9996365    ⇐ The GFI
:
```

following an "⇐" is not part of the file and is provided to help the reader understand the command.

```
;Rasch Calibration of Mathematics data
&INST                              ⇐ required (NAMELIST structure)
TITLE='rasch calibration math data'
NI=5                               ⇐ number of items
ITEM1=6                            ⇐ item responses begin in column 6
XWIDE=1                            ⇐ item responses occupy 1 column
CODES=01                           ⇐ possible item response codes; responses are binary
NCOLS=10                           ⇐ last column of item responses
MODELS=R                           ⇐ model declaration
STBIAS=Y                           ⇐ use bias correction factor[6]
GROUPS=0                           ⇐ part of model declaration
TABLES=1110011001101000100000     ⇐ specifying which output tables to produce
  :
&END                               ⇐ required (NAMELIST structure)
  :
```

For this example, a single file (MATH.CON) contains both the control information and the response data. Alternatively, we can keep the control information and the data in separate files. If the data reside in a separate file, our command file contains the DATA command followed by the data file name (e.g., DATA=MATH.DAT; it is assumed that all files reside in the same folder [i.e., subdirectory]). The number of items is identified with the NI command. The ITEM1 and XWIDE commands are used to define how the response data are read. For example, our ITEM1 and XWIDE commands indicate that the response vectors begin in column 6 and each response occupies one column, respectively. Because these data are already in a binary format, the CODES command simply identifies the values 0 and 1. However, if the data are not in a 0/1 format, then the response codes in the data file would be identified on the CODES command and a KEY1 command would be inserted into the command file to identify which responses should be converted to 1; by omission all other responses are converted to 0.

BIGSTEPS can produce a plethora of results. All results are presented in tables and the user can control which tables are presented in the output file by using the TABLES command. The TABLES command consists of 1s and 0s, where a 1 indicates that a table should be displayed in the output file, otherwise it should be suppressed. For instance, our TABLES command indicates that we want tables 1, 2, and 3 displayed in the output file, tables 4 and 5 should be suppressed, tables 6 and 7 should be shown in the output file, and so on.

The output file always contains two tables. These default tables, Table 0.1 and Table 0.2, appear at the end of the output file and are presented in Table 3.3. (We use the Courier font for BIGSTEPS' table labels.) Table 0.1 shows the program control parameter settings (e.g., convergence criterion, number of items, metric scaling, etc.), whereas Table 0.2 presents the iteration history. These tables should be the first tables examined.

TABLE 3.3. BIGSTEPS Abridged Program Control Parameters (Table 0.1) and Iteration History Table (Table 0.2)

```
TABLE 0.1 rasch calibration math data
---------------------------------------------------------------------------------
         TITLE= rasch calibration math data
CONTROL FILE: MATH.CON
 OUTPUT FILE: MATH.LST

CONTROL VARIABLES:
Input Data Format      PAIRED = N              Item Delete/Anchor
  DATA =               REALSE = N              IDFILE =
 NAME1 = 1             STBIAS = Y              IDELQU = N
NAMLEN = 5             ---------------         IAFILE =
 ITEM1 = 6             Misfit Selection        IANCHQ = N
 ITLEN = 30             FITI = 2.000           ---------------
    NI = 5              FITP = 2.000           Person Delete/Anchor
 XWIDE = 1             OUTFIT = Y              PDFILE =
:
:
PERSON = CASE          ---------------         RFILE =
 ASCII = Y             Convergence Control     SFILE =
---------------         MPROX = 10             XFILE =
User Scaling           MUCON = 25              ---------------
 UMEAN = .000          LCONV = .010            Data Reformat
USCALE = 1.000         RCONV = .500            FORMAT =
UDECIM = 2             TARGET = N              GRPFRM = N
 UANCH = Y             ---------------         KEYFRM = 0
---------------        Scale Structure         MODFRM = N
Adjustment             GROUPS = 0              RESFRM = N
EXTRSC = .500          MODELS = R              SPFILE =
 HIADJ = .250          STKEEP = N              ---------------
LOWADJ = .250          ---------------
19601 CASE   Records Input

TABLE 0.2 rasch calibration math data
INPUT: 19601 CASES, 5 ITEMS
---------------------------------------------------------------------------------
                              CONVERGENCE TABLE

+------------------------------------------------------------------------------+
|   PROX         ACTIVE COUNT       EXTREME 5 RANGE      MAX LOGIT CHANGE       |
| ITERATION   CASES  ITEMS  CATS    CASES    ITEMS      MEASURES     STEPS      |
| ---------------------------------------------------------------------------- |
|     1       19601    5     10      2.77     1.14        2.0650                |
|     2       15525    5     10      3.17     1.69         .8874                |
|     3       15525    5     10      3.58     1.76         .2125                |
| ---------------------------------------------------------------------------- |
|   UCON      MAX SCORE   MAX LOGIT   LEAST CONVERGED     CATEGORY     STEP     |
| ITERATION   RESIDUAL*    CHANGE   CASE  ITEM   CAT      RESIDUAL    CHANGE    |
| ---------------------------------------------------------------------------- |
|     1        428.35     -.1716      2    5*                                   |
|     2        153.49     -.0581      2    5*                                   |
|     3         92.02     -.0434      2    4*                                   |
|     4         58.32     -.0317      7    4*                                   |
|     5         39.53     -.0211      7    4*                                   |
|     6         26.04     -.0147    167    4*                                   |
|     7         16.26     -.0097    167    4*                                   |
|     8         11.04     -.0063    167    4*                                   |
|     9          5.72     -.0043    167    5*                                   |
|    10          4.40     -.0023      7    4*                                   |
|    11          2.74     -.0016    167    4*                                   |
|    12          1.24     -.0010    167    4*                                   |
|    13         -1.24     -.0006    167    3*                                   |
|    14           .94     -.0006    167    4*                                   |
|    15          -.66     -.0004    167    2*                                   |
|    16          -.65     -.0003    167    2*                                   |
|    17          -.49     -.0002    167    3*                                   |
+------------------------------------------------------------------------------+
Standardized Residuals N(0,1)  Mean:  .01 S.D.: 1.03
```

Table 0.1 should be inspected to verify that the program control parameters are correct and that the data have been read correctly. Subsequently, the iteration history (Table 0.2) should be examined to ensure that convergence is achieved.

BIGSTEPS (and WINSTEPS) uses a normal approximation estimation procedure called PROX as a preprocessing step to provide good starting values for the UCON procedure; PROX assumes a normal distribution of ability to simplify calculations. We see that PROX iterated three times before achieving convergence; Table 0.1 shows that the default maximum iterations for PROX (i.e., MPROX) is 10. The ACTIVE COUNT columns indicates how many persons, items, and categories (5 items * two categories: 0, 1) the program started with and how many remain after deletion of 0 and perfect response vectors (i.e., response vectors that contain all 0s or all 1s, respectively). After removing 4076 people (19,601 – 15,525) that had either 0 or perfect response vectors, there are 15,525 examinees remaining.[7] If the number of CASES under ACTIVE COUNT at the first iteration does not match the number of persons to be used in the calibration, then the data file was not correctly read. In this example the ACTIVE COUNT CASES column shows that the program read the correct number of individuals (i.e., 19,601). The EXTREME 5 RANGE columns provide an estimate of the dispersion between the mean $\hat{\theta}$ of the top 5 and the mean $\hat{\theta}$ of the bottom 5 persons (labeled CASES) as well as a current estimate of the spread between the mean $\hat{\delta}$ of the top 5 and the mean $\hat{\delta}$ of the bottom 5 (labeled ITEMS). Max Logit Change is the logit change across iterations for persons (labeled MEASURES) and, if relevant, for items (labeled STEPS). In a well-behaved situation these values should decrease as the number of iterations increases.

The bottom portion of Table 0.2 contains the iteration history for UCON. By default the maximum number of UCON iterations is unlimited, but we have it set to 25 (see Table 0.1: MUCON = 25) to avoid having to abort the program's execution in case of convergence problems. That is, if UCON performs a large number of iterations, then it is having difficulty converging to a solution. This may be due to many reasons, such as the data not conforming to the model or to a misspecified command file (e.g., the item responses are not in the columns specified in the command file). In this example UCON converged in 17 iterations. Convergence for UCON is controlled by criteria associated with MAX SCORE RESIDUAL and MAX LOGIT CHANGE columns. The MAX SCORE RESIDUAL is the maximum change in the residuals for an item or a person across iterations (i.e., the numerator of the step size discussed in Appendix A); the SCORE RESIDUAL is the difference between observed and expected scores (for a person or an item). In contrast, MAX LOGIT CHANGE is the maximum change in the location of a person or an item from one iteration to the next. Both of these should progressively decrease as the program iterates to a solution. Convergence is defined by RCONV for MAX SCORE RESIDUAL and by LCONV for MAX LOGIT CHANGE. In this example the (default) convergence criterion for items is 0.01 (see Table 0.1: LCONV = 0.010) and for persons it is 0.5 (see Table 0.1: RCONV = 0.500). We can see that both MAX SCORE RESIDUAL and MAX LOGIT CHANGE decrease as UCON iterated to convergence.

The LEAST CONVERGED columns present for persons (labeled CASE) the ordinal position of the person that is farthest from meeting convergence criterion and for items (labeled ITEM) the ordinal position of the item that is farthest from meeting the criterion.

With respect to persons individuals 2, 7, 167 and ITEMs 2 through 5 were identified. If we had experienced a convergence problem, then this information might be useful in rectifying the problem.

At the bottom of Table 0.2 we find the MEAN and standard deviation (S.D.) of the standardized residuals. These residuals should follow a normal distribution and have a mean close to 0.0 and a standard deviation of approximately 1.0. MEAN and S.D. values that are substantially different from these ideal values indicate that the data do not follow the Rasch model assumptions (Linacre & Wright, 2001). Moreover, if these descriptive statistics indicate a departure from the assumption that randomness is normally distributed, then the fit statistics, INFIT and OUTFIT, are adversely affected. Our descriptive statistics do not indicate any problems. Because Table 0.2's information does not show any difficulties in calibrating the data, we proceed to examine model–level fit and then item–level fit.

Model–Data Fit Assessment

Model Level Fit

BIGSTEPS' TABLE 3.1 (Table 3.4) contains model–level fit results. TABLE 3.1 is divided into a top half containing respondent information (labeled SUMMARY OF ... CASES) and a bottom-half containing item information (labeled SUMMARY OF ... ITEMS).

TABLE 3.1's second line (labeled INPUT:) indicates that 15,525 of 19,601 examinees and all five items were used for calibration (i.e., 4076 examinees were dropped, but no items were removed from the calibration). These 15,525 respondents are the NON EXTREME examinees. (In BIGSTEPS parlance respondents are classified as either EXTREME or NON EXTREME. An EXTREME respondent has either a zero or perfect observed score, whereas a NON EXTREME respondent does not.) From the top half of TABLE 3.1 we see why 4076 individuals were removed from the analysis. Specifically, 3385 of the 4076 dropped examinees obtained the MAXIMUM EXTREME SCORE of 5 (i.e., these persons correctly responded to all items, X = 5) and 691 obtained the MINIMUM EXTREME SCORE of 0 (i.e., these persons incorrectly responded to all items).

The MEAN observed score for the 15,525 individuals is 2.6 with an S.D. of 1.1. After removing the zero and perfect scores, the maximum (MAX.) and minimum (MIN.) observed scores are 4 and 1, respectively. The COUNT column refers to the number of items attempted. The COUNT column's MEAN and S.D. of 5 and 0, respectively, reflects that no items were omitted. These descriptive statistics are also presented in logits for both person $\hat{\theta}$s (labeled MEASURE) and their corresponding standard errors (labeled MODEL ERROR). The average person location estimate is 0.18 with an average standard error of 1.19; the standard deviation of the person location estimates is 1.39. The least able person is located at –2 (i.e., MIN) and the most able person is at 1.95 (i.e., MAX).

BIGSTEPS (and WINSTEPS) produces two fit statistics, INFIT and OUTFIT, for examining model–data fit. In the following paragraphs we define these statistics and then discuss them in the context of the example. INFIT and OUTFIT provide information concerning discrepancies in responses, depending on whether the discrepancies occur close to or farther away from the estimated parameter. These fit statistics are calculated for both persons

TABLE 3.4. Rasch (BIGSTEPS) Calibration Summary Results for the Mathematics Test Data

```
TABLE 3.1   rasch calibration math data
INPUT: 19601 CASES, 5 ITEMS  ANALYZED: 15525 CASES, 5 ITEMS, 10 CATS        v2.82
-------------------------------------------------------------------------------

          SUMMARY OF 15525 MEASURED (NON-EXTREME) CASES
+----------------------------------------------------------------------------+
|              RAW                        MODEL      INFIT        OUTFIT      |
|            SCORE      COUNT    MEASURE   ERROR   MNSQ  ZSTD    MNSQ  ZSTD    |
|          ------------------------------------------------------------------|
|  MEAN      2.6        5.0        .18     1.19    .98    .0    1.03    .1    |
|  S.D.      1.1         .0       1.39      .13    .66   1.0    1.40   1.2    |
|  MAX.      4.0        5.0       1.95     1.42   3.37   4.5    9.90   9.8    |
|  MIN.      1.0        5.0      -2.00     1.06    .28  -1.3     .16   -.7    |
|          ------------------------------------------------------------------|
|  REAL RMSE  1.34  ADJ.SD   .39  SEPARATION  .29  CASE   RELIABILITY  .08    |
| MODEL RMSE  1.19  ADJ.SD   .72  SEPARATION  .61  CASE   RELIABILITY  .27    |
|  S.E. OF CASE   MEAN   .01                                                  |
|  WITH  4076 EXTREME CASES  = 19601 CASES    MEAN   .53  S.D.   1.75         |
|  REAL RMSE  1.39  ADJ.SD  1.06  SEPARATION  .76  CASE   RELIABILITY  .37    |
| MODEL RMSE  1.28  ADJ.SD  1.19  SEPARATION  .93  CASE   RELIABILITY  .46    |
+----------------------------------------------------------------------------+

  MAXIMUM EXTREME SCORE: 3385 CASES
  MINIMUM EXTREME SCORE:  691 CASES

     SUMMARY OF     5 MEASURED ITEMS
+----------------------------------------------------------------------------+
|              RAW                        MODEL      INFIT        OUTFIT      |
|            SCORE      COUNT    MEASURE   ERROR   MNSQ  ZSTD    MNSQ  ZSTD    |
|          ------------------------------------------------------------------|
|  MEAN    8029.8    15525.0       .00      .02   1.00  -1.2    1.06   -.2    |
|  S.D.    3499.1         .0      1.24      .00    .11   7.3     .21   7.2    |
|  MAX.   14010.0    15525.0      1.27      .02   1.17   9.9    1.39   9.9    |
|  MIN.    4207.0    15525.0     -2.21      .02    .86  -9.9     .78  -9.9    |
|          ------------------------------------------------------------------|
|  REAL RMSE   .02  ADJ.SD  1.24  SEPARATION 68.25  ITEM   RELIABILITY 1.00  |
| MODEL RMSE   .02  ADJ.SD  1.24  SEPARATION 70.09  ITEM   RELIABILITY 1.00  |
|  S.E. OF ITEM   MEAN   .62                                                  |
+----------------------------------------------------------------------------+
```

and items at the individual person and item levels. Therefore, each individual and item has both an INFIT and OUTFIT statistic. For persons the statistics' calculations involve a sum across items, whereas for items the sum is across people.

INFIT is a *weighted* fit statistic based on the squared standardized residual between what is observed and what would be expected on the basis of the model (i.e., a chi-square-like statistic). These squared standardized residuals are information weighted and then summed across observations (i.e., items or people); the weight is $p_j(1 - p_j)$. These "chi-square" statistics are averaged to produce the INFIT mean-square statistic; the mean square is labeled MNSQ in the output.

OUTFIT is also based on the squared standardized residual between what is observed and what would be expected, but the squared standardized residual is not weighted when summed across observations (i.e., items or people). As such, OUTFIT is an *unweighted* standardized fit statistic. As is the case with the INFIT statistic, the OUTFIT statistic is transformed to a mean square and labeled MNSQ in the output.

These two statistics differ in their sensitivity to where the discrepancy between what is observed and what is expected occurs. For instance, and from a person fit perspective, responses on items located near the person's $\hat{\theta}$ that are in line with what would be expected produce INFIT values close to 1 (given the stochastic nature of the model). However, responses on items located near the person's $\hat{\theta}$ that are not *in* line with what would be expected lead to large *IN*FIT values. That is, INFIT is sensitive to unexpected responses near the person's $\hat{\theta}$. In contrast, OUTFIT has a value close to its expected value of 1 when responses on items located away from a person's $\hat{\theta}$ are consistent with what is predicted by the model (again, given the stochastic nature of the model). However, unexpected responses on items located away from a person's $\hat{\theta}$ (i.e., "*outlier*" responses) lead to *OUT*-FIT values substantially greater than 1. That is, OUTFIT is sensitive to, say, a high-ability person incorrectly responding to an easy item or a low-ability person correctly responding to a hard item. One has an analogous interpretation for these fit statistics when used for item fit analysis.

The range of INFIT and OUTFIT is 0 to infinity with an expectation of 1; their distributions are positively skewed. Values that are above or below 1 indicate different types of misfit. For example, values substantially less than 1 may be indicative of dependency or overfit, whereas values substantially greater than 1 may reflect noise in the data. Although there are various interpretation guidelines, one guideline states that values from 0.5 to 1.5 are "okay," with values greater than 2 warranting closer inspection of the associated person or item. Smith, Schumacker, and Bush (1998) state that using a common cutoff value does not necessarily result in correct Type I error rates. They echo Wright's suggestion (see Smith et al., 1998) to take sample size into account when interpreting INFIT and OUTFIT by using $1 \pm 2/\sqrt{N}$ and $1 \pm 6/\sqrt{N}$ as cutoff values, respectively.

Given INFIT's and OUTFIT's expectations and their range, it is clear that there is an asymmetry in their scales. Therefore, INFIT and OUTFIT are transformed to have a scale that is symmetric about 0.0. The result of this transformation is a standardized (0, 1) fit statistic, ZSTD. Such ZSTDs are obtained by using a cube root transformation of the MNSQs to make them normally distributed and to have a range from $-\infty$ to ∞. Good fit is indicated by INFIT ZSTD and OUTFIT ZSTD values close to 0. Because the ZSTDs are approximate t statistics, as sample size increases these "t statistics" approach z statistics. As such, values of ± 2 are sometimes used for identifying items or people that warrant further inspection; for inferential testing the null hypothesis is perfect model–data fit. In our output the standardized INFIT statistic is labeled INFIT ZSTD and the standardized OUTFIT statistic is labeled OUTFIT ZSTD. INFIT ZSTD and OUTFIT ZSTD correspond to the standardized INFIT MNSQ and OUTFIT MNSQ, respectively. See Linacre and Wright (2001) and Smith (1991, 2004) for more information on INFIT and OUTFIT and their transformations.

Returning to our example, one sees that the top half of BIGSTEPS' TABLE 3.1 (Table 3.4) contains descriptive statistics for the overall person fit, whereas the bottom half contains descriptive statistics associated with overall item fit. In general, because INFIT is weighted and is concerned with responses close to the person's estimated location, it should be looked at first. Because these mean INFIT MNSQ and OUTFIT MNSQ values are close to their expected value of 1.0, we conclude that most of the participants are behaving consistently with the model. The variability of these fit statistics (S.D. = 0.66 for INFIT and S.D. = 1.40 for OUTFIT) as well as the maximum fit statistics (e.g., maximum OUTFIT MNSQ =

9.9) indicate that not all individuals are responding consistently with the model. The reasons for these maxima are discussed below.

Additional fit information provided in TABLE 3.1 comes from REAL RMSE and MODEL RMSE. REAL RMSE and MODEL RMSE are calculated both with and without deleted persons (i.e., with and without the 4076 EXTREME CASES). REAL RMSE is the root mean squared error calculated from the perspective that misfit is due to departures in the data from model specifications, whereas MODEL RMSE is the same statistic, but calculated from the perspective that the data fit the model; "REAL" means that the statistics have been adjusted for misfit encountered in the data (Linacre & Wright, 2001). Both RMSEs are calculated for persons and items. The top half of TABLE 3.1 contains the calculations for people and the bottom half contains the calculations for items. Small values of these two statistics indicate a good situation, with large values of REAL RMSE reflecting departures in the data from the model. These statistics' values indicate that we're doing a better job with the items than with the people.

In general, one typically administers an instrument in order to differentiate between persons located at different points along the latent variable. However, we may also be interested in how well an instrument can separate or distinguish items in terms of their latent variable locations. In this regard, the program produces the SEPARATION index for persons and for items.

The person SEPARATION index gives an indication of how well the instrument can separate or distinguish persons in terms of their latent variable locations. Although this index has a lower bound of 0, it does not have an upper bound. Because the SEPARATION index does not have a finite upper bound, it is sometimes difficult to determine what is a good large value. In contrast, the related RELIABILITY index is more easily interpreted than the SEPARATION index. Similar to coefficient alpha, the person RELIABILITY tells us about the consistency of the measures (i.e., $\hat{\theta}$s). Its range is from 0 to 1, with values close to or at 1 considered better than values approaching or at 0. For our example, the RELIABILITY for the REAL RMSE (nonextreme) line is 0.08. This value indicates that the mathematics instrument does not appear to be doing a good job of distinguishing people. We conjecture that this is due, in part, to the instrument's length of five items. These indices are further discussed in Appendix E, "The Separation and Reliability Indices."

In the subsection entitled WITH . . . EXTREME CASES . . . the RMSEs, ADJ. SDs, SEPARATIONs, and RELIABILITYs are repeated using all 19,601 respondents (i.e., including the 4076 EXTREME persons). Some may find comparing these results with those from the NON EXTREME individuals useful in determining the effect of the EXTREME persons on the overall fit. However, we ignore these results because they are affected by the value used in the estimation of the EXTREME persons (i.e., the EXTRSC estimation adjustment criterion that is discussed below).

The bottom half of TABLE 3.1 (labeled SUMMARY OF 5 MEASURED ITEMS) presents analogous information for items; MEASURE in this section refers to $\hat{\delta}$. As is the case with the person half, descriptive statistics on the items both in raw score and logit units are provided. For example, the mean item location estimate in logits is 0.0, with a standard deviation (labeled S.D.) of 1.24. It can also be seen that the lowest item location estimate is –2.21 (labeled MIN.) and the highest is located at 1.27 (labeled MAX.). Comparing these minimum and maximum location estimates with those of the persons (minimum = −2 and maximum = 1.95) shows that there is a match at the lower end of the continuum between the instrument's $\hat{\delta}$ range and the persons location estimates, but not at the upper end. Overall, the INFIT/OUTFIT MNSQ values, their lack of variability, and their minima and maxima indicate that the instrument *as a whole* appears to have model–data fit. This does not necessarily mean that we have fit for each item. Therefore, in the next section we examine item-level fit.

Analogous to the person SEPARATION index, the item SEPARATION index gives an indication of how well the instrument can separate or distinguish items in terms of their latent variable locations. The premise of this index is that we would like our items to be sufficiently well separated in terms of their locations in order to identify the direction and the meaning of the latent variable (Wright & Masters, 1982). In addition, we would like to see little estimation error. This last aspect is assessed by the (item) RELIABILITY index. As is the case with the person SEPARATION and RELIABILITY indices, our item SEPARATION and RELIABILITY indices are related. Therefore, despite the lack of an upper bound for the item SEPARATION index, we can interpret the item RELIABILITY index. Our REAL ITEM RELIABILITY of 1.00 indicates that the instrument is creating a well-defined variable, although it apparently is not performing well with respect to these people. It should be noted that whether this instrument is measuring the latent variable that is intended requires a validity study.

Item Level Fit and Item Location Estimates

Table 3.5 contains two BIGSTEPS tables, TABLE 13.1 and TABLE 13.2. We examine the item information presented in Table 3.5 prior to the person information because the ratio of persons to items favors item estimation. If there had been problems in estimating the items, then these problems could have potentially affected the estimation of the persons. Therefore, there would have been little reason to examine the person estimation output.

The column in TABLE 13.1 labeled MEASURE contains the item location estimates, $\hat{\delta}$s, and the ERROR column contains the corresponding standard errors of estimate, $s_e(\hat{\delta})$s. The column labeled RAW SCORE is the observed item score (i.e., the number of correct responses on item j, q_j) and COUNT is the number of respondents to the item; RAW SCORE divided by COUNT gives the item's traditional item difficulty, P_j. This table is displayed in descending order of item difficulty (i.e., MEASURE ORDER). The item location estimates for our items are $\hat{\delta}_1 = -2.21, \hat{\delta}_2 = -0.26, \hat{\delta}_3 = 0.20, \hat{\delta}_4 = 1.01,$ and $\hat{\delta}_5 = 1.27$, each with a standard error of 0.02.

TABLE 13.1 also shows the values of the item-level fit statistics for each item in the INFIT MNSQ and OUTPUT MNSQ columns. Recall that values around 1 are considered good, with values substantially different from 1 indicating either dependency or noise. Following Smith et al.'s (1998) suggestion of using $1 \pm 2/\sqrt{N}$ and $1 \pm 6/\sqrt{N}$ for defining INFIT and OUTFIT cutoff values, the acceptable range for INFIT would be 0.9839 to 1.0161 (inclusive) and for OUTFIT the range would be 0.9518 to 1.0482 (inclusive). Using these criteria, and regardless of whether INFIT or OUTFIT is examined, items 1 and 5 would be flagged as exhibiting misfit and warranting further inspection. However, with a sample

TABLE 3.5. Rasch (BIGSTEPS) Item Location Estimates for the Mathematics Test Data

```
TABLE 13.1 rasch calibration math data
INPUT: 19601 CASES, 5 ITEMS  ANALYZED: 15525 CASES, 5 ITEMS, 10 CATS      v2.82
-----------------------------------------------------------------------------

           ITEMS STATISTICS:  MEASURE ORDER

+----------------------------------------------------------------------------+
|ENTRY   RAW                      |  INFIT  |  OUTFIT |PTBIS|               |
|NUMBR  SCORE  COUNT  MEASURE ERROR|MNSQ  ZSTD|MNSQ  ZSTD|CORR.| ITEMS  G   |
|----------------------------------+---------+---------+-----+---------     |
|    5   4207 15525     1.27   .02|1.17   9.9|1.39   9.9| -.07| ITEM5  0   |
|    4   4984 15525     1.01   .02| .98  -2.3|1.05   2.4|  .08| ITEM4  0   |
|    3   7709 15525      .20   .02| .93  -7.4| .91  -7.0|  .15| ITEM3  0   |
|    2   9239 15525     -.26   .02| .86  -9.9| .78  -9.9|  .22| ITEM2  0   |
|    1  14010 15525    -2.21   .02|1.07   3.7|1.17   3.4|  .02| ITEM1  0   |
|----------------------------------+---------+---------+-----+---------     |
|MEAN   8030.15525.      .00   .02|1.00  -1.2|1.06   -.2|     |            |
|S.D.   3499.    0.     1.24   .00| .11   7.3| .21   7.2|     |            |
+----------------------------------------------------------------------------+
                      :
TABLE 13.2 rasch calibration math data
INPUT: 19601 CASES, 5 ITEMS  ANALYZED: 15525 CASES, 5 ITEMS, 10 CATS      v2.82
-----------------------------------------------------------------------------

           ITEMS FIT GRAPH:  MEASURE ORDER

+--------------------------------------------------------------------+
|ENTRY| MEASURE | · INFIT MEAN-SQUARE  | OUTFIT MEAN-SQUARE  |        |
|NUMBR| -     + |0    0.7 1 1.3      2|0    0.7 1 1.3      2| ITEMS G|
|-----+---------+----------------------+---------------------+--------|
|    5|       * |    :   .* :         |      :   .   *      | ITEM5 0|
|    4|      *  |    : *. :           |      :   *  :       | ITEM4 0|
|    3|    *    |    : *. :           |      : *. :         | ITEM3 0|
|    2|  *      |    :* . :           |      *  . :         | ITEM2 0|
|    1|*        |    : *  :           |      :  .* :        | ITEM1 0|
+--------------------------------------------------------------------+
                      :
```

size of 15,525 persons these criteria result in very little tolerance of deviation from the expected value of 1. (There does not appear to be empirical justification for these sample size-dependent criteria.)

Additional item fit information is available in TABLE 13.2: ITEMS FIT GRAPH. In this graph the vertical lines consisting of colons delimit common cutoff points at 0.7 and 1.3. This graph shows that all the items fall within the 1 ± 0.3 interval. That is, there does not appear to be any apparent serious fit problems because the fit statistics are within acceptable bounds. (The use of a common cutoff ignores the fact that large samples tend to provide more accurate estimates than smaller samples, all things being equal. As such, some individuals do not consider these common cutoffs as useful as criteria that take into account sample size, like those in the previous paragraph.)

Although we feel comfortable with the above evidence supporting item-level data fit, our discussion continues in order to show one approach for diagnosing misfit. In practice, any item(s) flagged as potentially problematic would be examined in an attempt to determine the cause of the misfit. For example, is the misfit due to misfitting people, is it due to individuals located far away from the item's location not responding as expected, is the misfit due to a few individuals or many, is it due to poor item wording? Depending on the diagnosis we may need to consider eliminating the item from the instrument. If we eliminate one or more items, then it would be necessary to recalibrate the instrument, because each individual could have a potentially different observed score and the original estimate of the person's location could have been adversely affected by the deleted item(s).

In the current context, the items flagged for further inspection are the easiest (item 1) and hardest (item 5) items on the instrument. This finding may be related to the above-mentioned maximum person OUTFIT MNSQ value of 9.9 (OUTFIT ZSTD = 9.8). For example, the response patterns 00001 and 01111 would lead to misfitting persons. In fact, Table 2.1 (Chapter 2) shows that there are 184 persons with a pattern of 00001 and 40 with a pattern of 01111. For the 00001 pattern, the most difficult item is correctly answered (e.g., by guessing) and all easier items are not. This pattern is inconsistent with the model. Conversely, the 01111 shows that the easiest item is incorrectly answered (e.g., owing to inattentiveness), but the more difficult items are answered correctly. Again, this pattern is inconsistent with the model. Individuals providing either of these two patterns would most likely be identified as misfitting. As such, person misfit can impact item misfit.

In its TABLE 11.1 BIGSTEPS provides an *item's* response vector (i.e., all the responses to an item) with the corresponding standardized residuals to aid in diagnosing item misfit. Table 3.6 contains a small portion of TABLE 11.1. The format of this table is the item label (e.g., for item 5 the label is 5 ITEM5; "ITEM5" is a user supplied label) along with the item's location estimate ($\hat{\delta}_5 = 1.27$) and its INFIT ZSTD and OUTFIT ZSTD values. The subsequent line contains the responses from the first 25 persons to item 5 (i.e., persons 1–8 responded incorrectly to item 5, person 9 correctly responded, person 10 responded incorrectly, and so on. The next line shows the standardized residuals (Z-RESIDUAL) information corresponding to each of these responses. A positive number indicates an unexpected response from primarily lower-ability individuals (i.e., a correct response) and a negative value reflects an unexpected response from primarily higher-ability persons (i.e., an incorrect response); an X reflects that the person providing the response is an EXTREME individual. These latter two lines are repeated for the remaining persons in the data set.

We see from Table 3.6 that there are a number of standardized residuals of 2 and 5 for item 5, as well as –3, –5, and –9 for item 1. Matching the response data with the persons with Z-RESIDUALs of 5 shows that they come from individuals (persons 4,815 and 13,500) who provided the response vector 00001; the Z-RESIDUAL = 2 comes from individuals (persons 25, 38, etc.) with the response vector 10001. With respect to item 1, the Z-RESIDUAL of –9 (person 358) is associated with a response vector of 01111 (i.e., an incorrect response to the easiest item from a high-ability person), a Z-RESIDUAL of –5 (person 45) is associated with $\underline{x}$ = 01110, and Z-RESIDUAL of –3 (person 20) comes from $\underline{x}$ = 01010. In short, the largest absolute standardized residuals came from persons with response vectors that are inconsistent with the model. Using just this information (i.e., as opposed to the question's wording), we attribute items 1 and 5's fit issue to these individuals and do not consider it to be an issue. These individuals are further discussed below when we review individual person fit information.

TABLE 3.6. Abridged Item Misfit Information for Poorly Fitting Items 1 and 5

```
TABLE 11.1 rasch calibration math data
INPUT: 19601 CASES, 5 ITEMS  ANALYZED: 15525 CASES, 5 ITEMS, 10 CATS      v2.82
--------------------------------------------------------------------------------
TABLE OF POORLY FITTING ITEMS      (CASES   IN ENTRY ORDER)
NUMBER - NAME -- POSITION ------ MEASURE - INFIT (ZSTD) OUTFIT

    5 ITEM5                          1.27     9.9     A     9.9
        RESPONSE:    1:  0 0 0 0 0   0 0 0 1 0   1 0 1 0 1   1 0 0 0 0   1 1 0 0 1
        Z-RESIDUAL:                          X       X X     X                 X               2

        RESPONSE:   26:  0 1 0 1 0   0 0 1 0 0   0 0 1 0 0   1 1 0 0 0   0 0 0 0 0
        Z-RESIDUAL:               X           X                    2
        :

        RESPONSE:  201:  0 0 0 1 1   0 1 0 1 1   1 0 0 1 0   0 0 0 0 1   0 0 0 0 0
        Z-RESIDUAL:            X X     X           X   X               X   X     2
        :

        RESPONSE:  751:  1 1 1 1 1   1 0 1 0 1   0 0 0 1 1   0 0 0 0 0   0 0 0 0 1
        Z-RESIDUAL:               X           X   X               X
        :

        RESPONSE: 4801:  0 1 0 0 0   0 0 0 0 0   0 0 0 0 1   0 0 1 0 0   0 1 0 1 0
        Z-RESIDUAL:               X           X                    5       2            X 2
        :

        RESPONSE:13476:  1 1 0 0 1   1 1 0 1 1   1 0 1 0 0   1 1 0 0 0   0 1 1 0 1
        Z-RESIDUAL:            X   X X       2     X   X       X 2               X     5
        :

        RESPONSE:19601:  1
        Z-RESIDUAL:


    1 ITEM1                         -2.21     3.7     B     3.4
        RESPONSE:    1:  1 1 1 1 1   1 1 1 1 1   1 1 1 1 1   1 1 0 1 0   1 1 1 1 1
        Z-RESIDUAL:                          X       X X     X           -3   X

        RESPONSE:   26:  1 1 1 1 1   1 1 1 1 0   1 1 1 1 1   1 1 1 1 0   1 1 1 1 1
        Z-RESIDUAL:               X           X  -3                        -5
        :

        RESPONSE:  351:  1 1 1 1 1   1 1 0 1 1   1 1 1 1 0   1 1 1 1 1   1 1 1 1 1
        Z-RESIDUAL:            X X         X X-9 X       X             X           X X   X
        :

        RESPONSE:19601:  1
        Z-RESIDUAL:
```

Person Information

Table 3.7 (an abridged TABLE 17.1) shows the person location estimates and corresponding fit information. ENTRY NUMBER is the case's ordinal position in the file, RAW SCORE is the person's observed score (X), COUNT is the number of items answered, MEASURE is the person's location (proficiency) estimate with its corresponding standard error of estimate (ERROR). Only the unique θs are shown are shown in Table 3.7. For observed scores of 0, 1, 2, 3, 4, and 5, the corresponding person estimates, $\hat{\theta}$s, are –3.19 (1.72), –2.00 (1.42), –0.43 (1.13), 0.73 (1.06), 1.95 (1.21), and 2.86 (1.55), respectively; the associated $s_e(\hat{\theta})$s are in parentheses. Therefore, all individuals who got one item correct (i.e., X = 1) have an estimated mathematics proficiency of –2.00, all individuals who correctly answered two items have –0.43 as their person location estimate, and so on (i.e., every person with a given X receives the same $\hat{\theta}$).

It may have been noted that BIGSTEPS provided $\hat{\theta}$s for X = 0 and X = 5 despite the fact that in Chapter 2 we demonstrated that it is not possible to obtain finite estimates for zero or perfect scores using MLE. BIGSTEPS obtains these location "estimates" by using a kludge. Specifically, it subtracts a fractional score point from the perfect score and adds the same fractional score point to the 0 score in order to create scores that are estimable. By default this fractional score point is 0.5 (the control parameter EXTRSC can be used to change this value).[8] Therefore, for estimating these EXTREME persons the perfect score of 5 is converted to 4.5 and the zero score becomes 0.5. Hence, the $\hat{\theta}$ of –3.19 is *not* the MLE corresponding to zero score and the $\hat{\theta}$ of 2.86 is *not* the MLE for a perfect score. Rather, these are artifacts of the particular fractional score point value used; some may consider this modification of X to be a form of imputation. It should be recalled that these extreme persons (i.e., X = 0 and X = 5) are not used for estimating item locations. Therefore, the choice of the fractional value does not affect the item location estimates.

TABLE 3.7. Abridged Person Estimate Table

```
TABLE 17.1 rasch calibration math.data
 INPUT: 19601 CASES, 5 ITEMS  ANALYZED: 15525 CASES, 5 ITEMS, 10 CATS      v2.82
-------------------------------------------------------------------------------

       CASE STATISTICS:  MEASURE ORDER

+-----------------------------------------------------------------------+
|ENTRY  RAW                        |  INFIT   | OUTFIT  |PTBIS|          |
|NUMBR  SCORE  COUNT  MEASURE  ERROR|MNSQ  ZSTD|MNSQ  ZSTD|CORR.| CASE    |
|--------------------------------------+----------+----------+-----+------|
|    9     5     5     2.86    1.55| MAXIMUM ESTIMATED MEASURE |       9|
|  :                                                                     |

|    7     4     5     1.95    1.21| .72  -.5| .45  -.2| .55|       7|
|  :                                                                     |

|    2     3     5      .73    1.06| .49 -1.3| .40  -.5| .80|       2|
|  :                                                                     |

|    1     2     5     -.43    1.13| .55  -.8| .41  -.7| .84|       1|
|  :                                                                     |

|    3     1     5    -2.00    1.42| .28  -.8| .16  -.5| .85|       3|
|  :                                                                     |

|19414     0     5    -3.19    1.72| MINIMUM ESTIMATED MEASURE | 19414|
|19585     0     5    -3.19    1.72| MINIMUM ESTIMATED MEASURE | 19585|
|--------------------------------------+----------+----------+-----+------|
| MEAN    3.    5.     .18    1.19| .98   .0|1.03   .1|     |          |
| S.D.    1.    0.    1.39     .13| .66  1.0|1.40  1.2|     |          |
+-----------------------------------------------------------------------+
```

The individual person INFIT and OUTFIT (Table 3.7) are defined analogously to the way they are defined for items (cf. Linacre & Wright, 2001, pp. 92–93). We do not present this fit information for all persons because there are potentially unique INFIT and OUTFIT values for each of our 19,601 examinees. That is, even though all persons with the same observed score have the same estimated location (and error), this does not mean the fit is the same for all persons with the same observed score. For instance, a person with a pattern consistent with the model, such as 11110, would have INFIT and OUTFIT values of 0.72 and 0.45, respectively. However, a person with the same observed score, but with the pattern 11011, would have an INFIT value of 1.46 and an OUTFIT value of 1.36. The interpretation of INFIT and OUTFIT is similar to that used with the item-level analysis. The overall model-level person fit information presented in Table 3.4 is based on the individual-level fit statistics shown in Table 3.7. As shown below, this individual-level person fit information facilitates identifying person-level problems.

Above it is mentioned that BIGSTEPS' TABLE 3.1 shows a maximum person OUTFIT MNSQ value of 9.9 (OUTFIT ZSTD = 9.8). We can explore these results by using different BIGSTEPS tables. For instance, BIGSTEPS can provide tables containing a plot of each individual's INFIT and OUTFIT values against his or her $\hat{\theta}$; these are BIGSTEPS' Tables 4 and 5. These plots would graphically depict the extensiveness of person misfit and the point(s) (if any) along the continuum where misfit is occurring, as well as give a sense of the distribution of these fit statistics. In addition, BIGSTEPS provides a table (TABLE 7.1) that displays the poorly fitting individuals along with their response vectors, $\hat{\theta}$, and fit information. We can examine this information to identify the reason for misfit. A snippet of BIGSTEPS' TABLE 7.1 is shown in Table 3.8. The table's format contains a column labeled NUMBER that refers to the case's ordinal position in the file, followed by the person's label (if any), location estimate (MEASURE), and INFIT ZSTD and OUTFIT ZSTD values. The subsequent line beginning with RESPONSE contains the person's item responses, and the responses' corresponding residuals are on the line labeled Z-RESIDUAL. For example, the first person listed is person 358 with a $\hat{\theta}$ = 1.95, INFIT ZSTD = 1.5, OUTFIT ZSTD = 9.8, and a response pattern of 01111.

From Table 3.8 we see that the OUTFIT ZSTD value of 9.8 is associated with persons who, although they have high proficiency estimates ($\hat{\theta}$ = 1.95), incorrectly answered the easiest item ($\hat{\delta}_1$ = −2.21) and correctly answered the remaining more difficult items; Table 2.1 shows that there are 40 individuals with this response vector (i.e., 01111). The incorrect response to the easiest item may have been due to carelessness, inattentiveness, or another factor. The Z-RESIDUAL's negative value associated with item 1 indicates that, according to the model, these persons were expected to respond correctly but did not; the magnitude of Z-RESIDUAL indicates the degree of discrepancy.

What should we do with these 40 misfitting individuals? If we are concerned that these persons are adversely affecting the item location estimation, then these individuals could be removed, the instrument recalibrated, and these persons assigned the $\hat{\theta}$ for an observed score of 4 from the recalibration results. However, these 40 examinees represent 0.2% of the sample and so their removal's potential impact on the accuracy of item parameter estimation should be minimal. This should not be interpreted to mean that the item parameter

TABLE 3.8. Abridged Person Response Vector Misfit Information for Poorly Fitting People

```
TABLE 7.1 rasch calibration math data
 INPUT: 19601 CASES, 5 ITEMS  ANALYZED: 15525 CASES, 5 ITEMS, 10 CATS      v2.82
 --------------------------------------------------------------------------------

 TABLE OF POORLY FITTING CASES    (ITEMS   IN ENTRY ORDER)
 NUMBER - NAME -- POSITION ------ MEASURE - INFIT (ZSTD) OUTFIT

   358   358                        1.95    1.5   A    9.8
         RESPONSE:    1:  0 1 1 1 1
      Z-RESIDUAL:        -9

  1236 1,236                        1.95    1.5   B    9.8
         RESPONSE:    1:  0 1 1 1 1
      Z-RESIDUAL:        -9

  2022 2,022                        1.95    1.5   C    9.8
         RESPONSE:    1:  0 1 1 1 1
      Z-RESIDUAL:        -9

  2349 2,349                        1.95    1.5   D    9.8
         RESPONSE:    1:  0 1 1 1 1
      Z-RESIDUAL:        -9

  2800 2,800                        1.95    1.5   E    9.8
         RESPONSE:    1:  0 1 1 1 1
      Z-RESIDUAL:        -9
       :
       <more examinees>
       :
```

estimates themselves would not change. Most likely the removal of these individuals would affect the $\hat{\delta}_j$s and, as such, would also affect the fit statistics for all the items, not only those for item 1.[9] However, the INFIT ZSTD for these 40 persons is 1.5 and this indicates less reason to be concerned about these individuals. That is, these persons are responding relatively consistently to items near their estimated ability. Given this rationale and the fact that the person OUTFIT value's magnitude is being driven by an anomalous response to just one item, these examinees are retained.

Invariance Assessment

Theoretically, IRT item parameters are invariant. In this regard, *invariance* refers to one or more parameter metrics that are interchangeable within a permissible transformation (cf. Rupp & Zumbo, 2006). However, whether invariance is realized in practice (i.e., with parameter estimates) is contingent on the degree of model–data fit. Therefore, the presence of invariance can be used as part of a model–data fit investigation. The quality of model–data fit may be assessed by randomly dividing the calibration sample into two subsamples.[10] Each of these subsamples is separately calibrated and their item parameter estimates compared to determine their degree of linearity. Therefore, one measure of agreement between the two samples' estimates is the Pearson Product–Moment correlation coefficient.

The first step in using invariance for assessing model–data fit is to randomly divide the sample in half. One way to do this is to assign a uniform random number to each individual. To create two subsamples of approximately equal size, this random number is compared to 0.50. If the random number for a person is greater than 0.50, then the individual belongs to one subsample, otherwise the person belongs to the other subsample. Applying this process to the example data produced two subsamples, one with 9780 persons and the other with 9821 individuals. Independent calibrations of each subsample resulted in $\hat{\delta}_1 = -2.18, \hat{\delta}_2 = -0.31, \hat{\delta}_3 = 0.22, \hat{\delta}_4 = 1.02$, and $\hat{\delta}_5 = 1.26$ for subsample 1 and $\hat{\delta}_1 = -2.25, \hat{\delta}_2 = -0.22, \hat{\delta}_3 = 0.18, \hat{\delta}_4 = 1.02$, and $\hat{\delta}_5 = 1.27$ for subsample 2. Therefore, subsample 1's item location estimates are not equal to the corresponding estimates in subsample 2, although they show the same rank order. The Pearson correlation coefficient between these two sets of item parameter estimates is 0.9991. Therefore, we have evidence of invariance across these subsamples. This result provides additional evidence of model–data fit. (It should be noted that a large Pearson correlation coefficient is a necessary, but not a sufficient, condition for invariance; e.g., see Rupp & Zumbo [2004].) For completeness, the Pearson correlation coefficient between the first subsample's estimates and those of the "full" sample (N = 15,525) is 0.9998 and for the second subsample's $\hat{\delta}$s the correlation with the full sample $\hat{\delta}$s is 0.9998. The implication of the magnitude of these correlations is that we can use a linear transformation to convert the estimates on one metric to that of the other metric without any loss of information concerning model–data fit or person and item location estimates.

Why do the estimates across subsamples not agree with one another even though there is apparent model–data fit? The primary reason is that, as stated above, the latent variable continuum's metric is not absolute, but rather is defined with respect to the information available for estimation. Each sample defines the continuum's metric for the item location estimates. A second reason is that the estimates have some error as indicated by $s_e(\hat{\delta})$. The relative nature of the metrics is not problematic as long as the metrics are highly linearly related. When this is true, then we can use a linear transformation to convert from one metric to the other.

How do the "by hand" calculations from Chapter 2 (Table 2.3) compare with those of BIGSTEPS? A comparison of BIGSTEPS' $\hat{\delta}$s based on the full sample with those obtained by hand reveals that the values do not correspond exactly. For example, the estimated by-hand item 1 location is −2.5118, but BIGSTEPS estimated its location to be −2.18. However, the two sets of item parameter estimates are highly linearly related (r = 0.9999). The primary reason for the difference between our by-hand estimates and BIGSTEPS' is due to algorithmic differences. In essence, the hand calculations performed step 1 of the JMLE process and did not "ping-pong" between JMLE's steps 1 and 2. In addition, we used a stricter convergence criterion of 0.0001 in our hand-based calculations than did BIGSTEPS (i.e., LCONV= 0.01).

Of course, if the metric for the hand-based calculations does not match that of BIGSTEPS, then there is no reason to believe the hand-based $\hat{\theta}$s will be equal to BIGSTEPS' $\hat{\theta}$s (i.e., the $\hat{\theta}$s are on the same metric as the $\hat{\delta}$s). However, if the two metrics are highly linearly related, then so will the corresponding $\hat{\theta}$s be. A comparison of the $\hat{\theta}$s from Table 2.2 and those from BIGSTEPS (i.e., for X = 1, 2, 3, 4 the $\hat{\theta}$s are −2.00, −0.43, 0.73, and 1.95, respectively) shows that the two sets of estimates do not match. However, the two sets of $\hat{\theta}$s are highly linearly related (r = 0.9990).

Validity Evidence

Recall that prior to estimating the item and person locations we assumed that we had content validity evidence for our instrument. Stated another way, we subjected our instrument to a rational analysis to determine whether the items were measuring mathematics proficiency. Moreover, we examined the instrument to make sure that there were no items that, owing to nonmathematical proficiency factor(s), could disadvantage some individuals. Although we have successfully applied the Rasch model to the data set (i.e., we have model–data fit), it is still necessary to acquire additional validity evidence for the $\hat{\theta}$s in terms of the mathematics construct as well as criterion-related validity.

Obtaining construct- and criterion-related validity evidence may be accomplished via traditional validation approaches. For instance, if there were additional measures of mathematics proficiency that could serve as criteria (e.g., performance in mathematics courses), then one could obtain criterion-related validity evidence by regressing each of these measures on our instrument's $\hat{\theta}$s. Obtaining construct validity evidence can involve making predictions about differential performance between groups and determining whether the instrument correctly differentiates between the groups. For example, if the instrument purports to measure mathematics at and beyond algebra, then it should be able to correctly identify individuals who have a knowledge of algebra and higher-level mathematics from those who do not. Additional approaches may include the application of the multitrait–multimethod validity paradigm (Campbell & Fiske, 1959).

As part of this validation process we should also perform a *differential item functioning* (DIF) analysis (Chapter 12 contains an overview of DIF). The DIF analysis is used to determine whether performance on any of the items differs for certain groups of individuals (e.g., females vs. males) after controlling for differences in person location. Although this is discussed in greater detail in Chapter 12, for now suffice it to say that the premise of DIF is that if one matches, for example, males and females on mathematics proficiency, then the probability of correctly responding to an item should be the same for females and males. If we find that the probability of correctly responding to an item for males is less than that for females (or vice versa), then the item is functioning differentially across gender. In this case, the item would appear to be measuring not only the construct of interest, mathematics proficiency, but also an additional tangential or nuisance factor(s) associated with gender (see Ackerman, 1992; Kok, 1988).

Summary of the Application of the Rasch Model

In general, the application of the Rasch model proceeds by administering a set of items to a sample of individuals, performing a model–data fit analysis, and examining items and persons for poor model–data fit. The fit analysis is performed on the basis of both graphical and statistical fit indices. The examination of items flagged as poorly fitting is concerned with discovering why an item is identified as a poor fit to the model. For instance, if the item misfit is due to its unique discrimination capacity, then this may reflect an item that is being interpreted in more than one way by the respondents. Rewording the item could potentially eliminate this ambiguity. After this examination one may conclude that such poorly fitting items should be removed from the instrument. However, simply because an item is identified as exhibiting poor fit does not automatically result in its removal. It is the examination of the poorly fitting items that should lead to an item's retention or removal.

The argument for item removal relies on the observation that the item is not functioning in a fashion consistent with the model. Some have used the removal of items as a criticism of the Rasch model. However, this strategy is not different from that used in other routinely used techniques for instrument development. For example, if one performs a factor analysis and finds an item that has a low loading on the instrument's factors, then rather than introducing a single-item factor, the item is, typically, discarded. Similarly, in traditional item analysis items may be removed because of a valid negative biserial (i.e., the sign is not due to an incorrect keying of the correct response). In this situation the item is not behaving in a fashion consistent with conventional wisdom. In addition, one approach to scale development relies on discarding items in order to maximize the observed scores' reliability. Therefore, the removal of items to improve an instrument's psychometric properties is not without precedence and is considered acceptable with other psychometric analyses.

After the Rasch model–data fit process is completed, one has constructed a scale for measuring a variable. This scale fits the Rasch model to some degree in the same sense that Guttman (1950) accepted some degree of deviation from a perfect Guttman scale in his Scalogram method and Walker (1931) accepted deviation from a unig test. In other words, the Rasch approach to measurement can be found in other measurement procedures.

To summarize our analyses, the nonlinear factor analysis provided support that a unidimensional model of the data is a reasonable representation of the data. The INFIT and OUTFIT fit statistics at the individual item and person level, the subsequent response vector analysis to investigate large OUTFIT ZSTD values, and the invariance assessment all provide evidence supporting model–data fit. Presumably, validity evidence would also support the application of the Rasch model to our mathematics data. If so, then these data would have been successfully calibrated using the Rasch model. The calibration indicates that the instrument does and will perform comparatively better in estimating persons toward the middle and lower end of the mathematics continuum than those toward its upper end. (In Chapter 7 we introduce BIGSTEPS' Item-Person map (e.g., Table 7.5) as an aid in comparing the person distribution with the item location estimates and facilitating the foregoing interpretation.)

SUMMARY

Estimating item and person locations may be accomplished by various methods. One approach is to "simultaneously" estimate both item and person locations by maximizing the joint likelihood function of persons and items. This method is referred to as joint maximum likelihood estimation (JMLE). The procedure begins with provisional estimates of person locations, and these are treated as known for estimating the items' parameters via Newton's method. Once convergence is obtained for the item parameter estimates, these estimated item parameters are treated as "known" and the person locations are estimated via

Newton's method. Upon achieving convergence for the persons, these person locations are presumably more accurate than the provisional person location estimates initially used for item parameter estimation. Therefore, the improved person location estimates are treated as "known" and the item parameters reestimated. Similarly, the improved item parameter estimates are used to reestimate the person parameters. The JMLE method ping-pongs between the two stages until the difference between successive iterations is sufficiently small to satisfy the convergence criteria.

Theoretically, the person and item parameters are invariant. However, we have only estimates of these parameters. One implication of not knowing either the item or the person parameters is that the continuum's metric is indeterminate. If we knew either set of parameters (i.e., persons or items), then the metric would be determined by the parameters' values. However, because we do not know either set of parameters, the metric needs to be fixed in some fashion to identify the model. Two common approaches are person centering and item centering. In both approaches sample information is used for fixing the metric when estimating person and/or item parameters. Therefore, when different samples are used to estimate an instrument's item parameters, the resulting estimates may not necessarily be identical. However, if there is model–data fit, then the estimates are linearly related and one metric may be transformed to the other.

The application of an IRT model involves an analysis of model–data fit. All IRT models make dimensionality assumptions. Therefore, one of the first steps in our fit analysis is to determine whether, for example, a unidimensional model is an accurate representation of the data. Although there are various approaches that can be used for dimensionality assessment, with our binary response data we used a nonlinear factor analysis to mitigate the possibility of obtaining "difficulty" factors. (Obtaining validity evidence should be considered part of the dimensionality assessment.) Our second model–data fit step uses item/person/model fit measures. For instance, our calibration program's INFIT and OUTFIT indices are used to determine if the items and people were behaving consistently with the model. The third step in our model–data fit analysis looks at the degree of linearity between the item parameter estimates from the separate calibrations of subsamples. For example, if we randomly create two subsamples and calibrate each sample, then a large correlation between the item location estimates from the two subsamples would provide evidence of the invariance of our estimates. If our estimates are highly linearly related, then not only would we have evidence supporting the invariance of the parameter estimates, but also by implication, model–data fit.

In the next chapter a different approach for performing IRT parameter estimation, marginal maximum likelihood estimation (MMLE), is introduced. This approach is used in estimation programs such as BILOG-3 (Mislevy & Bock, 1997), BILOG-MG, MULTILOG, PARSCALE, ConQuest (Wu, Adams, & Wilson, 1997), and OPLM, to name a few. Unlike JMLE, MMLE separates item parameter estimation from person parameter estimation. Parallel to this chapter's structure, the MMLE estimation approach is discussed, followed by its application to the mathematics data using BILOG-MG. As part of this example, we introduce the comparison of predicted and observed IRFs as a model–data fit method. Within the context of this application the concepts of the alignment of metrics and an instrument's total characteristic curve are introduced.

NOTES

1. An alternative approach is to select an item, set its estimate to some fixed value, say 0.0, and then estimate the remaining items on the instrument keeping the target item fixed. This approach fixes the metric around the target item and thereby resolves the metric indeterminacy.

2. This recommendation is based on using JMLE. Moreover, Lord (1983a), using LOGIST, looked at the bias in estimating θ using either the 1PL model or a more complicated model, the two-parameter model (see Chapter 5). He concluded that for 10- to 15-item instruments the unweighted observed score (i.e., $X_i = \sum x_{ij}$) used in the 1PL model was slightly superior to the weighted observed score used in the two-parameter model when the item parameters were estimated on the basis of "less than 100 or 200" cases (Lord, 1983a, p. 58).

3. The raw product–moment matrix is obtained using the program PRODMOM (Fraser, 1988). The current available version of NOHARM does not provide the PRODMOM program. Therefore, to avoid repeatedly calculating the raw product–moment matrix, one would provide the binary response data for the first analysis and request that NOHARM print the $\underline{P}$ matrix to the output file or to a separate text (i.e., ASCII) file. This matrix could then be used for subsequent analyses of the data.

4. Performing more than a two-dimensional analysis with five items would not be meaningful. For example, with a three-dimensional solution one would have to allow items to cross-load, otherwise one factor would consist of only one item and would not be well defined. In addition, the number of independent parameters estimated with a three-dimensional solution would exceed the unique pieces of information (i.e., number of unique joint proportions).

5. When using NOHARM for dimensionality assessment, the results of the unidimensional solution also contain item parameter estimates. The model used for fitting the data is a two-parameter normal ogive model and is discussed in Appendix C. These item parameter estimates are not presented in Table 3.2. However, they are discussed in Appendix E, "Example: NOHARM Unidimensional Calibration." As a result, NOHARM can be used for both dimensionality assessment and item calibration for the one-, two-, and (modified) three-parameter models as well as their multidimensional versions.

6. It has been demonstrated that the location estimates are biased under JMLE (Wright & Douglas, 1977). By averaging the relative bias over observed scores and items, Wright and Douglas (1977) arrived at a correction factor, $(L - 1)/L$, that can substantially reduce the bias (assuming that the distribution of item locations and of persons over observed scores is somewhat uniform). In BIGSTEPS and WINSTEPS the implementation of this correction factor is accomplished by setting STBIAS to "yes" (i.e., STBIAS = Y); the default for STBIAS is "no." The effect of this correction is greatest for short instruments. Wright and Douglas (1977) suggest that for instruments of at least 30 items and item variability of about 1.0, there is little need for use of the correction factor.

7. As one removes either persons or items that have constant responses, it is possible to create additional response vectors that also have this characteristic for the remaining items and/or persons. For instance, assume that our data consist of the following binary response vectors from five persons on five items:

$$
\begin{array}{ll}
11111 & \Leftarrow \text{person 1} \\
00000 & \Leftarrow \text{person 2} \\
10111 & \Leftarrow \text{person 3} \\
11110 & \Leftarrow \text{person 4} \\
10000 & \Leftarrow \text{person 5}
\end{array}
$$

As we see, none of the *item* response vectors (i.e., the columns) have item scores of 0 or 5. However, the first two *person* response vectors (i.e., the rows) need to be deleted when using JMLE because person 1 has a perfect score of 5 and person 2 has a zero score. (Whenever one has zero variance for a binary response vector, it is not possible to use MLE for estimation.) After removing the first two cases item 1's item score is equal to 3 (i.e., the number of remaining cases) and is a zero variance binary response vector. Upon removing item 1 the last case (person 5) has an observed score of 0 and needs to be removed. Removing the last case leaves two persons responding to the remaining four items. Inspecting the response vectors for these two people shows that there are two items that have item scores equal to 2 and these two items need to be removed. Therefore, after culling all the zero-variance binary response vectors the data consist of two persons (persons 3 and 4) responding to two items that have item scores of 1 and both persons have the same observed score (X = 1). Applying this logic to a perfect Guttman scale leads to the conclusion that a perfect Guttman scale cannot be calibrated using JMLE.

8. A variation of this approach, sometimes referred to as the "half-item rule," has 0.5 assigned to the item with the smallest location value for a zero-score response vector and to the item with the largest location value for a perfect-score response vector. For example, assuming five items are in increasing order of their locations, then a zero-score response vector would become '0.5 0 0 0 0' and a perfect score vector would be '1 1 1 1 0.5.' These modified vectors could then be used to obtain MLE θs for persons with zero and perfect scores.

9. We conjecture that these 40 persons along with the 184 persons with $\underline{x}$ = 00001 could account for items 1 and 5's large OUTFIT ZSTD values. To verify this, these 224 persons are removed and the data recalibrated. This results in the OUTFIT ZSTD value for item 1 becoming 0.8 and that for item 5 falling to 0.5. The INFIT MNSQ value for item 1 decreases by 0.03 and for item 5 it increases by 0.03; the remaining items' INFIT MNSQ values change by less than 0.02. For completeness, $\hat{\delta}_1$ = −2.36, $\hat{\delta}_2$ = −0.26, $\hat{\delta}_3$ = 0.21, $\hat{\delta}_4$ = 1.04, and $\hat{\delta}_5$ = 1.36 with a corresponding standard error for each item of 0.02. Therefore, there is a slight change in location estimates owing to the use of different people, but minimal impact on the accuracy of the estimates. In general, comparing calibration results with and without problem respondents can provide useful information for determining the best course of action.

10. Alternative splits that could be used for examining invariance and that might be of specific interest would be gender, racial/ethnic background (e.g., majority group individuals versus minority group individuals), educational level, high versus low on the θ continuum (e.g., high-proficiency versus low-proficiency individuals), and so on. Depending on the particular context, it may also make sense to examine estimate invariance over time. In each of these situations we would perform separate calibrations for each group and then compare the results as we do in the examples in this chapter and in Chapter 5, or by using a statistic, such as the likelihood ratio statistic (Andersen, 1973).

4

Marginal Maximum Likelihood Parameter Estimation

In this chapter we present an alternative to JMLE that separates item parameter estimation from person parameter estimation. This alternative, marginal maximum likelihood estimation (MMLE), estimates only item parameters.[1] As such, after obtaining item parameter estimates and achieving satisfactory model–data fit, one typically proceeds to estimate the person parameters using either MLE (see Appendix A) or a Bayesian approach. In the following, we begin with a conceptual presentation of MMLE and then discuss the Bayesian *expected* a posteriori method for estimating person locations. As we did in Chapter 3, we then apply these methods to the data introduced in Chapter 2. Our fit analysis involves a graphical comparison of the empirical and predicted IRFs. In addition, the items' empirical IRFs provide us with evidence of the tenability of the model's functional form assumption. We end by discussing the conversion of estimates from one metric to a different metric and introduce the concept of an instrument's characteristic function.

MARGINAL MAXIMUM LIKELIHOOD ESTIMATION

In JMLE one is simultaneously determining the item and person parameter estimates that maximize the joint likelihood of the observed data. There are a number of practical implications of this approach. First, there is the statistical issue of trying to simultaneously estimate the item parameters and the person parameters. Andersen (1970) referred to this issue as estimating *structural parameters* (the item parameters) concomitant with *incidental parameters* (the person parameters). The gist of this issue is that one way of obtaining better (e.g., consistent, efficient) item parameter estimates is to increase the sample size. However, in JMLE increasing the sample size leads to an increase in the number of person parameters to be estimated. Therefore, there are more person parameters to estimate without additional (item) information with which to estimate the person parameters. Moreover, Neyman and

Scott (1948) argue that when structural parameters are estimated simultaneously with the incidental parameters, the maximum likelihood estimates (MLEs) of the structural parameters do not have to be consistent as sample size increases. de Gruijter (1990) has shown that these estimates are biased.

Second, there is an issue of efficiency. Because the item and person parameter estimations are coupled together, if one finds that one or more items do not exhibit model–data fit and removes the item(s), then the instrument has to be recalibrated. The recalibration is necessary to remove the adverse effect(s) of the bad item(s) from the person location estimates as well as from the metric. Unfortunately, in JMLE one has to estimate the person locations as part of the process of estimating the item locations. It would be far more efficient to uncouple the item and person parameter estimation phases. In that case, estimation of the person parameters would not occur until one achieves satisfactory model–data fit.

Third, separating the person parameter estimation from the item parameter estimation potentially improves the theoretical accuracy of the estimates for some instruments. That is, for short instruments, say of 15 items or fewer, JMLE produces biased person location estimates that then result in poorly estimated item locations (Lord, 1983b, 1986).

MMLE provides an estimation approach that addresses these issues. (Other alternatives for handling the structural/incidental parameter issue include a Bayesian approach presented by Swaminathan & Gifford [1982] as well as by Jannarone, Yu, & Laughlin [1990], and for the 1PL model the use of conditional maximum likelihood estimation.) In the following discussion we begin with an analogy to two sampling situations in which the ANOVA framework may be applied. We then proceed to discuss MMLE.

To begin, consider two independent variables and the selection of their corresponding levels. In one case, the independent variables' levels may be the only levels of interest. For example, for the first independent variable the levels are males and females and for the second independent variable the levels are treatment and control groups. These levels and their combination exhaust the set of levels to which we wish to make inferences. This situation may be analyzed using a fixed effects ANOVA model (see Hays, 1988; Scheffé, 1959).

Alternatively, the levels of one variable may be randomly sampled from a population of levels, whereas the second independent variable's levels are the only ones of interest. For instance, consider a repeated measures design in which we randomly sample the participants, but the independent variable, say *diet*, consists of two diet regimens. In this case, we are not only interested in making inferences to the specific treatment levels of the diet factor, but also want to be able to make inferences to the entire population of people from which the random sample is taken. The diet factor is a fixed effects factor and the person factor is a random effects factor. This situation may be analyzed using a mixed effects ANOVA model.

In the IRT context, the fixed effects model is analogous to JMLE (Bock & Aitkin, 1981; Bock & Lieberman, 1970). In JMLE the items are considered fixed because one is interested only in the particular items on the instrument and not in generalizing to other potential items that may have been included on the instrument. Persons are also considered fixed because it is only for the people in the calibration sample that one is interested in estimating person parameters. In contrast, Bock and Lieberman (1970) proposed the MMLE solution by assuming that people are randomly sampled from a population (e.g., a normal distribution). In MMLE the items are still considered fixed, but the persons are considered a "random effect." As such, the MMLE is analogous to a mixed effects ANOVA model.

In contrast to the ANOVA context where a random factor's function is to allow the making of inferences from the sample to the population, in MMLE the random factor is a mechanism for introducing population information into the estimation of the item parameters without having to directly estimate the person parameters. By invoking the idea that the calibration sample represents a random sample from a population, the estimation of the item parameters can be freed from the estimation of person locations. However, in this case the estimation of the item parameters is potentially dependent on the population distribution.

The introduction of a population from which respondents are randomly sampled changes the estimation equations shown in Chapter 3. To arrive at the MMLE equations we begin with the probability of the response vector $\underline{x}$:

$$p(\underline{x}|\theta, \underline{\vartheta}) = \prod_{j=1}^{L} p_j^{x_j}(1 - p_j)^{1-x_j} \tag{4.1}$$

where $p(\underline{x}|\theta, \underline{\vartheta})$ is conditional on the person location, θ, and on the item parameters ($\underline{\vartheta}$ is a matrix of item parameters [e.g., α and δ_js]), and L is the instrument's length.

Mathematically, the application of the idea of randomly sampling respondents from a population to Equation 4.1 requires that one integrate over the population distribution:

$$p(\underline{x}) = \int_{-\infty}^{\infty} p(\underline{x}|\theta, \underline{\vartheta}) \, g(\theta|\underline{\upsilon})d\theta \tag{4.2}$$

where $p(\underline{x}|\theta, \underline{\vartheta})$ is given by Equation 4.1 and $g(\theta|\underline{\upsilon})$ represents the continuous population distribution of individuals—$\underline{\upsilon}$ is a vector containing location and population scale parameters that are typically 0 and 1, respectively (Thissen, 1982).[2] Note that $p(\underline{x})$ is *not* conditional on θ (i.e., the individual has been eliminated). Rather, Equation 4.2 specifies the unconditional or marginalized probability of a randomly selected person from the population with a continuous latent distribution $g(\theta|\underline{\upsilon})$ providing the response vector $\underline{x}$ (Baker, 1992; Bock & Aitkin, 1981). Therefore, although an individual's θ is unknown, the probability of his or her possible θs can be determined on the basis of his or her responses, the item parameters, and $g(\theta|\underline{\upsilon})$. Equation 4.2 is referred to as the *marginal probability* of the response vector $\underline{x}$. It is from this marginal distribution that the item parameters are estimated. In effect, in MMLE one multiplies the likelihood of the observed data by the population distribution to eliminate the person location parameters. Subsequently, one obtains MLEs of the item parameters by maximizing the resulting marginal likelihood function (cf. Lord, 1986; Thissen, 1982).

Because persons are eliminated from the estimation process, increasing the sample size does not increase the number of person parameters in the (marginal) likelihood function. The population distribution may be assumed to have a specific form *a priori*, such as a normal distribution, or it may be estimated empirically (Mislevy & Bock, 1997). It should be noted that although IRT and JMLE do not make an assumption about the distribution of persons, MMLE does make an assumption about how individuals are distributed. Moreover, because this distributional assumption does not change from one individual to the next, all persons are considered to belong to the same distribution (cf. Appendix E, "Mixture Models").

As is seen, Equation 4.2 contains an integral. The gist of integration is to determine the area under a function. In Equation 4.2 this area corresponds to the probability of a person providing the response vector $\underline{x}$ when the person is randomly selected from a population with a continuous latent distribution $g(\theta|\underline{v})$. Stated another way, to determine this probability one needs to determine the area under the function defined in Equation 4.2. Various approaches to performing numerical integration with computers have been developed. Some of these approaches use the Hermite–Gauss quadrature or are based on the Newton–Cotes integration formulas (e.g., the trapezoidal rule or Simpson's rule). Because the technique typically associated with MMLE is the Hermite–Gauss quadrature method, this is the method we discuss.

The area defined by Equation 4.2 can be approximated by using a discrete distribution consisting of a series of rectangles (i.e., a histogram). The weighted sum of these rectangles provides an approximation to the area under the function (i.e., the probability). Obviously, for a given range on the continuum—say –4 to 4—the larger the number of rectangles, the narrower each rectangle becomes and the better the approximation. Each rectangle has a midpoint known as a *quadrature node* or *point* (X_r) and an associated *quadrature weight* ($A(X_r)$) that reflects the height of the function $g(\theta|\underline{v})$ around X_r. Figure 4.1 conceptually represents this idea for the unit normal distribution where a quadrature point is represented by a longish tick mark on the abscissa within each bar and the bar's area reflects the quadrature weight; there are 11 quadrature points represented in the graph.[3]

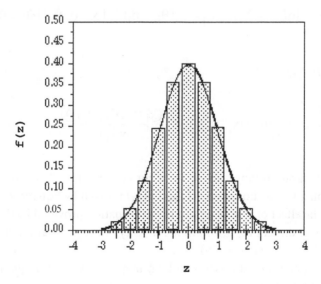

FIGURE 4.1. Conceptual representation of the quadrature concept with the unit normal distribution.

Applying the quadrature points and weights to Equation 4.2 simplifies the calculation of the probability to a simple weighted sum of the conditional probabilities:

$$p(\underline{x})^* \approx \sum_{r}^{R} p(\underline{x}|X_r, \underline{\vartheta}) A(X_r) \qquad (4.3)$$

where the weighting is accomplished by using the quadrature weights, the sum is across the R quadrature points, and the probabilities are calculated using the quadrature points (X_rs) in lieu of θ. The quantity $p(\underline{x})^*$ is the unconditional probability of a randomly selected person from the population providing the response vector $\underline{x}$. Equation 4.3 is the "quadrature form" of Equation 4.2 (i.e., the quadrature form of the equation uses quadrature nodes and weights). As such, the implementation of the Gaussian quadrature approximation results in the θ and the integral seen in Equation 4.2 being replaced by the quadrature points and a summation, respectively.

To apply the foregoing ideas to the entire N x L data matrix, we begin with the log likelihood of the marginalized likelihood function:

$$\ln L = \sum_{i}^{N} \ln p(\underline{x}) \qquad (4.4)$$

where $p(\underline{x})$ is given by Equation 4.2. By substitution and simplification we obtain the marginal likelihood equation to be solved for estimating an item's location based on individual response patterns:

$$\frac{\partial}{\partial \delta_j} \ln L = -\sum_{i}^{N} \int \{[x_{ij} - p_j(\theta_i)][p_j(\theta_i \mid \underline{x}_i, \underline{\vartheta}, \underline{v})]\} d\theta = 0 \qquad (4.5)$$

where $p(\theta \mid \underline{x}, \varphi, \underline{v})$ is given by

$$p(\theta_i|\underline{x}_i, \underline{\vartheta}, \underline{v}) = \frac{p(\underline{x}_i \mid \theta_i, \underline{\vartheta})g(\theta_i \mid \underline{\vartheta})}{p(\underline{x}_i)} \qquad (4.6)$$

we suppress the integration range of $-\infty$ to ∞ for convenience. The term $p(\underline{x}_i|\theta_i, \underline{\vartheta})$ is the likelihood function given by Equation 4.1, and $p(\underline{x}_i)$ is given by Equation 4.2. Conceptually, Equation 4.6 has the effect of spreading out the information provided by the response vector across the θ metric in direct proportion to the density of the population distribution (Baker, 1992; Harwell, Baker, & Zwarts, 1988).

Given the foregoing, Equations 4.5 and 4.6 may be rewritten in quadrature form. The quadrature form of Equation 4.5 is

$$\frac{\partial}{\partial \delta_j} \ln L = -\sum_r^R \sum_i^N [x_{ij} - p_j(X_r)] \, [p_j(X_r|\underline{x}_i, \underline{\vartheta}, \underline{\upsilon})] \, d\theta = 0 \qquad (4.7)$$

and in quadrature form Equation 4.6 becomes

$$p_j(X_r|\underline{x}_i, \underline{\vartheta}, \underline{\upsilon}) = \frac{L(X_r)A(X_r)}{\displaystyle\sum_s^R L(X_s)A(X_s)} \qquad (4.8)$$

where $L(X_r) = \displaystyle\prod^L p_j(X_r)^{x_{ij}} (1 - p_j(X_r))^{1-x_{ij}}$. The term $L(X_r)$ is the approximation of the likelihood function using the quadrature approach.

Equation 4.7 may be further simplified. First, expanding the product term in Equation 4.7 produces

$$\frac{\partial}{\partial \delta_j} \ln L = -\sum_r^R \sum_i^N \left[[x_{ij} * p_j(X_r | \underline{x}_i, \underline{\vartheta}, \underline{\upsilon})] - [p_j(X_r) * p(X_r | \underline{x}_i, \underline{\vartheta}, \underline{\upsilon})] \right] d\theta = 0 \quad (4.9)$$

Second, distributing the summation across people results in

$$\frac{\partial}{\partial \delta_j} \ln L = -\sum_r^R \left[[\sum_i^N x_{ij} * p_j(X_r | \underline{x}_i, \underline{\vartheta}, \underline{\upsilon})] - [p_j(X_r)\sum_i^N p(X_r|\underline{x}_i, \underline{\vartheta}, \underline{\upsilon})] \right] d\theta = 0 \quad (4.10)$$

Turning to the first term in Equation 4.10, let $\bar{c}_{rj} = \displaystyle\sum_i^N x_{ij} * p_j(X_r|\underline{x}_i, \underline{\vartheta}, \underline{\upsilon})$. By substitution of Equation 4.8 into $\bar{c}_{rj}$ we obtain

$$\bar{c}_{rj} = \sum_i^N x_{ij} * p_j(X_r|\underline{x}_i, \underline{\vartheta}, \underline{\upsilon}) = \sum^N \frac{x_{ij}L(X_r)A(X_r)}{\displaystyle\sum_s^R L(X_s)A(X_s)} \qquad (4.11)$$

Because $\bar{c}_{rj}$ contains the binary response to item j, x_{ij}, the sum "counts" only the responses of 1 to item j for "persons" at X_r. As such, it reflects the expected number of responses of 1 to item j at each quadrature node X_r and is an *expected* item score.

Now looking at the second term in Equation 4.10, let $\bar{n}_{rj} = \displaystyle\sum p_j(X_r|\underline{x}_i, \underline{\vartheta}, \underline{\upsilon})$. Again by substitution of Equation 4.8 we obtain

$$\bar{n}_{rj} = \sum^N p_j(X_r|\underline{x}_i, \underline{\vartheta}, \underline{\upsilon}) = \sum^N \frac{L(X_r)A(X_r)}{\displaystyle\sum_s^R L(X_s)A(X_s)} \qquad (4.12)$$

The term $\bar{n}_{rj}$ is the *expected* number of persons at each quadrature point X_r. Equations

4.11 and 4.12 distribute the observed response vector for a person over the R quadrature nodes in proportion to the likelihood of the person being at the node (Mislevy & Bock, 1985).

Therefore, by substitution of Equations 4.11 and 4.12 into Equation 4.10 the marginal likelihood equation that needs to be solved to estimate item j's location is

$$-\sum_{r}^{R} [\bar{c}_{rj} - \bar{n}_{rj}\, p_j(X_r)] = 0 \qquad (4.13)$$

where $p_j(X_r)$ comes from the model using X_r in lieu of θ_i (Baker, 1992; Bock & Aitkin, 1981; Harwell, Baker, & Zwartz, 1988, 1989). The difference in Equation 4.13 has the form of an expected "observed" item score minus an expected "predicted" correct. The value that minimizes the sum of these differences across the R quadrature points is the estimate of the item location, δ. (Quote marks are used to distinguish the term "observed" from the way the term is used throughout this book [e.g., Appendix A]. That is, the "observed" item score does not represent solely observed responses to item j, but is based, in part, on the latent population distribution.) Examination of Equation 4.13 shows that it does not contain any reference to the θs, therefore increasing the sample size does not lead to an increase in the number of parameters to be estimated; this has been true since the introduction of Equation 4.7.

Estimating δ_j for the Rasch model is an iterative process. This process begins with a provisional estimate of δ_j that is successively refined through a series of expectation and maximization cycles until Equation 4.13 is essentially 0.0 to a degree of accuracy determined by the convergence criterion. The Bock and Aitkin (1981) approach for MMLE is implemented through an extension to a procedure developed for obtaining maximum likelihood estimates for probability models in the presence of incomplete data known as the *EM algorithm* (Dempster, Laird, & Rubin, 1977). In the current context, the person parameters are treated as the missing data.

The essence of the EM algorithm is to calculate $\bar{n}_{rj}$ and $\bar{c}_{rj}$ in the expectation step (i.e., the E-step). In the maximization step (i.e., the M-step) the values from the E-step are used to estimate the item parameters through an evaluation of the (marginal) likelihood function through a process similar to that discussed in Appendix B (i.e., find the maximum of this marginal likelihood function). Subsequent to the M-step, the refined M-step estimates are compared to the item parameter estimates used in the E-step. If the difference between these two sets of item parameter estimates is greater than the convergence criterion (and the maximum number of cycles has not been reached), then another E–M cycle is executed; otherwise, convergence has been achieved and the estimation process has been completed.

Because the EM algorithm does not provide sample standard errors, some programs (e.g., BILOG-3, BILOG-MG, MULTILOG) perform a series of Newton–Raphson (i.e., Newton–Gauss, Fisher-scoring) steps to improve the estimates and to obtain standard errors. Bock and Aitkin (1981) suggest stopping the EM steps short of convergence and using one or two Newton–Raphson iterations to improve the nearly converged EM solution and provide the standard errors of the item parameter estimates.

The $\bar{c}_{rj}$s and $\bar{n}_{rj}$s are typically referred to as "artificial data" or "pseudo-data" because they reflect the expected frequency and expected sample size, respectively, at each quadrature node (cf. Baker, 1992; Mislevy, 1986a; Thissen, 1982). The R $\bar{n}_{rj}$s represent the discrete posterior θ distribution. It is on the basis of this posterior θ distribution that the indeterminacy of scale issue is addressed. This is done by using the $\bar{n}_{rj}$s to adjust the quadrature weights from the previous E-step. Subsequently, the adjusted weights, $A(X_r)$, are normalized by dividing each expected number of persons at each quadrature point by the observed sample size (i.e., $A(X_r) = \bar{n}_{rj}/N$) and then standardized (i.e., $\sum_r^R A(X_r)X_r = 0$ and $\sum_r^R A(X_r)$ $X_r^2 = 1$) to set the location and scale of the latent variable (Baker 1990; Mislevy & Bock, 1985). The process is repeated for each E-step. This strategy results in a "modified" person centering approach because it uses the posterior θ distribution rather than the distribution of individual $\hat{\theta}$s. (The individual $\hat{\theta}$s are not available at this point because of separation of the item parameter estimation from the person parameter estimation.) Baker (1992), Baker and Kim (2004), Bock and Aitkin (1981), Harwell and Baker (1991), Harwell et al. (1988) (cf. Harwell et al., 1989), and Thissen (1982) provide greater detail about MMLE; the Bock and Aitkin (1981) and Thissen (1982) presentations use the frequency of response patterns rather than individual case data.

The use of a finite number of quadrature nodes is tantamount to assuming that these points are the only values that the θs can take on (Mislevy & Stocking, 1989). Moreover, the statistical properties (e.g., consistent item parameter estimates) may not be realized if the assumed θ distribution is incorrect. There have been a number of studies to investigate the effects of various factors on MMLE (e.g., Drasgow, 1989; Harwell & Janosky, 1991; Zwinderman & van der Wollenberg, 1990). For instance, Zwinderman and van der Wollenberg (1990) found that violation of the distributional assumption led to a loss of efficiency and biased estimates. Such bias and precision loss are directly related to the degree of violation. Seong (1990a) compared the item and proficiency parameter estimates from BILOG's approach for determining the quadrature points and weights with those obtained by using the Stroud and Secrest values. Results showed that when a large number of quadrature points were used (e.g., 30, 40), the two methods estimated item and person location parameters equally well, but when a small number of quadrature points was specified (e.g., 10), the item and person parameter estimates were less accurate than when the Stroud and Secrest values were used. As is the case with MLE, it is not possible to estimate items that have zero variability in their binary response vectors (i.e., all responses to an item are 1 or are all 0).

ESTIMATING AN INDIVIDUAL'S LOCATION: EXPECTED A POSTERIORI

Application of MMLE to an instrument yields only item parameter estimates. Once we are satisfied with our degree of model–data fit we can proceed to obtain person location estimates. There are various person estimation approaches that we can use. One estimation approach is the MLE strategy introduced in Chapter 2 and covered in greater detail in Appendix A. However, in Chapter 2 it is shown that MLE cannot produce finite estimates of a person's location when he or she obtains either a zero score or a perfect score. When this issue was initially introduced we noted that additional information could reduce our uncertainty about a person's location. This additional information can come from previous experience or by making assumptions. For example, if we believe or are willing to assume that the construct of interest is normally distributed in the population, then the person could be considered to be sampled from a normal population. This in turn would provide information, in addition to the person's response vector, about where we would expect the person to be located. That is, assuming that one had a normal population, the probability of observing persons located between −1 and 1 would be more likely than, say, above 3. A mechanism for incorporating this ancillary information into the estimation of person locations comes from Bayes' theorem.

The essence of this Bayesian strategy is that one has person location information in terms of a probability distribution prior to obtaining any observational data. This distribution is known as a *prior distribution*. After administering the instrument one has observational data that is incorporated with the prior distribution information. The result of integrating the prior distribution with the observational data is a distribution referred to as the *posterior distribution*, because it comes after collecting the observations. It is on the basis of the posterior distribution that we obtain the estimate of a person's location. It should be noted that the terms *prior* and *posterior* are relative (i.e., the posterior distribution can serve as the prior distribution in a second estimation cycle, and so on).

Figure 4.2 contains a conceptual representation of incorporating a prior distribution into the observational data (i.e., a likelihood function) to produce the posterior distribution. In this case, we have the likelihood for the response pattern 110 (i.e., $\underline{x} = 110$). Assuming that a unit normal distribution is a reasonable prior to use, the result of incorporating this

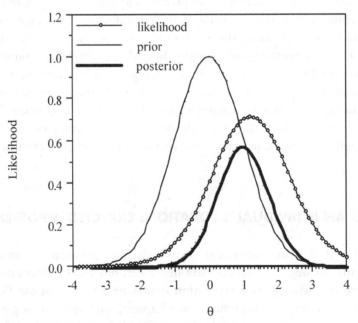

FIGURE 4.2. Conceptual presentation of the incorporation of a prior distribution into a likelihood function to produce the posterior distribution.

distribution information into the likelihood reduces the uncertainty about the person's loca-tion as reflected in the posterior distribution (the heights of the prior and posterior distribu-tion are an artifact of how the plot is created). Using this Bayesian strategy, the $\hat{\theta}$ would be approximately 0.90, the mean or mode of the posterior distribution. If instead of using the likelihood function for $\underline{x} = 110$ we had used the likelihood function for, say, a perfect score (e.g., Figure 2.8), then incorporating the prior distribution into this likelihood function would produce a posterior distribution that *had* a maximum and, as a result, its mean or mode could be used as $\hat{\theta}$. Other prior distributions are sometimes used in lieu of a normal distribution—for example, a beta distribution.

As mentioned, either the mean or the mode of the posterior distribution can be used to provide the person location estimate; in the case of a symmetric distribution both of these yield the same $\hat{\theta}$. In general, using the mean as the estimator minimizes the overall mean squared error of estimation, provided that the appropriate prior is used. This mean squared error is less than that obtained by using MLE, although there is a concomitant increase in the estimation bias known as regression toward the prior's mean (Lord, 1986). One can get a crude sense of this regression by returning to Figure 4.2. Assume that the person's true location is $\theta = 1.0$. The location of the maximum of L (the open circle line) is the MLE $\hat{\theta}$ and it has an approximate value of 1.20. However, the Bayesian estimate of 0.90 represents the estimate being pulled toward the prior's mean of 0.0. (This is a conceptual representation of the regression toward the prior's mean phenomenon and the value 0.9 is not a true Bayesian estimate.) The estimation bias is variable and depends on the magni-tude of the difference between the location of the prior and the $\hat{\theta}$. The estimation bias is magnified the farther away the prior's mean is from the $\hat{\theta}$, and minimized the closer the $\hat{\theta}$ is to the prior's mean. The general pattern is one of underestimating large θs and overes-timating low θs. Swaminathan and Gifford (1982) suggest that it is desirable to use priors that are neither too vague nor too specific. Selecting a somewhat diffuse prior mitigates to some extent the estimation bias.

The use of the mean or the mode of the posterior distribution as an estimate corre-sponds to the two primary Bayesian strategies. In *maximum a posteriori* (MAP; also known as *Bayes Modal Estimate*) one uses the mode of the posterior distribution as the $\hat{\theta}$ (e.g., Swa-minathan & Gifford, 1982) and in *expected a posteriori* (EAP, or *Bayes Mean Estimate*) one uses the mean of the posterior distribution as the $\hat{\theta}$ (Bock & Mislevy, 1982). The variability of the posterior distribution is used as an index of the error of estimation.

All three approaches for estimating a person's location (MLE, EAP, MAP) treat the item parameters' estimates as "known" and ignore their estimation error when estimating θ. Moreover, all three approaches can be modified to use *biweights* to reduce a person location estimate's sensitivity to responses that are inconsistent with an IRT model (Mislevy & Bock, 1982).[4] However, unlike MLE, both EAP and MAP can be used to obtain location estimates for all response patterns including zero and perfect scores. Therefore, the advantage of a Bayesian approach over MLE is that finite $\hat{\theta}$s are available for all individuals. That is, per-sons with perfect and zero scores would have finite $\hat{\theta}$s that are not artifacts dependent on an MLE correctional system (e.g., as in BIGSTEPS). The disadvantage of a Bayesian approach is the (potential) bias that arises from the possible mismatch between an individual's θ and the prior's mean.

MAP differs from EAP in various ways. First, the MAP approach is an iterative method like MLE, whereas EAP is noniterative and is based on numerical quadrature methods like those used in MMLE. Because of its noniterative (and efficient) nature it is potentially faster than either MLE or MAP in estimating person locations. Second, MAP uses a continuous prior distribution, whereas EAP uses a discrete prior distribution. Third, whereas MAP $\hat{\theta}$s exist for all response patterns, they suffer from greater regression toward the prior's mean than do the EAP estimates (Bock & Mislevy, 1982; Mislevy & Bock, 1997). Fourth, the average squared error for EAP estimates over the population is less than that for MAP (as well as MLE) person location estimates (Bock & Mislevy, 1982). A fifth difference has to do with implementation. Specifically, the mathematics required for deriving the computational forms for person location estimation with any IRT model are simpler with EAP than with MAP. In the following we discuss EAP; how to obtain MAP $\hat{\theta}$s is shown in Chapter 8.

The EAP estimate (Bock & Mislevy, 1982) of an individual's θ after administering L items is given by

$$\hat{\theta}_i = \frac{\sum_{r=1}^{R} X_r L(X_r) A(X_r)}{\sum_{r=1}^{R} L(X_r) A(X_r)} \tag{4.14}$$

and its posterior standard deviation is

$$PSD(\hat{\theta}) = \sqrt{\frac{\sum_{r=1}^{R} (X_r - \hat{\theta}_i)^2 L(X_r) A(X_r)}{\sum_{r=1}^{R} L(X_r) A(X_r)}} \tag{4.15}$$

where X_r, $A(X_r)$, and R are defined above and $L(X_r)$ is the likelihood function at X_r given the response pattern $\underline{x} = x_1, \ldots, x_L$ and a particular model,

$$L(X_r) = \prod_{}^{L} p_j(X_r)^{x_{ij}} (1 - p_j(X_r))^{(1-x_{ij})} \tag{4.16}$$

As an example, we obtain the EAP $\hat{\theta}$ for X = 2 and $\underline{x}$ = 11000 using 10 quadrature points and weights. Table 4.1 shows the relevant calculations. The likelihood function, $L(X_r)$, is obtained using the X_rs, the Rasch model, and the item parameter estimates ($\hat{\alpha}$ = 1.0, $\hat{\delta}_1$ = −2.155, $\hat{\delta}_2$ = −0.245, . . . , $\hat{\delta}_5$ = 1.211; these estimates come from our example calibration below). Dividing the sum of column 4 by that of column 5 produces an EAP $\hat{\theta}$ for X = 2 of −0.2271. The discrepancy between this $\hat{\theta}$ and each of the quadrature points is then used to modify the weighted likelihood to obtain the PSD($\hat{\theta}$). The PSD($\hat{\theta}$) corresponding to our $\hat{\theta}$ is

TABLE 4.1. EAP $\hat{\theta}$ for $\underline{x}$ = (11000)

X_r	$A(X_r)$	$L(X_r)$	$X_r L(X_r) A(X_r)$	$L(X_r) A(X_r)$	$(X_r - \hat{\theta}_j)^2 L(X_r) A(X_r)$
			header $\hat{\theta}$		$\text{PSD}(\hat{\theta})$
−4.0000	0.00012	0.0030369	−1.4456E-06	3.6139E-07	5.1444E-06
−3.1110	0.00281	0.0140101	−1.2226E-04	3.9298E-05	3.2684E-04
−2.2220	0.03002	0.0502904	−3.3546E-03	1.5097E-03	6.0082E-03
−1.3330	0.14580	0.1216368	−2.3640E-02	1.7735E-02	2.1690E-02
−0.4444	0.32130	0.1697289	−2.4235E-02	5.4534E-02	2.5753E-03
0.44440	0.32130	0.1178053	1.6821E-02	3.7851E-02	1.7067E-02
1.33300	0.14580	0.0382276	7.4296E-03	5.5736E-03	1.3565E-02
2.22200	0.03002	0.0064165	4.2801E-04	1.9262E-04	1.1554E-03
3.11100	0.00281	0.0006914	6.0338E-06	1.9395E-06	2.1612E-05
4.00000	0.00012	0.0000586	2.7884E-08	6.9711E-09	1.2456E-07
$\sum_{r=1}^{R}$:			−0.0266689	0.1174369	0.0624150

$$\hat{\theta} = \frac{-0.0266689}{0.1174369} = -0.2271 \qquad \text{PSD}(\hat{\theta}) = \sqrt{\frac{0.0624150}{0.1174369}} = 0.7290$$

($s_e(\hat{\theta})$ =) 0.7290. The use of the PSD($\hat{\theta}$) as the standard error is based on the fact that after 20 items the likelihood function and the posterior distribution are nearly identical and the PSD($\hat{\theta}$) is virtually interchangeable with the standard error (Bock & Mislevy, 1982); the PSD($\hat{\theta}$)s are labeled as standard errors in BILOG's EAP output.

Bock and Mislevy (1982) show that the EAP method produces reasonably accurate person location estimates. Seong (1990b) found that increasing the number of quadrature points from 10 to 20 produced more accurate $\hat{\theta}$s, regardless of sample size and appropriateness of the prior distribution (i.e., normal, positively skewed, and negatively skewed). Given that person locations are estimated independently of one another, it is not surprising that sample size did not have a significant effect on the accuracy of EAP $\hat{\theta}$s.

The accuracy of the EAP sample standard errors has been studied (e.g., De Ayala, Schafer, & Sava-Bolesta, 1995). The investigators found that using 10 quadrature points tended to result in EAP $s_e(\hat{\theta})$s that underestimated the observed standard error. These $s_e(\hat{\theta})$s gave the false impression that $\hat{\theta}$ was being estimated more accurately than, in fact, it was. Therefore, if these $s_e(\hat{\theta})$s are used to create confidence intervals (CIs), then the CIs would be erroneously narrower and classification decisions based on such CIs would potentially be incorrect. For instance, examinees may receive certification because their (erroneous) CIs fell above the criterion. For these applications it is recommended that one increase the number of quadrature points used in EAP estimation. A conservative approach would be to use 80 quadrature points because, overall, this level was found to provide the best agreement between the CIs and their expected values. However, unless one needs to be concerned with the accuracy of standard errors, there does not appear to be a compelling reason to use 20 or more quadrature points, given that using 10 quadrature points provides very good agreement between the EAP $\hat{\theta}$s and their corresponding θs (i.e., $r_{\theta\hat{\theta}}$) for symmetric distributions. If there is reason to suspect that the latent person distribution is skewed, then the use of $2\sqrt{L}$ quadrature points may be necessary (see Mislevy & Bock, 1997).

EXAMPLE: APPLICATION OF THE RASCH MODEL
TO THE MATHEMATICS DATA, MMLE

For this example assume that we have already engaged in the various categories of activities (e.g., checking data integrity, assessing dimensionality) performed in Chapter 3, "Example: Application of the Rasch Model to the Mathematics Data, JMLE." However, unlike our previous use of fit statistics as part of our model–data fit analysis, in this example we perform a graphical examination of fit by comparing empirical and predicted IRFs. Moreover, an item's empirical IRF allows us to determine whether our model's functional form assumption is tenable for the item. This graphical examination complements the use of fit statistics. It should be noted that in addition to the INFIT and OUTFIT fit statistics used in Chapter 3, there are other fit statistics that may be calculated. See Glas (2007), Glas and Dagohoy (2007), Glas and Verhelst (1995a, 1995b), McKinley and Mills (1985), Reise (1990), and van den Wollenberg (1988) for examples.

This example calibration of the mathematics data uses MMLE. One program that implements MMLE is BILOG-MG. BILOG-MG exists on the Windows/Intel and compatible chips (so-called PC) platforms. This program uses a GUI to create an input text command file. The GUI facilitates creating the command file by using a series of menus and dialogs to specify the data's characteristics, the model to be used for calibration, the changing of default values, the nature of $g(\theta|\underline{\upsilon})$, and so on. After completing the menus and corresponding dialogs, one selects BUILD SYNTAX from the RUN menu to create the command file. The command file (MATH.BLM) for our Rasch analysis is presented in Table 4.2; the data reside in a separate file called MATH.DAT. With BILOG-MG we can analyze either individual case data or pattern data like that presented in Table 2.1. For this example we analyze individual case data, but in Chapter 6 we analyze the pattern data from Table 2.1.

The GLOBAL command line specifies the use of the logistic version (i.e., LOGistic) of the one-parameter model (i.e., NPArm = 1). This line in conjunction with the CALIB

TABLE 4.2. BILOG Command File for Rasch Calibration

```
Example Rasch Calibration

>GLOBAL DFName = 'C:\Math.dat',
        NPArm = 1,
        LOGistic,
        SAVe;
>SAVE PARm = 'MATHRSCH.PAR';
>LENGTH NITems = (5);
>INPUT NTOtal = 5,
       NIDchar = 10;
>ITEMS ;
>TEST1 TNAme = 'TEST0001',
       INUmber = (1(1)5);
(10A1, T1, 5(1X,A1))
>CALIB ACCel = 1.0000,
       CHIsquare = (5, 8),
       PLOt = 1.0,
       RASch;
```

command line's use of the keyword RASch specifies a Rasch model calibration.[5] In addition, BILOG-MG is instructed to save the item parameter estimates to a file called MATHRSCH. PAR for future use (this requires the SAVe subcommand on the GLOBAL line and the file specification PARm='MATHRSCH.PAR' on the SAVE line). On the INPUT line the total number of unique items (i.e., NTOtal = 5) and the use of 10 characters as an identification field (i.e., NIDchar = 10) is specified. For our example the individual's response pattern is used as his or her identification field. This is accomplished by using the same first and last columns for the Case ID and Response String data fields in the Examinee Data dialog (accessed from the Data menu). This dialog creates the FORTRAN format (i.e., (10A1,T1,5(1X,A1))) used for reading the data. (On the FORTRAN format statement the first data field [i.e., prior to the first comma] is the identification field [i.e., "10A1"] and the second data field [i.e., "5(1X,A1)"] reflects the responses. FORTRAN formats are briefly discussed in Appendix E, "FORTRAN Formats.")

Although with fewer than 20 items the program's item fit chi-square statistics are unreliable, BILOG uses their probabilities to determine which empirical versus predicted IRFs to plot. Therefore, to obtain the IRF plots, we need to have BILOG calculate the item chi-squares. For our example, this is a two-step process. First, because by default BILOG-MG does not calculate the item chi-squares with fewer than 20 items, we need to tell BILOG to calculate the chi-square statistics with 5 items. We do this by inserting the subcommand CHIsquare = (5, 8) on the CALIB line; the 8 specifies the number of intervals to be used in calculating the chi-square value and can affect the appearance of the empirical IRF. Second, to have BILOG plot the empirical versus predicted IRFs for all the items, we increase the probability cutoff for display to 1 (i.e., PLOt = 1.0 on the CALIB line). In the following we ignore the calculated chi-squares. However, assuming that it is appropriate to use the chi-square statistic (e.g., $L \geq 20$), then this statistic tests the null hypothesis that an item's data are consistent with the model. Stated another way, we would like to see nonsignificant chi-square values. As is generally true, failure to reject the null hypothesis does not imply that the model is correct, but only that there is insufficient evidence to believe that it is incorrect.

BILOG presents its output in three phases. Phase 1 results are found in a file with the same name as the command file, but with the extension "PH1" (e.g., MATH.PH1). This phase contains information concerning the job setup, the reading of the data, and classical item statistics. Phase 2 contains the IRT calibration results, and Phase 3 contains person location estimates and related information.

Table 4.3 contains the BILOG-MG output for Phase 1. The Phase 1 output contains echoes of the commands shown in Table 4.2. The FILE ASSIGNMENT AND DISPOSITION section should be checked to ensure that the correct data file is being used: SUBJECT DATA INPUT FILE MATH.DAT. (The additional listed [scratch] files [e.g., MF.DAT, CF.DAT, etc.] are created in the command file's folder and are automatically erased upon successful completion of the run. If the program "crashes," then these files are found littering the folder.) The line labeled ITEM RESPONSE MODEL indicates that the 1 PARAMETER LOGISTIC model and the logistic metric (i.e., LOGIT METRIC) are being used for the calibration.

In the DATA INPUT SPECIFICATIONS section we find details about the data to

TABLE 4.3. BILOG Output: Phase 1

```
:
>GLOBAL DFName = 'C:\Math.dat',
        NPArm = 1,
        LOGistic,
        SAVe;

   FILE ASSIGNMENT AND DISPOSITION
   ================================
   SUBJECT DATA INPUT FILE      C:\MATH.DAT
   BILOG-MG MASTER DATA FILE    MF.DAT      WILL BE CREATED FROM DATA FILE
   CALIBRATION DATA FILE        CF.DAT      WILL BE CREATED FROM DATA FILE
   ITEM PARAMETERS FILE         IF.DAT      WILL BE CREATED THIS RUN
   CASE SCALE-SCORE FILE        SF.DAT
   CASE WEIGHTING                           NONE EMPLOYED
   ITEM RESPONSE MODEL                      1 PARAMETER LOGISTIC
                                            LOGIT  METRIC (I.E., D = 1.0)
   >SAVE PARm = 'MATHRSCH.PAR';

   BILOG-MG SAVE FILES
   [OUTPUT FILES]
   ITEM PARAMETERS FILE         MATHRSCH.PAR
:

   DATA INPUT SPECIFICATIONS
   =========================
   NUMBER OF FORMAT LINES                        1
   NUMBER OF ITEMS IN INPUT STREAM               5
   NUMBER OF RESPONSE ALTERNATIVES            1000
   NUMBER OF SUBJECT ID CHARACTERS              10
   NUMBER OF GROUPS                              1
   NUMBER OF TEST FORMS                          1
   TYPE OF DATA                       SINGLE-SUBJECT DATA, NO CASE WEIGHTS
   MAXIMUM SAMPLE SIZE FOR ITEM CALIBRATION  10000000
   ALL SUBJECTS INCLUDED IN RUN
:
   FORMAT FOR DATA INPUT IS:
   (10A1, T1, 5(1X,A1))

   OBSERVATION #     1  WEIGHT:     1.0000  ID :  0 0 0 1 1
   SUBTEST #:   1     TEST0001
    GROUP #:    1

     TRIED    RIGHT
    5.000    2.000
   ITEM     1     2     3     4     5
   TRIED  1.0   1.0   1.0   1.0   1.0
   RIGHT  0.0   0.0   0.0   1.0   1.0
:
   19601 OBSERVATIONS READ FROM FILE:   C:\MATH.DAT
:
   ITEM STATISTICS FOR SUBTEST TEST0001
                                                   ITEM*TEST CORRELATION
   ITEM   NAME      #TRIED    #RIGHT   PCT    LOGIT   PEARSON  BISERIAL
   ----------------------------------------------------------------------
      1   ITEM0001  19601.0   17395.0  88.7   -2.07    0.246    0.407
      2   ITEM0002  19601.0   12624.0  64.4   -0.59    0.439    0.564
      3   ITEM0003  19601.0   11094.0  56.6   -0.27    0.416    0.524
      4   ITEM0004  19601.0    8369.0  42.7    0.29    0.405    0.511
      5   ITEM0005  19601.0    7592.0  38.7    0.46    0.312    0.397
   ----------------------------------------------------------------------
:
```

be calibrated. The number of items calibrated is indicated on the line labeled NUMBER OF ITEMS IN INPUT STREAM. The line labeled NUMBER OF SUBJECT ID CHARACTERS shows the identification field width as 10. (This value is the first field in the FORTRAN format; the format is echoed following the FORMAT FOR DATA INPUT IS line.) The TYPE OF DATA line indicates that individual case data are being used (i.e., SINGLE-SUBJECT DATA, NO CASE WEIGHTS) rather than, for example, pattern data. For this example all of these are correct. The first two observations are echoed (only the first one is presented) and their inspection shows that the data are read correctly.

On the line OBSERVATIONS READ FROM FILE . . . BILOG indicates the number of cases it read. This value should always be checked to verify that it matches the number of cases that are in the data file. Although there are many reasons why there might be a mismatch, two common problems are a misspecified format statement and/or an incorrect data filename. In our example the correct number of cases are read from the correct file.

The ITEM STATISTICS section contains traditional item difficulty and discrimination statistics. If we had labeled the items, then their names would be found in the NAME column. Although knowing the proportion of people attempting an item is more useful than simply the number tried (#TRIED), the #TRIED column can provide information about potential speededness or instrument/person mismatch. For instance, omitted item(s) that occur at the end of an instrument may indicate that individuals were given insufficient time to respond; in this case the instrument is said to be *speeded*.[6] The ratio of the number right (#RIGHT) to #TRIED is presented in the percent column (labeled PCT). This column indicates the percentage of people correctly responding to an item. Dividing these percentages by 100% yields the traditional measure of an item's difficulty or P-value, P_j. In this case we see that 88.7% of the examinees correctly answered item 1 and, as a consequence, it may be considered an "easy" item for this sample. In contrast, item 5 is comparatively more difficult for this sample because only 38.7% correctly answered it. The logit column is a transformation from the proportion difficulty (P_j) metric to a more "IRT-like" metric (logit = $\ln(\frac{P_j}{1-P_j})$). To reconcile that the interpretation of the traditional difficulty metric is the reverse of the IRT metric (e.g., P_j values close to 1.0 and large *negative* IRT logit values represent "easy" items) the logits are transformed to their opposite sign by multiplying them by −1.

The last two columns are collectively labeled ITEM*TEST CORRELATION and contain two traditional measures of item discrimination. The second to the last column (labeled PEARSON) contains the point–biserial correlations, whereas the last column (labeled BISERIAL) contains the corresponding biserial correlations.[7] If we use principal axis for dimensionality analysis and there are indications of more than one factor underlying the data, then inspecting the biserials may provide a clue to the presence of curvilinearity factors. According to McDonald (1985), "extremely sharply discriminating items" (p. 199) may lead to factors of curvilinearity (also known as "difficulty factors").

The Phase 2 results are presented in Table 4.4. The beginning of this output contains information about the execution: the maximum number of EM cycles (MAXIMUM NUMBER OF EM CYCLES: 20), Newton–Gauss cycles (MAXIMUM NUMBER OF NEWTON CYCLES: 2), the convergence criterion (CONVERGENCE CRITERION: 0.01), the assumption of a Gaussian person prior (LATENT DISTRIBUTION: NORMAL PRIOR FOR EACH GROUP), and the quadrature points and corresponding weights (e.g., the first

TABLE 4.4. BILOG Output: Phase 2

```
:
                               *** PHASE 2  ***
Example Rasch Calibration

>CALIB ACCel = 1.0000,
       CHIsquare = (5, 8),
       PLOt = 1,
       RASch;

CALIBRATION PARAMETERS
======================
MAXIMUM NUMBER OF EM CYCLES:                    20

MAXIMUM NUMBER OF NEWTON CYCLES:                2
CONVERGENCE CRITERION:                          0.0100
ACCELERATION CONSTANT:                          1.0000

LATENT DISTRIBUTION:                 NORMAL PRIOR FOR EACH GROUP
:
METHOD OF SOLUTION:

EM CYCLES (MAXIMUM OF    20)
FOLLOWED BY NEWTON-RAPHSON STEPS (MAXIMUM OF    2)

QUADRATURE POINTS AND PRIOR WEIGHTS:
            1           2           3           4           5
POINT   -0.4000E+01 -0.3429E+01 -0.2857E+01 -0.2286E+01 -0.1714E+01
WEIGHT   0.7648E-04  0.6387E-03  0.3848E-02  0.1673E-01  0.5245E-01

            6           7           8           9          10
POINT   -0.1143E+01 -0.5714E+00 -0.8882E-15  0.5714E+00  0.1143E+01
WEIGHT   0.1186E+00  0.1936E+00  0.2280E+00  0.1936E+00  0.1186E+00

           11          12          13          14          15
POINT    0.1714E+01  0.2286E+01  0.2857E+01  0.3429E+01  0.4000E+01
WEIGHT   0.5245E-01  0.1673E-01  0.3848E-02  0.6387E-03  0.7648E-04

[E-M CYCLES]
-2 LOG LIKELIHOOD =      112092.890

CYCLE    1;   LARGEST CHANGE=  0.19046
-2 LOG LIKELIHOOD =      111293.340

CYCLE    2;   LARGEST CHANGE=  0.12708
-2 LOG LIKELIHOOD =      110963.903

CYCLE    3;   LARGEST CHANGE=  0.08050
-2 LOG LIKELIHOOD =      110842.600

CYCLE    4;   LARGEST CHANGE=  0.15630
-2 LOG LIKELIHOOD =      110780.672

CYCLE    5;   LARGEST CHANGE=  0.05751
-2 LOG LIKELIHOOD =      110778.567

CYCLE    6;   LARGEST CHANGE=  0.07970
-2 LOG LIKELIHOOD =      110777.950

CYCLE    7;   LARGEST CHANGE=  0.01872
-2 LOG LIKELIHOOD =      110774.876

CYCLE    8;   LARGEST CHANGE=  0.00745
[FULL NEWTON CYCLES]
-2 LOG LIKELIHOOD:        110774.2948

CYCLE    9;   LARGEST CHANGE=  0.00596

INTERVAL COUNTS FOR COMPUTATION OF ITEM CHI-SQUARES
-----------------------------------------------------------------------
        0.   691.  3099.  4269.  4116.  4041.  3385.     0.
-----------------------------------------------------------------------

INTERVAL AVERAGE THETAS
-----------------------------------------------------------------------
    ******* -2.025 -1.293 -0.632  0.019  0.713  1.520*******
-----------------------------------------------------------------------
```

cont.

TABLE 4.4. *cont.*

```
SUBTEST TEST0001;  ITEM PARAMETERS AFTER CYCLE   9
ITEM      INTERCEPT     SLOPE     THRESHOLD   LOADING   ASYMPTOTE    CHISQ    DF
            S.E.        S.E.        S.E.       S.E.       S.E.      (PROB)
```

ITEM	INTERCEPT S.E.	SLOPE S.E.	THRESHOLD S.E.	LOADING S.E.	ASYMPTOTE S.E.	CHISQ (PROB)	DF
ITEM0001	2.155 0.028*	1.000 0.016*	-2.155 0.020*	0.707 0.012*	0.000 0.000*	160.2 (0.0000)	4.0
ITEM0002	0.245 0.021*	1.000 0.016*	-0.245 0.015*	0.707 0.012*	0.000 0.000*	1285.5 (0.0000)	4.0
ITEM0003	-0.206 0.020*	1.000 0.016*	0.206 0.014*	0.707 0.012*	0.000 0.000*	625.6 (0.0000)	4.0
ITEM0004	-0.984 0.020*	1.000 0.016*	0.984 0.014*	0.707 0.012*	0.000 0.000*	367.6 (0.0000)	4.0
ITEM0005	-1.211 0.020*	1.000 0.016*	1.211 0.014*	0.707 0.012*	0.000 0.000*	264.3 (0.0000)	4.0

```
                                               * STANDARD ERROR
     LARGEST CHANGE =     0.005960             2702.9  20.0
                                               (0.0000)
```

```
NOTE: ITEM FIT CHI-SQUARES AND THEIR SUMS MAY BE UNRELIABLE
FOR TESTS WITH LESS THAN 20 ITEMS

PARAMETER       MEAN   STN DEV
-----------------------------------
THRESHOLD       0.000    1.340

QUADRATURE POINTS, POSTERIOR WEIGHTS, MEAN AND S.D.:
                    1            2            3            4            5
POINT        -0.4057E+01  -0.3477E+01  -0.2898E+01  -0.2318E+01  -0.1739E+01
POSTERIOR     0.5977E-04   0.5148E-03   0.3272E-02   0.1537E-01   0.5209E-01

                    6            7            8            9           10
POINT        -0.1159E+01  -0.5797E+00  -0.2245E-03   0.5793E+00   0.1159E+01
POSTERIOR     0.1228E+00   0.1979E+00   0.2246E+00   0.1890E+00   0.1184E+00

                   11           12           13           14           15
POINT         0.1738E+01   0.2318E+01   0.2897E+01   0.3477E+01   0.4056E+01
POSTERIOR     0.5372E-01   0.1742E-01   0.4042E-02   0.6735E-03   0.7979E-04

MEAN          0.00000
S.D.          1.00000
:
ITEM:  ITEM0001   CHISQ =    160.0  DF =   4.0  PROB< 0.0000
    1.00+-------------------------------------------------------------+
        |                                           X         ..........|
        |                                    X    ...|.......          |
    0.90|                                         |.....               |
        |                              X    ....|                      |
    0.80|                            ..|....                           |
        |                          ...                                 |
    0.70|                    X...                                      |
        |                  .|                                          |
    0.60|               ..                                             |
        |             ..                                               |
    0.50|          ..                                                  |
        |        ..                                                    |
    0.40|                                                              |
        |                                                              |
    0.30|                                                              |
        |                                                              |
    0.20|                                                              |
        |                                                              |
    0.10|                                                              |
        |                                                              |
    0.00|                                                              |
        +--+-----+-----+-----+-----+-----+-----+-----+-----+-----+---+
  THETA   -2.17 -1.74 -1.32 -0.89 -0.47 -0.04  0.39  0.81  1.24  1.66
```

quadrature node is X_1 = $-0.4000E+01$ = -4.0 and its weight $A(X_1)$ = $0.7648E-04$ = 0.0007648). Following this information is the calibration's iteration history. Given that the last changed across iterations (i.e., LARGEST CHANGE= 0.005) is less than the convergence criterion of 0.01 and the number of executed EM and Newton cycles are less than their corresponding maxima, we have a converged solution; the number of EM cycles is 8 with 1 Newton cycle. The -2 LOG LIKELIHOOD values show the expected progressively decreasing pattern of a well-behaved solution. The marginal maximum log likelihood function value (-2 LOG LIKELIHOOD) after the last cycle may be used for comparing relative model fit; this is done in Chapter 6.

The table subsequent to the iteration history contains the item parameter estimates. From Chapter 2 we know that the model may be written in a slope–intercept (i.e., linearized) form. In this form the intercept, γ, is a function of an item's discrimination and location parameters; Equation 2.3, $\gamma = -\alpha\delta$. The INTERCEPT column contains the estimated item intercepts, $\hat{\gamma}$s. The columns labeled SLOPE and THRESHOLD contain the fixed common discrimination parameter estimate, $\hat{\alpha}$, and item location parameter estimates, $\hat{\delta}$s, respectively.[8] The column labeled LOADING refers to the relationship between responses on item j and the (unidimensional) latent trait; it is obtained by $\alpha_j\sqrt{1+\alpha_j^2}$ and is discussed in Appendix C and Appendix E, "Using Principal Axis for Estimating Item Discrimination." The ASYMPTOTE column contains the estimates of the IRFs' lower asymptote. This lower asymptote (χ) is associated with the three-parameter model and is discussed in Chapter 6. For the 1PL model $\chi = 0.0$ for all items.

The CHISQ and DF columns contain the chi-square statistics used for fit assessment and their degrees of freedom, respectively. These chi-square statistics are based on combining individuals into, by default, 9 intervals on the basis of their Bayes location estimates (Mislevy & Bock, 1985). As mentioned above, we are ignoring these values because for our short instrument these values are suspect; their calculation is requested only as a means of obtaining the empirical versus predicted IRFs and for illustrative purposes.[9]

Given that this is a Rasch model calibration, our common discrimination parameter estimate is set to 1.0 (i.e., $\hat{\alpha} = 1.0$). As can be seen from the THRESHOLD column, the item location estimates are $\hat{\delta}_1 = -2.155, \hat{\delta}_2 = -0.245, \hat{\delta}_3 = 0.206, \hat{\delta}_4 = 0.984$, and $\hat{\delta}_5 = 1.211$. The sample standard errors for these estimates are $s_e(\hat{\alpha}) = 0.016, s_e(\hat{\delta}_1) = 0.02, s_e(\hat{\delta}_2) = 0.015$, and 0.014 for $s_e(\hat{\delta}_2), s_e(\hat{\delta}_3)$, and $s_e(\hat{\delta}_5)$). The mean and (inferential) standard deviation of the $\hat{\delta}$s are 0.0 and 1.340, respectively. (If we use the 1PL model for our calibration, then the $\hat{\alpha}$ column would potentially contain a value not equal to 1.0. Below, in the "Metric Transformation and the Total Characteristic Function" section, we provide the 1PL model estimates.)

Following the item parameter estimates table come the final adjusted quadrature weights and standardized quadrature points that determine the metric of the item parameter estimates. Comparing these adjusted weights and rescaled points with the initial $A(X_r)$s and X_rs we see only slight changes in the weights.

Subsequent to the adjusted quadrature weights and points are the empirical versus predicted IRF plots. Only item 1's figure is presented in Table 4.4. (Prior to BILOG-MG these IRFs plots were available only as the character-based graphics shown here. With BILOG-MG both character-based and bitmap graphics are available. A bitmap example of this type of plot is shown in Chapter 6, Figure 6.4.) The dotted line represents the model predicted IRF based on the item's parameter estimates. The Xs represent the proportion correct of a group of persons with approximately similar locations, whereas the vertical lines (error bands) represent a span of two standard errors around the expected group proportion tolerance interval (Mislevy & Bock, 1985). Collectively, these Xs are, in effect, the empirical IRF. If the Xs fall within the error bands, then there is agreement between the empirical IRF and the predicted IRF indicating item fit. For this particular item there is reasonable agreement, although for the other four items there is less agreement between the empirical and predicted IRFs. However, all empirical IRFs showed an ogival pattern consistent with the model's functional form assumption.

The degree of agreement between the empirical and predicted IRFs informs our judgment of fit, but is not the sole determinant of our judgment. For instance, sometimes we find that the Xs reflect an ogival pattern that shows close agreement with the predicted IRF for a substantial range of the continuum, but disagreement at, for example, the lower end of the continuum (say, below -2). Depending on the application, this lack of fit at and below -2 may not be reason for concern. In short, different situations may be more amenable to or accepting of a certain degree of less than perfect fit. Another consideration is the number of intervals used in calculating the chi-square value and in creating the empirical IRFs. That is, as mentioned above the number of intervals used can affect the appearance of these IRFs and, thereby, our interpretation. For example, with a small number of intervals we might observe strong agreement between the empirical and the predicted IRFs, but with a larger number of intervals the degree of agreement is not as strong, all other things being equal. Moreover, in making our judgment of fit we recognize that the choice of two standard errors for defining the error bands is a reasonable, but arbitrary, decision. As a result, what defines agreement between the predicted and empirical IRFs is not absolute. Again, all of this information is used to inform our judgment of fit along with the context (e.g., the number of items on the instrument, the number of items exhibiting "weak agreement," the number of respondents, the purpose of the application, etc.).

Figure 4.3 contains a Double-Y graph for the total information function ($I(\theta)$) and the corresponding sample SEEs for the instrument. The shape of the $I(\theta)$ is identical to that presented in Figure 2.11 (Chapter 2), although its maximum is located at different points along the θ continuum. This is due to the two metrics not being aligned with one another (i.e., this is a result of the indeterminacy of metric issue). However, we can linearly transform the Figure 4.3 metric to align with that in Figure 2.11. As such, the total information function is invariant within a linear transformation; this is also true for the item information functions. From Equation 2.15 (Chapter 2) we know that there is an inverse relationship between $I(\theta)$ and SEE. We see this relationship in Figure 4.3. Specifically, as the total information (the solid line) for estimating θ decreases, the $s_e(\hat{\theta})$s (the dashed line) for the $\hat{\theta}$s increases, and vice versa. On this metric this instrument provides comparatively more information for estimating person locations between -0.5 and 1.25 than it does outside this range. Moreover, this figure may be used to determine the total information available (or standard error) for a particular θ. For example, we see that for individuals located at -3, the total information (solid line) is about 0.34 (i.e., from the left ordinate scale) and that this corresponds to a standard error (dashed line) of approximately 1.72 (i.e., from the right ordinate scale).

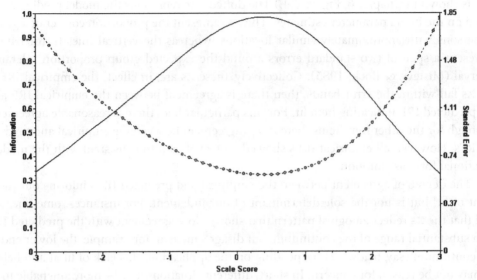

FIGURE 4.3. Total (test) information function (solid line) and standard error of estimate (dashed line).

Figure 4.4 presents the first item's IRF (the item's location estimate, $\hat{\delta}_1$, is identified by "b" on the abscissa; left panel) as well as its information function (right panel). As discussed in Chapter 2, for the 1PL model the item's maximum information occurs at the item's δ. Therefore, for the first item its maximum information occurs at $\hat{\delta}_1 = -2.155$. If we present the $I_j(\theta)$ plot for the second item, then its maximum information would be the same as that for item 1, albeit at a different location (i.e., at $\hat{\delta}_2 = -0.245$). As would be expected and can

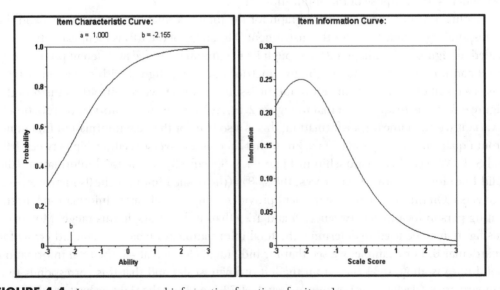

FIGURE 4.4. Item response and information functions for item 1.

be seen from the right panel, the maximum item information for this item as well as for the other items on the instrument is 0.25.

As done in Chapter 3, we would also want to examine model–data fit by verifying the invariance of the estimates by splitting the sample into, say, two randomly equivalent groups and calibrating each group independently. (Other nonrandomly equivalent groups [e.g., males vs. females] may also be examined.) BILOG has the capability of sampling the data file by specifying SAMPle on the INPUT line. The use of this feature for invariance assessment is demonstrated in Chapter 5.

In general, it is the constellation of item fit statistics, empirical versus predicted IRFs, and the tenability of assumptions that need to be considered in determining model–data fit. From the foregoing we conclude that, practically speaking, there is an acceptable degree of fit for the instrument using the Rasch model. However, this does not mean that we cannot obtain better model–data fit with an alternative model and hence revisit these data using a different model in Chapter 5.

As previously mentioned, in BILOG the indeterminacy of the metric is addressed by imposing constraints on the estimated densities at the quadrature nodes to standardize $g(\theta|\underline{\upsilon})$ (Mislevy & Stocking, 1989). Because of the differences in the way the indeterminacy of the metrics is addressed in BILOG and BIGSTEPS, we should not directly compare the $\hat{\delta}$s from the two calibrations without transforming one metric to the other. (Making comparisons across metrics is discussed later in this chapter.) However, theoretically and assuming model–data fit, the two δ metrics should be linearly related. Therefore, because the correlation is a standardized linear relationship index (i.e., it is not tied to a particular metric), it is possible to use it to assess the relative linear ordered agreement across the metrics. Given our conclusion that there is model–data fit, we would expect the BILOG and BIGSTEP δ metrics to be highly linearly related. Comparing the BILOG estimates with those of BIGSTEPS (Table 3.5) shows that although they are not exactly equal, they are very close to one another. In fact, the Pearson correlation between the BILOG and BIGSTEPS' sets of $\hat{\delta}$s is 0.9999. However, the variability of the BIGSTEPS $\hat{\delta}$s is larger (SD = 1.728) than with the BILOG estimates. Another difference between the calibrations is BILOG's use of all 19,601 examinees and BIGSTEPS use of 15,525; this is due to the programs' different estimation approaches (i.e., JMLE vs. MMLE).

Obtaining Person Location Estimates with BILOG-MG

Although we could obtain item and person parameter estimates in a single execution of BILOG, we separated the two stages for efficiency. That is, if the item fit analyses led to the removal of one or more item(s), then we would have had to reexecute BILOG on the reduced item set. Separating the item parameter estimation stage from person parameter estimation allowed us to avoid estimating the locations for 19,601 persons until after we had achieved a satisfactory level of model–data fit. We now turn to estimating the person locations.

In estimating the person θs we do not reestimate the item parameter estimates. Rather, we use our previously estimated items. That is, recall that the command file for estimating the item locations (Table 4.2) contained the SAVE subcommand on the GLOBAL command line and included the SAVe command (i.e., >SAVE PARm = 'MATHRSCH.PAR';). These keywords instruct BILOG to save the item parameter estimates to a file. It is this file's contents that we now use for obtaining the EAP person location estimates. Specifically, to estimate the person locations we change the GLOBAL command line to read the item parameter estimate file by inserting the subcommand IFNAME='MATHRSCH.PAR'. Therefore, our GLOBAL command reads both the data and the item parameter estimate files (i.e., >GLOBAL DFName='C:\Math.dat',IFName='C:\MATHRSCH.dat',NPA=1,LOG;). In addition, we suppress item parameter estimation by replacing the CALIB line with >CALIB SELECT=0; and we add the SCORE command with METHOD=2 to specify (default) EAP estimation (i.e., >SCORE MET=2;); MET=2 is specified for pedagogical reasons.

Although the person location estimates are found in the third phase listing (e.g., MATH. PH3) we would normally want to inspect the Phase 1 listing to make sure that the item parameter estimate file is correctly identified and read. For example, we would check the FILE ASSIGNMENT AND DISPOSITION section for the line ITEM PARAMETERS FILE 'MATHRSCH.PAR,' as well as a line that reads PREVIOUSLY-PREPARED ITEM FILE READ FROM FILE: 'MATHRSCH.PAR.'

Table 4.5 contains part of our person location estimation results. On the line "METHOD OF SCORING SUBJECTS: EXPECTATION A POSTERIORI," BILOG indicates that EAP estimation is performed. The section (GROUP SUBJECT IDENTIFICATION) contains the location estimates with two lines per person. The TRIED, RIGHT, and PERCENT columns contain the number of items attempted, the number of responses coded 1, and the percent of 1s, respectively. The ABILITY column contains the $\hat{\theta}$s, and the S.E. column the corresponding standard errors. As is the case above, we see that all individuals with the same observed score (i.e., the RIGHT column) obtain the same $\hat{\theta}$ regardless of the response pattern. Therefore, there are only six unique $\hat{\theta}$s for all 19,601 persons. For example, compare the last three persons in the table with X = 4. Because the individual's response pattern is used as his or her identification field, we see that for the first person with an X = 4 his or her $\underline{x}$ is 01111. Furthermore, because the items are ordered in terms of δ, we know that he or she incorrectly answered the easiest item and correctly answered the progressively more difficult items. The second of our three examinees had a response pattern of 10111, and the last person incorrectly responded to the hardest item, but correctly answered all the easier items (i.e., $\underline{x}$ =11110). All three obtained a location estimate of 0.8238 with an $s_e(\hat{\theta})$ of 0.7292. It may also be noted that individuals with zero (X = 0) and perfect (X = 5) scores had $\hat{\theta}$s of −1.3438 and 1.3685, respectively. Table 4.5 shows that the $\hat{\theta}$ for X =2 agrees with our hand calculations above, as does the corresponding $s_e(\hat{\theta})$; see Table 4.1.

The last column in Table 4.5 contains the response vector's marginal probability (MARGINAL PROB). Above we defined the marginal probability as the probability of observing a response vector for a person randomly sampled from the population with a distribution of $g(\theta|\underline{\upsilon})$. In the current context, the marginal probability is expressed in the denominators of Equations 4.14 and 4.15 (i.e., the MARGINAL PROB is given by $\Sigma L(X_r) A(X_r)$). Therefore, the individual's $\hat{\theta}$ is not used in calculating the probability of a particular response vector, $\underline{x}$. Rather, only the item parameter estimates and $g(\theta|\underline{\upsilon})$, as approximated by using the quadrature points and weights X_rs and $A(X_r)$s, are used for calculating the marginal probability of a response vector. The general pattern is that for a given observed score, the marginal probability is highest for the pattern that is consistent with intuition (i.e., an ideal response

TABLE 4.5. BILOG Output: Phase 3

```
:
    PARAMETERS FOR SCORING, RESCALING, AND TEST AND ITEM INFORMATION

    METHOD OF SCORING SUBJECTS:              EXPECTATION A POSTERIORI
                                             (EAP; BAYES ESTIMATES)
    TYPE OF PRIOR:                           NORMAL
    SCORES WRITTEN TO FILE                   MATH.PH3
    TYPE OF RESCALING:                       NONE REQUESTED
    ITEM AND TEST INFORMATION:               NONE REQUESTED
    DOMAIN SCORE ESTIMATION:                 NONE REQUESTED
:
    EAP SUBJECT ESTIMATION, SUBTEST:MATH
    QUADRATURE POINTS AND PRIOR WEIGHTS, MEAN AND S.D.:

                  1            2            3            4            5
    POINT    -0.4000E+01  -0.3111E+01  -0.2222E+01  -0.1333E+01  -0.4444E+00
    WEIGHT    0.1190E-03   0.2805E-02   0.3002E-01   0.1458E+00   0.3213E+00

                  6            7            8            9           10
    POINT     0.4444E+00   0.1333E+01   0.2222E+01   0.3111E+01   0.4000E+01
    WEIGHT    0.3213E+00   0.1458E+00   0.3002E-01   0.2805E-02   0.1190E-03

    MEAN         0.0000
    S.D.         1.0000

    GROUP    SUBJECT IDENTIFICATION                                   MARGINAL
    WEIGHT     TEST      TRIED  RIGHT  PERCENT   ABILITY    S.E.       PROB
    -----------------------------------------------------------------------
      1   1 1 0 0 0
      1.00   TEST0001     5      2     40.00  |  -0.2272    0.7291  |  0.117440
      1   1 0 0 0 0
      1.00   TEST0001     5      1     20.00  |  -0.7698    0.7457  |  0.150947
      1   1 1 1 0 0
      1.00   TEST0001     5      3     60.00  |   0.2984    0.7228  |  0.099142
      1   1 0 0 1 1
      1.00   TEST0001     5      3     60.00  |   0.2984    0.7228  |  0.010609
      1   0 0 1 1 1
      1.00   TEST0001     5      3     60.00  |   0.2984    0.7228  |  0.001001
      1   0 0 0 0 0
      1.00   TEST0001     5      0      0.00  |  -1.3438    0.7706  |  0.050159
    :
  <MANY MORE PERSONS>
    :
      1   1 1 1 1 1
      1.00   TEST0001     5      5    100.00  |   1.3685    0.7491  |  0.057713
      1   0 1 1 1 1
      1.00   TEST0001     5      4     80.00  |   0.8238    0.7292  |  0.002240
      1   1 0 1 1 1
      1.00   TEST0001     5      4     80.00  |   0.8238    0.7292  |  0.015124
      1   1 1 1 1 0
      1.00   TEST0001     5      4     80.00  |   0.8238    0.7292  |  0.064910
    -----------------------------------------------------------------------
    :
```

pattern) and decreases as the pattern becomes increasingly counterintuitive. For example, intuitively we would expect a person with an observed score of 3 to correctly answer the three easiest items (11100), rather than the three hardest items (00111). From Table 4.5 we see that a response vector of 11100 has a marginal probability of 0.099142, whereas the response vector of 00111 has a marginal probability of 0.001001. Therefore, given this instrument and the assumed distribution, the observed 11100 pattern is more probable than the 00111 response pattern. The other possible patterns with an X = 3 would have corresponding marginal probabilities between 0.099 and 0.001, with the values reflecting the degree of conformity to the 11100 pattern (e.g., 11010 would have a marginal probability greater than that for 11001).

Because the two calibration programs, BIGSTEPS and BILOG-MG, resolve the indeterminacy issue differently from one another, the MLE $\hat{\theta}$s and the EAP $\hat{\theta}$s are on different metrics and cannot be directly compared without a metric transformation. However, we can examine the relationship between the $\hat{\theta}$s for two estimation approaches. The Pearson correlation between the MLE and the EAP $\hat{\theta}$s corresponding to Xs of 1, 2, 3, 4 is 0.9978 and indicates the two metrics are highly linearly related.

METRIC TRANSFORMATION
AND THE TOTAL CHARACTERISTIC FUNCTION

In this as well as the preceding chapters, there have been situations where we wanted to compare estimates across different metrics—for example, directly comparing the BILOG estimates with those of BIGSTEPS or directly comparing estimates from different subsamples. Short of just making statements about the linear agreement of estimates across the two metrics, we could not directly compare the estimates from the two different metrics because of (potential) differences in the origins and units used. As a consequence, to make these comparisons we need to align the two metrics with one another to produce a common metric.

Although this idea is more fully examined in Chapter 11, we present the essence of it here. Typically, one chooses one metric to serve as the *target* metric onto which the other metric is transformed. This is analogous to choosing the Fahrenheit temperature scale as the target metric and transforming Celsius temperatures to Fahrenheit. (As is also true with the temperature scales in this analogy, the IRT metric is relative, not absolute.)

As previously mentioned, our continuum is determined up to a linear transformation. In general, the linear transformation from one metric to another metric for both person and item locations is given by

$$\xi^* = \zeta(\xi) + \kappa \tag{4.17}$$

where ξ is the δ_j (or θ) on the metric to be transformed (the *initial* metric) and ξ^* is the δ_j^* (or θ^*) on the target metric. Collectively, ζ and κ are called the *metric transformation coefficients* or *equating coefficients*. (In the Celsius/Fahrenheit analogy $\zeta = 1.8$ and $\kappa = 32$.)

To transform our other item parameter, item discrimination, we would use

$$\alpha^* = \frac{\alpha}{\zeta} \tag{4.18}$$

In terms of a slope–intercept parameterization, our intercept parameter is transformed by

$$\gamma^* = \gamma - \frac{\alpha(\kappa)}{\zeta} \tag{4.19}$$

In some situations the values of ζ and κ are given by the target metric's characteristics. For instance, if we are interested in converting our θs (or their estimates) to the T-score scale to enhance their interpretability, then the target metric is the T-score scale and, by definition, $\zeta = 10$ and $\kappa = 50$. In other situations, we might wish to align the metric from one calibration sample with that of another sample or align the Rasch calibration metric with a 1PL model calibration of the same data. (We refer to this alignment of metrics as *linking* and is discussed further in Chapter 11.) In these cases we need to estimate the values of ζ and κ.

There are multiple strategies that we can use to obtain the metric transformation coefficients. One simple approach is based on using the means and standard deviations of the item locations. In this approach the transformation coefficient ζ is obtained by taking the ratio of the target to initial metric item location standard deviations:

$$\zeta = \frac{s_{\delta^*}}{s_\delta} \qquad (4.20)$$

where s_{δ^*} is the standard deviation of the item locations on the target metric and s_δ is the standard deviation of the item locations on the initial metric. Once ζ is determined, the other transformation coefficient κ is obtained by

$$\kappa = \bar{\delta}_j{}^* - \zeta \bar{\delta}_j \qquad (4.21)$$

where $\bar{\delta}_j{}^*$ is the mean of the item locations on the target metric and $\bar{\delta}_j$ is the mean of the item locations on the initial metric. Equations 4.20 and 4.21 are the standard linear transformation equations one sees in an introductory statistics course. (An alternative approach for determining ζ and κ is discussed in Chapter 11.)

As an example, assume we wish to link the metric from our Rasch model calibration with that from a 1PL model calibration of the mathematics data. To obtain the 1PL model calibration estimates we remove the keyword RASch from the CALIB command line (Table 4.2) and reexecute BILOG. Our 1PL model item parameter estimates are $\hat{\alpha} = 1.421$, $\hat{\delta}_1 = -1.925, \hat{\delta}_2 = -0.581, \hat{\delta}_3 = -0.264, \hat{\delta}_4 = 0.284$, and $\hat{\delta}_5 = 0.443$. The mean and standard deviation of the $\hat{\delta}$s are -0.409 and 0.943, respectively. Table 4.4 shows that our Rasch model estimates are $\hat{\alpha} = 1.0, \hat{\delta}_1 = -2.155, \hat{\delta}_2 = -0.245, \hat{\delta}_3 = 0.206, \hat{\delta}_4 = 0.984$, and $\hat{\delta}_5 = 1.211$ with a mean $\hat{\delta}$ of 0.0. Comparing the two sets of estimates shows that the two metrics are not the same although they are highly linearly related ($r = 0.9999$).

To transform the Rasch model calibration metric (i.e., the initial metric) to that of the 1PL model calibration metric (i.e., the target metric), we apply Equations 4.17 and 4.18. Our metric transformation coefficients are obtained using the metrics' means and standard deviations. Given that the 1PL and Rasch models' $\hat{\delta}$s standard deviations are 0.943 and 1.340, respectively, we have

$$\zeta = s_{\delta^*}/s_\delta = 0.943/1.340 = 0.704$$

Because the respective initial and target metric means are 0.0 and -0.409, we have that

$$\kappa = \overline{\delta}_j{}^* - \zeta\overline{\delta}_j = -0.409 - 0.704\,(0) = -0.409$$

Therefore, the transformation equation for item (and person) location estimates is

$$\xi^* = \zeta(\hat{\xi}) + \kappa = (0.704)\,\hat{\zeta} + (-0.409)$$

and for the item discrimination parameter we use

$$\alpha^* = \frac{\alpha}{\zeta} = \frac{\alpha}{0.704}$$

For example, to transform the Rasch $\hat{\alpha}$ of 1.0 to the target (1PL model) metric we have

$$\hat{\alpha}^* = \frac{1.0}{0.704} = 1.421$$

Transforming the location estimate for item 1 to the target metric yields

$$\hat{\delta}_1^* = \hat{\delta}_1(\zeta) + \kappa = \hat{\delta}_1(0.704) + (-0.409) = -2.155(0.704) - 0.409 = -1.9257$$

For the other items, the transformed estimates are $\hat{\delta}_2^* = -0.5814$, $\hat{\delta}_3^* = -0.2640$, $\hat{\delta}_4^* = 0.2835$, and $\hat{\delta}_5^* = 0.4433$.

Of course, the correlation between the two metrics is still 0.9999. Now that we have aligned our metrics we can directly compare our 1PL model and Rasch model estimates to one another. As would be expected, given the mathematical equivalency of the Rasch and 1PL models, the two sets of estimates are the same. (Any differences in the transformed estimates and the target values are due to item parameter estimation error as well as rounding error.) Comparing our results, we see that the effect of having forced α to be 1.0 is to stretch out the metric relative to when α is estimated to be 1.421. Because α's value is absorbed into the metric, we can stretch or contract the metric by changing the value of α.

As mentioned above, another use of a metric transformation is to convert a metric to make it more meaningful or interpretable. Focusing on the person location estimates, we could convert our standard θ metric that is centered at 0.0 to a target metric that did not have negative values (e.g., a T-score scale, the College Entrance Examination Board [CEEB] scale, etc.). This would be done by using Equation 4.17 with ξ representing θ and the appropriate values for ζ and κ.

Another target metric that has intrinsic meaning for people is the total score metric. For instance, rather than informing a respondent that his or her $\hat{\theta}$ is 1.1746, which may or may not have any inherent meaning to the person, we can transform the individual's $\hat{\theta}$ to the more familiar total score metric.

We can perform this transformation through the *total characteristic function* (TCF):

$$T = \sum^{L} p_j \tag{4.22}$$

where T is the *expected trait score*, L represents the instrument's length, and p_j is the probability of a response of 1 according to a dichotomous IRT model; Equation 4.22 is also called the *test characteristic function*. In a proficiency assessment situation the total score metric indicates the number of expected correctly answered items.

From Equation 4.22 we see that θ and T represent the same concept, but on different metrics (Lord, 1980). That is, with θ we have an infinite metric $-\infty < \theta < \infty$, whereas with T and the 1PL model we have a bounded metric, $0 \leq T \leq L$. As a result, when $\theta = -\infty$, T equals 0, and when $\theta = \infty$, then T equals the number of items on the instrument (a perfect score). However, θ and T differ in that T's metric is dependent on the items on the instrument and the θ's metric is independent of the instrument's items. In addition, because the relationship between p_j and θ is nonlinear, the relationship between θ and T is also nonlinear.

In some cases, it may be desirable to convert θ to a proportion metric. To obtain an expected proportion equivalence for θ (i.e., the proportion of responses of 1), we divide T by L:

$$\mathcal{E}T = \frac{\Sigma p_j}{L} \tag{4.23}$$

The term $\mathcal{E}T$ is referred to as the *expected proportion trait score* or as a *domain score* (e.g., see Hambleton & Swaminathan, 1985; Lord, 1980). In proficiency assessment $\mathcal{E}T$ is the expected proportion of correct responses.

As an example, assume that we wish to report performance on our mathematics test on the total score metric (i.e., 0 to 5), but we also want to have the advantages that IRT provides over CTT. As a result, rather than reporting observed scores, we calibrate our data with the 1PL model and estimate our examinees' locations. To convert these $\hat{\theta}$s to the total score metric we use Equation 4.22. For instance, for individuals located at 1.1746 (i.e., $\hat{\theta} = 1.1746$) we calculate the probabilities of a response of 1 for each of our items. These probabilities are $p_1 = 0.9882$, $p_2 = 0.9255$, $p_3 = 0.8878$, $p_4 = 0.7841$, and $p_5 = 0.7434$. Therefore, all examinees with a location estimate of 1.1746 have a trait score of

$$T = 0.9882 + \ldots + 0.7434 = 4.3291$$

or, in terms of expected proportion correct, we have

$$\mathcal{E}T = \frac{4.3291}{5} = 0.87$$

That is, any person with a location estimate of 1.1746 would be expected to correctly answer 4.33 items, or 87% of the items, on our mathematics examination.

We can graphically represent the functional relationship between θ and T (i.e., Equation 4.22). This graphical relationship is referred to as a *total characteristic curve* (TCC) or *test characteristic curve*. For example, Figure 4.5 contains the TCC for our five-item mathematics instrument and shows the transformation of 1.1746 to its corresponding T. We can easily convert any $\hat{\theta}$ to its corresponding T by simply identifying the person's location on the abscissa, projecting from this point up to the TCC, and then proceeding to the ordinate. Moreover, the TCC graphical representation allows us to take any T and convert it to its corresponding θ.

From the foregoing we see that the total characteristic function not only specifies the

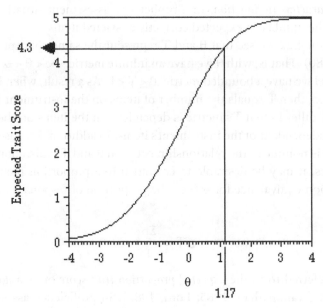

FIGURE 4.5. Total characteristic curve for the five-item instrument.

relationship between the trait score T and the IRT person location (or its estimate), but also facilitates the conversion of θ (or $\hat{\theta}$) to the total score metric. This function has one additional use. In Chapter 11 we use it to place different calibration results onto a common metric. This approach, known as *total characteristic function equating*, provides an additional method for obtaining our metric transformation coefficient values.

SUMMARY

In this chapter we presented a second method, marginal maximum likelihood estimation, for instrument calibration. This method separates the estimation of items from that of persons by assuming that persons are randomly sampled from some population. In this approach the original likelihood is multiplied by the population distribution and thereby eliminates, through integration, the person location parameters. MMLE then obtains MLEs of the item parameters by maximizing the (marginal) likelihood function. The numerical integration is accomplished by using a Gaussian quadrature approach. In short, the continuous population distribution is approximated by using a discrete distribution consisting of quadrature nodes and associated weights that reflect the density of the function around the node. As is the case with JMLE, MMLE is an iterative procedure. Once convergence is achieved, we assess model–data fit.

Because we separate item estimation from person estimation, we can use MLE or a Bayesian procedure, such as Bayes Modal Estimation or Bayes Mean Estimate (i.e., EAP), for estimating person locations. EAP is noniterative, and unlike MLE $\hat{\theta}$s, EAP location estimates are available for all response patterns, including zero and perfect score patterns.

In addition to the model–data fit methods introduced in previous chapters, in this chapter we introduced a graphical approach based on empirical and predicted IRFs. Specifically, if the predicted IRFs show close agreement with the observed IRFs, then we have evidence supporting model–data fit. Moreover, the tenability of our model's functional form assumption may be determined by examining the empirical IRFs. At this point in this book we have looked at model–data fit by using fit statistics and graphically, by determining the tenability of the dimensionality and functional form assumptions, and by examining the invariance of item parameter estimates.

In this chapter we introduced the transformation of one metric to another as well as the alignment or the linking of two metrics. Metric transformation can be used to enhance the interpretability of our results. For instance, we can transform the person location estimate through the instrument's total characteristic function to a total score metric that respondents may find inherently informative. The total characteristic function relates the θ continuum to the expected trait scores on the instrument. In terms of metric alignment we presented one approach for obtaining the metric transformation coefficients.

In the next chapter we relax the constraint that all items must have a common discrimination parameter. Eliminating this constraint yields the two-parameter model. In this model there is a parameter for the item's location and another for its discrimination capacity. Allowing the discrimination parameter to vary across items allows the modeling of items that differentially discriminate. Therefore, the number of situations in which we may obtain model–data fit is potentially greater than what is possible with the one-parameter model.

NOTES

1. An alternative to using JMLE or marginal maximum likelihood estimation is to use Markov chain Monte Carlo (MCMC) simulation methods. The gist of MCMC involves conducting a simulation in which one randomly samples from a particular distribution until convergence is achieved. The MCMC method uses a subset of the generated data for estimation of the parameters. The estimation of simple as well as complex models is comparatively easier with MCMC than with either JMLE or marginal maximum likelihood estimation because it does not require precalculation of derivatives (Patz & Junker, 1999a). However, MCMC implementation software is not as user-friendly as the software available for JMLE and marginal maximum likelihood estimation. Given this book's orientation, MCMC methods are not covered. Patz and Junker (1999a, 1999b) contain introductions to using MCMC methods with IRT models, and Baker and Kim (2004) discuss a particular MCMC method known as the Gibbs Sampler.

2. The symbol $\int_a^b f(x)dx$ means integrate the function $f(x)$ between a and b with respect to x; the dx means perform the integration with respect to x. The a and b are the limits of the integration. For example, the integral $\int_a^b \frac{1}{\sqrt{2\pi}}e^{-(z^2)/2}dz$ means integrate the expression $\frac{1}{\sqrt{2\pi}}e^{-(z^2)/2}$ over the range of values from a to b with respect to z. In integrating a function one is, in effect, finding the area under the function between a and b. Integrals are sometimes called antiderivatives.

3. Implied in Figure 4.1 is that the quadrature points have special locations to maximize the accuracy of the approximation. As a contrarian example, one would not expect that using 11 quadrature points located between 0 and 1 would lead to an accurate approximation of the area under the curve in Figure 4.1. The locations (X_rs) and their corresponding weights ($A(X_r)$s) may be obtained from tables provided by Stroud and Secrest (1966) for approximating the Gaussian error function.

The Stroud and Secrest Gauss–Hermite X_rs and $A(X_r)$s must be multiplied by $\sqrt{2}$ and $(1/\sqrt{\pi})$, respectively, to place them on the normal function metric (Bock & Lieberman, 1970). However, typically the Stroud and Secrest values are not used in programs that use MMLE, such as BILOG-3 , BILOG-MG, or MULTILOG. Rather, a specified range of the θ continuum (e.g., –4.0 to 4.0) is divided into R equidistant discrete points that serve as the X_rs, and the standard unit normal probability density is computed at each of the R points (i.e., $f(X_r) = \left[1/\sqrt{2\pi} \right] \exp(-X_i^2/2)$). The probability density at X_r is multiplied by the interval width (i.e., $X_r - X_{r+1}$) to obtain the quadrature weight $A(X_r)$. If the discrete (prior) distribution is symmetric, then the $A(X_r)$s need to be calculated only for the X_rs ≤ 0. The X_rs and $A(X_r)$s must satisfy the constraints that $\Sigma A(X_r) = 1.0$, $\Sigma X_r A(X_r) = 0.0$, and $\Sigma X_i^2 A(X_r) = 1.0$.

4. Alternative to using biweights or a Bayesian strategy is to use a *weighted MLE* approach for estimating θ (Warm, 1989) or an *AMT-Robustified Jackknife MLE* (Wainer & Wright, 1980). The former approach uses, in effect, the instrument's total information to reduce the bias inherent in MLE $\hat{\theta}$s. The latter approach uses the Jackknife procedure to accomplish the same thing when the bias is due to response aberrations. Wainer and Wright (1980) investigated the AMT-Robustified Jackknife MLE and found that it performed well in the context of guessing; the study assumed that reasonably good estimates of δ could be obtained, for example, by culling from the calibration sample persons with unusual response patterns.

5. Specifying a Rasch calibration with BILOG-MG version 3.0 requires, in addition to specifying the 1PL for Model in the SETUP menu's GENERAL dialog, that one also select "ONE PARAMETER LOGISTIC MODEL" [*sic*] from the TECHNICAL menu's CALIBRATION OPTIONS dialog. That is, the "ONE PARAMETER LOGISTIC MODEL" check box is mislabeled; the check box should read "Rasch Model." Selecting the "ONE PARAMETER LOGISTIC MODEL" check box to perform a Rasch calibration instructs the program to rescale the 1PL estimates so that $\alpha = 1$; the δ_js are also appropriately transformed. How this rescaling is performed is discussed in the "Metric Transformation and the Total Characteristic Function" section.

6. Although the presence of omitted item(s) at the end of an instrument may indicate speededness, their absence does not necessarily indicate that individuals had sufficient time to take the instrument. This is due to the fact that an individual realizing that administration time is about to expire may simply answer at random those items he or she has insufficient time to appropriately consider.

7. The biserial correlation coefficient (ρ_b) is a measure of the association between an artificially dichotomized variable and a continuous variable. With a ρ_b one has two normally distributed continuous variables, but for some reason one variable is reduced to two categories. The nondichotomized continuous variable may be the variable being measured by the instrument. In contrast, the point-biserial (ρ_{pb}) is an association index for a genuine dichotomous variable and a continuous variable; the point-biserial is a special case of the Pearson correlation coefficient. The continuous variable is assumed to be normally distributed. The relationship between these correlations is presented in Appendix C.

8. The term *threshold* should not be confused with the epidemiological use of *threshold* in logistic regression. In that context, a threshold is the point on a continuum where the response function first begins to increase rapidly. Therefore, the associated probability with this threshold is less than 0.5. In BILOG *threshold* refers to the item's location.

9. Some versions of BILOG, for example, BILOG-3, also contain a column labeled DISPERSION. DISPERSION is the item standard deviation when working with the normal ogive models and is equaled to $1/\alpha$; a normal ogive model is discussed in Appendix C.

5

The Two-Parameter Model

In Chapter 2 we developed a model on the premise that the distance between a person's location and an item's location is an important determinant of his or her response. However, when we examine a traditional discrimination index, such as the biserial correlation, we typically find that they vary across the items on the instrument. For instance, the biserials for the mathematics data vary from 0.397 to 0.564 (see Table 4.3). In this chapter we extend our distance idea to incorporate information about how well an item discriminates among individuals located at different points. We still use the distance between the person's and the item's locations, but we now weight this distance by how well the item discriminates. Thus, the probability of a response of 1 is a function of not only how far apart the person and the item are, but also how well the item differentiates among respondents located at different points on the continuum.

By taking into account how well an item discriminates we are relaxing the constraint that items must share a common slope. As a result, we are able to obtain model fit in a greater number of situations than with the Rasch model. Our relaxing of the common discrimination parameter constraint implies a philosophical shift. That is, with the Rasch model our interest is not so much in modeling the data, but rather in constructing an instrument that is consistent with the Rasch model.[1] With the two-parameter model our philosophical perspective is one of modeling the data. In the following discussion, we conceptually develop the two-parameter logistic model. Consistent with the previous three chapters, we then apply the model to the mathematics data introduced in Chapter 2. As part of our model fit analysis we revisit item parameter invariance and discuss strategies for its examination when item discrimination is allowed to vary across items. We end by discussing relative efficiency as an approach for simultaneously comparing multiple total information functions.

CONCEPTUAL DEVELOPMENT OF THE TWO-PARAMETER MODEL

As is true for the 1PL model, the data for the two-parameter model need to be dichotomous. Such data may come from, for example, a personality inventory, a depression scale, or an examination (cf. Reise & Waller, 1990; Schaeffer, 1988). In Chapter 2 we pointed out that we could potentially improve fit by varying the slope of the predicted IRF to more closely match that of the empirical IRF.

Figure 5.1 contains the IRFs for five items with different discrimination values, but located at the same point on the continuum. This common location corresponds to the intersection point of all five IRFs and is $\delta_1 = \delta_2 = \delta_3 = \delta_4 = \delta_5 = 1.0$. As can be seen, as the values of α change from 0.5 to 3.0 the corresponding IRFs become progressively steeper. For example, comparing item 1 ($\alpha_1 = 0.5$; solid line) with item 5 ($\alpha_5 = 3.0$; bold dashed line) one sees that item 1's slope is substantially less than that of item 5. These IRFs may be modeled by modifying the 1PL model to allow for α to vary across items. When this is done the 1PL model becomes the Birnbaum *two-parameter logistic* (2PL) model:

$$p(x_j = 1|\theta, \alpha_j, \delta_j) = \frac{e^{\alpha_j(\theta-\delta_j)}}{1+e^{\alpha_j(\theta-\delta_j)}} \qquad (5.1)$$

where θ is the person location parameter, and δ_j and α_j are item j's location and discrimination parameters, respectively; the subscript on α indicates that each item j has its own discrimination parameter. With the 2PL model the logistic deviate or logit, $\alpha_j(\theta - \delta_j)$, contains the item's two parameters, δ_j and α_j.[2] (The 2PL model may also be written to include the scaling constant, D; see Appendix C.) The 2PL model is predicated on a unidimensional latent space, conditional independence, and the functional form assumptions discussed in Chapter 2. The functional form assumption embodies an IRF with a lower asymptote of 0. For ease of presentation we use p_j instead of $p(x_j = 1|\theta, \alpha_j, \delta_j)$ in the following discussion.

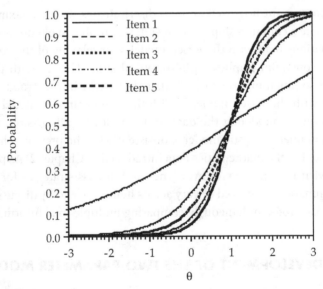

FIGURE 5.1. Item response functions for five items with the same location and different slopes ($\alpha_1 = 0.5$, $\alpha_2 = 1.5$, $\alpha_3 = 2.0$, $\alpha_4 = 2.5$, $\alpha_5 = 3.0$; $\delta = 1.0$ for all five items).

An item's α_j characterizes how well the item can differentiate among individuals located at different points on the continuum. As is the case with the 1PL model, α_j is proportional to the slope of the IRF at its inflexion point, δ_j. The slope at δ_j is $0.25*\alpha_j$.[3] As the value of α_j increases, the IRF's slope becomes steeper and the item's capacity to discriminate between individuals also increases. When items vary in their discrimination, then their corresponding IRFs cross one another at some point along the continuum.

The discrimination parameter can theoretically vary from $-\infty$ to ∞ with an $\alpha = \infty$ (or $\alpha = -\infty$) reflected in a step function IRF. Reasonably "good" values of α range from approximately 0.8 to about 2.5. A negative α_j reflects an item where individuals with lower θs have a higher probability of obtaining a response of 1 than individuals with higher θs (i.e., a monotonically nonincreasing IRF). As such, an item with a negative α_j is behaving in a counterintuitive fashion. Similar to a traditional negative discrimination index (e.g., a negative point biserial or biserial correlation), a negative α_j may indicate an item that should be discarded because its performance is inconsistent with the model or, in the case of proficiency assessment, an item that has its correct response incorrectly specified.

Figure 5.1 shows that a 2PL model's IRF share a similarity with those of the 1PL model. Namely, the item is located at the point where an individual randomly selected from all the persons located at the item's location has a 50:50 chance of obtaining a response of 1. Because this is also the point of maximum slope, the item location is also the point at which the item discriminates most effectively among respondents.

INFORMATION FOR THE TWO-PARAMETER MODEL

There is an indirect relationship between an item's α_j and how much it reduces our uncertainty about a person's location on the continuum. Stated another way, as an item's discrimination parameter increases, the maximum item information for estimating θ increases, and this in turn leads to a decrease in our uncertainty about a person's location when the item is located close to θ.[4] This increase in available information at δ_j is associated with a concomitant decrease in the standard error for our estimated person location at this point. The standard error is our measure of uncertainty. That is, because this asymptotic standard error reflects the variability of the $\hat{\theta}$s over an infinite number of independent administrations, a reduction in the standard error means that the $\hat{\theta}$s would be tightly clustered together about θ and we would have greater certainty about the person's true location.

The item information functions ($I_j(\theta)$s) corresponding to the items in Figure 5.1 are presented in Figure 5.2. As is the case with the 1PL model, Figure 5.2 shows that an item provides its maximum information at δ_j and that the distribution of information is unimodal and symmetric about δ_j. However, we see that for individuals located at or near $\delta = 1.0$ these items vary in their amount of information for estimating a person's location. In contrast to the 1PL model, the maximum amount of information provided by an item varies as a direct function of the magnitude of α_j. Item 5 with an $\alpha_5 = 3.0$ provides the greatest amount of information for distinguishing among individuals in the vicinity of δ_j, whereas item 1 with the smallest α ($\alpha_1 = 0.5$) provides the least information at δ.[5]

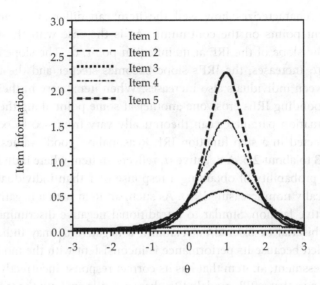

FIGURE 5.2. Item information functions for five items from Figure 5.1 ($\alpha_1 = 0.5$, $\alpha_2 = 1.5$, $\alpha_3 = 2.0$, $\alpha_4 = 2.5$, $\alpha_5 = 3.0$; $\delta = 1.0$).

In Chapter 2 a general formulation of item information is presented. Specifically, our item information is given by

$$I_j(\theta) = \frac{[p_j']^2}{p_j(1-p_j)} \tag{5.2}$$

Conceptually, Equation 5.2 can be interpreted as an item's information at θ equals how quickly the IRF changes over the (conditional) variance at θ.[6] Given that the first derivative for the 2PL model is

$$p_j' = \alpha_j p_j(1 - p_j) \tag{5.3}$$

its substitution for p_j' into Equation 5.2 produces the 2PL model item information function

$$I_j(\theta) = \alpha_j^2 p_j(1 - p_j) \tag{5.4}$$

Because when $p_j = (1 - p_j) = 0.5$ the product $p_j(1 - p_j)$ is at its maximum, our maximum item information is $\alpha_j^2 \, 0.25$. When an item is calibrated with the two-parameter model and $\alpha_j > 1.0$, then the item contributes more information for estimating θ than when the Rasch model is used for calibration. Moreover, we see that the 1PL model's item information, $\alpha^2 p_j(1 - p_j)$, is a special case of Equation 5.4. The total information for an instrument is defined as it is in Chapter 2 (i.e., the sum of the item information functions):[7]

$$I(\theta) = \frac{1}{\sigma_e^2(\theta)} = \sum_{j=1}^{L} I_j(\theta) \qquad (5.5)$$

CONCEPTUAL PARAMETER ESTIMATION FOR THE 2PL MODEL

If we were to graphically present the log likelihood function for estimating δ_j in the Rasch model, we would need only two dimensions because item discrimination is constant. That is, one axis would represent δ, whereas the other would reflect the log likelihood values. The resulting figure would look similar to the ln$L$ shown in Figure A.1 (Appendix A). However, when estimating an item's α_j and δ_j the graphical presentation of the (log) likelihood function requires three dimensions (Figure 5.3): one dimension for each parameter and the third to represent the (log) likelihood values. (This is analogous to having a regression line with one predictor [i.e., the Rasch model case], but requiring a regression plane with two predictors [i.e., the 2PL model case]. We can view the log likelihood function for estimating δ_j in the Rasch model as a "slice" through the surface [Figure 5.3] conditional on $\alpha = 1.0$.)

As we see, as α_j increases the surface becomes more peaked and, conversely, as α_j decreases the surface becomes less peaked. Therefore, as α_j decreases it becomes more difficult to obtain $\hat{\delta}_j$ and as α_j increases the estimation of δ_j becomes comparatively easier, all

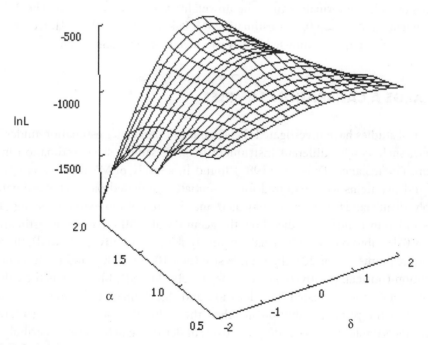

FIGURE 5.3. Log likelihood function for an item with $\alpha = 1.00$ and $\delta = 0.25$.

other things being equal. Conceptually, our estimation requires us to simultaneously determine the location of the maximum of this surface with respect to both the α and δ axes. The location of the maximum on the α axis is our estimate of α (i.e., $\hat{\alpha}_j$) and the location on the δ axis is our estimate of δ (i.e., $\hat{\delta}_j$). In Figure 5.3 the maximum of the $\ln L$ occurs at approximately $\hat{\alpha}_j = 0.98$ and $\hat{\delta}_j = 0.26$.

The 2PL model's log likelihood equation is similar to that seen in Chapter 2 (Equation 2.10), but with p_j determined by Equation 5.1. The general principles for parameter estimation that were outlined in Chapters 2 and 3 (as well as Appendices A and B) also apply here. The 2PL model's parameters may be estimated by several different methods, such as JMLE or MMLE. As is the case with the 1PL model, starting values for the estimation need to be provided. Equations C.12 and C.16 (Appendix C) can be used to provide these starting values for estimating α_j and δ_j, respectively. The mathematical details for 2PL model estimation are shown in Baker and Kim (2004).

The 2PL model, like the 1PL model, has sufficient statistics. For estimating a person i's location the sufficient statistic is the weighted sum of the item responses, $\sum \alpha_j x_{ij}$.[8] In general, this weighted sum provides more information than the unweighted sum (i.e., $\sum x_{ij}$) except when the two sums are identical or proportional (Lord, 1983a). One implication of weighting the item responses by the item discrimination parameters is that different patterns of responses, albeit with the same observed score (e.g., 11100 and 10011), result in different person location estimates. However, unlike the sufficient statistic for the 1PL model, the sufficient statistic for the 2PL model depends on the unknown discrimination parameters, α_js. In short, the sufficient statistic for estimating a person's location is not independent of the items because we need to know their α_js. If the estimates of the α_js are inaccurate, then the weighted sum is less informative than the unweighted sum (Lord, 1983a). The 2PL model has a sufficient statistic, $\sum p_j \theta_i$, for estimating α_j (Baker & Kim, 2004). However, this sufficient statistic also requires knowledge of a parameter—the person parameter.

HOW LARGE A CALIBRATION SAMPLE?

A number of studies have investigated the accuracy of parameter estimation under various conditions, such as with different instrument lengths, sample sizes, estimation methods, and so on. For instance, Drasgow (1989) found in a study of MMLE that as few as 200 persons and five items were required for "essentially" unbiased parameter estimates with reasonably small standard errors as long as α and δ were not too extreme. Seong (1990b), using a 45-item instrument, studied how the accuracy of MMLE parameter estimation was affected by θ distribution shape (normal, positively skewed, negatively skewed), the number of quadrature points (10 or 20), the sample size (N = 100 or 1000), and the assumed prior θ distribution (normal, positively skewed, negatively skewed); BILOG was the calibration program. Overall, the estimated item location and discrimination parameters were more accurate when the prior distribution matched the θ distribution than when there was a mismatch; the sample size was 1000. Moreover, under the match θ/prior distributions and N = 1000 condition the accuracy of the item parameter estimates could be improved by increasing the number of quadrature points. Seong suggested that the default normal prior distribution and quadrature points used in BILOG were reasonable choices for a small sample size.

In another Monte Carlo study, Stone (1992) examined the effect of instrument length (L = 10, 20, or 40), sample size (N = 250, 500, or 1000), and θ distribution shape (normal, positively skewed, or symmetric and platykurtic) on estimation accuracy with a MMLE program, MULTILOG. In general, he found that with 500 or more individuals and instruments of 20 or more items both item location and discrimination estimates were generally precise and stable. The effect of the θ distribution factor was ameliorated by using the 40-item instrument. In contrast, Harwell and Janosky (1991) looked at estimation accuracy in the context of prior distribution characteristics with BILOG. They found that for short instruments (15 items) and small samples (e.g., N = 75, 100, 150) the prior variances affected the accuracy of parameter estimation. Comparatively longer instruments (25 items) were not affected as much by the prior distribution variance when the sample sizes were greater than 100. They recommended that for 15-item instruments and fewer than 250 persons, a prior variance of 0.25 for α not be used; all simulees were randomly sampled from a normal distribution and restricted to the range −3 to 3.

Because these are fixed effects design studies, we should not generalize beyond the conditions that were investigated. However, these studies may still provide some guidance as to what one might anticipate to occur in somewhat similar situations. For example, the results indicate that there are a number of factors (e.g., instrument length, prior distributions, estimation method, etc.) that affect item parameter estimation accuracy and that need to be considered in determining calibration sample size. Additional factors to take into account in determining a desirable sample size target is the application's purpose, ancillary technique sample size requirements, model–data fit tolerance, the estimation method, instrument characteristics, the variability and distribution of respondents, and the amount of missing data. The interaction of these variables makes it difficult to provide a suggested sample size that would be applicable in all situations. However, to provide some guidance we offer an admittedly rough guideline.

Assuming MMLE, the use of a prior distribution for α, and favorable conditions (e.g., θ/prior distribution match, etc.), it appears that a calibration sample size of at least 500 persons and instruments of 20 or more items tend to produce reasonably accurate item parameter estimates. It must be noted that less favorable situations may necessitate larger sample sizes. However, it should also be noted that "it is not necessarily true that because the parameters of a fitted function are not well estimated that certain other characteristics of the function are unstable . . . like the information function" (Thissen & Wainer, 1982, p. 409). That is, there may be situations where even though item parameters may not be well estimated, the estimates may still be useful. Moreover, it may be anticipated that there is a sample size, say 1200, at which one reaches, practically speaking, a point of diminishing returns in terms of improvement in estimation accuracy, all other things being equal; this should not be interpreted as an upper bound. To reiterate, the caveats and considerations previously mentioned, as well as the need to avoid interpreting sample size guidelines as hard-and-fast rules, still apply to our recommendation.[9]

METRIC TRANSFORMATION, 2PL MODEL

Examination of the model in Equation 5.1 shows that the indeterminacy issue raised with the 1PL model also applies to the 2PL model. Namely, we can add or subtract a constant from θ and δ_j and not change the logistic deviate. As a result, the IRF is unaffected, although its location moves up or down the continuum. Stated another way, the origin of the metric is arbitrary. Similarly, multiplying θ and δ_j by a constant and dividing α_j by the same constant would leave $\alpha_j(\theta - \delta_j)$ unchanged. This implies that the unit for measuring θ and δ_j is also arbitrary. As discussed in Chapters 3 and 4, this indeterminacy is addressed in different ways, such as through person centering.

This metric indeterminacy facilitates the transformation of the metric to have certain characteristics. As discussed in Chapter 4, we can rescale our parameters or their estimates by using our metric transformation coefficient ζ and κ. The discrimination parameter (or its estimate) for each item is transformed by

$$\alpha_j^* = \frac{\alpha_j}{\zeta} \tag{5.6}$$

where α_j is item j's discrimination on the metric to be transformed (i.e., α_j is on the initial metric) and α_j^* is the transformed discrimination value (i.e., α_j^* is on the target metric). In terms of a slope–intercept parameterization, the itemwise transformation would be

$$\gamma_j^* = \gamma_j - \frac{\alpha_j(\kappa)}{\zeta} \tag{5.7}$$

In general, our linear transformation is $\xi^* = \zeta(\xi) + \kappa$, where ζ and κ are the unit and location of the new metric, respectively. Therefore, to transform our item locations, ξ represents δ_j (or its estimate) on the initial metric and ξ^* reflects δ_j^* (or its estimate) on the target metric

$$\delta_j^* = \zeta(\delta_j) + \kappa \tag{5.8}$$

In addition, we can transform the person locations by letting ξ be θ (or its estimate) on the initial metric with ξ^* representing the transformed person location θ^* (or its estimate). The values of ζ and κ may be given for a particular scale, such as the T-score scale, or they may be obtained by Equations 4.20 and 4.21. However, Equations 4.20 and 4.21 ignore information in the item discrimination parameters. Therefore, when item discrimination varies across items, a preferable method for determining the values of ζ and κ is the total characteristic function equating approach presented in Chapter 11.

As is the case with the 1PL model, with the 2PL model the instrument has a total characteristic curve that is bounded by 0 and the instrument's length, L. The nonlinear transformation of θ to the total score metric is accomplished, as shown in Chapter 4, by $T = \sum p_j$, where p_j is the 2PL model. As previously mentioned, all individuals with the same location obtain the same trait score, T.

EXAMPLE: APPLICATION OF THE 2PL MODEL
TO THE MATHEMATICS DATA, MMLE

For pedagogical reasons we use BILOG to perform a 2PL model calibration of the mathematics data from Chapter 2. However, various alternative programs could also be used, such as MULTILOG, XCALIBRE (Assessment Systems Corporation, 1997), MPLUS (Muthén & Muthén, 1998), SAS (SAS Institute, 2002), R (R Development Core Team, 2007), or NOHARM. The use of NOHARM for calibration is demonstrated in Appendix E, "Example: NOHARM Unidimensional Calibration."

In Chapter 3 we assessed the tenability of the unidimensionality assumption. In short, and in the current context, assessing this assumption is tantamount to asking the question, "Can we model our data with a unidimensional 2PL model?" For brevity we assume that the unidimensionality assumption is tenable for these data.[10] The command file for our calibration (Table 5.1) is similar to the one used for the 1PL model (Table 4.2) except for a few modifications. These changes include obtaining person parameter estimates as part of the item calibration and replacing NPARM = 1 with NPARM = 2 to specify the two-parameter model (GLOBAL line); LOG indicates the logistic version of the two-parameter model (i.e., a 2PL model calibration). In this example we perform person and item parameter estimation in a single run for two reasons. First, we want to show how to estimate the item and person parameters in a single run. Second, because in Chapters 3 and 4 we concluded that we have acceptable model–data fit with the Rasch model, we expect the less restrictive 2PL model to also show acceptable model–data fit. Therefore, our rationale in Chapter 4 for separating person and item parameter estimation is not applicable.

To estimate person locations we include the SCORE command line. Although both MAP and MLE are available (with or without the biweight modification), we use EAP person parameter estimation, >SCORE MET=2, NOPRINT;.[11] By default, BILOG prints all

TABLE 5.1. The BILOG Command File for the 2PL Model Item Calibration

```
2PL item calibration

>GLOBAL DFNAME='MATH.DAT', NPARM=2, NWGHT=0,LOG,SAVE;
>SAV PARM='MATH.PAR', SCO='MATH.SCO';
>LENGTH NITEMS=5;
>INPUT NTOT=5,NALT=2,NIDC=10,SAMP=20000,TYPE=1;
>ITEMS;
>TEST TNAMES='MATH',
      INumber = (1(1)5);
(10A1,T1,5(1X,1A1))
>CALIB CYCLES=20, NEWTON=20, CHI=(5,9), PLOT=1.0;
>SCORE MET=2,NOPRINT;
```

the $\hat{\theta}$s to the Phase 3 listing file. However, we do not want 19,601 $\hat{\theta}$s in our listing file and so we suppress this printing by using the subcommand NOPRINT on the SCORE line. Therefore, to see our $\hat{\theta}$s we instruct BILOG to save them to an alternative file by using the SAV command line with the subcommand SCO='MATH.SCO' and the SAVE subcommand on the GLOBAL line. This alternative file, MATH.SCO, can also be used in further statistical analyses of the $\hat{\theta}$s.

Table 5.2 contains the Phase 1 and 2 results. The line ITEM RESPONSE MODEL shows that the calibration is using the 2 PARAMETER LOGISTIC model. The Phase 2 output shows that the calibration converged in eight iterations. The item parameter estimates are found in the table following ITEM PARAMETERS AFTER CYCLE 8. This table has the format seen in Chapter 4. The estimates for the five items are $\hat{\alpha}_1 = 1.226, \hat{\delta}_1 = -2.107; \hat{\alpha}_2 = 1.992, \hat{\delta}_2 = -0.499; \ldots ; \hat{\alpha}_5 = 0.983$, and $\hat{\delta}_5 = 0.560$.[12] (The final column of the item parameter estimates table contains the chi-square statistics that, as discussed in the previous chapter, should be ignored because of the length of our instrument.) In terms of item discrimination, the estimated discrimination parameters are all reasonably good items. As is the case with the 1PL model calibration, if one would like to measure individuals at the upper end of the θ continuum, it would be necessary to have items that are located beyond item 5. It can be seen that the mean discrimination of 1.459 (SD = 0.381) is slightly greater than the common $\alpha = 1.421$ obtained with the 1PL model (Chapter 4). In effect, the 1PL model treated the item set as having a discriminating power equal to the "mean discrimination" across items.

The top half of Table 5.3 contains the Phase 3 abridged output. Because BILOG is instructed to send the EAP $\hat{\theta}$s to a separate file, the listing contains the line SCORES WRITTEN TO FILE MATH.SCO (i.e., the file name specified on the SAVE line). An example of the contents of this latter file is shown in the bottom half of Table 5.3.

The Phase 3 output is similar to that seen in Chapter 4. However, because of the NOPRINT subcommand on the SCORE line, the person table contains only information for the first three cases. The mean $\hat{\theta}$ for all 19,601 persons is −0.001 with a standard deviation of 0.7882. Following these descriptive statistics BILOG provides a summary of person parameter estimation accuracy. Although we can get a sense of the estimation accuracy at different points along the continuum (e.g., Figure 5.4), sometimes it is desirable to have a single bounded value that represents the quality of estimation for the entire continuum. One such index, the *empirical reliability*, is based on the ratio of the variance of the EAP $\hat{\theta}$s to the sum of the variance of the $\hat{\theta}$s and error variance (Zimowski et al., 2003). This index has a range from 0 to 1 with values that approach or are equal to 1.0 considered to be good values because they reflect small error variability. From Table 5.3 we have that the $\hat{\theta}$ VARIANCE is 0.6213 and the error variance of the EAP $\hat{\theta}$s is 0.3852 (i.e., VARIANCE of the SQUARE POSTERIOR STANDARD DEVIATIONS). Therefore, the

$$\text{EMPIRICAL RELIABILITY} = \frac{0.6213}{(0.6213 + 0.3852)} = 0.6173$$

This value may be considered marginally acceptable, given the instrument's length. Although a single accuracy value may be desirable, the tradeoff is that it may potentially be misinterpreted. For instance, given the nonuniformity in the total information function

TABLE 5.2. BILOG Output: Phases 1 and 2 (Abridged)

```
<Phase 1 results >
    :
FILE ASSIGNMENT AND DISPOSITION
================================
SUBJECT DATA INPUT FILE      MATH.DAT
BILOG-MG MASTER DATA FILE    MF.DAT
                                        WILL BE CREATED FROM DATA FILE
CALIBRATION DATA FILE        CF.DAT
                                        WILL BE CREATED FROM DATA FILE
ITEM PARAMETERS FILE         IF.DAT
                                        WILL BE CREATED THIS RUN
CASE SCALE-SCORE FILE        SF.DAT
CASE WEIGHTING                          NONE EMPLOYED
ITEM RESPONSE MODEL                     2 PARAMETER LOGISTIC
                                        LOGIT  METRIC (I.E., D = 1.0)
    :

    <Phase 2 results begin>
    :

DATA INPUT SPECIFICATIONS
=========================
    :
TYPE OF DATA                              SINGLE-SUBJECT DATA, NO CASE WEIGHTS
MAXIMUM SAMPLE SIZE FOR ITEM CALIBRATION  20000
ALL SUBJECTS INCLUDED IN RUN


    :
CYCLE     6;   LARGEST CHANGE=  0.01593
-2 LOG LIKELIHOOD =     110397.160
CYCLE     7;   LARGEST CHANGE=  0.00962

[FULL NEWTON CYCLES]
-2 LOG LIKELIHOOD:      110397.1034
CYCLE     8;   LARGEST CHANGE=  0.00305


INTERVAL COUNTS FOR COMPUTATION OF ITEM CHI-SQUARES
-------------------------------------------------------------------------
       0.   691.  2857.  2600.  3500.  2714.  3854.  3385.    0.
-------------------------------------------------------------------------


INTERVAL AVERAGE THETAS
-------------------------------------------------------------------------
   ******* -1.964 -1.336 -0.767 -0.339  0.160  0.762  1.472*******
-------------------------------------------------------------------------
```

```
SUBTEST MATH    ;  ITEM PARAMETERS AFTER CYCLE    8
```

ITEM	INTERCEPT S.E.	SLOPE S.E.	THRESHOLD S.E.	LOADING S.E.	ASYMPTOTE S.E.	CHISQ (PROB)	DF
ITEM0001	2.584	1.226	-2.107	0.775	0.000	164.8	5.0
	0.044*	0.047*	0.056*	0.030*	0.000*	(0.0000)	
ITEM0002	0.995	1.992	-0.499	0.894	0.000	2285.6	3.0
	0.032*	0.061*	0.013*	0.027*	0.000*	(0.0000)	
ITEM0003	0.394	1.551	-0.254	0.840	0.000	1174.8	5.0
	0.022*	0.041*	0.014*	0.022*	0.000*	(0.0000)	
ITEM0004	-0.416	1.544	0.270	0.839	0.000	362.8	5.0
	0.021*	0.039*	0.014*	0.021*	0.000*	(0.0000)	
ITEM0005	-0.551	0.983	0.560	0.701	0.000	1762.4	5.0
	0.018*	0.026*	0.021*	0.019*	0.000*	(0.0000)	

```
-------------------------------------------------------------------------
                                              * STANDARD ERROR

      LARGEST CHANGE =    0.003055                5750.4  23.0
                                                  (0.0000)
-------------------------------------------------------------------------
```

TABLE 5.2. *cont.*

```
NOTE: ITEM FIT CHI-SQUARES AND THEIR SUMS MAY BE UNRELIABLE
FOR TESTS WITH LESS THAN 20 ITEMS

PARAMETER       MEAN  STN DEV
--------------------------------
SLOPE          1.459   0.381
LOG(SLOPE)     0.350   0.267
THRESHOLD     -0.406   1.039

:
```

(Figure 5.4), this empirical reliability understates the accuracy in the center of the metric and overstates the estimation accuracy for $\hat{\theta}$s < −1.5 and $\hat{\theta}$s > 1.

The bottom half of Table 5.3 contains part of the MATH.SCO output file. As can be seen, the file contains only the title and the person estimate information; the first three lines match the cases displayed in the Phase 3 output. The layout of this file corresponds to the person table in the Phase 3 listing file. Recall that for the 2PL model the sufficient statistic for $\hat{\theta}$ is the weighted item responses, $\sum \alpha_j x_{ij}$. As a result, when item discrimination parameters (or their estimates) vary, different response patterns produce different $\hat{\theta}$s. In other words, the pattern of responses is important because providing a response of 1 on an item with a larger α_j is more influential in estimating θ than if the item has a smaller α_j. For instance, the patterns 11110, 11101, 11011, 10111, and 01111 all have the same observed score (i.e., X = 4), but the corresponding $\hat{\theta}$s are 0.7027, 0.4819, 0.4795, 0.3162, and 0.6047, respectively. In contrast, with the 1PL model all individuals with an X = 4 received the same $\hat{\theta}$ of 0.8238 (cf. Table 4.5) because the pattern of 1s and 0s is irrelevant. As we see, each estimate's SEE varies across the different response patterns for a given a observed score (e.g., the $s_e(\hat{\theta})$ for 11110 is 0.6404, but for 01111 it is 0.6284).

FIT ASSESSMENT: AN ALTERNATIVE APPROACH FOR ASSESSING INVARIANCE

In the previous two chapters we used fit statistics and empirical versus predicted IRF plots as part of our fit analysis. Moreover, we looked for the evidence of estimate invariance by examining the correlation between the $\hat{\delta}$s from two random subsamples. That is, if our estimates are invariant within a linear transformation, then we have evidence supporting model–data fit. All of the previously discussed methods for examining model–data fit are appropriate for the 2PL model. However, we now further develop our approach for obtaining evidence of invariance.

We start by subdividing our calibration sample into two random subsamples. With BILOG we use its SAMPLE subcommand on the INPUT command line to specify that a subsample be taken from the calibration sample. For instance, to create the first subsample we might specify that 10,000 cases be randomly sampled from our calibration sample by substituting the subcommand SAMP=10000 for the SAMP=20000 seen on the INPUT line

TABLE 5.3. BILOG Phase 3 (Abridged) Output (Top Half) and Abridged MATH.SCO Output File (Bottom Half)

```
  :
>SCORE MET=2,FIT,NOPRINT;
  :
METHOD OF SCORING SUBJECTS:          EXPECTATION A POSTERIORI
                                     (EAP; BAYES ESTIMATES)
TYPE OF PRIOR:                       NORMAL
SCORES WRITTEN TO FILE               MATH.SCO
SUBJECT FIT PROBABILITIES:           YES
TYPE OF RESCALING:                   NONE REQUESTED
ITEM AND TEST INFORMATION:           NONE REQUESTED
DOMAIN SCORE ESTIMATION:             NONE REQUESTED

              QUAD
TEST    NAME  POINTS
----------------------
   1    MATH    10

----------------------
  :
GROUP    SUBJECT IDENTIFICATION                              MARGINAL
WEIGHT    TEST      TRIED  RIGHT  PERCENT   ABILITY   S.E.    PROB
------------------------------------------------------------------------
   1  00000                                          |
  1.00   MATH        5      0     0.00    | -1.5821  0.6711 | 0.044414
   1  10000                                          |
  1.00   MATH        5      1    20.00    | -1.0752  0.6181 | 0.116346
   1  01000                                          |
  1.00   MATH        5      1    20.00    | -0.7957  0.5908 | 0.011625
------------------------------------------------------------------------

  :
MEANS AND STANDARD DEVIATIONS OF SCORE ESTIMATES:

TEST:              MATH
MEAN:             -0.0010
S.D.:              0.7882
VARIANCE:          0.6213

ROOT-MEAN-SQUARE POSTERIOR STANDARD DEVIATIONS

TEST:              MATH
RMS:               0.6206
VARIANCE:          0.3852

EMPIRICAL  RELIABILITY:      0.6173
  :
```

A bridged MATH.SCO output file:

```
2PL item calibration

1  00000
1.00 MATH      5    0     0.00   -1.582075   0.671065   0.000000   0.044414
1  10000
1.00 MATH      5    1    20.00   -1.075171   0.618089   0.000000   0.116346
1  01000
1.00 MATH      5    1    20.00   -0.795662   0.590771   0.000000   0.011625

   :
   <MANY MORE PERSONS>
   :
1  11000
1.00  MATH     5    2    40.00   -0.390327   0.566461   0.000000   0.074707

   <MANY MORE PERSONS>
   :
1  11100
1.00  MATH     5    3    60.00    0.125623   0.591210   0.000000   0.089643
   :
```

cont.

TABLE 5.3. *cont.*

```
    <MANY MORE PERSONS>
         :
1   11110
1.00   MATH      5    4    80.00    0.702708    0.640394    0.000000    0.110770
1   11101
1.00   MATH      5    4    80.00    0.481892    0.615527    0.000000    0.069513
1   11011
1.00   MATH      5    4    80.00    0.479453    0.615300    0.000000    0.030829
1   10111
1.00   MATH      5    4    80.00    0.316185    0.602409    0.000000    0.014184
1   01111
1.00   MATH      5    4    80.00    0.604702    0.628386    0.000000    0.004111
         :
    <MANY MORE PERSONS>
         :
1   11111
1.00  MATH       5    5    100.00   1.144288    0.702522    0.000000    0.157243
```

in Table 5.1. The second subsample is created by using the ISEED subcommand to specify the use of a different random number seed than the (default) seed value used for the first subsample. By using a different random number seed a different random sample is generated. For example, the INPUT line INPUT TOT=5,NALT=2,NIDC=10,ISEED=10,SAM P=10000,TYPE=1; would generate a different random subsample of 10,000 individuals. It should be noted that because BILOG performs the random sampling *in situ* there is always the possibility that some cases will appear in multiple subsamples.

To implement this process we create a command file for each subsample. Each command file has one of the above INPUT command lines. Further, we save the item parameter

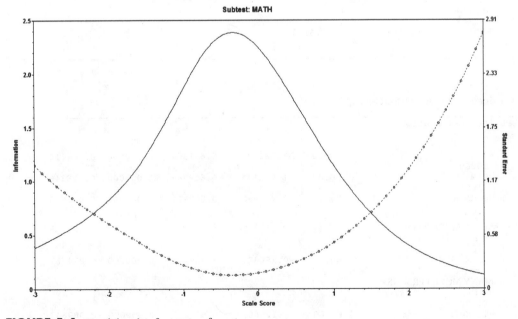

FIGURE 5.4. Total (test) information function.

estimates to separate files by using different file names on the SAV command line (e.g., PARM= 'MATH1.PAR' in subsample 1's command file and PARM='MATH2.PAR' in subsample 2's command file). These item parameter estimates files are used for our invariance analyses. After performing the separate calibrations we examine the DATA INPUT SPEC-IFICATIONS section of each phase 1 output to verify that the correct number of cases are sampled (i.e., MAXIMUM SAMPLE SIZE FOR ITEM CALIBRATION 10000).

With the two-parameter model there are two sets of parameter estimates with which we need to be concerned, $\hat{\alpha}_j$ and $\hat{\delta}_j$. The correlation between the two samples' parameter estimates is 0.956 for the $\hat{\alpha}_j$s and 0.997 for the $\hat{\delta}_j$s. These correlations show that the item discrimination and location estimates from the two samples are highly linearly related. Therefore, given the magnitude of these correlations, we have evidence supporting model–data fit.

With the 2PL model the correlation coefficients for the item discrimination and location estimates tell only part of the story because they do not fully reflect the interaction of these two types of parameters in describing an item. Therefore, we now present an additional (complementary) technique based on the difference in an item's response functions across subsamples. By using the IRF we are able to see whether the item discrimination and location parameter interaction causes the two subsamples to vary.

There are multiple ways for assessing the difference, or area, between two IRFs. Prior to their use one should align or link the subsample metrics to one another by, for example, the total characteristic function equating approach (Chapter 11). One approach for examining the difference between two IRFs is to use the root mean squared difference (RMSD) between the probabilities represented by the two IRFs.[13] In the current context one set of probabilities (p_{js}) is based on the parameter estimates from subsample s and the other probability set (p_{jt}) is based on the estimates from subsample t. The θs used in calculating p_{js} and p_{jt} would be a series reflecting a desired degree of accuracy. For instance, one might use –3.0, –2.95, . . . , 3.0 (i.e., 0.05 logit difference) or whatever θ range is of particular interest.[14] Decreasing the logit difference (e.g., from 0.05 to 0.005) will improve the index's accuracy as a measure of the difference between the two IRFs. The $RMSD_j$ statistic for item j is given by

$$RMSD_j = \sqrt{\frac{\sum (p_{js} - p_{jt})^2}{n}} \qquad (5.9)$$

where n is the number of θs used in calculating p_{js} and p_{jt}. For instance, if the range of θ is –3 to 3 in 0.05 increments, then n = 121. $RMSD_j$ has a range of 0 to 1 (inclusive) with small values indicating good agreement between the two IRFs. For example, if two IRFs are identical, then $RMSD_j$ equals 0.0. However, one should expect that even with perfect model–data fit, estimation error will be reflected in an item's nonzero, albeit small, $RMSD_j$ value. From this perspective, a small $RMSD_j$ reflects two IRFs that may be considered to be sufficiently similar to one another to not have reason for concern.

In those cases where one observes a large $RMSD_j$ there may be various reasons for its magnitude. For instance, the item may be poorly written and thereby interpreted differently across the subsamples or the model may have insufficient item parameters to accurately describe the item. Depending on the diagnosis of the cause(s) of the magnitude of $RMSD_j$, one may decide to omit the item from the instrument and retain only those items with small $RMSD_j$ values. $RMSD_j$ should be used in conjunction with a plot of the IRFs to determine whether the magnitude of these statistics is representative of a systematic difference across the continuum or reflects a difference for a particular portion of the continuum.

For our example, using the θ range -3 to 3 with a 0.05 increment we obtain $RMSD_j$s of 0.0429, 0.0150, 0.0080, 0.0119, and 0.0138 for items 1 through 5, respectively. For items 2–5 these $RMSD_j$s represent small (trivial) differences between the two subsamples' IRFs. Our largest $RMSD_j$ occurs for item 1 with a value of 0.0429. The corresponding IRF plot (not presented) shows that this item is slightly less discriminating and easier in subsample 2 than in subsample 1. Therefore, given that the correlations between the two subsamples' estimates are high and that four of the five $RMSD_j$s are small, we conclude that we have some evidence supporting the invariance of our estimates as well as model–data fit.

A more sophisticated approach for computing the area between two IRFs for the one-, two-, and three-parameter models as well as providing corresponding significance tests is offered by Raju (1990). However, given the sample sizes for some calibrations, the power associated with these statistical tests may render them not very meaningful; the null hypothesis is that there is no difference between the two IRFs. Moreover, if the subsamples contain cases in common, then the statistical test's probability is not correct.

For the 2PL model the unsigned area, UA_{22}, between two IRFs for item j is obtained by

$$UA_{22j} = \left| \frac{2(\hat{\alpha}_{jt}^* - \hat{\alpha}_{js})}{\hat{\alpha}_{js}\hat{\alpha}_{jt}^*} \ln\left\{1 + \exp\left[\frac{\hat{\alpha}_{js}\hat{\alpha}_{jt}^*(\hat{\delta}_{jt}^* - \hat{\delta}_{js})}{\hat{\alpha}_{jt}^* - \hat{\alpha}_{js}} \right]\right\} - (\hat{\delta}_{jt}^* - \hat{\delta}_{js}) \right| \quad (5.10)$$

(To simplify presentation "exp[z]" is used instead of "e^z".) Equation 5.10 simplifies to $\left|\hat{\delta}_{jt}^* - \hat{\delta}_{js}\right|$ when $\hat{\alpha}_{jt}^* = \hat{\alpha}_{js}$; Raju presents a version of UA_{22} for the three-parameter model (Chapter 6) for a common lower asymptote across subsamples.

For our instrument, and after transforming sample 2's metric to that of sample 1, we obtain UA_{22} values of 0.7470, 0.0005, 0.1731, 0.1460, and 0.0970 for items 1, 2, 3, 4, and 5, respectively. Although the agreement between UA_{22} and RMSD is not perfect (r = 0.9206), there is good agreement. Again, item 1 stands out as reflecting the greatest difference between the two samples' IRFs.

INFORMATION AND RELATIVE EFFICIENCY

Above it is mentioned that the mean α for the 2PL model calibration is greater than that of the 1PL model's α. The larger mean α for the 2PL model is reflected in an overall increase in the information available for estimating person locations. This increase may be represented graphically (e.g., Figures 5.2 and 5.4) or in terms of the *total information area* index, I_A. We introduce I_A to provide a complementary way of summarizing, in a single number, the total information available for estimation. The total information area index represents the area under the total information function. Because the items contribute independently to the total information function, the area under the total information function is the sum of the item information areas:

$$I_A = \sum_{}^{L} \alpha_j \iota = \sum_{}^{L} I_{A_j} \qquad (5.11)$$

and the average total information area, $\bar{I}_A$, is

$$\bar{I}_A = \frac{I_A}{L} \qquad (5.12)$$

where

$$\iota = \frac{\chi_j \ln(\chi_j) + 1 - \chi_j}{1 - \chi_j}$$

and χ_j is the IRF's lower asymptote. Further, whenever $\chi_j = 0$, then $\iota \equiv 1$. Because for both the 1PL and 2PL models $\chi_j = 0$ and $\iota = 1$, the *item information area* index (i.e., the area under the item information function) is

$$I_{A_j} = \alpha_j \iota \qquad (5.13)$$

Equations 5.11 to 5.13 provide a set of numerical indices that succinctly and nongraphically summarize the amount of information available for estimation without one's having to estimate person locations or make distributional assumptions.[15] All other things being equal, larger values of these indices indicate more information than do smaller values.

For instance, after linking the 1PL model's metric with that of the 2PL model, the 1PL model $\hat{\alpha} = 1.40$ and $I_A = L\hat{\alpha} = 5(1.40) = 7.0$. In contrast, for the 2PL model the area under the total information function is $I_A = \sum \hat{\alpha}_j = 1.226 + 1.992 + 1.551 + 1.544 + 0.983 = 7.296$. Therefore, for these data and metric the 2PL model calibration of this instrument results in about 4% more total information for person estimation than does the 1PL model calibration (i.e., $7.296/7 = 1.0423$).

In addition, we may examine the total information functions for the 1PL and 2PL models to see how the distributions of the total information compare with one another. For convenience the 1PL model's total information function is superimposed over that of the 2PL model in Figure 5.5. First, we see that the maximum of the total information with the 1PL model is approximately 1.927 at $\theta \cong -0.15$. However, with the 2PL model the maximum of the total information is about 2.385 at $\theta \cong -0.35$. Second, it can be seen that the 2PL model is able to provide more information than the 1PL model in the approximate range of −1.5 to

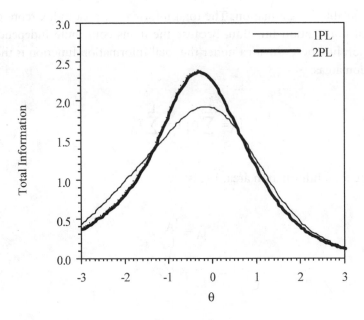

FIGURE 5.5. 1PL and 2PL models' total information functions.

0.5. At about –0.5 the 2PL model provides 20% more information than the 1PL model. However, outside this range the 1PL model provides more information than the 2PL model.[16]

An alternative way of simultaneously comparing multiple information functions is by using a *relative efficiency* plot. Lord (1980; also see Birnbaum, 1968) presents the relative efficiency (RE) of one score x to another score y as the ratio of their information functions:

$$RE\{x,y\} = \frac{I(\theta,x)}{I(\theta,y)} \tag{5.14}$$

The scores x and y may come from two different instruments that measure the same construct θ or may arise from scoring the same instrument in two different ways. In the current context, the same instrument is scored in two different ways (i.e., the 1PL and 2PL models). Figure 5.6 contains the RE plot for the 1PL and 2PL models' calibration of the mathematics instrument. It is created by taking the 2PL model's total information and dividing it by the 1PL model's total information at each θ and plotting this ratio as a function of θ; that is, x = 2PL, y = 1PL, and RE{2PL,1PL} = I(θ,2PL)/I(θ,1PL).

Figure 5.6 shows that the 2PL model is able to provide more information than the 1PL model in the approximate range of –1.5 to 0.5. In addition, at about –0.5 the 2PL model provides 20% more information than the 1PL model, but outside the range of –1.5 to 0.5 the 1PL model provides more information than the 2PL model. As the name would imply, the plot reflects the relative information as a function of θ. Therefore, one caveat in using RE plots is that although the magnitude of information may be quite small at a particular θ, this may not necessarily be evident from the plot. For instance, if the 2PL model provides 0.05

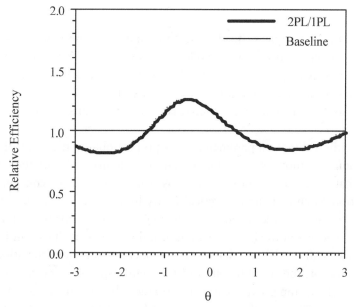

FIGURE 5.6. Relative efficiency plot for 1PL and 2PL models' calibrations.

information for estimating a person located at $\theta = 1.5$ and the 1PL model provides 0.025 at this same point, then the 2PL model provides twice as much information as the 1PL model at this θ, although both provide a negligible amount of information at $\theta = 1.5$.

Given that Figures 5.5 and 5.6 present similar information, one might ask, "What is the advantage of using a relative efficiency plot?" To help in understanding the benefit of an RE plot, the θ metric is transformed to a T-score scale. Recall that a T-score scale is defined as having an $M = 50$ and an $SD = 10$. Therefore, we can transform our θ metric to a T-score scale by applying Equations 5.6 and 5.8 and letting $\kappa = M$ and $\zeta = SD$.

The effect of this linear transformation on the metric is shown in Figure 5.7. This linear transformation does not affect the IRFs. Moreover, the shape of the information function is not affected by the linear transformation. However, it can be seen that the magnitude of information is affected by the transformation because the transformation affects the magnitude of the $\hat{\alpha}_j$s. For example, for the 1PL model the maximum information is 1.927 (Figure 5.5) at $\theta = -0.15$, whereas on the T-score scale the maximum information becomes 0.0193 at 48.5. Therefore, given the relationship between information and the metric-dependent standard error of estimate, the information functions' values are also metric dependent. However, the corresponding RE plot for the T-score transformation (Figure 5.8) is identical to that shown in Figure 5.6 except for the abscissa metric reflecting a T-score scale. Therefore, the benefit of an RE plot lies in its metric independence. In fact, relative efficiency is metric independent under any *monotonic* transformation of the metric (Lord, 1980). (See Appendix E, "Relative Efficiency, Monotonicity, and Information" for more information on RE plots.) Moreover, the ratio of the total information area indices still shows that the 2PL model provides about 4% more total information than does the 1PL model; that is, $I_{A,2PL}/I_{A,1PL} = 0.7296/0.7 = 1.0423$.

SUMMARY

Items may vary in their capacity to discriminate among respondents located at different points along a variable's continuum. Therefore, the use of an IRT model that captures this discrimination information may be useful for estimating a person's location. The two-parameter model is one such model because it allows for items to vary not only in their locations, but also in their capacity to differentiate among persons located at different points on the continuum.

Because the discrimination parameter, α_j, is proportional to the slope of the IRF at the point of inflexion, the most obvious manifestation of items with different discrimination parameters is that their corresponding IRFs cross somewhere on the continuum. Although the discrimination parameter can theoretically vary from $-\infty$ to ∞, items with positive α_js between approximately 0.8 and 2.5 are considered good values. For the 2PL model an IRF's point of inflexion occurs at the item's location δ, and the slope at this point is 0.25 α_j.

As is the case with the 1PL model, the 2PL model has sufficient statistics. For estimating a person's location the weighted sum of the item responses, $\sum \alpha_j x_{ij}$, is the sufficient statistic. This weighted sum provides more information than the unweighted sum used with the Rasch model except when the two sums are identical or proportional or when the $\hat{\alpha}$s are not accurate. However, unlike the sufficient statistics for the 1PL model, the sufficient statistics for the 2PL model depend on unknown parameters.

A simple (albeit incomplete) method to assess the invariance of the parameter estimates at an instrument level is by computing correlations between the parameter estimates across two subsamples. A complementary strategy is to examine the difference between IRFs using the parameter estimates from the two subsamples. One index of this difference is $RMSD_j$. $RMSD_j$ should be used in conjunction with the corresponding plots of the IRFs.

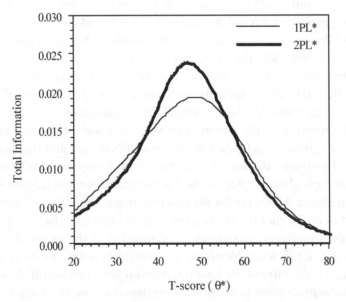

FIGURE 5.7. 1PL and 2PL models' total information functions for linearly transformed scale.

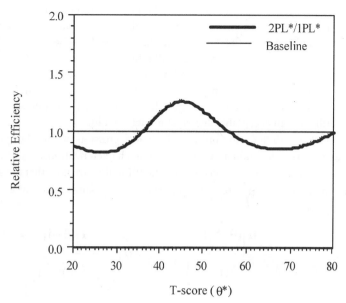

FIGURE 5.8. Relative efficiency plot for linearly transformed scale.

With the two-parameter model an item provides its maximum information at δ_j. In contrast to the one-parameter model, in the two-parameter model the maximum amount of item information may vary from item to item as α varies across items. To compare multiple information functions one can use the relative efficiency plot. This plot can be created by taking the total information of one instrument and dividing it by the total information of the other instrument at each θ and plotting this ratio as a function of θ. In addition, the total information area index is introduced to complement graphical information function representations. This index summarizes in a single value the amount of information that an instrument provides and that is represented in its information function graph.

The 1PL and 2PL models share the constraint that their IRFs' lower asymptotes need to be zero. In Chapter 6 we relax this constraint and obtain the three-parameter model. With this model there is a parameter for the item's location, another for its discrimination capacity, and a third for the IRF's lower asymptote. This lower asymptote parameter is called the item's *pseudo-guessing parameter*, χ_j. Allowing the pseudo-guessing parameter to be nonzero permits the modeling of situations where one observes chance success on an item by persons of very low θs. As such, the number of situations in which one may obtain model–data fit is potentially greater with the three-parameter model than with either the two- or one-parameter models.

NOTES

1. Successful Rasch model–data fit indicates a one-to-one correspondence between mathematical operations, such as addition or subtraction of the measured values and the "structure of the properties

of the objects that are measured" (Andrich, 1988, p. 17). (This correspondence is the gist of the concept of *fundamental measurement*.) From this perspective the Rasch model is "chosen to express our intentions and not to simply describe the data" (Andrich, 1988, p. 14). Use of the model is predicated on the assumption that only items with empirical IRFs that have *approximately* the same slope are useful for estimating person locations. That is, although the ideal under the Rasch model is an item set with a constant item discrimination, in practice a certain degree of variability from this ideal is expected and tolerated. In point of fact, even though the biserials for the mathematics data vary from 0.397 to 0.564, we still have an acceptable degree of model–data fit.

2. The 2PL model is, in effect, the ordinary logistic regression of the observed dichotomous responses on the latent person location and the latent item characterizations.

3. To determine the relationship between α_j and the IRF's slope we note that the slope is the same as the 2PL model's first derivative, $p'_j = \alpha_j p_j (1 - p_j)$. Therefore, by substitution of Equation 5.1 for p_j we have that the slope is

$$p'_j = \frac{e^{\alpha_j(\theta - \delta_j)}}{(1 + e^{\alpha_j(\theta - \delta_j)})(1 + e^{\alpha_j(\theta - \delta_j)})} = \alpha_j \frac{e^{\alpha_j(\theta - \delta_j)}}{\left[1 + e^{\alpha_j(\theta - \delta_j)}\right]^2} \qquad (5.15)$$

Because α_j is defined at $\theta = \delta$, the slope is

$$p'_j = \alpha_j \frac{e^{\alpha_j(0)}}{\left[1 + e^{\alpha_j(0)}\right]^2} = \frac{1}{4}\alpha_j = 0.25\alpha_j \qquad (5.16)$$

As a result, α_j is proportional to the slope of the tangent line to the IRF at δ_j and may be thought of as a rate of change indicator for the IRF in the neighborhood around δ_j. When using the D scaling constant the slope for the 2PL model is $0.25D\,\alpha_j = 0.425\,\alpha_j$.

4. As the distance between the person's and item's locations increases, a large α_j can lead to a loss of information away from δ_j because most of the information is concentrated in a neighborhood around δ_j. As α_j increases, the effective size of this neighborhood gets progressively smaller. For instance, in Figure 5.2 item 2 ($\alpha_2 = 1.5$) provides more information than does item 5 ($\alpha_5 = 3.0$) below approximately –0.05. This "attenuation paradox" (Lord & Novick, 1968) can be summarized as follows: If each α_j is extremely high, then one has virtually error-free discrimination between θ levels in a small neighborhood around each δ_j, but as one leaves this neighborhood there is "virtually no other information for discrimination or estimation" (p. 465).

5. The area under $I_j(\theta)$ is equal to α_j (with the D scaling constant the area is equal to $D\alpha_j$; Lord & Novick, 1968), that is,

$$\int_{-\infty}^{\infty} I_j(\theta) = \alpha_j$$

Moreover, the area under $\sqrt{I_j(\theta)}$ is equal to pi (Samejima, 1994).

6. The idea of "how quickly the IRF is changing" is captured by the slope of the IRF and is reflected in the model's first derivative, p'_j, whereas $p_j(1 - p_j)$ is the variance at θ.

7. The standard error for the person location estimate under the 2PL is

$$\text{SEE}(\hat{\theta}) = \frac{1}{\sqrt{\sum\limits_{j=1}^{L} \alpha_j^2 p_j(1-p_j)}} \tag{5.17}$$

where p_j is conditional on $\hat{\theta}_i$.

8. The sufficient statistic for estimating a person's location is a weighted composite, $\sum \alpha_j x_{ij}$, where the weights are given by the item discrimination parameters. From a more general perspective, one can write the weighted composite as $\sum w_j x_{ij}$. As a result, one might ask, "Is there a weight that will provide more information for estimating a person's location than that provided by α_j?" Lord (1980) shows that the information function for the weighted composite is the total information function and that this is the maximum information attainable by any scoring method. Therefore, the optimal scoring weight for an item j is

$$w_j(\theta) = \frac{p_j'}{p_j(1-p_j)} \tag{5.18}$$

Because the first derivative for the 2PL model is

$$p_j' = \alpha_j p_j (1-p_j)$$

one has by substitution and simplification that the optimal weight for the 2PL model is

$$w_j(\theta) = \frac{\alpha_j[p_j(1-p_j)]}{p_j(1-p_j)} = \alpha_j \tag{5.19}$$

Therefore, α_j is the optimal weight for maximizing information for locating persons. As would be expected, for the 1PL model $w_j(\theta) = \alpha$ and for the Rasch model $w_j(\theta) = 1$. With the scaling factor D we have that $w_j(\theta) = D\alpha_j$, $w_j(\theta) = D\alpha$, and $w_j(\theta) = D$ for the 2PL, 1PL, and Rasch models, respectively.

9. In general, one no longer sees JMLE used for parameter estimation for the two-parameter model. Nevertheless, for completeness we describe some of the parameter recovery research in this area. Hulin, Lissak, and Drasgow (1982) in a study of JMLE (specifically, LOGIST) conducted a Monte Carlo study to investigate the effects of four sample sizes (N = 200, 500, 1000, or 2000) and three instrument lengths (L = 15, 30, or 60 items) on the accuracy of parameter estimation. They found that the average error (i.e., root mean squared) for instruments of at least 30 items was no greater than 0.05 for a sample size of 1000 and less than 0.07 with 500 cases. Lim and Drasgow (1990) found that samples of 250 tended to result in greater biased item parameter estimates and standard errors than did the larger sample size of 750 persons. In general, JMLE parameter and standard error estimates were not as accurate as those of MMLE even when using a 25-item instrument and a sample size of 1000. It may be conjectured that these results are due to the ping-pong nature of estimating persons and item parameters. That is, less accurate $\hat{\theta}$s at one stage (e.g., due to an instrument's length) affect the accuracy of the $\hat{\alpha}$s and $\hat{\delta}$s, which then in turn affect the accuracy of the subsequent $\hat{\theta}$s, and so on. In short, the estimation errors are compounded and/or propagated through each stage of estimating the persons and items. On the basis of these results it appears that instruments of 25 items or more with sample sizes of at least 1000 persons should be used when using JMLE.

10. In addition to the unidimensionality assumption, we should also determine the tenability of

the conditional independence assumption. We investigate this assumption's tenability for the mathematics data in Chapter 6. Although the approach we use is applicable for the 1PL and 2PL models, Glas (1999) has developed an alternative procedure specifically for the two-parameter model.

11. If we had used MLE for estimating the person locations, then we would not be able to obtain MLE estimates for individuals with zero scores or perfect scores. In Chapter 3 two approaches were mentioned that could be used for these cases; the half-item rule and the addition of a constant (e.g., 0.5) to a zero score and its subtraction from a perfect score. With the two-parameter model there is an additional rule one could use. Individuals with zero scores are assigned a value equal to $\alpha_{min}/2$ (i.e., $X = \alpha_{min}/2$), and for persons with perfect scores the observed score, X, equals $\Sigma\alpha - \alpha_{max}/2$, where α_{min} and α_{max} are the minimum and maximum α_js, respectively, for the administered instrument.

12. When all individuals respond the same way to an item (e.g., all responses are 1s), then it is not possible to obtain estimates of the item's parameters using either MLE or MMLE. In the case of MMLE this demonstrates that MMLE is not a Bayesian procedure. However, if one requests that BILOG-MG (version 3) save the item parameter estimates to an external file (i.e., the ".PAR" file) the item(s) with the zero variance will have item parameter "estimates" in the file (albeit with an extreme location estimate), although the Phase 2 output will not have an entry for the zero variance item(s). If there is a need to obtain estimates when all persons correctly respond to an item, then a kludge (i.e., "work around") is to randomly select a case and change the response to be an omitted response (e.g., changing the observed correct response to blank). This allows the item's parameters to be estimated. By randomly selecting the case one can treat the "omitted" response as missing completely at random. In the case of the 1PL model the location estimate may be "comparatively" extreme. With the 2PL model the estimates may be reasonable, depending on the sample size.

13. This approach is similar to the UA and SOS differential item functioning measures presented in Shepard, Camilli, and Averill (1981) as well as Shepard, Camilli, and Williams (1984).

14. The θ range used for the calculating RMSD should be the range of interest. For instance, in a particular application we might focus on a range of θ around a cutpoint, θ'. Therefore, we would be most concerned with the similarity between IRFs within this range around θ' and less concerned with discrepancies that occurred farther away from θ'.

15. On the normal metric the total information area and item information area indices are

$$I_A = D\sum_{}^{L}\alpha_j\iota \tag{5.21}$$

and

$$I_{A_j} = D\alpha_j\iota$$

respectively; $D = 1.702$.

16. These statements are tied to this particular metric. As a result, the 2PL and 1PL models' metrics were linked with one another prior to superimposing the two information functions. This is accomplished by using the total characteristic function equating approach to place the 1PL model estimates (i.e., the initial metric) on the 2PL model metric (i.e., the target metric); this approach is discussed in Chapter 11. The metric transformation coefficients are $\zeta = 1.0150$ and $\kappa = 0.0037$. These values indicate that the two metrics are in very close alignment even before linking, because values of $\zeta = 1$ and $\kappa = 0$ would indicate perfect alignment between the metrics. After linking, the 1PL estimates become $\hat{\alpha} = 1.40$, $\hat{\delta}_1 = -1.950$, $\hat{\delta}_2 = -0.586$, $\hat{\delta}_3 = -0.264$, $\hat{\delta}_4 = 0.292$, and $\hat{\delta}_5 = 0.453$.

6

The Three-Parameter Model

In this chapter we present a model for addressing chance success on an item. This chance success is reflected in an IRF with a nonzero lower asymptote. To model this lower asymptote we extend the 2PL model to produce the three-parameter model. Parallel to the structure of the chapters discussing the 1PL and 2PL models, we present an example of a three-parameter model calibration using the mathematics data set introduced in Chapter 2.

Through the previous chapters we have developed a "toolbox" of model-fit techniques. This toolbox includes methods for assessing the tenability of various assumptions. To summarize these approaches, the unidimensionality assumption can be assessed using nonlinear factor analysis, linear factor analysis, and structural equation modeling. We can assess the tenability of the functional form assumption by examining the empirical IRFs. Moreover, model–data fit can be assessed through fit statistics (e.g., INFIT and OUTFIT chi square), comparing the predicted and empirical IRFs, as well as by obtaining evidence of item parameter estimate invariance through the use of correlations and RMSD. We have also examined person fit through fit statistics.

In this chapter we add to our toolbox. Specifically, (1) we introduce the likelihood ratio, AIC, and BIC statistics for making model comparisons, (2) we use Q_3 for assessing the tenability of the conditional independence assumption, and (3) we discuss the appropriateness of a person's estimated location as a measure of his or her true location. Although for pedagogical reasons we have presented the model-fit techniques separately, it should be noted that in practice they would be used collectively. The last topic we cover in this chapter is the handling of missing data.

CONCEPTUAL DEVELOPMENT OF THE THREE-PARAMETER MODEL

Individuals at the lower end of the latent continuum may be expected to have a high probability of providing a response of 0. For example, examinees who have low mathematics proficiency may be expected to incorrectly respond to, say, a topology question on a mathematics examination. If this mathematics examination uses a multiple-choice item format, then some of these low-proficiency individuals may select the correct option simply by guessing. Similarly, people administered a neuroticism inventory using a true/false response format and who are low in neuroticism may be expected to respond "False" to a question depicting a neurotic behavior. However, owing to inattention or fatigue some of these individuals may respond "True" to the question. In these cases the item's response function has a lower asymptote that may not be asymptotic with 0.0, but with some nonzero value. The three-parameter model addresses this nonzero lower asymptote.

To develop the three-parameter model we need to be concerned with two cases. The first case is, "What is the probability of a response of 1 on an item when an individual responds consistently with his or her location on θ?" Our answer is that the probability of the response of 1 is modeled by the 2PL model.

The second case to consider is, "What should be the probability of a response of 1 on an item due to chance alone?" To answer this question, let us symbolize this probability as χ_j. Therefore, when a person can be successful on item j on the basis of chance alone (i.e., irrespective of the person's location), then the corresponding probability is given by $\chi_j[1 - p_j]$. In this case as θ becomes progressively more negative, then p_j approaches 0.0 and $\chi_j[1 - p_j]$ simplifies to χ_j. Stated another way, the probability of a response of 1 for an individual with an infinitely low location is χ_j. As such, χ_j represents the IRF's lower bound or asymptote.

Putting these two (mutually exclusive) cases together we can obtain the probability of a response of 1 from

$$p_j^* = p_j + \chi_j[1 - p_j] \tag{6.1}$$

where p_j is given by the 2PL model. Equation 6.1 may be rearranged to be

$$p_j^* = \chi_j + (1 - \chi_j)p_j \tag{6.2}$$

By substitution of the 2PL model for p_j we obtain the *three-parameter logistic* (3PL) model:

$$p(x_j = 1|\theta, \alpha_j, \delta_j, \chi_j) = \chi_j + (1 - \chi_j) \frac{e^{\alpha_j(\theta - \delta_j)}}{1 + e^{\alpha_j(\theta - \delta_j)}} \tag{6.3}$$

Although, strictly speaking, Equation 6.3 is not in logistic form, it is referred to as a logistic model. (Because there is a normal ogive version of the three-parameter model Equation 6.3 is sometimes presented incorporating the scaling factor D.) As is the case with the 1PL and 2PL models, δ_j represents item j's location and α_j reflects its discrimination parameter. The additional parameter, χ_j, is referred to as the item's *pseudo-guessing* or *pseudo-chance* parameter and equals the probability of a response of 1 when θ approaches $-\infty$ (i.e., $\chi_j = p(x_j = 1|\theta \rightarrow -\infty)$). Therefore, with the 3PL model there are three parameters characterizing the item j (i.e., $\alpha_j, \delta_j, \chi_j$).

The 3PL model is based on the same assumptions discussed in Chapter 2 with the 1PL model. Specifically, these assumptions are a unidimensional latent space, conditional independence, and a specific functional form. For brevity we use p_j instead of $p(x = 1|\theta, \alpha_j, \delta_j, \chi_j)$ in the following.

Examples of the 3PL model's IRF are given in Figure 6.1. The two items shown in the figure have the same discrimination and location parameters, but have different values χ_j. For item 1, $\chi_1 = 0.1$, and for item 2, $\chi_2 = 0.05$. We see that the IRFs have nonzero lower asymptotes and that an IRF is asymptotic with its corresponding χ_j value. In addition, we see that item 1 with the larger χ_j value has the higher IRF. In general, as χ_j increases so does p_j, all other things being equal. In the context of proficiency assessment, this means that items with larger χ_js are easier than those with smaller χ_js. The figure shows that the valid range for χ_j is 0.0 to 1.0.

As is the case with the 1PL and 2PL models, the IRF's slope is at a maximum at the item j's location. This point of inflexion occurs midway between the lower and upper asymptotes. The lower asymptote is the floor of the IRF and represents the smallest probability for a response of 1, whereas the upper asymptote is the ceiling for the IRF and reflects the largest probability of a response of 1. If we let ε_j denote item j's upper asymptote, then a general expression for determining the midpoint (i.e., the probability at δ_j) for any of our dichotomous models is $(\varepsilon_j + \chi_j)/2$. For example, with the 1PL and 2PL models the lower asymptote is 0 and the upper asymptote is 1. Therefore, for the 1PL and 2PL models we have that $\chi_j = 0.0$, $\varepsilon_j = 1.0$, and the probability of a response of 1 at δ_j is $(1 + 0.0)/2 = 0.50$. For the 3PL model, if χ_j is greater than 0.0, then the probability of a response of 1 at δ_j is greater than 0.50. For example, if $\chi_j = 0.20$ and $\varepsilon_j = 1.0$, then the probability of a response of 1 at δ_j is $(1 + \chi_j)/2 = (1 + 0.2)/2 = 0.6$.[1] Moreover, as is true with the 1PL and 2PL models,

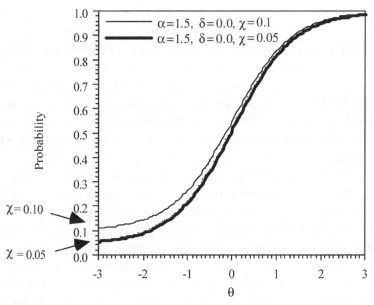

FIGURE 6.1. 3PL model IRFs for two items with $\alpha_1 = 1.5$, $\delta_1 = 0.0$, $\chi_1 = 0.1$, and $\alpha_2 = 1.5$, $\delta_2 = 0.0$, $\chi_2 = 0.05$.

the 3PL model's discrimination parameter is proportional to the slope at the inflexion point. However, the relationship between α_j and the slope now involves χ_j. Specifically, the slope for the 3PL model is $0.25\ \alpha_j(1 - \chi_j)$.[2] Therefore, unlike our previous models, an item's discriminatory effectiveness is affected by the magnitude of χ_j. Specifically, as χ_j increases, an item's discriminatory effectiveness decreases, all other things being equal. For example, we see from Figure 6.1 that item 1's discriminatory effectiveness (reflected in its IRF's slope) is less than that for item 2.

ADDITIONAL COMMENTS ABOUT THE PSEUDO-GUESSING PARAMETER, χ_j

In regard to the pseudo-guessing parameter, our first comment is about the different labels used for χ_j. Originally, χ_j was referred to as the item's guessing parameter (e.g., Lord, 1980, p. 12). However, because χ_j is typically lower than what would be predicted by a random guessing model (i.e., the reciprocal of the number of multiple-choice options), χ_j is now referred to as the pseudo-guessing parameter. This difference between χ_j and the random guessing model prediction is due to differential option attractiveness. That is, the random guessing model assumes that all options are equally attractive. Yet we know from traditional item analyses that item alternatives vary in their degree of attractiveness to persons. For instance, using keywords in alternatives is a typical tactic to increase the attractiveness of alternatives. Moreover, test taking preparation instructs examinees who do not know the answer to a question to select the longest option because it is usually the correct response. As such, the random guessing model's assumption is not reflected in the response data.

Our second comment concerns the nature of χ_j. As mentioned above, χ_j's function in the model is to reflect that some individuals with infinitely low locations may obtain a response of 1 when, according to the 2PL model, they should not. These responses are a manifestation of the interaction between person and item characteristics (including item format). In the case of proficiency instruments, person characteristics include not only a person's θ, but also his or her test-wiseness and "risk-taking" tendencies. These last two factors are tangential latent person variables. Therefore, although χ_j is considered to be an *item* parameter, it may be more reflective of a *person* characteristic (i.e., another person parameter) rather than an item characteristic or, at least, an interaction between person and item characteristics.

Our final comments concern the implicit assumption made by the use of χ_j and the effect of χ_j on estimation. In regard to the former, we see from Equation 6.3 that the presence of χ_j in the model assumes that, regardless of a person's location, his or her propensity to "guess" is constant across the continuum (i.e., χ_j does not vary as a function of θ). This assumption may or may not be reasonable in all situations. With respect to effects, nonzero χ_js lower the estimate of a person's location (Wainer, 1983) and reduce the amount of item information.[3] Thus, although we are modeling nonzero χ_js, it is very desirable that our χ_js be close to zero. In this case, a 2PL model may provide a sufficiently reasonable representation of the data.

CONCEPTUAL PARAMETER ESTIMATION FOR THE 3PL MODEL

The estimation of item parameters proceeds as discussed in previous chapters. However, unlike the 1PL and 2PL models, the 3PL model does not have sufficient statistics for parameter estimation (Baker, 1992; Lord, 1980). The (log) likelihood surface for an item with three item parameters would require four dimensions to graphically represent it. However, the general idea can be represented as a series of static multiple surfaces similar to the one presented in Figure 5.3, but with each surface slightly different from one another. Each surface would be associated with a particular value of χ_j (e.g., 0.0, 0.01, 0.02, etc.). (Obviously, the discrete nature of this series of surfaces does not accurately reflect the continuous nature of χ_j.) The essence of the estimation process would be to identify across these "multiple surfaces" the values of α_j, δ_j, and χ_j that maximize the log likelihood for an item.[4]

In some cases distinguishing between these multiple surfaces may be problematic. For instance, if there are insufficient data at the lower end of the continuum, then there may be multiple sets of α_j, δ_j, and χ_j that may account for the data in this region. As such, the corresponding IRFs are similar to one another in this region (cf. Mislevy, 1986a). As an example, assume that in a given calibration sample everyone is located above -1. As a result, there is insufficient data to estimate the lower asymptote (i.e., χ_j's value from very low values of θ). Figure 6.2 presents two competing IRFs that can account for the empirical data. One IRF is based on $\alpha = 0.8$, $\delta = -0.05$, and $\chi = 0.435$, whereas the other has the item parameter values of $\alpha = 0.56$, $\delta = -1.8$, and $\chi = 0.0$. As can be seen, these two IRFs are very similar to one another above -1 and, in fact, differ by less than 0.01 in the θ range -1 to 1 and by less than 0.018 in the range -1 to 3. Without additional information (e.g., persons located around -3, or prior information) it is not possible to determine whether χ_j should be 0.435 or 0. In terms of

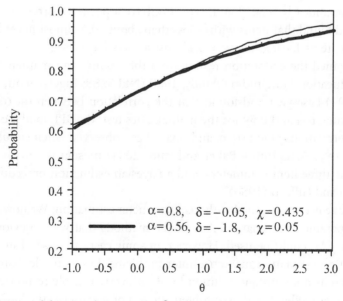

FIGURE 6.2. 3PL model IRFs when $\alpha = 0.8$, $\delta = -0.05$, $\chi = 0.435$ and when $\alpha = 0.56$, $\delta = -1.8$, $\chi = 0.0$.

our "multiple surfaces" analogy, we cannot distinguish between the (log) likelihood surface associated with $\chi = 0.435$ and the one when $\chi = 0.0$. Therefore, if the respondents are located above -1, it is difficult to determine which of these two sets of item parameter estimates is "best" and we have difficulty obtaining a converged solution for the item.[5]

In general, the estimation of χ_j may be problematic for some items because of the paucity of persons at the lower end of the continuum, because the items are located at the lower end of the continuum (e.g., very easy items), and/or because the items have low estimated discrimination parameters. Problems in estimating χ_j can influence the estimation of the item's other parameters. In these situations a criterion may be used to determine whether χ_j should be estimated. For instance, LOGIST uses the "stability" criterion of $(\delta_j - 2/\alpha_j)$. Specifically, χ_j is estimated only when $(\delta_j - 2/\alpha_j) > -2.5$; -2.5 is the default value and may be changed. The stability criterion is the location on the θ continuum "at which the proportion of correct responses is only about 0.03 above the lower asymptote" (Wingersky et al., 1982, p. 21). Alternative strategies are to fix χ_j to a specific value or to impose a prior distribution. In regard to the former, the selection of a constant (common) value for χ may be done arbitrarily (e.g., LOGIST's $(1/m - 0.05)$ where m is the number of item options) by averaging the nonproblematic $\hat{\chi}_j$s, by averaging the $\hat{\chi}_j$s for items located at the lower end of the continuum (i.e., the so-called easy items), or by fixing the lower asymptote to some nonzero value determined by inspecting the lower asymptote of empirical IRFs.

We may also use a prior distribution with the χ_js. de Gruijter (1984) has demonstrated that the use of a prior distribution for estimation of χ_j can lead to reasonable parameter estimates for the model. The regression toward the mean phenomenon that typically occurs when using a prior distribution is not as problematic in estimating χ_j as it is when estimating person and item location parameters (Lord, 1986). In general, we recommend the use of a prior on the χ_js as the first strategy to facilitate the estimation of the lower asymptote.

In regard to the item's other parameters, empirical data calibration has shown that the $\hat{\alpha}_j$s and $\hat{\delta}_j$s are nonlinearly related and, typically, have a positive correlation (Lord, 1975). In addition, Lord found that items with $\hat{\delta}$s less than about -0.5 almost never have $\hat{\alpha}$s greater than 1 and that items located above 0.5 almost always have $\hat{\alpha}$s greater than 1.0. In this regard, we examined the calibration results from the reading and mathematics tests from the National Education Longitudinal Study, 1988 (NELS: 88; Ingels, Scott, Rock, Pollack, & Rasinski, 1994) base year and found that the correlation between the $\hat{\alpha}$s and the $\hat{\delta}$s is 0.25 for the reading test and 0.59 for the mathematics test; the 3PL model calibration used LOGIST. Intercorrelations among $\hat{\alpha}$, $\hat{\delta}$, and $\hat{\chi}$ have been observed when simulated data have been calibrated (e.g., Yen, 1987). Baker and Kim (2004) present the mathematics for the estimation of the three item parameters, and a Bayesian estimation procedure is presented in Swaminathan and Gifford (1986).

So far we have been concerned with item parameter estimation. We now turn our attention to person parameter estimation. Any of the methods that were previously discussed, such as MLE or EAP, could be used. However, in some cases the use of unrestricted MLE for person location estimation may encounter problems. For example, Samejima (1973a) showed that there is not a unique solution for θ for every possible response pattern under the three-parameter model. For these problematic response patterns the likelihood function may have more than one maximum. For example, assume we have a two-item instrument with $\alpha_1 = 2.0$, $\delta_1 = 0.0$, $\chi_1 = 0.25$ for the first item and $\alpha_2 = 1.0$, $\delta_2 = -0.5$, $\chi_2 = 0.0$ for the second item. On these two items, assume that a person has a response of 1 on item 1 and a response of 0 on item 2 (Samejima, 1973a). Assuming a proficiency testing situation, then this response pattern reflects a person correctly answering the "harder/more discriminating" item (possibly by guessing) and incorrectly answering the "easier/less discriminating" item. The corresponding likelihood function is presented in Figure 6.3.

As we see, the likelihood function has a *local* maximum at approximately –0.05, and as θ becomes progressively smaller the likelihood function begins to approach an asymptote of 0.25. Therefore, this likelihood function is asymptotic with a value 0.25 and without a unique person location estimate. Stated another way, these types of response vectors do not have a *global* maximum and have multiple maxima. In these cases, the use of standard MLE with the three-parameter model may yield a $\hat{\theta}$ that turns out to be a local, not a global, maximum. When a local maximum is suspected, then using a different starting/provisional estimate for the MLE algorithm (see Appendix A) might produce a different $\hat{\theta}$. (In fact, the presence of multiple solutions for a given response vector is evidence indicating that one or more of the solutions represent local maxima.)

Although the example only uses two items Samejima (1973a) speculated that "the likelihood function may be more complicated, with possibly more than one local maximum in addition to a terminal maximum" (p. 225). We have empirical support for the occurrence of multimodal likelihood functions from the work of Yen, Burket, and Sykes (1991). Specifically, in an analysis of 14 empirical data sets they found that as many as 3.1% of the examinees had response vectors whose likelihoods functions had multiple maxima (cf. Fischer, 1981).

The multimodal likelihood function seen in Figure 6.3 is due to the specific $\underline{x}$ and

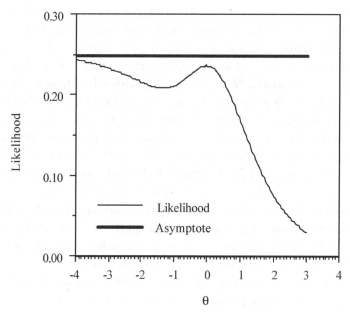

FIGURE 6.3. Likelihood function for a two-item instrument with no unique maximum, $\underline{x} = \{1, 0\}$.

the particular relationship among the α_j, δ_j, and χ_j. However, if $\chi_j = 0$ for both items (i.e., the 1PL and 2PL models), then the likelihood function has a unique solution. Therefore, one possibility of addressing these multimodal likelihood function situations is to use the *truncated 2PL model* (Samejima, 2001) for person parameter estimation. The truncated 2PL model capitalizes on the fact that the 2PL model's IRF (with appropriate item parameter values) is virtually indistinguishable from that of the 3PL model above a critical value, θ_g. Below θ_g the probability of a response of 1 is 0 for the truncated 2PL model (i.e., the IRF is truncated at θ_g). Therefore, for the truncated 2PL model there are two conditions: (1) for $-\infty < \theta < \theta_g$ we have that $p_j = 0$; and (2) for $\theta_g < \theta < \infty$, we have p_j given by the 2PL model (Equation 5.1). Samejima (1973a) shows that $\theta_g = 0.5 \ln(\chi_j) + \delta_j$. An alternative approach for handling multimodal likelihood functions is to use a Bayesian person estimation technique (e.g., EAP).

HOW LARGE A CALIBRATION SAMPLE?

The answer to the question of how large a sample is needed depends, in part, on the estimation procedure, instrument characteristics (e.g., the distribution of item parameter estimates, instrument length, etc.), response data characteristics (e.g., amount of missing data), and person distribution. In general, attempts at answering this question have involved conducting simulation studies where the parameter estimates can be compared, directly or indirectly, with the corresponding parameters.

For example, Yen (1987) investigated the parameter recovery of MMLE and JMLE as implemented in BILOG and LOGIST, respectively, using a fixed sample size of 1000. In this Monte Carlo study she investigated three different instrument lengths (10, 20, and 40 items) and different θ distributions: normal (0, 1), negatively skewed (skew = –0.4/kurtosis = –0.1), positively skewed (skew = 0.4/kurtosis = –0.1), and platykurtic (skew = 0.1/kurtosis = –0.4). In general, she found that MMLE estimates were more accurate than those of JMLE, particularly at the 10-item instrument length. With respect to MMLE, the item discrimination estimation results using the 20- and 40-item instruments were comparable to one another in terms of their root mean squared deviation (RMSD) with values ranging from 0.09 to 0.20. Moreover, the correlations between $\hat{\alpha}$ and α (i.e., $r_{\hat{\alpha}\alpha}$) ranged from 0.88 to 0.94, regardless of the normality or nonnormality of the θ distribution. For the 10-item length the RMSD doubled to 0.48 and $r_{\hat{\alpha}\alpha}$ decreased to 0.84. In terms of item location estimation, the 20- and 40-item instruments had correlations (i.e., $r_{\hat{\delta}\delta}$) from 0.97 to 0.99 with RMSDs of 0.07 to 0.16; the 10-item length had an $r_{\hat{\delta}\delta}$ of 1.00 and RMSDs of 0.18. In general, item location is better estimated than item discrimination. The lower asymptote showed $r_{\hat{\chi}\chi}$s between 0.11 to 0.54 and RMSDs of 0.03 to 0.08 across the various instrument lengths and irrespective of the type of θ distribution. Although not a formal parameter recovery study, Mislevy (1986a) presents results that indicate that BILOG does a reasonably good job in recovering item parameters with a sample size of 1000 and a 20-item instrument.

On the basis of this research it appears that for MMLE a sample of 1000 persons may lead to reasonably accurate item parameter estimates with the 3PL model under favorable conditions (e.g., a symmetric θ distribution, an instrument length of 20 items, etc.). This (rough) guideline assumes the use of prior distributions for χ_j and α_j. However, it is strongly recommended that calibration sample sizes exceed 1000 to mitigate the convergence problems that sometimes plague 3PL model calibrations. In fact, Thissen and Wainer (1982) suggest trying to avoid estimating χ_j if possible under unrestricted MLE and also suggest that the use of a prior distribution when estimating χ_j seems "to offer some hope" (p. 410). In cases where one has a smallish sample size and/or one experiences difficulty in estimating the item parameters with the 3PL model, then fixing the lower asymptote to a reasonable nonzero value for some or all the items may help. In addition, some convergence problems (e.g., $-2\ln L$ values that oscillate across iterations) may sometimes be rectified by using the RIDGE subcommand available in BILOG and PARSCALE. The calibration sample size caveats and considerations previously mentioned in Chapters 3 and 5, such as model–data misfit tolerance, ancillary technique sample size requirements, the amount of missing data, and so on are also applicable to the three-parameter model.[6]

ASSESSING CONDITIONAL INDEPENDENCE

In Chapter 2 we stated that one assumption underlying IRT models is that the responses to one item are not related to those on any other item conditional on $\theta(s)$. This assumption is the conditional (or local) independence assumption. When this assumption is violated, then the accuracy of our item parameter estimates is affected and the total instrument information is overestimated (Chen & Thissen, 1997; Oshima, 1994; Sireci, Wainer, & Thissen, 1991; Thissen, Steinberg, & Mooney, 1989). As such, any subsequent use of the item parameter estimates for, say, equating (see Chapter 11), will be potentially adversely affected. In the following we discuss some causes of item *dependence*, some ways to handle this dependence, and then a statistic for identifying local dependent items postadministration.

Violation of the conditional independence assumption may occur for various reasons, such as physical dependence among items, content clues, instrument length, insufficient allotted time to complete an instrument (i.e., speededness), and/or an insufficient number of latent variables in the IRT model. Examples of items with physical dependence are a set of survey questions that all refer to the same, say, life-changing event (e.g., a diagnosis of cancer, contracting HIV, etc.), comprehension questions that use the same reading passage, or trigonometry problems based on a common figure. In all of these cases one may see local dependence. In addition, when there is insufficient time to respond to all the items on an instrument the items affected by the lack of time may exhibit dependence. As a consequence, their corresponding parameter estimates are adversely affected. Conversely, when there is sufficient time to respond to an instrument but the instrument is very long, one may observe local dependence due to fatigue or diminished motivation. Practice effects may also lead to local dependence.

For some of these causes it is possible to identify the items that may be prone to local dependence prior to administering the instrument. In general, an instrument should be inspected for connections between the items. This inspection involves looking for similarity in the questions' text, an item providing a cue(s) as to how to respond to another item(s), the items sharing grammatical inconsistencies or common information (e.g., a passage or a figure), the items sharing a nesting/hierarchical relationship, and so on. Depending on the outcome of this inspection, rewriting the items may be sufficient to address the anticipated dependency. In other cases, the items cannot be rewritten because they need to be logically related or physically dependent. In these cases the dependent items may be combined to form a testlet (Thissen et al., 1989; Wainer & Kiely, 1987; Wainer & Lewis, 1990).

A testlet (also known as an item bundle) is a group of interdependent items. A testlet may be created pre- or postadministration. There are at least two ways to score a testlet. In one approach each item in the testlet provides an item score and the score on the testlet is, for example, the sum of these item scores. For instance, if a testlet consists of three 1-point items, then the possible scores on the testlet would be 0, 1, 2, 3. In effect, the testlet is treated as a single "item" for estimating a person's location. One way of utilizing this testlet score is to use a model that can handle both dichotomous and polytomous responses. Models that can address not only polytomous responses, but also dichotomous responses, are presented in the following chapters.

In the foregoing polytomous model approach to handling testlets there is some loss of information. For example, a testlet score does not say anything about the response pattern that produced the score. Whether this an important issue is context-specific. However, if the loss of this information is important, then an alternative approach to scoring a testlet is to use a model that incorporates a parameter that reflects the dependency among items within the testlet. Bradlow, Wainer, and Wang (1999) developed such a model by augmenting the 2PL model. The augmentation is a random effect parameter that reflects a person-specific testlet effect. The Bradlow et al. model may be applied to both items that are independent and those in testlets; one- and three-parameter models also exist (see Wang & Wilson, 2005; Wainer, Bradlow, & Du, 2000). This *testlet model* and its variants form the basis of the evolving testlet response theory (Wainer, Bradlow, & Wang, 2007).

Various indices have been developed for identifying local dependence. A review of some of these indices and an examination of which index works best may be found in Kim, De Ayala, Ferdous, and Nering (2007); also see Glas (1999), Glas and Falcón (2003), Orlando and Thissen (2000), and Rosenbaum (1984) for related indices. One of these indices is Yen's (1984) Q_3 index. Although no index may be considered to be the best in terms of combining high power to detect conditional item dependence with low false positive rates, the Q_3 index works reasonably well (e.g., see Kim et al., 2007). Because of Q_3's simplicity and its comparative good performance we use it to demonstrate evaluating the conditional independence assumption with our mathematics data example.

Q_3 is the correlation between the residuals for a pair of items. The residual for an item is the difference between an individual's observed response and his or her expected response on the item. Therefore, after fitting the model the Pearson correlation coefficient is used to examine the linear relationship between pairs of residuals. In the current context, the observed response is either a 1 or a 0 and the expected response is the probability according to the 3PL model. Symbolically, the residual for person i on item j is

$$d_{ij} = x_{ij} - p_j(\hat{\theta}_i)$$

and for item k it is

$$d_{ik} = x_{ik} - p_k(\hat{\theta}_i)$$

Q_3 is the correlation between d_{ij} and d_{ik} across respondents:

$$Q_{3jk} = r_{d_j d_k} \qquad\qquad (6.4)$$

If $|Q_3|$ equals 1.0, then the two items are perfectly dependent. In contrast, a Q_3 of 0.0 is a necessary, but not sufficient condition for independence because a $Q_3 = 0$ can be obtained when the items in the pair are independent of one another *or* because they exhibit a nonlinear relationship. Therefore, Q_3 is useful for identifying items that exhibit item *dependence*. Under conditional independence Q_3 should have an expected value of $-1/(L - 1)$ (Yen, 1993).

As mentioned above, in some cases one can explain item dependence in terms of multidimensionality. That is, the dependency between two items is due to a common additional latent variable such as test-wiseness. If two items are independent, then their interrelationship is completely explained by the latent structure of the model. If one applies a unidimensional model when two dimensions are called for, then the items that are influenced by both latent variables show a negative local dependence and items that are affected by only one of the two latent variable show a positive local dependence (Yen, 1984). However, if only one of the latent variables is used, then the items that are influenced only by that underlying variable show a slight negative local dependence. To obtain a large Q_3 value for an item pair we need to have similarity of parameters for the items in question and the items need to share one or more unique dimensions. Therefore, similarity of parameters is a necessary, but not sufficient condition for obtaining a large Q_3 value.

Some research (e.g., Yen, 1984) has found that although the value of Q_3 is not as much influenced by the sample size as other measures, it is affected by the instrument's length. This may be due to the fact that item scores are involved in both x_{ij} and (implicitly) $p_j(\hat{\theta}_i)$. As a result, Q_3 may tend to be slightly negative due to part–whole contamination (Yen, 1984). The implication of this is that for short instruments one would expect to see substantially more negative Q_3s than for longer instruments. In this case, these negative values may, in part, be artifacts due to the instrument's length.

There are various ways to use Q_3 to identify locally dependent items. First, we can use Q_3 in a statistical z-test (Yen, 1984). This would require that Q_3 be transformed by the Fisher r-to-z transformation (z_{Q_3}) and then used in a z-test, $z = z_{Q_3}/\sqrt{1/(N-3)}$; z_{Q_3} has a mean of 0.0 and a variance of $1/(N - 3)$. The standard unit normal table can provide critical values for identifying items with z_{Q_3} values that are unlikely to be observed owing to chance alone. However, because the typical calibration sample size will result in a test with a great deal of power, we will most likely reject the null hypothesis of independence for trivially small correlations. An additional issue to consider is that the sampling distribution of Q_3 may not be symmetric (Chen & Thissen, 1997). That is, because the Q_3 sampling distribution may not approximate the standard normal very well, the critical values would be inappropriate. Because of this the Q_3 empirical Type I error rates do not match the nominal significance level α that one would expect under normal curve theory. Therefore, rather than using the critical values in a strict statistical fashion it is preferable to use them as guidelines for informed judgment.

A second way of using Q_3 is to take advantage of the fact that Q_3 is a correlation. Specifically, because Q_3 is a correlation coefficient, the square of Q_3 (Q_3^2) may be interpreted as a measure of the amount of residual variance shared by an item pair. Therefore, item pairs with a large proportion (e.g., 5% or greater) of shared variability would indicate dependent items.

Alternatively, one could compare Q_3 to a cutpoint. That is, an observed Q_3 that is larger than the cutpoint would indicate item dependence. One such cutpoint is suggested by Yen (1993); her suggestion was in the context of instruments with a minimum of 17 items. Specifically, a Q_3 screening value of 0.2 can be used to identify items exhibiting dependence (i.e., $|Q_3| > 0.2$ indicates local item dependence). Although this cutpoint has been found to produce small Type I error rates, it also leads to comparatively lower power than other detection methods (Chen & Thissen, 1997).

In our example below we use a different cutpoint strategy. That is, rather than using the suggested 0.2 criterion, we empirically determine the screening value for our instrument and estimated parameters through a simulation. From this simulation we are able to identify the Q_3 value(s) that would cut off, say, 5% of the Q_3 value, and that would serve as our screening value.

EXAMPLE: APPLICATION OF THE 3PL MODEL TO THE MATHEMATICS DATA, MMLE

There are a number of programs that perform 3PL model calibration, including, but not limited to, BILOG-MG, MULTILOG, XCALIBRE, and NOHARM. However, for comparison of the 3PL model calibration results with those of the 1PL and 2PL models we use BILOG.

In our previous 1PL and 2PL model calibrations we used the individuals' response vectors (i.e., case data). In this example we demonstrate how to analyze response pattern data. Response pattern data consist of the unique response patterns and their corresponding frequencies. As mentioned in Chapter 2, with five binary items there are $2^L = 2^5 = 32$ potential patterns, and these 32 patterns are enumerated in Table 2.1. The command file for performing the calibration of our response pattern data is shown in Table 6.1. The GLOBAL subcommands of NPARM=3, NWGHT=3, LOG specify the use of the three-parameter model, "case weighting," and the logistic metric, respectively. By using case weighting we are specifying the analysis of our pattern data where the response pattern frequency is the weight.

Table 6.2 contains the corresponding abridged Phase 1 and 2 output. The echo of the program parameters indicates that the intended model (3 PARAMETER LOGISTIC) and the logistic metric (LOGIT METRIC) are being used. The echo of the Phase 2 program parameters shows the maxima of 20 EM and 10 Newton cycles (CALIB line) as well as the default convergence criterion of 0.01. Moreover, the output indicates the use of prior distributions for the estimation of α_j and χ_j (i.e., CONSTRAINT DISTRIBUTION ON SLOPES and CONSTRAINT DISTRIBUTION ON ASYMPTOTES, respectively).

TABLE 6.1. The BILOG Command File for the 3PL Model Item Calibration

```
3PL CALIB & EAP ABILITY EST,PATTERN DATA

>GLOBAL DFNAME='MATHPAT.DAT',NPARM=3, NWGHT=3,LOG,SAVE;
>SAV  PARM='MATH3pls.PAR';
>LENGTH NITEMS=5;
>INPUT NTOT=5,NALT=2, NIDC=2, SAMP=20000, TYP=2;
>ITEMS;
>TEST TNAMES=MATH,
     INumber=(1(1)5);
     (2A1,T5,F4.0,T11,5A1)
>CALIB CYC=20, NEW=10, CHI=(5,10),PLOT=1.0;
>SCORE MET=2;
```

The Phase 2 results show that 20 EM cycles and 6 Newton cycles were executed. Given that the LARGEST CHANGE at cycle 20 (i.e., 0.01563) is greater than the EM convergence criterion, we did not achieve EM convergence; the Newton step converged. Because we do not have EM convergence we ignore remaining portion of the Phase 2 output and modify the command file. To increase the maximum number of EM cycles, for example to 50, we substitute CYC=50 for CYC=20 on the CALIB line; no other changes are made. With this revised command file BILOG-MG is re-executed. The second calibration converged in 23 EM cycles with 5 Newton cycles.

The item parameter estimates from the converged solution are presented in Table 6.3. (The converged solution's parameter estimates are only slightly different from those of the nonconverged solution.) The item discrimination, location parameter, and pseudo-guessing parameter estimates are obtained from the SLOPE, THRESHOLD, and ASYMPTOTE columns, respectively. For instance, for item 1 the item discrimination estimate $(\hat{\alpha}_1)$ is 1.921, the item location estimate $(\hat{\delta}_1)$ is -1.052, with a pseudo-guessing parameter estimate $(\hat{\chi}_1)$ of 0.486. By and large, the $\hat{\chi}_j$s for items 2–4 are acceptable, although item 1's value is considered to be surprisingly large.[7]

As part of our model–data fit analysis we compare the empirical and predicted IRFs for each of our items. Figure 6.4 shows item 3's empirical and predicted IRFs. The estimate of the item's pseudo-guessing parameter is identified by the symbol c instead of χ and the item's location by b. As can be seen, there is a close correspondence between the empirical and predicted IRFs. This correspondence provides evidence of data fit for this item. Figure 6.4 is typical of the other empirical versus predicted IRFs plots. Item 3's IRF and information function are presented in the left and right panels, respectively, of Figure 6.5. From the right panel we see that the item's information function is not quite centered about the item's location. This is true for all items calibrated with the 3PL model and is due to the influence of a nonzero lower asymptote. The actual location of the maximum of the item information is discussed below.

Fit Assessment: Conditional Independence Assessment

We use Q_3 for evaluating the conditional independence assumption. As noted above, Yen's (1993) suggested 0.2 screening criterion was in the context of instruments that had at least

TABLE 6.2. BILOG Output: Phases 1 and 2 (Abridged); Run 1, Nonconverged Solution

```
     <Phase 1 results>
       :
>GLOBAL DFNAME='MATHPAT.DAT', NPARM=3, NWGHT=3, LOG, SAVE;

FILE ASSIGNMENT AND DISPOSITION
================================
SUBJECT DATA INPUT FILE       MATHPAT.DAT
BILOG-MG MASTER DATA FILE     MF.DAT
                                        WILL BE CREATED FROM DATA FILE

CALIBRATION DATA FILE         CF.DAT
                                        WILL BE CREATED FROM DATA FILE

ITEM PARAMETERS FILE          IF.DAT
                                        WILL BE CREATED THIS RUN

CASE SCALE-SCORE FILE         SF.DAT
CASE WEIGHTING                          FOR SUBJECT STATISTICS AND
                                        ITEM CALIBRATION
ITEM RESPONSE MODEL                     3 PARAMETER LOGISTIC
                                        LOGIT  METRIC (I.E., D = 1.0)

       :
     <Phase 2 results begin>
       :
CALIBRATION PARAMETERS
======================
MAXIMUM NUMBER OF EM CYCLES:            20
MAXIMUM NUMBER OF NEWTON CYCLES:        10
CONVERGENCE CRITERION:                 0.0100
LATENT DISTRIBUTION:                    NORMAL PRIOR FOR EACH GROUP
CONSTRAINT DISTRIBUTION ON ASYMPTOTES:  YES
CONSTRAINT DISTRIBUTION ON SLOPES:      YES
CONSTRAINT DISTRIBUTION ON THRESHOLDS:  NO
SOURCE OF ITEM CONSTRAINT DISTIBUTION
        MEANS AND STANDARD DEVIATIONS:  PROGRAM DEFAULTS
       :
METHOD OF SOLUTION:

EM CYCLES (MAXIMUM OF    20)
FOLLOWED BY NEWTON-RAPHSON STEPS (MAXIMUM OF   20)
       :
[EM STEP]

         -2 LOG LIKELIHOOD =    118043.518
CYCLE  1:    LARGEST CHANGE =   2.60459
       :
         -2 LOG LIKELIHOOD =    110088.005
CYCLE 20:    LARGEST CHANGE =   0.01563

====> NOTE: CONVERGENCE HAS NOT BEEN REACHED TO CRITERION =   0.01000

[FULL NEWTON STEP]
         -2 LOG LIKELIHOOD =    110077.0063
CYCLE 21:    LARGEST CHANGE =   0.11455
-2 LOG LIKELIHOOD:       110065.0330
CYCLE    25;   LARGEST CHANGE=   0.01206

-2 LOG LIKELIHOOD:       110064.9312
CYCLE    26;   LARGEST CHANGE=   0.00615
       :
```

TABLE 6.3. BILOG Output: Phase 2 (Abridged); Run 2, Converged Solution

:

ITEM	INTERCEPT S.E.	SLOPE S.E.	THRESHOLD S.E.	LOADING S.E.	ASYMPTOTE S.E.	CHISQ (PROB)	DF
ITEM0001	2.021	1.921	-1.052	0.887	0.486	192.4	4.0
	0.251*	0.196*	0.223*	0.090*	0.092*	(0.0000)	
ITEM0002	0.613	2.936	-0.209	0.947	0.172	2706.9	3.0
	0.111*	0.245*	0.052*	0.079*	0.030*	(0.0000)	
ITEM0003	-0.369	2.446	0.151	0.926	0.209	59.3	5.0
	0.130*	0.198*	0.043*	0.075*	0.021*	(0.0000)	
ITEM0004	-1.485	2.768	0.537	0.941	0.149	554.2	5.0
	0.182*	0.257*	0.023*	0.087*	0.012*	(0.0000)	
ITEM0005	-1.459	1.637	0.892	0.853	0.161	335.5	5.0
	0.159*	0.139*	0.033*	0.073*	0.016*	(0.0000)	

```
                                          * STANDARD ERROR
      LARGEST CHANGE =    0.007188         3848.3  22.0
                                          (0.0000)
```

NOTE: ITEM FIT CHI-SQUARES AND THEIR SUMS MAY BE UNRELIABLE
FOR TESTS WITH LESS THAN 20 ITEMS

:

17 items (i.e., an expected Q_3 value of $-1/(L - 1) = -0.0625$). However, the expected Q_3 value for our 5-item mathematics test is -0.25. This value is substantially farther away from 0 than the expected Q_3 value in Yen's (1993) study. Therefore, although a ±0.2 screening criterion may be useful when the expected Q_3 value is comparatively close to 0 (e.g., with 35 or more items), with only 5 items this criterion is less useful. As a result, rather than use the 0.2 screening criterion we empirically determined the screening value for our 5-item instrument. To identify our screening criterion we conducted a simulation that showed the magnitude of Q_3s that might be expected to be observed if the data conformed to the model's conditional independence assumption.[8] From this simulation the screening value is determined to be -0.2961.

With a five-item instrument there are 10 Q_3 values (i.e., $L(L - 1)/2$) to calculate. Although a statistical package can be used to calculate Q_3, we used a spreadsheet program. To calculate Q_3 we need to have estimates of the person locations in order to determine the expected responses, p_js. We reexecuted BILOG requesting only the EAP $\hat{\theta}$s and that these estimates be saved to their own file (this is demonstrated in Chapter 5). These $\hat{\theta}$s along with the response data and the item parameter estimates were entered into a spreadsheet program and the residuals determined. The Pearson product–moment correlation function is used to calculate the correlations (i.e., the Q_3s) among the unique residual pairings. Table 6.4 contains these Q_3s for the mathematics data example; the scatterplots (not presented) corresponding to these values were inspected for anomalies, but none were found. Not surprisingly, given the instrument's length, only one of the Q_3s is positive; the average Q_3 is -0.1799.

Our Q_3s show that two item pairs (items 1 and 4; items 2 and 5) have *absolute* values exceeding the screening value of 0.2961. That is, after fitting the unidimensional 3PL model to the data the items in these two item pairs had slightly more than 10% of their residual variability in common. (These item pairs may or may not be found to exceed the screening criterion with either the 1PL or 2PL models.) Although these two item pairs may be considered to be exhibiting item dependence, evidence of conditional dependence in the remaining eight pairs is absent.

How one deals with items that are considered sufficiently dependent to be problematic postadministration is contingent on what one believes is the cause of the dependency. Again, inspection of the items exhibiting local dependence may be useful (e.g., the local dependence may be related to the locations of the items in the instrument, their text, etc.). In some cases where there is a great deal of dependence it may be necessary to remove one of the dependent items for pragmatic reasons and because it is not clear as to why there is a dependency between the items. Because highly dependent items are in a sense redundant, the removal of one of the dependent items may not be problematic. In other cases, the items may be combined to form a testlet. In either case the instrument would need to be recalibrated.

For this example the local dependence exhibited by the two item pairs could be addressed by forming a testlet for each pair. Testlet 1 would consist of items 1 and 4, whereas testlet 2 would involve items 2 and 5. Each testlet would have possible testlet scores of 0 through 2

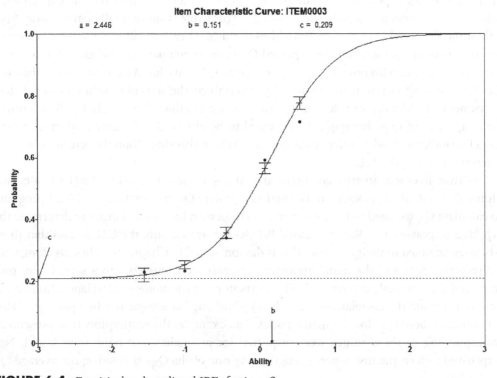

FIGURE 6.4. Empirical and predicted IRFs for item 3.

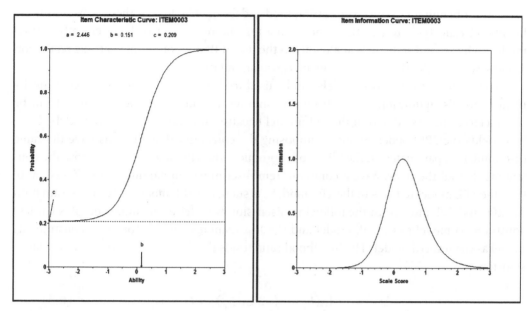

FIGURE 6.5. Item response and item information functions for item 3.

and the instrument would consist of three "items" (i.e., testlet 1, testlet 2, and item 3). The corresponding response data could be calibrated using, for example, the polytomous partial credit model discussed in Chapter 7.

Fit Assessment: Model Comparison

In this and in previous chapters our focus has been on whether a particular model is exhibiting model–data fit. We now present three model–data fit statistics that can be used for making model comparisons and selection. These complementary procedures should be

TABLE 6.4. Q_3 Statistics for the Math Data Set

	Items 1	2	3	4	5
1	1.0000				
2	-0.1549 (0.0240)	1.0000			
3	-0.0844 (0.0071)	-0.1201 (0.0144)	1.0000		
4	-0.3567 (0.1273)	-0.1357 (0.0184)	-0.2740 (0.0751)	1.0000	
5	0.0008 (0.0000)	-0.3199 (0.1023)	-0.2105 (0.0443)	-0.1218 (0.0148)	1.0000

Note. Q_3^2s are in parentheses.

used after obtaining evidence supporting model–data fit. The first of these is based on the likelihood ratio (G^2) test statistic for comparing the relative fit of hierarchically related models. The second statistic is analogous to the use of R^2 for comparing various regression models, whereas the third is based on an information criterion.

The change in G^2 across models can be used to determine whether two hierarchically related models significantly differ from one another. For instance, the 2PL model can be considered to be nested within the 3PL model because constraining the 3PL model's χ_js to be 0 yields the 2PL model. Similarly, imposing the constraint that all items have the same discrimination parameter on the 2PL model produces the 1PL model. If we impose the constraints that all the items have a common item discrimination parameter and χ_js equal 0, then the 3PL model reduces to the 1PL model. As such, the 1PL model is nested within both the 2PL and 3PL models. In the following discussion we refer to the more complex (or less constrained) model as the *full* model and the less complex/simpler (or more constrained) model as the *reduced* model. The likelihood ratio test is the difference between two deviance statistics:

$$\Delta G^2 = -2 \ln(L_R) - (-2 \ln(L_F)) = G_R^2 - G_F^2 \qquad (6.5)$$

where L_R is the maximum of the likelihood for the reduced model and L_F is the maximum of the likelihood for the full model. (Note that the log likelihood, $\ln L$, is typically multiplied by -2 when it is provided in output. In these cases the minus sign in "$-2\ln L$" represents a label and not a mathematical operation to be performed in Equation 6.5.) The degrees of freedom (df) for evaluating the significance of ΔG^2 is the difference in the number of parameters between the full model and the reduced model.[9] This statistic is distributed as an X^2 when the sample size is large and the full (nesting) model holds for the data. A nonsignificant statistic indicates that the additional complexity of the nesting model is not necessary. For instance, if a comparison of the 2PL model with the 3PL model is not significant, then the additional estimation of the pseudo-guessing parameters (i.e., the increased model complexity) is not necessary to improve model–data fit over and above that obtained with the 2PL model.

Table 6.5 contains the values of the -2 log likelihoods (i.e., $-2 \ln L$) for the 1PL, 2PL, and 3PL models from our BILOG calibrations. The $-2 \ln L$ is the last entry from the converged solution's iteration history and is labeled -2 LOG LIKELIHOOD: in the output. As can be seen, as the models increase in complexity, the corresponding G^2s decrease. The difference between the 1PL and 2PL models is

$$\Delta G^2 = -2 \ln(L_R) - (-2 \ln(L_F)) = 110{,}774.295 - 110{,}397.103 = 377.1914$$

with 4 df. Therefore, at the instrument level the 2PL model represents a significant ($\alpha = 0.05$) improvement in fit over the 1PL model. An analogous comparison between the 2PL and 3PL models also shows a significant ($\alpha = 0.05$) improvement in fit by the 3PL model over the 2PL model. Therefore, the 3PL model fits significantly better than either the 2PL or 1PL model.

Our second model comparison statistic is complementary to ΔG^2. This approach uses

TABLE 6.5. Model Fit Statistics

Model	−2 lnL	df	Relative change	Number of parameters	AIC	BIC
1PL[a]	110,774.295	25		6	110,784.295	110,823.711
2PL	110,397.103	21	0.0034	10	110,417.103	110,495.937
3PL	110,064.926	16	0.0030	15	110,094.926	110,213.176

[a]Five item locations plus a common α.

G^2 in a manner analogous to comparing various regression models' R^2s. (That is, the change in R^2s may be used for assessing the relative improvement in the proportion of variability accounted for by one model over another model.) In the current context, our strategy is to calculate the relative reduction in G^2s (Haberman, 1978). For instance, for the comparison of the 2PL model (G_F^2) with the 1PL model (G_R^2) we would calculate

$$R_\Delta^2 = \frac{(G_R^2 - G_F^2)}{G_R^2} = \frac{110774.295 - 110397.103}{110774.295} = 0.0034$$

This R_Δ^2 indicates that the 2PL model results in a 0.34% improvement in fit over the 1PL model. Comparing the 3PL and 2PL models we have

$$R_\Delta^2 = \frac{110397.103 - 110064.929}{110397.103} = 0.003$$

Therefore, using the more complex 3PL model results in an improvement of fit of 0.3% over the 2PL model. We do not consider this to be a meaningful improvement in fit vis-à-vis the increase in model complexity. Summarizing the results so far, we have that the 3PL model fits significantly better than the 2PL and 1PL models, but it does not result in a *meaningful* improvement of fit of over either model.

Because models with more parameters tend, in general, to fit a data set better than models with fewer parameters, it is advisable to consider the additional parameters when examining model–data fit. By taking into account the number of parameters used to achieve a particular degree of fit, one can reduce the tendency toward model overparameterization. To this end we have our third model comparison statistic. Schwarz (1978) introduced the *Bayesian information criterion* (BIC) as a criterion for model selection. BIC is an outgrowth of another information criterion, the *Akaike information criterion* (AIC) (Akaike, 1974) is:

$$AIC = -2\ln L + 2*Nparm \tag{6.6}$$

where Nparm is the number of parameters being estimated. The BIC statistic takes the number of parameters estimated by a model (Nparm), weights it by the transformed sample size (N), and then "penalizes" the log likelihood:

$$BIC = -2\ln L + \ln(N)*Nparm \qquad (6.7)$$

· where N is the number of persons. The model with the smallest BIC indicates the model with the "best" comparative fit and tends to favor constrained models.

Table 6.5 shows the AIC and BIC values for the three models. As is the case with ΔG^2 above, we see that even taking the 3PL model's additional complexity into account (i.e., relative to the 1PL and 2PL models) these statistics indicate that it is the best fitting of these three models.

A fourth statistic that could be used for model fit and selection belongs to the family of limited information goodness-of-fit statistics from Maydeu-Olivares and Joe (2006). In particular, their M_2 statistic maintains appropriate Type I error rates under varying degrees of model misspecification. Their M_2 is asymptotically distributed as an X^2 with, for binary data, $df = 2^L - $ (number of item parameters) $- 1$. Although it shows promise, M_2 is not yet readily available.

Although our triangulation with ΔG^2, AIC, and BIC shows that the 3PL model is the best-fitting model of the three considered, our R_Δ^2 shows that the differences are slight. In fact, the correlation between the 1PL model-based $\hat{\theta}$s and those of the 2PL model is 0.9907, and for the $\hat{\theta}$s from the 2PL and 3PL models the correlation is 0.9859; the lowest correlation is between the 1PL and 3PL models' $\hat{\theta}$s, $r = 0.9764$. That is, although the 3PL model is the best fitting of the three models, we have a high degree of linear agreement in the ordering of individuals across the three models. Based solely on the R_Δ^2, the magnitude of the $\hat{\theta}$ intercorrelations, the variability in the $\hat{\alpha}_j$s (both this chapter and Chapter 5), and the axiom "Make everything as simple as possible, but not simpler" (Albert Einstein), we would select the 2PL model for modeling these data. (However, we believe that a reasonable argument can be made for selecting the 1PL model.) Regardless of the model chosen item 1 should be more closely examined, given its $\hat{\chi}_1$ of 0.486. Additional points to consider in model selection are presented below in the section "Issues to Consider in Selecting among the 1PL, 2PL, and 3PL Models."

ASSESSING PERSON FIT: APPROPRIATENESS MEASUREMENT

Various person fit measures have been previously discussed. From one perspective, these measures are trying to determine whether the person is behaving in a fashion consistent with the model. Alternatively, one may ask, what is the *appropriateness* of a person's estimated location, $\hat{\theta}$, as a measure of his or her true location (θ)? For instance, imagine that a person has a response pattern of missing easy items and correctly answering more difficult items. Did this pattern arise from the person's correctly guessing on some difficult items and incorrectly responding to easier items, or does this reflect a person who was able to copy the answers on some items? Various statistically based indices have been developed to measure the degree to which an individual's response pattern is unusual or is inconsistent with the model used for characterizing his or her performance. These indices of person fit are examples of *appropriateness measurement* (e.g., Levine & Drasgow, 1983; Meijer & Sijtsma, 2001).

One index, l_z, has been found to perform better than other person fit measures (cf. Drasgow, Levine, & McLaughlin, 1987). This index is based on a standardization of the person log likelihood function to address the interaction of $\ln L$ and θ. As such, this standardization of log likelihood allows us to compare individuals at different θ levels on the basis of their l_z values.

In order to present l_z we start with the log likelihood function for a person i's response vector:

$$\ln L(\underline{x_i}|\theta, \underline{\alpha}, \underline{\delta}, \underline{\chi}) = \sum_{j=1}^{L} [x_{ij} \ln(p_j) + (1 - x_{ij}) \ln(1 - p_j)] \quad (6.8)$$

To standardize $\ln L$ we need both its variance and mean (i.e., the expected value). The expected value of the $\ln L$ is given by

$$\mathcal{E}(\ln L) = \sum_{j=1}^{L} \left\{ p_j \ln(p_j) + (1-p_j)\left[\ln(1-p_j)\right] \right\} \quad (6.9)$$

and its variance by

$$\text{Var}(\ln L) = \sum_{j=1}^{L} \left\{ p_j(1-p_j)\left[\ln \frac{p_j}{(1-p_j)}\right]^2 \right\} \quad (6.10)$$

Using Equations 6.8–6.10 and the z-score formula we obtain

$$l_z = \frac{\ln L - \mathcal{E}(\ln L)}{\sqrt{\text{Var}(\ln L)}} \quad (6.11)$$

In practice, we use $\hat{\theta}$ in lieu of θ in the calculation of p_j.

Although l_z is purported to have a unit normal distribution, this has not necessarily been true for instruments of different lengths (Drasgow et al., 1987; Levine & Drasgow, 1983). Therefore, using the standard normal curve for hypothesis testing with l_z may be inadvisable in some situations. Nevertheless, various guidelines exist for using l_z for informed judgment. In general, a "good" l_z is one around 0.0. An l_z that is negative reflects a relatively unlikely response vector (i.e., inconsistent responses), whereas a positive value indicates a comparatively more likely response vector than would be expected on the basis of the model (i.e., hyperconsistent responses). Also see Appendix E, "The Person Response Function," for a graphical approach that can be used for detecting aberrant response vectors.

INFORMATION FOR THE THREE-PARAMETER MODEL

The amount of information an item provides for estimating θ under the 3PL model is

$$I_j(\theta) = \alpha_j^2 \left[\frac{(p_j - \chi_j)^2}{(1 - \chi_j)^2} \right] \left[\frac{(1 - p_j)}{p_j} \right] \qquad (6.12)$$

Because guessing behavior reflects "noise," it may be intuited that one effect of a nonzero χ_j is to reduce the amount information available for locating people on the θ continuum.[10] Equation 6.12 shows that this is indeed the case. For a given α_j and δ_j an item provides more information for person estimation when $\chi_j = 0$ than when it is nonzero. Therefore, for the 3PL model the upper limit of $I_j(\theta)$ is given by the more restrictive 2PL model. If one sets $\chi_j = 0$ and simplifies, then Equation 6.12 reduces to Equation 5.4.

In contrast to the 1PL and 2PL models with their maximum item information at δ_j, Figure 6.5 shows that for the 3PL model the peak of the item information does not occur at δ_j, but slightly above it. This offset from δ_j is given by[11]

$$\frac{\ln\left[\frac{1}{2} + \frac{\sqrt{1 + 8\chi_j}}{2} \right]}{\alpha_j}$$

At this location the maximum item information value is (Lord, 1980)

$$\text{Max}(I_j(\theta)) = \frac{\alpha_j^2}{8(1 - \chi_j)^2} [1 - 20\chi_j - 8\chi_j^2 + (1 + 8\chi_j)^{1.5}] \qquad (6.13)$$

As has previously been the case, the total information for an instrument is the sum of the item information:

$$I(\theta) = \frac{1}{\sigma_e^2(\theta)} = \sum_{j=1}^{L} I_j(\theta) \qquad (6.14)$$

In the foregoing we have focused on the amount of information an item provides for estimating a person's location.[12,13] However, we can also look at how much information the calibration sample provides for estimating a particular item parameter.[14] The information functions for estimating α_j, δ_j, and χ_j are, respectively (Lord, 1980):

$$I_{\alpha\alpha} = \frac{1}{(1 - \chi_j)^2} \sum_{i}^{N} (\theta_i - \delta_j)^2 (p_j - \chi_j)^2 \frac{(1 - p_j)}{p_j} \qquad (6.15)$$

$$I_{\delta\delta} = \frac{\alpha_j^2}{(1-\chi_j)^2} \sum_i^N (p_j - \chi_j)^2 \frac{(1-p_j)}{p_j} \tag{6.16}$$

and

$$I_{\chi\chi} = \frac{1}{(1-\chi_j)^2} \sum_i^N \frac{(1-p_j)}{p_j} \tag{6.17}$$

The application of Equations 6.15–6.17 to our example's five-item instrument is shown in Figures 6.6–6.8, respectively. As we see from Figure 6.6, the information function for estimating α_j is bimodal. The different modal values are a reflection of the magnitude of the nonzero χ_js. It is also apparent that the modes occur on opposite sides of the item's location, with the leftmost mode always less than the rightmost mode; these characteristics are most easily seen with item 5. This characteristic is a reflection of positive α_js (i.e., if the α_js are negative, then the leftmost mode would be greater than the rightmost mode). The location of the minimum of the information function between the two modes corresponds to the item's δ_j; this minimum information is 0.

Figure 6.7 shows that the information function for estimating δ_j is unimodal with the mode located at the item's δ_j. Therefore, individuals around the item's location provide the greatest information for estimating δ. As is the case with Figure 6.6, the different heights of the modes across the items is a reflection of the interaction among the item's parameters as

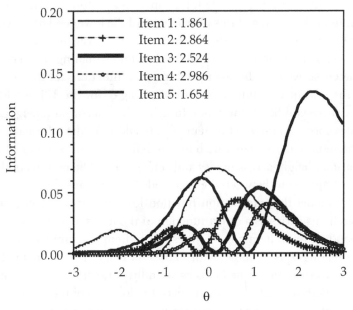

FIGURE 6.6. Information for estimating α_j for each of five items.

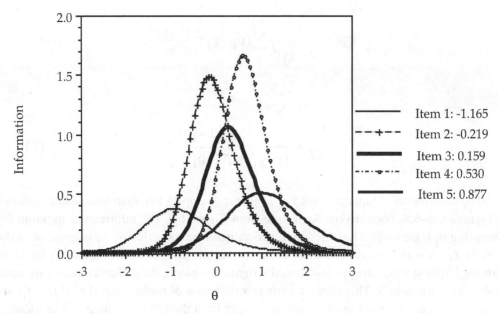

FIGURE 6.7. Information for estimating δ_j for each of five items.

well as their different values across items. In short, poor estimation of one or more of the parameters (e.g., χ_j) affects the estimation of the item's other parameter(s).

With respect to χ_j one sees (Figure 6.8) that most information for estimating χ_j comes from the lower end of the θ continuum. Depending on the particular item, there is virtually no useful information for estimating χ_j from individuals located above 2.0. However, the information function plateaus show that even at the lower end of the θ continuum there is a finite amount of information available for estimating χ_j. Moreover, the larger the χ_j, the greater the shift in the beginning of this plateau toward the lower end of the continuum than when χ_j is smaller. We also see that the larger the χ_j, the lower the plateau, indicating less information for estimating these large χ_j values than for estimating smaller χ_j values.

For completeness, we now discuss the information functions for the 1PL and 2PL models. If we plot the information functions for estimating δ_j for the 1PL model, we find that across items the corresponding information functions have a constant height, with the location of the modes corresponding to the items' δ_js. In addition, the information functions for estimating a common α across items are bimodal, but unlike the 3PL model case, the functions have a constant height across modes and across items. The minima of the information functions are zero and occur between the two modes at the items' δ_js.

For the 2PL model the information function for estimating the δ_j is also unimodal. Its height across items varies as a direct function of the items' α_js, with the location of the modes corresponding to an item's δ_j. With respect to item discrimination, the information function for estimating α_j is bimodal, with a constant height across the modes for an item. However, the modes vary across the items as an indirect function of the value of the items' α_js. As is the case with the 1PL and 3PL models, the location of the minimum of the information function between the two modes corresponds to the item's δ_j and has a value of 0.

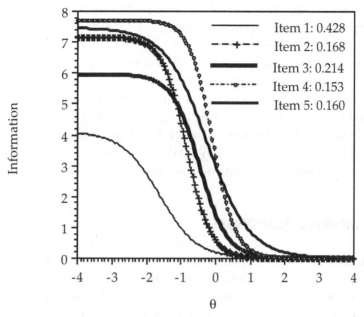

FIGURE 6.8. Information for estimating χ_j for each of five items.

METRIC TRANSFORMATION, 3PL MODEL

Linear rescaling of α_j and δ_j (or their estimates) is accomplished as performed with the 2PL model. Because the pseudo-guessing parameter is on the probability scale, it does not have an indeterminacy in its scale and there is no need to rescale χ_j. Person location parameters (or their estimates) are transformed by $\theta^* = \zeta(\theta) + \kappa$.

The total characteristic curve for the 3PL model is determined as shown, for example, in Chapter 4. As is the case with the 1PL and 2PL models, all individuals with the same location, θ, obtain the same expected trait score, T. Furthermore, neither θ nor T depends on the distribution of persons. However, unlike the case with the previous models, the TCC under the 3PL model has a lower bound of the sum of the χ_js and an upper bound equal to the instrument's length. As an example, the expected trait score for individuals with a $\hat{\theta}$ of 1.1746 on our mathematics test would be

$$T = \sum_{}^{L} p_j = 0.9927 + \ldots + 0.6813 = 4.4952$$

Therefore, a person with an estimated location of 1.1746 would be expected to obtain almost 4.5 correct answers on the mathematics test. Figure 6.9 contains the TCC with the transformation of $\hat{\theta} = 1.1746$ to its corresponding T identified. Comparing this figure with the TCC for the 1PL model (Chapter 4, Figure 4.5) shows that it is steeper than the 1PL model's. The steepness of the TCC is a function of not only the discrimination parameter estimates (for the 3PL model the mean α is 2.3778 and for the 1PL model the common α

is 1.421), but also the variability of the δ_js as well as the magnitude of the χ_js. As is seen, the lower asymptote of the TCC approaches the $\sum\chi_j = 1.230$ and its upper asymptote is the instrument's length, because $\varepsilon = 1$ for all IRFs.

Typically, the TCC is depicted as ogival shaped and resembling an IRF. However, the TCC's shape is a function of not only the number of items, but also the calibration model and the distribution/characteristics of the item parameter estimates. For example, if our $\hat{\delta}_j$s are more widely spaced than those used in Figure 6.9, the TCC's shape would change. Figure 6.10 contains the TCC for a five-item set that contains the same $\hat{\alpha}_j$s and $\hat{\chi}_j$s used in Figure 6.9, but with $\hat{\delta}_1 = -3.0$, $\hat{\delta}_2 = -2.5$, $\hat{\delta}_3 = 0.0$, $\hat{\delta}_4 = 0.5$, and $\hat{\delta}_5 = 3.0$. Clearly, this TCC is still monotonically nondecreasing, but also contains ridges.

HANDLING MISSING RESPONSES

From the preceding discussion, we know that IRT models are concerned with modeling *observed* responses. However, in working with empirical data one will, at times, encounter situations where some items do not have responses from all individuals in the calibration sample. Some of these missing data may be considered to be missing by design or structurally missing. For example, one may administer an instrument to one group of people and an alternate form of the instrument to another group. If these two forms have some items in common, then the calibration sample can consist of both groups. As a result, our data contain individuals who have not responded to all items. Figure 11.1 in Chapter 11 contains a graphical depiction of this. In situations where the nonresponses are missing by design, these missing data may be ignored because of the IRT properties of person and item parameter

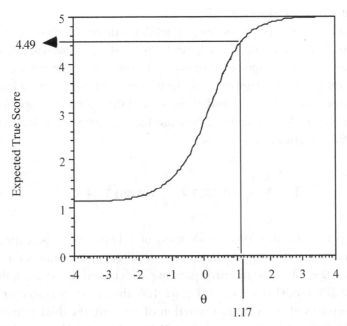

FIGURE 6.9. TCC for the five-item mathematics instrument calibrated with the 3PL model.

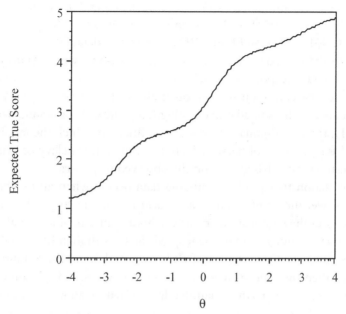

FIGURE 6.10. TCC for widely spaced δs.

invariance. However, when nonresponses are not structurally missing, then one needs to consider how to treat these nonresponses. We begin with a brief overview of a taxonomy for missing data and then address handling missing data in the IRT context.

In general, missing data (e.g., omitted responses) may be classified in terms of the mechanism that generated the missing values. According to Little and Rubin (1987) missing data may be classified as *missing completely at random* (MCAR), *missing at random* (MAR), and *nonignorable*. MCAR refers to data in which the missing values are statistically independent to the values that could have been observed, as well as to other variables. In contrast, when data are MAR, then the missing values are conditionally independent on one or more variable(s). In both of these cases the data are missing at random either unconditionally (MCAR) or conditionally on one or more variables (MAR). If the data are neither MCAR nor MAR, then the missing values are considered to be nonignorable. Nonignorable missing values are data for which the probability of omission is related to what the response would be if the person had responded.

Various approaches for handling missing data have been developed. Some of these approaches share the goal of creating "complete data," so standard analysis techniques may be applied. For instance, complete data may be created by deleting either the case that contains the missing value(s) either in its entirety or some subset of the case, or by replacing the missing value(s) by estimate(s) of what the missing value could have been. The replacement of the missing values by estimates is, in general, known as imputation. There are a number of single imputation methods (e.g., cold-deck imputation, hot-deck imputation, mean substitution) as well as multiple imputation methods. Multiple imputation methods differ from single imputation methods by creating multiple (imputed) complete data sets in order to model the uncertainty in sampling from a population, whereas only one complete data set is created with single imputation. Other missing data methods are maximum likelihood-based. See C. H. Brown (1983); R. L. Brown (1994); Dillman, Eltinge, Groves, and Little (2002); Enders (2001, 2003); and Roth (1994) for greater detail.

Returning to the IRT context, there are various reasons why an individual's response vector may not contain responses to each item. We present three conditions that lead to missing data. The first condition is mentioned above. In the *missing by design* case (e.g., *not-presented* items), such as in adaptive testing (Appendix D) or simultaneous calibration (see Chapter 11), the nonresponses represent conditions in which the missingness process may be ignored for purposes of person location estimation (Mislevy & Wu, 1988, 1996). Therefore, the estimation is based only on the observed responses.

A second situation that produces missing data occurs when an individual has insufficient time to answer the item(s). These *not-reached* items are (typically) identified as collectively occurring at the end of an instrument (this assumes the individual responds to the test items in a serial fashion) and represent *speededness*. Although IRT should be applied to unspeeded tests, Lord (1980) stated that if we knew which items the examinee did not have time to consider, then these not-reached items may be ignored for person location estimation because they contain no readily quantifiable information about the individual's location (e.g., his or her proficiency). Therefore, when one has (some) missing data due to not-reached items, then the person's location is estimated using only the observed responses. However, this should not be interpreted as indicating that one should apply IRT to speeded instruments nor that these not-reached items are unaffected by being speeded. Speeded situations may lead to violation of the unidimensionality assumption and biased item parameter estimates. Research has shown that the speeded items' α_js and δ_js are overestimated and the χ_js are underestimated (Oshima, 1994). Because of the overestimation of α_j the corresponding item information and, therefore, the instrument's total information becomes inflated. Identifying the speeded items as not-reached within BILOG mitigates the bias in item parameter estimation.

The third situation that produces missing data occurs when an examinee intentionally chooses to not respond to a question for which he or she does not know the answer. These *omitted responses* represent nonignorable missing data (Lord, 1980; Mislevy & Wu, 1988, 1996). Again, assuming that an individual responds in a serial fashion to an instrument, omitted responses may be distinguished from not-reached items because omits appear throughout the response vector and not just at the end of the vector. Lord (1980) has argued that omitted responses should not be ignored, because an individual could obtain as high a proficiency estimate as he or she wished by simply answering only those items the individual had confidence in correctly answering. This idea has found some support in Wang, Wainer, and Thissen's (1995) study on examinee item choice.

The effect of omitted responses on EAP person location estimates has been studied (De Ayala, Plake, & Impara, 2001). Results show that for dichotomous data, omits should not be treated as incorrect nor should they be ignored; also see Lord (1974a, 1983c). However, using a fractional value of 0.5 in place of omitted values leads to improved person location estimation, compared with treating the omits as incorrect or using a fractional value equal to the reciprocal of the number of item options (i.e., $1/m$ where m is the number of item options). (The $1/m$ approach assumes that an individual responds randomly to a multiple-choice item format and was suggested by Lord [1974a, 1980].) The results also seem to indicate that this would be true for MLE person location estimation. By using this fractional value, one is simply imputing a response for a binomial variable and thereby "smoothing" irregularities in the likelihood function. Although this research was conducted using the 3PL model, it appears that the results would apply to both the 1PL and 2PL models.

A different imputation approach using a "marginalized" likelihood procedure has been found to work well (De Ayala, 2006). In this approach the various possible responses are substituted for each omitted response and the likelihood of the resulting response pattern calculated. These likelihood functions are combined to create a single likelihood function that reflects the likelihoods of all possible patterns. Although this study used ordered polytomous data, presumably this approach would also work with dichotomous data. Because this approach is based on response patterns, this method is limited by the number of items and number of omissions. An alternative approach that may be fruitful in some situations is to treat omission as its own response category and apply a polytomous model such as the multiple-choice model or the nominal response model; both models are discussed in Chapter 9. In addition, SAS's PROC MI or SPSS's MISSING VALUE ANALYSIS-EM (SPSS Incorporated, 2006) can be used to impute values for the omitted responses. These complete data may then be calibrated.

There are some issues in the treatment of omits of which the practitioner should be aware. For instance, in the context of proficiency assessment all imputation procedures that produce complete data for analysis are, in effect, giving partial credit for an omitted response. For example, Lord's (1974a, 1980) suggested use of $1/m$ gives an individual partial credit worth, say 0.2 (i.e., $m = 5$), for having omitted an item. A second issue to be aware of is that using the same imputed value for all omits assumes that individuals located at different points can all be treated the same. These issues are raised so that the practitioner understands the assumptions that are being made with some of the missing data approaches discussed. However, these may or may not be of concern to a particular practitioner. Moreover, when IRT is used in personality testing or with attitude or interest inventories, these may be nonissues. A third issue that should be noted is that omits tend to be associated with personality characteristics, demographic variables, and proficiency level (Mislevy & Wu, 1988; Stocking, Eignor, & Cook, 1988). Thus, in those situations where information on these variables is available one may wish to use this information as covariates in the imputation process; use of these covariate(s) may or may not have any meaningful impact on the person location estimates.

It is good practice when calibrating a data set to identify items without responses by some code. For instance, in the data file not-reached items may be identified by a code of, say 9, not-presented items by a code of 8, omitted items by a code of 7. With certain calibration programs (e.g., BILOG 3, BILOG-MG, MULTILOG) any ASCII character may be used (e.g., the letters "R" for not-reached, "P" for not-presented, and "O" for omit). In these cases, the code used must be identified for the program. With BILOG one would use the KFName, NFName, and/or OFName subcommands on the GLOBAL or INPUT command line depending on the version of BILOG one is using. For BILOG omitted responses must be identified as such, whereas with other programs (e.g., MULTILOG) any response code encountered in the data file that is not identified as a valid response is considered to reflect an omitted item. Omitted responses that have been identified by an omitted response code are, by default, treated as incorrect by BILOG.

ISSUES TO CONSIDER
IN SELECTING AMONG THE 1PL, 2PL, AND 3PL MODELS

The issues to be considered in selecting among the 1PL, 2PL, and 3PL models involve, in part, one's philosophy of whether the data should fit the model or vice versa (see Chapter 2) as well as the application context (e.g., sample size, instrument characteristics and considerations, assumption tenability, political realities, etc.). Given that the 1PL model is the most restrictive of the three models, there have been a number of studies investigating the use of the 1PL model when it misfits. For instance, Forsyth, Saisangjan, and Gilmer (1981) investigated the robustness of the Rasch model when the dimensionality and constant α assumptions are violated. Because their empirical data came from an examination using a multiple-choice item format, it was assumed that some examinees would engage in guessing. Forsyth et al. concluded that "the Rasch model does yield reasonably invariant item parameter and ability estimates . . . even though the assumptions of the model are not met" (p. 185). Similar results were obtained by Dinero and Haertel (1977) using simulation data.

Wainer and Wright (1980) stated, "It seems that the Rasch model yields rather good estimates of ability and difficulty even when its assumption of equal slopes is only roughly approximated" (p. 373). Furthermore, Lord and Novick (1968) stated, "It appears that if the number of items is very large, then inferences about an examinee's ability based on his total test score will be very much the same whether" (p. 492) the Rasch model or the 3PL model is used. In this regard, recall that for the mathematics data example the Pearson correlation between the $\hat{\theta}$s based on the 1PL and the 3PL models' $\hat{\theta}$s for the example's data is 0.9764. For the other model combinations we have a correlation of 0.9907 for the 1PL and the 2PL models' $\hat{\theta}$s, and for the 2PL and the 3PL models' $\hat{\theta}$s the correlation is 0.9859. Although these are all reasonably strong correlations, the correlations among the standard errors, $s_e(\hat{\theta})$s, for the various model combinations paint a different picture. The correlation between the 1PL model standard errors and those of the 2PL model is 0.9721, between the 1PL model and the 3PL model the correlation is 0.3318, and for the 2PL and the 3PL models' standard errors it is 0.2275. Therefore, in situations where confidence bands about $\hat{\theta}$ are used for classification decisions, the same individual would be classified differently depending on the model used. Presumably, using longer instruments would allow for greater agreement among the standard errors. Moreover, the magnitude of the correlations between the 1PL, 2PL, and 3PL models' $\hat{\theta}$s would be affected by the correlation between α_j and δ_j (Yen, 1981).

For samples of 200 or fewer Lord (1983a) found that the Rasch model was slightly superior to the 2PL model in terms of person estimation. As previously mentioned, Thissen and Wainer (1982) studied the asymptotic standard errors of the one-, two-, and three-parameter models. On the basis of their results, Thissen and Wainer suggested fitting the 1PL model first and examining its model–data fit. If only a few items misfitted and they could be omitted without adversely affecting the instrument (e.g., the validity of the $\hat{\theta}$s), then one should consider removing them. However, if the omission of these misfitting items is problematic, then one should increase the sample size and try to fit the 2PL model (presumably the item(s) misfit is due to varying item discrimination). In contrast, Gustafsson (1980) suggested grouping the items into homogeneous subsets rather than removing them from the instrument. For instance, looking at the mathematics 2PL model calibration example, we see that in terms of the $\hat{\alpha}_j$s there are three groupings of items. Items 3 and 4 are very similar in terms of their $\hat{\alpha}_j$s, items 1 and 5 are somewhat similar to one another, and item 2 is substantially different from the other four items. Therefore, three subsets could be created for the mathematics data example. Assuming item misfit is due to varying item discrimination, another alternative is to use the OPLM model approach in which the item locations are estimated but the item discrimination(s) are imputed (Verhelst & Glas, 1995; Verhelst et al., 1995). The use of mixture models (see Appendix E, "Mixture Models"), as well as some of the models presented in von Davier and Carstensen (2007), may also provide additional solutions. (It should be noted that the desirable properties of the Rasch model [e.g., specific objectivity] hold only when one has model–data fit.)

Yen (1981) advocates a process of first fitting all three models (i.e., 1PL, 2PL, 3PL) to the empirical data set of interest. Subsequently, simulation data sets are generated based on item parameter distributions that are similar to those found with the calibration of the empirical data set. For example, we would generate a data set using the 1PL model, another with the 2PL model, and so on. The final step involves comparing the fit analyses across models in conjunction with the fit analysis of the empirical data to facilitate model selection.

In a simulation study Yen (1981) generated different data sets based on various models and compared the fit of the 1PL, 2PL, and 3PL models to these data. When she used the 3PL model for data generation, she found that the 2PL model fitted the data almost as well as the 3PL model did, although the item parameters estimates were not the same across the two models. She noted that when an item was difficult and had a moderate to high discrimination, it was difficult for the 2PL to model a nonzero lower asymptote. She concluded that although the 2PL model performed almost as well as the 3PL model in modeling the response vectors, one might observe sample dependency when difficult items have their discrimination parameters estimated with low-proficiency-level examinees.

As may be inferred from the above there are variants of the dichotomous models. For instance, it is possible to constrain the 3PL model to produce modified versions—such as, constraining the α_js to a constant value as well as the χ_js to a nonzero value. This model is sometimes referred to as a modified 1PL model (Cressie & Holland, 1983; also see Kubinger & Draxler, 2007). Further, one may use the 3PL model with the χ_js for certain problematic items fixed to a constant nonzero value, whereas χ_j is estimated for other items. In general, for those situations where one is not holding χ_js fixed it would be prudent to use a prior distribution on the χ_js when estimating the lower asymptotes. In addition, with some data one may obtain unreasonably large estimates of α_j (e.g., greater than 3). For these situations the use of a prior distribution on the α_js may be in order.

As discussed in this chapter and the preceding chapters, it is the validity of the person location estimates that is paramount. From a pragmatic perspective, if convincing validity evidence can be accrued for person location estimates using a particular model in a particular application, then it would seem that the above arguments, although interesting in their own right, are somewhat irrelevant.[15]

SUMMARY

The 3PL model attempts to obtain useful information from a response pattern over and above that contained in response vector's observed score. To achieve this objective the 3PL model contains parameters that reflect the item's location and discrimination as well as the lower asymptote of the IRF. As is true with the 2PL model's IRFs, the 3PL model's IRFs may potentially cross because the 3PL model allows for varying discrimination. With the 3PL model item discrimination is proportional to the slope of the IRF at the point of inflexion and is equal to $0.25\alpha_j(1 - \chi_j)$. In addition, the 3PL model's IRFs may cross because the model allows for the lower asymptote parameters, χ_js, to vary across items. The lower asymptote parameter is restricted to the range 0 to 1 (inclusive) and reflects the probability of obtaining a response of 1 by individuals who are extremely low on the latent variable continuum. The lower asymptote parameter is referred to as the pseudo-guessing parameter.

In previous chapters fit is investigated in terms of item statistics, empirical and predicted IRFs, and by examining the invariance of item parameter estimates across random calibration subsamples. Building on this foundation, we introduced additional approaches for assessing model–data fit. For instance, the likelihood ratio and the AIC and BIC statistics were presented as approaches for assessing model–level fit. Moreover, we introduced an appropriateness index to gauge person fit and the Q_3 statistic for assessing the tenability of the conditional independence assumption. The Q_3 statistic may be useful for identifying sets of items that are exhibiting item dependence. When items are found to be interdependent it may make sense to bundle the items together and obtain an item score for the item bundle or testlet. This item score is polytomous and ordinal in nature (i.e., a larger item score reflects more of the latent variable than a smaller value). The analysis of these data can sometimes be accomplished through the use of a polytomous model.

Chapter 7 introduces polytomous models that are derived from the Rasch model. These models, the partial credit and rating scale models, are appropriate for ordinal polytomous data. As is the case with the Rasch model, these models assume that the items on an instrument are equally effective in discriminating among individuals. As the models' names imply, the partial credit model can be used with data that reflect degrees of response correctness, whereas the rating scale model can be used with data from response formats, such as the Likert or summated ratings format. In actuality, both models are applicable to data that reflect degrees of response endorsement, but differ from one another in the models' respective simplifying assumptions. In Chapter 8 the use of polytomous models for ordinal data continues, but with models that are not based on the Rasch model.

NOTES

1. Although the three-parameter model allows for the possibility that the lower asymptote is nonzero, the upper asymptote is still 1.0. That is, as θ approaches positive infinity the probability of

a response of 1 is 1.0 or, symbolically, $p(x = 1|\theta \to \infty) \to 1$. An alternative model, the *four-parameter logistic* model (Barton & Lord, 1981), extends the three-parameter model to allow for the possibility that persons with very large θs may still not have a success probability equal to 1 (see McDonald, 1967). The motivation behind the model's development was to improve person location estimation. For instance, if a person with a very large θ makes a clerical error on an easy item, then his or her estimate would be more drastically lowered using a model with an upper asymptote of 1 than when this asymptote was less than 1 (Barton & Lord, 1981). To address this situation, Barton and Lord (1981) introduced a parameter, ε_j, that reflected the IRF's upper asymptote into the 3PL model. As a consequence, as θ approaches ∞ the probability of a response of 1 is ε_j or, symbolically, $p(x = 1|\theta \to \infty) \to \varepsilon$. The *four-parameter logistic* (4PL) model is

$$p(x_j=1|\theta, \alpha_j, \delta_j, \chi_j, \varepsilon_j) = \chi_j + (\varepsilon_j - \chi_j) \frac{e^{\alpha_j(\theta-\delta_j)}}{1+e^{\alpha_j(\theta-\delta_j)}} \qquad (6.18)$$

Barton and Lord (1981) compared the model in Equation 6.18 to the 3PL model using empirical data. They found that the 3PL model did as well or better than the 4PL model. Barton and Lord concluded that "there is no compelling reason to urge the use of this <4PL> model" (p. 6). However, it should be noted that although the α_js, δ_js, and χ_js were estimated (using JMLE), the ε_js were *not* estimated. Rather, the ε_js were held fixed at either 0.98 or 0.99. Given the study's design decisions, it is doubtful that this one study should be considered definitive.

2. The first derivative of the 3PL model is

$$p_j' = \alpha_j (1 - p_j) \frac{(p_j - \chi_j)}{(1 - \chi_j)}$$

where

$$(1 - p_j) = 1 - \left[\chi_j + (1 - \chi_j) \frac{e^{\alpha_j(\theta-\delta_j)}}{1+e^{\alpha_j(\theta-\delta_j)}} \right] = 1 - \left[\chi_j + \frac{(1-\chi_j)}{1+e^{-\alpha_j(\theta-\delta_j)}} \right]$$

Because by definition α_j is defined at $\theta = \delta_j$, p_j simplifies to

$$p_j = \chi_j + (1 - \chi_j) \frac{e^{\alpha_j(\theta-\delta_j)}}{1+e^{\alpha_j(\theta-\delta_j)}} = \chi_j + \frac{(1-\chi_j)}{1+e^0} = \chi_j + \frac{(1-\chi_j)}{2} = \frac{2\chi_j+1-\chi_j}{2} = \frac{1+\chi_j}{2}$$

and $(1 - p_j)$ simplifies to

$$(1 - p_j) = 1 - \left[\chi_j + \frac{(1-\chi_j)}{1+e^{-\alpha_j(\theta-\delta_j)}} \right] = 1 - \left[\frac{1+\chi_j}{2} \right] = \frac{2-(1+\chi_j)}{2} = \frac{1-\chi_j}{2}$$

By substitution for p_j in p_j' we obtain

$$p_j' = \alpha_j (1 - p_j) \frac{(p_j - \chi_j)}{(1 - \chi_j)} = \alpha_j \left[\frac{1-\chi_j}{2} \right] \left[\frac{(\frac{1+\chi_j}{2} - \chi_j)}{(1-\chi_j)} \right] = \alpha_j \left[\frac{(\frac{1+\chi_j}{2} - \chi_j)}{2} \right] = 0.25\alpha_j \left(1-\chi_j\right)$$

When the D scaling constant is used, then the slope for the 3PL model is $0.25D\,\alpha_j(1-\chi_j) = 0.425\,\alpha_j(1-\chi_j)$.

3. For example, assume we have a two-item instrument with $\alpha_1 = 2.0, \delta_1 = 0.0, \chi_1 = 0.25$ for the first item and $\alpha_2 = 1.0, \delta_2 = -0.5, \chi_2 = 0.0$ for the second item. According to the 3PL model a person with the response vector $\underline{x} = \{0, 1\}$ will have an $\hat{\theta}$ of -0.55. However, if we use the 2PL model (i.e., $\chi_1 = \chi_2 = 0.0$), then our $\hat{\theta}$ is -0.1558. For the Rasch model (i.e., $\alpha_1 = \alpha_2 = 1.0$ and $\chi_1 = \chi_2 = 0.0$), our $\hat{\theta}$ is approximately -0.25. Comparing these $\hat{\theta}$s shows that one effect of including a nonzero χ_j in our model is to reduce the $\hat{\theta}$ relative to not including χ_j.

4. Some users of the Rasch model have argued that the item discrimination parameter cannot be estimated as is done with the 2PL and 3PL models (e.g., see Wright, 1977b). According to Gustafsson (1980), when one has unequal discriminations the item locations are related to the calibration sample's characteristics on the latent variable (e.g., a high- or low-proficiency group). In fact, he states that "it is difficult to make a distinction between the assumption of unidimensionality and the assumption of homogeneous item discrimination" (p. 208). A similar opinion is expressed by Lumsden (1978): "Test scaling methods are self-contradictory if they assert both unidimensionality and different slopes for the ICC. . . . If the unidimensionality requirement is met, the Rasch (1960) one-parameter model will be realized" (p. 22). (Lumsden also suggested abandoning the two- and three-parameter normal ogives.) Gustafsson (1980) suggests that it may be prudent to investigate the robustness of the Rasch model in the face of varying item discriminations for specific applications.

5. According to Holland (1990a) there can be at most two parameters per item and "models that contain three or more parameters per item can only estimate these parameters successfully for one of two reasons; either they are not applied to a large enough item set or the test is not unidimensional" (p. 17); also see Cressie and Holland (1983) and Holland (1990b). As such, there appear to be more parameters in the 3PL model than can be supported by a unidimensional test.

6. As is true with the two-parameter model, JMLE no longer seems to be used for parameter estimation with the three-parameter model. However, for completeness, we describe some of the past research in this area. The Hulin et al. (1982) study of JMLE presented in Chapter 5 also examined parameter estimation accuracy for two models (2PL, 3PL); this study had the additional factors of sample sizes (200, 500, 1000, 2000) and instrument length (15, 30, 60 items). They found that for a given condition the 2PL model results were better than those for the 3PL. However, for both models, and not surprisingly, the larger the sample size and the longer the instrument, the more accurate the estimates. In addition, the average error (i.e., root mean squared) in recovering the true IRFs for both models and using at least 30 items was no greater than 0.05 for a sample size of 1000 and less than 0.07 with 500 cases. In general, increasing the instrument's length for a given sample size resulted in more accurate estimates. A similar finding is reported by Skaggs and Stevenson (1989) using LOGIST. They also found that the average error in recovering the true IRFs for the 15-item instrument was about 0.07 and for the 30-item length the average error was slightly below 0.055 when using a sample size of 500. These average errors decreased to about 0.05 and about 0.037 for the 15- and 30-item lengths, respectively, when the sample was quadrupled to 2000 cases. Lord (1968) suggests that the sample size be greater than 1000 and that instruments be at least 50 items long when using LOGIST. However, Swaminathan and Gifford (1983) found that reasonably good estimates can be obtained with a 1000-person sample and a 20-item instrument. Therefore, it appears that samples of a 1000 or more with instruments of at least 20 items, and preferably longer, should be used with JMLE as implemented in LOGIST. However, work by Thissen and Wainer (1982) calls this sample size suggestion into question. For example, applying their observations to the 3PL model for an item with α_j of 1.5, $\delta_j = 2$ (or $\delta_j = -2$), and $\chi_j = 0.1$ would require 97220, 22142, and 46743 individuals in order to estimate the item's δ_j, α_j, and χ_j, respectively, with an accuracy of one-tenth. Therefore, the calibration sample size would be 97,220.

7. Although the same calibration sample is used for the 1PL, 2PL, and 3PL model calibrations, the different models produced different estimates. The mean item location estimate for the 1PL, 2PL, and 3PL models are -0.403, -0.400, and 0.036, respectively. Moreover, the mean discrimination estimate of 2.342 for the 3PL model is substantially greater than the common $\hat{\alpha} = 1.421$ found with the 1PL model or the 2PL model's mean discrimination estimate of 1.459. This is due to the nonzero lower asymptote as well as to differences in metrics. With respect to the former explanation, we see from a comparison of the 2PL and 3PL models' $\hat{\alpha}_1$s that the 2PL model accommodates the nonzero asymptote by decreasing $\hat{\alpha}$ relative to what is obtained when we estimate the lower asymptote; for the 2PL model $\hat{\alpha}_1$ is 1.226 and for the 3PL model $\hat{\alpha}_1 = 1.921$. In fact, for all the items the 2PL model's $\hat{\alpha}_j$s are less than the corresponding 3PL model's $\hat{\alpha}_j$s. These lower 2PL model $\hat{\alpha}_j$s are associated with a metric that, relative to the 3PL model's $\hat{\delta}_j$s, is stretched out and located lower than that of the 3PL model. In short, we have different metrics for the different model calibrations of the data. As such, the differences in the estimates across models for corresponding item parameters is partly due to a difference in metrics. Therefore, strictly speaking, we need to link the various metrics before directly comparing individual item parameter estimates across models.

8. To determine an empirical screening criterion value we conducted a simulation study to identify the magnitude of Q_3s that we could expect to see if the data conformed to the model's conditional independence assumption. This simulation can be conducted with a statistical package (e.g., SAS) or a programming language (e.g., the freeware language R). The simulation consists of randomly sampling 1000 standard unit normal zs from a normal distribution. These zs are considered to be the persons' θs and these "persons" are referred to as simulees. To generate a simulee's item response we use the item's parameter estimates from Table 6.3 and the simulee's θ to calculate the probability of a response of 1 according to the 3PL model. This probability is compared with a uniform random number. If the uniform random number is less than or equal to the calculated probability, then the simulee's response to the item is coded as 1, otherwise it is coded as 0. This process is repeated for each item and for each simulee. Because in practice we have only an estimate of θ, we obtain each simulee's EAP location estimate using the item parameter estimates. These EAP $\hat{\theta}$s are used to determine the expected response for each item for each simulee. The expected responses are compared with the simulated response data to determine the residuals for each item. The intercorrelations among these item residuals are calculated and recorded. The entire process, from sampling the 1000 simulees to calculating the Q_3s, is repeated 5000 times. With five items there are 10 unique Q_3s (i.e., $L(L-1)/2$) or $10 * 5000 = 50,000$ Q_3s across the 5000 replications. The Q_3 value corresponding to the bottom 5% (i.e., 5% total) of the Q_3 (null) distribution is -0.2961; the minimum and the maximum Q_3s are -0.4096 and 0.0656, respectively. We use the 5% lower tail Q_3 screening value because the upper tail covers 0.0.

9. A complementary approach for determining the df for evaluating ΔG^2 is to use the difference in the model's dfs. The df for a model is given by $2^L -$ (number of item parameters) $- 1$, where L is the number of items on the instrument and the number of item parameters is based on the model and the number of items. For example, for the 3PL model there are three item parameters (α_j, δ_j, and χ_j) and for a, say, five-item instrument the number of items parameter is $3 \times 5 = 15$. Therefore, for the 3PL model the $df = 32 - 15 - 1 = 16$. For the 2PL model there are two item parameters (α_j and δ_j) and with a five-item instrument the $df = 32 - 10 - 1 = 21$. With the 1PL model each item has a location (δ_j) and all items have a common α. Therefore, with a five-item instrument there are six parameters that are estimated and the model's $df = 32 - 6 - 1 = 25$. With BILOG, if one uses the keyword RASch the program performs 1PL estimation and then rescales the common α to be 1 and adjusts all the δ_js accordingly; how this is done is demonstrated in Chapter 4. Therefore, with BILOG there are six, not five, item parameters estimated with the Rasch model. In contrast, a program like BIGSTEPS (or

WINSTEPS) does not estimate a common α and, as a result, there are only five δ_js estimated; that is, the $df = 32 - 5 - 1 = 26$.

10. From Lord and Novick (1968) we have that the area under the item information function is

$$\int_{-\infty}^{\infty} I_j(\theta) = \alpha_j \frac{\chi_j \ln(\chi_j) + 1 - \chi_j}{1 - \chi_j}$$

With the use of the D scaling constant in the 3PL model, the item information is

$$I_j(\theta) = \frac{D^2 \alpha_j^2 (1 - p_j)(p_j - \chi_j)^2}{(1 - \chi_j)^2 p_j} \tag{6.19}$$

and the corresponding area under the item information function is equal to

$$\int_{-\infty}^{\infty} I_j(\theta) = D\alpha_j \frac{\chi_j \ln(\chi_j) + 1 - \chi_j}{1 - \chi_j}$$

11. To determine where an item has its maximum information, recall that α_j is proportional to the slope of the IRF at δ_j (i.e., the slope at δ_j is $0.25\alpha_j(1 - \chi_j)$). The offset from δ_j to where an item has its maximum information is obtained from the item information equation. By substituting $0.25\alpha_j(1 - \chi_j)$ into Equation 6.12 and rearranging terms (and for convenience dropping the item index j) we have

$$I_j(\theta) = \alpha^2 \frac{e^{-\alpha(\theta-\delta)}}{1 + e^{-\alpha(\theta-\delta)}} (1 - \chi) \frac{e^{\alpha(\theta-\delta)-\ln\chi}}{1 + e^{\alpha(\theta-\delta)-\ln\chi}}$$

Following Lord and Novick (1968) and maximizing $I_j(\theta)$ with respect to $\alpha(\theta - \delta)$ leads to

$$\frac{\partial}{\partial\alpha(\theta-\delta)} \ln I_j(\theta) = \frac{\partial}{\partial\alpha(\theta-\delta)} \left[\ln\left(\frac{e^{-\alpha(\theta-\delta)}}{1 + e^{-\alpha(\theta-\delta)}}\right) + \ln\left(\frac{e^{\alpha(\theta-\delta)-\ln\chi}}{1 + e^{\alpha(\theta-\delta)-\ln\chi}}\right) \right]$$

$$= 2 \left[\frac{e^{-\alpha(\theta-\delta)}}{1 + e^{-\alpha(\theta-\delta)}} \right] - 1 + \frac{e^{-\alpha(\theta-\delta)+\ln\chi}}{1 + e^{-\alpha(\theta-\delta)-\ln\chi}}$$

$$= \frac{2}{1 + e^{-\alpha(\theta-\delta)}} - 1 + \frac{1}{1 + e^{-\alpha(\theta-\delta)/\chi}}$$

$$= \frac{1 - e^{\alpha(\theta-\delta)}}{1 + e^{\alpha(\theta-\delta)}} + \frac{\chi}{\chi + e^{\alpha(\theta-\delta)}}$$

$$= \frac{2\chi + e^{\alpha(\theta-\delta)} - e^{2(\alpha(\theta-\delta))}}{(\chi + e^{\alpha(\theta-\delta)})(1 + e^{\alpha(\theta-\delta)})}$$

To find the maximum of this last equation, its derivative is set to 0 and we solve for $\alpha(\theta - \delta)$:

$$\frac{2\chi + e^{\alpha(\theta-\delta)} - e^{2(\alpha(\theta-\delta))}}{(\chi + e^{\alpha(\theta-\delta)})(1 + e^{\alpha(\theta-\delta)})} = 0$$

Because this equation is equal to 0.0 when its numerator equals zero we only need to be concerned with the numerator:

$$2\chi + e^{\alpha(\theta - \delta)} - e^{2(\alpha(\theta - \delta))} = 0$$

This last equation is in the form of a quadratic (i.e., $f(x) = ax^2 + bx + c$, where a, b, and c are real constants and $x = e^t$; therefore, $2c + e^t + e^{2t}$). We can solve this last equation by using the quadratic formula:

$$x = \frac{-b \pm \sqrt{b^2 - 4ac}}{2a}$$

with $a = -1$, $b = 1$, and $c = 2\chi$. Because in this case, $a < 0$, we have two solutions: $1 + 4(2c) > 0$ and $x = -1/2(-1) = 0.5$. Using the quadratic formula, we obtain by substituting the values for a, b, and c:

$$x = \frac{-1 \pm \sqrt{(-1)^2 - 4(-1)(2c)}}{2(-1)} = \frac{-1 \pm \sqrt{1 + 8c}}{-2}$$

The solutions are

$$x = \frac{-1 + \sqrt{1 + 8c}}{-2} = \frac{1}{2} - \frac{\sqrt{1 + 8c}}{2} \quad \text{and} \quad x = \frac{-1 - \sqrt{1 + 8c}}{-2} = \frac{1}{2} + \frac{\sqrt{1 + 8c}}{2}$$

We can eliminate

$$\frac{1}{2} - \frac{\sqrt{1 + 8c}}{2}$$

because it leads to having to take the log of a negative number. Therefore, we have $x = e^{\alpha(\theta - \delta)}$ and $\ln(x) = \alpha(\theta - \delta)$. By substitution:

$$\ln\left(\frac{1}{2} + \frac{\sqrt{1 + 8c}}{2}\right) = \alpha(\theta - \delta)$$

$$\frac{\ln\left(\frac{1}{2} + \frac{\sqrt{1 + 8c}}{2}\right)}{\alpha} = (\theta - \delta)$$

The item has the location of its maximum information at

$$\frac{\ln(\frac{1}{2} + \frac{\sqrt{1+8\chi}}{2})}{\alpha} + \delta$$

and the offset is

$$\frac{\ln(\frac{1}{2} + \frac{\sqrt{1+8\chi}}{2})}{\alpha}$$

That is, an item provides its maximum information at a location slightly higher than its δ. When $\chi_j = 0$ the offset equals 0.

12. The standard error for the person location estimate under the 3PL is

$$SEE(\hat{\theta}_i) = \sqrt{\sum_{j=1}^{L} \left\{ \frac{p_j(1-\chi_j)^2}{\alpha_j^2(1-p_j)(p_j-\chi_j)^2} \right\}} \tag{6.20}$$

where p_j is conditional on $\hat{\theta}_i$.

13. In Chapter 5 it is mentioned that the maximum information attainable by any scoring method is given by the total information function. Therefore, the optimal scoring weight for an item j is given by Equation 5.18:

$$w_j(\theta) = \frac{p_j'}{p_j(1-p_j)}$$

Given that the first derivative for the 3PL model is

$$p_j' = \frac{\alpha_j(p_j - \chi_j)(1-p_j)}{(1-\chi_j)} \tag{6.21}$$

we have by substitution of Equations 6.21 into Equation 5.18 that the optimal scoring weight for the 3PL model is (Lord, 1980)

$$w_j(\theta) = \frac{\alpha(p_j - \chi_j)}{(p_j - \chi_j)} = \frac{\alpha_j}{(1 + \chi_j e^{-\alpha_j(\theta - \delta_j)})} \tag{6.22}$$

Therefore, the optimal weight is a function of not only the item parameters, but also the person's location. As a result, with the 3PL model it is not possible to know the optimal scoring weight for an individual. Equation 6.22 shows that when $\chi_j = 0$, then $w_j(\theta) = \alpha_j$. Similarly, whenever θ is very large (i.e., $\theta \to \infty$), then the item's optimal weight approaches its discrimination (i.e., $w_j(\theta) \to \alpha_j$). In contrast, whenever θ is very small (i.e., $\theta \to -\infty$), then $p_j \to \chi_j$ and $w_j(\theta) \to 0$. In this latter condition, the respondent's location makes the item ineffective. With the scaling constant, D, Equation 6.22 becomes

$$w_j(\theta) = \frac{D\alpha_j}{1 + \chi_j e^{-D\alpha_j(\theta - \delta_j)}}$$

14. On the normal metric the corresponding item parameter information formulas are (Lord, 1980)

$$I_{\alpha\alpha} = \frac{D^2}{(1-\chi_j)^2} \sum_i^N (\theta_i - \delta_j)^2 (p_j - \chi_j)^2 \frac{(1-p_j)}{p_j} \tag{6.23}$$

$$I_{\delta\delta} = \frac{D^2\alpha_j^2}{(1-\chi_j)^2} \sum_i^N (p_j - \chi_j)^2 \frac{(1-p_j)}{p_j} \tag{6.24}$$

and

$$I_{\chi\chi} = \frac{1}{(1-\chi_j)^2} \sum_i^N \frac{(1-p_j)}{p_j} \tag{6.25}$$

As mentioned above, the various item parameters are interrelated. Therefore, one also has

$$I_{\alpha\delta} = -\frac{D^2\alpha_j}{(1-\chi_j)^2} \sum_i^N (\theta_i - \delta_j)^2 (p_j - \chi_j)^2 \frac{(1-p_j)}{p_j} \tag{6.26}$$

$$I_{\alpha\chi} = \frac{D}{(1-\chi_j)^2} \sum_i^N (\theta_i - \delta_j)(p_j - \chi_j) \frac{(1-p_j)}{p_j} \tag{6.27}$$

and

$$I_{\delta\chi} = -\frac{D\alpha_j}{(1-\chi_j)^2} \sum_i^N (p_j - \chi_j) \frac{(1-p_j)}{p_j} \tag{6.28}$$

15. Based on the work of Yen (1981), it appears that whenever one applies an inappropriate model to a data set one may obtain *sample-dependent* estimates (i.e., a contradiction to one of IRT's potential advantages). Therefore, adopting a model that expresses one's intentions and does not simply describe the data appears to be a prudent strategy. From a philosophical perspective, because all models are partially false, then this begs the question as to whether one may obtain sample-independent estimates in any truly absolute fashion. It is conjectured that, most likely, the best that one may be able to achieve is sample-independent estimates for a particular range of data (as demonstrated in Chapter 3). If these data represent the situations that one is primarily interested in, then whether one may obtain sample independent estimates in an absolute fashion may be academic.

7

Rasch Models
for Ordered Polytomous Data

The models discussed so far are appropriate for dichotomous response data. This type of data can be obtained either directly by using a two-option item (e.g., the true/false item format used with the MMPI [Swenson, Pearson, & Osborne, 1973]) or indirectly by recoding an individual's actual response as 0 or 1 (e.g., by implementing a scoring paradigm or by passing judgment on the individual's response). The response of 0 reflects the absence of some characteristic or, in the case of proficiency testing, an incorrect response. Conversely, the response of 1 is the complement of a 0 response. As such, it represents the presence of the characteristic, a respondent's endorsement, or in the case of proficiency testing, a correct response. However, in some situations our data may have more than two response categories. For instance, judges may rate a person's performance on a rating scale, a Likert scale allows varying degrees of agreement to an item, or we can assign codes that reflect an answer's degree of correctness.

In these examples the data are by nature polytomous (i.e., more than two response categories) as well as inherently ordered. By "ordered" we mean that some responses indicate more (or less) of what is being measured than other responses. For example, assume that we allow a person to respond to the statement "The Congress should legislate that English be the national language of the United States" by using one of four possible response categories, such as "strongly agree," "agree," "disagree," "strongly disagree." These response categories, and therefore the person's response, are ordered on a scale that represents a favorable to an unfavorable attitude. As another example, assume that the amount of credit an answer is given is directly related to the degree of correctness of the response. As a result, higher credit indicates greater, say mathematics proficiency, than does lower credit.

Below we discuss models derived from the Rasch model that are appropriate for the above examples of ordered polytomous data. In the subsequent chapter we present two additional models, the generalized partial credit and graded response models, that may also be used for the analysis of ordered polytomous data. Models for unordered polytomous data are discussed in Chapter 9.

CONCEPTUAL DEVELOPMENT OF THE PARTIAL CREDIT MODEL

The example data used in previous chapters contain examinee responses to a mathematics examination. The test administrator took the examinees' observed responses and classified them into one of two categories, correct or incorrect. This dichotomization treats all the incorrect answers as equivalent to one another. As such, all the mathematical operations required to answer an item are considered *una voce* (i.e., as a "single operation"). If an examinee correctly performs all the operations, then he or she performs "one correct operation" and the response is categorized in the correct category with an assigned value of 1. Otherwise, his or her response is categorized as incorrect and it receives a value of 0. Therefore, the value assigned to the examinee responses reflects *only* whether the examinee has correctly performed (heuristically) one "operation." In contrast, consider the item

$$(6/3) + 2 = ?$$

A scoring rubric for this item might be based on the assumptions that to correctly answer this item certain operations must be performed correctly and that it is not possible to correctly guess on these operations. The first operation is the evaluation of the quotient 6/3 and the second operation is the addition of the numeral 2 to the first operation's result. Zero points would be assigned for incorrectly performing the first operation. Because this item consists of two operations we can assign partial credit (e.g., 1 point) for correctly performing only the first operation and full credit for correctly performing the first and second operations (i.e., the 2 points reflects the number of correctly performed operations). We believe that if some credit is assigned for partially correct responses, the partially correct responses can provide useful information for estimating a person's location.

Implied in this rubric is that one cannot obtain 1 point for correctly performing *only* the second operation. That is, the only way to obtain 1 point is by successfully performing only the first operation. Therefore, for this item j there are three possible integer scores (x_j) of 0, 1, 2 (i.e., $x_j = \{0, 1, 2\}$). These scores are called *category scores* and can be taken to indicate the number of or a count of the successfully performed operations. As a result, higher-category scores indicate a higher level of overall performance than do lower-category scores. In this approach, and in general, the examinees' responses are categorized into $m_j + 1$ scores (i.e., $x_j = \{0, 1, \ldots, m_j\}$), where m_j is the number of "operations" to correctly answer item j. For the above example item $m_j = 2$.

One approach for modeling ordered polytomous data involves decomposing the responses into a series of ordered pairs of adjacent categories or category scores and then successively "applying" a dichotomous model to each pair. This is the approach that Masters (1982) used in developing his partial credit model and that is described below.

Assume that there is a point on the latent variable continuum below which an individual provides a particular response (e.g., $x_j = 0$) and above which the person provides the *next* higher response (e.g., $x_j = 1$). As such, this point indicates the transition from one category score to the next category score. In the current context, a polytomously scored item has multiple ordered response categories (or category scores) with adjacent categories separated by such a transition point. Let each transition point be indexed by h and the *loca-*

tion of each transition point h on the continuum for item j be represented by δ_{jh} (i.e., the *transition location parameter*). For the example item these two transition points would be symbolized as δ_{j1} and δ_{j2}; they are interpreted below.

Generally speaking, the Rasch model specifies the probability, p_j, of the occurrence of an event b and $(1 - p_j)$ specifies the probability of b's complementary event $\bar{b}$ (e.g., $b = 1$ and $\bar{b} = 0$); the events b and $\bar{b}$ are mutually exclusive and jointly exhaustive. (Sometimes the events b and $\bar{b}$ are referred to as success and "not success," respectively.) When we apply the Rasch model to ordered polytomous data the events are the adjacent category scores or the adjacent response categories. For instance, for the example item, $(6/3) + 2 = ?$, we have two pairs of adjacent category scores. Pair one consists of $x_j = \{0, 1\}$ and the second pair is $x_j = \{1, 2\}$. Each pair of adjacent category scores has a transition point. The first transition point (δ_{j1}) reflects the shift in pair one from $x_j = 0$ to $x_j = 1$, whereas the second transition point (δ_{j2}) is for the progression in pair two from $x_j = 1$ to $x_j = 2$. In terms of the events terminology, for pair one the event $\bar{b}$ reflects $x_j = 0$ and the event b represents $x_j = 1$ (i.e., b reflects a successful transition from 0 to 1). For the second pair, the event $\bar{b}$ reflects $x_j = 1$ and the event b represents $x_j = 2$ (i.e., b represents a successful transition from 1 to 2). The pair's corresponding (transition) location parameter can be used in the Rasch model to calculate the probability of event b.

Given that the Rasch model can be used to calculate the probability of the successful transition from one category score to the next category score, its complement specifies the probability of an individual who is *not* successful in the transition from one category score to the next category score. For presentation ease we drop the subscript j on δ in the following. For example, if an individual is *not* successful in the transition from $x_j = 0$ to $x_j = 1$, then the corresponding probability according to the Rasch model is

$$p(x_j = 0) = 1 - p(x_j = 1) = 1 - \left[\frac{e^{(\theta - \delta_1)}}{1 + e^{(\theta - \delta_1)}}\right] = \frac{1}{1 + e^{(\theta - \delta_1)}} = \frac{e^0}{e^0 + e^{(\theta - \delta_1)}}$$

More generally, we may write

$$p(x_j = 0) = \frac{e^0}{\varphi}$$

where φ reflects all the possible outcomes. In contrast, if the individual is successful in the transition from $x_j = 0$ to $x_j = 1$ (i.e., pair one from above), then based on the distance between the person's location and the (transition) location parameter for $x_j = \{0, 1\}$ we have

$$p(x_j = 1 \mid x_j = 0) = \frac{e^{(\theta - \delta_1)}}{\varphi}$$

This may be interpreted as the probability of observing a category score of 1 *rather* than a category score of 0. Similarly, for pair two we have the probability of observing a category score of 2 *rather* than a category score of 1 as

$$p(x_j = 2 | x_j = 1) = \frac{e^{(\theta - \delta_2)}}{\varphi}$$

In the preceding we have applied the Rasch model to the separate dichotomizations, but have not considered the ordinal relationship between the three possible outcomes. These separate calculations may be "aggregated" by invoking this ordinal relationship. In the following we temporarily omit displaying the denominator, φ; however, the appropriate denominator is *implied* for the statements that read "the probability of . . ."

If an individual *fails* to make the transition from $x_j = 0$ to $x_j = 1$, then the probability of this event is e^0. However, for an individual to obtain an $x_j = 1$, then this person needs to "pass through" a response of 0 *and* the first transition point, δ_1. The probability of both of these is given by adding the (mutually exclusive) events of 0 and 1, that is, $e^0 + e^{(\theta - \delta_1)}$.

In a similar fashion, for a person to obtain an $x_j = 2$, then this person needs to "pass through" the second transition point, δ_2. However, to get to δ_2 he or she would have to pass through a category score of 1 (i.e., the first transition point); this idea is embodied in the phrasing above, "category score of 2 *rather* than a category score of 1." To pass through δ_1 the person would have to pass through a response of 0. Therefore, to obtain an $x_j = 2$ the individual passes through $x_j = 0$ (i.e., e^0), passes through $x_j = 1$ (i.e., $e^0 + e^{(\theta - \delta_1)}$), *and* then passes through the second transition point (i.e., $e^0 + e^{(\theta - \delta_1)} + e^{(\theta - \delta_2)}$). Therefore, the probability of $x_j = 2$ is given by $e^0 + e^{(\theta - \delta_1)} + e^{(\theta - \delta_2)}$. Figure 7.1 contains a schematic representation of these sequences where (a), (b), and (c) conceptually reflect the processes for the attainment of the category scores of 0, 1, and 2, respectively. As can be seen, the category score determines the number of aggregated distances between a person's location and the (transition) location parameter(s).

When each of the three terms (i.e., e^0, $e^0 + e^{(\theta - \delta_1)}$, $e^0 + e^{(\theta - \delta_1)} + e^{(\theta - \delta_2)}$) is divided by φ one obtains the probability of the category scores of 0, 1, and 2, respectively.

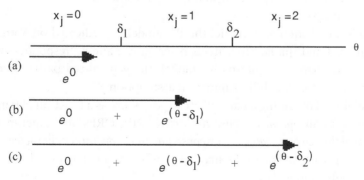

FIGURE 7.1. Schematic representation of the processes for obtaining the category scores of 0, 1, and 2.

Consistent with the definition of a probability the denominator ϕ is the sum of the three mutually exclusive outcomes.

A general expression that incorporates the principles just outlined is given by the *partial credit* (PC) model (Masters, 1982). The PC model specifies that the conditional probability that an examinee with latent location θ obtains a category score of x_j is

$$p(x_j|\theta, \delta_{jh}) = \frac{\exp\left[\sum_{h=0}^{x_j}(\theta - \delta_{jh})\right]}{e^0 + \sum_{k=1}^{m_j}\exp\left[\sum_{h=0}^{k}(\theta - \delta_{jh})\right]} = \frac{\exp\left[\sum_{h=0}^{x_j}(\theta - \delta_{jh})\right]}{\sum_{k=0}^{m_j}\exp\left[\sum_{h=0}^{k}(\theta - \delta_{jh})\right]} \quad (7.1)$$

For convenience $\sum_{j=0}^{0}(\theta - \delta_{jh}) \equiv 0$ and for notational ease "exp[z]" is used in lieu of "e^z." The transition location parameter for item j, δ_{jh}, is sometimes referred to as a "step difficulty" parameter or "step parameter."[1] Because the PC model may be applied to noncognitive assessment, as well as to avoid a sequential steps interpretation, we call δ_{jh} the *transition location* parameter. In effect, δ_{jh} reflects the relative difficulty in endorsing category h over category (h – 1). The use of a subscript on m (i.e., m_j) reflects that the number of category scores may vary across items. Therefore, the PC model may be applied to items that are polytomously scored with a varying number of category scores, are dichotomously scored, or consist of both dichotomous and polytomously scored items.[2] In the following p_{x_j} is used for $p(x_j|\theta, \delta_{jh})$.

Although for the PC model the response categories must be ordered, this does not mean that the transition locations are necessarily ordered. This is easiest to see in the context of proficiency assessment. For instance, it is obvious for the example item above that the second operation (i.e., the addition of 2) is a comparatively easier operation than is the first operation (i.e., the division of 6 by 3). Therefore, the corresponding δ_{jh}s are not in increasing order. Moreover, it is important to note that the δ_{jh}s are conditionally defined and cannot be interpreted simply as independent pieces of an item. Masters (1988) states that the δ_{jh}s "are more appropriately interpreted as a set of parameters associated with item <j>, none of which can be interpreted meaningfully outside the context of the entire item in which it occurs" (p. 23).

As an extension of the Rasch model the PC model is predicated on a unidimensional construct of interest and the fact that items discriminate among respondents to the same degree. In the next chapter an alternative model, the generalized partial credit model, is presented that relaxes the equal discrimination assumption.

The probability of obtaining a particular category score as a function of θ may be graphically represented in an *option response function* (ORF); ORFs are sometimes referred to as *category probability curves*, *category response functions*, *operating characteristic curves*, or *option characteristic curves*. The ORFs may be viewed as an extension of the dichotomous models' IRFs to polytomous data.

Figure 7.2 contains the ORFs for an item j worth 2 points ($m_j = 2$) with ordered transition locations. The first transition location occurs at –1.0 (i.e., δ_{j1} = –1.0) and the second transition location at 1.0 (i.e., δ_{j2} = 1.0). An example of an item that would produce ordered transition locations is an item such as (8 + 4)/3 = ?. For this item the sum of 8 and 4 is the first operation and the second, more difficult, operation is the division of this sum by 3; m_j = 2. The proficiency required to correctly perform the first operation and obtain a category score of 1 (x_i = 1) is less than that required to correctly perform the second operation to obtain a category score of 2 (x_j = 2). As a result, the corresponding transition locations would reflect this ordering of proficiencies.

As can be seen from Figure 7.2, the transition location parameter is the point of transition from one category (score) to the next. Stated another way, the transition location is the point where the probability of responding in two adjacent categories is equal. This is a reflection that an individual's response mechanism is really a binary "choice" between two adjacent categories. That is, the probability of selecting a particular response category over the previous one is governed by the dichotomous Rasch model. For example, the transition location at –1.0 is the transition between a category score of 0 and that of 1, whereas the transition location at 1.0 represents the transition between the (partial credit) score of 1 and that of the (full credit) score of 2 on this item. As one moves in either direction away from a transition location, the probability of obtaining one particular category score increases while the probability of obtaining the other category scores decreases.

One may interpret these ORFs as indicating that individuals located below –1.0 are most likely to obtain a category score of 0 (i.e., the solid nonbold line). However, some of the examinees located below –1.0 may obtain a score of 1 (i.e., the squared line segment below –1.0), albeit with a lower probability than a score of 0. Moreover, there is a substantially smaller probability that individuals located below –1.0 will correctly respond to this item (i.e., a category score of 2; the portion of the solid bold line below –1.0). Persons

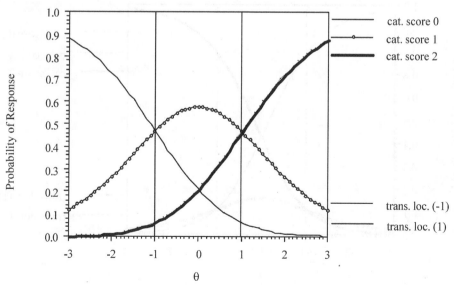

FIGURE 7.2. PC model ORFs for a two-point item j with δ_{j1} = –1.0 and δ_{j2} = 1.0.

located between −1.0 and 1.0 are most likely to obtain a category score of 1 (e.g., correctly performing one operation) and those located above 1.0 are increasingly likely to obtain a category score of 2 (e.g., correctly perform two operations). In each of these latter cases there is some nonzero probability that persons will not respond in the most likely category. The sum of the probabilities across category scores for a given θ is 1.0.[3]

In contrast to the ordered transition locations seen in Figure 7.2, Figure 7.3 contains the ORFs for a 2-point item in which the transition locations are in reverse order. (When adjacent transition locations are in decreasing order we call it a "*reversal*" [e.g., see Dodd, 1984].) For this item the transition from no credit (i.e., a category score of 0) to that of partial credit (1 point) occurs at 1.0. However, the transition from partial credit to full credit (2 points) occurs at −1.0. If this is a proficiency item, then the first transition from a category score of 0 to that of 1 would be substantially more difficult than the second transition from a category score of 1 to that of 2 because the first transition is located to the right of the second transition location. The item (6/3) + 2 = ? is an example of this situation (i.e., the first operation, (6/3), is more difficult than the second operation, the addition of 2).

Because of the transition location reversal this item is functioning very similarly to a dichotomous item. Below θ = 0.0 persons are most likely to provide a category score of 0 (e.g., obtain no credit on this item; solid nonbold line) and individuals above this point are most likely to respond with a category score of 2 (e.g., obtain full credit on this item; solid bold line). Comparatively speaking, the probability that persons will obtain a category score of 1 (e.g., obtain partial credit on this item; circle line) is less than that for the other two possibilities. Intuitively, this makes some sense. That is, if one has the capability to correctly perform the more difficult first operation on this item, then it is very likely that one would successfully perform the second and easier operation.

The ORFs for any item always consist of, at a minimum, one monotonically nondecreas-

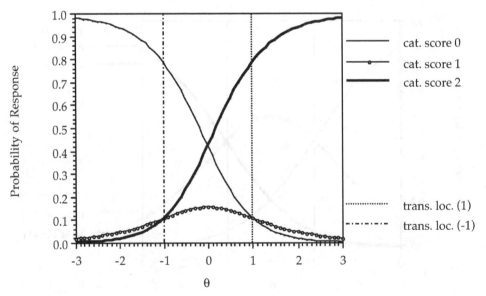

FIGURE 7.3. PC model ORFs for a two-point item j with $\delta_{j1} = 1.0$ and $\delta_{j2} = -1.0$.

ing ORF and one monotonically nonincreasing ORF. With dichotomous data the monotonically nondecreasing ORF represents a category score of 1 and has a positive α (i.e., this ORF is the IRF). The monotonically nonincreasing ORF reflects a category score of 0 and has the negative of α. Because the two ORFs intersect at the item's location, we can consider δ to be the threshold or transition location between a response of 0 and a response of 1. For items with more than two response categories we potentially have one unimodal ORF for each additional response category score.

CONCEPTUAL PARAMETER ESTIMATION OF THE PC MODEL

The general principles presented in Chapters 2 through 4 as well as Appendices A and B are applicable for estimating the multiple item and person parameters. In general, one obtains the likelihood function for the response data. The person and item values that maximize the likelihood function are taken as the estimates of the person and item locations. With the PC model this estimation capitalizes on the existence of sufficient statistics. With respect to persons, the observed score is a sufficient statistic for estimating a person's location. Therefore, individuals who obtain the same observed score (i.e., the simple unweighted sum of their item responses) obtain the same location estimate and an individual's pattern of responses does not provide any more information for estimating the person's location than does his or her observed score. In regard to items, it is the simple count of the number of respondents for each category score, not the actual response pattern across individuals, that contains all the information required for estimating the transition locations. Stated another way, the counts are sufficient statistics for estimating the transition locations for an item. Therefore, item categories that have the same count have the same transition location estimate. The details of the estimation for the PC model may be found in Wright and Masters (1982) and Masters (1982); also see Wilson and Adams (1993).[4]

EXAMPLE: APPLICATION OF THE PC MODEL TO A REASONING ABILITY INSTRUMENT, MMLE

As mentioned in the previous chapter examples, one would examine the tenability of the dimensionality assumption prior to performing the calibration. For brevity, assume that we have evidence supporting our unidimensional model as a reasonable representation of the data. In addition, assume that we have validity evidence supporting the use of our instrument. Although we could use BIGSTEPS (or WINSTEPS) for performing our calibration, the MULTILOG program is used instead. MULTILOG implements MMLE for parameter estimation for the dichotomous models that have been discussed so far, as well as for polytomous models such as the graded response, nominal response, and multiple-choice models; these polytomous models are discussed in subsequent chapters.[5]

The example data concern reasoning ability and come from the General Social Science survey (National Opinion Research Center, 2003). The instrument consists of a series of questions that ask how two things are alike. For instance, "In what way are an orange and a banana alike?" or "In what way are a dog and a lion alike?" The responses were graded in three categories (incorrect—0 points, partially correct—1 point, and correct—2 points) according to the quality of the response. Specifically, the rubric emphasized the response's degree of abstraction in determining the response score. Two points were awarded for pertinent general categorizations; one point for the naming of one or more common properties or functions of the members of a pair (this is considered a more concrete problem-solving approach); and 0 points for the naming of specific properties of each member of the pair, generalizations that were incorrect or not pertinent, differences between the members of the pair, or clearly wrong responses. For example, to the question "In what way are an orange and a banana alike?" 2 points would be awarded if the response is "both are fruit," 1 point for a response such as "both are food," and 0 points for a response such as "both are round." There are eight such items on the instrument.

As is the case with BILOG, estimation of the item parameters may proceed independently of estimation of the person parameters. MULTILOG 7's interface is similar to that of BILOG's in the use of menus and dialogs to facilitate the creation of an input (control) file. This file is subsequently processed by MULTILOG.

The command file for the PC calibration of the reasoning ability data is shown in Table 7.1. All command lines begin with the symbol ">," are terminated by a semicolon, and contain a series of subcommands; in general, commands and subcommands can be abbreviated to two or three characters. Briefly, in the problem line (PROBLEM or PRO) one describes some of the data's characteristics. For instance, the INDIVIDUAL subcommand specifies that individual case data (rather than pattern data) are being used, that there are at most 3000 examinees (NEXAMINEES=3000; one may use this subcommand to restrict the number of cases read), that eight items are to be calibrated (NITEMS=8), and the RANDOM subcommand indicates that one is assuming that the individuals are randomly sampled from the population of interest and that one is performing item parameter estimation. In addition, each examinee case uses 15 characters as an identification label (NCHARS=15).

To obtain estimates for the PC model we need to impose constraints on the nominal response model; the nominal response model is discussed in Chapter 9. Therefore, the TEST line instructs the program to obtain estimates for all items (ALL) on the instrument using the nominal response model (NOMINAL). Each of the eight items consists of three response categories (i.e., NC=(3(0)8)), and the keyword HIGH=(3(0)8) indicates that response category 3 is the highest category for each of the eight items. This notation of "(3(0)8)" is MULTILOG's (and BILOG's) shorthand way of indicating an integer set without having to individually indicate each value in the set. For example, NC=(3(0)8) indicates eight 3s and is equivalent to NC=(3,3,3,3,3,3,3,3).

Subsequent to the TEST command is where we specify the constraints on the nominal response model to obtain the PC model. That is, the TMATRIX, EQUAL, and FIX lines impose the appropriate constraints on the nominal response model to obtain PC model estimates. These constraints implement the contrasts among the various nominal response model parameters to obtain PC model estimates. Thissen and Steinberg (1986) as well as Muraki (1992) contain technical details on these constraints. Because the PC model states that all items have the same discrimination, we need to use the line EQUAL ALL AK=1 to instruct MULTILOG to constrain all the $\hat{\alpha}_j$s to be equal to one another, although not neces-

TABLE 7.1. Command File for the MULTILOG PC Model Calibration Example

```
MULTILOG for Windows 7.00.2327.2
ALIKE, 8 ITEMS, PC                    ⇐ title^a
>PROBLEM RANDOM,                       ⇐ Problem description line
        INDIVIDUAL,
        DATA = 'Alike.DAT',
        NITEMS = 8,
        NGROUPS = 1,
        NEXAMINEES = 2942,
        NCHARS = 15;
>TEST ALL,                            ⇐ Instrument description line
     NOMINAL,                         ⇐ Specification of NO model
     NC = (3(0)8),
     HIGH = (3(0)8);
>TMATRIX ALL AK POLY;                 ⇐ constraints for PC^b
>EQUAL ALL AK=1;                      ⇐ constraints for PC^b
>FIX ALL AK=2 VALUE=0.0;              ⇐ constraints for PC^b
>TMATRIX ALL CK TRIANGLE;             ⇐ constraints for PC^b
>EST NC=100 IT=25;
>END ;                                ⇐ Terminates command section
3                                     ⇐ Number of response categories
012                                   ⇐ The response code line
11111111                              ⇐ The 0s are recoded to be 1s for all eight items
22222222                              ⇐ The 1s are recoded to be 2s for all eight items
33333333                              ⇐ The 2s are recoded to be 3s for all eight items
(15A1,T1,8(A1,1X))                    ⇐ The format for reading the data
```

^aThe text following the ⇐ is provided to help the reader understand the corresponding input.
^bThese lines are inserted in the main MULTILOG window.

sarily equal to 1. (If this line is omitted, each item's α_j would be estimated and the calibration model would be the generalized partial credit model [Chapter 8].)[6]

On the EST NC=100 IT=50 line the maximum number of EM cycles that can be executed is set to 100 (NC=100) and the maximum number of M-step iterations is specified to be 25 (IT=25). Following the END command line is the description of the response data. There are three response categories with the codes 0, 1, and 2; therefore, these values are listed on the response code line (i.e., the line 012). Because with polytomous models MULTILOG internally uses category 0, we need to recode these response data. We recode the data by specifying that the response of 0 for each of the eight items should be recoded to 1 (i.e., the line 11111111). Similarly, we recode the response codes of 1 and 2 to be 2 and 3, respectively (i.e., the lines 22222222 and 33333333, respectively). The final line contains the FORTRAN format for reading the response data. In this example each individual's response vector is used as his or her character identification code. Therefore, the '15A1' in the format is associated with the NCHARS=15 case identification subcommand on the PROBLEM line, whereas the '8(A1,1X)' is the format for reading the eight item responses; 'T1' tells the program to return to the first column. (FORTRAN formats are briefly discussed in Appendix E, "FORTRAN Formats.")

The output presented in Table 7.2 begins with the specification of the number of exam-

inees, number of items, and number of response codes, along with other logistical information. For example, the program read 2942 cases, there are eight items, and so on. The next
section, ESTIMATION PARAMETERS, contains information concerning the calibration
parameters. It shows that the maximum number of EM cycles is 100 (i.e., NC=100) and the
maximum number of M-steps is 25 (i.e., IT=25). For the EM cycles and M-steps phases the
convergence criteria are 0.001 and 0.0001, respectively. In addition, the line NUMBER OF
FREE PARAMETERS IS: specifies the number of parameters estimated for this calibration. This information is useful for calculating degrees of freedom (e.g., for use with ΔG^2).
In this case, there are 17 parameters being estimated (8 items * 2 transition locations, δ_{j1}
and δ_{j2}, per item plus the common α). Following the ESTIMATION PARAMETERS section is the response codes section, CODE CATEGORY. One should inspect these codes to
ensure that the codes used are the ones that are intended to be used and that there are as
many codes as there are items. Similarly, the FIRST OBSERVATION AS READ should
be verified to be correct. Given that the value of FINISHED CYCLE is less than 100 (i.e.,
FINISHED CYCLE is 11) and the MAXIMUM INTERCYCLE PARAMETER CHANGE is
less than the convergence criterion we have a converged solution.

The ITEM SUMMARY section contains the PC model item parameter estimates under
the heading CONTRAST-COEFFICIENTS. From ITEM 1 we see that the common item
discrimination estimate, $\hat{\alpha}$, for all items is 0.84. Item 1's first transition location $(\hat{\delta}_{11})$ is estimated to be –1.30 and the second one $(\hat{\delta}_{12})$ is –2.06; the standard errors for $\hat{\alpha}, \hat{\delta}_{11}$, and $\hat{\delta}_{12}$,
are 0.01, 0.12, and 0.08, respectively. The section OBSERVED AND EXPECTED COUNTS/
PROPORTIONS IN contains the response frequency for each response category 0, 1, 2 (in
the output these are labeled 1, 2, and 3, respectively). For instance, of the 2942 persons
in the calibration sample, 201 did not receive any credit, 351 received partial credit, and
81.24% or 2390 received full credit on item 1 (i.e., the traditional item difficulty for item 1,
P_1, is 2390/2942 = 0.8124). This is a relatively easy item for this sample. It is important to
examine the observed frequencies (or proportions) section because it allows one to determine the distribution of (category) scores on an item, whether there are some scores that are
not observed, or whether there are infrequently given scores on a particular item. In these
latter cases the corresponding transition location may not be well estimated.

Returning to item 1's CONTRAST-COEFFICIENTS section, one sees that each estimate has a parameter number label (i.e., P(#)). For example, the common $\hat{\alpha}$ of 0.84 has
the parameter number label of 1. Throughout the output all items that share a common $\hat{\alpha}$
(i.e., the items that are involved in the equality constraint) have the corresponding param-
eter estimate labeled 1. The transition location estimates for item 1, $\hat{\delta}_{11}$ and $\hat{\delta}_{12}$, have the
parameter numbers 2 and 3, respectively. If item 2's estimates were presented, then $\hat{\delta}_{21}$
would have the parameter number 4 and $\hat{\delta}_{22}$ would have the parameter number 5; the common $\hat{\alpha}$ would still have the parameter number 1. This characteristic can be seen with the
results for the eighth item. The common $\hat{\alpha}$ has the same parameter number as it did for the
first item and the $\hat{\delta}_{81}$ =1.27 and $\hat{\delta}_{82}$ = 1.36 have parameter numbers labels of 16 and 17,
respectively. That is, δ_{82} is the 17th parameter referred to in the line NUMBER OF FREE
PARAMETERS IS:17.

The line labeled @THETA: INFORMATION shows item 1's information function; the
@THETA is labeled with a θ range that specifies the corresponding location for the item

TABLE 7.2. Abridged Output from the MULTILOG PC Model Calibration Example

```
       :
<echo of command file>
       :
  DATA PARAMETERS:
   NUMBER OF LINES IN THE DATA FILE: 2942
   NUMBER OF CATEGORICAL-RESPONSE ITEMS:    8
   NUMBER OF CONTINUOUS-RESPONSE ITEMS, AND/OR GROUPS:    1
   TOTAL NUMBER OF "ITEMS" (INCLUDING GROUPS):    9
   NUMBER OF CHARACTERS IN ID FIELDS: 15
   MAXIMUM NUMBER OF RESPONSE-CODES FOR ANY ITEM:   3
   THE MISSING VALUE CODE FOR CONTINUOUS DATA:  9.0000
   THE DATA WILL BE STORED IN MEMORY

  ESTIMATION PARAMETERS:
   THE ITEMS WILL BE CALIBRATED--
     BY MARGINAL MAXIMUM LIKELIHOOD ESTIMATION
   MAXIMUM NUMBER OF EM CYCLES PERMITTED: 100
   NUMBER OF PARAMETER-SEGMENTS USED IS:   9
   NUMBER OF FREE PARAMETERS IS:   17
   MAXIMUM NUMBER OF M-STEP ITERATIONS IS  25 TIMES
     THE NUMBER OF PARAMETERS IN THE SEGMENT
   THE M-STEP CONVERGENCE CRITERION IS: 0.000100
   THE EM-CYCLE CONVERGENCE CRITERION IS: 0.001000
   THE RK CONTROL PARAMETER (FOR THE M-STEPS) IS:  0.9000
   THE RM CONTROL PARAMETER (FOR THE M-STEPS) IS:  1.0000
   THE MAXIMUM ACCELERATION PERMITTED IS:  0.0000
   THETA-GROUP LOCATIONS WILL REMAIN UNCHANGED
  :
  KEY-
  CODE   CATEGORY
    0     11111111                    ⇐ The recodings to 1 for a response of 0ᵃ
    1     22222222                    ⇐ The recodings to 2 for a response of 1
    2     33333333                    ⇐ The recodings to 3 for a response of 2
  :
  FIRST OBSERVATION AS READ-
  ID       1 1 2 0 0 0 0 0
  ITEMS 11200000                      ⇐ The  response pattern for the first person
  NORML      0.000

  FINISHED CYCLE  11                   ⇐ Number of iterations
  MAXIMUM INTERCYCLE PARAMETER CHANGE=   0.00055 P(  17)


  ITEM SUMMARY

  ITEM   1:      3 NOMINAL CATEGORIES,   3 HIGH
   CATEGORY(K): 1      2      3
     A(K)     -0.84   0.00   0.84
     C(K)      0.00   1.30   3.36

              CONTRAST-COEFFICIENTS (STANDARD ERRORS)
     FOR:          A               C
   CONTRAST P(#)  COEFF.[POLY.]  P(#)  COEFF.[ TRI.]
       1      1   0.84 (0.01)     2   -1.30 (0.12)
       2     18   0.00 (0.00)     3   -2.06 (0.08)

  @THETA:     INFORMATION:   (Theta values increase in steps of 0.2)
  -3.0 - -1.6  0.352  0.404  0.451  0.489  0.514  0.523  0.513  0.487
  -1.4 -  0.0  0.448  0.400  0.349  0.298  0.251  0.209  0.172  0.141
   0.2 -  1.6  0.115  0.093  0.076  0.062  0.051  0.042  0.034  0.028
   1.8 -  3.0  0.023  0.019  0.016  0.013  0.011  0.009  0.008

  OBSERVED AND EXPECTED COUNTS/PROPORTIONS IN
  CATEGORY(K):   1       2       3
  OBS. FREQ.    201     351     2390
  OBS. PROP.  0.0683  0.1193  0.8124
  EXP. PROP.  0.0669  0.1203  0.8128
  :

  ITEM   8:      3 NOMINAL CATEGORIES,   3 HIGH
   CATEGORY(K): 1      2      3
     A(K)     -0.84   0.00   0.84
     C(K)      0.00  -1.27  -2.63
```

cont.

TABLE 7.2. cont.

```
          CONTRAST-COEFFICIENTS (STANDARD ERRORS)
    FOR:           A                    C
    CONTRAST P(#)  COEFF.[POLY.]  P(#)  COEFF.[ TRI.]
       1       1   0.84 (0.01)     16   1.27 (0.06)
       2      39   0.00 (0.00)     17   1.36 (0.09)

    @THETA:     INFORMATION:   (Theta values increase in steps of 0.2)
    -3.0 - -1.6  0.017  0.020  0.023  0.028  0.033  0.040  0.047  0.057
    -1.4 -  0.0  0.068  0.081  0.096  0.115  0.137  0.163  0.192  0.226
     0.2 -  1.6  0.262  0.301  0.341  0.379  0.413  0.439  0.455  0.460
     1.8 -  3.0  0.452  0.433  0.404  0.369  0.330  0.290  0.252

    OBSERVED AND EXPECTED COUNTS/PROPORTIONS IN
    CATEGORY(K):  1       2       3
    OBS. FREQ.   2043     616     283
    OBS. PROP.   0.6944  0.2094  0.0962
    EXP. PROP.   0.6947  0.2079  0.0974

    ITEM   9: GRP1, N[MU:  0.00 SIGMA:  1.00]
       P(#);(S.E.):   43; (0.00)    44; (0.00)
  :

    TOTAL TEST INFORMATION

    @THETA:     INFORMATION:
    -3.0 - -1.6  1.831  1.972  2.124  2.283  2.444  2.602  2.755  2.898
    -1.4 -  0.0  3.031  3.153  3.264  3.365  3.457  3.538  3.604  3.651
     0.2 -  1.6  3.669  3.654  3.602  3.513  3.390  3.240  3.071  2.889
     1.8 -  3.0  2.704  2.523  2.350  2.190  2.044  1.913  1.798

    @THETA:     POSTERIOR STANDARD DEVIATION:
    -3.0 - -1.6  0.739  0.712  0.686  0.662  0.640  0.620  0.603  0.587
    -1.4 -  0.0  0.574  0.563  0.554  0.545  0.538  0.532  0.527  0.523
     0.2 -  1.6  0.522  0.523  0.527  0.534  0.543  0.556  0.571  0.588
     1.8 -  3.0  0.608  0.630  0.652  0.676  0.699  0.723  0.746

    MARGINAL RELIABILITY:     0.6986

    NEGATIVE TWICE THE LOGLIKELIHOOD=      -7624.1
    (CHI-SQUARE FOR SEVERAL TIMES MORE EXAMINEES THAN CELLS)
```

[a]The text following the ⇐ is provided to help the reader understand the corresponding input.

information value. For example, the first line specifies the range from −3 to −1.6; therefore the information at $\theta = -3$ is 0.352, at $\theta = -2.8$ it is 0.404, and so on. From the θ range provided it be can be seen that item 1 provides most of its information in a neighborhood around −2 and then steadily decreases for the rest of the continuum.

For contrast purposes, item 8's information is presented. This item is correctly answered by only 9.62% of the sample and its item information function peaks in the vicinity of 1.6. Given the model, its $\hat{\alpha}$ is the same as that of item 1 and its corresponding transition locations, $\hat{\delta}_{81} = 1.27$ and $\hat{\delta}_{82} = 1.36$, are relative to item 1's transition locations, at the opposite end of the θ continuum. ("Item 9" is not really an item but is concerned with whether the sample comes from a [prior] normal distribution with mean 0 and variance 1.)

Figure 7.4 contains the ORFs and information functions for item 1; the PLOT menu item on the RUN menu produced this figure. Given the reversal in $\hat{\delta}$s for item 1 (i.e., $\hat{\delta}_{11} = -1.30$ and $\hat{\delta}_{12} = -2.06$), it is not surprising that respondents located above (approximately) −2.0 are more likely to receive full credit (ORF labeled "3") rather than partial credit (ORF labeled "2"; left panel of Figure 7.4). Similarly, respondents located below −2.0 have a higher probability of receiving no credit (ORF labeled "1") rather than partial credit. Although the OBSERVED AND EXPECTED COUNTS indicate that each of the category scores are being utilized, the ORFs show that, in effect, this item is primarily behaving like a dichotomous item. For most of the respondents this is a relatively easy item. The @THETA: INFORMA-TION section of the output shows that at approximately –2.0 this item provided its maximum information. This is confirmed by the item information function in the right panel of Figure 7.4.

Figure 7.5 contains the ORFs for all the items on the instrument. Four of the items have a tendency to behave in a dichotomous way (items 1, 2, 5, and 7), whereas items 3, 4, 6, and 8 are trichotomous. It is also seen that items 1, 2, and 3 are useful for assessing people located in the lower half of the θ continuum, items 4, 5, and 7 provide information in the middle of the continuum, and items 6 and 8 are tapping the upper half of the continuum. Therefore, the instrument gives relatively broad capacity to measure reasoning ability.

The sum of the item information functions is captured by the instrument's total information (in Table 7.2, labeled TOTAL TEST INFORMATION); these values have 1.0 added to them. This table, read similarly to that of the item information, indicates that the maximum information for locating individuals occurs in the neighborhood of $\theta = 0.2$. A graphical depiction of this information function is shown in Figure 7.6; the PLOT menu item on the RUN menu produced this figure. This double-Y graph overlays the corresponding standard errors for persons as a function of θ on the total information function (the right side ordinate provides the scale for interpreting the standard errors); similar information is provided in the table entitled @THETA: POSTERIOR STANDARD DEVIATION in the output (Table 7.2). As can be seen, the accuracy of person location estimation varies as a function of the specific location. Specifically, this instrument does a comparatively better job

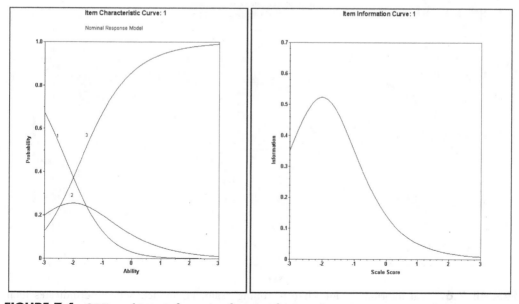

FIGURE 7.4. ORFs and item information function for item 1.

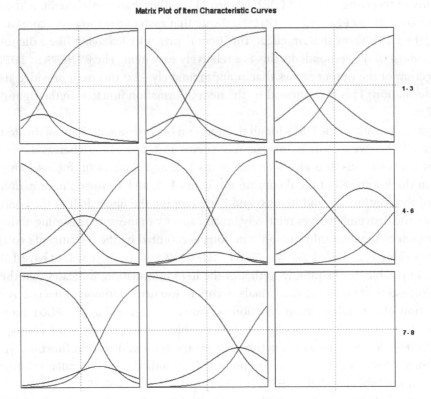

FIGURE 7.5. ORFs for all eight Alike items. Items are read left to right, top to bottom. For example, for row 1 item 1 is left, item 2 is center, item 3 is right; for row 2 item 4 is left, item 5 is center, and so on.

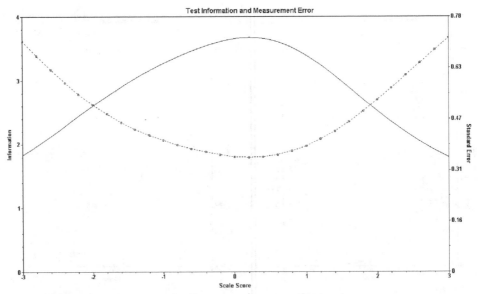

FIGURE 7.6. Total information for Alike reasoning exam, PC model. Solid line indicates total information; dotted line indicates standard error.

of estimating a person's location from around –0.5 to 1.0 and a progressively poorer job as one approaches 2 or –2.

Most practitioners and consumers of psychometrics are familiar with traditional estimators of the reliability of an instrument's scores (e.g., coefficient alpha [Guttman, 1945][7]). Therefore, in some situations it may be desirable to have a single numerical value that "captures" the accuracy of the person location estimation. Green, Bock, Humphreys, Linn, and Reckase (1984) present an average or marginal measurement error index, the *marginal reliability*, that is unitless and is bounded by 0 and 1. MULTILOG presents a MARGINAL RELIABILITY on the output. The marginal reliability for the $\hat{\theta}$s from this instrument is 0.6986 and it reflects an average accuracy across the continuum. However, it is only when the total information function is somewhat uniformly distributed that this value accurately characterizes the precision of measurement across the continuum. In our example, the total information function is peaked and, as a result, the marginal reliability is underrepresenting the accuracy in the vicinity of the peak and overrepresenting accuracy in the tails of the information function.[8]

In terms of model-level fit information MULTILOG provides –2ln*L* at the end of its output (i.e., NEGATIVE TWICE THE LOGLIKELIHOOD). (The value printed is negative 2 times the log of a number that is proportional to the likelihood [Thissen et al., 2003].) With individual case data, as we have in this example, the –2ln*L* value of –7624.1 is not useful and is ignored. However, when pattern data are calibrated, this index may be used for an overall assessment of model–data fit as well as model comparisons; this assumes that most or all of the possible patterns are observed. Chapters 8 and 9 contain examples using pattern data with MULTILOG.

Because MULTILOG 7 (and earlier versions) does not provide item-level tests of fit we use another program, MODFIT (Levine, Drasgon, & Stark, 2001), to obtain this fit information. As mentioned above, the sample sizes typically seen in calibrations result in potentially powerful statistical fit tests. As such, significant statistical tests should be interpreted in conjunction with graphical displays. In this regard, MODFIT provides both the empirical and predicted ORFs, as well as the item fit statistics (e.g., X^2). (MODFIT is limited to 40 two- to seven-option items and 3000 cases. It can produce these graphs for dichotomous as well as polytomous models; the technical details may be found in Drasgow, Levine, Tsien, Williams, & Mead [1995].)

Figure 7.7 contains the empirical and predicted ORFs for each option for item 1 using MODFIT. As can be seen from panel A, the predicted ORF (labeled ORF 1-0; symbol = diamond) falls within the 95% error bars of the empirical ORF (labeled EMP 1- 0; symbol = circle) for the incorrect response (i.e., option 0). Similarly, the partially correct response (i.e., option 1) shows some congruence between the predicted (ORF 1-1) and empirical (EMP 1- 1) ORFs (panel B), but not as well as for option 0. The same may be said for the correct response, option 2 (panel C). Panel C shows that for part of the continuum the predicted (ORF 1-2) does not fall within the error bars of the empirical ORF (EMP 1- 2), indicating a lack of agreement. Examination of the empirical and predicted ORFs for the other items shows better agreement between the empirical and predicted ORFs than seen in Figure 7.7; this is true for all of the remaining items except for item 3. However, overall we consider the agreement between the empirical and predicted ORFs to be sufficiently good

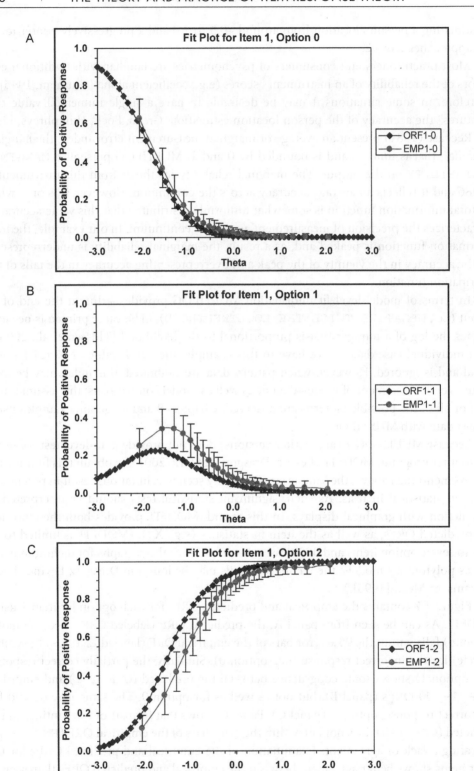

FIGURE 7.7. Empirical and predicted ORFs for item 1.

to believe that we have model–data fit with the PC model. (In the next chapter a model that allows items to vary in terms of their discrimination is applied to these data to see if model–data fit may be improved.)

It is good practice that model–data fit analysis include examinations of the invariance and conditional independence assumptions. The corresponding evidence would aid in supporting (or not) the above conclusion of model–data fit with the PC model. Because MULTILOG does not have BILOG's random sampling capability (e.g., see Chapter 5) we would use the sampling procedure presented in Chapter 3 to investigate invariance with the PC model. Analogous to what was done in Chapter 3, this invariance investigation would use the correlations between corresponding $\hat{\delta}_{jh}$s across the two groups.

With respect to conditional independence one could use Q_3 or some other similar index. Recall from Chapter 6 that Q_3 is the correlation between the residuals for a pair of items. In the case of the PC model the residual for an item is the difference between an individual's observed category score and the individual's expected category score on the item. As such, after fitting the model the Pearson correlation coefficient is used to examine the linear relationship between pairs of item residuals. In the current situation, the observed category score is a 0, 1, or 2 and the expected response is given by the weighted sum of the response category probabilities according to the PC model (i.e., $\mathcal{E}(x_j|\hat{\theta}_i) = \sum_{k=0}^{m} k * p(x_j|\hat{\theta}_i, \delta_{jh})$). Symbolically, the residual for person i for item j is $d_{ij} = x_{ij} - \mathcal{E}(x_j|\hat{\theta}_i)$ and for item z it is $d_{iz} = x_{iz} - \mathcal{E}(x_z|\hat{\theta}_i)$. Q_3 is the correlation between d_{ij} and d_{iz} across persons.

THE RATING SCALE MODEL

In contrast to proficiency testing, some applications are focused on assessing an individual's attitude toward some concept (e.g., immigration), whereas in others one is interested in personality assessment (e.g., social anxiety). These situations tend to use instruments that rely, in part or in whole, on a response format developed by Rensis Likert (1932). This response format typically consists of a series of ordinal categories that range from strongly disagree to strongly agree. This "Likert scale" may contain an even (e.g., 4) or an odd number (e.g., 5 or 7) of response categories. Andrich's (1978b, 1978c; also see Andersen, 1977; Masters, 1982) *rating scale* (RS) model is one model that is appropriate for modeling Likert response scale data as well as performance rating data.

The RS model uses responses that come from a series of ordered categories and assumes that these ordered categories are separated from one another by a series of ordered *thresholds*. Each threshold, τ_h, is on the latent variable's continuum and separates adjacent response categories. For example, assume we are interested in assessing attitudes toward condoms. One of our items is "I prefer to use condoms over other methods of birth control" and uses a four-category Likert response scale. Figure 7.8 shows how the thresholds relate to the response categories. For the moment, assume that the item itself has a location (δ) value of 0. Conceptually, when a person, with location θ, encounters this item the probability of responding in, for example, the "strongly disagree" category or the "disagree" category depends on whether the person is located below or above τ_1. If $\theta < \tau_1$, then the person responds in the "strongly disagree" category, otherwise he or she doesn't. If the person is

I prefer to use condoms over other methods of birth control.

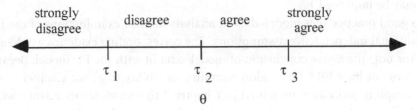

FIGURE 7.8. Representation of item parameter characterization for the RS model (m = 3).

located above τ_1, then following a similar process the person's response of "disagree" would be determined by whether $\theta < \tau_2$. If $\theta > \tau_2$, then according to this response mechanism a response of "strongly agree" would occur if the person is located above τ_3, otherwise the response would be "agree." Thus, the person "passes through" one or more of the thresholds to arrive at his or her response. The number of thresholds passed is represented by x_j. Therefore, x_j may take on the values from 0 thresholds passed up to and including the mth threshold. When the respondent has passed zero thresholds (i.e., $x_j = 0$), then he or she remains in the first or lowest category (e.g., strongly disagree). In contrast, if the respondent has passed all m thresholds (i.e., $x_j = m$), then he or she has responded in the last or highest category (e.g., strongly agree). Assuming, for instance, that the respondent "agreed" to this example item, then he or she would have had to pass two thresholds (τ_1 and τ_2) to arrive at the "agree" category and $x_j = 2$.

From Figure 7.8 we see that that there is always one fewer thresholds than there are response categories (i.e., there are m + 1 response categories). Unlike the PC model in which m is subscripted (i.e., m_j) to reflect that items can differ in terms of the number of operations, with the RS model all items must have the same number of thresholds (i.e., the same number of response categories).[9] These thresholds have the same values for all items. However, this does not mean that the thresholds are at the same *locations* on the continuum for all items. Recall that with the Rasch model items on the instrument may have different locations, δ_js, along the latent variable continuum. The threshold values may be viewed as offsets from an item's location. As a result, it is the combination of the item's location and the threshold (offset) value that determines the threshold's location on the continuum.

As an example, assume we have two items for assessing attitudes toward condom use, "Most of your friends think that condoms are uncomfortable" and "It's embarrassing to buy condoms," using the same 4-point Likert scale described above. On a continuum of not favorable to favorable attitudes toward condom use, there is no reason to believe that across a sample of individuals these two items must be located at the same point on the continuum. Figure 7.9 graphically shows the locations of these two items, δ_1 and δ_2, and how the thresholds for the 4-point Likert item relate to these two item locations. As can be seen, the differences between the τ_hs (i.e., $\tau_1 - \tau_2$, $\tau_1 - \tau_3$, and $\tau_2 - \tau_3$) remain constant across the items. However, the thresholds' actual locations on the continuum vary as a function of the item's location (i.e., δ_1 or δ_2). For example, let τ_1, τ_2, τ_3 have the values of –0.8, –0.2 and 0.5, respectively, and let $\delta_1 = -1$ and $\delta_2 = 1$. Then the actual location of a threshold h

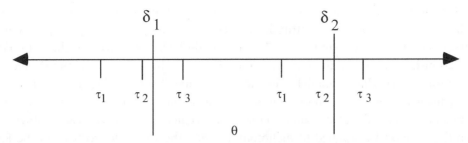

FIGURE 7.9. Graphical representation of item locations and thresholds for two items.

on the continuum for a particular item j would be $\delta_{jh} = \delta_j + \tau_h$. In this example, the first threshold's location (h = 1) on the continuum with respect to item 1 would be $\delta_{11} = \delta_1 + \tau_1$ = −1 − 0.8 = −1.8 and for the second item the first threshold's location would be $\delta_{21} = \delta_2 + \tau_1$ = 1 − 0.8 = 0.2. In a similar fashion we can determine the actual locations for the second and third thresholds for these two items.

The above ideas and principles may be incorporated into the Rasch model to obtain the RS model:

$$p(x_j|\theta, \delta_j, \underline{\tau}) = \frac{\exp\left[\sum_{h=0}^{x_j}(\theta-(\delta_j+\tau_h))\right]}{\sum_{h=0}^{m}\exp\left[\sum_{h=0}^{k}(\theta-(\delta_j+\tau_h))\right]} = \frac{\exp\left[-\sum_{h=0}^{x_j}\tau_h+x_j(\theta-\delta_j)\right]}{\sum_{h=0}^{m}\exp\left[-\sum_{h=0}^{k}\tau_h+k(\theta-\delta_j)\right]} \quad (7.2)$$

where $p(x_j|\theta, \delta_j, \underline{\tau})$ is the probability for a person with location θ passing x_j number of thresholds (i.e., responding in a particular category) on an item j located at δ_j with threshold set $\underline{\tau}$; m is the number of thresholds. The range of x_j is the integer values from 0 to m (i.e., $x_j = \{0, 1, \ldots, m\}$). The sum of the thresholds is constrained to be zero, $\sum^m \tau_h = 0$.

Equation 7.2 may be simplified by letting κ_{x_j} represent

$$-\sum_{h=0}^{x_j}\tau_h$$

By substitution of κ_{x_j} into Equation 7.2 one obtains the typical presentation of the RS model (Andrich, 1978b, 1978c):

$$p(x_j|\theta, \delta_j, \underline{\kappa}) = \frac{\exp[\kappa_{x_j}+x_j(\theta-\delta_j)]}{\sum_{k=0}^{m}\exp[\kappa_k+k(\theta-\delta_j)]} \quad (7.3)$$

where the new term, κ_{x_j}, is referred to as a *category coefficient* and is a function of the τ_js. By definition, $\kappa_{x_j} = 0$ when x_j is zero, otherwise $\kappa_{x_j} = -\sum_{h=1}^{x_j}\tau_h$ with x_j taking on a value from 1 up to the m*th* threshold. In the context of the RS model the person's location (θ) may be interpreted as his or her attitude and the item's location (δ_j) may be interpreted as the item's affective value (Andrich, 1978c) or the difficulty of endorsing the item. Given the relationship between Equations 7.2 and 7.3, it may be evident that the RS model is an extension of the Rasch model. Therefore, the model's underlying assumptions are a unidimensional latent space and that items have a similar capacity to discriminate among respondents; there is also an assumption that there is equal discrimination at the thresholds. When the RS model is applied to dichotomous data, the RS model reduces to the Rasch model (i.e., there is one threshold, m = 1, $\tau_1 = \delta_j$). For convenience p_{x_j} is used in lieu of $p(x_j|\theta, \delta_j, \underline{\kappa})$ in the following discussion.

As is the case with the PC model, each response category has an ORF. Moreover, the ORFs for any item always consist of at least one monotonically nondecreasing ORF and one monotonically nonincreasing ORF. There is typically a unimodal ORF for each additional response category. Figures 7.10 and 7.11 contain example ORFs for two items. These two items use a four-category Likert response scale (strongly disagree, disagree, agree, strongly agree) and come from an instrument designed to measure attitude toward condom use. Such an instrument might be used, for example, as part of an HIV awareness program. Item 1 asks the respondents whether condoms offer good protection and item 2 asks if they are embarrassed to purchase condoms. Assume that item 1 is located at ($\delta_1 =$) –0.98 and item 2 has a δ_2 of 0.70. For these two items, as well as all the other items on the instrument, the thresholds have the values of $\tau_1 = -0.30$, $\tau_2 = -0.02$, and $\tau_3 = 0.32$. Using these values with the model in Equation 7.3 produced the ORFs in Figures 7.10 and 7.11. As can be seen, each item has a monotonically nondecreasing ORF and a monotonically nonincreasing ORF

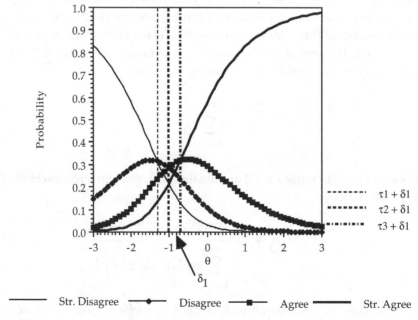

FIGURE 7.10. RS model ORFs for a four-category Likert item with $\delta_1 = -0.98$.

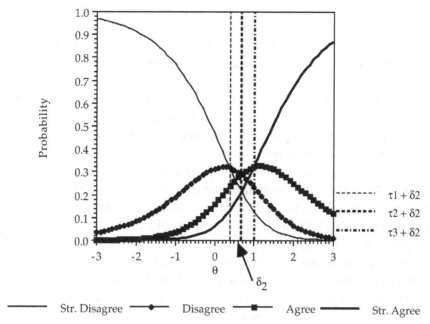

FIGURE 7.11. RS model ORFs for a four-category Likert item with $\delta_2 = 0.70$.

representing the strongly agree and strongly disagree response categories, respectively. The agree and disagree response categories are reflected in ORFs that are unimodal and symmetric.[10]

The ORFs in Figure 7.10 may be interpreted as indicating that individuals in the narrow band between –1.28 and –1.0 are likely to disagree with this item. Similarly, respondents in the range –1.0 to –0.67 are likely to agree with the item. Outside this range of approximately six tenths of a logit (i.e., from –0.67 to –1.28) respondents will, by and large, have a higher probability of strongly disagreeing with this item if their attitudes are below –1.28 or strongly agreeing with this item if their attitudes are above –0.67.

Comparing Figure 7.10 with Figure 7.11 shows the same pattern, albeit at a different point along the continuum. If the right side of the continuum reflects people who have negative attitudes toward condom use, then item 2 ("It's embarrassing to buy condoms") is an item that individuals who have relatively negative attitudes toward condom use (e.g., located above 1.0) will tend to strongly agree with or to strongly endorse. In contrast, a comparatively large portion of the continuum reflects individuals who are comfortable in purchasing condoms even though some of them have average/neutral or somewhat positive attitudes toward condom use.

Similarly, given item 1's location, respondents who are somewhat below average, as well as those who are positive in their attitude toward condom use, will tend to strongly agree that condoms offer good protection. Overall, and given the threshold values, the nature of this item set is that there is a tendency to either strongly disagree or strongly agree with an item. That is, this item set has a strong tendency to polarize individuals and the four response categories behave almost, but not quite, as two categories.

One might ask, "Where on the continuum does the probability of strongly disagreeing equal the probability of disagreeing with item 1?" (this point is represented by the vertical nonbold dashed line in Figure 7.10). In other words, what is the location of τ_1, given item 1's location? To determine the threshold's location on the continuum one simply adds the threshold's value to the item's location. Therefore, we have $\delta_1 + \tau_1 = -0.98 + (-0.30) = -1.28$ as the point of intersection of the strongly disagree ORF and the disagree ORF. With respect to this item, the second and third threshold locations would be located at -1.0 and -0.67, respectively. In a similar fashion, we may determine the thresholds' locations on the continuum for the second item (Figure 7.11).

From Figure 7.10 it can be seen that the relative locations of the thresholds (i.e., with respect to item 1's location) correspond to the transitions between the ORFs of adjacent categories. This is identical to the PC model's transition locations interpretation. In terms of the PC model notation the actual location of threshold 1 for item 1 would be $\delta_{11} = \delta_1 + \tau_1$ or, generically, $\delta_{jh} = \delta_j + \tau_h$. Masters (1982) has shown that his PC model subsumes the RS model; also see Masters and Wright (1984) and Wright and Masters (1982). Moreover, under certain constraints the RS model is a special case of Bock's nominal response model; the nominal response model is discussed in Chapter 9. As is the case with the PC model, the sum of the probabilities across response categories for a fixed θ equals 1.0.

CONCEPTUAL ESTIMATION OF THE RS MODEL

The formulae for the RS model estimation may be found in Andrich (1978c). As is the case with the PC and Rasch models, the principle of maximizing a likelihood function is used. Two common approaches that can be used to obtain the parameter estimates are JMLE (UCON) (see Chapter 3) and MMLE (see Chapter 4). For estimation purposes, a person's observed score (i.e., the simple unweighted sum across items of the number of thresholds passed) is a sufficient statistic for estimating the person's location on the continuum. As is the case with the other members of the Rasch family, individuals who obtain the same observed score have the same location on the continuum. Furthermore, the item score (i.e., the unweighted sum of responses across people) is a sufficient statistic for estimating the item j's location, δ_j. As a result, for the RS model items that have the same item score have the same location. With respect to the category coefficient, the total number of responses with respect to all respondents and all items that are associated with category x is a sufficient statistic for estimating the corresponding κ_x (Andrich, 1978c). One implication of a common set of thresholds across items is that the thresholds need only be estimated once for an item set.

EXAMPLE: APPLICATION OF THE RS MODEL TO AN ATTITUDES TOWARDS CONDOMS SCALE, JMLE

The example's data come from the Voluntary HIV Counseling and Testing Efficacy Study performed by the Center for AIDS Prevention Studies (2003). This study was concerned with the effectiveness of HIV counseling and testing for the prevention of new HIV infections. As part of this study, respondents were surveyed about their attitudes toward condoms. Six items from the survey are used in this example. The six items are statements people had made about condoms. Respondents were asked how much they agreed with each of the statements on a 4-point response scale (1="strongly disagree," 2="disagree more than I agree," 3="agree more than I disagree," 4="strongly agree").[11] Given the ("negative") wording of the statements, a respondent who strongly agreed with a statement was indicating a less favorable attitude toward condom use. We assume that we have evidence supporting the tenability of a unidimensional latent space. This evidence might be obtained, for example, through the factor analysis of a polychoric item correlation matrix; SAS's `plcorr` keyword with `proc freq` can be used to obtain these coefficients. As mentioned above, the validity of the measures provides additional information concerning this assumption.

Among other programs, BIGSTEPS, WINSTEPS, and PARSCALE can be used to obtain item parameter estimates for the RS model. For pedagogical reasons we use BIGSTEPS for obtaining the parameter estimates for the Attitude Toward Condoms scale. Because this example builds on the program's features that are introduced in Chapter 3, we now focus on new aspects of the output. (On the author's website is the output from the analyis of these data using the generalized rating scale model and PARSCALE.)

Table 7.3 contains the command file for specifying the BIGSTEPS calibration of the Attitude Toward Condoms scale. The layout of this file is similar to that shown in Chapter 3; however, with this example we introduce user-specified item labeling. Specifically, the items' text is paraphrased to be used as the items' labels. The CODES line specifies the observed response values of 1 through 4, and MODELS=R specifies our model.

Table 7.4 shows that PROX and UCON converged; PROX iterated 4 times and UCON iterated 19 times. By looking at the PROX iteration history we see that 219 respondents were dropped from the analysis. Inspection of the data shows that 119 of these individuals responded "strongly disagree" to all items (i.e., all 1s) and the remaining 100 responded "strongly agree" to each item (i.e., all 4s).

Because our calibration involves a polytomous model, the CONVERGENCE TABLE contains information not seen in Chapter 3 (cf. Table 3.3). For instance, the Max Logit Change columns now contain information not only about persons (MEASURES), but also about items (STEPS). This additional item information is due to the model's transition locations. In a well-behaved situation the values in both MEASURES and STEPS should decrease with increasing iterations. In this example both of these show this decrease. The CATEGORY RESIDUAL and STEP CHANGE columns indicate the difference between the observed and expected count for any category and the maximum logit change, respectively. The CATEGORY RESIDUAL and STEP CHANGE are expected, as they do here, to decrease across iterations. In addition to information indicating the person (CASE) and item (ITEM) that are farthest from meeting the convergence criterion, we have information about the ordinal position of the response category, CAT, that is farthest from meeting the criterion. As stated in Chapter 3, if the standardized residuals have a mean close to zero with a standard deviation (i.e., S.D.) of approximately 1.0, then this indicates that the data are following Rasch model assumptions. If the mean and SD are substantially different from 0 and 1, respectively, then there is a departure from the assumption that randomness is normally distributed and this affects the fit statistics.

Table 7.5 shows a BIGSTEPS table not presented in Chapter 3, the Item-Person Map

TABLE 7.3. BIGSTEPS Command File for RS Model Calibration of the Attitude Towards Condoms Scale

```
;RS Calibration of Attitude Towards Condoms data
&INST
TITLE='Attitude Towards Condoms'
NI=6
ITEM1=5
CATEGS=4
XWIDE=1
CODES=1234
NCOLS=10
MISSING=8
MODELS=R
CURVES=111
CATREF=0
STBIAS=Y
TABLES=1110011001001000100000
NORMAL=Y
NAME1=1
PERSON=CASE                      ⇐ person label[a]
ITEM=item                        ⇐ general item label
PFILE=HIV00COM.PF
IFILE=HIV00COM.IF
&END
EMBARRASS BUY CONDOM             ⇐ item label for item 1
CONDOM NOT GOOD FEEL             ⇐ item label for item 2
EMBARRASS TO PUT ON CONDOM       :
CONDOMS BREAK/SLIP OFF           :
PARTNER WANTS CONDOM CHEAT       :
FRIENDS CONDOM UNCOMFORTABLE     ⇐ item label for item 6
END NAMES
```

[a]The text following the ⇐ is provided to help the reader understand the corresponding input.

(also known as a Variable Map). The Item-Person Map shows how the distributions of respondents and items relate to one another. Because persons and items are located on the same continuum, the term MEASURE refers to either $\hat\theta$ or $\hat\delta$. The numerical demarcations indicate logits. The left side of the leftmost panel shows the distribution of respondents (symbolized by either "#" or a "."; at the bottom of the table the legend indicates that each "#" represents 30 individuals, and each "." indicates from 1 to 29 persons). Respondents who were likely to "strongly agree" to the items are located toward the top of this distribution, whereas those who were likely to "strongly disagree" are located toward the bottom of the table's left panel. Given the negative wording of the items, the top represents a less favorable attitude toward condom use and the bottom reflects a positive attitude toward condom use. As can be seen, the majority of individuals tend to fall between 0.0 and the positive attitude toward condom use end of the continuum.

The next three panels show how the items' (transition) locations relate to the person distribution. Each item's location is symbolized by an X. The first item panel (labeled ITEMS BOTTOM) "locates" the items by using the inflexion point of the IRF corresponding to the bottommost category (i.e., the "strongly disagree" category), the second item panel (labeled ITEMS CENTER) shows the location of the items at the center of the rating scale (i.e., where

TABLE 7.4. Abridged Program Control Parameters (Table 0.1) and Iteration History Table (Table 0.2)

```
TABLE 0.1 Attitude Towards Condoms
-------------------------------------------------------------------------------

        TITLE= Attitude Towards Condoms
CONTROL FILE: condom.con
 OUTPUT FILE: condom.lis

CONTROL VARIABLES:
Input Data Format      PAIRED = N              Item Delete/Anchor
  DATA =               REALSE = N              IDFILE =
 NAME1 = 1             STBIAS = Y              IDELQU = N
NAMLEN = 4             ---------------         IAFILE =
 ITEM1 = 5             Misfit Selection        IANCHQ = N
 ITLEN = 30             FITI = 2.000           ---------------
   NI = 6               FITP = 2.000           Person Delete/Anchor
 XWIDE = 1             OUTFIT = Y              PDFILE =
 INUMB = N             LOCAL = N              PDELQU = N
:
PERSON = CASE                                  RFILE =
 ASCII = Y             ---------------         SFILE =
---------------        Convergence Control     XFILE =
User Scaling           MPROX = 10             ---------------
 UMEAN = .000          MUCON = 0               Data Reformat
USCALE = 1.000         LCONV = .010            FORMAT =
UDECIM = 2             RCONV = .500            GRPFRM = N
 UANCH = Y             TARGET = N              KEYFRM = 0
---------------        ---------------         MODFRM = N
Adjustment             Scale Structure         RESFRM = N
EXTRSC = .500          GROUPS =                SPFILE =
 HIADJ = .250          MODELS = R             ---------------
LOWADJ = .250          STKEEP = N
 3473 CASE   Records Input
```

```
-------------------------------------------------------------------------------
                            CONVERGENCE TABLE
+-----------------------------------------------------------------------------+
|   PROX         ACTIVE COUNT       EXTREME 5 RANGE     MAX LOGIT CHANGE       |
| ITERATION   CASES   ITEMS   CATS    CASES   ITEMS     MEASURES    STEPS      |
|  ---------------------------------------------------------------------------  |
|        1     3473     6      5      4.23     .73        3.1355   1.1028      |
|        2     3373     6      4      5.86    1.16       -2.0426   -.5026      |
|        3     3254     6      4      6.15    1.28        -.1464   -.1740      |
|        4     3254     6      4      6.26    1.30        -.0519   -.0291      |
|  ---------------------------------------------------------------------------  |
|   UCON      MAX SCORE   MAX LOGIT   LEAST CONVERGED    CATEGORY    STEP       |
| ITERATION   RESIDUAL*    CHANGE    CASE   ITEM    CAT  RESIDUAL   CHANGE      |
|  ---------------------------------------------------------------------------  |
|        1     543.93     .9585       3     3*     1    -445.05    .1709       |
|        2     367.56     .2833     562     3*     4     366.01    .0854       |
|        3     257.23    -.1632      37     3*     4     388.41    .1430       |
|        4     217.48    -.1456      18     3*     4     216.10   -.0637       |
|        5     157.73    -.0920      18     3*     4     149.73   -.0423       |
|        6     108.77    -.0597      18     3*     4      99.81   -.0274       |
|        7      72.83    -.0386      18     3*     4      64.54   -.0177       |
|        8      47.98    -.0249      18     3*     4      40.99    .0115       |
|        9      31.30    -.0160      18     3*     4      25.59    .0079       |
|       10      20.17    -.0101      18     3*     4      16.19    .0059       |
|       11      12.91    -.0063      18     3*     4      10.30    .0038       |
|       12       8.20     .0040     695     3*     4       6.87    .0020       |
|       13       5.33    -.0026      18     3*     4       4.66   -.0013       |
|       14       3.49    -.0018      18     3*     4       3.13   -.0009       |
|       15       2.23    -.0012      18     3*     4       1.86   -.0005       |
|       16       1.43    -.0007      18     3*     4       1.08    .0003       |
|       17        .92    -.0005      18     3*     4        .85    .0002       |
|       18        .59    -.0003      18     3*     4        .53    .0002       |
|       19        .39    -.0002      18     3*     4        .31    .0001       |
+-----------------------------------------------------------------------------+
Standardized Residuals N(0,1)  Mean: -.02 S.D.: 1.01
```

TABLE 7.5. RS (BIGSTEPS) Item-Person Map for the Attitude Towards Condoms Scale

```
TABLE 1.1 Attitude Towards Condoms FIFTEEN SUBPARTS
INPUT: 3473 CASES, 6 ITEMS  ANALYZED: 3254 CASES, 6 ITEMS, 4 CATS
------------------------------------------------------------------------
                      MAP OF CASES    AND ITEMS
 MEASURE            |            P=50%|           P=50%|        P=50% MEASURE
 <more> ------CASES -+-ITEMS BOTTOM+-ITEMS CENTER+-ITEMS  TOP -- <rare>
  2.0         .### +           +              +               2.0
                  |            |              |
             .#   |            |              |
:                 |            |              |
             ##   |            |              |
                  |            |              |
  1.0           + |           +              + X             1.0
             .#### |            |              X
                  |            |              |
             .##   |            |              |
                  |            |         X    |
             .###  |            |         X    |
            .######## |         |              |
            .###### |          |              X
            .###### | X        |              |
                  | X         |             XX
  .0  .############ +         +              +               .0
            .######## |        | X           |
                  |          |            X
           .######### |        | XX         |
                  |          |              |
         .############ | X     |            |
            .######## |        | X          |
                  | XX       |              |
            .###### |         |              |
                  |          |              |
            .######## | X      |             |
 -1.0           + |           +              +              -1.0
                  |            |              |
             .#### |            |              |
                  |            |              |
:                 |            |              |
                  |            |              |
             .##   |            |              |
                  |            |              |
:                 |            |              |
 -2.0        .### +           +              +              -2.0
  <less> ------CASES -+-ITEMS BOTTOM+-ITEMS CENTER+-ITEMS  TOP -- <frequ>
   EACH '#' IN THE CASE  COLUMN IS  30 CASES ; EACH '.' IS 1 TO  29 CASES
```

responding in the top and bottom categories is equally probable [Linacre & Wright, 2001]), and the third (rightmost) item panel (labeled ITEMS TOP) "locates" the items by using the inflexion point of the IRF of the topmost category (i.e., "strongly agree"); the location of the inflexion point (i.e., p = 0.5) does not necessarily correspond to δ_{jh}. As a result, with the RS model the topmost X in each panel reflects the same item (i.e., the topmost Xs in the first, second, and third panels may be connected by a diagonal line to represent the item). Similarly, the second to the top X in each panel represents another item, and the second to the top X in each panel may be connected by another diagonal line to represent this item, and so on for the remaining four items on the scale. For instance, the topmost X in each panel represents item 3, the second to the topmost X in each panel represents item 2, and the bottommost X in each panel reflects item 6; the identification of which X represents which item comes from the output discussed below. Figure 7.12 shows how these X locations for the ITEMS BOTTOM and ITEMS TOP relate to item 6's ORFs. The ITEMS BOTTOM and ITEMS TOP locations are sometimes called category boundaries (Masters, 1982).

By comparing the item locations to the person distribution one can obtain an idea of how well the items are functioning in measuring the people. For example, we see from the lowest X in the rightmost panel that roughly half the respondents (i.e., people located slightly below 0.0 and above) have a probability of at least 0.5 of responding in the "strongly agree" category for item 6. Conversely, there are more than 270 persons with locations of about –1 or less who have a probability of at least 0.5 of responding in the item's "strongly disagree" category (i.e., the lowest location X in the first item panel). It can be seen from Table 7.5 that, given the distribution of respondents, the items (collectively) cover most

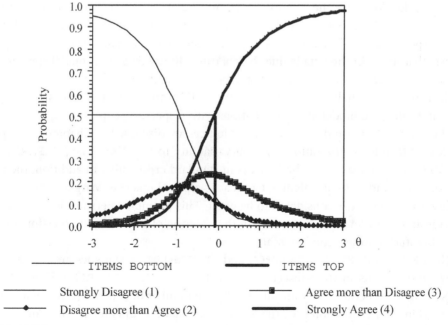

FIGURE 7.12. RS model ORFs for item 6 with ITEMS BOTTOM and ITEMS TOP locations identified.

of the attitudinal range where people are located. Moreover, it may be anticipated that the range of attitude will facilitate the estimation the item δ_{jh}s. In short, this table not only allows one to see how well the respondents' distribution matches the range of the instrument, but also provides an idea of how well the items are distributed. Using this information one may anticipate where on the θ continuum one may experience greater difficulty in estimating person as well as item locations.

Table 7.6 (BIGSTEPS' TABLE 3.1) shows descriptive statistics for the calibration as well as information about how well the test separates the respondents' measures. Recall from our Chapter 3 discussion of this table that the top half of the table presents summary information on the respondents, whereas the bottom half presents summary information on the items.

In the top half (i.e., SUMMARY OF ... CASES) we see descriptive statistics on the observed score (labeled RAW SCORE). Because the observed score, X, is the sum of the item responses and we have six four-category items, the range of X is from 6 to 24 (i.e., 6 * 1 = 6 and 6 * 4 = 24, where 1 = strongly disagree, 4 = strongly agree). The mean observed score for the 3254 NON-EXTREME respondents is 14.1 with a range from 7 to 23.

We know from the iteration history (see Table 7.4) that only 3254 of the 3473 respondents persons are used in the calibration. We now see that of the 3473 respondents 100 obtained the MAXIMUM EXTREME SCORE of 24 and 119 persons obtained the MINIMUM EXTREME SCORE of 6; these 219 respondents are considered EXTREME CASES. The columns labeled MEASURE and MODEL ERROR refer to $\hat{\theta}$ and its standard error, respectively. Therefore, across the 3254 persons the mean person location estimate is –0.16 with a standard deviation 0.64, and the smallest and the largest $\hat{\theta}$s are –1.71 and 1.78, respectively. In general, individuals tend to be slightly favorably predisposed toward condom use.

We would like to see the INFIT MNSQ and OUTFIT MNSQ values be close to 1 (or 0 for the INFIT ZSTD and OUTFIT ZSTD).[12] At the model level we have model fit with respect to persons. Recall that the REAL RMSE is the root mean squared error calculated on the basis that misfit in the data is due to departures in the data from model specifications, whereas MODEL RMSE is the same statistic, but calculated on the basis that the data fit the model. In the person half of TABLE 3.1 the RMSEs are calculated across people. Small RMSEs indicate good model–data fit situations with respect to people.

The SEPARATION and RELIABILITY indices are discussed in Chapter 3. The person SEPARATION index is the ratio of person variability to the RMSE (i.e., SEPARATION = ADJ.SD/RMSE) and, as such, the index is in standard error units. In addition, the person RELIABILITY index is equivalent to Cronbach's alpha (Linacre & Wright, 2001), with values close to or equal to 1 considered to be good. This example's person RELIABILITY of 0.44 indicates a low level of consistency in the ordering of person location estimates across different attitudes toward condom scales.

The RMSE, ADJ.SD, SEPARATION and RELIABILITY statistics are repeated using all 3473 respondents in the subsection entitled WITH ... EXTREME CASES. These results are ignored because they are affected by the number of extreme respondents and the value used in their estimation (i.e., the EXTRSC estimation adjustment criterion).

The bottom half of TABLE 3.1 (SUMMARY OF ... ITEMS) contains the same statistical indices as used for describing the respondents, but now focused on the items. The

TABLE 7.6. RS (BIGSTEPS): Calibration Results—Overall

```
TABLE 3.1 Attitude Towards Condoms
INPUT: 3473 CASES, 6 ITEMS  ANALYZED: 3254 CASES, 6 ITEMS, 4 CATS
```

SUMMARY OF 3254 MEASURED (NON-EXTREME) CASES

	RAW SCORE	COUNT	MEASURE	MODEL ERROR	INFIT MNSQ	ZSTD	OUTFIT MNSQ	ZSTD
MEAN	14.1	6.0	-.16	.43	1.00	.0	1.01	.0
S.D.	3.9	.0	.64	.10	.57	1.1	.76	1.1
MAX.	23.0	6.0	1.78	.88	3.25	5.3	6.04	6.1
MIN.	7.0	6.0	-1.71	.37	.03	-2.2	.03	-2.0

```
REAL RMSE   .48 ADJ.SD   .43 SEPARATION  .89 CASE  RELIABILITY  .44
MODEL RMSE  .44 ADJ.SD   .47 SEPARATION 1.08 CASE  RELIABILITY  .54
S.E. OF CASE   MEAN    .01
WITH   219 EXTREME CASES   = 3473 CASES   MEAN   -.16  S.D.    .85
REAL RMSE   .56 ADJ.SD   .63 SEPARATION 1.12 CASE  RELIABILITY  .55
MODEL RMSE  .53 ADJ.SD   .66 SEPARATION 1.24 CASE  RELIABILITY  .61
```

```
MAXIMUM EXTREME SCORE:  100 CASES
MINIMUM EXTREME SCORE:  119 CASES
```

SUMMARY OF   6 MEASURED ITEMS

	RAW SCORE	COUNT	MEASURE	MODEL ERROR	INFIT MNSQ	ZSTD	OUTFIT MNSQ	ZSTD
MEAN	7622.8	3254.0	.00	.02	1.00	.0	1.01	.8
S.D.	1425.7	.0	.42	.00	.05	2.4	.09	2.8
MAX.	9465.0	3254.0	.62	.02	1.10	4.9	1.12	4.5
MIN.	5573.0	3254.0	-.54	.02	.95	-2.4	.89	-2.8

```
REAL RMSE   .02 ADJ.SD   .42 SEPARATION 23.86 ITEM  RELIABILITY 1.00
MODEL RMSE  .02 ADJ.SD   .42 SEPARATION 24.06 ITEM  RELIABILITY 1.00
S.E. OF ITEM   MEAN    .19
```

columns labeled MEASURE and MODEL ERROR refer to the $\hat{\delta}$s and their standard errors. As would be expected from a program that uses item centering, the mean $\hat{\delta}$ is 0 with a standard deviation of 0.42. The minimum $\hat{\delta}$ is –0.54 and the maximum $\hat{\delta}$ is 0.62. Although not indicated in this table, in Table 7.8 (BIGSTEPS' TABLE 10.1) we see that the minimum $\hat{\delta}$ is item 6, whereas the maximum is item 3's $\hat{\delta}$. The results indicate that, overall, there is model–data fit from an item perspective (INFIT MNSQ and OUTFIT MNSQ), that there is little error in the estimation (REAL RMSE and MODEL RMSE), and that we have a good item RELIABILITY value indicating that the instrument is creating a well-defined variable.

Table 7.7 contains item threshold-level calibration information and summary information about the response categories. The CATEGORY LABEL column contains the CODES labels, where 1 = "strongly disagree," 2 = "disagree more than I agree," 3 = "agree more than I disagree," and 4 = "strongly agree." For each category the sum across items of the number of persons responding in each category is presented in the OBSERVED COUNT column (e.g., for CATEGORY LABEL 1, the OBSERVED COUNT is the sum of the frequency of 1 across all 6 items). The AVERAGE MEASURE and its EXPected value are defined in the table's legend, where Bn is the person location estimate, $\hat{\theta}$, and Di is the item location estimates, $\hat{\delta}$s.

TABLE 7.7. RS (BIGSTEPS) Calibration Summary Results for the Attitude Towards Condoms Scale

```
TABLE 3.2 Attitude Towards Condoms
INPUT: 3473 CASES, 6 ITEMS  ANALYZED: 3254 CASES, 6 ITEMS, 4 CATS
-------------------------------------------------------------------------


SUMMARY OF MEASURED STEPS
+----------------------------------------------------------------------+
|CATEGORY OBSERVED|AVERAGE EXP.| COHERENCE|INFIT OUTFIT| STEP     |
| LABEL    COUNT  | MEASURE    | EXP% OBS%| MNSQ  MNSQ |CALIBRATN |
|-----------------+------------+----------+------------+--------- |
|    1      8004  | -.67  -.65 | 85%  39% | .99   1.07 | NONE     |
|    2      2608  | -.24  -.29 | 18%  52% | 1.00   .99 | .65      |
|    3      3131  |  .13   .07 | 23%  48% | .86    .83 | -.29*    |
|    4      5781  |  .41   .44 | 71%  22% | 1.04  1.03 | -.36*    |
+----------------------------------------------------------------------+
AVERAGE MEASURE is mean of (Bn-Di), EXP. is expected value.
EXP% = (expected & observed)/(all expected) [MEASURE->RATING?]
OBS% = (expected & observed)/(all observed) [RATING->MEASURE?]


+----------------------------------------------------------+
|CATEGORY    STEP    STEP | SCORE-TO-MEASURE |THURSTONE |
| LABEL    CALIBRATN S.E. | AT CAT. ----ZONE----|THRESHOLD |
|-------------------------+------------------+--------- |
|    1      NONE          |( -1.31) -INF   -.85|          |
|    2       .65     .02  |  -.37   -.85   -.02| -.38     |
|    3      -.29     .02  |   .33   -.02    .84| -.05     |
|    4      -.36     .02  |( 1.34)   .84   +INF|  .40     |
+----------------------------------------------------------+
```

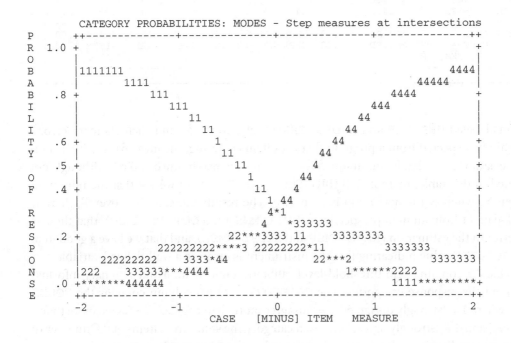

This AVERAGE MEASURE column shows that, on average, as one progresses from "strongly disagree" to "strongly agree" there is an increase in the respondents' (less positive) attitudes toward condom use.

The COHERENCE EXP% and COHERENCE OBS% are ratios focused on the degree of agreement between what is observed for a response category and what would be expected for that category. In this situation, 100% represents the best-case scenario and values less than 50% are considered to be "inferential insecure" (Linacre & Wright, 2001). These ratios differ from one another only in their respective denominators. For both indices the numerators reflect the number of times an observation and its expectation fell within the same response category. For COHERENCE EXP% a response category's count is divided by all *expectations* in the response category, whereas for COHERENCE OBS% a response category's count is divided by all *observations* in the response category. Linacre and Wright (2001) state that COHERENCE EXP% assesses the extent that measures corresponding to a response category predict ratings in it. In contrast, COHERENCE OBS% is concerned with the extent to which ratings in a response category predict measures corresponding to it. It can be seen that the "strongly disagree" and "strongly agree" response categories do a good job of predicting the ratings within them (COHERENCE EXP%), whereas the "disagree more than I agree" and "agree more than I disagree" ratings do comparatively better in predicting the measures corresponding a response category (COHERENCE OBS%) than vice versa. The INFIT MNSQ and OUTFIT MNSQ values for the items are relatively close to or equal to their expected value of 1, indicating consistency between the data and the RS model. That is, a common set of thresholds (τ_hs) for the entire item set appears to be appropriate.

The STEP CALIBRATION column contains the estimated transition location for the category of interest *relative* to the transition location from the category below the one of interest. For example, assume that the category of interest is "disagree more than I agree." Therefore, the transition from "strongly disagree" to "disagree more than I agree" occurs at the relative position of 0.65; the lowest category, 1 ("strongly disagree"), has no *prior* transition location and is shown as NONE. The transition from "disagree more than I agree" to "agree more than I disagree" occurs at the relative position of –0.29, and the last transition from "agree more than I disagree" to "strongly agree" occurs at the relative position of –0.36. Therefore, the estimates of the τs are $\hat{\tau}_1 = 0.65$, $\hat{\tau}_2 = -0.29$, and $\hat{\tau}_3 = -0.36$, each with a $s_e(\hat{\tau}_h)$ of 0.02. To determine the actual, not relative, location on the continuum of the transition from, say, "strongly disagree" to "disagree more than I agree" for a particular item, would require also knowing the item's location; this is demonstrated below. As we would expect, the sum of the $\hat{\tau}$s is 0.0. As we see, the differences between successive $\hat{\tau}$s are not equal (i.e., $|\hat{\tau}_1 - \hat{\tau}_2| \neq |\hat{\tau}_2 - \hat{\tau}_3|$).

The τs are expected to increase across the response categories and when there is a reversal in their order, as with categories 3 and 4, they are flagged with an "*". A reversal indicates that the corresponding category is not as likely to be chosen as the other categories. In this case, given the number of reversals relative to the number of response categories, these items are behaving primarily in a dichotomous, not polytomous, fashion. Given these $\hat{\tau}$s, it is not surprising that the CATEGORY PROBABILITIES plot shows that persons responding to these items are primarily using just the "strongly disagree" and "strongly agree" response categories. For completeness, the THURSTONE THRESHOLD indicates the location of the

TABLE 7.8. RS (BIGSTEPS) Item Location Estimates for the Attitude Towards Condoms Scale

```
TABLE 10.1 Attitude Towards Condoms
INPUT: 3473 CASES, 6 ITEMS  ANALYZED: 3254 CASES, 6 ITEMS, 4 CATS
-------------------------------------------------------------------------------
           ITEMS STATISTICS:  MISFIT ORDER
+-----------------------------------------------------------------------------+
|ENTRY  RAW                       | INFIT  | OUTFIT |PTBIS|                     |
|NUMBR  SCORE  COUNT  MEASURE  ERROR|MNSQ ZSTD|MNSQ ZSTD|CORR.| ITEMS          |
|----------------------------------+---------+---------+-----+-----------------|
|    5   8444   3254    -.25    .02|1.10  4.9|1.12  4.5|A .23| PARTNER WANTS CONDOM CHEAT |
|    4   8585   3254    -.29    .02|1.02   .9|1.11  3.9|B .17| CONDOMS BREAK/SLIP OFF     |
|    6   9465   3254    -.54    .02| .95 -2.4|1.05  1.7|C .21| FRIENDS CONDOM UNCOMFORTABLE|
|    1   7773   3254    -.06    .02| .97 -1.3| .99  -.4|c .27| CONDOM NOT GOOD FEEL       |
|    3   5573   3254     .62    .02| .98  -.9| .91 -2.2|b .34| EMBARRASS TO PUT ON CONDOM |
|    2   5897   3254     .51    .02| .97 -1.2| .89 -2.8|a .34| EMBARRASS BUY CONDOM       |
|----------------------------------+---------+---------+-----+-----------------|
| MEAN  7623.  3254.     .00    .02|1.00   .0|1.01   .8|     |                  |
| S.D.  1426.     0.     .42    .00| .05  2.4| .09  2.8|     |                  |
+-----------------------------------------------------------------------------+


TABLE 10.2 Attitude Towards Condoms
INPUT: 3473 CASES, 6 ITEMS  ANALYZED: 3254 CASES, 6 ITEMS, 4 CATS
-------------------------------------------------------------------------------
           ITEMS FIT GRAPH:  MISFIT ORDER
+-----------------------------------------------------------------------------+
|ENTRY| MEASURE | INFIT MEAN-SQUARE | OUTFIT MEAN-SQUARE |                     |
|NUMBR|  -   + |0    0.7 1 1.3    2|0    0.7 1 1.3    2| ITEMS                |
|-----+--------+--------------------+--------------------+---------------------|
|   5 |*       |         :  * :     |A    :  .* :        | PARTNER WANTS CONDOM CHEAT |
|   4 |*       |         :  * :     |B    :  .* :        | CONDOMS BREAK/SLIP OFF     |
|   6 |*       |         : *. :     |C    :  *  :        | FRIENDS CONDOM UNCOMFORTABLE|
|   1 |  *     |         : *. :     |c    :  *. :        | CONDOM NOT GOOD FEEL       |
|   3 |      * |         : *. :     |b    :  *. :        | EMBARRASS TO PUT ON CONDOM |
|   2 |     *  |         : *. :     |a    :*  . :        | EMBARRASS BUY CONDOM       |
+-----------------------------------------------------------------------------+


TABLE 10.3 Attitude Towards Condoms
INPUT: 3473 CASES, 6 ITEMS  ANALYZED: 3254 CASES, 6 ITEMS, 4 CATS
-------------------------------------------------------------------------------
           ITEMS OPTION/DISTRACTOR FREQUENCIES:  MISFIT ORDER
+-----------------------------------------------------------------------------+
|  NUM NONMISS|MISSING R% SCR|   1   % SCR |   2   % SCR |   3   % SCR |
|             |       4   % SCR|           |             |             |
|-------------+--------------+-------------+-------------+-------------|
|  5A   3473  |    0   0  **| 1243  35   1 |  380  10   2 |  440  12   3 |
|             | 1410  40   4|             |             |             |
|  4B   3473  |    0   0  **|  956  27   1 |  596  17   2 |  728  20   3 |
|             | 1193  34   4|             |             |             |
|  6C   3473  |    0   0  **|  744  21   1 |  451  12   2 |  774  22   3 |
|             | 1504  43   4|             |             |             |
|  1D   3473  |    0   0  **| 1338  38   1 |  492  14   2 |  602  17   3 |
|             | 1041  29   4|             |             |             |
|  3E   3473  |    0   0  **| 2280  65   1 |  344   9   2 |  272   7   3 |
|             |  577  16   4|             |             |             |
|  2F   3473  |    0   0 ·**| 2157  62   1 |  345   9   2 |  315   9   3 |
|             |  656  18   4|             |             |             |
+-----------------------------------------------------------------------------+


TABLE 10.4 Attitude Towards Condoms
INPUT: 3473 CASES, 6 ITEMS  ANALYZED: 3254 CASES, 6 ITEMS, 4 CATS
-------------------------------------------------------------------------------
MOST MISFITTING RESPONSE STRINGS
ITEM               OUTMNSQ |CASE
                           |33333333333333332222222222222111  33221  22211
                           |30444433222221097665543110920960041494110446553 42
                           |85430076988620802636164849072224178924957646970224
                           |05515233886758140573163768306787671441040776979582
                      high-------------------------------------------------------
   5 PARTNER WANTS    1.12 A|..11.11..1.1..1111.11.111.1..1....................
   4 CONDOMS BREAK    1.11 B|........11....11....1..1....1.1..................
   6 FRIENDS CONDO    1.05 C|22..1..1..1.......................1.1111..........
   3 EMBARRASS TO      .91 b|.......................................44444.44.4..
   2 EMBARRASS BUY     .89 a|...............................4444......4..4.33
                           -------------------------------------------------low
                           |33333333333333332222222222222211196332219422116553242
                           |30444433222221097665543110920220041424110446970524
                           |85430076988620802636164849072784178941957646979 82
                           |05515233886758140573163768306  76714  04077
```

TABLE 7.8. *cont.*

```
TABLE 10.5 Attitude Towards Condoms
INPUT: 3473 CASES, 6 ITEMS  ANALYZED: 3254 CASES, 6 ITEMS, 4 CATS
------------------------------------------------------------------------
MOST UNEXPECTED RESPONSES
ITEM                    MEASURE |CASE
                                |33333333333333322222222222111  33221  22211
                                |30444433222221097665543110920960041494110446553 42
                                |85430076988620802636164849072224178924957646970224
                                |05515233886758140573163768306787671441040776979582
                        high----------------------------------------------------
      6 FRIENDS CONDO   -.54 C|22..1..1..1...........1.1111................
      4 CONDOMS BREAK   -.29 B|........1...11....1..1...1.1...............
      5 PARTNER WANTS   -.25 A|..11.11..1.1..1111.11.111.1..1.............
      2 EMBARRASS BUY    .51 a|................................4444.....4..4.33
      3 EMBARRASS TO     .62 b|..................................44444.44.4..
                              |----------------------------------------------low
                              |33333333333333322222222222111196332219422211 6553242
                              |30444433222221097665543110920202200414241104 46970524
                              |85430076988620802636164849072784178941957646979 82
                              |0551523388675814057316376 8306  76714  04077
```

```
TABLE 13.1 Attitude Towards Condoms
INPUT: 3473 CASES, 6 ITEMS  ANALYZED: 3254 CASES, 6 ITEMS, 4 CATS
------------------------------------------------------------------------
        ITEMS STATISTICS:  MEASURE ORDER
+--------------------------------------------------------------------------------+
|ENTRY  RAW                    |   INFIT  |  OUTFIT  |PTBIS|                       |
|NUMBR  SCORE  COUNT MEASURE ERROR|MNSQ ZSTD|MNSQ ZSTD|CORR.| ITEMS                 |
|------------------------------+---------+---------+-----+-----------------------|
|    3  5573  3254    .62   .02| .98  -.9| .91 -2.2| .34 | EMBARRASS TO PUT ON CONDOM|
|    2  5897  3254    .51   .02| .97 -1.2| .89 -2.8| .34 | EMBARRASS BUY CONDOM      |
|    1  7773  3254   -.06   .02| .97 -1.3| .99  -.4| .27 | CONDOM NOT GOOD FEEL      |
|    5  8444  3254   -.25   .02|1.10  4.9|1.12  4.5| .23 | PARTNER WANTS CONDOM CHEAT|
|    4  8585  3254   -.29   .02|1.02   .9|1.11  3.9| .17 | CONDOMS BREAK/SLIP OFF    |
|    6  9465  3254   -.54   .02| .95 -2.4|1.05  1.7| .21 | FRIENDS CONDOM UNCOMFORTABLE|
|------------------------------+---------+---------+-----+-----------------------|
|MEAN 7623. 3254.     .00   .02|1.00   .0|1.01   .8|     |                       |
|S.D. 1426.    0.     .42   .00| .05  2.4| .09  2.8|     |                       |
+--------------------------------------------------------------------------------+
```

median probability. That is, at these locations the probability of observing the categories below equals the probability of observing the categories equal to or above. This is the point on the variable at which the category interval begins (Linacre & Wright, 2001).

The $\hat{\delta}$s are presented in BIGSTEPS' TABLE 10.1:ITEMS STATISTICS:MISFIT ORDER (see Table 7.8); TABLE 13.1 presents the same information as TABLE 10.1, but in descending order of $\hat{\delta}$. Because the output is presented in misfit (MNSQ) order, we need to examine the ENTRY NUMBR column to determine the item number for a given $\hat{\delta}_j$ (labeled MEASURE). As can be seen, item 1 is located at $\hat{\delta}_1 = -0.06$ with an $s_e(\hat{\delta}_1) = 0.02$, item 2 is located at $(\hat{\delta}_2) = 0.51$ with an $s_e(\hat{\delta}_2) = 0.02$, and so on. As we would expect from an item-centering approach, the mean $\hat{\delta}$ is (approximately) 0.0.

By combining the $\hat{\tau}$s from BIGSTEPS' TABLE 3.2 with the $\hat{\delta}$s we can calculate the $\hat{\delta}_{jh}$s as well as produce the items' ORFs. For example, for item 1 the transition from "strongly disagree" to "disagree more than I agree" is

$$\hat{\delta}_{11} = \hat{\delta}_1 + \hat{\tau}_1 = -0.06 + 0.65 = 0.59$$

the transition from "disagree more than I agree" to "agree more than I disagree" occurs at

$$\hat{\delta}_{12} = \hat{\delta}_1 + \hat{\tau}_2 = -0.06 + (-0.29) = -0.35$$

and the transition from "agree more than I disagree" to "strongly disagree" has a location for item 1 at

$$\hat{\delta}_{13} = \hat{\delta}_1 + \hat{\tau}_3 = -0.06 + (-0.36) = -0.42$$

Figure 7.13 contains the ORFs for item 1 based on these intersection points. As can be seen, the interpretation of the CATEGORY PROBABILITIES from TABLE 3.2 applies to the ORFs for item 1; this is also the interpretation for all the items.

The items' INFIT MNSQ and OUTFIT MNSQ values are provided in this table, although the corresponding graphical presentation (TABLE 10.2) is easier to interpret. The interpretation of these indices is discussed in Chapter 3. From the information presented in TABLE 10.1 and TABLE 10.2 we conclude that the items are behaving in a fashion consistent with the model.

With polytomous data it is useful to produce TABLE 10.3 because it provides a breakdown of the respondents' use of each response category for each item. This information is useful for diagnosing estimation problems and/or for identifying items that should be rewritten. As is the case with Tables 10.1-10.4, the items are listed in order of their misfit. This table's layout has the item number first (NUM) followed by the number of respondents to the item (NONMISS). The next three columns contain the number of omissions (MISSING), the percentage of omission (R%), and the code (SCR) used to represent missing. The remaining columns present the category frequency, the percentage of respondents in the category, and the code representing the category response for each of the categories. In this example, the information "wraps around" and the fourth response cat-

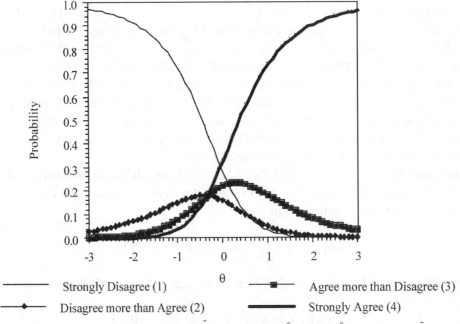

FIGURE 7.13. RS model ORFs for item 1 ($\hat{\delta}_1 = -0.06$ with $\hat{\tau}_1 = 0.65$, $\hat{\tau}_2 = -0.29$, and $\hat{\tau}_3 = -0.36$).

egory is listed in the second panel (i.e., MISSING R% SCR) that contains the missing data information. This is why below the "MISSING R% SCR" label we find the fourth response category's "4 % SCR" label.

Interpreting BIGSTEPS' TABLE 10.3, we have that the first item listed is item 5 and there are 3473 respondents to this item with 0 MISSING and the percentage missing (R% =) is 0%; the "**" indicates that no code is used to represent missing. Of the 3473 respondents, 1243 (% = 35%) responded in the first category (i.e., SCR = 1), 380 (10%) responded in category 2, 440 (12%) responded in category 3, and, wrapping around, 1410 or 40% responded in the fourth category ("strongly agree"). Therefore, each item presented actually occupies two lines in the table. The next item presented is item 4, and its information is listed on the third and fourth lines of the table's body. This pattern is continued for the remaining items.

As we can see, each response category attracted at least 272 respondents. As such, the thresholds should be well estimated. In general, the first and fourth response categories had the largest number of respondents regardless of the item. The only exception to this occurred with item 6 and the "agree more than I disagree" response (category 3). From these frequencies we see that each response category is being used. However, from Figure 7.13 we know that the items are primarily functioning in a dichotomous fashion.

If we had fit problems with one or more items, then BIGSTEPS' TABLE 10.4 and TABLE 10.5 can be useful for diagnostic purposes (TABLE 10.4 differs from TABLE 10.5 in that TABLE 10.4 contains the items in terms of their OUTFIT values, whereas TABLE 10.5 contains the items in terms of their locations). As an example, in TABLE 10.4 the first case listed has the id of #3380 (one reads across the rows within a column of the CASE panel to determine the id code). We know from the person estimates that this respondent is estimated to be located at $\hat\theta_{3380}$ = 1.26 (OUTFIT = 3.66); to save space the estimated person locations output is not shown. This person's response of 2 is the most misfitting response to item 6. Item 6 had an OUTFIT of 1.05 value and is estimated to be located at –0.54. Therefore, given the item and person estimated locations, it is expected that this person would have provided a response of 3 or 4. That is, it is expected that this person, who is located toward the "less favorably predisposed toward condom use" end of the continuum, would have agreed or strongly agreed with the item that condoms are uncomfortable. Instead, this person indicated that he or she disagreed more than agreed with the item. The transition location estimate for "strongly agree" on this item is $\hat\delta_{63} = \hat\delta_6 + \hat\tau_3$ = –0.54 – 0.36 = –0.90 and this is more than 2.1 logits (–90 – 1.26 = –2.16) *below* the person's estimate location. (The next individual listed, #3055, has the same estimated location as #3380.)

The last person in the table, #242, is estimated to be located at $\hat\theta_{242}$ = –1.24 (OUTFIT = 3.38). This person is located toward the "more favorably predisposed toward condom use" end of the continuum. However, he or she provided a response of 3 ("agree more than disagree") to item 2 ($\hat\delta_2$ = 0.51), "It's embarrassing to buy condoms." That is, we expect that this respondent would *not* select the "agree more than disagree" response, given that he or she is located more than two logits below the transition location estimate of ($\hat\delta_{21}$) 1.16. Rather, this person is expected to "strongly disagree" or "disagree" more than "agree" with this item (i.e., to select category 1 or 2).

As discussed above, our model–data fit analysis should include examinations of the invariance and conditional independence assumptions. The invariance procedure presented in Chapter 3 would be applied to the $\hat{\delta}_{jh}$s. In terms of conditional independence one could use Q_3, that is, the correlation between the residuals for a pair of items. With the RS model the residual for an item is the difference between an individual's observed response and the individual's expected (category) response on the item. In our example, the observed responses are 1 through 4, and the expected response is given by the weighted sum of the response category probabilities according to the RS model, that is

$$\mathcal{E}(x_j|\hat{\theta}_i) = \sum_{k=1}^{m+1} k * p(x_j|\hat{\theta}_i)$$

If a 0-based counting system is used (e.g., Dodd, 1990), then

$$\mathcal{E}(x_j|\hat{\theta}_i) = \sum_{k=0}^{m} k * p(x_j|\hat{\theta}_i)$$

The Pearson correlation coefficient would be applied to the residuals for items j and z; $d_{ij} = x_{ij} - \mathcal{E}(x_j|\hat{\theta}_i)$ and $d_{iz} = x_{iz} - \mathcal{E}(x_z|\hat{\theta}_i)$.

Once the researcher achieves satisfactory model–data fit with a scale, the IRT advantages over traditional approaches, such as the capacity to estimate a person's attitude free of a scale's characteristics, are available to the researcher as part of his or her study. In fact, subsequent administrations of the scale do not necessarily require that the new response data be recalibrated to obtain person attitudinal estimates. Instead, one may take advantage of the fact that, with the Rasch family of models, all individuals with the same observed score receive the same $\hat{\theta}$ in order to create a concordance table using the satisfactory calibration results. This table would contain the possible observed scores and their corresponding $\hat{\theta}$s. In this way, subsequent administrations would only require determining the respondent's observed score and then using the table to determine the corresponding $\hat{\theta}$.

HOW LARGE A CALIBRATION SAMPLE?

In contrast to the dichotomous models, the polytomous PC and RS models contain (potentially) more item parameters to estimate. Given these additional item parameters, one might expect that the sample size recommendations for dichotomous models may not apply to polytomous models. Therefore, in the following we discuss some of the relevant research.

Walker-Bartnick (1990) studied the stability of PC model item parameter estimates using MSTEPS. (MSTEPS [Wright, Congdon, & Shultz, 1988] is a precursor to BIGSTEPS and uses JMLE.) She found that a 2:1 or larger ratio of persons to item parameters produced stable item and person parameter estimates, regardless of the number of response categories. Choi, Cook, and Dodd (1997) investigated the parameter recovery for the PC model using MULTILOG (i.e., MMLE) for instruments of varying lengths and two levels of the number of response categories for an item. They suggested that the sample size ratio could be a more complete guideline if it took into account the number of transition locations per item. For instance, although they obtained accurate estimation with a sample size of 250, they recommended that, for a given number of total parameters, the sample size to number of item parameters ratio needed to be larger if there were a large number of response categories than if there were a small number of categories.

With respect to the RS model, French and Dodd (1999) studied how well the item and person parameters were estimated under various sample sizes, θ distributions, and δ distributions. Although they kept instrument length fixed at 30 items, they varied the number of response categories (m = 4 and m = 5). They used PARSCALE (MMLE) for parameter estimation. Consistent with the findings of others (e.g., Reise & Yu, 1990), they found that sample size does not appear to impact the recovery of person locations (i.e., when MMLE is used for estimation). Moreover, with a minimum sample size ratio of approximately 1.8:1 PARSCALE was able to recover the item parameters very well.

Given the foregoing, then, for example, a 30-item instrument with a four-category response scale and using the Walker-Bartnick (1990) 2:1 ratio, we would expect stable results with 180 people (30 items * 3 transition location parameters * 2 = 180). Assuming that the respondents distributed themselves uniformly across the response categories, then a 2:1 ratio would lead to the expectation that each category would have approximately 45 respondents (180 people/4 categories = 45). However, a uniform distribution of individuals across response categories is not likely to occur in practice. Therefore, with smaller samples it is more likely that certain response categories would not have any, or would have a relatively small number of, respondents and, as such, their parameter estimates would be adversely affected. In addition, fit analyses may be adversely affected by smaller sample sizes. For example, fit statistics will have less power and the creation of empirical/predicted ORFs for fit analysis will be problematic with the small sample sizes produced by the above sample size ratios. As mentioned in previous chapters, sample size requirements for the use of ancillary methods is also a consideration. For instance, if factor analysis is used in dimensionality assessment, then its rules of thumb would be a factor determining the calibration sample size.

Because of the interaction of the distribution of the respondents across the response categories, as well as across the items, it is difficult to arrive at a hard-and-fast guideline that would be applicable in all situations. However, this is of little consolation to the practitioner. Therefore, for guidance we provide very rough guidelines. Assuming MMLE, a symmetric θ distribution, and that the respondents distribute themselves across the response categories in reasonable numbers, we suggest that the minimum sample size be, say 250, in order to address the issues raised above (e.g., fit analysis, facilitating dimensionality assessment, ensuring that there are respondents in each category, etc.). Moreover, it may be anticipated that there is a sample size, say 1200, at which one reaches, practically speaking, a point of diminishing returns in terms of improvement in estimation accuracy, all other things being equal. (This should not be interpreted as an upper bound.) If one adopts a sample size ratio for sample size determination (e.g., 5 persons for every parameter estimated), then it is probably more useful closer to the lower bound of 250 than to the 1200 value (i.e., when the sample size is large, then the sample size ratio becomes less important). These suggestions are tempered by the purpose of the administration (e.g., survey, establishing norms, equating, item pool development/maintenance, etc.), the estimation approach, the application's characteristics (e.g., the distribution and range of transition locations, instrument length, latent distribution shape, etc.), ancillary technique sample size requirements, and the amount of missing data. As previously mentioned, sample size guidelines should not be interpreted as hard-and-fast rules.

INFORMATION FOR THE PC AND RS MODELS

With polytomous models it is possible to determine the amount of information provided by each response category. The sum of these weighted *option information functions* or *category information functions*, $I_{x_j}(\theta)$, across the graded categories (or category scores) is the item information (Samejima, 1969):

$$I_j(\theta) = \sum_{x_j=0}^{m_j} I_{x_j}(\theta) p_{x_j} = \sum_{x_j=0}^{m_j} \frac{\left\{p_{x_j}'\right\}^2}{p_{x_j}} \qquad (7.4)$$

where p_{x_j} is the probability of obtaining x_j conditional on θ, and p_{x_j}' is the first derivative of p_{x_j}.[13] The term p_{x_j} may be the PC model or the RS model. For dichotomous data Equation 7.4 simplifies to the item information formula presented in Chapter 2 (Samejima, 1969). Samejima (1969) shows that there is an increase in item information if a response category is added between two adjacent categories. In short, one obtains greater item information when treating an item in a polytomous fashion than in a dichotomous fashion. As seen in previous chapters (e.g., Chapter 2), the sum of the item information functions yields the instrument's total information:

$$I(\theta) = \sum_{j=1}^{L} I_j(\theta) \qquad (7.5)$$

For the PC model item information is

$$I_j(\theta) = \sum_{k=1}^{m_j} k^2 p_{x_j} - \left(\sum_{k=1}^{m_j} k p_{x_j}\right)^2 \qquad (7.6)$$

and for the RS model item information is given by

$$I_j(\theta) = \left(\sum_{x=0}^{m} x p_{x_j}\right)^2 - \left(\sum_{x=0}^{m} x^2 p_{x_j}\right) \qquad (7.7)$$

The distribution of item information for the PC and RS models differs from than that seen with the dichotomous models.[14] For instance, with the 1PL model item information has a fixed maximum value that occurs at δ_j. However, for the PC model, items with the same number of score categories provide the same total amount information, although items that have more score categories yield more information across θ than do items with fewer categories (Dodd & Koch, 1987). Moreover, the maximum item information occurs within the range of transition locations. However, the distribution of item information is affected by the range of the transition locations, the number of reversals of transition locations, and the distance between the reversed transition locations. In general, for a fixed distance between the first and last transition locations, an item that has more transition locations that are in sequential order, and the greater the distance between transition locations that are out of order, the more peaked is the item information function (Dodd & Koch, 1987).

With respect to the RS model's information functions, the location of the maximum of the item information function is affected by the symmetry of the thresholds about the item location, the number of thresholds, and the range of the thresholds. In general, items with four thresholds produce more total information across the continuum than items with three thresholds. Therefore, only items with the same number of thresholds produce the same total information across the θ continuum (Dodd, 1987). The location of the item information maximum is affected by whether the thresholds are symmetrically or asymmetrically distributed about the item's location and whether there is an odd or even number of thresholds. When there is an odd number of asymmetric thresholds (e.g., three) the location of the maximum information shifts away from the item location in the direction of the dominant sign of the thresholds. With an even number of thresholds (e.g., four), the degree of shift in the location of the item information maximum is directly related to the distance between adjacent thresholds. Specifically, the greater the distance between the two middle thresholds, the greater the shift (Dodd & De Ayala, 1994). A different pattern occurs with symmetric thresholds. With an odd number of thresholds that are symmetric about the item's location, the peak of the item information occurs at δ_j. For items with four thresholds that are symmetric about the item's location, the distance between the middle two thresholds affects the shape as well as the location of the information function's maximum. If the range between the middle two thresholds is less than 2 logits, then the peak of the information function occurs at the item location. However, if the middle two thresholds are greater than 2 logits apart, then the item information may be asymmetrically bimodal. In general, rating scales with thresholds that span a small θ range produce a more peaked information function than when the thresholds have a wider θ range (Dodd, 1987; Dodd & De Ayala, 1994).

METRIC TRANSFORMATION, PC AND RS MODELS

The principles outlined in previous chapters for metric conversion apply to both the PC and RS models. That is, the location parameters, δ_{jh}s (or their estimates), are transformed by $\xi^* = \zeta(\xi) + \kappa$. Person location parameters (or their estimates) are transformed by $\theta^* = \zeta(\theta) + \kappa$. The methods presented in Chapter 11 can be used to determine the values of ζ and κ.

If one desires to convert PC or RS model-based person locations (or their estimates) to their corresponding expected trait scores and the lowest and highest response categories are represented as 0 and m, respectively, then one would use

$$T = \sum^{L} \left[\sum_{k=0}^{m_j} k * p_{x_j} \right] \qquad (7.8)$$

The range of T is 0 to $\sum^{L} m_j$. When Equation 7.8 is applied to the RS model where 1 indicates the lowest response category, then the limits of summation for the inside-the-brackets summation would be 1 and m + 1; the range of T is L to L(m + 1).

SUMMARY

The partial credit model is applicable to situations in which one has ordered response data. For example, ordered polytomous data arise in the assignment of partial credit or Likert response data. With the PC model the ordered responses to an item are referred to as *category scores*. For instance, in a situation where partial credit is assigned the category scores could be 0, 1, and 2 for "no credit," "partial credit," and "full credit," respectively. With the PC model items may vary from one another in terms of the number of category scores. Each of these category scores has an associated option response function that describes the probability of obtaining the category score as a function of θ. The intersection of adjacent ORFs (e.g., the ORFs for scores of 0 and 1) occurs at the item's transition locations (δ_{jh}s). The number of transition locations is always one less than the number of category scores. These transition locations do not have to be ordered in terms of their magnitude. For instance, for an item from a proficiency test the transition from no credit to receiving partial credit may be more difficult than the transition from partial to full credit.

With the RS model, responses are assumed to represent a series of ordered categories (e.g., strongly disagree, disagree, agree, strongly agree). The adjacent response categories are separated by a series of thresholds. In contrast to those of the PC model, these thresholds are constant across items. Therefore, the number of response categories is the same for all items modeled by the rating scale model. Although the thresholds have the same values for all items, their locations on the continuum may vary across the items. The rating scale model is a special case of the partial credit model and both are members of the Rasch family of models. As such, the partial credit model may be applied to ratings or Likert response scale data. Both the partial credit and rating scale models reduce to the Rasch model when one has two response categories. Moreover, because both models are extensions of the simple Rasch model, they assume that all items are equally effective in discriminating among respondents and neither model addresses the possibility of examinees guessing on items.

In Chapter 8 we present two models that relax the requirement of a common item discrimination. Although the two models differ from one another in how they conceptualize the response process, they both allow item discrimination to vary across items and have item location parameters associated with the response categories. For comparative purposes we apply one model, the generalized partial credit model, to the same example data used with the PC model. Further, the second model, the graded response model, is used with the Attitudes Toward Condoms scale that we analyzed using the RS model. For continuity with this chapter's examples we continue to use MULTILOG. In previous chapters the EAP and MLE person location estimation approaches are discussed. In Chapter 8 a third approach for person location estimation, *maximum a posteriori* (MAP), is introduced.

NOTES

1. The literature sometimes refers to m_j as the number of "steps" required to correctly answer an item. The term *operation* is used for *step* in the following because the "step" terminology may invite a "sequential steps" interpretation, which contradicts the fact that the partial credit model does not model sequential steps (Masters, 1988; Tutz, 1990).

2. For a two-category item (i.e., $x_j = \{0, 1\}$). Given that

$$\sum_{j=0}^{0} (\theta - \delta_{jh}) \equiv 0$$

then the probability of responding in the highest category (i.e., $x_j = 1$) is

$$p_{x_j} = \frac{\exp\left[\sum_{h=0}^{x_j} (\theta - \delta_{jh})\right]}{\sum_{k=0}^{m_j} \exp\left[\sum_{h=0}^{k} (\theta - \delta_{jh})\right]} = \frac{e^{0+(\theta-\delta_1)}}{e^{\sum_{j=0}^{0}(\theta-\delta_{jh})} + e^{\sum_{j=0}^{1}(\theta-\delta_{j1})}} = \frac{e^{0+(\theta-\delta_{j1})}}{e^0 + e^{0+(\theta-\delta_{j1})}}$$

$$= \frac{e^{(\theta-\delta_{j1})}}{1 + e^{(\theta-\delta_j)}} \tag{7.9}$$

Because when there are two categories there is only one transition location from the lowest category ($x_j = 0$) to the highest category ($x_j = 1$), the subscript h on δ_{jh} may be omitted. The model in Equation 7.9 may be recognized as the Rasch model and indicates that the PC model subsumes the dichotomous Rasch model.

3. To obtain the ORFs presented in Figure 7.2 we calculate the probability of responding in each category as a function of θ. As an example of the relevant calculations, assume that a person is located at 0.0 (i.e., $\theta = 0.0$) and that the transition location points are $\delta_{j1} = -1$ and $\delta_{j2} = 1$ for an item with $m = 2$; $x_j = \{0, 1, 2\}$. Therefore, the probability of this individual obtaining a category score of 0 is

$$p(x_{j0} = 0) = \frac{\exp\left[\sum_{h=0}^{x_j} (\theta - \delta_{jh})\right]}{\sum_{h=0}^{m_j} \exp\left[\sum_{h=0}^{k} (\theta - \delta_{jh})\right]} = \frac{e^0}{e^0 + e^{0+(0-(-1))} + e^{0+(0-(-1))+(0-1)}}$$

$$= \frac{1}{4.7183} = 0.2119$$

(The numerator is e^0 because

$$\sum_{j=0}^{0} (\theta - \theta_{jh}) \equiv 0.)$$

The probability of this person obtaining a category score of 1 is

$$p(x_{j1} = 1) = \frac{e^{\sum\limits_{k=0}^{x_k} (\theta - \delta_k)}}{\sum\limits_{k=0}^{m_j} \exp\left[\sum\limits_{h=0}^{k} (\theta - \delta_{jh}) \right]} = \frac{e^{0+(0-(-1))}}{e^0 + e^{0+(0-(-1))} + e^{0+(0-(-1))+(0-1)}}$$

$$= \frac{2.7183}{4.7183} = 0.5761$$

For category score 2 we have

$$p(x_{j2} = 2) = \frac{e^{\sum\limits_{k=0}^{x_k} (\theta - \delta_k)}}{\sum\limits_{k=0}^{m_j} \exp\left[\sum\limits_{h=0}^{k} (\theta - \delta_{jh}) \right]} = \frac{e^{0+(0-(-1))+(0-1)}}{e^0 + e^{0+(0-(-1))} + e^{0+(0-(-1))+(0-1)}}$$

$$= \frac{1}{4.7183} = 0.2119$$

The sum of these probabilities across these category scores conditional on $\theta = 0.0$ is $0.2119 + 0.5761 + 0.2119 = 1.0$.

4. In general, it is not possible to estimate the parameters for a category that does not have any observations. However, by reparameterizing the PC model Wilson and Masters (1993) provide a solution for estimating item parameters for these categories with zero frequencies (i.e., "null" categories).

5. MULTILOG does not use the scaling constant D in its estimation. As a result, the item parameter estimates are on the logistic metric. To place them on the normal metric we would transform the discrimination estimates using

$$\hat{\alpha}_j^* = \frac{\hat{\alpha}_j}{D}$$

6. Because the constant α across items may not be equal to 1, the relationship between the MULTILOG PC model and the Masters PC model is analogous to the relationship between the 1PL and Rasch models. That is, mathematically, the MULTILOG PC model and the Masters PC model are equivalent: The values from one model can be converted into the other by appropriate rescaling. However, if one wants to directly estimate the Masters PC model, then a program such as BIGSTEPS, WINSTEPS, or ConQuest can be used.

7. Guttman's (1945) L_3 formula is identical to Cronbach's (1951) α formula.

8. Green et al. (1984) define the marginal reliability as

$$\rho_{marg} = \frac{\sigma_\theta^2 - \sigma_{em}^2}{\sigma_\theta^2}$$

where σ_θ^2 is the variance of the observed person locations, σ_{em}^2 is the marginal measurement error

$$\sigma_{em}^2 = \int_{-\infty}^{\infty} \sigma_e^2(\theta)g(\theta)d\theta \Big/ \int_{-\infty}^{\infty} g(\theta)d\theta$$

and $g(\theta)$ is the person distribution that, when $g(\theta)$ is normally distributed, can be evaluated using a Gaussian quadrature approach.

As an alternative to an index for the entire metric, one may calculate the *conditional reliability* (Green et al., 1984) at a θ point. They define conditional reliability as

$$\rho(\theta) = \frac{\sigma_\theta^2 - \sigma_e^2(\theta)}{\sigma_\theta^2} \qquad (7.10)$$

where σ_θ^2 is the variance of the observed person locations and $\sigma_e^2(\theta)$ is the expected variance error of estimate. The term $\rho(\theta)$ specifies "the reliability if everyone were measured with the same precision as those persons" (p. 353) located at θ. In addition, the graphing of $\rho(\theta)$ as a function of θ would allow an assessment of the estimation properties of the instrument at various levels of θ on a bounded and potentially more easily interpreted (ordinate) scale from 0 to 1 than that used with the total information function. An additional reliability index is provided by Bock and Mislevy (1982). Their reliability coefficient for the EAP location estimate, $\rho = 1 - \text{PSD}(\hat{\theta})^2$, is based on the assumption that the latent variable is normally distributed in the population with mean 0 and variance 1.

9. Although the model requires that each item have the same number of categories, it is also important to note that, conceptually, the items should have response scales that are *functionally* equivalent. For example, consider an instrument that uses a four-category response scale. For some items, this 4-point scale is a Likert scale with the labels of 0 = "strongly disagree," 1 = "disagree," 2 = "agree," 3 = "strongly agree," whereas for other items a 0 represents "never," a 1 represents "sometimes," a 2 reflects "often," and a 3 indicates "always." These two response scales differ functionally from one another. Therefore, it may be argued that whenever the response scale changes across an item set one might be measuring a different construct or least a different facet of the construct. In these situations dimensionality analysis may reveal a multidimensional situation. If each dimension consists of items that share a common response scale, then the RS model could be applied to each dimension.

10. To obtain the ORFs presented in Figures 7.10 and 7.11 we calculate the probability of responding in each category as a function of θ. To demonstrate this, assume that an individual is

located at $\theta = 0.0$, our item is located at -0.98 ($\delta_1 = -0.98$), and that the thresholds have values of $\tau_1 = -0.30$, $\tau_2 = -0.02$, and $\tau_3 = 0.32$.

For convenience of presentation the category coefficient values (κ_{x_j}s) are determined first, followed by calculating the denominator of the RS model. From the above we have that

$$\kappa_{x_j} = -\sum_{h=1}^{x_j} \tau_h$$

and that $\kappa_{x_0} = 0$ when $x = 0$. For $x = 1$ this means that

$$\kappa_{x_1} = -(0 + (-0.30)) = 0.30$$

for $x = 2$ we have

$$\kappa_{x_2} = -(0 + (-0.30) + (-0.02)) = 0.32$$

and for $x = 3$ we have

$$\kappa_{x_3} = -(0 + (-0.30) + (-0.02) + 0.32) = 0$$

The denominator, Y, is the sum of the four possible numerators:

$$Y = e^{[0 + 0(0 - (-0.98))]} + e^{[0.30 + 1(0 - (-0.98))]} + e^{[0.32 + 2(0 - (-0.98))]} + e^{[0 + 3(0 - (-0.98))]}$$
$$= e^0 + e^{1.28} + e^{2.28} + e^{2.94} = 33.2892$$

Therefore, the probability of responding in the "strongly disagree" category for an individual located at $\theta = 0.0$ is

$$p(x_j | \theta = 0.0, \delta_1, \tau_0) = \frac{\exp[\kappa_{x_j} + x_j(\theta - \delta_j)]}{\sum_{k=0}^{m} \exp[\kappa_k + k(\theta - \delta_j)]} = \frac{\exp[0 + 0(0 - (-0.98))]}{Y} \frac{1}{33.2892} = 0.0300$$

The probability of this individual responding in the "disagree" category ($x = 1$) is

$$p(x_j | \theta = 0.0, \delta_1, \tau_1) = \frac{\exp[0.30 + 1(0 - (-0.98))]}{Y} = \frac{3.5966}{33.2892} = 0.1080$$

For the "agree" category ($x = 2$) the probability is

$$p(x_j | \theta = 0.0, \delta_1, \tau_2) = \frac{\exp[0.32 + 2(0 - (-0.98))]}{Y} = \frac{9.7767}{33.2892} = 0.2937$$

and for the "strongly agree" category (x = 3) we have

$$p(x_j | \theta = 0.0, \delta_1, \tau_3) = \frac{\exp[0 + 3(0 - (-0.98))]}{Y} = \frac{18.9158}{33.2892} = 0.5682$$

The sum of these probabilities across these category scores conditional on $\theta = 0.0$ is $0.0300 + 0.1080 + 0.2937 + 0.5682 = 1.0$.

11. Some authors use the coding $0, \ldots, 3$ rather than $1, \ldots, 4$ to be consistent with the model's presentation. For example, see Andrich (1978c) and Dodd (1990).

12. INFIT and OUTFIT MNSQs can be transformed into either z (ZSTD) or t distributions. In these cases the range for these transformed fit statistics is $-\infty$ to ∞ with an expectation of 0. However, the interpretation of ZSTD depends on whether rescaling is done, and if so, the type of scaling. The LOCAL keyword is used to specify rescaling. If LOCAL = N, then no rescaling is performed and ZSTD should be ignored. If LOCAL = Y, then the MNSQs are rescaled to reflect their level of significance in the context of the degree of error in the data. In this case, negative ZSTD values indicate a response string close to a Guttman pattern and positive values indicate more variation than would be predicted by the Rasch model. If LOCAL = L, then the MNSQs are logarithmically rescaled. For this example TABLE 0.1 shows that LOCAL = N, so the ZSTDs are ignored (see Table 7.4). See Linacre and Wright (2001) for more information on this issue.

13. When one scores an item in a graded fashion (and assuming the operating characteristic of the graded response is twice-differentiable), then the information function for the graded response is (Samejima, 1969):

$$I_{x_j}(\theta) = \left\{ -\frac{\partial^2 \ln p_{x_j}}{\partial \theta^2} \right\} p_{x_j} = \frac{\left\{ p_{x_j}' \right\}^2}{\left\{ p_{x_j} \right\}^2} - \frac{p_{x_j}''}{p_{x_j}} \tag{7.11}$$

where p_{x_j} is the probability of obtaining x_j conditional on θ, p_{x_j}' is the first derivative of p_{x_j}, and p_{x_j}'' is the second derivative of p_{x_j}. $I_{x_j}(\theta)$ is the option information function. The sum of these option information functions across the categories (or category scores) is defined by Samejima (1969) as the item information, $I_j(\theta)$:

$$I_j(\theta) = -\mathcal{E}\left\{ \frac{\partial^2 \ln p_{x_j}}{\partial \theta^2} \right\}$$

$$= \sum_{x_j=0}^{m_j} I_{x_j}(\theta) p_{x_j} = \sum_{x_j=0}^{m_j} \left\{ \frac{\left[p_{x_j}' \right]^2}{p_{x_j}} - p_{x_j}'' \right\}$$

$$= \sum_{x_j=0}^{m_j} \frac{\left\{P_{x_j}'\right\}^2}{p_{x_j}} - \sum_{x_j=0}^{m_j} p_{x_j}'' \qquad (7.12)$$

However, because the sum of the second derivatives across m_j graded categories is 0, Equation 7.12 simplifies to Equation 7.4.

   14. The standard error for the person location estimate under the PC model is

$$SEE(\hat{\theta}_i) = \frac{1}{\sqrt{\sum_{j=1}^{L}\left\{\sum_{k=1}^{m_j} k^2 p_{x_j} - \left(\sum_{k=1}^{m_j} k p_{x_j}\right)^2\right\}}} \qquad (7.13)$$

and for the RS model it is

$$SEE(\hat{\theta}_i) = \frac{1}{\sqrt{\sum_{j=1}^{L}\left\{\left(\sum_{x=0}^{m} x p_{x_j}\right)^2 - \left(\sum_{x=0}^{m} x^2 p_{x_j}\right)\right\}}} \qquad (7.14)$$

For both Equations 7.13 and 7.14 p_{x_j} is conditional on $\hat{\theta}_i$.

8

Non-Rasch Models for Ordered Polytomous Data

The models for ordered polytomous data in Chapter 7 are extensions of the dichotomous Rasch model. In this chapter we present two models that relax the assumption of equal item discrimination and that are applicable to ordered polytomous data.[1] These two models, the generalized partial credit and the graded response models, differ from one another in their conceptualization of the operating characteristic function. We begin with the generalized partial credit model and apply it to the reasoning ability instrument from Chapter 7. Subsequently, the graded response model is presented. As part of this presentation, the Attitudes Toward Condoms scale from Chapter 7 is used to demonstrate applying the graded response model. In this example we use *maximum a posteriori* (MAP) for person location estimation. With the presentation of MAP we have presented the three common ability estimation approaches (EAP, MAP, MLE).

THE GENERALIZED PARTIAL CREDIT MODEL

As mentioned in Chapter 7, the PC model states that all items on an instrument have equal discrimination. Muraki's (1992) *generalized partial credit* (GPC) model relaxes this assumption. Muraki developed his model using, in essence, Masters' (1982) approach, by assuming that the probability of selecting a particular response category over the previous one is governed by a dichotomous model. However, instead of using the dichotomous Rasch model as Masters did, Muraki used the 2PL model. The application of this process leads to a model that specifies the probability of providing a response in item j's *kth* category, x_{jk}

$$p(x_{jk}|\theta, \alpha_j, \delta_{jk}) = \frac{\exp\left[\sum_{h=1}^{k_j} \alpha_j(\theta - \delta_{jh})\right]}{\sum_{c=1}^{m_j} \exp\left[\sum_{h=1}^{c} \alpha_j(\theta - \delta_{jh})\right]} \tag{8.1}$$

where θ is the latent trait, α_j is the item discrimination, δ_{jh} is the transition location parameter between the hth category and the $h - 1$ category (i.e., the intersection point of adjacent ORFs), m_j is the number of categories, and $k = \{1, \ldots, m_j\}$. Given that Muraki (arbitrarily) defines the first boundary location as zero (i.e., $\delta_{j1} \equiv 0$), there are $m_j - 1$ transition locations. (Note that we use the italicization of "m" to indicate the number of response categories, not the number of transition locations.) For example, a four-response category item would have $m_j = 4$ and three transition location parameters labeled δ_{j2}, δ_{j3}, and δ_{j4}. As is the case with the PC model, the δ_{jh}s do not have to be in sequential order. Some (e.g., Yen, 1993) refer to the model in Equation 8.1 as the two-parameter partial credit (2PPC) model.

As previously mentioned, Masters (1982) shows that the RS model can be obtained from his PC model by decomposing an item's δ_{jk}s into an item location parameter and a threshold component. Similarly, the transition locations in Equation 8.1 may be decomposed into an item location component and a threshold parameter to obtain a formulation of the GPC that is analogous to the RS model, but that models items with varying discrimination. By substituting $\delta_{jk} = \delta_j - \tau_k$ into Equation 8.1 we obtain a model that specifies the probability of responding in category k, x_{jk}, on an item j as

$$p(x_{jk}|\theta, \alpha_j, \delta_j, \underline{\tau}) = \frac{\exp\left[\sum_{h=1}^{k_j} \alpha_j(\theta - \delta_j + \tau_h)\right]}{\sum_{c=1}^{m} \exp\left[\sum_{h=1}^{c} \alpha_j(\theta - \delta_j + \tau_h)\right]} \qquad (8.2)$$

where m is the number of response categories, $k = 1, \ldots, m$, and $\tau_1 \equiv 0$. As can be seen, this parameterization of the GPC model is similar to the RS model, but without the constraint that item discriminations be equal to 1 for all items. Muraki (1992) considers the model in Equation 8.2 to be the GPC model "unless its rating aspect is specifically emphasized" (p. 165). Therefore, although both Equations 8.1 and 8.2 may be considered the GPC model, because Equation 8.2 is the "rating formulation" of the GPC model, we refer to it as the *generalized rating scale* (GRS) model; also see Muraki (1990). In the following discussion, p_{xj} is used for $p(x_{jk}|\theta, \alpha_j, \delta_j, \underline{\tau})$ and $p(x_{jk}|\theta, \alpha_j, \delta_{jk})$.

In Equations 8.1 and 8.2 the discrimination parameter, α_j, "indicates the degree to which categorical responses vary among items as θ changes" (Muraki, 1992, p. 162). Although α_j has a range from $-\infty$ to ∞, its acceptable range consists of positive values. Muraki interprets the τ_h in Equation 8.2 as the relative difficulty of "step" h "in comparing other steps within an item" (p. 165); "difficulty" may also be interpreted as the difficulty of endorsing a particular category. Moreover, the τ_hs do not need to be sequentially ordered for $k = 1, \ldots, m$. Parameter estimation for the GRS model may be accomplished using PARSCALE.

To demonstrate the impact of a varying discrimination parameter and transition point locations we present a series of ORFs. Consistent with the partial credit terminology used in Chapter 7, we use the category scores of 0, 1, and 2 for no credit, partial credit, and full credit, respectively. In terms of the GPC model's parameterization in Equation 8.1, the response categories of 1, 2, 3 correspond to the figures' labeled category scores of 0, 1, and 2, respectively.

Figures 8.1 to 8.3 show the ORFs for 3 three-category items with identical transition locations, but with different discrimination values; $\alpha_1 = 0.50$, $\alpha_2 = 1.0$, and $\alpha_3 = 2.0$ for Figures 8.1 to 8.3, respectively. Because δ_{j1} is defined as equal to 0, the intersections of the ORFs are labeled (generally speaking) δ_{j2} and δ_{j3}, with $\delta_{j2} = -1.0$ and $\delta_{j3} = 1.0$. Comparing the three figures one sees that as the item discrimination value increases, the ORFs for the zero and full-credit scores (i.e., category scores of 0 and 2) are steeper. As is the case with the PC model, the ORFs for any item always consist of one monotonically nondecreasing ORF (e.g., category 2) and one monotonically nonincreasing ORF (e.g., category 0), with typically one unimodal ORF for each additional response category.

Figures 8.3 and 8.4 contain the ORFs for two items with the same α, but with transition parameters farther apart in Figure 8.4 than they are in Figure 8.3. Contrasting these two figures, we see that when the transition parameters are in increasing order and become farther apart, the probability of obtaining a category score of 1 increases throughout the continuum, as compared with when the δ_{jh}s are closer together.

To understand the effect of item discrimination on the ORFs for the nonzero/non-full-credit category scores, we need to attend to whether the transition locations are in increasing order, as well as to the distance between transition location parameters. Figures 8.5 and 8.3 represent items with the same discrimination, but with the transition parameters reversed. For Figure 8.5, $\delta_{52} > \delta_{53}$, but for Figure 8.3 we have $\delta_{32} < \delta_{33}$. When the transition locations are in sequential order (i.e., $\delta_{32} < \delta_{33}$), then as α increases, the ORF(s) for the nonzero/non-full-credit response categories become more peaked (cf. Figures 8.1 and 8.3).

When there is a reversal in the transition locations (e.g., $\delta_{52} = 1.0$ and $\delta_{53} = -1.0$, as in Figure 8.5), then the probability of obtaining a category score of 1 is substantially

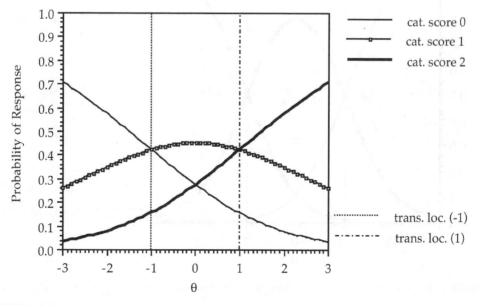

FIGURE 8.1. GPC model ORFs for a three-category item with $\alpha_1 = 0.50$, $\delta_{12} = -1.0$, and $\delta_{13} = 1.0$.

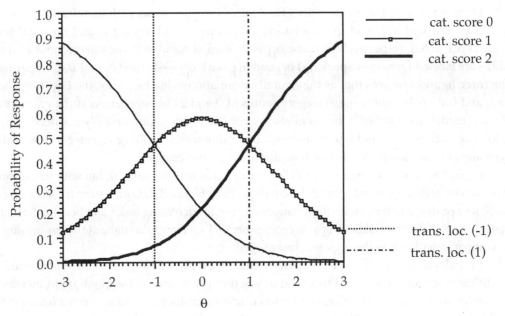

FIGURE 8.2. GPC model ORFs for a three-category item with $\alpha_2 = 1.00$, $\delta_{22} = -1.0$, and $\delta_{23} = 1.0$.

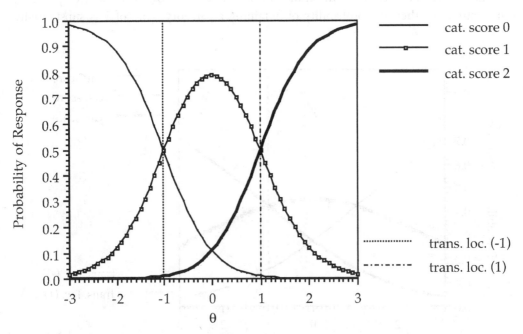

FIGURE 8.3. GPC model ORFs for a three-category item with $\alpha_3 = 2.0$, $\delta_{32} = -1.0$, and $\delta_{33} = 1.0$.

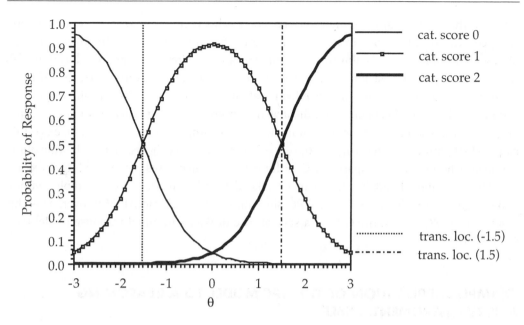

FIGURE 8.4. GPC model ORFs for a three-category item with $\alpha_4 = 2.0$, $\delta_{42} = -1.5$, and $\delta_{43} = 1.5$.

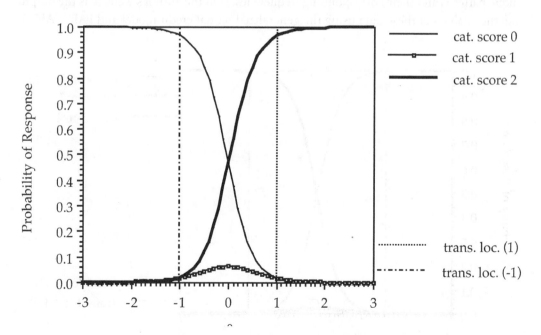

FIGURE 8.5. GPC model ORFs for a three-category item with $\alpha_5 = 2.0$, $\delta_{52} = 1.0$, and $\delta_{53} = -1.0$.

less than that of obtaining a score of either 0 or 2. This is the same pattern observed with reversed transition locations in the PC model and shown in Figure 7.3. In effect, the item represented in Figure 8.5 is almost functioning as a binary item with an item location of 0 (i.e., $\delta_{52} + \delta_{53}$)/2). Consistent with this interpretation is the observation that the ORF for the response category of 1 is not very effective at attracting respondents. Despite this observation, recall that α reflects how well the *item* discriminates among different values of θ, not how well *each* response category discriminates. Contrasting Figure 8.5 ($\alpha_5 = 2.0$, $\delta_{52} = 1.0$, $\delta_{53} = -1.0$) with Figure 8.6 ($\alpha_6 = 2.0$, $\delta_{62} = 1.5$, $\delta_{63} = -1.5$) shows that as the transition parameters become farther apart, the ORF for category 1 decreases, while holding α fixed.

The GPC model can be shown to be related to other models. For example, with a two-category item (i.e., $m_j = 2$) the GPC simplifies to the 2PL model. Moreover, as is the case with the PC model, the GPC is a special case of Bock's nominal response model (see Chapter 9).

EXAMPLE: APPLICATION OF THE GPC MODEL TO A REASONING ABILITY INSTRUMENT, MMLE

As an example, we apply the GPC model to the Alike Reasoning data calibrated with the PC model in Chapter 7. Although PARSCALE could be used to perform this calibration, for comparison purposes with the PC model results we use MULTILOG. In addition, we demonstrate the analysis of pattern data with MULTILOG. Pattern data consist of all the unique patterns and their corresponding frequencies. (On the author's website is the output from the analysis of these data using the generalized partial credit model and PARSCALE.)

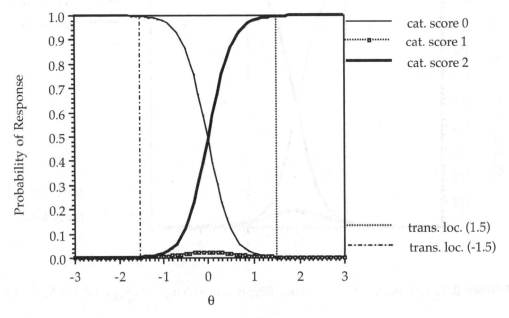

FIGURE 8.6. GPC model ORFs for a three-category item with $\alpha_j = 2.0$, $\delta_{j2} = 1.5$, and $\delta_{j3} = -1.5$.

The command file is identical to that used for the PC calibration (Table 7.1) except for three changes. First, to use pattern data we make two changes to the PROBLEM line: (1) the keyword PATTERNS is used in lieu of INDIVIDUAL, and (2) NPATTERNS = 6561 is specified instead of NEXAMINEES=3000. (Given the number of individuals, we do not observe all of the 3^8 = 6561 possible patterns; only 904 unique patterns are observed.) The third change is that the line 'EQUAL ALL AK=1' used in the PC calibration is omitted to allow for the discrimination parameter estimates, $\hat{\alpha}_j$s, to vary across items. The output file has the same appearance as that of the PC model calibration except for the additional output containing the EAP $\hat{\theta}$ for each pattern. That is, when MULTILOG calibrates pattern data it produces item and person parameter estimates in a single calibration run.

Table 8.1 contains the abridged output. As can be seen from the ESTIMATION PARAM-ETERS section, the NUMBER OF FREE PARAMETERS is 24 (i.e., each item has 3 parameters (2 transition locations, δ_{j1} and δ_{j2}, plus 1 α_j) times 8 items). The first line in the data file consists of a response vector of all zeros (i.e., ITEMS 00000000) and there are 53 persons (i.e., WT/CR 53) who provided this set of responses. Convergence is achieved in 16 iterations.

As done in Chapter 7, the item parameter estimates are read from the CONTRAST-COEFFICIENTS table. The rest of the item parameter estimate output is similar to that seen with the PC model and is interpreted the same way. Table 8.2 contains the item parameter estimates and their corresponding standard errors for all the items on the instrument. The $\hat{\alpha}_j$ column shows that the items differ in their discrimination. By and large, the transition locations are found to fall between −2.24 and 2.42 and so it is not surprising that the total information function (Figure 8.7) indicates that this instrument tends to do a better job estimating individuals located within this range than outside of it. In addition, the GPC total information maximum is located around −1.2 and is more peaked than that observed with the PC model.

MULTILOG provides −2lnL at the end of its output (i.e., NEGATIVE TWICE THE LOGLIKELIHOOD). As mentioned in Chapter 7, when pattern data are calibrated this index is positive and may be used for an overall assessment of model–data fit; this assumes that most or all of the possible patterns are observed (i.e., there are very few cells with zero frequencies in the contingency table made up of m^L cells). With pattern data the −2lnL value can be interpreted as a chi-square with df = [(number of patterns) − (number of estimated item parameters) − 1], where the number of estimated item parameters can be determined by the user or obtained from the line 'NUMBER OF FREE PARAMETERS IS' and the (number of patterns) = m^L. For example, with four three-response category items, L = 4 and m = 3, the number of patterns is 3^4 = 81. The null hypothesis is that the data are consistent with a general multinomial model. In our example the combination of the number of items, the number of response categories, and the sample size result in a contingency table that is quite sparse (i.e., there are many cells with zero frequencies and small expected frequencies) and the −2lnL is not distributed as a chi-square.

Alternatively, as shown in Chapter 6, the difference in −2lnLs from two hierarchically nested models is distributed as a chi-square with df equal to the difference in the number of parameters between the Full model and the Reduced model, given that the Full model holds for the data. The calibration of these pattern data with the PC model produces a −2lnL of 3148.7 with 17 free parameters. Given that the PC model is nested within the GPC model,

TABLE 8.1. Abridged Output from the MULTILOG GPC Model Calibration Example

```
     :
DATA PARAMETERS:
  NUMBER OF LINES IN THE DATA FILE: 6561
  NUMBER OF CATEGORICAL-RESPONSE ITEMS:    8
  NUMBER OF CONTINUOUS-RESPONSE ITEMS, AND/OR GROUPS:    1
  TOTAL NUMBER OF "ITEMS" (INCLUDING GROUPS):    9
  NUMBER OF CHARACTERS IN ID FIELDS:   8
  MAXIMUM NUMBER OF RESPONSE-CODES FOR ANY ITEM:   3
  THE MISSING VALUE CODE FOR CONTINUOUS DATA:  9.0000
  RESPONSE-PATTERN FREQUENCIES WILL BE READ
  THE DATA WILL BE STORED IN SCRATCH FILES ON DISK

ESTIMATION PARAMETERS:
  THE ITEMS WILL BE CALIBRATED--
    BY MARGINAL MAXIMUM LIKELIHOOD ESTIMATION
  MAXIMUM NUMBER OF EM CYCLES PERMITTED: 100
  NUMBER OF PARAMETER-SEGMENTS USED IS:   8
  NUMBER OF FREE PARAMETERS IS:   24
  MAXIMUM NUMBER OF M-STEP ITERATIONS IS  50 TIMES
    THE NUMBER OF PARAMETERS IN THE SEGMENT
  THE M-STEP CONVERGENCE CRITERION IS: 0.000100
  THE EM-CYCLE CONVERGENCE CRITERION IS: 0.001000
     :
KEY-
CODE   CATEGORY
  0      11111111
  1      22222222
  2      33333333
     :
FIRST OBSERVATION AS READ-
ID    00000000
ITEMS 00000000
NORML     0.000
WT/CR    53.00
     :
FINISHED CYCLE  16
MAXIMUM INTERCYCLE PARAMETER CHANGE=   0.00059 P(   2)
     :
ITEM   1:       3 NOMINAL CATEGORIES,  3 HIGH
  CATEGORY(K): 1        2        3
    A(K)    -1.30    0.00    1.30
    C(K)     0.00    2.00    4.24

            CONTRAST-COEFFICIENTS (STANDARD ERRORS)
  FOR:                A                    C
  CONTRAST P(#)  COEFF.[POLY.]   P(#)  COEFF.[ TRI.]
     1      1    1.30 (0.07)      2   -2.00 (0.16)
     2     25    0.00 (0.00)      3   -2.24 (0.09)

@THETA:      INFORMATION:    (Theta values increase in steps of 0.2)
-3.0 - -1.6 0.327 0.433 0.566 0.722 0.887 1.037 1.139 1.168
-1.4 -  0.0 1.114 0.993 0.835 0.671 0.521 0.397 0.298 0.223
 0.2 -  1.6 0.166 0.125 0.093 0.070 0.053 0.040 0.031 0.023
 1.8 -  3.0 0.018 0.014 0.011 0.008 0.006 0.005 0.004

OBSERVED AND EXPECTED COUNTS/PROPORTIONS IN
CATEGORY(K):   1        2        3
OBS. FREQ.    201      351     2390
OBS. PROP.  0.0683  0.1193  0.8124
EXP. PROP.  0.0668  0.1210  0.8122

   :

@THETA:      INFORMATION:
-3.0 - -1.6 1.777 1.970 2.206 2.486 2.798 3.118 3.411 3.646
-1.4 -  0.0 3.801 3.879 3.895 3.872 3.827 3.774 3.721 3.665
 0.2 -  1.6 3.601 3.520 3.416 3.286 3.132 2.959 2.776 2.593
 1.8 -  3.0 2.416 2.251 2.102 1.970 1.854 1.753 1.664

@THETA:      POSTERIOR STANDARD DEVIATION:
-3.0 - -1.6 0.750 0.713 0.673 0.634 0.598 0.566 0.541 0.524
-1.4 -  0.0 0.513 0.508 0.507 0.508 0.511 0.515 0.518 0.522
 0.2 -  1.6 0.527 0.533 0.541 0.552 0.565 0.581 0.600 0.621
 1.8 -  3.0 0.643 0.667 0.690 0.712 0.734 0.755 0.775

MARGINAL RELIABILITY:     0.7058
```

TABLE 8.1. *cont.*

OBSERVED(EXPECTED)		STD. RES. :	EAP (S.D.) :	PATTERN :
53.0(	24.9)	5.62 :	-2.13 (0.60) :	11111111
2.0(	1.9)	0.08 :	-1.91 (0.57) :	11111112
0.0(	0.2)	-0.42 :	-1.70 (0.55) :	11111113
0.0(	0.9)	-0.94 :	-1.84 (0.56) :	11111121
0.0(	0.1)	-0.28 :	-1.63 (0.54) :	11111122
0.0(	0.0)	-0.09 :	-1.44 (0.53) :	11111123
0.0(	0.2)	-0.44 :	-1.57 (0.54) :	11111131
0.0(	0.0)	-0.14 :	-1.38 (0.53) :	11111132
0.0(	0.0)	-0.05 :	-1.20 (0.52) :	11111133
12.0(	8.2)	1.31 :	-1.92 (0.57) :	11111211
:				
8.0(	7.6)	0.16 :	2.11 (0.67) :	33333333

NEGATIVE TWICE THE LOGLIKELIHOOD=   3071.4
(CHI-SQUARE FOR SEVERAL TIMES MORE EXAMINEES THAN CELLS)

the difference between their respective $-2\ln Ls$ is distributed as a chi-square with a value of 77.2 with 7 degrees of freedom; we assume that we would observe GPC model–data fit with a larger sample. Therefore, the GPC model fits these data significantly better than does the PC model. One reason for the GPC's better fit is its capability to capture the variability in the item discriminations. As mentioned above, as part of any model–data fit analysis one should compare the empirical and predicted ORFs. The program MODFIT could be used for this purpose with the GPC model.

CONCEPTUAL DEVELOPMENT OF THE GRADED RESPONSE MODEL

The PC and GPC models take one approach to characterizing the graded scoring of an item. Specifically, the approach used is one of a series of dichotomous models that govern the probability of responding in one category versus the next adjacent category; the dichotomous models underlying the PC and GPC models are the Rasch and 2PL models, respectively. As an example, and given the category scores for the item "(6/3) + 2 = ?" (i.e., 0, 1, 2 for incorrect, partially correct, and correct responses, respectively), we can focus on the probability of obtaining a category score of 0 versus a score of 1 or the probability of

TABLE 8.2. Item Parameter Estimates from the MULTILOG GPC Model Calibration Example

Item	$\hat{\alpha}_j$	$s_e(\hat{\alpha}_j)$	$\hat{\delta}_{j2}$	$s_e(\hat{\delta}_{j2})$	$\hat{\delta}_{j3}$	$s_e(\hat{\delta}_{j3})$
1	1.30	(0.07)	-2.00	(0.16)	-2.24	(0.09)
2	1.06	(0.06)	-0.64	(0.10)	-1.34	(0.07)
3	0.84	(0.05)	-1.04	(0.09)	-0.24	(0.05)
4	0.67	(0.04)	-0.22	(0.06)	0.51	(0.06)
5	0.87	(0.04)	1.57	(0.09)	-1.21	(0.08)
6	0.63	(0.05)	-0.16	(0.05)	2.42	(0.11)
7	0.88	(0.05)	1.60	(0.07)	0.03	(0.09)
8	0.66	(0.05)	1.24	(0.05)	1.18	(0.10)

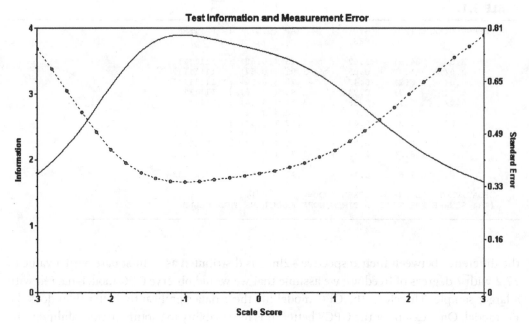

FIGURE 8.7. Total information for Alike reasoning exam, GPC model. Solid line indicates total information; dotted line indicates standard error.

obtaining a score of 1 versus a score of 2. In this fashion we have a series of dichotomous choices. However, this is not the only approach one could use.

An alternative method is used by Samejima (1969) in her extension of Thurstone's method of successive intervals (Masters, 1982). In her approach there is a boundary above which a person is expected to obtain certain category score(s) as opposed to lower category score(s). The important distinction from the PC/GPC models is in the plurality of the choice. For instance, given the three category scores for the item "(6/3) + 2 = ?," we can focus on the probability of obtaining a score of 1 *or higher* versus a score of 0, or the probability of obtaining a score of 2 versus a score of 0 or 1. In effect, the polytomous scores have been turned into a series of *cumulative* comparisons (i.e., below a particular category versus *at and above* this category). We can then trace each of these cumulative probabilities with a dichotomous model. This is the approach used in the *graded response* (GR) model (Samejima, 1969).

The GR model specifies the probability of a person responding with category score x_j *or higher* versus responding in lower category scores. Stated another way, the GR model specifies the probability of a person responding in category k or higher versus responding in categories lower than k. (Because the GR model is applicable to situations where partial credit scoring is used as well as Likert response data, we use the terms *category scores* and *categories* interchangeably in the following.) As is the case with the PC model, responses to item j are categorized into $m_j + 1$ categories, where higher categories indicate more of the latent trait. Associated with each of item j's response categories is a category score, x_j, with integer values 0, 1, . . . , m_j. According to the GR model the probability of obtaining x_j *or higher* is given by

$$P_{x_j}^*(\theta) = \frac{e^{\alpha_j(\theta - \delta_{x_j})}}{1 + e^{\alpha_j(\theta - \delta_{x_j})}} \qquad (8.3)$$

where θ is the latent trait, α_j is the discrimination parameter for item j, δ_{x_j} is the *category boundary location* for category score x_j, and $x_j = \{0, 1, \ldots, m_j\}$; also see Samejima (1973b). Alternatively, the category boundary location may be viewed as the boundary between categories k and k − 1 (Masters, 1982).[2] As is the case with the PC and GPC models, the number of categories may vary across items. In the GR model the δ_{x_j}s are always in increasing order and there are m_j category boundary locations for item j. For simplicity of presentation $P_{x_j}^*$ is used for $P_{x_j}^*(\theta)$ in the following.

The model in Equation 8.3 may be recognized as, in essence, the 2PL model. As such, the GR model is the successive application of the 2PL model to an ordered series of bifurcated responses (e.g., 0 vs. 1,2; 0,1 vs. 2). Generally speaking, the 2PL model specifies the probability, p_j, of the occurrence of event *b* and $(1 - p_j)$ specifies the probability of *b*'s complementary event $\bar{b}$ (e.g., $b = 1$ and $\bar{b} = 0$); the events $\bar{b}$ and *b* are mutually exclusive and jointly exhaustive. In the GR model context, the events $\bar{b}$ and *b* reflect subsets of the x_j (set of) responses. For example, for $m_j = 3$ we have $x_j = \{0, 1, 2, 3\}$. For $x_j = 0$ we have P_0^* with $\bar{b} = \{0, 1, 2, 3\}$ and *b* is the null set, for $x_j = 1$ we have P_1^* with $\bar{b} = \{0\}$ and $b = \{1, 2, 3\}$, for $x_j = 2$ we have P_2^* with $\bar{b} = \{0, 1\}$ and $b = \{2, 3\}$, and for $x_j = 3$ we have P_3^* with $\bar{b} = \{0, 1, 2\}$ and $b = \{3\}$. Each $P_{x_j}^*$, except for P_0^*, is given by the 2PL model using the x_j category boundary location. By definition, the probability of responding in the lowest category 0 *or higher* is 1.0 (i.e., $P_0^* \equiv 1$) and the probability of responding in category $m_j + 1$ *or higher* is 0.0 (e.g., for this item $P_4^* \equiv 0$). In other words, the definition for P_0^* states that the response has to be within one of the categories, whereas the latter definition (e.g., P_4^*) states that the probability of responding beyond the highest category is zero.[3]

From this perspective it is not surprising that when $P_{x_j}^*$ is displayed as a function of θ, one obtains an ogive. The plot of these cumulative probabilities, sometimes referred to as *category boundary curves, cumulative probability curves, category characteristic curves* (Dodd, 1984), or *boundary characteristic curves* (Baker, 1992), is similar to a series of IRFs with lower and upper asymptotes of 0.0 and 1.0, respectively. An example of these category boundary curves for an item with three category scores (i.e., $x_j = \{0, 1, 2\}$; $m_j = 2$) and $\alpha = 1.5$, $\delta_1 = -1.0$, and $\delta_2 = 1.0$ is shown in Figure 8.8. As can be seen, P_1^* (dashed line) specifies the probability of a score of 0 versus 1 or 2, and P_2^* (solid bold line) indicates the probability of a score of 0 or 1 versus 2. Figure 8.8 also shows that the point of inflexion of a boundary curve is located at δ_{x_j}. As such, the probability of obtaining a category score x_j or higher is 0.50 at δ_{x_j}. The slopes of the boundary curves at δ_{x_j} are proportional to α_j.

As may be clear from the preceding discussion, the model in Equation 8.3 specifies the probability, $P_{x_j}^*$, of an individual obtaining category score x_j *or higher* on item j, *not* the probability of obtaining a specific category score or responding in a particular category, p_{x_j}. To calculate the probability of an individual obtaining a *particular* category score x_j or responding in a *particular* category k, p_k, we must take the difference between the cumulative probabilities for adjacent categories. That is,

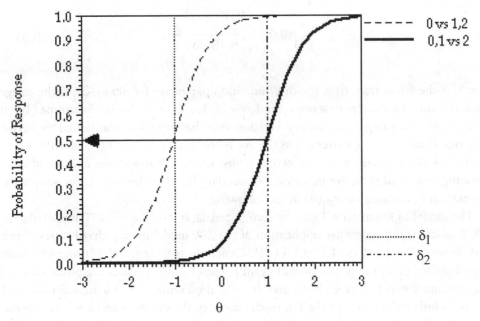

FIGURE 8.8. Category boundary curves for a three-category response item with $\alpha = 1.5$, $\delta_1 = -1.0$, and $\delta_2 = 1.0$.

$$p_k = P_k^* - P_{k+1}^*$$ (8.4)

where P_k^* is $P_{x_j}^*$ from Equation 8.3; note the use of lowercase "p" to indicate the probability of responding in a *particular* category and (capital) "P*" to indicate *cumulative* probabilities.

By way of an example, assume that an item has three response categories (i.e., $x_j = \{0, 1, 2\}$; $m_j = 2$). By definition, P_0^* is equal to 1 (i.e., $P_0^* \equiv 1.0$) and specifies the probability of responding in category 0, 1, or 2. The term P_1^* is the probability of responding in category 1 or 2 rather than in category 0 (i.e., $k = 1$ or $x_j = 1$). Also, P_2^* is the probability of responding in category 2 rather than in category 0 or 1 (i.e., $k = 2$ or $x_j = 2$) and $P_3^* \equiv 0$. Therefore, the probability of responding in category 0 (i.e., $x_j = 0$) is given by

$$P_0 = P_0^* - P_1^* = p(x_j = \{0, 1, 2\}|\theta) - p(x_j = \{1, 2\}|\theta) = 1.0 - \frac{e^{\alpha_j(\theta-\delta_1)}}{1+e^{\alpha_j(\theta-\delta_1)}}$$

the probability of responding in category 1 (i.e., $x_j = 1$) is

$$P_1 = P_1^* - P_2^* = p(x_j = \{1, 2\}|\theta) - p(x_j = 2|\theta) = \frac{e^{\alpha_j(\theta-\delta_1)}}{1+e^{\alpha_j(\theta-\delta_1)}} - \frac{e^{\alpha_j(\theta-\delta_2)}}{1+e^{\alpha_j(\theta-\delta_2)}}$$

and the probability of responding in category 2 (i.e., $x_j = 2$) equals

$$P_2 = P_2^* - P_3^* = p(x_j = 2|\theta) - p(x_j > 2|\theta) = \frac{e^{\alpha_j(\theta - \delta_2)}}{1 + e^{\alpha_j(\theta - \delta_2)}} - 0 = P_2^*$$

The sum of the p_ks across the response options for a fixed value of θ is 1.0, that is

$$\sum_{x_j=0}^{m_j} p_k = 1$$

The plots of the p_{x_j}s as a function of θ for each option (i.e., the ORFs) for the item in Figure 8.8 are shown in Figure 8.9. Note that the δ_{x_j}s do not necessarily correspond to the points of intersection of adjacent ORFs. Rather, for the lowest and highest categories the δ_{x_0} and δ_{x_m}, respectively, correspond to where the probability of responding in the given category is 0.5. For the other ORF(s) the δ_{x_j}s specify the mode of the ORF such that the $\text{mode}_{x_j} = (\delta_{k+1} + \delta_k)/2$, where $k = 1, \ldots, m_j - 1$ and $x_j = \{0, 1, \ldots, m_j\}$. For instance, the mode of the ORF for $x_j = 1$ is $(\delta_2 + \delta_1)/2 = (1 + (-1))/2 = 0$ (the dotted line in Figure 8.9). As a second example, Figure 8.10 contains the ORFs for a four-response category item with $\alpha = 1.5$, $\delta_1 = -1.0$, $\delta_2 = 1.4$, and $\delta_3 = 2$. The modes of the ORFs for $x_j = 1$ and 2 are $(\delta_2 + \delta_1)/2 = (1.4 + (-1))/2 = 0.2$ (the dotted line) and $(2 + 1.4)/2 = 1.7$ (dashed line), respectively. As is also seen, the probability of responding $x_j = 0$ is 0.5 at δ_1 and the probability of responding $x_j = 3$ is 0.5 at δ_3.

Given that with the GR model we can have only sequentially ordered δ_{x_j}s, it is not possible to inspect the δ_{x_j}s for an indication of which categories are unlikely to be chosen.

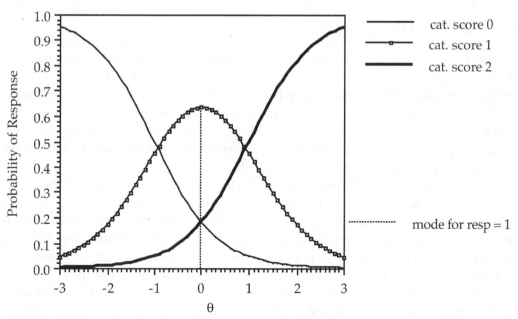

FIGURE 8.9. ORFs for a three-category response item with $\alpha = 1.5$, $\delta_1 = -1.0$, and $\delta_2 = 1.0$.

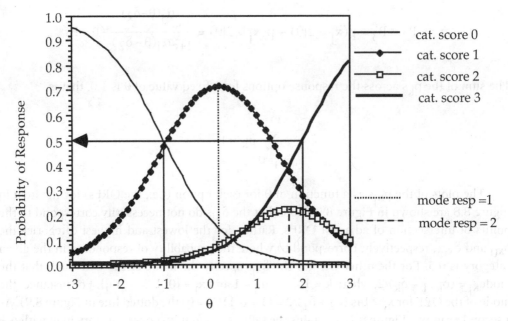

FIGURE 8.10. ORFs for a four-response category item with α = 1.5, δ_1 = –1.0, δ_2 = 1.4, and δ_3 = 2.

Thus, for the GR model it is necessary to plot the ORFs to determine which categories (if any) are less likely to be chosen. For example, Figure 8.11 contains the ORFs for an item with the same slope as the item in Figure 8.9, but with different category boundary locations. As can be seen, although the δ_{x_j}s are in sequence, the corresponding ORFs show that the item is behaving primarily as a dichotomous item, with a category score of 1 being less likely than a category score of 0 or 2.

It can be seen from Figure 8.8 that the boundary curves are parallel. This parallelism reflects the assumption in Equation 8.3 that discrimination is constant across the graded response categories (i.e., α_j is constant within an item across thresholds, but not necessarily across items). This is sometimes referred to as the *homogeneous* GR model and is the model most typically used. In contrast, α_j may be allowed to vary across the graded response categories as well as across items. This second variant may be called the *heterogeneous* GR model; see Samejima (1969, pp. 19–20). These models may be seen as special cases of the *continuous response* model (Samejima, 1973b).

As is true with the PC, RS, and GPC models, the GR model can be used with both cognitive and attitude measurement. For instance, Samejima (1969) applied the GR model to the analysis of non-verbal reasoning ability, Koch (1983) has used the model for the analysis of teacher attitudes to the communication skills of school administrators, and Steinberg (2001) examined the context effects of anger experience and anger expression questions through the GR model. Dodd (1984) provided a comparative analysis of the GR and PC models for attitude measurement. She found that, in general, using the PC and GR models for attitude assessment produced results that were highly related to traditional analysis methods while also providing the advantages of (1) knowing the precision of the measurement attained by the attitude scale for each individual and (2) facilitating the development of sample-independent scales. The GR model has also been applied to indirect measures of writing assessment (Ackerman, 1986) and to computerized adaptive testing (CAT; Samejima, 1976).

HOW LARGE A CALIBRATION SAMPLE?

In a study of parameter recovery in the GR model, Reise and Yu (1990) found that sample size did not affect estimation of the person location parameter, but did affect estimation of the item parameters. They recommended that at least 500 respondents were needed to achieve an adequate calibration with the GR model. Their study was conducted with 25 five-response category items and, therefore, their guidelines (strictly speaking) are appropriate only for instruments of this length.

As is the case with the PC and RS models, because of the interaction of the distribution of the respondents across the response categories, as well as across the items, it is difficult to arrive at a hard-and-fast guideline that would be applicable in all situations. However, for guidance we provide very rough guidelines. Assuming MMLE, a symmetric θ distribution, and that the respondents distribute themselves across the response categories in reasonable numbers, we suggest that the minimum sample size be, say 500. This value is a quasi-lower bound that serves to address the issues of fit analysis, dimensionality assessment, ensuring that there are respondents in each category, difficulty in estimating discrimination parameters, and so on. As stated in the previous chapter, it may be anticipated that there is a sample size, say 1200, at which one reaches, practically speaking, a point of diminishing returns in

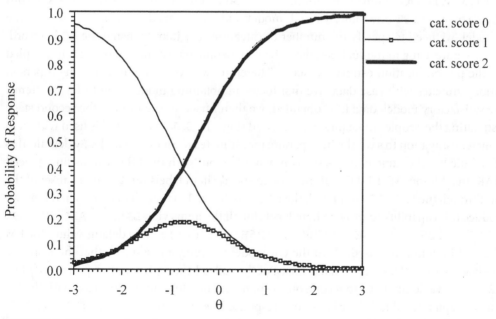

FIGURE 8.11. ORFs for a three-category response item with $\alpha = 1.5$, $\delta_1 = -1.0$, and $\delta_2 = -0.5$.

terms of improvement in estimation accuracy. (As previously stated, this 1200 should not be interpreted as an upper bound.) If one adopts a sample size ratio for sample size determination (e.g., 5 persons for every parameter estimated), then it is probably more useful closer to the lower bound than to the 1200 value (i.e., when the sample size is large, then the sample size ratio becomes less important). As previously mentioned, these sample size guidelines should not be interpreted as hard-and-fast rules and these suggestions are tempered by the purpose of the administration (e.g., survey, establishing norms, equating, item pool development/maintenance, etc.), the estimation approach, the application's characteristics (e.g., distribution and range of transition/category boundary locations, instrument length, latent distribution shape, etc.), ancillary technique sample size requirements, the use of a prior distribution for estimating α, and the amount of missing data.

EXAMPLE: APPLICATION OF THE GR MODEL TO AN ATTITUDES TOWARDS CONDOMS SCALE, MMLE

In Chapter 7 we apply the RS model to survey data from an attitudes toward condoms instrument. We now revisit these data. Recall that our instrument contains six statements people have made about condoms. The respondents are asked how much they agree with each of the statements on a 4-point Likert response scale (1="strongly disagree," 2="disagree more than I agree," 3="agree more than I disagree," 4="strongly agree"). Because the six statements are "negatively" worded, a respondent who strongly agrees with a statement is indicating a less favorable attitude toward condom use. As we did in Chapter 7, we assume that we have evidence supporting the tenability of the unidimensionality assumption. We use MULTILOG to perform our calibration.

The MULTILOG command file for this calibration is presented in Table 8.3. The keyword GRADED on the TEST line indicates a GR model calibration. In addition, as we did with the PC model, we need to specify the number of categories per item by using the NC keyword. Because we are using individual case data, the item parameter estimation phase is uncoupled from the person location estimation stage. Therefore, we now show how to obtain person location estimates with case data. We first focus on obtaining model–data fit for the items. Once satisfactory model–data fit is obtained, we then turn our attention to the second stage of estimating the people. To facilitate this second stage the SAVE command is used with item parameter estimation to save the item parameter estimates to an external file. By default, this external file has the same name as the command file, but with the MLG extension replaced by PAR. In addition, MULTILOG allows one to specify item labels for ALL or a subset of the items through the LABELS command; the labels are limited to four characters. Therefore, we introduce this capability to provide item labels for all the items via >LABELS ALL, NAMES= ('I26B','I26C','I26E','I26G','I26H','I26K');. The default values for EM cycles and iterations are used. With the GR model the program assumes that the response codes begin with 1. Because our data consist of the codes 1 through 4, our response code line is 1234 and we do not have to recode our responses. Therefore, unlike the case with the PC model (Chapter 7, Table 7.1), each of our response lines (i.e., the lines 111111, 222222, and so on) matches the values in the response code line.

TABLE 8.3. Command File for the MULTILOG GR Model Calibration Example

```
MULTILOG for Windows 7.00.2327.2
Attitudes toward condoms
>PROBLEM RANDOM, INDIVIDUAL, DATA = 'C:CONDOMS.DAT',NITEMS = 6, NGROUPS = 1,
        NEXAMINEES = 3473, NCHARS = 4;
>TEST ALL,
        GRADED,                              ⇐ Specification of GR model[a]
        NC = (4(0)6);
>LABELS ALL,NAMES=('I26B','I26C','I26E', 'I26G','I26H','I26K');
>SAVE ;
>END ;
4                               ⇐ Number of response categories
1234                            ⇐ The response code line
111111                          ⇐ The 1s are coded to be 1s for all six items
222222                          ⇐ The 2s are coded to be 2s for all six items
333333                          ⇐ The 3s are coded to be 3s for all six items
444444                          ⇐ The 4s are coded to be 4s for all six items
(4A1,6A1)
```

[a]The text following the ⇐ is provided to help the reader understand the corresponding input.

The output is presented in Table 8.4. The listing shows that the MAXIMUM NUMBER OF EM CYCLES PERMITTED is 25 and that MULTILOG executed 23 (i.e., FINISHED CYCLE 23). Therefore, convergence is achieved. (If convergence is not achieved, then we would modify the command file by, for example, inserting the line >EST NC=999 IT=250; directly preceding the >END; line to increase the number of EM cycles and iterations and reexecute the program.) The NUMBER OF FREE PARAMETERS IS: 24 and reflects that there are 3 δ_{xj}s plus one α_j for each of the six items.

The item parameter estimates for the first item are presented to show the their presentation format. The MULTILOG GR model estimates are on the logistic metric. The first line labeled A provides the item's $\hat{\alpha}$, and the following lines labeled B(1), B(2), and B(3) are the $\hat{\delta}_{11}, \hat{\delta}_{12}$, and $\hat{\delta}_{13}$, respectively (i.e., $\hat{\alpha}_1 = 1.02, \hat{\delta}_{11} = -0.55, \hat{\delta}_{12} = 0.13, \hat{\delta}_{13} = 1.00$). As would be expected, the $\hat{\delta}_{xj}$s are in sequential order. Table 8.5 contains all the item parameter estimates. Most items show reasonable discrimination capacity and, it appears, that the instrument should perform well in estimating individuals in the approximate range of –1.88 to 1.23. This belief may be verified by examining the total information function.

As discussed above, the item parameter estimates are followed by two tables containing the item's information as well as the observed and expected proportions for each category. Comparing the expected and observed proportions shows that there is relatively close agreement between the observed proportion within a category and what would be predicted on the basis of the model using these parameter estimates. As mentioned in previous chapters, our fit analysis should include a comparison of empirical and predicted ORFs. Although MULTILOG does not provide these graphs, the program MODFIT can be used for this purpose with the GR model.

The ORFs for the first item are presented in Figure 8.12. This figure's left panel shows that this item ("Sex doesn't feel as good when you use a condom") is behaving primarily as a dichotomous item. Below approximately $\theta = 0.33$ a respondent is most likely to "strongly disagree" with the statement, and above this point would most likely "strongly agree" with the statement. The figure's right panel shows that this item provides most of its information

TABLE 8.4. Abridged Output from the MULTILOG GR Model Calibration Example

```
:
ESTIMATION PARAMETERS:
 THE ITEMS WILL BE CALIBRATED--
   BY MARGINAL MAXIMUM LIKELIHOOD ESTIMATION
 MAXIMUM NUMBER OF EM CYCLES PERMITTED:  25
 NUMBER OF PARAMETER-SEGMENTS USED IS:  15
 NUMBER OF FREE PARAMETERS IS:   24
 MAXIMUM NUMBER OF M-STEP ITERATIONS IS   4 TIMES
   THE NUMBER OF PARAMETERS IN THE SEGMENT
 THE M-STEP CONVERGENCE CRITERION IS: 0.000100
 THE EM-CYCLE CONVERGENCE CRITERION IS: 0.001000
:
FINISHED CYCLE  23
MAXIMUM INTERCYCLE PARAMETER CHANGE=   0.00070 P(    9)

ITEM SUMMARY

ITEM   1: I26B  4 GRADED CATEGORIES
       P(#) ESTIMATE (S.E.)
A        1    1.02  (0.05)
B( 1)    2   -0.55  (0.05)
B( 2)    3    0.13  (0.05)
B( 3)    4    1.00  (0.07)

@THETA:      INFORMATION:   (Theta values increase in steps of 0.2)
-3.0 - -1.6  0.073 0.087 0.103 0.120 0.139 0.159 0.181 0.202
-1.4 -  0.0  0.224 0.245 0.264 0.280 0.294 0.305 0.313 0.317
 0.2 -  1.6  0.319 0.318 0.314 0.306 0.296 0.283 0.267 0.249
 1.8 -  3.0  0.229 0.207 0.186 0.164 0.143 0.124 0.106

OBSERVED AND EXPECTED COUNTS/PROPORTIONS IN
CATEGORY(K):   1       2      3      4
OBS. FREQ.   1338     492    602    1041
OBS. PROP.  0.3853 0.1417 0.1733 0.2997
EXP. PROP.  0.3858 0.1411 0.1725 0.3007
:
@THETA:      INFORMATION:
-3.0 - -1.6  1.384 1.428 1.476 1.529 1.586 1.650 1.722 1.806
-1.4 -  0.0  1.907 2.031 2.189 2.393 2.653 2.974 3.347 3.739
 0.2 -  1.6  4.099 4.377 4.539 4.579 4.500 4.300 3.984 3.580
 1.8 -  3.0  3.139 2.715 2.345 2.045 1.811 1.634 1.500

@THETA:      POSTERIOR STANDARD DEVIATION:
-3.0 - -1.6  0.850 0.837 0.823 0.809 0.794 0.778 0.762 0.744
-1.4 -  0.0  0.724 0.702 0.676 0.646 0.614 0.580 0.547 0.517
 0.2 -  1.6  0.494 0.478 0.469 0.467 0.471 0.482 0.501 0.529
 1.8 -  3.0  0.564 0.607 0.653 0.669 0.743 0.782 0.816

MARGINAL RELIABILITY:    0.6706
```

around 0.2, although not a large amount relative to the other items on the instrument. For example, Figure 8.13's right panel shows that item 2 provides substantially more information for estimating a person's location than does item 1. This difference in the amount of available information is directly related to the items' $\hat{\alpha}_j$s; $\hat{\alpha}_1 = 1.02$ and $\hat{\alpha}_2 = 2.09$. This item ("It's embarrassing to buy condoms") also behaves primarily as a dichotomous item (the left panel). The ORFs show that individuals who hold positive attitudes toward condom use (the left side of the continuum), as well as "somewhat" neutral attitudes, are most likely not to find the purchase of condoms embarrassing. In other words, persons with θs below approximately 0.8 are most likely to "strongly disagree" with the statement "It's embarrassing to buy condoms."

Although our examination of item 1's ORFs shows that the item is behaving primarily as a dichotomous item, this observation cannot be gleaned from the OBSERVED AND EXPECTED COUNTS/PROPORTIONS table nor from examining the $\hat{\delta}_{xj}$s (Table 8.5); this is also true for item 2. Therefore, it is recommended that standard practice with the GR model be to obtain the ORFs for all items on the instrument. For completeness, our examination of the ORFs for the remaining items on the instrument reveals the same dichotomous-like pattern of ORFs seen with items 1 and 2. If these data were from a pilot test of the instrument, then the instrument's author(s) might want to consider modifying the statements.

For pedagogical reasons, we assume that we have model–data fit analysis and that there is no concern with the dichotomous-like nature of the items. Therefore, the six-item scale is used to estimate the respondents' attitudes toward condoms. In previous chapters both the MLE and EAP approaches to person location estimation have been used. This time we use *maximum a posteriori* (MAP). (MAP is discussed in Chapter 4.) Recall that like EAP, MAP provides a Bayes estimator that is typically regressed toward the mean of the prior distribution. However, whereas EAP uses the mean of the posterior distribution, MAP uses its mode. As a Bayesian approach, MAP provides person location estimates for all response patterns.

To obtain the person estimates with individual case data requires a second execution of MULTILOG. In this second execution we may choose to reestimate the item parameters or we can provide the item parameter estimates and estimate only the people. Because in our item parameter calibration stage we saved the item parameter estimates to an external file, we estimate only the people in our second execution.

To estimate the person locations we modify the command file presented in Table 8.3. The PROBLEM RANDOM, ... line in the command file in Table 8.3 is replaced with PROBLEM SCORE, ... The subcommand SCORE on the PROBLEM line instructs MULTILOG to calculate person location estimates. We use MAP estimation with the default normal prior with a mean of 0.0.[4] To read the previously saved item parameter estimates file, the START command is used. Specifically, >START ALL,PARAM='C:CONDOMS.PAR'; instructs MULTILOG to use the item parameter values in the file CONDOMS.PAR for all the items; this file's name is created in the item parameter estimation stage. (If the START command

TABLE 8.5. GR Model Item Parameter Estimates for the Attitude Towards Condoms Six-Item Scale

Item	$\hat{\alpha}_j$	$s_e(\hat{\alpha}_j)$	$\hat{\delta}_{j1}$	$s_e(\hat{\delta}_{j1})$	$\hat{\delta}_{j2}$	$s_e(\hat{\delta}_{j2})$	$\hat{\delta}_{j3}$	$s_e(\hat{\delta}_{j3})$
1	1.02	(0.05)	−0.55	(0.05)	0.13	(0.05)	1.00	(0.07)
2	2.09	(0.08)	0.39	(0.03)	0.74	(0.03)	1.13	(0.04)
3	2.15	(0.09)	0.50	(0.03)	0.87	(0.03)	1.23	(0.04)
4	0.67	(0.04)	−1.57	(0.12)	−0.34	(0.07)	1.07	(0.10)
5	0.90	(0.05)	−0.74	(0.06)	−0.15	(0.05)	0.51	(0.06)
6	0.77	(0.05)	−1.88	(0.12)	−0.93	(0.08)	0.40	(0.07)

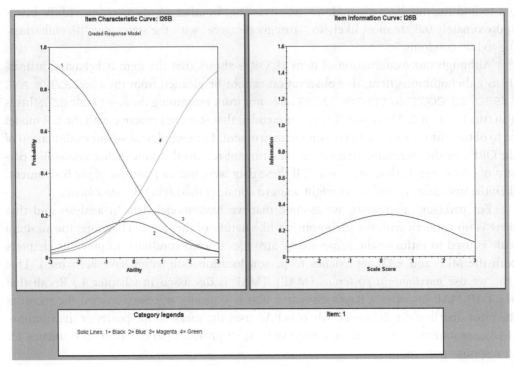

FIGURE 8.12. ORFs and item information function for item 1.

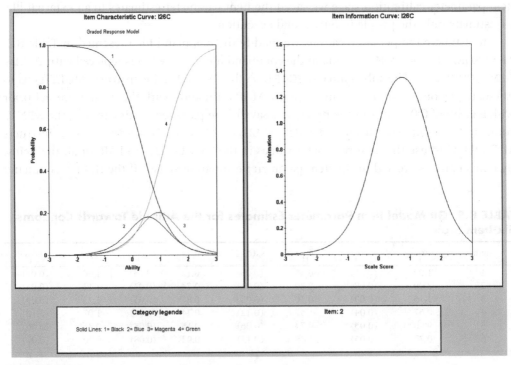

FIGURE 8.13. ORFs and item information function for item 2.

had been omitted, then MULTILOG would have reestimated the item parameters in the process of estimating the person locations, but would not have displayed the item parameter estimates. In this context, the use of the SAVE command would instruct MULTILOG to save the person, not item, parameter estimates to an external file with the same file name as the command file, but with the extension SCO.) The command file for person parameter estimation is presented in Table 8.6.

Table 8.7 contains some of the output. The file has the format previously seen, except that the item parameter values read from the external file are echoed to the output file. These should be checked to ensure that they are correct. The line MODAL THETAS WILL BE ESTIMATED indicates person location estimation; with MULTILOG 7.03 this line does not indicate MAP estimation because it is also displayed when MLE is used. In addition, the line THE MODAL THETAS WILL BE PRINTED states that the person location estimates are displayed in the output file as opposed to being saved to an external file (i.e., through the use of the SAVE command).

It can be seen from the FIRST OBSERVATION AS READ line that the first person responded "strongly disagree" to all six items (i.e., the person's response vector is 111111). Although estimating this person's location with MLE would not have been possible, with MAP this individual receives a location estimate of −1.883 with a standard error of 0.661.[5] This person is almost 2 logits below the mean. In terms of the instrument's purpose this person has a positive attitude toward condom use. In contrast, the last person responded "strongly agree" to all items and obtained a $\hat{\theta}$ of 1.883 with the same standard error as the first person; the response vector is determined by looking at the data file. This $\hat{\theta}$ of 1.883 indicates that the person has a negative attitude toward condom use. The standard error is, in part, a function of the instrument's length as well as the quality of the items comprising the scale. Given the instrument's total information function, we would expect, by and large, that the standard errors would be smaller for $\hat{\theta}$s around the center of the attitude toward condoms continuum than at the extremes of this latent variable.

TABLE 8.6. Command File for the MULTILOG GR Model Calibration Example—MAP Estimation

```
MULTILOG for Windows 7.00.2327.2
Attitudes toward condoms; used previously save item param estimates
>PROBLEM SCORE, INDIVIDUAL, DATA = 'C:CONDOMS.DAT',NITEMS = 6, NGROUPS = 1,
     NEXAMINEES = 3473, NCHARS = 4;
>TEST ALL,
     GRADED,                               ⇐ Specification of GR model[a]
     NC = (4(0)6);
>START ALL,PARAM='C:CONDOMS.PAR';
>END ;
4
1234
111111
222222
333333
444444
(4A1,6A1)
```

[a]The text following the ⇐ is provided to help the reader understand the corresponding input.

TABLE 8.7. Abridged MAP Output from the MULTILOG GR Model Calibration Example

```
:
>START ALL,PARAM='C:CONDOMS.PAR';
            PARAMETER VALUES
:
< Estimates from external file displayed>
:
 DATA PARAMETERS:
  NUMBER OF LINES IN THE DATA FILE: 3473
:

 ESTIMATION PARAMETERS:
   MODAL THETAS WILL BE ESTIMATED

 OUTPUT-CONTROL PARAMETERS
  THE MODAL THETAS WILL BE PRINTED
:
 FIRST OBSERVATION AS READ-

 ID       1
 ITEMS 111111
 NORML      0.000

 SCORING DATA...

   THETAHAT      S.E.   ITER      ID FIELD
    -1.883      0.661     6          1
    -1.883      0.661     6          2
    -1.315      0.658     4          3
    -1.883      0.661     6          4
    -1.883      0.661     6          5
      :
     1.883      0.661     6       3471
     1.883      0.661     6       3472
     1.883      0.661     6       3473
```

INFORMATION FOR GRADED DATA

As discussed in Chapter 7, with polytomous models it is possible to determine the amount of information provided by each response category. When one scores an item in a graded way, the information function for the graded response is (Samejima, 1969)

$$I_{x_j}(\theta) = \left\{-\frac{\partial^2 \ln p_k}{\partial \theta^2}\right\} p_k \tag{8.5}$$

That is, each graded response (potentially) contributes some information for estimating a person's location. The sum of these option information functions, $I_{x_j}(\theta)$, equals the item's information, $I_j(\theta)$. That is, item information is defined as

$$I_j(\theta) = \sum_{x_j=0}^{m_j} I_{x_j}(\theta) = \sum_{x_j=0}^{m_j} \frac{\left\{P_{x_j}'\right\}^2}{P_{x_j}} \qquad (8.6)$$

When applied to dichotomous data Equation 8.6 simplifies to the item information formula presented in Chapter 2.

As seen in previous chapters, the sum of the item information yields the instrument's total information:

$$I(\theta) = \sum_{j=1}^{L} I_j(\theta) \qquad (8.7)$$

In the case of the GR model, and given Equation 8.4, the option information function is

$$I_{x_j}(\theta) = \frac{\left\{P_{x_j}'\right\}^2}{P_{x_j}} = \frac{\left[P_{x_j}^* - P_{x_{j+1}}^*\right]^2}{\left\{P_{x_j}^* - P_{x_{j+1}}^*\right\}} \qquad (8.8)$$

where $P_{x_j}^*$ is given by Equation 8.3 and $P_{x_j}^{*\prime}$ is its first derivative. As mentioned above, $P_{x_j}^*$ is, in effect, the 2PL model and in Chapter 5 we stated that the first derivative of the 2PL model is $\alpha_j p_j(1 - p_j)$. As a result, we have that $P_{x_j}^{*\prime} = \alpha_j P_{x_j}^*(1 - P_{x_j}^*)$.

By way of an example, let $m_j = 2$, and for ease of presentation, let $\varphi_{x_j} = (1 + \exp(\alpha_j(\theta - \delta_{x_j})))^2$. In the following we first concentrate on the bracketed term in the numerator of Equation 8.8 and then proceed to calculate the option and item information.

When $x_j = 0$, then we have that $P_0^* \equiv 1.0$ and our

$$\varphi_1 = \left[1 + e^{\alpha_j(\theta - \delta_1)}\right]^2$$

so that

$$P_0' = \left[P_0^{*\prime} - P_1^{*\prime}\right] = 0 - \alpha_j \left(\frac{e^{\alpha_j(\theta - \delta_1)}}{\varphi_1}\right) = -\alpha_j \left(\frac{e^{\alpha_j(\theta - \delta_1)}}{\varphi_1}\right)$$

For the category score $x_j = 1$ we have that

$$\varphi_2 = \left[1 + e^{\alpha_j(\theta - \delta_2)}\right]^2$$

and

$$P_0' = \left[P_0^{*'} - P_1^{*'} \right] = \alpha_j \left(\frac{e^{\alpha_j(\theta-\delta_1)}}{\varphi_1} \right) - \alpha_j \left(\frac{e^{\alpha_j(\theta-\delta_1)}}{\varphi_1} \right)$$

$$= \alpha_j \left[\left(\frac{e^{\alpha_j(\theta-\delta_1)}}{\varphi_1} \right) - \left(\frac{e^{\alpha_j(\theta-\delta_2)}}{\varphi_2} \right) \right]$$

For the last category score, $x_j = 2$, we have that $P_3^* \equiv 0$. Therefore,

$$P_2' = \left[P_2^{*'} - P_3^{*'} \right] = \alpha_j \left(\frac{e^{\alpha_j(\theta-\delta_2)}}{\varphi_2} \right) - 0 = \alpha_j \left(\frac{e^{\alpha_j(\theta-\delta_2)}}{\varphi_2} \right)$$

To obtain the item's information we square each of these first derivatives, divide it by the probability of responding in the corresponding category, and then sum the quotients:

$$I_j(\theta) = \sum_{x_j=0}^{2} \frac{\left\{ P_{x_j}' \right\}^2}{P_{x_j}} = \frac{\left[P_0' \right]^2}{P_0} + \frac{\left[P_1' \right]^2}{P_1} + \frac{\left[P_2' \right]^2}{P_2}$$

where each quotient is the option information function for the corresponding x_j.

Figure 8.14 contains the option and item information functions for the item shown in Figures 8.8 and 8.9. Given Equation 8.6, it is not surprising that the item information (solid bold line) for this item is greater than the individual option information functions. These individual option information functions vary not only in their individual contributions to the item information, but also in how their information is distributed across θ. For example, the option information functions for $x_j = 0$ and 2 are unimodal, whereas for $x_j = 1$ the function is bimodal with a minimum around 0.0. Because the maxima of the option information functions for $x_j = 0$ and 2 are in the vicinity of 0.0, this item is able to provide a somewhat uniform amount of information for estimating individuals between roughly −1.5 and 1.5. The distribution of information is a function of the distances between δ_{x_j}s (Samejima, 1969).

Samejima (1969) shows that there is an increase in item information if a response category is added between two adjacent categories. Therefore, the amount of item information available by treating an item in a polytomous graded fashion is at least equal to, and more likely greater than, the amount of item information available when the item is scored in a dichotomous fashion. We can see this in Figure 8.14. The dashed line in the figure shows the information available when this item is dichotomously scored (i.e., $x_j = 0$ or 1 is considered to be incorrect). As can be seen, the graded scoring results in greater information

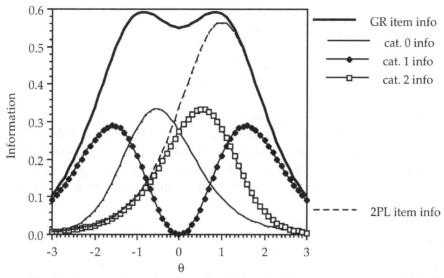

FIGURE 8.14. Category and item information functions for a three-category response item with $\alpha = 1.5$, $\delta_1 = -1.0$, and $\delta_2 = 1.0$ and a dichotomous item ($\alpha = 1.5$ and $\delta_2 = 1$).

than when the item is dichotomously scored. Moreover, this information is over a broader range of θ than when the item is scored dichotomously. In general, polytomously scored items tend to provide greater information toward the lower end of the continuum than when dichotomously scored. For our example item, we see that the graded scoring results in greater information, particularly below the item's location of 1, than when the item is dichotomously scored.

METRIC TRANSFORMATION, GPC AND GR MODELS

To transform the item parameter estimates one uses $\alpha^*_j = \alpha_j / \zeta$ for the discrimination parameters (or their estimates) and $\delta^*_{x_j} = \zeta(\delta_{x_j}) + \kappa$ for the category location parameters (or their estimates). The θ metric can be transformed to another metric that in itself would be useful (e.g., an "attitude toward condoms" metric that has some arbitrary mean and unit) by using $\theta^* = \zeta(\theta) + \kappa$.

Alternatively, we can convert the person locations (or their estimates) to their corresponding expected trait scores through the sum of the expected item responses. For the GPC model where 1 indicates the lowest response category we use

$$T = \sum^{L} \left[\sum_{k=1}^{m_j} k * p(x_{jk} \mid \theta) \right] \tag{8.9}$$

T has a range from L to $\sum^{L} m_j$ and the bracketed term is expected item response.

For the GR model with 0 to represent the lowest response category we use

$$T = \sum_{}^{L} \left[\sum_{k=0}^{m_j} k * p(x_{jk} | \theta) \right] \tag{8.10}$$

and the bracketed term is expected item response. In this case T's range is from 0 to $\sum^{L} m_j$. When 1 represents the lowest response category (e.g., as might be used with a Likert response scale) the limits of summation for the inside-the-brackets summation would be changed to 1 and $(m_j + 1)$; the range of T is L to $\sum^{L} m_j + L$. The expected item response from either Equation 8.9 or 8.10 can be used with Q_3 to examine conditional dependence.

SUMMARY

The generalized partial credit model relaxes the equal item discrimination assumption of the partial credit model. That is, the GPC model contains a discrimination parameter that indicates the degree to which an item can differentiate among different values of θ. As in the partial credit model, the points of intersection of adjacent ORFs are the transition location parameters, δ_{jh}s. These transition locations do not need to be sequentially ordered. The model's ORFs reflect an interaction between the item's transition location parameters and discrimination parameter. The GPC may be applied to situations where ordered response data arise through either partial credit scoring, ratings, or through the use of a Likert response format. In this latter case, the GPC may be referred to as the generalized rating scale model. Therefore, the GRS model allows for the modeling of Likert response data where items are allowed to vary in their discrimination.

The partial credit model is (mathematically) a special case of the generalized partial credit model in the same way that the Rasch model is a special case of the 2PL model. However, some individuals consider the partial credit model to represent a philosophical approach to measurement that is not reflected in the generalized partial credit. (This philosophical difference is the same one presented with the Rasch model in Chapter 2.) The GPC model simplifies to the 2PL model in the two category (dichotomous) case. As is the case with the partial credit and rating scale models, the generalized partial credit model is a special case of the nominal response model.

Another model for ordered polytomous data that allows items to vary in their discrimination is the graded response model. Both Masters (1982) and Muraki's (1992) original formulations of their models are in terms of a series of dichotomous models that govern the probability of responding in one category versus the next adjacent category. In contrast, the formulation of the graded response model involves specifying the probability that a respondent would obtain a given category score or higher versus lower category score(s). As such, the model provides the cumulative probabilities of obtaining different subsets of category scores. To obtain the probability of responding in a particular category, one subtracts the cumulative probabilities for adjacent scores from one another. Unlike the case with the partial credit, rating scale, and generalized partial credit models, the category boundary location parameters are sequentially ordered in the graded response model. Given this characteristic, we need to examine the ORFs to determine whether each response category is the most likely response at some point along the continuum. The GR model simplifies to the two-parameter model when applied to dichotomous data. It should be noted that in the context of proficiency assessment, neither the GPC model nor the GR model addresses the possibility of examinees guessing on items.

In the next chapter we present two models for polytomous responses that are not inherently ordered. Such data may arise, for example, in proficiency testing (e.g., analogy items using a multiple-choice item format) or with attitudinal or survey instruments that use a nonordered response format (e.g., "Yes," "No," "Unsure"). These models, the nominal response model and the multiple-choice model, contain two parameters for each response category to reflect the attractiveness of each category as well as how well each category differentiates among θs. As mentioned above, the nominal response model can be constrained to subsume the GPC, GRS, PC, and RS models as well as the two-parameter model.

NOTES

1. The models are, in essence, *ordinal logistic regression* models using latent person and item characterizations. In the case of the graded response model, a probit link function is used in lieu of the logit link function. That is, the function used is the cumulative density function of the normal distribution. Therefore, "probit[p(b)]" is used in lieu of "logit[p(b)]," so that we have probit[p(b)] = $\gamma + \alpha\theta$ instead of logit[p(b)] = $\gamma + \alpha\theta$.

2. Samjima's (1969) development is based on the two-parameter normal ogive model (see Appendix C). As such, the presentation of the GR model typically includes the scaling constant D:

$$P_{x_j}^*(\theta) = \frac{e^{D\alpha_j(\theta-\delta_{x_j})}}{1+e^{D\alpha_j(\theta-\delta_{x_j})}} \tag{8.11}$$

However, the perspective in this book is that the logistic metric is intrinsically useful and we are not concerned with approximating the normal metric. Therefore, the GR model in Equation 8.3 does not include D.

3. When the GR model is applied to dichotomous data, the GR model simplifies to the two-parameter model. When an item has only two possible scores (e.g., $x_j = 0$ or 1), then $m_j = 1$ and the probability of a response of 1, p_1, equals

$$p_1 = P_1^* - P_2^* = P_1^* - 0 = \frac{e^{\alpha_j(\theta-\delta_{x_1})}}{1+e^{\alpha_j(\theta-\delta_{x_1})}} - 0 = \frac{e^{\alpha_j(\theta-\delta)}}{1+e^{-\alpha_j(\theta-\delta)}} \tag{8.12}$$

because $P_2^* \equiv 0$ and the probability of a response of 0 is

$$p_0 = P_0^* - P_1^* = 1.0 - P_1^* = 1 - \frac{e^{\alpha_j(\theta-\delta)}}{1+e^{\alpha_j(\theta-\delta)}} = \frac{1}{1+e^{-\alpha_j(\theta-\delta)}} \tag{8.13}$$

because $P_0^* \equiv 1$. Equation 8.12 is the 2PL model and shows that the GR model is equivalent to the two-parameter model when an item has only two response categories; with only two categories there is only one δ and the category subscript on δ is dropped. If discrimination is held constant across items, then Equation 8.12 becomes the one-parameter model.

4. If we want MLE person location estimates, then the PROBLEM line would also include the subcommands NOPOP and CRITERION (i.e., PROBLEM SCORE, ..., NOPOP, CRITERION;) In addition, the response vectors would need to be augmented to have a criterion value (e.g., 0.0) or at least as many blanks spaces as specified in the format statement. For example, the first case would be "ƀƀƀ1111111ƀ0.0" where the ƀ indicates a blank space (i.e., x = "   1111111 0.0"). As a result, the corresponding format statement would need to include an additional field to read the criterion value, say F4.0, so that the format statement is (4A1,6A1,F4.0). Because the output file contains one or more lines for each case, we recommend that the SAVE command be used if the estimates are to be used for further analysis. When MLE is not possible for a case, then the output file contains an indication that the estimation is not possible (i.e., DID NOT CONVERGE, SUBJECT - <case number>) on one line, followed on the subsequent line by the case's response vector. If the SAVE command is used, then only the nonconverged information is presented in the output file. However, if the SAVE command is not used, then the output file contains nonconverged cases intermixed with the converged cases. For the converged cases, the $\hat{\theta}$, its standard error, the number of iterations required to achieve convergence, and the case identification are presented.

5. As is true with dichotomous models, using MLE for estimating a respondent's location in this example will not provide a finite estimate for either a response vector of all 1s or of all 4s (i.e., response vectors that consist only of the minimum or only of the maximum response categories). However, MLE respondent location estimates are available for the other (nonminimum or nonmaximum) constant response vectors of, for example, all 2s or all 3s, assuming a four-category score item. To understand why this is so, consider the ORFs for a three-category score item with category scores of 1, 2, and 3. The ORF for $x_j = 1$ is asymptotic with 1 and 0, whereas the ORF for $x_j = 3$ is asymptotic with 0 and 1. Conceptually speaking, the likelihood function for a response vector of all 3s can be envisioned as the multiplication of the corresponding ORFs L times. As a result, the likelihood function looks like the ORF for a category score of 3 and does not have a mode. Conversely, the likelihood function for a response vector of all 1s is the multiplication of the corresponding ORFs L times and looks like the ORF for a category score of 1 and does not have a mode. In neither case can MLE provide a finite estimate of θ. However, for $x_j = 2$ we have an ORF with a mode. Therefore, when one has a response vector of 2s, the product of the corresponding ORFs results in a likelihood function that has a mode. In this case, MLE can provide a finite estimate of θ.

9

Models for Nominal Polytomous Data

In this chapter we discuss two models, the nominal response and multiple-choice models, that can be used with nominal polytomous data. Unlike ordered polytomous data, with nominal data the item responses are not inherently ordered. As a result, one does not have a direct, nor an inverse, relationship between the observed responses and the magnitude of θ. However, it is still possible to capture information in each of the possible responses. Therefore, in addition to the previously mentioned advantages of IRT over classical test theory (CTT), with the nominal response and multiple-choice models we can obtain a person location estimate that is directly based on the individual's nominal response data. In contrast, because the sum of nominal polytomous responses has no inherent meaning vis-à-vis the variable being measured, the traditional approach of using a total score as a person measure would be meaningless. The best that one can do in the traditional sense is to sum the *dichotomized* polytomous responses to obtain a potentially meaningful total score.

Nominal response data (also known as categorical response data) may arise in a number of situations. For instance, in the social sciences scales will sometimes incorporate variables that use categorical polytomous response formats. Responses to these variables constitute nominal polytomous response data. For example, consider the following three-item scale for measuring compulsive behavior using a categorical response format.

1. Whenever I leave the house I feel a need to check at least five times that I locked each door and window.

    ☐ Yes ☐ No ☐ Maybe ☐ Won't Say

2. I need to wash my hands at least five times before I can eat.

    ☐ Yes ☐ No ☐ Maybe ☐ Won't Say

3. Whenever I mail a check to pay a bill I will verify that I have signed the check at least five times before mailing it.

    ☐ Yes ☐ No ☐ Maybe ☐ Won't Say

None of the previously discussed models would be appropriate for modeling all four categorical responses to these items. In other situations we might specifically design questions to incorporate useful information for locating an individual. For instance, research on student misconceptions in solving mathematics problems (e.g., Brown & Burton, 1978; Brown & VanLehn, 1980; Tatsuoka, 1983) has shown that incorrect responses can be due to more than just one kind of misconception. As such, items may be designed to incorporate these misconceptions rather than simply providing arbitrary or plausible incorrect alternatives. However, it may not be possible to order the item alternatives to reflect different degrees or severity of misconceptions. If this is the case, then one would have categorical response data. As an example of an item that is constructed to incorporate misconceptions, consider the following item whose alternatives reflect the application of erroneous rules of signed-number subtraction (Tatsuoka, 1983):

1. $-6 - (-10) = ?$

    a. -16

    b. -4

    c. 4

These alternatives potentially provide useful information, not only for locating individuals, but also for the diagnosis of mathematical misconceptions. If we dichotomized the responses to this item into incorrect and correct responses, then we would be discarding this information. Because the incorrect alternatives do not represent partially correct answers, the use of models for ordered polytomous data (e.g., the PC, GPC, or GR models) would be inappropriate for modeling this item and others like it.

CONCEPTUAL DEVELOPMENT OF THE NOMINAL RESPONSE MODEL

With categorical polytomous data one has a set of mutually exclusive unordered response categories. These response categories may correspond to (1) item options from a multiple-choice item format, (2) response options from a survey or attitude instrument, (3) rater judgments (rater judgments do not necessarily result in ordered ratings), to name just a few possibilities. Figure 9.1 contains a graphical depiction of the response format for the item from the above compulsive behavior scale, "I need to wash my hands at least five times before I can eat." In the figure the ellipse represents the item, and the response categories are presented as not being contiguous with one another to avoid implying that they are inherently ordered.

    Conceptually, each of the item's response categories has an associated probability such that the sum of these response probabilities across the categories is 1.[1] For example, when this item is administered to an infinitely large sample, the relative frequency of individuals responding "yes," "no," "maybe," and "won't say" might be, for example, 0.50, 0.25, 0.20, and 0.05, respectively. Let p_1, p_2, p_3, and p_4 be the probabilities associated with the responses "yes," "no," "maybe," and "won't say," respectively (i.e., $p_1 = 0.50$, $p_2 = 0.25$, etc.). Based on this set of probabilities we can determine the odds of one response versus

2. I need to wash my hands at least five times before I can eat.

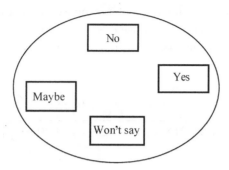

FIGURE 9.1. Schematic of categorical response categories.

another. For example, the odds of a response being a "no" as opposed to a "yes" are the odds$_{2,1}$ = (p_2/p_1) = 1/2. That is, a response of "no" is half as likely as a response of "yes," or we expect to see one "no" for every two "yes's." (Appendix E, "Odds, Odds Ratios, and Logits," contains an introduction to odds.)

As mentioned in Chapter 2, for convenience odds can be transformed to a logarithmic scale and thereby give the log odds (i.e., the logit). As an example, given that the response is either a "no" or a "yes," then the log odds of a response being a "no" as opposed to a "yes" are $\log(p_2/p_1)$. Moreover, this logit transformation allows one to express the log odds of a response being a "no" as opposed to a "yes" in terms of a predictor X (e.g., an individual's compulsive behavior):

$$\log(p_2/p_1) = \gamma_2 + \alpha_2 X$$

where α_2 and γ_2 characterize the "no" response category. (The term "$\gamma + \alpha X$" is the slope-intercept parameterization form of the logit seen in Chapter 2.) The symbol γ is the intercept and reflects the propensity to respond in one category over the other category regardless of X (i.e., γ is the baseline log odds—a model without a predictor). Further, α is the slope or the change in the log odds, or the logit, for this response as the predictor X changes by one unit. If $\alpha = 0$, then the log odds do not change as X changes.

Similarly, the log odds of a response being a "maybe" as opposed to a "yes" may be obtained by

$$\log(p_3/p_1) = \gamma_3 + \alpha_3 X$$

and the log odds of a response being a "won't say" as opposed to a "yes" is

$$\log(p_4/p_1) = \gamma_4 + \alpha_4 X$$

The above three logit equations use the "yes" response category as a *baseline* response category (i.e., the odds or log odds are with respect to the baseline category). This category may be one of specific interest or may be the category that has the largest frequency (Agresti, 1990).

Rather than talking about the log odds of a response in one category over another category, the probability of a particular response can be directly expressed by using the above logits.[2] Using these logit equations, the conditional probability for each response category, given X, are

$$p(x = 4|X) = \frac{e^{\gamma_4 + \alpha_4 X}}{e^{\gamma_1 + \alpha_1 X} + e^{\gamma_2 + \alpha_2 X} + e^{\gamma_3 + \alpha_3 X} + e^{\gamma_4 + \alpha_4 X}}$$

$$p(x = 3|X) = \frac{e^{\gamma_3 + \alpha_3 X}}{e^{\gamma_1 + \alpha_1 X} + e^{\gamma_2 + \alpha_2 X} + e^{\gamma_3 + \alpha_3 X} + e^{\gamma_4 + \alpha_4 X}}$$

$$p(x = 2|X) = \frac{e^{\gamma_2 + \alpha_2 X}}{e^{\gamma_1 + \alpha_1 X} + e^{\gamma_2 + \alpha_2 X} + e^{\gamma_3 + \alpha_3 X} + e^{\gamma_4 + \alpha_4 X}}$$

and

$$p(x = 1|X) = \frac{e^{\gamma_1 + \alpha_1 X}}{e^{\gamma_1 + \alpha_1 X} + e^{\gamma_2 + \alpha_2 X} + e^{\gamma_3 + \alpha_3 X} + e^{\gamma_4 + \alpha_4 X}}$$

More generally, letting m represent the number of response categories, we have that the probability of a response, k, conditional on X is

$$p(x = k|X) = \frac{e^{\gamma_k + \alpha_k X}}{\sum\limits_{h=1}^{m} e^{\gamma_h + \alpha_h X}} = \frac{e^{\gamma_k + \alpha_k X}}{1 + \sum\limits_{h=2}^{m} e^{\gamma_h + \alpha_h X}} \tag{9.1}$$

To identify this model we may set the baseline response category's α and γ to 0 (i.e., $\alpha_1 = \gamma_1 = 0$). As a result, there are $m - 1$ unique logit equations with $(m - 1)$ α_ks and $(m - 1)$ γ_ks. In other words, there are $(m - 1)$ potentially nonzero α_ks, $(m - 1)$ potentially nonzero γ_ks, and one α_k and one γ_k that are each equal to zero. The probability for the baseline category may be obtained by subtracting the sum of the probabilities for the other categories from 1.

The $(m - 1)$ α_ks may be transformed to obtain an α_k that is potentially nonzero for each of the m response categories. Similarly, the $(m - 1)$ γ_ks may be transformed so that each of the m γ_ks is potentially nonzero. (Note that we use italicization/nonitalicization to distinguish between the estimated slopes and intercepts [i.e., the $(m - 1)$ α_ks and $(m - 1)$ γ_ks] and the transformed slopes and intercepts [i.e., the m α_ks and m γ_ks].) With these transformations the $\alpha_1 = \gamma_1 = 0$ constraint will "translate" into the m α_ks, collectively summing to zero, and the m γ_ks, as a set, will be constrained to sum to zero (i.e., the model is still identified). These transformations are accomplished by using the appropriate transformation matrix.[3]

As an example of these transformations, assume a four-response category item ($m = 4$) with α_ks of {0.44, –0.55, –0.60} and γ_ks of {0.37, –0.74, –0.34}. (These α_k and γ_k values come from Table 9.2.) If we use the transformation matrix, $\underline{T}$, with the values of

$$\underline{T} = \begin{bmatrix} -0.25 & 0.75 & -0.25 & -0.25 \\ -0.25 & -0.25 & 0.75 & -0.25 \\ -0.25 & -0.25 & -0.25 & 0.75 \end{bmatrix}$$

then we obtain (through matrix algebra) that

$$\alpha_1 = 0.44*(-0.25) + (-0.55*-0.25) + (-0.60*-0.25) = 0.18$$

$$\alpha_2 = 0.44*(0.75) + (-0.55*-0.25) + (-0.60*-0.25) = 0.62$$

$$\alpha_3 = 0.44*(-0.25) + (-0.55*0.75) + (-0.60*-0.25) = -0.37$$

$$\alpha_4 = 0.44*(-0.25) + (-0.55*-0.25) + (-0.60*0.75) = -0.42$$

The sum of these α_ks is 0.0. For the intercepts we have

$$\gamma_1 = 0.37*(-0.25) + (-0.74*-0.25) + (-0.34*-0.25) = 0.18$$

$$\gamma_2 = 0.37*(0.75) + (-0.74*-0.25) + (-0.34*-0.25) = 0.55$$

$$\gamma_3 = 0.37*(-0.25) + (-0.74*0.75) + (-0.34*-0.25) = -0.56$$

$$\gamma_4 = 0.37*(-0.25) + (-0.74*-0.25) + (-0.34*0.75) = -0.16$$

the sum of these γ_ks also equals 0; the nonitalicized α_ks and γ_ks reflect the transformed italicized α_ks and γ_ks. Therefore, with the α_ks and γ_ks we potentially have a nonzero slope–intercept pair for each response category.

Equation 9.1 can be cast into the context of a latent person location variable and latent item parameters. The result is Bock's (1972) *nominal response* (NR) model (also called the *nominal categories* model). According to the NR model the probability of a person located at θ responding in the kth category of item j is given by

$$p_j(x = k | \theta, \underline{\alpha}, \underline{\gamma}) = \frac{e^{\gamma_{jk} + \alpha_{jk}\theta}}{\sum\limits_{h=1}^{m_j} e^{\gamma_{jh} + \alpha_{jh}\theta}} \tag{9.2}$$

where α_{jk} and γ_{jk} are the slope and the intercept parameters, respectively, of the response function associated with the kth indexed category of item j, and m_j is the number of response categories of item j (i.e., $k = \{1, \ldots, m_j\}$). (Note that the italicized "*m*" indicates the number of response categories, not the number of transition locations as seen with, say, the PC model.) The symbol k simply indexes the response categories and does not imply that the categories are ordered. Unlike the model in Equation 9.1, the NR model in Equation 9.2 is in terms of the *transformed* α_ks and γ_ks. For item j, γ_{jk} reflects the individual's propensity to use response category k, and α_{jk} reflects, in part, the option's discrimination capacity. The magnitude of the α_{jk}s also reflects the "order" of the categories because of the constraint mentioned above and discussed below. For brevity we use p_{jk} in lieu of $p_j(x = k|\theta, \underline{\alpha}, \underline{\gamma})$ in the following.

Given the NR model's parameterization, the description of an item's alternatives consists of m_j slope and intercept parameters. For convenience these are sometimes collected into vectors and represented in vector notation: $\underline{\alpha} = (\alpha_{j1}, \ldots, \alpha_{jm})$ and $\underline{\gamma} = (\gamma_{j1}, \ldots, \gamma_{jm})$. To address the indeterminacy issue discussed in previous chapters, two constraints are imposed on the parameters: (1) the sum of the α_{jk}s equals zero (i.e., $\sum^{m_j} \alpha_{jh} = 0$), and (2) the sum of γ_{jk}s equals zero (i.e., $\sum^{m_j} \gamma_{jh} = 0$); alternatively, the α and γ for the baseline response category may be set to 0. As a result of these constraints the number of estimated category slopes and intercepts for an item is $2(m_j - 1)$.

As discussed in connection with Equation 9.1 these constraints are implemented by using a transformation matrix, $\underline{T}$, on the *unconstrained* slope, α_{jk}, and *unconstrained* intercept, γ_{jk}, parameters; the italicization of α_{jk} and γ_{jk} reflects that they are unconstrained parameter estimates. By unconstrained, we mean the slope and intercept parameters prior to imposing the constraints or prior to being transformed by $\underline{T}$. We can collect these unconstrained discrimination parameters into a vector $\underline{\alpha} = (\alpha_{j1}, \ldots, \alpha_{jm-1})$. Similarly, the unconstrained intercept parameters may be placed in a vector $\underline{\gamma} = (\gamma_{j1}, \ldots, \gamma_{jm-1})$.

To obtain the *constrained* set of slopes ($\underline{\alpha}$) and intercepts ($\underline{\gamma}$), one postmultiplies the corresponding estimated unconstrained parameter estimate vectors by $\underline{T}$:

$$\underline{\alpha} = \underline{\alpha}' \, \underline{T}$$

and

$$\underline{\gamma} = \underline{\gamma}' \, \underline{T}$$

That is, we can obtain the constrained slope and intercept parameter estimates from the estimated unconstrained slope and intercept parameters. (The prime symbol on $\underline{\alpha}$ and $\underline{\gamma}$ indicates that $\underline{\alpha}'$ and $\underline{\gamma}'$ are row vectors as opposed to column vectors.) As a result, for each item we have m_j constrained α_{jk}s and γ_{jk}s parameters where the *m*th discrimination parameter, α_{jm}, is equal to $1 - \sum^{m_j-1} \alpha_{jh}$ and the *m*th intercept parameter, γ_{jm_j}, is $1 - \sum^{m_j-1} \gamma_{jh}$ for $h = \{1, \ldots, m_j\}$. The transformation matrix $\underline{T}$ is referred to as the TMATRIX in MULTILOG's parlance. This is the matrix seen in the PC model calibration (see Table 7.1). MULTILOG produces both the constrained and unconstrained parameter estimates. See Bock (1972) as well as Thissen et al. (2003) for greater detail.

Equation 9.2 is sometimes written in a multivariate logit (Bock, 1972) or multinomial logit (Bock, 1997) form:

$$P_{jk} = \frac{e^{z_{jk}(\theta)}}{\sum\limits_{h=1}^{m_j} e^{z_{jh}(\theta)}} \qquad (9.3)$$

where $z_{jk}(\theta) = \gamma_{jk} + \alpha_{jk}\theta$ and is the multivariate or multinomial logit. In this form the constraints of $\Sigma\alpha_{jh} = 0$ and $\Sigma\gamma_{jh} = 0$ become $\sum^{m_j} z_{jh}(\theta) = 0$ for h= {1, . . . , m_j}.

To aid in interpreting these parameters we present a logit space plot of the logit (i.e., $\gamma_{jk} + \alpha_{jk}\theta$) as a function of θ for a three-category ($m_j = 3$) item in Figure 9.2; $\underline{\alpha} = (-0.75, -0.25, 1.0)$ and $\underline{\gamma} = (-1.5, -0.25, 1.75)$. Recall from Chapter 2 that the lines in this graph are logit regression lines. As can be seen, the γ_{jk} value is the y-intercept (i.e., when $\theta = 0.0$) and α_{jk} is the slope of the corresponding logit regression line and indicates how the log odds for response category k change as the individual's θ increases. Because category 3 has the largest α_{jk}, its corresponding logit regression line has the steepest positive slope. Conversely, the largest negative α_{jk} is associated with category 1 and its logit regression line has the maximal negative slope. Of the three options, category 3 differentiates the best. For this category an increase from $\theta = 0$ to 1 corresponds to an increase in the log odds for this category from 1.75 to 2.75 (i.e., the difference is the value of α_3). Furthermore, we see that the log odds of persons located in the upper end of the continuum favor selecting category 3 over the other response categories. Conversely, it can be seen that individuals located at the lowest end of

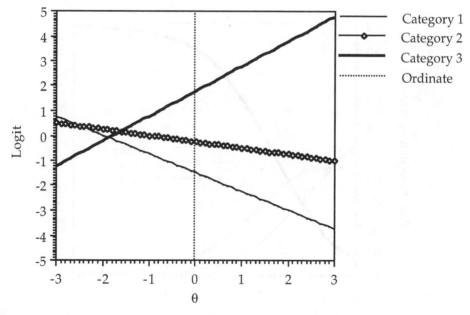

FIGURE 9.2. NR model logit regression lines for a three-category item with $\underline{\alpha} = (-0.75, -0.25, 1.0)$ and $\gamma = (-1.5, -0.25, 1.75)$.

the scale will tend to select category 1 over categories 2 and 3, although there is a strong tendency for these individuals to also select category 2. Further, as an individual's location increases there is a decrease in the tendency to select either categories 1 and 2.

In general, Figure 9.2 is somewhat typical of the logit space plot for an item. However, if the α_{jk}s for two or more response categories are equal and these categories have unequal γ_{jk}s, then the corresponding logit regression lines are parallel. In contrast, and as one would expect, if the α_{jk}s for two or more response categories are equal and have equal γ_{jk}s, then the response categories collapse into a single category.

Although Figure 9.2 tells us the log odds of selecting a category as a function of θ, it is sometimes difficult to look at a logit regression line and get a sense of the probability of responding in the corresponding category. For this purpose we can examine the item's ORFs. Figure 9.3 contains the ORFs corresponding to the item shown in Figure 9.2; these ORFs are obtained by using Equation 9.2.

A comparison of Figures 9.2 and 9.3 shows that the points of intersection of the logit regression lines correspond to the transition points among the ORFs. In general, with the NR model an item has one category ORF that has a maximal positive slope (monotonically increasing) and one that has a maximal negative slope (monotonically decreasing). The former is typically the correct response and/or the category with the highest frequency. The other response category(ies) have usually, but not always, a unimodal pattern. However, the overall pattern of an item's ORFs as well as their points of intersection reflect an interaction among the item's α_{jk}s and γ_{jk}s. In addition, if the α_{jk}s for two or more response categories are equal and have unequal γ_{jk}s, then the corresponding ORFs do not intersect and the response category with the larger γ_{jk} envelops the other(s). In this case, the response categories discriminate the same as one another, but are differentially attractive. Unless there is a

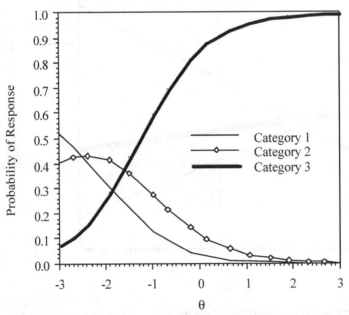

FIGURE 9.3. NR model ORFs for the three-category item shown in Figure 9.2.

substantive reason to maintain separate response categories, one might consider combining these response categories. When response categories have equal α_{jk}s as well as equal γ_{jk}s, then these response categories have collapsed into a single category with a single ORF.

We can formulate category location parameters in two ways. The first approach is analogous to that of the PC model (Chapter 7) in which the location parameters are defined at the intersection of ORFs. However, this does not mean that we are assuming that the response categories are ordered. The ORFs' intersection point can be obtained by setting the corresponding category multivariate logits equal to one another and solving for θ. Therefore, after simplification, noting that θ and δ are on the same scale, and dropping the item subscript for convenience, we have that for any item with $m_j \geq 2$, $k^* < k$, and $\alpha_{k^*} \neq \alpha_k$ that the transition point between categories k^* and k is

$$\delta_{k^*,k} = \frac{\gamma_{k^*} - \gamma_k}{\alpha_k - \alpha_{k^*}} \tag{9.4}$$

As is true for the PC and GPC models, with the NR model there are $m_j - 1$ transition location parameters across categories. If $\alpha_{k^*} = \alpha_k$, then the k^*th ORF does not intersect with the kth ORF and $\delta_{k^*,k}$ is undefined. For a binary item (i.e., $m_j = 2$) the 2PL and NR models are equivalent and the transition point is given by δ. Therefore, the NR model can model both dichotomous and polytomous data. As mentioned in the previous chapters, the PC, RS, and GPC models are special cases of the NR model. Thissen and Steinberg (1986) show that when the α_{jk}s are forced to increase in steps of one, the NR model becomes the PC/GPC models; also see Sijtsma and Hemker (2000) and Muraki (1992). As such, the NR model may also be applied to ordinal data. In fact, Mellenbergh (1995) shows different ways of preserving the order of the response categories for use with the NR model. These methods yield different types of models (e.g., adjacent-category models and cumulative probability models); also see Samejima (1979).

As an example of using Equation 9.4 to obtain transition points, we use the item shown in Figure 9.3. With $\underline{\alpha}$ = (−0.75, −0.25, 1.0) and $\underline{\gamma}$ = (−1.5, −0.25, 1.75) the intersection of categories 1 and 2 ($k^* = 1$ and $k = 2$) occurs at

$$\delta_{1,2} = \frac{-1.5 - (-0.25)}{-0.25 - (-0.75)} = -2.5$$

for categories 2 and 3 ($k^* = 2$ and $k = 3$) intersect at

$$\delta_{2,3} = \frac{-0.25 - 1.75}{1.0 - (-0.25)} = -1.6$$

and the transition point between categories 1 and 3 ($k^* = 1$ and $k = 3$) is

$$\delta_{1,3} = \frac{-1.5 - 1.75}{1.0 - (-0.75)} = -1.86$$

These values match the transition points among the three ORFs shown in Figure 9.3.

The second formulation of a location parameter establishes one location parameter for each response category. Using the relationship between the intercept and location parameters from Chapter 2 (Equation 2.5, $\delta = -\gamma/\alpha$), Baker (1992) reparameterized the model in Equation 9.2 to be

$$p_{jk} = \frac{e^{\alpha_{jk}(\theta - \delta^*_{jk})}}{\sum\limits_{h=1}^{m_j} e^{\alpha_{jh}(\theta - \delta^*_{jh})}} \qquad (9.5)$$

where $\delta^*_{jk} = -\gamma_{jk}/\alpha_{jk}$. This reparameterization presents the NR model in a format that is similar to that seen with the dichotomous IRT models.

Applying the δ^*_{jk} formulation to the example item from Figure 9.3 and dropping the item subscript, we have

$$\delta^*_1 = -\frac{-1.5}{-0.75} = -2.0$$

$$\delta^*_2 = -\frac{-0.25}{-0.25} = -1.0$$

and

$$\delta^*_3 = -\frac{1.75}{1.0} = -1.75$$

Figure 9.3 shows that these δ^*_k s do not correspond to the inflexion points of the ORFs nor do they correspond to points of ORF intersection. Only with a two-category item can one interpret the δ^*_k s as the point on the θ scale at which an individual has a probability of 0.50 of simultaneously responding in two categories (i.e., δ^*_1 is the transition point between category 0 and category 1).

HOW LARGE A CALIBRATION SAMPLE?

Because of the interaction between the α_{jk}s and the γ_{jk}s, as well as the effect of the distribution of respondents across categories, calibration sample size recommendations should be seen simply as rough guidelines. One guideline suggests a minimum ratio of 10:1 respondents to the total number of item parameters when the respondents are normally distributed, but a larger ratio if the respondents are not normally distributed (De Ayala & Sava-Bolesta, 1999).

DeMars (2003) investigated parameter recovery using two sample sizes (600 and 2400), two levels of the number of parameters per item (6 and 12; that is, three- and six-response category items), two levels of the total number of item parameters across all items, and three different respondent population distributions (normal, skewed, uniform). Her results showed that, on average, the estimation of γ_{jk}s was better than that of the α_{jk}s, decreasing the number of item parameters per item from 12 to 6 led to more accurate α_{jh} and γ_{jk} estimates, and that the 2400 sample size led to smaller root mean squared error (RMSE) than did a sample size of 600 for corresponding conditions. She suggested that one should focus on the ratio of sample size to number of categories, although she did not give a specific ratio because of the complex nature of the relationship of a sample's distribution to locations, category discrimination, and the degree of acceptable error. The DeMars' (2003) study replicated the De Ayala and Sava-Bolesta (1999) finding that normally distributed respondents led to, overall, the best results. In this regard, she showed that it is possible to obtain acceptable estimation accuracy (RMSE < 0.10) for both the α_{jh}s and the γ_{jk}s with 600 respondents, provided one has a normal (or a uniform) distribution of respondents and three category items. However, DeMars's best results (i.e., RMSE < 0.10) for both α_{jh}s and γ_{jk}s were obtained with sample size ratios of 10:1 and 20:1 and either normally or uniformly distributed respondents. The De Ayala and Sava-Bolesta and DeMars studies show that the match between the prior distribution used in estimation and the respondents' distribution is important for accurately estimating the item parameters. For those cases where respondents are not normally distributed, then modifying the prior distribution used in estimation may improve the accuracy of the estimated item parameters.

As we have done in previous chapters, here we provide very rough sample size guidelines. Assuming MMLE, a symmetric θ distribution, and that the respondents distribute themselves across the response categories in reasonable numbers, we suggest that the minimum sample size be 600. However, it may be anticipated that there is a sample size, say 1500 or so, at which one reaches, practically speaking, a point of diminishing returns in terms of improvement in estimation accuracy. (The value of 1500 should not be interpreted as an upper bound.) For instance, we conducted a small illustrative simulation in which three sample sizes were generated for a four-item instrument; $m_j = 4$. With four 4-choice items there are 256 possible response patterns, and for each sample size all the patterns were observed. Increasing the sample size from 973 cases to 1799 resulted in the corresponding item parameter estimates changing by an amount from 0 up to 0.07. In general, most of the changes between the two calibrations were on the order of 0.01 to 0.03; MULTILOG provides item parameter estimates to only two decimal places. However, "doubling" the sample size from 1799 to 3599 yielded no change in the item parameter estimates, thereby providing some support for the diminishing returns assertion.

If one adopts a sample size ratio for sample size determination (e.g., 10 persons for every parameter estimated), then it is probably more useful closer to the lower bound than to the value of 1500 (i.e., when the sample size is large, then the sample size ratio becomes less important). These suggestions are tempered by the purpose of the administration (e.g., survey, establishing norms, equating, item pool development/maintenance, etc.), the application characteristics (e.g., distribution and range of item parameter estimates, instrument length, latent distribution shape, etc.), ancillary technique sample size requirements, and the amount of missing data. As previously mentioned, sample size guidelines should not be interpreted as hard-and-fast rules.

EXAMPLE: APPLICATION OF THE NR MODEL TO A SCIENCE TEST, MMLE

The data for our example come from the Third International Mathematics and Science Study (TIMSS; Gonzalez et al., 1998) database. Using the responses from the 1995 Canadian examinees, four physical science items were selected. Three of the items are in a multiple-choice format (four options), whereas the fourth item is open-ended and scored using a four-point rubric. The three multiple-choice items' options constitute nominal response categories, and we initially treat the fourth item as such. The responses to each item are labeled 1 through 4. It should be noted that the toolbox of model–data fit methods summarized in Chapter 6 is still relevant and would be used in practice. We assume a unidimensional latent space and conditional independence.

Rather than analyzing individual case data in this example, we use pattern data. With four items, each with four possible "options," there are $4^4 = 256$ possible patterns (i.e., number of patterns $= m^L$). Of these 256 possible patterns we observed 233. The observed patterns indicate that for each item there is a response to each option. We use MULTILOG for calibrating these data. As mentioned in Chapter 8, when pattern data are calibrated MULTILOG automatically produces the EAP $\hat{\theta}$s.

The command file for the NR model calibration of the physical science test is shown in Table 9.1. Most of this file is described in Chapters 7 and 8. On the PROBLEM line we use PATTERNS to indicate the calibration of pattern data and NPATTERNS to specify the number of patterns. On the TEST line we specify that each of the four items consists of four response categories (i.e., NC=(4(0)4)) as well as which option has the highest frequency for each item (i.e., HIGH=(2,3,4,3)). For example, the HIGH subcommand indicates that item 1's highest frequency is category 2; that for item 2, category 3 has the highest frequency; and so on. (These highest frequency categories specify the item's baseline response category.) In our example the HIGH category is also the correct response. We set the number of EM cycles to 500 and the number of M-STEPS to 25 by using subcommands NC=500 and IT=25, respectively, on the EST line. Similar to what has been done in previous examples, the unique response pattern and its frequency are used as the person identification field. Therefore, the FORTRAN format's first field (9A1) refers to the person identification field, the actual item responses occupy the first four columns and are read by 4A1, and the field F5.0 is used to read the pattern frequencies.

Table 9.2 contains the abridged output. With four 4-option items there are L*2(m – 1) = 4*2(3) = 24 parameters being estimated and we see that this is the value on the NUMBER OF FREE PARAMETERS line. The identification field shows that the first observation is the pattern 1111 and that this pattern occurred once in the data. Convergence is achieved in 29 cycles.

In the ITEM SUMMARY section we find our item parameter estimates. For item 1 there are four possible options (i.e., 4 NOMINAL CATEGORIES) and the response of 2 has the highest frequency (i.e., 2 HIGH); this option is also the correct option. The constrained category discrimination parameter estimates are read from the A(K) line. That is, $\hat{\alpha}_{11} =$

TABLE 9.1. Command File for the MULTILOG NR Model Calibration Example

```
MULTILOG for Windows 7.00.2327.2
NR CALIBRATION, 4 PHYSICAL SCIENCE ITEMS
>PROBLEM RANDOM,
           PATTERNS,                      ⇐ Specification that pattern data are being used[a]
           DATA = 'C:SCIENCE.PAT',
           NITEMS = 4,
           NGROUPS = 1,
           NPATTERNS = 256,               ⇐ Number of possible patterns[b]
           NCHARS = 9;
>TEST ALL,
       NOMINAL,                           ⇐ Specification of NR model
       NC = (4(0)4),
       HIGH = (2,3,4,3);                  ⇐ Ordinal position of highest frequency category
>EST NC=500 IT=25;                        ⇐ Changing the number of EM and M-Step iterations
>END ;
4                                         ⇐ Number of response categories
1234                                      ⇐ The response code line
1111                                      ⇐ The 1s are coded to be 1s for all four items
2222                                      ⇐ The 2s are coded to be 2s for all four items
3333ˈ                                     ⇐ The 3s are coded to be 3s for all four items
4444                                      ⇐ The 4s are coded to be 3s for all four items
(9A1,T1,4A1,F5.0)
```

[a]The text following the ⇐ is provided to help the reader understand the corresponding input.
[b]The nonobserved patterns are added to the data file with corresponding frequencies of zero.

0.18, $\hat{\alpha}_{12} = 0.61$, $\hat{\alpha}_{13} = -0.37$, and $\hat{\alpha}_{14} = -0.42$ or $\hat{\underline{\alpha}} = (0.18, 0.61, -0.37, -0.42)$. The constrained intercept estimates are listed on the C(K) line with $\hat{\gamma}_{11} = 0.18$, $\hat{\gamma}_{12} = 0.55$, $\hat{\gamma}_{13} = -0.56$, and $\hat{\gamma}_{14} = -0.16$ or $\hat{\underline{\gamma}} = (0.18, 0.55, -0.56, -0.16)$. The unconstrained discrimination and intercept parameters are found in the section labeled "CONTRAST-COEFFICIENTS (STANDARD ERRORS)." The columns labeled A and C contain the $m_j - 1$ discrimination and intercept parameter estimates, respectively. For example, for item 1 option 1 we have $\hat{\alpha}_{11} = 0.44$ and $\hat{\gamma}_{11} = 0.37$.

Following the unconstrained parameter estimate section are the item's information values. These would be interpreted as done in Chapter 7. For this item as well as for the other items, we can see that the expected and observed proportions show good agreement for all categories (i.e., the difference between "OBS. FREQ." and "EXP. PROP." is about 1/10,000*th*).

In some situations one or more of an item's response categories may not be attractive and may never be chosen. These are sometimes referred to as *null* categories. In these cases one does not have data to estimate the category's parameters. In short, the item is functioning with fewer categories than are specified for the calibration. This situation would reveal itself by the null category's corresponding observed proportion and frequency being zero, as well as by the absence of an ORF for the null category in the item's ORF plot. If a null category occurs, then one should ignore the null category's parameter estimates and recalibrate the item set specifying the appropriate number of observed categories for each item. For instance, assume that item 4's fourth option is not selected by any individuals. Therefore, this item is functioning as a three-category item. To specify that item 4 has only three observed categories, we change the NC specification on the TEST line to indicate three cat-

TABLE 9.2. Abridged Output from the NR Model Calibration Example

```
     :
<echo of command file>
  NUMBER OF FREE PARAMETERS IS:   24
     :
FIRST OBSERVATION AS READ-

ID     1111    1
ITEMS 1111
NORML     0.000
WT/CR     1.00

FINISHED CYCLE 29
MAXIMUM INTERCYCLE PARAMETER CHANGE=   0.00082 P(   21)
     :
ITEM SUMMARY
     :
ITEM    1:      4 NOMINAL CATEGORIES,   2 HIGH
  CATEGORY(K): 1      2      3      4
   A(K)      0.18   0.61  -0.37  -0.42
   C(K)      0.18   0.55  -0.56  -0.16

          CONTRAST-COEFFICIENTS (STANDARD ERRORS)
   FOR:              A                 C
   CONTRAST P(#)  COEFF.[ DEV.]  P(#)  COEFF.[ DEV.]
      1       1    0.44 (0.09)     4    0.37 (0.08)
      2       2   -0.55 (0.12)     5   -0.74 (0.11)
      3       3   -0.60 (0.11)     6   -0.34 (0.10)

@THETA:       INFORMATION:    (Theta values increase in steps of 0.2)
-3.0 - -1.6  0.077  0.086  0.096  0.107  0.118  0.129  0.140  0.151
-1.4 -  0.0  0.161  0.170  0.178  0.183  0.187  0.188  0.187  0.184
 0.2 -  1.6  0.179  0.172  0.163  0.153  0.143  0.132  0.121  0.110
 1.8 -  3.0  0.100  0.090  0.081  0.073  0.065  0.058  0.052

OBSERVED AND EXPECTED COUNTS/PROPORTIONS IN
CATEGORY(K):    1        2        3        4
OBS. FREQ.     456      723      245      375
OBS. PROP.   0.2535   0.4019   0.1362   0.2084
EXP. PROP.   0.2535   0.4020   0.1362   0.2084
     :
TOTAL TEST INFORMATION
@THETA:       INFORMATION:
-3.0 - -1.6  1.380  1.424  1.471  1.521  1.572  1.624  1.674  1.721
-1.4 -  0.0  1.763  1.797  1.822  1.837  1.841  1.834  1.817  1.792
 0.2 -  1.6  1.759  1.722  1.681  1.638  1.595  1.551  1.509  1.468
 1.8 -  3.0  1.429  1.392  1.358  1.325  1.295  1.268  1.242
     :
MARGINAL RELIABILITY:     0.4142
     :
 OBSERVED(EXPECTED)    STD. :     EAP (S.D.)  :  PATTERN
                       RES. :                 :

     1.0(     0.7)     0.40 :    -0.97 ( 0.75) :  1111
     2.0(     0.8)     1.33 :    -0.45 ( 0.75) :  1112
     0.0(     1.0)    -1.01 :    -0.61 ( 0.75) :  1113
     2.0(     0.5)     2.00 :    -0.18 ( 0.75) :  1114
     :
NEGATIVE TWICE THE LOGLIKELIHOOD=      288.4
 (CHI-SQUARE FOR SEVERAL TIMES MORE EXAMINEES THAN CELLS)
```

egories for item 4 (i.e., NC = (4,4,4,3)); in this case the corresponding HIGH category identification does not need to be changed (i.e., HIGH = (2,3,4,3)).

The parameter estimates for all the items are presented in Table 9.3. As would be expected, the sum of the constrained $\hat{\alpha}_{jk}$s for an item is 0.0 and this is also the case for an item's $\hat{\gamma}_{jk}$s. Looking at item 1, one sees that category 2 does the best of the item's response categories in discriminating among the individuals ($\hat{\alpha}_{12} = 0.61$) and it is also the most attractive ($\hat{\gamma}_{12} = 0.55$). Because the γs are associated with category frequencies, the category with the largest frequency has the largest positive γ and the category with smallest frequency is associated with the most negative γ. (If a category has its α equal to zero, then its corresponding γ is poorly defined and has a tendency to drift. In this situation the calibration may not converge, but according to Thissen there is little loss of fit by allowing the calibration to stop because of reaching the maximum number of iterations.) The $-2\ln L$ for this calibration is 288.4 (BIC = 468.2797); we use the $2\ln L$ value below.

The corresponding ORFs for item 1 (Figure 9.4, left panel) shows that category 2 is most useful for persons located above approximately -0.69 and that category 4 is attractive for persons located below approximately -0.69. That is, the intersection between categories 2 and 4 is

$$\delta_{2,4} = \frac{0.55 - (-0.16)}{-0.42 - 0.61} = -0.69$$

MULTILOG's graph uses a red line to identify the HIGH category (i.e., category 2). According to the ORF pattern this item functions primarily as a two-category item with categories 2 and 4 being the primary categories. The item's information function (Figure 9.4, right panel) shows that this item is most useful for estimating persons located around -0.5.

The matrix plot feature simultaneously presents the ORFs for all the items and is shown in Figure 9.5. This figure shows that item 2 (top right) is behaving as a binary item. The relatively "flat" ORF reflects a category (specifically, category 1) that is not very discriminating (this is also reflected in its $\hat{\alpha}_{21} = -0.07$) and is not, comparatively speaking, attracting very many respondents; the latter interpretation comes from the magnitude of its $\hat{\gamma}_{21} = -1.19$. Item 3 is functioning as a three-, not four-, category item. As mentioned in previous chapters, a fit analysis should involve a comparison of empirical and predicted ORFs. The program MODFIT could be used for this purpose with the NR model.

EXAMPLE: MIXED MODEL CALIBRATION OF THE SCIENCE TEST—NR AND PC MODELS, MMLE

The calibration examples in the previous chapters have applied a single model to an instrument because the instrument used a single-item response format. However, some

TABLE 9.3. Constrained Item Parameter Estimates for Science Items—NR Model

Item	Discrimination				Intercept			
	$\hat{\alpha}_{j1}$	$\hat{\alpha}_{j2}$	$\hat{\alpha}_{j3}$	$\hat{\alpha}_{j4}$	$\hat{\gamma}_{j1}$	$\hat{\gamma}_{j2}$	$\hat{\gamma}_{j3}$	$\hat{\gamma}_{j4}$
1	0.18	0.61	−0.37	−0.42	0.18	0.55	−0.56	−0.16
2	−0.07	−0.29	0.54	−0.18	−1.19	−0.03	0.76	0.46
3	−0.45	−0.66	0.29	0.82	−0.76	−0.47	0.53	0.70
4	−0.73	−0.18	−0.10	0.66	−0.58	0.25	0.33	0.00

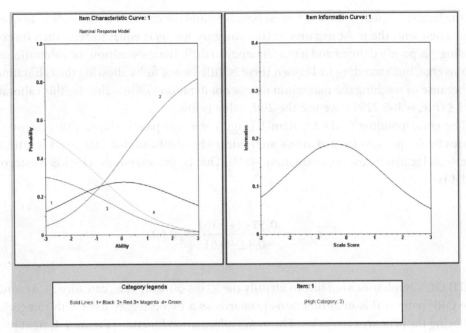

FIGURE 9.4. ORFs and item information function for item 1.

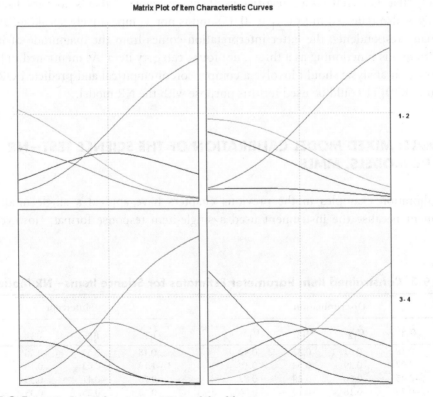

FIGURE 9.5. ORFs for all four items, NR model calibration.

instruments may contain various response formats. In these cases, and provided that the IRT assumptions are met for the entire instrument, one may apply multiple models to the data and still perform a single calibration of the instrument. In this example we apply two models, the NR and PC models, to the science test. As previously mentioned, the PC model is subsumed by the NR model. Therefore, this mixed model calibration involves a nested model and we are able to compare the fit of this mixed model calibration with that of the NR model calibration.[4]

In the previous example we mentioned that item 4 is an open-ended question. This question is concerned with whether the combined weight of two objects would change if one object is placed inside the other as opposed to remaining separate. The rubric identified the correct answer and various incorrect answers. One may consider some of these incorrect answers to reflect a better understanding of the physical sciences than do the other incorrect answers. For example, answering that the combined weight is zero when one of the objects is placed inside the other reflects a greater lack of understanding than some nonzero value. Therefore, responses to this item are scored by giving no credit, varying degrees of partial credit, and full credit. In this example we treat this item as a four-category partial credit item. Specifically, a value of 4 is assigned to a correct response, a value of 3 for a partially correct response, a value of 2 for a response that does not indicate an understanding as good as a value of 3, and a 1 for an incorrect response. We could have coded these as 3, 2, 1, and 0, respectively. However, we would then have had to recode these values to be 1 through 4 to perform a PC model calibration because a code of 0 is used internally by MULTILOG. To summarize our data, items 1 through 3 are considered to be nominally scored and item 4 is scored in a graded fashion. To accommodate these different scoring paradigms we apply two models to the four-item instrument. The NR model is used for items 1 through 3 and the PC model is applied to item 4. The command file for this calibration is shown in Table 9.4.

Because the PC model is nested within the NR model we use a single TEST line to identify the model, but then invoke the PC model constraints on the appropriate item (i.e., item 4). These constraints (i.e., the TMATRIX and FIX lines) are similar to those that we used in Chapter 7 (Table 7.1), although the ITEMS subcommand is used in lieu of ALL to specify that the constraints should be applied only to item 4. (If we had more than one item to be calibrated using the PC model and wanted them to all have a common $\hat{\alpha}$, then it would be necessary to also include the command line >EQUAL ITEMS=<item list>, AK=1; as well as to specify the items with the ITEMS subcommand.) The corresponding output is found in Table 9.5.

MULTILOG took 36 cycles to achieve convergence. For the NR model we have 2*(4 − 1) = 6 parameters per item, and with three items this yields 18 parameters. With the PC model there are 4 parameters, one α and 3 transition location parameters. Therefore, the total number of parameters estimated by both models is 18 + 4 = 22. This corresponds to the NUMBER OF FREE PARAMETERS listed in the output. The estimates for items 1 through 3 are not dramatically different from those observed when all the items were treated nominally. Using the PC model, item 4 has an estimated item discrimination of 0.33 with transition location estimates of $\hat{\delta}_{41} = -0.68$, $\hat{\delta}_{42} = -0.10$, and $\hat{\delta}_{43} = 0.28$.

We can conceive of the NR–PC mixed model calibration as nested within the NR model calibration from the previous example. Calibrating all four items using only the NR model produced a $-2\ln L$ of 288.4 with 24 free parameters (or 256 − 24 − 1 = 231 degrees of free-

TABLE 9.4. Command File for the NR and PC Mixed Model Calibration

```
MULTILOG for Windows 7.00.2327.2
MIX NR & PC MODELS; ITEM 4 - PC MODEL
>PROBLEM RANDOM,
        PATTERNS,
        DATA = 'C:SCIENCE.PAT',
        NITEMS = 4,
        NGROUPS = 1,
        NPATTERNS = 256,
        NCHARS = 9;
>TEST ALL,
      NOMINAL,
      NC = (4(0)4),                    ⇐ That is, NC = (4, 4, 4, 4)ᵃ
      HIGH = (2,3,4,4);
>TMATRIX ITEMS=4,AK,POLYNOMIAL;        ⇐ This line and the next 2 impose the constraints
>FIX     ITEMS=4,AK=(2,3),VALUE=0.0;        on the NR model to obtain the PC model
>TMATRIX ITEMS=4,CK,TRIANGLE;
>EST NC=500 IT=25;
>END;
    :
```

ᵃThe text following the ⇐ is provided to help the reader understand the corresponding input.

---

dom) and a BIC of 468.2797. With the mixed NR–PC model, calibration –2lnL increased to 320.5 with 22 free parameters or 233 degrees of freedom; BIC = 485.3897. The difference between these two -2lnLs is distributed as an X^2 with two degrees of freedom (i.e., 233 – 231 = 24 – 22 = 2); we assume that the Full (nesting) model holds for the data. Because the critical X^2 with two degrees of freedom ($\alpha = 0.05$) is 5.99 and the difference between the –2lnLs is 32.1, we observe a significant increase in misfit by using the PC model for the last item. Further, according to the BIC values the NR model is favored over the NR–PC mixed model calibration. Therefore, from a statistical perspective the NR model calibration is preferred to the NR–PC mixed model calibration. However, in some applications there may be pragmatic reasons for preferring the NR–PC mixed model calibration. For example, conceptually it may be more appealing to the various constituencies to treat item 4 in a graded fashion, particularly in light of the fact that the NR model does not fit the data in an absolute sense.

Figure 9.6 contains the ORFs for all the items using this mixed model approach; Figure 9.5 contains the corresponding ORFs based on the NR calibration. As would be expected, the ORFs for items 1 through 3 are very similar to those using the NR model. Item 4's ORFs show a slight spreading out, such that some of the response categories (e.g., category 3) have a wider θ range over which they are the most probable response category than when the item is treated nominally.

EXAMPLE: NR AND PC MIXED MODEL CALIBRATION OF THE SCIENCE TEST, COLLAPSED OPTIONS, MMLE

Inspection of the science test items' ORFs (e.g., Figure 9.5) indicate that item 2 contains a response option that is not very informative. Specifically, option 1 shows little discrimination

TABLE 9.5. Abridged Output for the NR and PC Mixed Model Calibration Example

```
    :
  NUMBER OF FREE PARAMETERS IS:    22
    :
  FINISHED CYCLE 36
    :
  ITEM SUMMARY
    :
  ITEM   1:       4 NOMINAL CATEGORIES,   2 HIGH
    CATEGORY(K): 1       2       3       4
     A(K)       0.21    0.68   -0.51   -0.38
     C(K)       0.20    0.55   -0.62   -0.13

                CONTRAST-COEFFICIENTS (STANDARD ERRORS)
     FOR:              A                   C
     CONTRAST P(#)  COEFF.[ DEV.]   P(#)   COEFF.[ DEV.]
        1      1    0.47 (0.09)      4     0.36 (0.07)
        2      2   -0.72 (0.12)      5    -0.82 (0.12)
        3      3   -0.60 (0.11)      6    -0.33 (0.10)

  @THETA:      INFORMATION:    (Theta values increase in steps of 0.2)
  -3.0 - -1.6  0.083  0.094  0.106  0.119  0.133  0.148  0.163  0.177
  -1.4 -  0.0  0.191  0.203  0.214  0.221  0.226  0.228  0.226  0.221
   0.2 -  1.6  0.213  0.203  0.190  0.177  0.162  0.148  0.134  0.120
   1.8 -  3.0  0.108  0.096  0.085  0.075  0.067  0.059  0.052

  OBSERVED AND EXPECTED COUNTS/PROPORTIONS IN
  CATEGORY(K):  1       2       3       4
  OBS. FREQ.    456     723     245     375
  OBS. PROP.   0.2535  0.4019  0.1362  0.2084
  EXP. PROP.   0.2535  0.4020  0.1362  0.2084
    :
  ITEM   4:       4 NOMINAL CATEGORIES,   4 HIGH
    CATEGORY(K): 1       2       3       4
     A(K)      -0.50   -0.17    0.17    0.50
     C(K)       0.00    0.68    0.78    0.50

                CONTRAST-COEFFICIENTS (STANDARD ERRORS)
     FOR:              A                   C
     CONTRAST P(#)  COEFF.[POLY.]   P(#)   COEFF.[ TRI.]
        1      19   0.33 (0.04)     20    -0.68 (0.11)
        2      32   0.00 (0.00)     21    -0.10 (0.09)
        3      33   0.00 (0.00)     22     0.28 (0.09)

  @THETA:      INFORMATION:    (Theta values increase in steps of 0.2)
  -3.0 - -1.6  0.078  0.082  0.086  0.089  0.093  0.097  0.100  0.103
  -1.4 -  0.0  0.105  0.108  0.109  0.111  0.111  0.112  0.111  0.110
   0.2 -  1.6  0.109  0.107  0.105  0.102  0.099  0.096  0.092  0.088
   1.8 -  3.0  0.084  0.080  0.076  0.072  0.068  0.065  0.061

  OBSERVED AND EXPECTED COUNTS/PROPORTIONS IN
  CATEGORY(K):  1       2       3       4
  OBS. FREQ.    288     507     551     453
  OBS. PROP.   0.1601  0.2818  0.3063  0.2518
  EXP. PROP.   0.1601  0.2818  0.3063  0.2518
    :
  MARGINAL RELIABILITY:    0.3945
    :
  OBSERVED(EXPECTED)    STD.  :    EAP (S.D.)  :  PATTERN
                        RES.  :                :
       1.0(     0.6)    0.51  :   -0.83 ( 0.77) :  1111
       2.0(     0.9)    1.10  :   -0.64 ( 0.76) :  1112
       0.0(     0.9)   -0.93  :   -0.44 ( 0.76) :  1113
       2.0(     0.6)    1.85  :   -0.25 ( 0.77) :  1114
    :
  NEGATIVE TWICE THE LOGLIKELIHOOD=        320.5

  (CHI-SQUARE FOR SEVERAL TIMES MORE EXAMINEES THAN CELLS)
```

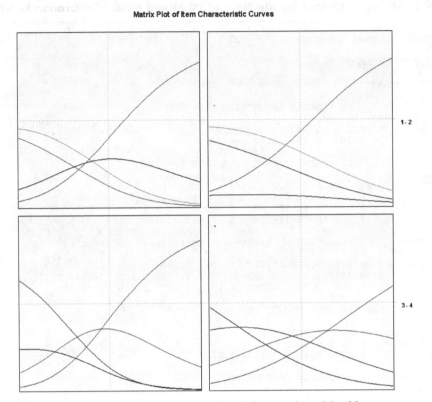

FIGURE 9.6. ORFs for all four items from the NR and PC mixed model calibration.

capacity, and this option's frequency is substantially smaller than those of the item's other response options. As such, it is not very attractive to the examinees. Therefore, unless there are substantive reasons for maintaining four options for this item, one might consider collapsing option 1 with another option. In this example, we collapse item 2's option 1 with its option 2. As a result, the test consists of items 1 and 3, each with four nominal response options, item 2 with three nominal response options, and item 4 with four graded options. As in the previous example, the NR model is used for items 1 through 3, whereas the PC model is applied to item 4. Although we can edit the data file and recode item 2's options (i.e., option 2 becomes 1, option 3 becomes 2, and option 4 becomes 3), it is less error-prone to have MULTILOG do the recoding. The recoding within MULTILOG is performed similarly to what is done in the PC model calibration example (Chapter 7). That is, in the command file section that specifies which codes to use for which items, one substitutes the new codes for the old response codes. Recall that this section's format is that the columns represent the items and the rows represent each identified response code. Here is the basic structure of the command file's response code section:

                                                        :

Number of response categories $\Rightarrow$ 4
Response code line (i.e., the codes in the data) $\Rightarrow$ 1234

Codes to use for the identified response of "1" for each item $\Rightarrow$ 1111
Codes to use for the identified response of "2" for each item $\Rightarrow$ 2122
Codes to use for the identified response of "3" for each item $\Rightarrow$ 3233
Codes to use for the identified response of "4" for each item $\Rightarrow$ 4344
                                                                          :
                                                                          ⇑

Columns represent items 1 through 4

In the current context, the second column (representing item 2) reflects the recoding of the observed codes of 4, 3, and 2 to be 3, 2, and 1, respectively (i.e., item 2's original response codes become 1, 2, and 3). After this recording, item 2 consists of three response categories, and this is reflected in the NC as well as the HIGH specifications on the TEST command line. The command file for this analysis is shown in Table 9.6, with the corresponding abridged output in Table 9.7.

Convergence is achieved in 36 cycles. The number of parameters estimated is 20 (i.e., $2(3 - 1) = 4$ for item 2, 4 for item 4 , plus 12 for items 1 and 3). The item parameter estimates for items 1, 3, and 4 are, within rounding, the same as those from the NR–PC mixed model calibration. The combining of item 2's options 1 and 2 results in the item's OBS. FREQ of 457. Because this number reflects the sum of the uncombined options 1 and 2's frequencies, we have assurance that the options were correctly combined. The previous calibration showed that the standard errors for the item parameter estimates were in the range of 0.15 to 0.16. As can be seen, by combining these two options the standard errors have decreased to

TABLE 9.6. Command File for the NR and PC Mixed Model Calibration—Collapsed Options

```
MULTILOG for Windows 7.00.2327.2
MIX NR & PC MODELS; ITEM 4 PC MODEL; ITEM 2-3 OPTIONS
>PROBLEM RANDOM,
        PATTERNS,
        DATA = 'C:SCIENCE2.PAT',
        NITEMS = 4,
        NGROUPS = 1,
        NPATTERNS = 256,
        NCHARS = 9;
>TEST ITEMS=(1,2,3,4),
     NOMINAL,
     NC = (4,3,4,4),
     HIGH = (2,2,4,4);
>TMATRIX ITEMS=4,AK,POLYNOMIAL;
>FIX     ITEMS=4,AK=(2,3),VALUE=0.0;
>TMATRIX ITEMS=4,CK,TRIANGLE;
>EST NC=500 IT=25;
>END ;
4                              ⇐ Number of response categories[a]
1234                           ⇐ The response code line
1111                           ⇐ Response code substitution for item 2: 1 stays as 1
2122                           ⇐ Response code substitution for item 2: 2 becomes 1
3233                           ⇐ Response code substitution for item 2: 3 becomes 2
4344                           ⇐ Response code substitution for item 2: 4 becomes 3
(9A1,T1,4A1,F5.0)
```

[a]The text following the ⇐ is provided to help the reader understand the corresponding input.

TABLE 9.7. Abridged Output for the NR and PC Mixed Model Calibration Example—Collapsed Options

```
    :
  NUMBER OF FREE PARAMETERS IS:   20
    :
  FIRST OBSERVATION AS READ-

  ID     1111    4
  ITEMS  1111
  NORML     0.000
  WT/CR     4.00

  FINISHED CYCLE  36
    :
  ITEM SUMMARY
    :
  ITEM   1:      4 NOMINAL CATEGORIES,  2 HIGH
    CATEGORY(K): 1      2       3      4
    A(K)      0.20   0.68   -0.50  -0.38
    C(K)      0.20   0.55   -0.62  -0.13

            CONTRAST-COEFFICIENTS (STANDARD ERRORS)
    FOR:              A                   C
    CONTRAST P(#)  COEFF.[ DEV.]  P(#)  COEFF.[ DEV.]
       1       1    0.48 (0.09)      4   0.36 (0.09)
       2       2   -0.70 (0.12)      5  -0.81 (0.12)
       3       3   -0.58 (0.11)      6  -0.33 (0.10)

    @THETA:     INFORMATION:   (Theta values increase in steps of 0.2)
    -3.0 - -1.6  0.081 0.092 0.104 0.117 0.130 0.144 0.159 0.173
    -1.4 -  0.0  0.187 0.199 0.210 0.218 0.223 0.225 0.224 0.220
     0.2 -  1.6  0.212 0.203 0.191 0.178 0.164 0.150 0.136 0.123
     1.8 -  3.0  0.110 0.098 0.087 0.077 0.068 0.061 0.054

    OBSERVED AND EXPECTED COUNTS/PROPORTIONS IN
    CATEGORY(K):  1        2        3        4
    OBS. FREQ.   456      723      245      375
    OBS. PROP.  0.2535 0.4019 0.1362 0.2084
    EXP. PROP.  0.2535 0.4020 0.1362 0.2084

  ITEM   2:      3 NOMINAL CATEGORIES,  2 HIGH
    CATEGORY(K): 1      2       3
     A(K)     -0.25   0.45   -0.20
     C(K)     -0.25   0.28   -0.03

            CONTRAST-COEFFICIENTS (STANDARD ERRORS)
    FOR:              A                   C
    CONTRAST P(#)  COEFF.[ DEV.]  P(#)  COEFF.[ DEV.]
       1       7    0.71 (0.09)      9   0.52 (0.08)
       2       8    0.06 (0.09)     10   0.21 (0.09)

    @THETA:     INFORMATION:   (Theta values increase in steps of 0.2)
    -3.0 - -1.6  0.038 0.043 0.047 0.052 0.058 0.063 0.069 0.075
    -1.4 -  0.0  0.081 0.087 0.092 0.098 0.102 0.106 0.110 0.112
     0.2 -  1.6  0.114 0.114 0.114 0.112 0.110 0.106 0.102 0.098
     1.8 -  3.0  0.092 0.087 0.081 0.075 0.069 0.063 0.058

    OBSERVED AND EXPECTED COUNTS/PROPORTIONS IN
    CATEGORY(K):  1        2        3
    OBS. FREQ.   457      785      557
    OBS. PROP.  0.2540 0.4364 0.3096
    EXP. PROP.  0.2540 0.4364 0.3096
    :
  ITEM   4:      4 NOMINAL CATEGORIES,  4 HIGH
    CATEGORY(K): 1      2       3      4
     A(K)     -0.50  -0.17    0.17   0.50
     C(K)      0.00   0.68    0.78   0.50

            CONTRAST-COEFFICIENTS (STANDARD ERRORS)
    FOR:              A                   C
    CONTRAST P(#)  COEFF.[POLY.]  P(#)  COEFF.[ TRI.]
       1      17    0.33 (0.04)     18  -0.68 (0.11)
       2      29    0.00 (0.00)     19  -0.10 (0.09)
       3      30    0.00 (0.00)     20   0.28 (0.09)
```

TABLE 9.7. *cont.*

```
@THETA:       INFORMATION:    (Theta values increase in steps of 0.2)
-3.0 - -1.6  0.078  0.082  0.086  0.090  0.094  0.097  0.101  0.104
-1.4 -  0.0  0.106  0.108  0.110  0.111  0.112  0.112  0.112  0.111
 0.2 -  1.6  0.110  0.108  0.106  0.103  0.100  0.096  0.093  0.089
 1.8 -  3.0  0.085  0.081  0.077  0.073  0.069  0.065  0.061

             OBSERVED AND EXPECTED COUNTS/PROPORTIONS IN
             CATEGORY(K):  1       2       3       4
             OBS. FREQ.    288     507     551     453
             OBS. PROP.    0.1601 0.2818 0.3063 0.2518
             EXP. PROP.    0.1601 0.2818 0.3063 0.2518
      :
@THETA:       INFORMATION:
-3.0 - -1.6  1.315  1.353  1.395  1.440  1.487  1.536  1.586  1.633
-1.4 -  0.0  1.677  1.714  1.743  1.763  1.772  1.770  1.758  1.737
 0.2 -  1.6  1.708  1.673  1.634  1.593  1.551  1.510  1.469  1.430
 1.8 -  3.0  1.393  1.359  1.327  1.297  1.270  1.244  1.222
      :
MARGINAL RELIABILITY:      0.3938
      :
OBSERVED(EXPECTED)     STD.  :    EAP (S.D.)  :  PATTERN
                      RES.  :              :

        1.0(      3.0)   -1.14  :    -0.94 ( 0.77) :  1111
        2.0(      4.4)   -1.15  :    -0.75 ( 0.77) :  1112
        0.0(      3.9)   -1.99  :    -0.55 ( 0.77) :  1113
        2.0(      2.6)   -0.35  :    -0.35 ( 0.77) :  1114
      :
NEGATIVE TWICE THE LOGLIKELIHOOD=         -171.2
      :
```

the range of 0.08 to 0.09. Therefore, by combining these low-frequency options we are able to obtain more accurate estimates. For completeness the ORFs are presented in Figure 9.7. As would be expected, except for item 2, these match those presented in Figure 9.6. Items 1 and 2 still show that they are behaving in a binary fashion (i.e., in general, examinees are either correctly answering the question or they are not). In Appendix E, "Example: Mixed Model Calibration of the Science Test—NR and 2PL Models, MMLE," we explore the effect of dichotomizing items 1 and 2.

Rather than using MULTILOG to recode item 2, if one edits the original response data to recode item 2 to have the three response categories described above, then one obtains 192 patterns. The calibration of these data yields the same item parameter estimates as shown in Table 9.7. However, we now obtain a valid $-2\ln L$ of 219.6 with a BIC of 369.4997 and 20 estimated parameters. These values reflect a substantial improvement in fit over simply using only the NR model or the mixed NR–PC model's calibrations.

INFORMATION FOR THE NR MODEL

As is true with the previous polytomous models, we can determine the amount of information for estimating a person's location provided by a particular item response category. For the NR model the option information function (Bock, 1972) is

$$I_{jk}(\theta) = \underline{\alpha W \alpha}' p_{jk} \qquad (9.6)$$

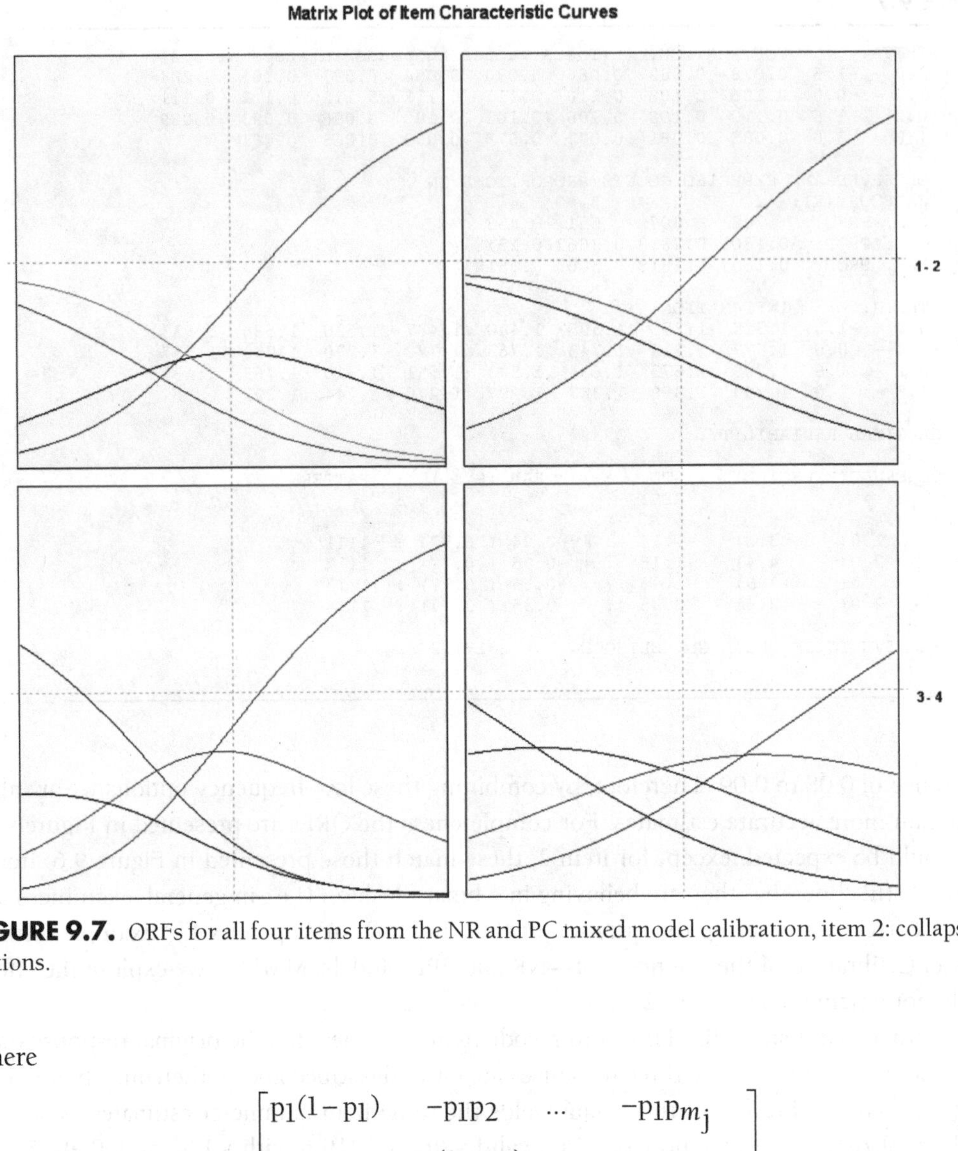

Matrix Plot of Item Characteristic Curves

FIGURE 9.7. ORFs for all four items from the NR and PC mixed model calibration, item 2: collapsed options.

where

$$
\underline{W} = \begin{bmatrix}
p_1(1-p_1) & -p_1p_2 & \cdots & -p_1p_{m_j} \\
-p_2p_1 & p_2(1-p_2) & \cdots & -p_2p_{m_j} \\
\cdot & \cdot & \cdots & \cdot \\
\cdot & \cdot & \cdots & \cdot \\
\cdot & \cdot & \cdots & \cdot \\
-p_{m_j}p_1 & -p_{m_j}p_2 & \cdots & p_{m_j}(1-p_{m_j})
\end{bmatrix}
$$

The sum of these option information functions provides the item information function

$$
I_j(\theta) = \sum_{k=1}^{m_j} \underline{\alpha W \alpha}'p_{jk} = \underline{\alpha W \alpha}' \tag{9.7}
$$

As is true for every model discussed in previous chapters, the total information provided by an instrument, $I(\theta)$, is the sum of the individual item information functions, $I_j(\theta)$.

In general, the distribution of information is affected by the distance between the item's γ_{jk}s, whether the γ_{jk}s are ordered in terms of magnitude, and the number of item alternatives (De Ayala, 1992). As is the case for the ordinal models, the information provided by the individual response categories does not have to be equal across response categories. Moreover, it is possible to obtain bimodal item information functions. The relationship between dichotomous and ordered polytomous models' information functions that we saw with the GR model also appears with the NR model. For example, Thissen's (1976) application of the NR model to the Ravens Progressive Matrices showed that the NR model provided more information than did a dichotomous model, particularly for individuals at the lower end of the scale.

METRIC TRANSFORMATION, NR MODEL

The principles outlined in previous chapters for metric conversion apply to the NR model. The intercept parameters (or their estimates) are transformed by $\gamma^*_{jk} = \gamma_{jk} - \dfrac{\alpha_{jk}}{\zeta}\kappa$ and the category slope parameters (or their estimates) by $\alpha^*_{jk} = \dfrac{\alpha_{jk}}{\zeta}$. Person location parameters (or their estimates) are transformed by $\theta^* = \zeta(\theta) + \kappa$. Because of the unordered nature of the response categories, it is not possible to convert the person location (estimates) to expected trait scores on the instrument without dichotomizing the responses.

CONCEPTUAL DEVELOPMENT OF THE MULTIPLE-CHOICE MODEL

The NR model states that examinees purposefully select an item's response option. Moreover, as shown in Figure 9.3, as an examinee's location decreases one particular response category will become increasingly more attractive, to the point where it is the most likely response. For example, in Figure 9.3 this is reflected by category 1's monotonically decreasing ORF. In contrast, in the context of proficiency assessment and a multiple-choice item format, conventional wisdom states that some individuals with very low proficiencies will randomly guess on some items. (This is, in fact, the thinking that led to the development of the 3PL model.) However, according to the NR model individuals with very low proficiencies will pick a particular option rather than randomly guess at the item's options. As such, the NR model does not address the possibility of examinee guessing behavior.

If one believes that individuals with very low θs will randomly select an item's option, then the observed nominal response data reflect a mixture of individuals who purposefully select the option and those who randomly select the option, with probability $1/m_j$ (i.e., the reciprocal of the item's number of options). Samejima (1979) proposed a solution to the issue of guessing in polytomous data by suggesting that these individuals who do not have the proficiency to even recognize the plausibility of a distractor guess randomly on an item and thereby select the item's options with equal probability $1/m_j$. This idea is incorporated into extensions of both the GR and NR models (normal ogive and logistic versions) by creating a "no recognition" category (labeled 0) to reflect the individuals who do not have the proficiency to even recognize the plausibility of an item's distractor and therefore guess at random on the item. This "no recognition" category has an ORF that is strictly decreasing with respect to θ and is asymptotic with 1 and 0. However, because the individuals who belong to this category are assumed to randomly guess on the m_j options, the "no recognition" ORF "disappears" and the other options are affected by this random guessing. As such, in Samejima's approach the "no recognition" category (category 0) might be considered to be a latent response category. In the context of nominal polytomous response data, this random guessing is modeled by modifying the NR model. Samejima (1979) refers to this modified model as the *Bock–Samejima model for multiple-choice items* (BS; also known as Type I Model C).[5] The BS model specifies the probability of an individual located at θ responding in category k of item j, given the item's $\underline{\alpha}$, $\underline{\gamma}$, and m_j as

$$p_j(x = k|\theta, \underline{\alpha}, \underline{\gamma}, m_j) = \frac{e^{\gamma_{jk}+\alpha_{jk}\theta} + (1/m_j)e^{\gamma_{j0}+\alpha_{j0}\theta}}{\sum\limits_{h=0}^{m_j} e^{\gamma_{jh}+\alpha_{jh}\theta}} \qquad (9.8)$$

where $\alpha_{j0} < \alpha_{j1} < \alpha_{j2} < \ldots < \alpha_{jm_j}$. The fixed proportion, $1/m_j$, is incorporated into each of the observed categories by the second term in the numerator of Equation 9.8, and if $\alpha_{j0} = \gamma_{j0} = 0$, then the model simplifies to the NR model (Thissen, Steinberg, & Fitzpatrick, 1989).

A second approach to modeling nominal polytomous data in the presence of guessing is presented by Thissen and Steinberg (1984). As is the case with the Bock–Samejima model, they conceptualized a latent response category for the "no recognition" individuals; they refer to these individuals as "don't know" individuals. However, in contrast to Samejima they felt that these "don't know" individuals would not guess with the equal probability of $1/m_j$ and presented data that supported their contention. Therefore, they modified Equation 9.8 to allow the proportion of "don't know" individuals to vary across an item's options. Their model is called the *multiple-response model* or the *multiple-choice* (MC) *model*. According to the MC model, the probability of a person located at θ responding in the kth category of item j is given by

$$p_j(x = k|\theta, \underline{\alpha}, \underline{\gamma}, \underline{\phi}) = \frac{e^{\gamma_{jk}+\alpha_{jk}\theta} + \phi_{jk}e^{\gamma_{j0}+\alpha_{j0}\theta}}{\sum\limits_{h=0}^{m_j} e^{\gamma_{jh}+\alpha_{jh}\theta}} \qquad (9.9)$$

where m_j, θ, α_{jk} and γ_{jk} are defined above, $k = \{1, \ldots, m_j\}$, and the model's new parameter, ϕ_{jk}, is associated with the latent "don't know" response category and is labeled 0 (i.e., α_{j0}, γ_{j0}). This unobserved response category is sometimes also referred to as category 0 (Thissen & Steinberg, 1997). For convenience we use p_{jk} for $p_j(x = k|\theta, \underline{\alpha}, \underline{\gamma}, \underline{\phi})$ in the following.

To summarize, in certain situations (e.g., proficiency assessment) the respondents to an item are assumed to consist of a mixture of two classes of individuals: those who choose specific item options and those who, because they "don't know," randomly choose among the response categories. Therefore, conceptually one is faced with the task of "unmixing" the respondents for each response category. The ϕ_{jk} parameter represents the proportion of respondents who "don't know" and select category k on item j; ϕ_{jk} is a function of the estimated parameters (Thissen & Steinberg, 1984; Thissen et al., 1989a). As previously done with the α_{jk}s and the γ_{jk}s, we can collect the m_j ϕ_{jk}s into a vector $\underline{\phi} = (\phi_{j1}, \ldots, \phi_{jm})$.

The model presented in Equation 9.9 is in terms of the *transformed* α_ks, γ_ks, and ϕ_ks. That is, similar to the case with the NR model, the α_ks, γ_ks, and ϕ_ks in Equation 9.9 are the result of transformations to address the indeterminacy issue and identify the model. These transformations of the estimated (unconstrained) parameters impose the constraints

$$\sum_{h=0}^{m_j} \alpha_{jh} = 0$$

$$\sum_{h=0}^{m_j} \gamma_{jh} = 0$$

and

$$\sum_{h=1}^{m_j} \phi_{jh} = 1$$

As is the case with the NR model, the first two constraints are imposed by applying the transformation matrix, $\underline{T}$, to the unconstrained slope, α_{jk}, and intercept, γ_{jk}, parameters (i.e., $\underline{\alpha} = \underline{\alpha}' \underline{T}$ and $\underline{\gamma} = \underline{\gamma}' \underline{T}$). (As done above, we use italicized symbols to represent the unconstrained parameters and nonitalicized symbols to reflect the constrained parameters.) The last constraint is imposed using a transformation matrix, but this matrix is smaller in dimensions than $\underline{T}$. This transformation matrix, $\underline{T}_\phi$, is applied to the unconstrained "don't know" parameters, ϕ_{jh}s (i.e., $\underline{\phi} = \underline{\phi}' \underline{T}_\phi$). As a result, the number of unconstrained (free) parameters per item is $3m_j - 1$ (i.e., m_j α_{jk}s, m_j γ_{jk}s, and $(m_j - 1)$ ϕ_{jk}s). In addition, for each item j there are $(m_j + 1)$ constrained α_{jk}s $(m_j + 1)$ constrained γ_{jk}s, and m_j constrained ϕ_{jk}s. If $\underline{\phi}'$ is fixed as a null vector (i.e., $\underline{0}$), then each of the ϕ_{jk}s equals $1/m_j$ and the MC model simplifies to the BS model (Thissen & Steinberg, 1984).

EXAMPLE: APPLICATION OF THE MC MODEL TO A SCIENCE TEST, MMLE

As an example, we reanalyze the science test data used in the NR model example. Recall that these data involved four physical science items and responses from 1799 examinees.

We observed 233 of the 256 possible patterns. Three of the items were in a multiple-choice format with four options, and the fourth item was open-ended and scored using a 4-point rubric. We use MULTILOG to perform our calibration.

Table 9.8 contains the command file. To instruct MULTILOG to use the MC model, the TEST line contains the keyword BS (B for Bock and S for Samejima). Given that a code of 1 represents the latent "don't know" category, we need to recode the observed responses of 1, 2, 3, 4 to be 2, 3, 4, and 5, respectively. This implies that one needs to count the "don't know" category when specifying the number of categories on the TEST line (i.e., NC=(5,5,5,5)) and when specifying the HIGH category for each of the items. Recoding of the responses is accomplished as done with the PC model calibration example (Chapter 7).

The corresponding output is presented in Table 9.9. We see that the response codes are correctly recoded (see the VECTOR OF CATEGORIES FOR CODE= and the CODE CATEGORY sections). The program took 253 cycles to achieve convergence. The calibration output format is similar to that of the NR model except for the inclusion of an additional line titled D(K) that contains the $\hat{\phi}_{jk}$s as well as a column labeled D. The item parameter estimates for item 1 are $\hat{\underline{\alpha}}$ = (−10.81, 3.16, 3.81, 1.10, 2.75), $\hat{\underline{\gamma}}$ = (−5.95, 1.65, 1.83, 1.31, 1.16), and $\hat{\underline{\phi}}$ = (0.24, 0.29, 0.04, 0.43) with $\Sigma\hat{\alpha}_{jh} = 0$, $\Sigma\hat{\gamma}_{jh} = 0$, and $\Sigma\hat{\phi}_{jh} = 1$. With respect to the $\hat{\phi}_{jk}$s we see that 24% of the individuals who "don't know" selected the first option (labeled 2 in the output) and 29% of those who "don't know" correctly responded (labeled 3 in the output) on this item. A similar interpretation would be used for the other options. This model's unequal $\hat{\phi}_{jk}$s indicate that examinees of very low proficiency are not randomly selecting among item 1's options. From the OBSERVED AND EXPECTED COUNTS/PRO-

TABLE 9.8. Command File for the MC Model Calibration

```
MULTILOG for Windows 7.00.2327.2
MC CALIBRATION, 4 PHYSICAL SCIENCE ITEMS
>PROBLEM RANDOM,
         PATTERNS,
         DATA = 'C:SCIENCE.PAT',
         NITEMS = 4,
         NGROUPS = 1,
         NPATTERNS = 256,
         NCHARS = 9;
>TEST ALL,
      BS,                          ⇐ Specification of MC model[a]
      NC = (5,5,5,5),              ⇐ "Five" categories/item counting the "don't know" category
      HIGH = (3,4,5,4);            ⇐ Ordinal position of highest-frequency category with
                                     respect to "five"-category scale
>EST NC=500 IT=25;
>END ;
4                                  ⇐ Specification of the number of codes in the data file,
                                     not counting the "don't category"
1234                               ⇐ The response code line
2222                               ⇐ The 1s are recoded to be 2s for all four items
3333                               ⇐ The 2s are recoded to be 3s for all four items
4444                               ⇐ The 3s are recoded to be 4s for all four items
5555                               ⇐ The 4s are recoded to be 5s for all four items
(9A1,T1,4A1,F5.0)
```

[a]The text following the ⇐ is provided to help the reader understand the corresponding input.

TABLE 9.9. Abridged Output from the MC Model Calibration Example

```
     :
<echo of command file>

 NUMBER OF CODES  4

1234
  VECTOR OF CATEGORIES FOR CODE=1
2222
  VECTOR OF CATEGORIES FOR CODE=2
3333
  VECTOR OF CATEGORIES FOR CODE=3
4444
  VECTOR OF CATEGORIES FOR CODE=4
5555
     :
  MAXIMUM NUMBER OF EM CYCLES PERMITTED: 500
  NUMBER OF PARAMETER-SEGMENTS USED IS:   4
  NUMBER OF FREE PARAMETERS IS:    44
  MAXIMUM NUMBER OF M-STEP ITERATIONS IS  25 TIMES
     :
  KEY-
 CODE   CATEGORY
   1     2222
   2     3333
   3     4444
   4     5555
     :
 FINISHED CYCLE 253
 MAXIMUM INTERCYCLE PARAMETER CHANGE=   0.00000 P(  44)
     :
 ITEM SUMMARY
     :
 ITEM   1:       5 NOMINAL CATEGORIES,  3 HIGH
   CATEGORY(K): 1       2       3       4       5
     A(K)    -10.81    3.16    3.81    1.10    2.75
     C(K)     -5.95    1.65    1.83    1.31    1.16
     D(K)              0.24    0.29    0.04    0.43

                 CONTRAST-COEFFICIENTS (STANDARD ERRORS)
 FOR:              A                    C                    D
 CONTRAST P(#)  COEFF.[ DEV.]  P(#)  COEFF.[ DEV.]  P(#)  COEFF.[ DEV.]
     1        1  13.97 (8.10)     5   7.60 (5.15)     9   0.18 (0.19)
     2        2  14.62 (8.07)     6   7.78 (5.15)    10  -1.70 (0.49)
     3        3  11.92 (8.21)     7   7.25 (5.09)    11   0.57 (0.18)
     4        4  13.56 (8.04)     8   7.11 (5.20)

@THETA:     INFORMATION:    (Theta values increase in steps of 0.2)
-3.0 - -1.6  0.000  0.000  0.000  0.000  0.000  0.000  0.000  0.000
-1.4 -  0.0  0.000  0.002  0.208  5.973  4.107  0.781  1.089  0.951
 0.2 -  1.6  0.771  0.605  0.468  0.362  0.284  0.227  0.186  0.155
 1.8 -  3.0  0.132  0.114  0.099  0.086  0.076  0.066  0.058

 OBSERVED AND EXPECTED COUNTS/PROPORTIONS IN
 CATEGORY(K): 1       2       3       4       5
 OBS. FREQ.      0     456     723     245     375
 OBS. PROP.  0.0000 0.2535 0.4019 0.1362 0.2084
 EXP. PROP.  0.2412 0.2534 0.4019 0.1363 0.2084
     :
 ITEM   4:       5 NOMINAL CATEGORIES,  4 HIGH
   CATEGORY(K): 1       2       3       4       5
     A(K)     -1.83   -4.47    0.25    2.46    3.59
     C(K)      2.38   -4.28    2.36    0.23   -0.69
     D(K)              0.32    0.00    0.44    0.24

                 CONTRAST-COEFFICIENTS (STANDARD ERRORS)
 FOR:              A                    C                    D
 CONTRAST P(#)  COEFF.[ DEV.]  P(#)  COEFF.[ DEV.]  P(#)  COEFF.[ DEV.]
     1       34  -2.64 (1.50)    38  -6.66 (3.47)    42  -6.83 (****)
     2       35   2.08 (0.30)    39  -0.02 (0.15)    43   0.34 (0.17)
     3       36   4.28 (0.48)    40  -2.15 (0.51)    44  -0.27 (0.19)
     4       37   5.41 (0.50)    41  -3.07 (0.51)
```

cont.

TABLE 9.9. *cont.*

```
@THETA:        INFORMATION:   (Theta values increase in steps of 0.2)
-3.0 - -1.6  0.759  0.920  0.961  0.846  0.629  0.418  0.282  0.233
-1.4 -  0.0  0.253  0.323  0.433  0.570  0.712  0.809  0.786  0.596
 0.2 -  1.6  0.400  0.608  1.261  1.799  1.866  1.574  1.176  0.829
 1.8 -  3.0  0.575  0.403  0.290  0.215  0.164  0.128  0.101

OBSERVED AND EXPECTED COUNTS/PROPORTIONS IN
CATEGORY(K):  1      2      3      4      5
OBS. FREQ.    0     288    507    551    453
OBS. PROP.   0.0000 0.1601 0.2818 0.3063 0.2518
EXP. PROP.   0.4490 0.1601 0.2815 0.3064 0.2521
  :
MARGINAL RELIABILITY:     0.7012
  :
NEGATIVE TWICE THE LOGLIKELIHOOD=       259.3
(CHI-SQUARE FOR SEVERAL TIMES MORE EXAMINEES THAN CELLS)
```

PORTIONS section one sees that approximately 24% of the individuals are expected to be in "category 1." All of the item parameter estimates are presented in Table 9.10.

The overall model fit is $-2\ln L = 259.3$ with a BIC = 589.0794 and 44 estimated parameters (i.e., for each item we have 4 α_{jks}, 4 γ_{jks}, and $(4-1)$ ϕ_{jks} for 11 estimated parameters or 44 parameters for the four items). This value of 44 matches the output's NUMBER OF FREE PARAMETERS IS: line. Compared to the NR model ($-2\ln L = 288.4$, BIC = 468.2797; see Table 9.2) the difference chi-square is $288.4 - 259.73 = 29.1$ with $44 - 24 = 20$ degrees of freedom; alternatively, we have for the NR model $df = 256 - 24 - 1 = 231$ and for the MC model $df = 256 - 44 - 1 = 211$. With a critical X^2 of 31.4 ($\alpha = 0.05$) the MC model almost provided a significantly better fit than did the NR for these data; we assume that the Full model holds for the data.

The ORFs for item 1 are presented in the left panel of Figure 9.8; the response code of 1 is represented by the line labeled 2, the response code of 2 is represented by the line labeled 3, and so on. These ORFs appear different from those seen above. For example, the correct response for this item (the "high" category with ORF labeled 3) does not have a strictly monotonically increasing ORF as seen with the NR model. Instead, its ORF contains a "dip" around −0.5. However, the "high" is always associated with the largest $\hat{\alpha}_{jks}$ for an item. In general, whenever the $\hat{\alpha}_{jks}$ are positive (i.e., categories 2–5) one sees that the $\hat{\phi}_{jks}$ reflect the lower asymptotes of the ORFs; see items 1–3 in Figure 9.9. For instance, item 1's ORF, labeled 2, has a lower asymptote of approximately 0.24, which is

TABLE 9.10. Item Parameter Estimates for Science Items—MC Model

k	Item 1			Item 2			Item 3			Item 4		
	$\hat{\alpha}_{jk}$	$\hat{\gamma}_{jk}$	$\hat{\phi}_{jk}$	$\hat{\alpha}_{jk}$	$\hat{\gamma}_{jk}$	$\hat{\phi}_{jk}$	$\hat{\alpha}_{jk}$	$\hat{\gamma}_{jk}$	$\hat{\phi}_{jk}$	$\hat{\alpha}_{jk}$	$\hat{\gamma}_{jk}$	$\hat{\phi}_{jk}$
1	−10.81	−5.95		−6.69	−8.06		−12.34	−15.16		−1.83	2.38	
2	3.16	1.65	0.24	1.77	0.65	0.18	2.75	3.12	0.23	−4.47	−4.28	0.32
3	3.81	1.83	0.29	1.26	2.16	0.00	1.62	3.32	0.00	0.25	2.36	0.00
4	1.10	1.31	0.04	2.20	2.77	0.29	3.73	4.28	0.46	2.46	0.23	0.44
5	2.75	1.16	0.43	1.45	2.48	0.53	4.24	4.45	0.30	3.59	−0.69	0.24

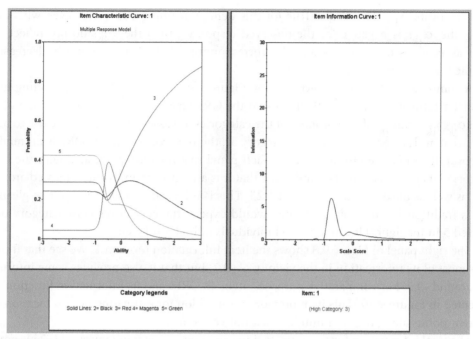

FIGURE 9.8. MC model ORFs and item information function for item 1.

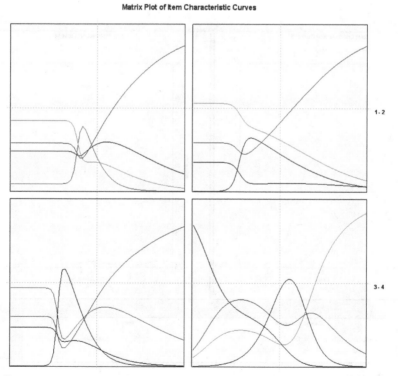

FIGURE 9.9. ORFs for all four items, MC model calibration.

the value of its $\hat{\phi}_{12}$. This is also true for this item's remaining ORFs. However, whenever one of the $\hat{\alpha}_{jk}$s is negative for the observed responses, then the $\hat{\phi}_{jk}$s do not reflect the lower asymptotes of the ORFs and the corresponding ORF is monotonically decreasing (see the ORFs for item 4; Figure 9.9).

A comparison of the item ORF plots in Figure 9.9 along with the corresponding item parameter estimates (Table 9.10) shows that the ORF shape is a complex interaction of an item's $\hat{\alpha}_{jk}$, $\hat{\gamma}_{jk}$, and $\hat{\phi}_{jk}$. If one or more of the categories are associated with $\hat{\phi}_{jk}$s close to zero (e.g., see item 1, category 4 or item 4, category 3), then the corresponding ORF is unimodal. Moreover, it can be seen from the figure's left panel that the ORF associated with the high category (labeled 4) is bimodal, indicating that it is attractive to individuals located around –1.5, as well as to some located around 1.25. This is information that could not be gleaned from a traditional item analysis. As one would expect, the correct response category of 4 (labeled 5 in the figure) is attractive to individuals of high proficiency.

The right panel of Figure 9.8 shows the item information for item 1. We see that it provides most of its information in the vicinity of -0.7, but that it also provides some information around -0.2. For comparative purposes, item 4's ORFs and its information function are presented in Figure 9.10. This item provides information for estimating person locations at different points along the continuum, albeit not very much.

The total information for this four-item instrument is shown in Figure 9.11. This graph shows that this instrument provides most of its information around –1.4, although it also has a small second mode in the vicinity of –0.7.

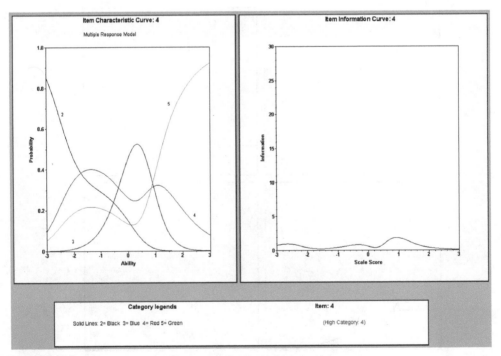

FIGURE 9.10. ORFs and item information function for item 4.

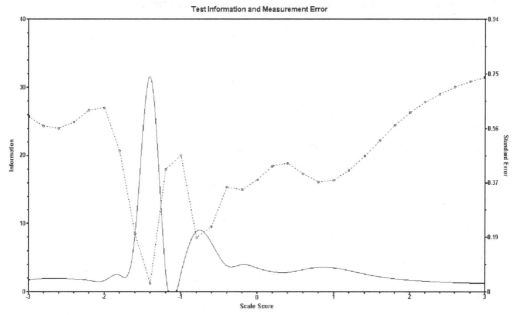

FIGURE 9.11. Total information function for MC model calibration. Solid line indicates total information; dotted line indicates standard error.

EXAMPLE: APPLICATION OF THE BS MODEL TO A SCIENCE TEST, MMLE

For this example we explore whether the proportion of "don't know" individuals is constant and equal to $1/m_j$. To investigate this, the data used in the MC model example are reanalyzed using the BS model and the fit of the models is compared. Because the data involve four 4-option items using (primarily) a multiple-choice response format, $1/m_j = 0.25$. To perform the BS model calibration we modify the command file for the MC model analysis (Table 9.8). Specifically, the modification is the insertion of the command line `>FIX ITEMS=(1,2,3,4), DK=(1,2,3), VALUE=0.0;` to impose the constraint that the "don't know" proportions (i.e., DK) are constrained to be $1/m_j = 0.25$ for all options across the four items. This line is inserted before the `>END;` line. Table 9.11 contains the corresponding output.

In contrast to the 253 cycles required for convergence with the MC model calibration of these data, the BS model required 337 to converge to a solution. The output format is identical to that seen with the MC model. Because of the imposed constraint, the line labeled `D(K)` (correctly) shows that each of the $\hat{\phi}_{jk}$s equals 0.25 and the column labeled `D` contains the constraint's value of 0.0. For item 1 the item parameter estimates are $\hat{\alpha}$ = (–0.60, 0.82, 1.34, –0.73, –0.84), $\hat{\gamma}$ = (2.44, 0.86, 1.33, –4.94, 0.31), and $\hat{\phi}$ = (0.25, 0.25, 0.25, 0.25) with $\Sigma\hat{\alpha}_{jh} = 0$, $\Sigma\hat{\gamma}_{jh} = 0$, and $\Sigma\hat{\phi}_{jh} = 1$.

Item 1's ORFs are presented in the left panel of Figure 9.12. As is the case with the NR model and the NR–PC mixed model calibrations, this item is primarily functioning in a

TABLE 9.11. Abridged Output from the BS Model Calibration Example

```
    :
MAXIMUM NUMBER OF EM CYCLES PERMITTED: 500
NUMBER OF PARAMETER-SEGMENTS USED IS:   4
NUMBER OF FREE PARAMETERS IS:   32
MAXIMUM NUMBER OF M-STEP ITERATIONS IS  25 TIMES
    :
FINISHED CYCLE 337
MAXIMUM INTERCYCLE PARAMETER CHANGE=  0.00051 P(  29)
    :
ITEM SUMMARY
    :
ITEM   1:      5 NOMINAL CATEGORIES,  3 HIGH
  CATEGORY(K): 1     2      3      4      5
    A(K)     -0.60   0.82   1.34  -0.73  -0.84
    C(K)      2.44   0.86   1.33  -4.94   0.31
    D(K)              0.25   0.25   0.25   0.25

                CONTRAST-COEFFICIENTS (STANDARD ERRORS)
    FOR:           A                    C                   D
  CONTRAST P(#)  COEFF.[ DEV.]  P(#)  COEFF.[ DEV.]  P(#)  COEFF.[ DEV.]
      1      1   1.42 (0.48)      5  -1.58 (1.27)     33   0.00 (0.00)
      2      2   1.94 (0.38)      6  -1.12 (1.03)     34   0.00 (0.00)
      3      3  -0.14 (****)      7  -7.39 (****)     35   0.00 (0.00)
      4      4  -0.24 (0.92)      8  -2.14 (1.72)

@THETA:      INFORMATION:    (Theta values increase in steps of 0.2)
-3.0 - -1.6  0.004  0.004  0.004  0.004  0.005  0.005  0.006  0.009
-1.4 -  0.0  0.012  0.018  0.028  0.045  0.073  0.115  0.172  0.241
 0.2 -  1.6  0.313  0.373  0.407  0.409  0.382  0.336  0.282  0.229
 1.8 -  3.0  0.182  0.143  0.112  0.088  0.070  0.056  0.046

  OBSERVED AND EXPECTED COUNTS/PROPORTIONS IN
  CATEGORY(K): 1      2      3      4      5
  OBS. FREQ.      0    456    723    245    375
  OBS. PROP.  0.0000 0.2535 0.4019 0.1362 0.2084
  EXP. PROP.  0.5437 0.2542 0.4011 0.1363 0.2084
    :
ITEM   4:      5 NOMINAL CATEGORIES,  4 HIGH
  CATEGORY(K): 1      2      3      4      5
    A(K)      2.35 -12.61   3.22   2.77   4.27
    C(K)      5.12 -17.46   4.34   4.53   3.47
    D(K)              0.25   0.25   0.25   0.25

                CONTRAST-COEFFICIENTS (STANDARD ERRORS)
    FOR:           A                    C                   D
  CONTRAST P(#)  COEFF.[ DEV.]  P(#)  COEFF.[ DEV.]  P(#)  COEFF.[ DEV.]
      1     25  -14.95 (****)    29  -22.58 (****)    45   0.00 (0.00)
      2     26   0.87 (0.25)     30  -0.78 (0.20)     46   0.00 (0.00)
      3     27   0.42 (0.23)     31  -0.59 (0.17)     47   0.00 (0.00)
      4     28   1.93 (0.30)     32  -1.65 (0.33)

@THETA:      INFORMATION:    (Theta values increase in steps of 0.2)
-3.0 - -1.6  0.000  0.000  0.000  0.000  0.008  0.161  3.209 34.849
-1.4 -  0.0  8.934  0.097  0.017  0.017  0.021  0.029  0.043  0.066
 0.2 -  1.6  0.102  0.151  0.210  0.274  0.334  0.382  0.412  0.420
 1.8 -  3.0  0.407  0.378  0.339  0.295  0.250  0.208  0.170

  OBSERVED AND EXPECTED COUNTS/PROPORTIONS IN
  CATEGORY(K): 1      2      3      4      5
  OBS. FREQ.      0    288    507    551    453
  OBS. PROP.  0.0000 0.1601 0.2818 0.3063 0.2518
  EXP. PROP.  0.3921 0.1609 0.2823 0.3062 0.2506
    :
MARGINAL RELIABILITY:    0.4962
    :
NEGATIVE TWICE THE LOGLIKELIHOOD=      277.7
(CHI-SQUARE FOR SEVERAL TIMES MORE EXAMINEES THAN CELLS)
```

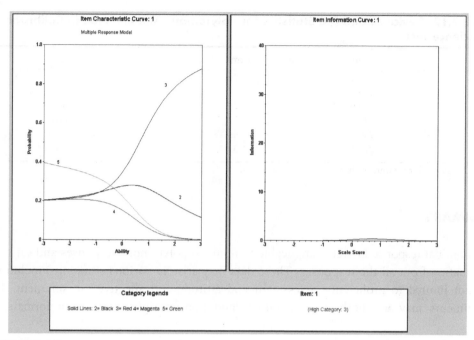

FIGURE 9.12. BS model ORFs and item information function for item 1.

dichotomous fashion. It may also be seen that if individuals below −2 did not select option 5, then they were equally likely to select among the remaining options. The item's information function (right panel) shows that this item is not providing very much information, and substantially less than that provided by this item using the MC model (cf. Figure 9.8). It should be noted that for each calibration the graphing routine imposes a common axis scale across items to facilitate comparisons. Therefore, when we compare figures across calibrations (e.g., Figures 9.8 and 9.12) we need to attend to the scaling differences of the ordinate. In the case of the BS model, item 4's information function has a maximum value of approximately 34.8 and so the maximum for the ordinate scale is set on this item's basis. Although this could potentially invite misleading interpretations of the amount of information an item provides, comparing the values in the @THETA:INFORMATION section of the outputs (Tables 9.9 and 9.11) substantiates the above conclusion. The ORFs for all four items are presented in Figure 9.13. As can be seen, for item 3 there is no single option that is preferred over the other options by individuals of low θ.

The overall BS model fit is $-2\ln L = 277.7$ with a BIC = 517.5396 and 32 estimated parameters (i.e., for each item there are 4 α_{jk}s and 4 γ_{jk}s, or 32 parameters for the four items). This deviance statistic is not significantly different from that for the MC model, although the BS model's BIC is about 12% smaller; we assume that the Full model holds for the data. Therefore, the BS model may be preferred to the MC model for these data. Table 9.12 contains the deviance and BIC statistics for the various polytomous model and model combinations that were applied to these data. According to its $-2\ln L$ and BIC values, the NR–PC mixed model calibration, where item 2's options 1 and 2 were combined, provides the best fit to these data.

TABLE 9.12. Deviance and BIC Statistics for Polytomous Models Used in Calibrating the Science Test

Model	$-2\ln L$	Number of estimated parameters	BIC
NR	288.4	24	468.2797
NR-PC	320.5	22	485.3897
NR-PC^{a}	219.6	20	369.4997
NR-GR	322.2	22	487.0897
MC	259.3	44	589.0794
BS	277.7	32	517.5396

^{a}Item 2 collapsed from four to three response categories.

SUMMARY

The nominal response model is applicable to nominal polytomous responses and captures information from all the responses. These data may arise in various situations, including, but not limited to proficiency assessment and attitude and affective measurement. The instruments may use both multiple-choice and non-multiple-choice item formats. In

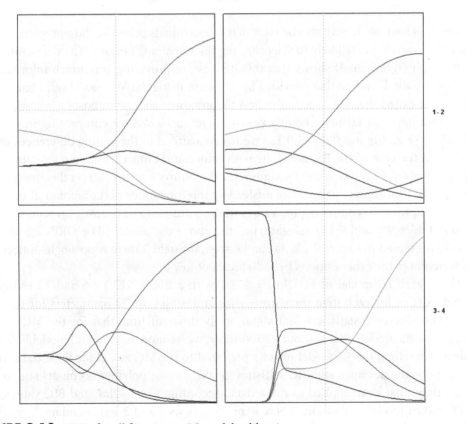

Matrix Plot of Item Characteristic Curves

FIGURE 9.13. ORFs for all four items, BS model calibration.

addition, the NR model may be applied to dichotomous data and, with the appropriate constraints, to ordinal data. The NR model subsumes the partial credit, generalized partial credit, and two-parameter models.

The NR model contains a slope, α_{jk}, and an intercept, γ_{jk}, parameter for each response category for an item. As is the case with previously discussed polytomous models, each response category has an associated option response function. Because the slope parameters for an item are constrained to sum to zero across categories, one category always has a monotonically increasing ORF and one a monotonically decreasing ORF. This latter characteristic implies that a particular (e.g., incorrect) response option should be preferred to the remaining responses for individuals with very low θs. This may be an inappropriate assumption in certain applications. In short, when the NR model is applied to proficiency assessment it does not address the possibility of examinees guessing on items. Stated another way, the NR model states that all individuals that are "randomly guessing" on an item will select the same distractor. In those cases where guessing may be an issue, then the multiple-choice (MC) or Bock–Samejima (BS) model may be preferred to the NR model.

The BS model is an extension of the NR model and incorporates a random guessing component. This model states that "don't know" individuals will guess on the options with the equal probability of $1/m_j$. In contrast, the MC model allows for the possibility that the "don't know" individuals will guess on the options with potentially unequal probability. As a result, in addition to the NR model's slope and intercept parameters, the MC model contains a new parameter, ϕ_{jk}, that represents the proportion of respondents who "don't know" and selected category k on item j. Conceptually, the respondents consist of a mixture of individuals who chose a specific option and those who guessed on each of the response options.

The models presented in the previous chapters are applicable to dichotomous, ordered polytomous, and nominal polytomous data. In many respects, all of the models presented may be viewed as either extensions of the two-parameter model or subsumed by the two-parameter model. As such, we view the two-parameter model as the "nexus model." In this regard, these models share the two-parameter model's assumption that a single latent trait underlies the data. In the next chapter we extend the two-parameter model to allow for the possibility of multiple latent traits underlying the response data.

NOTES

1. For a categorical response variable with m response categories, let $\{p_1, \ldots, p_m\}$ contain the corresponding set of response probabilities. Furthermore, across the m categories these probabilities sum to 1. Given that a random sample of N independent cases is drawn from a population with $\{p_1, \ldots, p_m\}$, then the probability distribution for the sample's observed frequency distribution across the m responses is called a multinomial distribution. (The binomial distribution is a special case of the multinomial distribution when $m = 2$.) For the example we are assuming a multinomial distribution.

2. This is accomplished by using the *multinomial logit model* to predict the observed data (cf. Agresti, 1990) . The nominal response model may be considered an example of multinomial logistic regression using the person's latent location and the items' latent characterizations. When $m = 2$ (i.e., binary response data), then we have a single logit equation and the analysis simplifies to ordinary logistic regression; $\log(p_1/p_0) = \log(p_1) = \gamma + \alpha X$.

3. In general, the transformation matrix, $\underline{T}$, with $(m_j - 1)$ rows and m_j columns contains the following deviation contrasts:

$$\underline{T} = \begin{bmatrix} -\dfrac{1}{m_j} & \dfrac{(m_j - 1)}{m_j} & \cdots & -\dfrac{1}{m_j} & -\dfrac{1}{m_j} \\ -\dfrac{1}{m_j} & -\dfrac{1}{m_j} & \cdots & -\dfrac{1}{m_j} & -\dfrac{1}{m_j} \\ \vdots & \vdots & \vdots & \vdots & \vdots \\ -\dfrac{1}{m_j} & -\dfrac{1}{m_j} & \cdots & \dfrac{(m_j - 1)}{m_j} & -\dfrac{1}{m_j} \\ -\dfrac{1}{m_j} & -\dfrac{1}{m_j} & \cdots & -\dfrac{1}{m_j} & \dfrac{(m_j - 1)}{m_j} \end{bmatrix}$$

The first column is equal to the negative of the sum of the following $(m_j - 1)$ columns and, as a result, the row sum is 0.0. For example, for a three-response category ($m_j = 3$) item the corresponding $\underline{T}$ would be

$$\underline{T} = \begin{bmatrix} -0.33333 & 0.66667 & -0.33333 \\ -0.33333 & -0.33333 & 0.66667 \end{bmatrix}$$

Bock's (1972) presentation of $\underline{T}$ has elements whose signs are the opposite of those above. The matrix above corresponds to that used by Thissen et al. (2003).

4. It is possible to use non-nested mixed models in a single calibration. For instance, we might use the GR model instead of the PC model for this example. However, because the example treats only one item in a graded fashion, there is no inherent benefit in using a model that allows items to vary in their discrimination over a model that constrains them to all be the same. We present the NR and GR mixed model calibration for the science test in Appendix E, "Example: Mixed Model Calibration of the Science Test—NR and GR Models, MMLE."

5. For ordered polytomous data (i.e., graded response data) Samejima (1979) proposed that the probability of a person located at θ responding in category k on item j in the presence of guessing is

$$p_{jk} = \frac{1 - \exp\{-\alpha_j(\delta_{j,k+1} - \delta_{j,k})\}}{[1 + \exp\{-\alpha_j(\theta - \delta_{j,k})\}][1 + \exp\{\alpha_j(\theta - \delta_{j,k+1})\}]} + \frac{1}{m_j\{1 + \exp[\alpha_j(\theta - \delta_{j,1})]\}} \quad (9.10)$$

where $\alpha_j > 0$, $-\infty < \delta_{j,1} < \delta_{j,2} < \ldots < \delta_{j,m_j} < \delta_{j,m_j+1} < \infty$, and $x_j = \{0, 1, \ldots, m_j\}$. The model in Equation 9.10 is called Type I Model B by Samejima (1979); her presentation uses $D\alpha_j$ in lieu of our α_j. (Type I Model A is the normal ogive version of Equation 9.10.) For Equation 9.10, the ORF when k = 0 is strictly decreasing in θ and represents the "no recognition" category. Therefore, the observed responses are $x_j = \{1, \ldots, m_j\}$ with the ORF being strictly increasing in θ when k = m_j and is the item's correct answer. Both the "k = 0" and k = m_j ORFs have asymptotes of 0 and 1. The ORFs for $x_j = \{1, \ldots, m_j - 1\}$ are unimodal and asymptotic to 0.

10

Models for Multidimensional Data

The models presented in the previous chapters contained a single parameter, θ, to reflect a person's location on a continuous latent variable. As a consequence, these models were predicated on a unidimensional latent space. However, in some situations it may be more realistic to hypothesize that a person's response to an item is due to his or her locations on multiple latent variables. In these situations we have a *multidimensional* latent space. In this chapter we present models that use multiple person location parameters to describe an individual's response behavior.

CONCEPTUAL DEVELOPMENT OF A MULTIDIMENSIONAL IRT MODEL

There are various situations in which one might encounter multidimensionality. For instance, consider an instrument designed to measure self-efficacy in overcoming barriers to healthy eating. If, theoretically, healthy eating self-efficacy involves cognitive and affective dimensions, then responses to this instrument are a function of a respondent's locations on these dimensions. A second example of multidimensionality is performance on a mathematical word problem. In this case, we may have, for example, two dimensions that underlie the response data. One dimension would reflect mathematics proficiency and the other reading proficiency.

These two examples describe two possible multidimensional scenarios that differ from one another in how the latent person variables interact to produce the observed responses. In the second example, an individual with highly developed reading proficiency might be able to compensate, to some extent, for his or her lower mathematics proficiency in order to correctly respond to a mathematical word problem. In contrast, with our self-efficacy example a respondent's location on the cognitive dimension could not compensate for his or her location on the affective dimension. In short, the mathematical word problem scenario reflects a compensatory multidimensional situation where a person's location(s) on one or more dimension(s) can compensate for his or her location(s) on other latent variable(s).

Conversely, the self-efficacy example presents a noncompensatory multidimensional case. In this case a person's location on one (or more) latent variable(s) does not compensate for his or her location(s) on other latent variable(s). Given these possibilities, the modeling of these types of data requires distinguishing between compensatory and noncompensatory multidimensional situations.

Models for noncompensatory multidimensional scenarios are called *noncompensatory* models, whereas models for compensatory multidimensional scenarios are referred to as *compensatory* multidimensional models. Examples of noncompensatory models may be found in Sympson (1978) and Whitely (1980). These models have not seen as much attention as the compensatory models, in part, because of estimation difficulties; also see Spray, Davey, Reckase, Ackerman, and Carlson (1990). In the following discussion we focus on two common compensatory models.

To develop a *multidimensional item response theory* (MIRT) model we assume for simplicity, but without loss of generalizability, that we are interested in modeling a two-dimensional latent space. It is possible to generalize the model to more than two dimensions, although graphical depiction becomes problematic with more than two dimensions.

From Chapters 2 and 5 we know that with dichotomous unidimensional models the probability of a response of 1 is a function of the unweighted or weighted distance between item j's location and person i's location (e.g., $\alpha_j(\theta_i - \delta_j)$). This idea may be extended to the two-dimensional latent space; in the following the second subscript indicates the dimension. At the simplest level, the probability of a response of 1 is a function of the difference between item j's location and person i's location on dimension 1 (e.g., $(\theta_{i1} - \delta_{j1})$) *and* the difference between the item's location and the person's location on dimension 2 (e.g., $(\theta_{i2} - \delta_{j2})$). However, simply using $(\theta_{i1} - \delta_{j1})$ and $(\theta_{i2} - \delta_{j2})$ in the logistic function implies that the item's relationship to each dimension is the same for both dimensions. This may not be the case in all situations. For instance, assume that an examination consists of algebra word problems. One question may require greater algebra knowledge than it does reading proficiency. As a result, the algebra dimension is a stronger determinant of a response of 1 on this item than is the reading proficiency dimension, although both are required to answer the question. In contrast, another item may require less algebra knowledge than it does reading proficiency to be correctly answered. Therefore, to reflect that an item's relationship to a dimension may vary across dimensions, these logits must be weighted to represent these item–dimension relationships.

A mechanism for weighting the logits for a dimension comes from factor analysis. Recall that in factor analysis the item's loading on a factor reflects the relationship between the item and the dimension. As presented in Appendix C, an item's loading is related to its discrimination parameter. Therefore, using the item's discrimination provides a mechanism to capture the item's relationships to the underlying dimensions. Specifically, an item's discrimination on each dimension can serve as a weight for the logit for that dimension. Incorporating these ideas into the logistic function produces

$$p(x_{ij} = 1 \mid \theta_{i1}, \theta_{i2}, \alpha_{j1}, \alpha_{j2}, \delta_{j1}, \delta_{j2}) = \frac{e^{\alpha_{j1}(\theta_{i1}-\delta_{j1})+\alpha_{j2}(\theta_{i2}-\delta_{j2})}}{1+e^{\alpha_{j1}(\theta_{i1}-\delta_{j1})+\alpha_{j2}(\theta_{i2}-\delta_{j2})}} \quad (10.1)$$

where α_{j1} and α_{j2} are item j's discrimination parameters on dimension 1 and 2, respectively. The model in Equation 10.1 states that the probability of a response of 1 is a function of the distance between person i and item j's locations on each dimension and the item's relationship to each dimension. Equation 10.1 may be seen as a generalization of the 2PL model to a two-dimensional latent space.[1] As such, items may vary in their discrimination parameters.

Alternatively, Equation 10.1 may be reparameterized into a slope–intercept form by introducing an intercept parameter, γ_j. Recall that in the unidimensional case this parameter reflects the interaction between an item's location and its capacity to discriminate among individuals (e.g., Chapter 2, Equation 2.3). Applying this idea to the two-dimensional case, Equation 10.1 becomes

$$p(x_{ij} = 1| \theta_{i1}, \theta_{i2}, \alpha_{j1}, \alpha_{j2}, \gamma_j) = \frac{e^{(\alpha_{j1}\theta_{i1}+\alpha_{j2}\theta_{i2})+\gamma_j}}{1+e^{(\alpha_{j1}\theta_{i1}+\alpha_{j2}\theta_{i2})+\gamma_j}} \quad (10.2)$$

where

$$\gamma_j = -(\alpha_{j1}\delta_{j1} + \alpha_{j2}\delta_{j2}) = -\sum_{f=1}^{2} \alpha_{jf}\delta_{jf}$$

One may generalize from the two-dimensional situation to F latent variables or dimensions. Applying this generalization to Equation 10.2 yields the (compensatory) *multidimensional two-parameter logistic* (M2PL) model (McKinley & Reccase, 1983a; Reccase, 1985):

$$p(x_{ij} = 1| \underline{\theta}_i, \underline{\alpha}_j, \gamma_j) = \frac{e^{\Sigma\alpha_{jf}\theta_{if}+\gamma_j}}{1+e^{\Sigma\alpha_{jf}\theta_{if}+\gamma_j}} = \frac{e^{\underline{\alpha}'_j\underline{\theta}_i+\gamma_j}}{1+e^{\underline{\alpha}'_j\underline{\theta}_i+\gamma_j}} \quad (10.3)$$

where $p(x_{ij} = 1| \underline{\theta}_i, \underline{\alpha}_j, \gamma_j)$ is the probability of a response of 1 on item j by person i, given his or her locations on each of the F-dimensions and the item characteristics of $\underline{\alpha}_j$ and γ_j. The (column) vector $\underline{\theta}_i$ contains person i's location parameters on each of the F-dimensions (i.e., $\underline{\theta}_i = (\theta_{i1}, \dots, \theta_{if}, \dots, \theta_{iF})$). The item is characterized by a vector, $\underline{\alpha}_j$, containing item j's discrimination parameters on each of the F-dimensions (i.e., $\underline{\alpha}_j = (\alpha_{j1}, \dots, \alpha_{jf}, \dots, \alpha_{jF})$) and an intercept parameter, γ_j; the prime symbol on $\underline{\alpha}_j$ in Equation 10.3 indicates that $\underline{\alpha}'_j$ is a row vector. The discrimination parameters indicate the sensitivity of the item to differences in person locations in the latent space in a particular direction (e.g., along the θ_1-axis). The intercept, γ_j, reflects the interaction of the item's location and discrimination parameters. In a proficiency assessment situation γ_j would be interpreted as *related* to an item's difficulty, although the two are opposite in sign. Analogous to Equation 2.3, the intercept parameter in the F-dimensional case is given by

$$\gamma_j = -\sum_{f=1}^{F} \alpha_{jf}\delta_{jf} \quad (10.4)$$

The number of elements in $\underline{\theta}_i$, and therefore $\underline{\alpha}_j$, equals the number of interpretable dimensions underlying the data. In the following we use p_j in lieu of $p(x_{ij} = 1|\ \underline{\theta}_i, \underline{\alpha}_j, \gamma_j)$.

Graphically, Equation 10.3 (or Equations 10.1 or 10.2) would produce a sigmoidal-shaped analog to the IRF. This analog is called the *item response surface* (IRS). For a two-dimensional situation (i.e., F = 2) we need three dimensions to display the IRS where two of the axes represent the two latent person variables and the third axis reflects the probability of a response of 1.

Figure 10.1 contains an example of an IRS for the two-dimensional case where $\alpha_{j1} = 2.0$, $\alpha_{j2} = 0.5$, $\delta_{j1} = -1.25$, and $\delta_{j2} = 1$ (or $\gamma_j = 2$). We see that the probability of a response of 1 increases as θ increases along each dimension. Conversely, as θ decreases we see that the surface becomes asymptotic with $p_j = 0$ (the foreground). Furthermore, we see that the IRS has different (conditional) slopes. This observation is easy to demonstrate by taking "slices" out of the IRS. For instance, for a person located at $\theta_1 = -1.2$, our slice through the IRS results in a conditional trace line along θ_2 (i.e., a line from the foreground to the background when $\theta_1 = -1.2$). We can take a second conditional trace line by slicing through the IRS along dimension 1 for $\theta_2 = -1.8$ (i.e., a line from the left side to the right side when $\theta_2 = -1.8$). These two conditional trace lines are shown in Figure 10.2, with the solid and dashed lines representing the first and second conditional trace lines, respectively. Our second conditional trace line has a substantially greater slope than does the first conditional trace line. These different slopes reflect that, in part, the item's relationship to dimension 1 is different from its relationship to dimension 2.

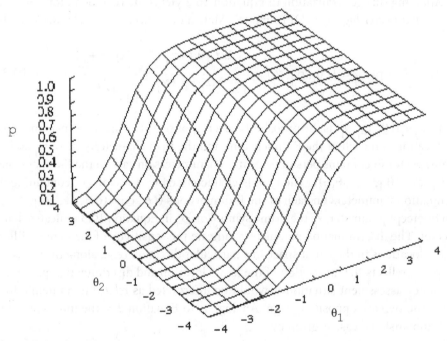

FIGURE 10.1. Item response surface for a two-dimensional item ($\alpha_{j1} = 2.0$, $\alpha_{j2} = 0.5$, and $\gamma_j = 2.0$).

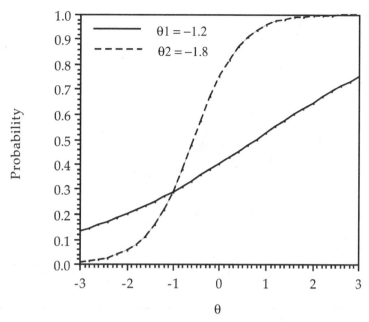

FIGURE 10.2. Conditional trace lines of the IRS shown in Figure 10.1.

With the 2PL model the probability of a response of 1 on item j equals 0.5 whenever $\theta = \delta_j$ (i.e., the logit equals 0). Similarly, with the M2PL model whenever the logit equals 0, then the probability of a response of 1 on item j equals 0.5. However, across the two dimensions there are multiple combinations of θs that for a given item parameter set result in the logit equaling 0.0. As such, and unlike the unidimensional case where there is a single point where $p_j = 0.5$, in the multidimensional situation there is a line of points for which $p_j = 0.5$. We refer to this line of points as the *inflexion line*. This property is easily shown using a contour plot to represent the IRS.

With a contour plot the contour lines represent points of equal probability. Figure 10.3 contains the contour plot corresponding to the IRS shown in Figure 10.1. As indicated by the legend, each contour line shows a different level of p_j as well as the various combinations of θs that interact with the item's parameters to produce these different p_js. The pattern we see is that the probabilities increase as one moves from left to right in the graph. For example, the rightmost line traces the various combinations of θ_1 and θ_2, which, given this item's parameters, results in a $p_j = 0.95$. The fourth contour line from the left reflects a p_j of 0.5 and is the IRS's inflexion line. The steepness of an IRS is represented by the proximity of the contour lines. The steeper the IRS, the closer the corresponding contour lines are to one another and, conversely, contour lines that are comparatively farther apart reflect a less steep portion of the IRS. This item shows a relatively steep (discriminating) portion in the center of the band of contour lines.

Analogous to the approach in Chapters 2 and 9, we use a logit space plot to help discuss the intercept parameter in the multidimensional case. Figure 10.4 shows the logit space plot for the item shown in Figures 10.1 and 10.3. Rather than the logit regression line seen with

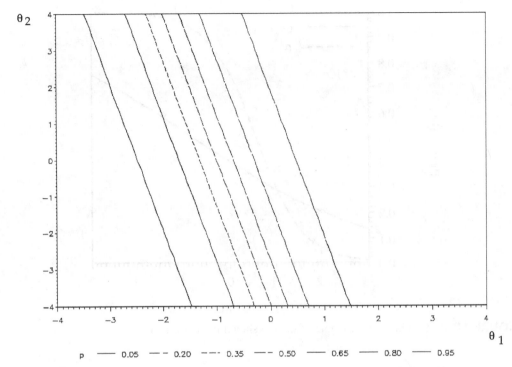

FIGURE 10.3. Contour plot of IRS in Figure 10.1 ($\alpha_{j1} = 2.0$, $\alpha_{j2} = 0.5$, and $\gamma_j = 2.0$).

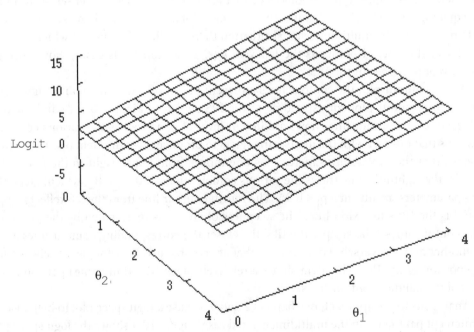

FIGURE 10.4. Multivariate logit space plot of the item in Figure 10.1 ($\alpha'_j = (2.0, 0.5)$ and $\gamma_j = 2.0$).

the unidimensional models, we now have a *logit regression plane*. This plane is analogous to the regression plane for a two-predictor multiple regression model. (To facilitate interpreting the ordinate, the axes have been truncated to begin at 0.0 and the θ_2 axis has been reversed from the way it is shown in Figure 10.1.) We see that not only does the plane have a steeper slope along dimension 1 than along dimension 2, reflecting that α_{j1} is four times larger than α_{j2}, but that the plane intersects the ordinate at $\gamma_j = 2$. Given that α_{j1} is larger than α_{j2}, we know that this item is better at discriminating among respondents on θ_1 than on dimension 2. One implication of this is that this item provides greater information for locating individuals along dimension 1 than along dimension 2.

MULTIDIMENSIONAL ITEM LOCATION AND DISCRIMINATION

Because γ_j involves both discrimination and location parameters, we cannot interpret γ_j as a location parameter. However, we can calculate an index, the *multidimensional item location* (Δ_j), that can be interpreted as a location parameter. In an analogous fashion we can determine an item's capacity to discriminate individuals across all dimensions. This index is item j's *multidimensional item discrimination* parameter, A_j. Therefore, although an item may not be a pure measure of a single latent dimension, A_j and Δ_j provide a form of data reduction of the item's multidimensional characterizations. That is, regardless of the number of dimensions, A_j provides a single (i.e., scalar) value that represents the best that item j can discriminate across all the dimensions. Similarly, the item's location in the multidimensional space is given by a single value, its Δ_j, and its direction cosine(s). The calculation of an item's A_j is informed by its Δ_j, and the calculation of Δ_j uses A_j. In the following we begin with the concept of a multidimensional item location and then discuss an item's multidimensional discrimination parameter.

Item j's multidimensional item location is given by

$$\Delta_j = \frac{-\gamma_j}{A_j} \qquad (10.5)$$

where all terms are defined above. An item's multidimensional item location indicates the *distance* from the origin in the $\underline{\theta}$ space to the point of maximum slope (i.e., the item's maximum discrimination) in a *particular direction* from the origin; Equation 10.5 is also called the item's *multidimensional item difficulty*.[2] This definition is based on the assumption that the most reasonable point to use in defining item j's Δ_j is the point where the item is most discriminating (Reckase, 1985).

Ignoring the directionality issue for now, Δ_j's definition is analogous to how the unidimensional item location is defined. That is, δ_j is the point where the IRF has its maximum slope—its inflexion point. Furthermore, a negative sign on Δ_j corresponds to a unidimensional model's negative location parameter, whereas a positive Δ_j reflects a unidimensional model's positive δ_j. Moreover, because A_j represents the item's discrimination capacity, Equation 10.5 is analogous to defining an item's unidimensional location in terms of its intercept and discrimination parameters (cf. Equation 2.5 in Chapter 2). As a result, if we rearrange Equation 10.5 we can obtain an expression of the intercept in terms of the multidimensional item location and multidimensional discrimination parameters:

$$\gamma_j = -A_j \Delta_j \tag{10.6}$$

Equation 10.6 is analogous in form to the intercept's definition with, say, the 2PL model where $\gamma_j = -\alpha_j \delta_j$.

With an IRS there any many possible slopes that can be calculated. That is, the slope of the IRS at a particular point may vary from that at another point, depending on where we are on the surface. This is easily seen from Figure 10.2 where the conditional trace lines reflect two different directions along the IRS. As we see, the slopes of the conditional trace lines at the intersection point differ from one another. Implied in these figures is that the slope is a change in the surface for a unit change in the θ_1–θ_2 plane in a particular direction. To determine this direction we need a reference or starting point for the path that we take across the surface and along which we calculate the unit change. Stated another way, there are many different starting points to proceed from across the surface, and the slope along and across each of these paths varies. By convention, the origin of the space serves as the reference point of interest (i.e., the point defined by $\theta_1 = \ldots = \theta_F = 0$; Reckase, 1985). From the origin we can determine the IRS's maximum slope in an infinite number of directions. It is the maximum value of these maxima that is used in defining item j's Δ_j.

Conceptually, to determine the IRS's point of maximum slope we first determine the slopes' values in the different directions. Once we know these, we can determine where the slopes are maximized and the direction of the maximum with respect to the origin. Let ω_{jf} represent a direction or angle from the fth dimension to a point of maximum slope for item j. For the M2PL model the *value* of the slope in the direction given by ω_{jf} is (Reckase, 1985)

$$p_j(1 - p_j) \sum_f^F \alpha_{jf} \cos \omega_{jf} \tag{10.7}$$

Given that at the inflexion line (i.e., $p_j = 0.5$) the slope in the direction given by the ω_{jf} is at its maximum, then the slope's value at a point on the inflexion line equals

$$0.25 \sum_f^F \alpha_{jf} \cos \omega_{jf} \tag{10.8}$$

Hypothetically, if we apply Equation 10.8 to angles from 0° to 90° with respect to the fth dimension, we obtain a series of corresponding slope values that represent the maximum at that angle (i.e., direction). We are interested in the maximum of these values and its direction. For instance, for our example item with $\underline{\alpha} = (2.0, 0.5)$ and the angles from 12° to 16° (with respect to the dimension θ_1) in one degree increments, the application of Equation 10.8 gives us the corresponding slope values of (0.51506, 0.51530, 0.51539,

0.51532, 0.51509); that is, the slope at 12° is 0.51506, at 13° it is 0.51530, and so on. The maximum (slope) of these maxima is 0.51539.

To determine the location of *the* maximum value of the series of slopes given by Equation 10.8, we need to identify its direction. The direction of the maximum slope from the origin is

$$\cos \omega_{jf} = \frac{\alpha_{jf}}{\sqrt{\sum_{f=1}^{F} \alpha_{jf}^2}} \qquad (10.9)$$

or, alternatively, the angle is

$$\omega_{jf} = \arccos \left(\frac{\alpha_{jf}}{\sqrt{\sum_{f=1}^{F} \alpha_{jf}^2}} \right) \qquad (10.10)$$

(In vector geometry Equation 10.9 is sometimes referred to as a direction cosine.) For our example item with $\underline{\alpha}$ = (2.0, 0.5), the maximum slope of 0.51539 occurs at an angle of approximately 14° with respect to θ_1 (below we show the calculation to obtain the angle). Therefore, the distance from the origin to the maximum slope of 0.51539 in the direction of 14° with respect to θ_1 is the item's Δ_j. We determine this distance below.

As mentioned above, the value of the slope at the inflexion point in a direction given by ω_{jf} is obtained by Equation 10.8. Equation 10.9 tells the specific direction to find the maximum slope of the maxima slopes. Therefore, by substitution of Equation 10.9 into Equation 10.8 *the* maximum slope is

$$0.25 \sum_{f}^{F} \alpha_{jf} \cos \omega_{jf} = 0.25 \sum_{f}^{F} \alpha_{jf} \left[\frac{\alpha_{jf}}{\sqrt{\sum_{f=1}^{F} \alpha_{jf}^2}} \right] = 0.25 \sqrt{\sum_{f}^{F} \alpha_{jf}^2} \qquad (10.11)$$

That is, Equation 10.11 directly gives the maximum slope of the maxima obtained through Equation 10.8. For example, applying Equation 10.11 to our example item yields, as identified above, that the maximum slope is 0.51539. Equation 10.11 shows that, analogous to the 2PL model, the item's α_{jf}s are related to the maximum slope at the inflexion line (McKinley & Reckase, 1983a; Reckase, 1985).

Because we now know the direction in which to proceed to calculate Δ_j, we can now discuss the other aspect of Δ_j's definition, the item's multidimensional discrimination capacity, A_j. We can determine item j's capacity to discriminate individuals across all F-dimensions by calculating its multidimensional item discrimination parameter (Reckase & McKinley, 1991)[3]:

$$A_j = \sqrt{\sum_{f=1}^{F} \alpha_{jf}^2} \qquad\qquad (10.12)$$

Reckase and McKinley (1991) define A_j to be a function of the slope of the IRS defined by the model at the steepest point in the direction indicated by the multidimensional item location, Δ_j. As stated above, the slope at the "steepest point" is the maximum of the slope maxima and occurs on the IRS's inflexion line. The larger the value of A_j, the greater item j's discrimination capacity across the F-dimensions. For an item that measures only one dimension, A_j reduces to the unidimensional α_j because the α_{jf}s for the other dimensions would be equal to 0. As is the case with the α_{jf}s, A_j is equal to four times the maximum slope.

For the example item shown in Figures 10.1 and 10.3, its multidimensional discrimination would be

$$A_j = \sqrt{\sum_{f=1}^{F} \alpha_{jf}^2} = \sqrt{2.0^2 + 0.5^2} = 2.062$$

Given that the item's $\gamma_j = 2$, then this item's multidimensional item location is

$$\Delta_j = \frac{-\gamma_j}{A_j} = \frac{-2.0}{2.062} = -0.9701$$

in a direction given by

$$\cos\overset{\circ}{\omega}_{j1} \cong \frac{\alpha_{j1}}{\sqrt{\sum_{f=1}^{F} \alpha_{jf}^2}} = \frac{2.0}{2.062} = 14°$$

with respect to dimension 1. Alternatively, with respect to dimension 2, the direction of maximum slope is

$$\cos\overset{\circ}{\omega}_{j2} \cong \frac{\alpha_{j2}}{\sqrt{\sum_{f=1}^{F} \alpha_{jf}^2}} = \frac{0.5}{2.062} = 76°$$

Therefore, if we proceed from the origin in a direction of 14° a distance of –0.9701 logits, then we arrive at the item's point of maximum slope; the slope's value at this point is 0.51539. Because of the magnitude of this angle this item primarily measures θ_1. If this is an proficiency item, then it might be considered to be somewhat easy and reasonably discriminating.

The A_j of 2.062 is the maximum discrimination capacity on the inflexion line. This can be shown by applying Equation 10.8 and multiplying the corresponding slope values by 4. (In the following all angles are with respect to the θ_1 dimension.) For example, if we increase the angle to 45°, then the item's discrimination capacity decreases from 2.062 to 1.7678. If we continue until the angle is 90°, then the item's discrimination capacity would decrease further to 0.50 (i.e., α_{j2}'s value). Conversely, if our angle is 0° (i.e., the θ_1 axis), then the item's discrimination capacity is (α_{j1} =) 2.0.

It should be noted that we should compare items' A_js only when they are measuring in the same direction (cf. Reckase & McKinley, 1991). To compare the discrimination capacity of items that are measuring in different directions we need to select a common direction ω and then calculate the *directional discrimination*, A_ω:

$$A_\omega = \sum_{f=1}^{F} \alpha_{jf} \cos(\omega_{jf}) \qquad (10.13)$$

ITEM VECTORS AND VECTOR GRAPHS

By using traditional multivariate graphical techniques we can combine A_j and Δ_j to simultaneously represent the discrimination(s) and location(s) of one or more items. Although IRS depictions (e.g., Figure 10.1) are useful, they can become cumbersome when one wants to simultaneously present multiple items. We can simplify the presentation of multidimensional item characteristics by using a vector graph. This type of graph allows us to simultaneously present not only an item's location and how well it discriminates, but also which dimension, if any, it measures best. This graph may be used to present the multidimensional item characteristics for all items on an instrument. Historically, multivariate techniques such as factor analysis have used vector graphs to represent how well items load on different factors (e.g., see Thurstone, 1947). These graphs use a vector to represent an item. A vector is typically represented by an arrow that has a starting point, a specified length, and points in a particular direction.

To graph an item vector we need to know its starting point, its length, and its direction in the multidimensional space. The item vector's starting point is given by Δ_j (i.e., the distance from the **θ** space's origin to the point of maximum slope) and its length by A_j.[4] In general, the direction of the vector with respect to a particular dimension f is given by Equation 10.10. For our purposes we use the horizontal axis to represent θ_1 and this also serves as our reference axis. The angle ω (in degrees) from this axis to the vector can be calculated by modifying Equation 10.10 to obtain

$$\omega_{j1}^{\circ} = \arccos\left(\frac{\alpha_{j1}}{A_j}\right) \qquad (10.14)$$

Once we know an item's A_j, Δ_j, and ω_{jf}, then we have all the components necessary to represent the item as a vector. For example, the item shown in Figure 10.1 has an angle of

$$\overset{\circ}{\omega}_{j1} = \arccos\left(\frac{\alpha_{j1}}{A_j}\right) = \arccos\left(\frac{2.0}{2.062}\right) = 14.0362°$$

with respect to the reference axis, θ_1; above we said this angle was approximately 14°. Therefore, for this item if we proceed from the origin a distance of $\Delta_j = -0.9701$ at an angle of $\overset{\circ}{\omega}_{j1} = 14.036°$, we come to the item's location as well as the IRS's point of maximum slope. If we proceed an additional distance of $A_j = 2.062$, then we have traversed the item's multidimensional discrimination capacity.

In Figure 10.5 we graphically represent how Δ_j, A_j, and ω_j relate to define an item vector. Before discussing the item vectors we describe the figure's layout. The graph is divided into four quadrants and uses the standard quadrant notation; the quadrants are labeled in their respective outside corners. The point of origin for this two-dimensional space is in the center of graph where all four quadrants meet and the θ_1 and the θ_2 continua intersect; the metrics for θ_1 and θ_2 are on the bottom and left margins of the graph, respectively. Item vectors representing two items are presented as bold arrows; the double-headed arrows indicate

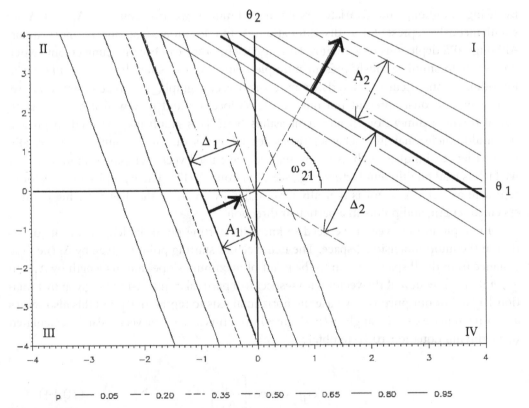

FIGURE 10.5. Vector plot for two items with different Δ_js, A_js, and ω_js.

distances. The contour plot for item 1 primarily occupies quadrants II and III, whereas item 2's contour plot primarily occupies quadrant I. For each contour plot the IRS's inflexion line is in bold. Although we have overlaid the items' contour plots to help clarify the relationship between an item's vector representation and its Δ_j, A_j, and ω_j values, vector plots do not normally have contour plots embedded in them (e.g., see Figure 10.8). In a proficiency assessment situation items in the top right corner of quadrant I would be considered to be difficult items and those in the bottom left corner of quadrant III would be considered to be easy items.

The item vector for item 2 appears in quadrant I (i.e., the upper right part of the figure). Recall that with the 2PL model the item's location is defined at the IRF's point of the inflexion. Analogously, with the M2PL model the multidimensional item location is defined at the IRS's line of inflexion. If we project from the origin to the closest point on the line of inflexion, then this distance is item 2's multidimensional item location, Δ_2. As we see, the item vector begins on the item's inflexion line (i.e., where $p_j = 0.5$). The angle between this projection and our reference axis is ω_{21}°. The length of item 2's vector is the item's multidimensional discrimination capacity, A_2, and reflects how well the item discriminates across the F-dimensional space. This depiction shows that item 2 is closer to θ_2 than it is to θ_1 and, as a result, it is primarily measuring θ_2 and discriminating best along this dimension. (If the item had measured *only* θ_2, then ω_{j1} would have been 90°, and if it had measured *only* θ_1, then ω_{j1} would have been 0°.)

Item 1 is shown as falling in quadrant III. As is the case with item 2, the item vector's starting point is on the inflexion line. The perpendicular distance from this line to the origin is its Δ_1 and the length of the vector is its A_1. (We do not show ω_{11}°, but it could be depicted as a convex arc facing left falling between the item vector and dimension 1.) Because of item 1's proximity to dimension 1, it is primarily measuring θ_1. Moreover, item 1 is more useful in assessing individuals whose θ_1 locations are in the general neighborhood of −1 to 0 than outside this range. In a proficiency assessment situation item 1 would be considered to be of average difficulty.

Given that items 1 and 2's vectors are not perpendicular to one another, we know that θ_1 and θ_2 are related to some degree. Each item is measuring a composite of θ_1 and θ_2, albeit to different degrees, and this degree is reflected, in part, in ω. In general, item vectors that are clustered together and that are pointing in the same direction are measuring the same relative combination of the F-dimensions. Similarly, a different cluster of item vectors would be measuring a different combination of the F-dimensions. An extreme condition occurs when the item clusters are orthogonal to one another. In this case, the two clusters are measuring completely differently from one another. Implied in the foregoing is that although θ_1 and θ_2 are oriented at 90° to one another, this does not mean that θ_1 and θ_2 are not interrelated or are independent of one another. Rather, it is the item vectors' orientation that represents the interrelationship of θ_1 and θ_2. This is similar to our use of a scatterplot to graphically depict the interrelation between two variables.

In addition to allowing the simultaneous presentation of the locations and discrimination capacity of an item set, a vector plot may be extended to accommodate representing three latent variables. In contrast, with an IRS it is difficult to depict a three-latent-person continua situation (i.e., θ_1, θ_2, θ_3). Using Figure 10.4 as an example of a three-dimensional figure, we would use θ_3 in lieu of the logit axis (e.g., the X axis would be θ_1, the Y axis would be θ_3, and θ_2 would be on the Z axis). Equation 10.10 is used to determine the angles of the item vector with respect to a reference plane, such as the θ_1–θ_2 plane. With these angles and the item's Δ_j and A_j we would be able to locate the item in the three-dimensional space. We could also extend this single item representation to an item set.

THE MULTIDIMENSIONAL THREE-PARAMETER LOGISTIC MODEL

In the preceding discussion we have focused on the M2PL model. However, the principles outlined can be generalized to other MIRT models. For instance, the M2PL model may be extended to create a multidimensional version of the three-parameter model. This model, the (compensatory) *multidimensional three-parameter logistic* (M3PL) model, is

$$p(x_{ij} = 1|, \underline{\theta}_i, \underline{\alpha}_j, \gamma_j, \chi_j) = \chi_j + (1 - \chi_j)\frac{e^{\underline{\alpha}'_j\theta_i + \gamma_j}}{1 + e^{\underline{\alpha}'_j\theta_i + \gamma_j}} \qquad (10.15)$$

where α_{jf} and γ_j are defined above, and χ_j is the pseudo-guessing parameter for item j. The χ_j is interpreted analogously to the way it is with the 3PL model.[5] That is, χ_j is the probability for a response of 1 when an individual is extremely low on *all* θs (i.e., $\theta_i = -\infty$). As such, the IRS is asymptotic with χ_j. When $\chi_j > 0$, then the corresponding IRS is raised above the "floor "of the graph by an amount equal to χ_j; the graph's floor is the θ_1–θ_2 plane. Analogous to the situation with the 3PL model, with the M3PL model the inflexion line for the surface corresponds to a probability of $(\chi_j + 1)/2$.

ASSUMPTIONS OF THE MIRT MODEL

As is true with the unidimensional models, MIRT models make a functional form assumption. This assumption states that the data follow the function specified by the model. For instance, for Equation 10.3 the functional form states that the probability of a response of 1 increases monotonically when there is an increase in any one or any combination of a person's θs and that for infinitely low θs the probability of $x_j = 1$ approaches zero.

A second assumption is the conditional independence assumption that is seen with the unidimensional models. It states that for any group of individuals that are characterized by the same values of $\theta_1, \theta_2, \ldots, \theta_F$, the conditional distributions of the item responses are all independent of each other (Lord & Novick, 1968). Therefore, whatever relationship exists among the items disappears when one conditions on $\underline{\theta}$.

The third assumption is a dimensionality assumption. This assumption states that the observations on the manifest variables are a function of a set of continuous latent person variables. As is the case with the unidimensional models, the proper application of a MIRT model involves dimensionality assessment to determine the number of latent variables in the set. For instance, if the true state of nature is that the item responses are a function of three latent variables, then the dimensionality assessment should facilitate correctly specifying that the model have three latent person variables and not, for example, two. As is the case with the unidimensional models, violation of the dimensionality assumption is a matter of degree, and whether the resulting $\underline{\theta}$s are useful and psychologically meaningful is a validity question.

ESTIMATION OF THE M2PL MODEL

There are several approaches available for estimating the M2PL model's item parameters. One approach uses JMLE (e.g., McKinley & Reckase, 1983b); the equations that need to be solved are presented in McKinley and Reckase (1983a); also see Carlson (1987). A second approach is presented by Bock and Aitkin (1981). Their approach applies MMLE to estimating the item parameters of a multidimensional two-parameter normal ogive model and is implemented in TESTFACT.[6] MMLE has also been applied to directly estimate the M2PL model (McKinley, 1987; cited in McKinley & Kingston, 1988).

A third approach involves fitting a polynomial that approximates the multidimensional two-parameter normal ogive model. (The extension of the two-parameter normal ogive model to its multidimensional equivalent is discussed in Appendix C.) The multidimensional two-parameter normal ogive model is the multidimensional analog to Equation C.9 (see Appendix C) and is the normal ogive version of the model in Equation 10.3. The multidimensional two-parameter normal ogive model states that the proportion of individuals responding 1 on item j, $\pi(x_j = 1)$, is given by

$$\pi(x_j = 1|\underline{\theta}) = \Phi(\gamma_j + \underline{\alpha}_j'\underline{\theta}) \qquad (10.16)$$

where $\Phi(\cdot)$ is the cumulative normal distribution function (e.g., see Fraser & McDonald, 1988; McDonald, 1997, 1999). As explained in Appendix C, the proportion of individuals responding 1 on item j is a function of the area under the unit normal distribution cutoff by the item's threshold, τ_j. By using sample information we can obtain an initial estimate of τ_j that is subsequently refined to provide an estimate of the intercept (Fraser & McDonald, 2003; McDonald, 1997). Obtaining estimates of the $\alpha_j$fs involves the observed joint proportion of 1s for items j and v. Specifically, unweighted least squares is used to minimize the squared discrepancies between the observed joint proportion of 1s for items j and v, p_{jv}, and what would be the predicted joint proportion of 1s for items j and v, $\pi_{jv}^{(r)}$:

$$F = \sum_{j \neq v} (p_{jv} - \pi_{jv}^{(r)})^2 \qquad (10.17)$$

where the term $\pi_{jv}^{(r)}$ is given by an r-term polynomial series with coefficients defined by normalized Hermite–Tchebycheff polynomials (Fraser & McDonald, 1988; McDonald, 1997). (Fraser and McDonald [1988] state that a four-term polynomial is used to determine $\pi_{jv}^{(r)}$.) This approach is implemented in the program NOHARM; see Fraser and McDonald

(2003) for the specifics on the polynomials series. Therefore, when we use NOHARM for parameter estimation we are, in addition to employing the assumptions mentioned above, assuming that θ is random with an F-variate normal distribution.

In general, NOHARM and TESTFACT are the programs used for MIRT item parameter estimation. When appropriately scaled these estimates can be used for the model in Equation 10.3 (i.e., the programs' estimates are on the normal metric). Knol and Berger (1991) found that compared with other programs NOHARM performed well in item parameter recovery.

INFORMATION FOR THE M2PL MODEL

With the unidimensional models our items are graphically depicted by their IRFs. Moreover, our items' information for estimating a person's location is a function of their response functions' slopes. In the current context, rather than a response function for describing our item we have a response surface. Conceptually, this IRS can be viewed as a collection of IRFs that are conditional on a particular direction from the origin. That is, there is a conditional IRF for 1°, another conditional IRF for 2°, and so on. Applying the item information function from, for example, Chapter 2, Equation 2.16, to each of these conditional IRFs results in a series of item information functions that are conditional on a direction from the origin. This conceptualization may be extended to a multidimensional space. That is, with MIRT models one has a conditional item information *surface* that is called the *multidimensional item information surface*. A graphical depiction of a multidimensional item information surface for the item presented in Figure 10.1 is shown in Figure 10.6.

In the unidimensional case, the relationship between an item's information and the IRF's slope is that, all things being equal, the steeper the IRF's slope, the greater the item information. Conversely, as the slope becomes less steep, one sees a reduction in item information. Similarly, in the multidimensional situation there is a direct relationship between the slope of the IRS and the amount of item information. However, the multidimensional situation differs from the unidimensional case because one can calculate different slopes for a point in the $\underline{\theta}$ space contingent upon the direction one uses to traverse the IRS (cf. Figure 10.2).

Recall that through Equation 10.7 we can calculate the value of the slope of the IRS in a direction given by ω_f. Therefore, by extending the unidimensional item information function (Chapter 5, Equation 5.4) to the multidimensional situation and taking into account the directional aspect of determining a slope given by Equation 10.7, we obtain an item's *multidimensional item information*, $I_{j\omega}(\underline{\theta})$ (Reckase & McKinley, 1991):

$$I_{j\omega}(\underline{\theta}) = p_j(1-p_j)\left(\sum_f^F \alpha_{jf}\cos\,\omega_f\right)^2 \tag{10.18}$$

where p_j is given by the MIRT model and all other terms have been defined above.[7] Equation 10.18 tells us how much information item j can provide for estimation in the

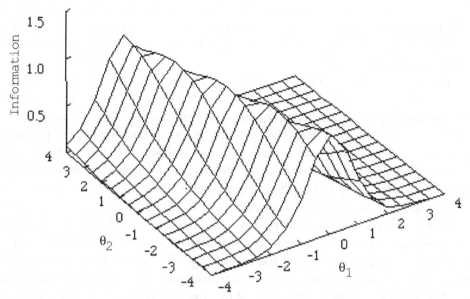

FIGURE 10.6. Multidimensional item information surface for the item in Figure 10.1, $\omega_1 = 14.0362°$. The irregularity along the crest of the surface is an artifact of the algorithm used to render the surface, given the number of data points used.

direction given by ω_f. This formula shows that item information is calculated with respect to the slope in the direction given by ω_f at the point given by $\underline{\theta}$. As such, to create the multidimensional item information surface shown in Figure 10.6 we chose its direction to be consistent with the item's vector. Selecting a different direction would potentially result in a different multidimensional item information surface. Therefore, unlike the case with unidimensional models, with MIRT models an item has multiple multidimensional item information surfaces corresponding to different ω_fs. To simultaneously display an item's multiple $I_{j\omega}(\underline{\theta})$s one may use a "clamshell" plot (e.g., Reckase & McKinley, 1991; Yao & Schwarz, 2006). (It should be noted that Equation 10.18 does not take into account the lack of conditional independence that arises from specifying a direction; Ackerman (1994) discusses this issue and presents a solution.)

As is true with the unidimensional models, one may sum the item information to produce a *total multidimensional information* for the instrument, $I_\omega(\underline{\theta}) = \Sigma\, I_{j\omega}(\underline{\theta})$. However, because the $I_{j\omega}(\underline{\theta})$s are defined with respect to a direction, the total multidimensional information is also defined with respect to the direction used to determine the multidimensional item information. One may graphically represent the total multidimensional information for the instrument with a *total multidimensional information surface* in the direction ω_f.

INDETERMINACY IN MIRT

With MIRT there are two sources of indeterminacy. As is the case with the unidimensional models' identification, our first source of indeterminacy in the M2PL model is the indeterminacy of the metric. As discussed in Chapter 3, we don't have a metric with an intrinsic origin or unit (i.e., the continuum's metric is not absolute, but rather relative). In the MIRT context, this means we have multiple latent person dimensions, each with an indeterminacy of metric issue.

To help conceptualize this metric indeterminacy issue with multiple dimensions, consider Figure 10.4. If we multiply each θ_f by a nonfractional constant (i.e., stretch out the θ_f metric) and divide the corresponding α_{jf}s by the same constant, then the plane's orientation in the three-dimensional space does not change. As a consequence, the probabilities do not change and the corresponding IRS is the same as shown in Figure 10.1. (This would also be true if we contract the metric by dividing each θ_f by a nonfractional constant and multiply the corresponding α_{jf}s by the same constant.) If we add a constant to γ_j and subtract from each $\alpha_{jf}\theta_f$ the ratio of the constant to F, then the plane simply moves up in the three-dimensional space. Because the plane's orientation does not change, the probabilities do not change and the corresponding IRS is the same as shown in Figure 10.1. Similarly, if we subtract a constant from γ_j and add to each $\alpha_{jf}\theta_f$ the ratio of the constant to F, then the plane simply moves down but does not change its orientation in the three-dimensional space. Therefore, we can change the values of the α_{jf}s, γ_j, and $\boldsymbol{\theta}$ without affecting the probability of a response of 1.

As is true with the unidimensional models, how this metric indeterminacy is addressed depends on the estimation approach. For instance, with the JMLE the $\hat{\theta}$s are rescaled to have a mean of zero and a variance of 1 (i.e., standardized) for each dimension, the $\hat{\alpha}_{jf}$s are multiplied by the standard deviation of the corresponding dimension's $\hat{\theta}$s, and the $\hat{\gamma}_j$s are adjusted by $\sum \hat{\alpha}_{jf}\bar{\hat{\theta}}_f$. One program for performing MIRT calibrations, NOHARM, addresses the indeterminacy of the metric by ensuring that each component of θ has a mean of zero and a variance of 1 (McDonald, 1997). A second program that can be used for MIRT calibration, TESTFACT, uses MMLE for estimation. As a result, it addresses the indeterminacy of metric issue in a fashion analogous to that discussed in Chapter 4, but applied to each dimension. However, rather than assuming that θ is from a unit normal distribution, TESTFACT assumes that $\boldsymbol{\theta}$ is multivariate normal with mean $\boldsymbol{0}$ and standard deviations of 1 (i.e., SD is the identity matrix, $\boldsymbol{I}$); NOHARM assumes the multivariate unit normal distribution for $\boldsymbol{\theta}$.

The second source of indeterminacy is *rotational indeterminacy*. Analogous to factor analysis, the axes' orientation in, say Figure 10.5, are not unique. Rotational indeterminacy, as well as metric indeterminacy, is a reflection of the fact that we have only an internal frame of reference. To understand rotational indeterminacy, consider, by way of analogy, a directional compass. Without a magnetic North the compass's needle would freely rotate about its spindle, indicating that "North" is in any direction. As such, if we use this compass to indicate the direction to, say, a mountain, we may find that on its first use the needle points toward the mountain. However, on the compass's second use the needle may point at an angle 25° from where it previously pointed, and with a third use the needle may point 75° from its first orientation. In each instance, if we take into account the magnitude of the angle, we can arrive at the mountain.

In our current context, the axes that represent our latent variables are free to rotate about their origin (i.e., the compass's spindle) because we do not have an external frame of reference to fix their orientation (i.e., we do not have a magnetic North). However, just as in our analogy, if we take into account the angle of orientation, we arrive at the same probability of a response of 1 (i.e., the mountain in the analogy).

For instance, using our example item from Figure 10.1 with $\underline{\alpha}'_j$ = (2.0, 0.5) and γ_j = 2.0, our probability of a response of 1 is 0.989 when $\underline{\theta}'$ = (1.5, –1). Let us rotate our θ-axes by 25°. When we rotate, our θ-axes our $\underline{\alpha}_j$ and $\underline{\theta}$ are affected. Therefore, after rotation our transformed discrimination parameters become α^*_{j1} = 2.0239 and α^*_{j2} = 1.2984. Applying the rotation to the θ′s yields θ^*_1 = 2.7724 and θ^*_2 = –2.3962. Using these transformed discriminations and thetas, $\underline{\alpha}^*_j$ and $\underline{\theta}^*$, the probability of a response of 1 is the same as obtained with the unrotated parameters, 0.989. If we further rotated the axes by 75°, then our $\underline{\alpha}^{*\prime}_j$ = (1.006, 2.0613) and $\underline{\theta}^{*\prime}$ = (–1.5636, 1.9719). Using these α_js and this $\underline{\theta}^*$ in Equation 10.3 results in a p_j = 0.989. The foregoing shows that we do not have a unique set of $\underline{\alpha}_j$ and $\underline{\theta}^*$ because of rotational indeterminacy. Stated another way, we can produce an infinite number of θ–α combinations that lead to the same p_j by rotating the axes. Figure 10.7 depicts the rotation of the axes by an angle of ∠ as well as the change in item j's vector before and after the rotation (i.e., j*).[8]

To solve the rotational indeterminacy within our compass analogy one could, say, fix the North/South axis to always point North. By fixing this axis, then the East/West axis would also be fixed. Similarly, in the multidimensional context a strategy for addressing rotational indeterminacy is to fix the axes by setting one of the items' estimated parameters on one axis to zero. Fixing one axis fixes the other axis.

Although the preceding discussion has presented the rotational indeterminacy identification problem in terms of two dimensions, the issue applies to more than two dimensions. Addressing the problem for more than two dimensions may be accomplished the way it is done for two dimensions. Specifically, for three factors one would restrict one item's estimates on the F – 1 factors to be zero, and for a second item one constrains the Fth estimate to be 0.

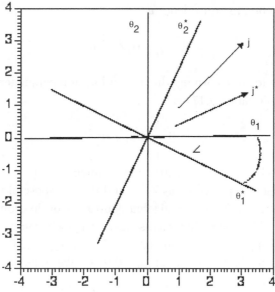

FIGURE 10.7. Axis rotation of two-dimensional structure and its effect on item j.

With 4 factors (F − 1 =) three items would be necessary to address the rotational indeterminacy. Therefore, for one item its loadings on the F − 1 factors are restricted to be zero, on a second item one constrains F-2 loadings to be 0, and for a third item one constrains the Fth loading to be 0. This is how NOHARM addresses the rotational indeterminacy issue.

METRIC TRANSFORMATION, M2PL MODEL

The metric transformation equations for the M2PL model are the matrix equivalents of those presented with the two-parameter model (Chapter 5). For example, from Equation 5.6 we have that

$$\alpha_j^* = \frac{\alpha_j}{\zeta}$$

The matrix algebra equivalence for transforming the $\alpha_j$fs (or their estimates) from their initial metric to a target metric is

$$\underline{\alpha}_j^* = (\underline{Z}^{-1})' \, \underline{\alpha}_j \tag{10.19}$$

To transform the unidimensional intercepts we use

$$\gamma_j^* = \gamma_j - \frac{\alpha_j(\kappa)}{\zeta}$$

In terms of matrix algebra, its equivalence is

$$\gamma_j^* = \gamma_j - \underline{\alpha}_j' \underline{Z}^{-1} \, \underline{\kappa} \tag{10.20}$$

The matrix equivalent for transforming the person location parameters (or their estimates) of $\theta^* = \zeta(\theta) + \kappa$ (e.g., Equation 4.17) is

$$\underline{\theta}_i^* = \underline{Z} \, \underline{\theta}_i + \underline{\kappa} \tag{10.21}$$

For Equations 10.19–10.21 $\underline{Z}$ is a matrix with dimensions F × F containing the unit adjustments, its inverse is represented as $\underline{Z}^{-1}$, and the transpose of the inverse is $(\underline{Z}^{-1})'$. (The inverse of a matrix is the matrix algebra equivalent of division.) The vector $\underline{\kappa}$ is of length F and consists of location adjustments; also see Hirsch (1989).

As an example of applying Equations 10.19–10.21, let $\underline{\alpha}' = (2.0, 0.5)$, $\gamma = 2.0$, and $\underline{\theta}' = (1.5, -1.0)$. According to the M2PL model, $p_j = 0.9890$. We transform these parameters by shifting the metric by 1.5 and adjusting the unit by 2. Our metric transformation matrix and vector are

$$\underline{Z} = \begin{bmatrix} 2 & 1 \\ 1 & 2 \end{bmatrix} \text{ and } \underline{\kappa} = \begin{bmatrix} 1.5 \\ 1.5 \end{bmatrix}$$

The inverse of $\underline{Z}$ is

$$\underline{Z}^{-1} = \begin{bmatrix} 0.6667 & -0.3333 \\ -0.3333 & 0.6667 \end{bmatrix}$$

In this example the transpose of $\underline{Z}^{-1}$ is the same as $\underline{Z}^{-1}$ (i.e., $(\underline{Z}^{-1})' = \underline{Z}^{-1}$). Applying Equation 10.19 to transform the $\alpha_j$fs we obtain

$$\underline{\alpha}^* = (\underline{Z}^{-1})' \underline{\alpha} = \begin{bmatrix} 0.6667 & -0.3333 \\ -0.3333 & 0.6667 \end{bmatrix} \begin{bmatrix} 2.0 \\ 0.5 \end{bmatrix} = \begin{bmatrix} 1.1667 \\ -0.3333 \end{bmatrix}$$

and for the intercept term we have

$$\gamma^* = \gamma - \underline{\alpha}' \underline{Z}^{-1} \underline{\kappa} = 2.0 - \begin{bmatrix} 2.0 & 0.5 \end{bmatrix} \begin{bmatrix} 0.6667 & -0.3333 \\ -0.3333 & 0.6667 \end{bmatrix} \begin{bmatrix} 1.5 \\ 1.5 \end{bmatrix} = 0.75$$

Transforming our θs produces

$$\underline{\theta}^* = \underline{Z} \underline{\theta} + \underline{\kappa} = \begin{bmatrix} 2 & 1 \\ 1 & 2 \end{bmatrix} \begin{bmatrix} 1.5 \\ -1.0 \end{bmatrix} + \begin{bmatrix} 1.5 \\ 1.5 \end{bmatrix} = \begin{bmatrix} 3.5 \\ 1.0 \end{bmatrix}$$

As would be expected, given the invariance of our parameters, when we use $\underline{\alpha}^*, \gamma^*$, and $\underline{\theta}^*$ with the M2PL model, our $p_j = 0.9890$.

With the 2PL model the total characteristic curve could be used to transform our θ (or its estimate) to an expected trait score. For the M2PL model the total characteristic curve becomes the *total characteristic surface*. This surface is defined as

$$\mathcal{E}T = \frac{\Sigma p_j}{L} \tag{10.22}$$

where p_j is a MIRT model (Reckase, 1997a; Reckase, Ackerman, & Carlson, 1988).

EXAMPLE: APPLICATION OF THE M2PL MODEL, NORMAL-OGIVE HARMONIC ANALYSIS ROBUST METHOD

Assume that we have a 10-item instrument designed to measure interpersonal engagement behavior and we administer it to 1000 individuals. This instrument uses a true/false response format. Item responses are assumed to be a function of an individual's locations on "love" and "dominance" dimensions. As such, we assume that there are two dimensions underlying the response data. (In practice, we would assess the fit of models with a varying number of latent variables to the data to acquire evidence supporting our two-dimensional hypothesis.)

We use NOHARM to fit a two-dimensional two-parameter model to the data. As described in Chapter 3, we prepare a text (i.e., ASCII) input file (Table 10.1) that is subsequently submitted to NOHARM. The first command line in the input file contains a title for the analysis, with the remaining lines specifying the analysis setup. The second line "10 2 1000 0 1 0 0 0" specifies that there are 10 items and a two-dimensional analysis based on 1000 cases, that the input data consist of binary responses, to perform an exploratory analysis, and that NOHARM should generate its starting values and print the correlation, covariance, and residual matrices, respectively. The subsequent line allows the user to provide the IRF's lower asymptote value for each of the 10 items.[9] Because we are fitting a two-parameter model this line contains one zero for each item. Following this line are the binary responses for the 1000 individuals. (Note that when the data consist of binary response vectors, the number of cases specified on line 2 is used for reading the data. If the number of cases specified on line 2 does not match the number of response lines, then an error will occur [i.e., "Unexpected end-of-file when . . ."].)

Table 10.2 contains the corresponding output. The beginning of the output contains echoes of the input specifications, initial starting values, the covariance matrix, and so on, followed by the `Results` section. We first discuss model–data fit before returning to the item parameter estimates.

As mentioned in Chapter 3, NOHARM produces a residual matrix to facilitate assessing model–data fit. The residual matrix is the discrepancy between the observed covariances and those of the items after the model is fitted to the data. Therefore, the ideal situation is where these discrepancies are zero. Our residuals are comparatively small vis-à-vis the observed item covariances, with almost all residual magnitudes in the thousandths' place or

TABLE 10.1. Two-Dimensional Input Command File

```
    Interpersonal Ex, 2 dimensions, raw data input, exploratory
    10   2   1000   0   1   0   0   0
    0 0 0 0 0 0 0 0 0 0
1 1 1 0 1 0 0 0 0 0
1 1 0 1 1 0 0 0 0 0
1 1 1 0 0 0 0 0 0 1
1 1 0 1 0 0 1 0 0 0
1 1 0 1 0 0 0 1 0 0
:
```

Note. Name = `intrprsnl.inp`.

TABLE 10.2. Output for the Self-Efficacy: Interpersonal Engagement Behavior Instrument

```
                              N O H A R M
                   Fitting a (multidimensional) Normal Ogive
                       by Harmonic Analysis - Robust Method

        Input File : intrprsnl.inp

        Title :     Interpersonal Ex, 2 dimensions, raw data input, exploratory

        Number of items      = 10
        Number of dimensions = 2
        Number of subjects   = 1000

        An exploratory solution has been requested.

Sample Product-Moment Matrix
         1       2       3       4       5       6       7       8       9
   1   0.704
   2   0.460   0.557
   3   0.505   0.403   0.614
   4   0.480   0.380   0.426   0.608
   5   0.415   0.323   0.356   0.346   0.511
 :

Item Covariance Matrix
         1       2       3       4       5       6       7       8       9
   1   0.208
   2   0.068   0.247
   3   0.073   0.061   0.237
   4   0.052   0.041   0.053   0.238
   5   0.055   0.038   0.042   0.035   0.250
 :

                          =======
                          Results
                          =======

Success. The job converged to the specified criterion.

Final Constants
     1       2       3       4       5       6       7       8       9       10
```
0.911   0.177   0.382   0.324   0.031 -0.828 -0.520 -0.627 -0.992 -1.018$\Leftarrow \hat{\gamma}_j$s

```
Final Coefficients of Theta
```
$\Leftarrow \hat{\alpha}_{jf}$s
```
         1       2
   1   1.374   0.0
   2   0.724  -0.024
   3   0.858  -0.020
   4   0.581   0.254
 , 5   0.494   0.079
   6   0.739   0.562
   7   0.650   0.610
   8   0.538   0.505
   9   0.591   0.587
  10   0.606   0.288

Final Correlations of Theta
         1       2
   1   1.000
   2   0.0     1.000


Residual Matrix (lower off-diagonals)
         1       2       3       4       5       6       7       8       9
   2  -3.1e-4
   3   0.002  -0.002
   4   0.003   0.002  -0.005
   5  -0.005   0.003   0.002   0.001
   6  -0.002  -0.001   0.002   0.001  -3.1e-4
   7  -0.001   0.002  -0.001   0.008  -0.005  -0.004
   8   0.002   7.0e-5   0.003  -0.006  -1.6e-4   0.003   0.002
   9   2.9e-4  -0.003  -0.001  -0.002   0.005   1.8e-5  -0.004   0.003
  10   0.001  -0.002  -4.3e-4  -0.005   0.004   0.003   0.004  -0.010   0.004

   Sum of squares of residuals (lower off-diagonals)   =    0.0005057
   Root mean square of residuals (lower off-diagonals) =    0.0033523        ⇐ The RMS
   Tanaka index of goodness of fit                     =    0.9984227        ⇐ The GFI
```

cont.

TABLE 10.2. cont.

Threshold Values

1	2	3	4	5	6	7	8	9	10
0.536	0.143	0.290	0.274	0.028	-0.607	-0.388	-0.504	-0.762	-0.845

Unique Variances

1	2	3	4	5	6	7	8	9	10
0.346	0.656	0.576	0.714	0.800	0.537	0.557	0.647	0.590	0.689

Factor Loadings

	1	2
1	0.809	0.0
2	0.586	-0.019
3	0.651	-0.015
4	0.490	0.214
5	0.442	0.071
6	0.542	0.412
7	0.485	0.455
8	0.433	0.407
9	0.454	0.451
10	0.503	0.239

Varimax Rotated Factor Loadings

	1	2
1	0.739	0.327
2	0.544	0.220
3	0.602	0.249
4	0.362	0.394
5	0.375	0.243
6	0.328	0.596
7	0.259	0.613
8	0.231	0.547
9	0.233	0.596
10	0.364	0.422

Varimax Rotated Coefficients of Theta

	1	2
1	1.257	0.557
2	0.672	0.271
3	0.793	0.329
4	0.428	0.467
5	0.420	0.272
6	0.448	0.813
7	0.348	0.821
8	0.288	0.680
9	0.303	0.776
10	0.438	0.509

Promax (oblique) Rotated Factor Loadngs

	1	2
1	0.810	-0.001
2	0.610	-0.031
3	0.670	-0.025
4	0.241	0.329
5	0.360	0.108
6	0.062	0.632
7	-0.045	0.699
8	-0.041	0.625
9	-0.071	0.693
10	0.225	0.367

Factor Correlations

	1	2
1	1.000	
2	0.760	1.000

Promax Rotated Coefficients of Theta

	1	2
1	1.376	-0.002
2	0.753	-0.038
3	0.883	-0.033
4	0.285	0.389
5	0.402	0.121
6	0.084	0.863
7	-0.061	0.937
8	-0.051	0.776
9	-0.093	0.901
10	0.271	0.442

[a]The text following the ⇐ is provided to help the reader understand the corresponding input.

less. To summarize the residual matrix, NOHARM provides the root mean square (RMS). As discussed in Chapter 3, the RMS is the square root of the average squared difference between the observed and predicted covariances. Therefore, small values of RMS are indicative good fit. This overall measure of model–data misfit may be evaluated by comparing it to four times the reciprocal of the square root of the sample size (i.e., the "typical" standard error of the residuals). For these data this criterion is 0.1265. The observed RMS of 0.0033523 indicates that we have evidence of model–data fit.

NOHARM also produces a goodness-of-fit (GFI) index. This goodness-of-fit index involves the sample covariance matrix, $\underline{C}$, and the residual covariance matrix, $\underline{C}_{res}$ (McDonald & Mok, 1995). This index, labeled Tanaka index of goodness of fit in the output, is

$$GFI = 1 - \frac{Tr(\underline{C}_{res}^2)}{Tr(\underline{C}^2)} \tag{10.23}$$

where Tr is the matrix's trace (i.e., the sum of the main diagonal's elements). A GFI of 1 indicates perfect fit. McDonald (1999) suggests that a minimum GFI of 0.90 indicates an acceptable level of fit and a minimum value of 0.95 indicates "good" fit. To summarize, for this example the residual matrix, the RMS, and the GFI all indicate good model–data fit. Therefore, we proceed to examine the item parameter estimates.

The items' intercept (constant) estimates, $\hat{\gamma}_j$s, are found in the section titled "Final Constants." This section shows that the estimates of γ_j are $\hat{\gamma}_1 = 0.911, \hat{\gamma}_2 = 0.177, \ldots,$ $\hat{\gamma}_{10} = -1.018$. The items' discrimination parameter estimates, $\hat{\alpha}_{jf}$s, are (first) shown in the "Final Coefficients of Theta" section. As would be expected from the discussion of indeterminacy, one sees that the first item's value on the second factor is fixed to zero to address the solution's rotational indeterminacy. The item discrimination parameter estimates for the first dimension are $\hat{\alpha}_{11} = 1.374, \hat{\alpha}_{21} = 0.724, \ldots, \hat{\alpha}_{10,1} = 0.606$ (i.e., column 1). For the second dimension the estimates of the discrimination parameters are $\hat{\alpha}_{12} = 0, \hat{\alpha}_{22} = -0.024, \ldots, \hat{\alpha}_{10,2} = 0.587$. Because these estimates are on the normal metric, we need to multiply them by $D = 1.702$ to place them on the logistic metric of the M2PL model. The "Final Correlations of Theta" section gives the correlation between the θ_fs. Table 10.3 presents the estimates and other summary information. As is clear from the output, NOHARM does not provide standard errors for its estimates. If standard errors are desired, they can be obtained by using the standard errors formulas provided by Maydeu-Olivares (2001) or by using the bootstrap methodology (Efron & Tibshirani, 1993).

The output following the residual matrix contains the common factor parameterization of the MIRT model. Whether this information is used depends on one's purpose (e.g., see McDonald, 1997; Reckase, 1997a). The sections labeled "Factor Loadings," "Varimax Rotated Factor Loadings," "Unique Variances," and "Promax (oblique) Rotated Factor Loadngs" [sic] contain the values based on the common factor model. Intermixed within these sections are two additional sections titled "Varimax Rotated Coefficients of Theta" and "Promax Rotated Coefficients of Theta" that contain the common factor model's reparameterization into the MIRT model.

TABLE 10.3. Summary Statistics for the Interpersonal Engagement Behavior Instrument

	Normal metric						Logistic metric	
	α_{j1}	α_{j2}	γ_j	A_j	Δ_j	ω°_{j1}	α_{j1}	α_{j2}
1	1.374	0	0.911	1.374	−0.663	0.0	2.339	0.000
2	0.724	−0.024	0.177	0.724	−0.244	1.9	1.232	−0.041
3	0.858	−0.020	0.382	0.858	−0.445	1.3	1.460	−0.034
4	0.581	0.254	0.324	0.634	−0.511	23.6	0.989	0.432
5	0.494	0.079	0.031	0.500	−0.062	9.1	0.841	0.134
6	0.739	0.562	−0.828	0.928	0.892	37.3	1.258	0.957
7	0.650	0.610	−0.520	0.891	0.583	43.2	1.106	1.038
8	0.538	0.505	−0.627	0.738	0.850	43.2	0.916	0.860
9	0.591	0.587	−0.992	0.833	1.191	44.8	1.006	0.999
10	0.606	0.288	−1.018	0.671	1.517	25.4	1.031	0.490

The estimated MIRT model is a reparameterization of the common factor model (see Appendix C). Therefore, the common factor model's loadings may be related to the MIRT model item parameters through the item unique variances. The items' unique variances are given on the line labeled "Unique Variances" and are equal to an item's communality subtracted from 1 (i.e., from Appendix C: unique variance = $1 - \rho_j' \Sigma \rho_j$). For example, for item 1 we have that its loadings on factors 1 and 2 are 0.809 and 0.0, respectively. Therefore, its estimated communality is $\hat{h}^2 = 0.809^2 + 0.0^2 = 0.654$ and its unique item variance is $1 - 0.654 = 0.346$. This is item 1's value in the "Unique Variances" section.

Dividing each item's estimated "Threshold Values" (i.e., from Appendix C) by the square root of its corresponding unique variance yields the item's intercepts (i.e., Equation C.29). As an example, for item 1 we have that its estimated threshold $\hat{\tau}_1 = 0.536$ and, as a result, its

$$\hat{\gamma}_1 = 0.536/\sqrt{0.346} = 0.911$$

(i.e., item 1's value in the "Final Constants" section). In terms of the "Factor Loadings" matrix, we can divide each item's factor loading by the square root of its unique variance to obtain the item's estimated discrimination parameter on the corresponding dimension (i.e., Equation C.30). For instance, item 2's loading on dimension 1 is $\hat{\rho}_{21} = 0.586$ and its

$$\hat{\alpha}_{21} = 0.586/\sqrt{0.656} = 0.724$$

For this item's relationship to the second dimension, we have $\hat{\rho}_{22} = -0.019$ and its

$$\hat{\alpha}_{22} = -0.019/\sqrt{0.656} = -0.024$$

Both of these α_{jf} estimates are found in the "Final Coefficients of Theta" matrix. Similarly, dividing the "Varimax Rotated Factor Loadings" by the corresponding square root of the item's unique variance yields the "Varimax Rotated Coefficients of Theta." The entries in this latter matrix yield the same p_j as those from the "Final Coefficients of Theta" section after accounting for rotation. For example, if $\underline{\theta} = (1.5, -1.0)$, then using the estimated parameters for items 1 and 2 one obtains $p_1 = 0.95129$ and $p_2 = 0.78364$. Rotating the "Factor Loadings" matrix by approximately 23.872° yields the values in the "Varimax Rotated Factor Loadings" matrix and, as a result, this rotation angle is reflected in the "Varimax Rotated Coefficients of Theta." Therefore, after rotating the $\underline{\theta}$ by this amount, our rotated person locations are $\underline{\theta}^* = (2.6417, -2.2626)$. Using this $\underline{\theta}^*$ and the rotated item parameter estimates for items 1 and 2, we obtain $p_1^* = 0.95129$ and $p_2^* = 0.78364$. As such, the "Varimax Rotated Coefficients of Theta" values may be more meaningful in some situations.

To summarize, NOHARM provides multiple estimates in one analysis and the user is left to select the appropriate results for his or her purpose. Depending on whether one is performing an exploratory or confirmatory analysis and whether one believes that the dimensions are orthogonal, then certain output tables are of value, whereas others may not be of any value. For example, if we believe that the dimensions are not orthogonal, then the section "Promax Rotated Coefficients of Theta" contains the appropriate discrimination parameter estimates.

Figure 10.8 contains the vector plot summarizing the instrument. As can be seen, we have a cluster of items in quadrant I that are measuring both dimensions to about the same degree for individuals who are above average in their interpersonal engagement. Most of the

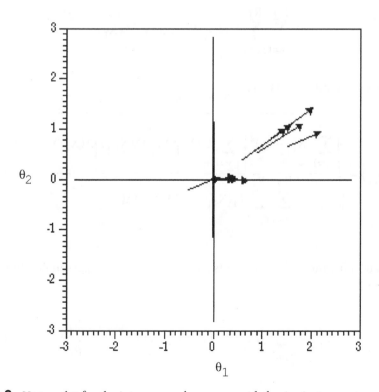

FIGURE 10.8. Vector plot for the interpersonal engagement behavior instrument.

remaining items are primarily assessing θ_1 and are located near the origin. In this exploratory situation we can attach meaning or labels to θ_1 and θ_2 by interpreting the rotated loadings.

OBTAINING PERSON LOCATION ESTIMATES

Once we have satisfactory model–data fit we can estimate the person locations by using, for example, EAP (Bock & Aitkin, 1981). For instance, assuming a two-dimensional latent space, the EAP estimate of person's i location on dimension 1 is

$$\hat{\theta}_{i1} = \sum_{r_1=1}^{R_1} X_{r_1} \left[\sum_{r_2=1}^{R_2} L_i(X_{r_1}, X_{r_2}) A(X_{r_2}) \right] \frac{A(X_{r_1})}{\tilde{p}_i} \qquad (10.24)$$

where the number of quadrature points on dimensions 1 and 2 are R_1 and R_2, respectively, X_{r_1} is the rth quadrature point on dimension 1 with corresponding weight $A(X_{r_1})$, X_{r_2} is the rth quadrature point on dimension 2 with corresponding weight $A(X_{r_2})$, L_i is the likelihood function for person i based on the model and evaluated at the X_{r_1} and X_{r_2} points, and $\tilde{p}_i$ is the unconditional probability of person i's response vector and is calculated using a two-dimensional Gauss–Hermite quadrature:

$$\sum_{r_2=1}^{R_2} \sum_{r_1=1}^{R_1} L_i(X_{r_1}, X_{r_2}) A(X_{r_1}) A(X_{r_2}) \qquad (10.25)$$

The estimate's standard error is given by

$$PSD(\hat{\theta}_{i1}) = \sqrt{\frac{\sum_{r_1=1}^{R_1} (X_{r_1} - \hat{\theta}_i)^2 \left[\sum_{r_2=1}^{R_2} L_i(X_{r_1}, X_{r_2}) A(X_{r_2}) \right] A(X_{r_1})}{\sum_{r_2=1}^{R_2} \sum_{r_1=1}^{R_1} L_i(X_{r_1}, X_{r_2}) A(X_{r_1}) A(X_{r_2})}} \qquad (10.26)$$

By appropriate substitution for the points and weights we have person i's estimated location on dimension 2:

$$\hat{\theta}_{i2} = \sum_{r_2=1}^{R_2} X_{r_2} \left[\sum_{r_1=1}^{R_1} L_i(X_{r_1}, X_{r_2}) A(X_{r_1}) \right] \frac{A(X_{r_2})}{\tilde{p}_i} \qquad (10.27)$$

SUMMARY

Some data cannot be appropriately modeled by one of our unidimensional IRT models. In some cases, the (*between-item*) multidimensionality may be addressed by decomposing the instrument into multiple unidimensional components and utilizing a unidimensional model with each component. In other situations, it is not possible to decompose the instrument into unidimensional components because the response to each item requires more than one latent continuous variable (i.e., *within-item multidimensionality*). Data of this type may be more appropriately modeled by using a multidimensional IRT model.

When more than one latent variable is necessary to respond to an item, there is the possibility that a person's location on one latent variable may compensate for his or her location on other latent variable(s). Data of this type are modeled using a compensatory MIRT model. In contrast, when a person's location on one latent variable does not compensate for his or her location on other latent variable(s), then one has a noncompensatory situation. Although noncompensatory MIRT and partial compensatory models exist, these models have not seen as much attention as the compensatory models. In addition to the models discussed in this chapter, there are a number of other models for multidimensional data (e.g., Bock & Aitkin, 1981; Embretson, 1997; Fischer & Seliger, 1997; Sympson, 1978; Whitely, 1980; also see Mislevy, 1986b). This chapter has focused on the compensatory multidimensional extensions of the 2PL and 3PL models.

The M2PL model is applicable to compensatory multidimensional data. This model is typically presented in a linearized form with an item discrimination parameter for each dimension and an intercept parameter, γ_j. As is true with the unidimensional models, one cannot directly interpret γ_j as a location parameter. In order to provide an interpretation analogous to a unidimensional model's location parameter, we must calculate the item's multidimensional item location, Δ_j. An item's multidimensional item location indicates the distance from the origin in the latent space to the item's point of maximum discrimination in a particular direction from the origin. With the M2PL this point of maximum discrimination occurs when $p_j = 0.5$.

Although the discrimination parameters can be interpreted as they are in the unidimensional models, sometimes it is useful to have a single value that represents an item's discrimination power in the multidimensional space. This value is reflected in the item's multidimensional discrimination parameter, A_j. The larger the value of A_j, the greater item j's discrimination capacity across the F-dimensions. Moreover, analogous to the unidimensional models, the greater the item's discrimination capability, the greater the item's multidimensional information in a particular direction.

MIRT models have two sources of indeterminacy that need to be addressed when estimating parameters. As is the case with the unidimensional models' identification, our first source of indeterminacy is the indeterminacy of the metric. The second source of indeterminacy is rotational indeterminacy. How these indeterminacies are addressed depends on the calibration program.

Graphical representation of an MIRT model's functional form is typically done by using an item response surface plot and/or contour plot. With a contour plot the contours represent the points of equal probability. Vector plots are typically used to display item characteristics for item sets. Vector plots are used to simultaneously present not only an item's location and how well it discriminates (i.e., Δ_j and A_j), but also which dimension, if any, it measures best.[10,11]

The preceding chapters have been devoted to presenting various IRT models for different types of data. As part of this presentation we have made comparisons with CTT and pointed out the advantages of IRT models over the true score model. One of these IRT advantages is the model's capacity to predict how individuals located at a particular point on a continuum would be expected to respond. Thus, we can administer only those items that provide the most information for estimating an individual's location. This is the premise of computerized adaptive testing and is discussed in Appendix D. A second advantage is, given that one has model–data fit, the invariance of the parameter estimates. This property facilitates the creation of item banks with desirable characteristics as well as multiple forms of an instrument. The creation of multiple forms is useful for maintaining the veracity of person location estimates and for tracking changes in performance over time. The creation of item pools and multiple forms requires that one be able to link the various instrument administrations onto a common metric. The next chapter addresses the creation of a common metric across multiple forms and/or samples of individuals.

NOTES

1. A number of model misspecification studies have examined the use of a unidimensional IRT model when the model should contain two dimensions. In general, when the true model is a compensatory two-dimensional IRT model, then the unidimensional $\hat{\delta}_j$ is found to be an estimate of the average of the δ_js across the dimensions, the unidimensional $\hat{\alpha}_j$ is an estimate of $(\alpha_{j1} + \alpha_{j2})$, and the estimated person location is an average of the true θs across the dimensions. In contrast, when the true model is a noncompensatory model, then the $\hat{\delta}_j$ is an overestimate of or correlated more highly with one dimension δ_{jf} than with the other δ_{jf}, $\hat{\alpha}_j$ is an estimate of the average of the true α_js, and θ is an estimate of the average true θs (Ackerman, 1989; Way, Ansley, & Forsyth, 1988; Reckase, 1979). Wang (1986, 1987) analytically determined that the "unidimensional estimates of item parameters are obtained with reference to a weighted composite of underlying latent traits" where the weights are "primarily a function of the discrimination vectors for the items, the correlations among the latent traits and, to a lesser extent, the difficulty parameters of the items" (Wang, 1987, p. 3). In short, the parameter estimates reflect a reference composite or trait (Wang, 1987).

2. An item's multidimensional item location is typically symbolized as D_j or MID_j (e.g., Reckase, 1985; Reckase & McKinley, 1991). For consistency with our convention of using Greek letters for parameters the uppercase delta, Δ, is used to represent an item j's multidimensional item location (Δ_j).

3. An item's multidimensional discrimination parameter is typically symbolized as $MDISC_j$ (e.g., Reckase & McKinley, 1991; Reckase, 1986), but in keeping with our convention of using Greek letters for parameters the uppercase alpha, A, is used to symbolize item j's multidimensional discrimination parameter (A_j).

4. From this item vector perspective we see that Equation 10.12 is the application of the Pythagorean theorem to determining a vector's length. That is, the vector is the hypotenuse of a right triangle. As such, an item's multidimensional discrimination parameter is analogous to the square root of the item's communality from a principal axis analysis.

5. As is the case with the 2PL and 3PL models, there are normal ogival forms of the M2PL and M3PL models (e.g., see Bock & Aitkin, 1981; Mislevy, 1986b; Samejima, 1974).

6. This approach assumes that $\underline{\theta}$ is multivariate normal with mean $\underline{0}$ and covariance matrix $\underline{I}$. This is an additional assumption to those presented above. Because the MMLE implementation uses the frequencies of response patterns and the pairwise proportions of 1s and 0s, the approach is sometimes called full-information factor analysis (FIFA).

7. An item's multidimensional information is typically symbolized as MINF (e.g., Reckase & McKinley, 1991), but in keeping with our convention of using I to symbolize the concept of information, we symbolize item j's multidimensional information as $I_{j\omega}(\underline{\theta})$.

8. The axes' rotation is accomplished by using a transformation matrix, $\underline{T}$. Specifically, the discrimination parameters are transformed (Hirsch, 1989) by

$$\underline{\alpha}_j^{*'} = \underline{\alpha}_j' \underline{T} \qquad (10.28)$$

and the person locations by

$$\underline{\theta}^* = (\underline{T}^{-1})\underline{\theta} \qquad (10.29)$$

where $\underline{T}^{-1}$ is the inverse of $\underline{T}$. For our example the transformation matrix is

$$\underline{T} = \begin{bmatrix} \cos\angle_{11*} & \cos\angle_{12*} \\ \cos\angle_{21*} & \cos\angle_{22*} \end{bmatrix} \qquad (10.30)$$

where $\cos\angle_{11*}$ is the cosine of the angle of rotation between the unrotated θ_1 and its rotated position θ_1^* (e.g., 25°) and $\cos\angle_{22*}$ is the cosine of the angle of rotation between the unrotated θ_2 and its rotated position θ_2^*.

Equations 10.28 and 10.29 show why the rotational transformation leaves the logit unchanged. Following Hirsch (1989), the substitution of Equations 10.28 and 10.29 into the exponent of the model in Equation 10.3 yields

$$\underline{\alpha}_j^{*'} \underline{\theta}^* + \gamma_j = \underline{\alpha}_j' \underline{T}\,(\underline{T}^{-1})\underline{\theta} + \gamma_j = \underline{\alpha}_j'\underline{\theta} + \gamma_j$$

because $\underline{T}\,(\underline{T}^{-1}) = \underline{I}$.

9. For the M3PL model we would provide an estimate of the lower asymptotes on this line. These estimates may be obtained by calibrating the data with the 3PL model and using the corresponding χ_j estimates as input for the M3PL model calibration. This approach has been found to work well with two-dimensional data, but not as well with four-dimensional data (DeMars, 2007).

10. As Rost (1990) indicates, "multidimensionality is often seen as the only way out of the inaccuracies of unidimensional models" (p. 281). Therefore, as a counterpoint to the preceding models, we present mixture models in Appendix E, "Mixture Models." These models may be useful in some multidimensional situations.

11. Reckase et al. (1988) show how a multidimensional calibration can be used to find clusters of items that measure the same weighted composite of traits that *meet* the assumption of unidimensionality. Therefore, it is possible to apply a unidimensional model to these item clusters. Their approach exploits the fact that "any item that can be described by the M2PL model is unidimensional in that it is equivalent to an item described by a unidimensional model with the <latent variable> scale equal to a weighted composite of the elements of the θ-vector" (p. 195).

11

Linking and Equating

In the preceding chapters we have had situations where we wanted to directly compare the item parameter estimates from different samples or models. However, because these estimates were on different metrics they could not be directly compared with one another. The process of aligning different metrics is known as *linking*. When the purpose of aligning the metrics is to compare person location estimates, then the process is known as *equating*. In this chapter we begin by first discussing the general process, including data collection approaches, and then present different methods for transforming different metrics to a common metric.

EQUATING DEFINED

Equating refers to a family of procedures for adjusting person location estimates that are on different metrics in order to place the estimates on a common metric.[1] Therefore, the purpose of equating is to facilitate comparing individuals. For instance, we may be interested in assessing change over a year. As part of our study we assess our participants quarterly, but to minimize carryover effects we administer multiple forms of our instrument. In practice it is impossible, in terms of statistical characteristics, to create precisely identical forms. In addition, differences in administration conditions may affect the individuals' performances on the forms and thereby affect the forms' statistical characteristics. These (albeit) slight differences in forms affect the person location estimates (e.g., X or $\hat{\theta}$). By equating the person location estimates across forms we can (reasonably) eliminate the forms' differences in order to compare individuals. If an equating is successful, then it should not in principle make any difference to individuals as to which form they are administered (Lord, 1980). This is the overarching goal of equating.

Livingston (2004) provides a simple general definition of *equating*: A score on a new form and a score on another form are equivalent in a group of individuals that have taken the form if they represent the same *relative position* in the group. How "relative position"

306

is operationalized differs across equating methods. For example, assume that we have two alternate forms of an instrument. Some equating approaches (e.g., *mean equating*) would consider the scores on the two forms to be equated when the adjustment makes the mean of, for example, the observed scores, on one form equal to the mean on the other form. Therefore, in mean equating the relative position of equated scores is defined in terms of the number of points the scores are from their respective means (Livingston, 2004). In other cases, such as *linear equating*, equating concerns itself with making the mean and standard deviation of, for example, the observed scores, on one form equal to those on the other form. Therefore, in linear equating the "relative position" of equated scores is defined in terms of the number of standard deviation units the scores are from their respective means. Stated another way, in mean equating the observed scores on one form are assumed to differ by a constant amount from those on the other form, whereas in linear equating the observed scores on one form may differ from those on the other form by different amounts, depending on their location on the observed score scale. A third strategy, *equipercentile equating*, operationalizes "relative position" in terms of the observed scores' percentile ranks on the two forms. Specifically, scores are considered equated across the two forms if they have the same percentile rank on both forms. When equipercentile equating is successful both instruments' distributions have approximately the same mean, standard deviation, and distributional shape.

This chapter is concerned with IRT equating and linking. The reader is referred to Angoff (1984), Holland and Rubin (1982), and Kolen and Brennan (1995, 2004) for detailed information on the traditional equating methods and their variants. It is noted for convenience that, although these procedures may be performed using a statistical package (e.g., equipercentile equating with cubic spline smoothing may be performed using SAS), specialized programs for performing traditional equating are available. For instance, to perform equipercentile equating one might use RAGE and RGEQUATE (Zeng, Kolen, Hanson, Cui, & Chien, 2004). Von Davier, Holland, and Thayer (2004) use KE to implement a kernel method approach to test equating.

Implicit in equating is that the multiple forms are all measuring the same construct and that these forms have been created to the same content and statistical specifications (Angoff, 1984; Kolen & Brennan, 1995). As a contrarian example, one should not equate the scores on an algebra test to those on an art history test or on an androgyny scale. In addition, the transformation should be independent of the groups of individuals used to develop the transformation (i.e., the transformation is unique; Angoff, 1984).

The equating process itself may be seen as consisting of a data collection phase followed by a transformation phase. The transformation phase would involve the application of an equating technique (e.g., equipercentile equating, total characteristic function or characteristic function equating). We discuss these two phases in order.

EQUATING: DATA COLLECTION PHASE

There are multiple data collection approaches or *equating designs*. Some of these strategies use a single sample (group) of individuals, whereas others use two samples. One of these single sample methods is sometimes referred to as the *single group with counterbalancing* (e.g., Kolen & Brennan, 1995) or *counterbalanced random-groups design* (Petersen, Kolen, & Hoover, 1989). In this approach we administer the two forms of an instrument to a single group of individuals. The administration uses counterbalancing of the form administration to control for order effects (e.g., fatigue, practice effects, etc.). For example, the single group would be decomposed into two subgroups. Subgroup 1 would receive form 1 followed by form 2 (form set 1), whereas subgroup 2 would receive form 2 followed by form 1 (form set 2). In practice, the counterbalancing is augmented by interleaving the form sets for administration. This interleaving is called *spiraling* and results in the first individual receiving form set 1, the second individual receiving form set 2, the third individual receiving form set 1, and so on (Angoff, 1984; Petersen et al., 1989). Because the same individuals are administered both forms there is common information across the forms that can be used for performing the equating. In some situations it may not be practical to use this data collection strategy because it requires a doubling of administration time.

A second single-group design creates *randomly equivalent groups* (also known as *random groups* or *random subgroups*) from the single sample. In this approach half of the group is randomly assigned one form and the remaining half is assigned the other form. The spiraling approach discussed above would be used to administer the forms (i.e., the first person receives form 1, the second person receives form 2, the third person receives form 1, and so on). This approach has the advantage of requiring half the administration time of the single group with counterbalancing design because each individual takes only one form. However, one also has less common information for performing the equating than with the single group with counterbalancing. For both the randomly equivalent groups and the single group with counterbalancing designs it is necessary that both forms be available to be administered at the same time. As defined, the common information across forms is assumed to exist owing to the application of random assignment. However, there is a variant of this data collection design that involves constructing the forms to have some items in common. This design is known as the *common-item random groups design* (Kolen & Brennan, 1995, 2004). In this approach the common items across the two forms provide additional information for performing the equating.

A third data collection strategy, the *common-item nonequivalent groups* design, involves using two samples of individuals with each sample being administered one of the forms; this is also called the nonequivalent groups with anchor test (NEAT) design. As the name implies, the forms are created to contain some items in common. These common items are also referred to as *anchor items*, as a *common test*, or as an *anchor test* (Angoff, 1984; Kolen & Brennan, 1995, 2004; Lord, 1980; Petersen et al., 1989). The information used for equating the forms comes from the common items.

There are two variants of the common-item nonequivalent groups design. The first variant, *internal common items*, includes the performance on the common items as part of the observed score. In the second variant, *external common items*, the individuals' performance on the common items is not considered part of their observed scores. With internal common items the items are typically distributed throughout the instrument in the same general locations on both forms, whereas with external common items they are typically presented after the noncommon items are administered (Lord, 1980). When administering the external common items in this way, fatigue, speededness, motivation, learning, practice, and so on, may have more of an impact on the equating than when using the internal common item approach.

The term *anchor test* implies how one should consider these common items. The common items should form a "miniversion" of the test or instrument (Klein & Jarjoura, 1985). That is, these items should be measuring the same construct, the same content specifications, and the same contextual effects as the noncommon items on the instrument (Angoff, 1984; Klein & Jarjoura, 1985; Kim & Cohen, 1998; Kolen & Brennan, 1995, 2004). An additional criterion for anchor tests to satisfy is that they have the same range of item locations as the total test. However, there may be some latitude with this criterion. For example, Sinharay and Holland (2007) found that anchor tests with a range smaller than the total test, but that had been appropriately centered, performed as well as anchor tests that had the same item location range as the total test. Because their study used external common items and equipercentile equating, their results may not generalize to other equating procedures and/or the use of internal common items. An additional consideration for anchor tests in the context of IRT is that the model's assumptions be tenable for the common items and that these items not exhibit differential item functioning (Chapter 12). Typically, the anchor test size should be at least 20 items or no less than 20% of the instrument length (whichever is larger) (Angoff, 1984). In contrast to the single-group designs, this two-group strategy does not require that both forms be available for administration at the same time.[2]

EQUATING: TRANSFORMATION PHASE

The transformation phase of the equating process involves the application of one or more of the transformation procedures identified above to the response data that have been collected. In the context of IRT we can consider this phase as consisting of potentially two steps. Assuming that one does not have item parameter estimates, then the first step involves obtaining model–data fit as well as item parameter estimates for the administrations and the linking of the metrics. The second step is the actual application of the equating method to the person location estimates. Each of these is treated in turn.

Recall that as a result of the indeterminacy of the latent variable's metric, the continuum's metric needs to be defined in the estimation process. This metric definition is addressed by the calibration program's centering strategy, as well as the calibration model, and is unique to a calibration sample. Therefore, if we administer the same instrument to two different groups, then each group defines its own metric for the latent continuum.[3] As mentioned above, when one has model–data fit, these two metrics are linearly related. This linear relationship is used to align metrics to form a common metric, and the alignment process is referred to as linking (cf. Koch & Reckase, 1979; Ree & Jensen, 1983).

One may perform linking in a number of ways. For example, one approach for when one has administered different forms to different groups is *simultaneous calibration* (also known as *concurrent calibration*). In this approach, both samples' response data are concatenated and calibrated in one analysis. The result is that all the items are on the same metric—the one defined by all the individuals combined. If these item parameter estimates are then used to estimate the person locations, then the person locations are all on the same metric regardless of which form the person took (i.e., the individuals are equated). Figure 11.1 shows a visual representation of the structure of the input data file; for presentation purposes all the common items in form 1 are shown as falling at the end of the form and all the common items in form 2 are depicted as falling at the beginning of the form. The vertical aspect of the figure represents the two calibration samples—one for form 1 and another for form 2. The horizontal aspect reflects the items on the two forms. If we visually inspected the data file, we see a series of responses reflecting the responses to form 1 followed by blank spaces (or not-presented codes). Conversely, if one scrolled down through the file one would find blank spaces (or not-presented codes) below form 1's responses, but upon scrolling across one would encounter form 2's responses. The simultaneous calibration strategy can be used with any of the equating designs mentioned above; depending on the design the data file's structure may not conform to that shown in Figure 11.1. In some contexts this strategy may not be practical because of the number of samples and/or their size or because one wishes to maintain a particular baseline metric.

A second approach makes use of previously obtained item parameter estimates for one of the forms. When the data for the second form are calibrated, the item parameter estimates from the first form are provided as input to the calibration and are held fixed (i.e., not reestimated). In effect, this *fixed item parameter* approach augments the second form's calibration by the first form's item calibration results. As a result, the second form's metric is aligned with the first form's metric. If these item parameter estimates are then used to estimate the person locations, then the person locations are on the same metric and the individuals are equated.

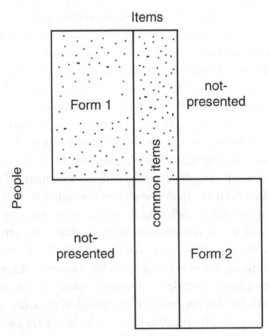

FIGURE 11.1. Graphical depiction of input data file for simultaneous calibration.

A third strategy involves using *metric transformation coefficients*. As mentioned in previous chapters, the continuum is determined up to a linear transformation. In general, the linear transformation from one metric to another for both person and item locations (or their estimates) is

$$\xi^* = \zeta(\xi) + \kappa \tag{11.1}$$

where ζ and κ are the unit and location coefficients, respectively. Typically, ζ and κ are referred to as *equating coefficients*. In this book they are referred to as metric transformation coefficients because they may or may not be used for equating. The symbol ξ represents the parameter (or its estimate) on the untransformed or *initial metric*, and ξ^* represents the same parameter (or its estimate) transformed to the *target metric*. The target metric or common metric is the metric onto which all other metrics are transformed.

For linking metrics ξ represents δ_j (or $\hat{\delta}_j$) on the initial metric and ξ^* is δ_j^* (or $\hat{\delta}_j^*$) on the target metric. For instance, by substitution into Equation 11.1 we have

$$\delta_j^* = \zeta(\delta_j) + \kappa \tag{11.2}$$

To transform the initial metric's item discrimination parameter, α_j, to the target item discrimination parameter metric, α_j^*, we use

$$\alpha_j^* = \frac{\alpha_j}{\zeta} \tag{11.3}$$

or in the slope–intercept parameterization

$$\gamma_j^* = \gamma_j - \frac{\alpha_j}{\zeta}(\kappa) \tag{11.4}$$

The discrimination, location, and intercept parameters' estimates may be used in lieu of α, δ, and γ, respectively. The IRFs' lower asymptote parameters, χ_js (or their estimates), are on a common [0, 1] metric and do not need to be transformed. To equate the person locations (or their estimates) Equation 11.1 is used with ξ representing the initial metric person locations (or their estimates) and ξ^* reflecting the target metric person locations (or their estimates).

Multiple approaches for determining the values of ζ and κ have been developed and are based on using common items. One approach, *linear equating* (e.g., Ree & Jensen, 1983) obtains the metric transformation coefficients by using the mean and standard deviations of the common items. Specifically, the equating coefficient ζ is obtained by taking the ratio of the target to initial metric standard deviations (s) of the locations:

$$\zeta = s_{\delta^*}/s_\delta \tag{11.5}$$

where $s_{\delta*}$ is the standard deviation of the item locations (or their estimates) on the target metric and s_δ is the standard deviation of the of the item locations (or their estimates) on the initial metric. Once ζ is determined the other equating coefficient, κ, is obtained by

$$\kappa = \overline{\delta}_j^* - \zeta\,\overline{\delta}_j \qquad (11.6)$$

where $\overline{\delta}_j^*$ is the mean of the item locations (or their estimates) on the target metric and $\overline{\delta}_j$ is the mean of the item locations (or their estimates) on the initial metric. This is the approach used in Chapter 4 and is applied to temperatures in Appendix E, "Linking: A Temperature Analogy Example."

Once the metric transformation coefficients are obtained, then the linking of the separate metrics is performed by applying Equations 11.2 and 11.3 (or Equation 11.4) itemwise (or category/intersection-wise in the case of polytomous models) to the item parameter estimates. To equate the person locations across the metrics we apply $\theta_i^* = \zeta(\theta_i) + \kappa$ to each individual's person location or its estimate. Either a program like SAS or specialized software (e.g., the ST program by Hanson and Zeng, 2004) can be used to implement this approach.

In contrast to linear equating's use of only the item location parameter estimates' standard deviations and means, a second approach, *total characteristic function equating*, uses all the item parameter estimates to determine the values of ζ and κ. The objective in this method (also known as *true score equating*, *test characteristic curve equating*) is to align as closely as possible the initial metric's total characteristic function (TCF) with that of the target metric. The metric transformation coefficients are the values of ζ and κ that satisfy this objective.

One variant of the total characteristic function equating method was proposed by Haebara (1980) and another by Stocking and Lord (1983). EQUATE (Baker, 1993b) implements the Stocking and Lord approach, and ST (Hanson & Zeng, 2004) and POLYST (Kim & Kolen, 2003) implement the Stocking and Lord approach as well as the Haebara approach. EQUATE and POLYST can be used with dichotomous and polytomous IRT models (e.g., the GPC, GR, NR models), whereas ST is for used with dichotomous models. These programs require that the two metrics to be linked have either all or a subset of items in common. That is, the information in the common items is used to determine the metric transformation coefficient values for adjusting the item parameter estimates and/or equating the person location estimates in order to align the two total characteristics curves.

Stocking and Lord (1983) show that if the estimates are error free, then the proper choice of the metric transformation coefficients results in the total characteristic curves from the two forms being linked to coincide. Baker (1996) found that the metric transformation coefficients' sampling distributions are "well behaved." As a consequence, one may have confidence in the reasonableness of the metric transformation coefficients; also see Baker (1997). Kaskowitz and De Ayala (2001) studied the impact of error on the total characteristic function method and found the method to be robust to estimation errors. Additional work by Baker and Al-Karni (1991) concluded that the Stocking and Lord total characteristic function procedure is the de facto standard against which other procedures for computing metric transformation coefficients should be compared.

The effect of the metric transformation coefficient κ is to shift the total characteristic function up or down the continuum, whereas the effect of the ζ coefficient is to change the slope of the total characteristic curve. For example, assume that we have two forms whose TCFs are perfectly aligned. If we apply $\kappa = -1$ and $\zeta = 1$ to Form 2's total characteristic function, then its TCF (the bold line) shifts down the continuum by one logit (Figure 11.2); Form 1 is our target metric. If we change κ to be 1.5, then Form 2's total characteristic curve shifts up the scale from its current location by one and one-half logits (Figure 11.3). By changing ζ to 0.5, Form 2's total characteristic curve becomes steeper (Figure 11.4). Therefore, by proper choice of κ and ζ we can align Form 2's total characteristic function with that of Form 1 on our target metric.

The gist of the total characteristic function approach is to determine the values of κ and ζ that come closest to superimposing the two forms' total characteristic functions. Specifically, ζ and κ are chosen to minimize the difference between the expected trait score estimates from two forms by using an appropriate function. Stocking and Lord (1983) suggested minimizing the quadratic loss function:

$$F = \frac{1}{N} \sum_{i=1}^{N} (\hat{T}_i - \hat{T}_i^*)^2 \qquad (11.7)$$

where N is the number of participants and $\hat{T}_i$ and $\hat{T}_i^*$ are the expected trait score estimates from two forms.[4]

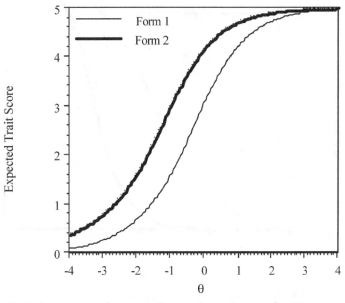

FIGURE 11.2. Total characteristic functions for two forms ($\kappa = -1$, $\zeta = 1$).

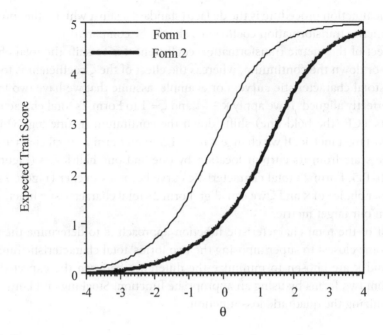

FIGURE 11.3. Total characteristic functions for two forms ($\kappa = 1.5$, $\zeta = 1$).

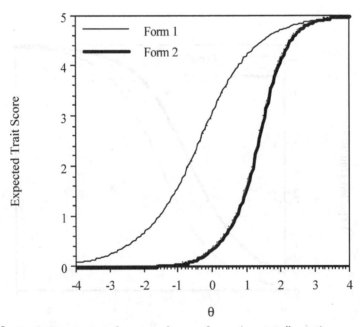

FIGURE 11.4. Total characteristic functions for two forms ($\kappa = 1.5$, $\zeta = 0.5$).

Equation 11.7 is minimized when

$$\frac{\partial F}{\partial \zeta} = \frac{\partial F}{\partial \kappa} = 0$$

and is solved by a system of simultaneous equations (Baker, 1993b). In contrast to Stocking and Lord's (1983) multivariate search method approach, Baker, Al-Karni, and Al-Dosary (1991) solved for the metric transformation coefficients by using the Davidon–Fletcher–Powell technique. To minimize F, $\hat{T}_i$ and $\hat{T}_i^*$ are evaluated for an arbitrary set of points along the latent variable continuum.

One may visualize the result of the minimization of the difference between two total characteristic functions by returning to the TCFs shown in Figures 11.2 through 11.4. For instance, if we apply the metric transformation coefficients $\kappa = -0.005$ and $\zeta = 0.95$ to Form 2's estimates (i.e., through Equations 11.2 and 11.3), then we can transform Form 2's (initial) metric to Form 1's (target) metric. Figure 11.5 shows that after this transformation Form 2's TCF is virtually identical with that of Form 1.

For MIRT models, multidimensional linking may be accomplished in various ways. For example, one might use the total characteristic function method, the item response function method, or the equated function method. (The item response function method is analogous to the total characteristic function approach, but is focused on minimizing the differences between item response surfaces, and the equated function method is similar to linear equating.) Oshima, Davey, and Lee (2000) studied four different approaches for performing multidimensional linking and found that the total characteristic function and

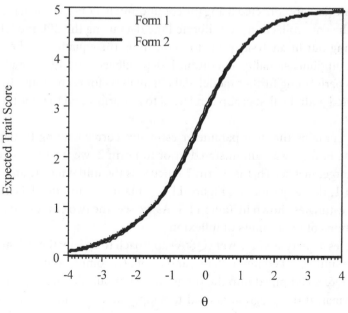

FIGURE 11.5. Total characteristic functions for two forms ($\kappa = -0.005$, $\zeta = 0.95$).

the item response function provided the most stable results, although all four approaches were comparable to one another. They suggested that selecting among the approaches be based on the purpose of performing the linking. For example, if the purpose is to achieve the equivalence of respondents' trait scores regardless of which form is used, then the total characteristic function approach may be the preferred method. However, if one's focus is on differential item functioning (see Chapter 12), then the item response function may be the best choice. (Also see Davey, Oshima, & Lee, 1996, and Hirsch, 1989, for greater detail on multidimensional equating.) Oshima et al.'s (2000) results were for a two-dimensional situation and may or may not hold for higher dimensional latent spaces.

EXAMPLE: APPLICATION OF THE TOTAL CHARACTERISTIC FUNCTION EQUATING METHOD

To demonstrate the total characteristic function method for linking and equating we administered a positivist psychology scale to two groups of respondents. This scale consists of 20 items using a true/false response format. The freeware EQUATE program (Baker, 1993b) is used to perform the linking and equating of the two samples.

The EQUATE program (Baker, 1993b, 1996) implements the total characteristic function equating technique. The program estimates the ζ and κ coefficients as well as the value of the loss-function F for these estimates; in the program ζ is denoted as A, κ is symbolized as K, and these are referred to as METRIC TRANSFORMATION COEFFICIENTS. In addition to calculating the ζ and κ coefficients, the program transforms the item and person parameter estimates from the initial to the target metric. These transformations are the implementations of Equations 11.2 and 11.3 using the values for ζ and κ from the program output.

Our response data are collected using the common-item nonequivalent groups approach. Subsequent to the data collection we calibrated the data using the 2PL model. Although we are not presenting our fit analysis, prior to performing the equating of the two groups we evaluated IRT's unidimensionality, condition independence, and functional form assumptions, as well as performing further model–data fit analysis for each group. In the following, the data associated with the first group is referred to as Form 1 and that for the second group as Form 2.

Table 11.1 contains the item parameter estimates corresponding to the two administrations. Because Form 1 was administered prior to Form 2, we treat the metric defined by Form 1 as our target metric. That is, Form 2's metric is the initial metric and is transformed to that of Form 1, the target metric. Figure 11.6 contains the unlinked TCFs based on the item parameter estimates shown in Table 11.1. As we see, the two curves vary in their slopes and in the locations of their points of inflection.

EQUATE uses a query-and-answer (Q&A) approach to specify the IRT model, the number of items, the number of common items, and so on. (A command input file could be used in place of this Q&A and piped into the program.) All input files are expected to be in text (i.e., ASCII) format. If the program is used to simply link two metrics, then one has only two input files containing the item parameter estimates on the target and initial metrics. In EQUATE's parlance, Form 2's (initial) metric is the "FROM" metric and Form 1's target

TABLE 11.1. Item Parameter Estimates for Two Forms

	Form 1 (target metric)			Form 2 (initial metric)	
Item	$\hat{\alpha}$	$\hat{\delta}$	Item	$\hat{\alpha}$	$\hat{\delta}$
1	1.6294	0.9824	1	1.3035	0.9780
2	1.6524	-0.1374	2	1.3219	-0.4218
3	2.3076	0.3471	3	1.8461	0.1839
4	1.9813	0.2589	4	1.5850	0.0736
5	1.9402	0.8661	5	1.5522	0.8326
6	2.3441	-0.0576	6	1.8753	-0.3220
7	1.8026	-0.3314	7	1.4421	-0.6643
8	2.1991	0.4043	8	1.7593	0.2554
9	1.6872	-0.0025	9	1.3498	-0.2531
10	2.2024	-0.4674	10	1.7619	-0.8343
11	2.0272	-0.5324	11	1.6218	-0.9155
12	2.3754	0.4611	12	1.9003	0.3264
13	1.6993	-1.1129	13	1.3594	-1.6411
14	1.8613	0.9174	14	1.4890	0.8968
15	2.4440	-0.2271	15	1.9552	-0.5339
16	1.6719	-0.8176	16	1.3375	-1.2720
17	1.6596	0.7683	17	1.3277	0.7104
18	1.6236	1.6089	18	1.2989	1.7611
19	2.3181	2.3312	19	1.8545	2.6640
20	1.9266	0.5202	20	1.5413	0.4003

metric is the "TO" metric. However, because we are using EQUATE for both linking and equating, we have a third file containing the Form 2 person location estimates to be used in equating. Specifically, one of our item parameter estimate files is called FORM1.TXT and contains the item parameter estimates that define the target metric (i.e., the "TO" metric). Our other item parameter estimate file, FORM2.TXT, contains the item parameter estimates that are on the initial metric (i.e., the "FROM" metric). The third file that we need, THE-TAEST2.TXT, contains the person location estimates from the Form 2 administration and, as a result of being obtained using Form 2, are on the initial metric.

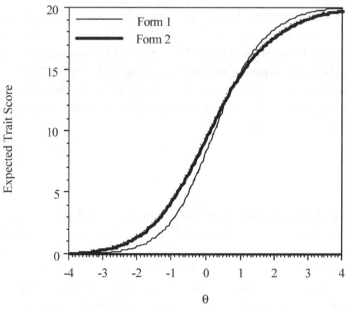

FIGURE 11.6. Unlinked total characteristic functions for the two forms shown in Table 11.1.

Table 11.2 contains the Q&A session for specifying the analysis. As can be seen, we start with the analysis's title and specify that EQUATE should use 50 points in its minimization of Equation 11.7 (i.e., ENTER NUMBER OF ABILITY SCALE POINTS N=). The subsequent queries allow us to specify the IRT model, the number of items, and the FOR-TRAN format for the initial metric. (FORTRAN formats are briefly discussed in Appendix E, "FORTRAN Formats.") Following the initial metric information we provide analogous information for the target metric. We instruct the program to create a file, called LINKED. TXT, that will contain the linked Form 2 estimates. Because we want EQUATE to also perform equating we answer "yes" (i.e., "Y") to the TRANSFORM THETAS? Y/N prompt. As a result, we identify the file containing the person location estimates on the initial metric, THETAEST2.TXT, as well as specify a file, XFRMTEST.TXT, for the equated person location estimates. At the end of the Q&A we are prompted to provide the positions of the common items on the initial (i.e., SPECIFY ANCHOR ITEM IDs FOR THE "FROM" INSTRUMENT) and target (i.e., SPECIFY ANCHOR ITEM IDs FOR THE "TO" MET-RIC) metrics. In this example, we are treating all items as common items. However, to be clear, the common items approach does not require that all items be in common, but only that some subset of the items on the instrument be in common.

After the Q&A session EQUATE performs its analysis. The abridged output is presented in Table 11.3 and the linked item parameter estimates and equated person locations estimates are shown in Table 11.4. EQUATE echoes the input specifications and its initial (start) values for κ and ζ; κ is symbolized as K and ζ is denoted as A. After iterating twice, the program provides its estimates for the metric transformation coefficients, $\kappa = 0.2$ and $\zeta = 0.8$. Descriptive statistics for our Form 2 item parameter estimates, after being placed on the target metric, are provided along with similar statistics for the equated person location estimates.

The left panel of Table 11.4 shows the results of Form 2's item parameter estimates after they have been linked to the target (Form 1's) metric; this is the contents of the file LINKED.TXT. These values are obtained by using $\kappa = 0.2$ and $\zeta = 0.8$ in Equations 11.2 and 11.3 with the item parameter estimates listed in the right panel of Table 11.1. Table 11.4's right panel contains the unequated ($\hat{\theta}$) and the equated person location estimates ($\hat{\theta}^*$) for the first 20 cases (i.e., this is part of the contents of file XFRMTEST.TXT). Using the linked Form 2 item parameter estimates (i.e., $\hat{\alpha}^*$ and $\hat{\delta}^*$) and Form 1's item parameter estimates to calculate $\hat{T}_i$ and $\hat{T}_i^*$, we see that the two corresponding TCFs are indistinguishable (Figure 11.7).

SUMMARY

Whenever we use different forms of an instrument and/or different groups of people, then our estimates will potentially and most likely be on different metrics. If we need to align the different item parameter estimate metrics with one another, then the process is referred to as linking. Equating is used when different groups of people are on different metrics and we wish to place all the individuals on a common metric. Therefore, the focus of linking is to adjust item parameter estimates, and the focus of equating is to adjust person

TABLE 11.2. EQUATE's Query-and-Answer Session

```
TYPE A TITLE FOR THE COMPUTER RUN
Example TCF equating, 2PL                          ⇐ input title[a]

ENTER NUMBER OF ABILITY SCALE POINTS N=
50                                                ⇐ number of points used in the minimization
RESPONSE MODE DICHOTOMOUS, GRADED OR NOMINAL? D/G/N
D                                                 ⇐ type of model: 2PL is a dichotomous model
ENTER NUMBER OF PARAMETERS IN ICC MODEL 1,2,3:
2

ENTER NAME OF "FROM METRIC" ITEM PARAMETER FILE
FORM2.TXT                                         ⇐ the initial metric (untransformed)

ENTER FORMAT OF "FROM METRIC FILE"
(3X,F6.4,1X,F7.4)                                 ⇐ FORTRAN format where α is read as F6.4 and
                                                    δ is read as F7.4
ENTER NUMBER OF ITEMS IN "FROM" TEST
20
IS FROM METRIC LOGISTIC OR NORMAL? L/N
L

ENTER NAME OF "TO METRIC" ITEM PARAMETER FILE
FORM1.TXT                                         ⇐ the target metric

ENTER FORMAT OF "TO METRIC FILE"
(3X,F6.4,1X,F7.4)                                 ⇐ FORTRAN format where α is read as F6.4 and
                                                     δ is read as F7.4
ENTER NUMBER OF ITEMS IN "TO" TEST
20
IS TO METRIC LOGISTIC OR NORMAL? L/N
L

ENTER NAME OF FILE TO STORE TRANSFORMED ITEM PARAMETERS
LINKED.TXT                                        ⇐ the file containing Form 2's transformed item
                                                    parameter estimates
TRANSFORM THETAS? Y/N
Y                                                 ⇐ perform equating

ENTER NAME OF "FROM" THETA FILE
THETAEST2.TXT                                     ⇐ file containing the (untransformed) person
                                                    location estimates on the initial metric
                                                    (i.e., person who took Form 2)
ENTER FORMAT OF "FROM" THETA FILE
(F7.4)                                            ⇐ FORTRAN format to read θ̂ s

ENTER NUMBER OF EXAMINEES
40                                                ⇐ number of individuals that will be
                                                    transformed
ENTER NAME OF FILE FOR TRANSFORMED THETAS
XFRMTEST.TXT                                      ⇐ file containing the (transformed) person
                                                    location estimates on the target metric
ARE THESE SPECIFICATIONS OK? Y/N
Y

SPECIFY ANCHOR ITEM IDs FOR THE "FROM" INSTRUMENT
ENTER LIST OF ANCHOR ITEMS SEPARATE WITH COMMAS TERMINATE WITH COLON
1-20:                                             ⇐ ordinal positions of common items. In this
                                                    case, all items on Form 2 are common items
SPECIFY ANCHOR ITEM IDs FOR THE "TO" METRIC
ENTER LIST OF ANCHOR ITEMS SEPARATE WITH COMMAS TERMINATE WITH COLON
1-20:                                             ⇐ ordinal positions of common items. In this
                                                    case, all items on Form 1 are in common
                                                    with those on Form 2
```

[a]The text following the ⇐ is provided to help the reader understand the corresponding input.

TABLE 11.3. Abridged EQUATE's Output

```
Example TCF equating, 2PL
   NUMBER OF ABILITY SCALE POINTS=    50
   DICHOTOMOUS RESPONSE MODEL
   ICC MODEL HAS    2 PARAMETERS

   :                                        ⇐ Echoing of input specifications[a]

   INITIAL VALUE FOR A=    0.5000  INITIAL VALUE FOR K=    0.1000
   FUNCTION AT INITIAL VALUES =      0.000000
   NUMBER OF ITERATIONS PERFORMED =    2
   METRIC TRANSFORMATION COEFFICIENTS ARE
   A=    0.8000  K=      0.2000            ⇐ The metric transformation coefficients: A is
                                             ζ and K is κ
   FUNCTION VALUE =      0.000000

     SUMMARY STATISTICS FOR TRANSFORMED ITEMS
        MEAN B=    0.289 VARIANCE B=    0.680  STD DEV B=    0.825
        MEAN A=    1.968 VARIANCE A=    0.084  STD DEV A=    0.289

     SUMMARY STATISTICS OF TRANSFORMED ABILITIES
               MEAN =    0.266269
           VARIANCE=    0.493555
     STANDARD DEVIATION=    0.702535
   :
```

[a]The text following the ⇐ is provided to help the reader understand the corresponding input.

location estimates. Placing the items or the individuals on a single metric allows us to make comparisons among the items or the individuals. The equating of multiple forms assumes that all the forms are measuring the same construct and that these forms have been created to the same content and statistical specifications.

The linking and equating processes consist of a data collection phase followed by a

TABLE 11.4. Transformed Form 2 Item Parameter Estimates and Equated Person Location Estimates

Item	Form 2 (linked) $\hat{\alpha}*$	Form 2 (linked) $\hat{\delta}*$	Unequated $\hat{\theta}$	Equated $\hat{\theta}*$
1	1.629	0.982	0.4452	0.556
2	1.652	-0.137	0.9714	0.977
3	2.308	0.347	1.5351	1.428
4	1.981	0.259	-0.0640	0.149
5	1.940	0.866	-0.3916	-0.113
6	2.344	-0.058	-0.5673	-0.254
7	1.803	-0.331	1.0645	1.052
8	2.199	0.404	-0.5360	-0.229
9	1.687	-0.002	-1.2148	-0.772
10	2.202	-0.467	-0.1990	0.041
11	2.027	-0.532	-0.6351	-0.308
12	2.375	0.461	0.8015	0.841
13	1.699	-1.113	0.1356	0.308
14	1.861	0.917	-0.9618	-0.569
15	2.444	-0.227	1.6185	1.495
16	1.672	-0.818	0.9273	0.942
17	1.660	0.768	0.8810	0.905
18	1.624	1.609	-1.1468	-0.717
19	2.318	2.331	0.5105	0.608
20	1.927	0.520	0.2059	0.365

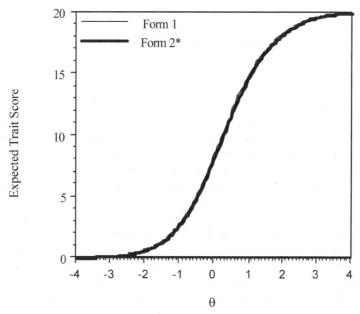

FIGURE 11.7. TCFs after initial metric (Form 2) is linked to the target metric (Form 1).

transformation phase. There are multiple data collection approaches, such as the single group with counterbalancing method and the common-item nonequivalent groups method. Once the data are collected, then we apply a transformation procedure to align the different metrics. These transformation procedures may be classified as traditional approaches (e.g., linear equating, equipercentile equating) or modern approaches (e.g., total characteristic function equating).

In the context of IRT, the transformation procedure requires determining the metric transformation coefficients ζ and κ to transform the item parameters and person parameters (or their estimates). Two common approaches for determining the metric transformation coefficients are linear equating and total characteristic function equating. The former uses the standard deviations and means of the item location parameters (or their estimates), whereas the latter uses all the item parameters (or their estimates) to determine the metric transformation coefficients. In general, if we are using a model with a constant discrimination parameter, then linear equating may be a useful approach. However, whenever item discrimination is allowed to vary across items, then the total characteristic function approach is the preferred technique.

In the next chapter we revisit a model–data fit issue, differential item functioning (DIF). DIF occurs when different groups of individuals perform differently on an item even after we control for or take into account differences in the latent variable, θ. In short, individuals in one group can have a more difficult time endorsing a particular response than those in the other group for reasons that have nothing to do with their positions on the latent variable. There are multiple approaches for identifying the presence of DIF. Some of these require that the item parameter estimates from the different groups first be linked before applying the DIF method. We discuss both non-IRT- and IRT-based methods.

NOTES

1. The process discussed is sometimes referred to as *horizontal equating*. In horizontal equating we are interested in adjusting person location scores for slight differences in, for example, difficulty across forms. If the procedure is successful in disentangling form differences from person differences, then the equated forms are *interchangeable*. A related procedure is *vertical scaling*; this procedure is sometimes called *vertical equating*, although vertical scaling is the preferred term. In vertical scaling we are interested in creating a common metric for comparing individuals across different educational levels (e.g., grades). Because the examinations are developed to be appropriate for a specific education level, they are most likely inappropriate for other education levels. As such, the instruments are *not interchangeable* even after the procedure is completed. For this reason the term *equating* is reserved for those techniques that result in an *interchangeability* of forms. Vertical scaling is considered to be a method for *scaling to achieve comparability* (AERA, APA, NCME, 1985). In situations involving children and a wide range of education levels, developmental changes in the children may adversely affect the creation of a meaningful common scale. Petersen et al. (1989) discuss issues that are relevant to vertical scaling in the context of grade equivalent scales; also see Baker (1984). A related issue is scale shrinkage (Yen, 1985). As originally defined, *scale shrinkage* refers to a pattern of increasing mean discrimination and decreasing item/person location variability as educational level increases after the tests have been vertically scaled. Camilli (1988, 1999) differentiates between within-education level shrinkage and between-education levels shrinkage. In both cases, one sees the pattern of decreasing variances across equated/scaled tests. Changes in dimensionality, reliability, and scaling procedures have been invoked to explain the possible occurrence of scale shrinkage.

2. The preceding has assumed that all items administered make up the *operational* set of items. In the ability/achievement context there may be additional item sets administered to the examinees. The examinees' performance on these additional sets are not used in determining their scores on the instrument. These *nonoperational* item sets are included to gather information on the items' characteristics as part of pretesting the items, for their calibration, or as part of a preequating design. For more information on preequating see Kolen and Brennan (1995, 2004) or Lord (1980).

3. There are a number of additional situations that would lead to metrics being unaligned. For example, because different programs may use different approaches for resolving the indeterminacy issues (e.g., person vs. item centering) the corresponding estimates are on different metrics even when the same calibration sample is used. A second example involves the creation of an item bank from which we would develop multiple forms. For security reasons we would continuously be developing new items for addition to the bank. Because these new items would most likely be administered to a different group of individuals than those used in creating the item bank, these new items would not be on the item bank's metric. Rather, the new items would be on the metric defined by the individuals used in their calibration and this metric would have to be linked to that of the item bank. However, any instruments developed from the item bank will yield estimated person locations that are on the same continuum as the item bank.

4. Haebara's (1980) method differs from the Stocking and Lord approach by using a slightly different criterion function that is focused on the IRFs from the two metrics. Divgi (1985) suggested a different criterion that could be solved using a minimum chi-square approach.

12

Differential Item Functioning

In this chapter we discuss items that behave one way for one group of respondents and in a different way for a different group of respondents. As an example of this type of item, assume that we have developed the following item to assess general vocabulary knowledge.

> What does *alto* mean?
> a. again
> b. also
> c. countertenor
> d. high
> e. in addition

If our respondents to this item are divided into Hispanic and non-Hispanic subgroups, we might find that Hispanics may select option *d*, whereas non-Hispanics may select option *c*, even after we control for differences in vocabulary proficiency. (In fact, some Hispanics of Mexican origin may think that the best answer, *stop*, is not even provided.) Therefore, performance on this item is a function not only of the respondent's English vocabulary proficiency, but also of a tangential variable—the respondent's ethnic group (specifically, the person's Spanish proficiency). Various approaches have been developed to try to identify items that function differently across groups. In the following we discuss some of these approaches. These differential item functioning techniques should be considered a standard part of our toolbox of model–data fit methods. We begin with a discussion of item bias and how it relates to differential item functioning, after which we present three techniques for performing differential item functioning analyses. Parallel to the structure of previous chapters, we then provide a demonstration of a differential functioning analysis.

DIFFERENTIAL ITEM FUNCTIONING AND ITEM BIAS

Although the term *bias* has a statistical interpretation, the systematic under- or overestimation of a parameter, in the layperson's mind bias is typically associated with the issue of unfairness. That is, an instrument that has an adverse impact on different ethnic or racial groups. As such, the terms *item bias* and *test bias* have certain culturally negative connotations. Despite efforts to disentangle these connotations from the term (e.g., Jensen, 1980) such perceptions have continued. Psychometrically, the definition of bias has evolved from instrument-focus to item-focus. Camilli and Shepard (1994), Holland and Wainer (1993), and Zumbo (2007) present the history of bias in testing as well as approaches for the analysis of bias scores.

Current practice for determining whether an instrument is biased is to examine the instrument at the item level to see whether one or more items may be considered biased. To identify items as biased involves using *differential item functioning* (DIF) methods to detect items that are functioning differently across manifest groups of individuals (e.g., Hispanics and non-Hispanics). An item identified as exhibiting DIF is reviewed by a panel of experts to determine whether the source of an item's differential performance is relevant or irrelevant to the construct being measured; this review is also known as "logical evidence of bias." It is the panel's conclusion that determines whether an item exhibiting DIF is also considered biased. It should be noted that, in practice, items are subjected to sensitivity reviews to remove material that may be considered offensive or demeaning to particular groups, regardless of DIF analyses (Camilli & Shepard, 1994). For example, the term *colored people* is considered offensive in the United States, but not necessarily in other countries (i.e., different cultures).

In the following discussion we focus on methods for identifying DIF. Although our presentation revolves around proficiency assessment, this should not be interpreted to mean that DIF is a concern only in proficiency assessment. For instance, attitude and personality inventories may contain items that inadvertently assume that the respondents have certain knowledge or a particular background in order to understand the items as intended. However, because of ethnic/racial, gender, and/or cultural differences in the respondents, this may not be true.

DIF is defined as an item that displays different statistical properties for different manifest groups after the groups have been matched on a proficiency measure (Angoff, 1993). For instance, assuming binary data and an IRT framework, DIF is reflected as a difference between the conditional probabilities of a response of 1 for two manifest groups (e.g., females and males). In the DIF nomenclature one of the manifest groups is known as the *focal group*, whereas the other is called the *reference group*. The focal group (e.g., females) is the one being investigated to see if it is disadvantaged by the item. The reference group is the comparison group (e.g., males). In some item bias literature the focal group is called the "minority" (membership) group and the reference group is the "majority" (membership) group.

Graphically, DIF can be represented as the difference between two IRFs. One IRF is based on the item's parameter estimate(s) from the focal group and the other IRF is based on the item's parameter estimate(s) from the reference group. If an item is not exhibiting DIF, then the groups' IRFs would be superimposed on one another (i.e., within sampling error) after we link the two groups' metrics. However, if the item is exhibiting DIF, then the two IRFs are not superimposed after we link the two groups' metrics. Figure 12.1 contains an example of an item exhibiting DIF.

The item shown in Figure 12.1 favors members of the reference group (nonbold line) over those from the focal group (bold line). In other words, we see that throughout the θ continuum the probability of a response of 1 is higher for reference group members than for focal group members. This form of DIF is known as *uniform DIF*. If this is a proficiency item, then the item is easier for members of the reference group than for focal group members.

The second type of DIF is *nonuniform DIF*. With this type, members of the reference group perform better than focal group members for part of the θ continuum, but this relationship is reversed for a different part of the continuum. Graphically, an item that exhibits nonuniform DIF has IRFs that cross. Figure 12.2 contains an example of an item exhibiting nonuniform DIF. Above θ = –0.5 reference group members have a higher probability of responding with a 1 than do members of the focal group. However, below θ = –0.5 focal group members have a higher probability of responding with a 1 than do members of the reference group. With nonuniform DIF it is possible that DIF for one group (positive DIF) may be wholly or partially compensated for by DIF against that group (negative DIF) at another point along the latent variable continuum. To summarize, in nonuniform DIF an item's IRFs differ in their slopes and potentially their locations, whereas with uniform DIF an item's IRFs differ only in their locations.

One explanation for why an item exhibits DIF is based on multidimensionality. That is, DIF can be conceptualized as a form of multidimensionality that occurs when an item measures multiple dimensions and when the manifest groups differ in their relative locations

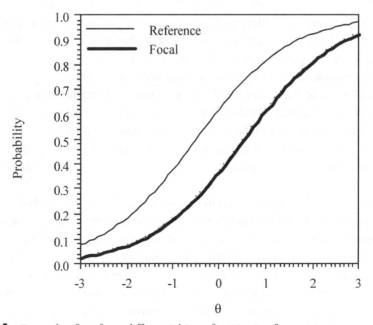

FIGURE 12.1. Example of uniform differential item functioning for one item.

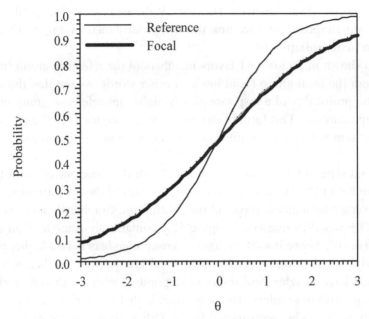

FIGURE 12.2. Example of nonuniform differential item functioning for one item.

to one another on the nonprimary latent variable(s). If the two groups do not differ in their relative locations on the nonprimary dimension(s), then neither group benefits from the nonprimary dimension and DIF does not occur even though the data are multidimensional (cf. Ackerman, 1992).

There are three additional issues we need to discuss. As noted above, once an item is identified as exhibiting DIF its text is subjected to panel review to determine if the wording of the item may explain the differential performance. If an acceptable explanation is not forthcoming, then the item is not considered biased, although it may be eliminated from the instrument for exhibiting DIF. In short, flagging an item as exhibiting DIF is a necessary but not sufficient condition for the item being considered to be biased.

The second issue is the degree of DIF. As we know, in hypothesis testing a statistically significant result does not necessarily mean that the result is meaningful. This concept may be applied to DIF analysis. For instance, at the Educational Testing Service (ETS) the practice is to classify items exhibiting DIF into three categories, depending on the significance of the test statistic and the magnitude (i.e., degree) of the DIF (Dorans & Holland, 1993; Zieky, 1993).

The third issue is the impact of an item exhibiting DIF on the analysis itself. That is, because DIF is defined as a difference between conditional probabilities, then one can ask about the impact of one or more DIF items on the conditioning variable (e.g., the observed score, X) used in the DIF analysis. Camilli and Shepard (1994) strongly recommend that the items exhibiting the greatest DIF, and that have been determined to be biased, be removed from the calculation of the conditioning variable and the DIF analysis be reperformed. Using this iterative process, the conditioning variable is "purified." The procedure's premise is that using this purified conditioning variable will identify the same items as exhibiting significant DIF while also helping to reveal whether there are other DIF items that were masked by the contaminated conditioning variable. Holland and Thayer (1988) conjectured "that it is correct to *include* the studied item in the matching criterion when it is being analyzed for DIF, but if it has substantial DIF then that item should be *excluded* from the criterion used to match examinees for any *other* studied item" (p. 143). Their reasoning is that including the item controls the size of the test, whereas the removal of the item prevents large DIF items from reducing the power of the test.

From an IRT perspective, the existence of DIF means that the DIF item's parameter estimates are not invariant across the manifest groups (i.e., item–data misfit).[1] It is this lack of invariance that is interpreted as evidence of DIF. There have been various IRT-based indices created for DIF detection and some are based on detecting this lack of invariance.

Among the DIF approaches based on IRT are the likelihood ratio (TSW-ΔG^2) method by Thissen, Steinberg, and Wainer (1988, 1993); Lord's Chi-Square (Lord, 1980); and the Exact Signed Area and H Statistic approaches (Raju, 1988, 1990).[2] Non-IRT-based approaches include but are not limited to the nonparametric Mantel–Haenszel Chi-Square (MH) statistic (Holland & Thayer, 1988), log linear modeling (Mellenbergh, 1982), and the use of logistic regression (Swaminathan & Rogers, 1990).

Below we discuss three approaches for DIF detection: the MH statistic, the TSW-ΔG^2, and the logistic regression approach. Each approach is implemented by examining each item on an instrument for DIF. Although we do not discuss Lord's Chi-Square or Raju's Exact Signed Area and H Statistics, it should be noted that these DIF indices require that the groups' metrics be linked prior to the technique's application; this is done by using one of the approaches discussed in Chapter 11. In the following discussion, we assume that the reference group is coded 0, the focal group is coded 1, and that we are working with dichotomous response data.

MANTEL–HAENSZEL CHI-SQUARE

The *Mantel–Haenszel* statistic (MH; Mantel & Haenszel, 1959) is used for determining whether two variables are independent of one another while conditioning on a third variable (i.e., the analysis of a three-way contingency table). As applied to DIF detection, the MH statistic consists of the sum of a series of 2 × 2 contingency tables where each table is based only on persons who received the same observed score. Typically, the conditioning variable is the observed score or some modification of the observed score. Each table is the cross-classification of an item's binary responses with group membership. Because for a zero observed score or a perfect observed score the 2 × 2 table collapses to have a single column that represents responses of 0 or 1, respectively, there are always one fewer tables than the maximum possible observed score on the instrument. For example, assuming a four-item instrument with observed scores of 0 to 4, we have three 2 × 2 tables. One 2 × 2 table is for an observed score of 1, another is for an observed score of 2, and a third table is for an observed score of 3.

To calculate the MH statistic we need to create each of the 2 × 2 tables conditioned on the observed scores. Let t represent the *t*th observed score where t = 1, . . . , (L −1) and L is the instrument's length. Then, for the item of interest and the tth observed score, the following 2×2 table of manifest groups by item response can be formed:

For the tth observed score:

<table>
<tr><td rowspan="5" style="writing-mode: vertical-rl">Manifest groups</td><td></td><td colspan="3" align="center">Item response</td></tr>
<tr><td></td><td align="center">0</td><td align="center">1</td><td align="center">Total</td></tr>
<tr><td>Reference</td><td align="center">B_t</td><td align="center">A_t</td><td align="center">n_{Rt}</td></tr>
<tr><td>Focal</td><td align="center">D_t</td><td align="center">C_t</td><td align="center">n_{Ft}</td></tr>
<tr><td>Total</td><td align="center">m_{0t}</td><td align="center">m_{1t}</td><td align="center">T_t</td></tr>
</table>

where A_t, B_t, C_t, and D_t are the frequencies for the corresponding cells, n_{Rt} and n_{Ft} are, respectively, the number of reference and focal group respondents that obtained the tth observed score, m_{1t} is the number of responses of 1, m_{0t} is the number of responses of 0, and T_t is the number of respondents in tth table. Because we create this 2×2 table for each of the remaining observed scores, each table is conditioned on an observed score.

The MH statistic allows us to determine if the responses to an item are independent of group membership after conditioning on the observed scores. Therefore, the null hypothesis is one of conditional independence. Following Holland and Thayer (1988), we can calculate MH by

$$\text{MH}_\chi 2 = \frac{\left\{ \left| \sum_{t=1}^{(L-1)} [A_t - \mathcal{E}(A_t)] \right| - 0.5 \right\}^2}{\sum_{t=1}^{(L-1)} \text{var}(A_t)} \tag{12.1}$$

where

$$\text{var}(A_t) = \frac{n_{Rt} n_{Ft} m_{1t} m_{0t}}{T_t^2 (T_t - 1)}$$

and the conditional expectation of A_t is that the responses and group membership are independent for the tth observed score:

$$\mathcal{E}(A_t) = \frac{n_{Rt} m_{1t}}{T_t}$$

The value of 0.5 in Equation 12.1 is Yates's correction for continuity.

$\text{MH}_\chi 2$ is evaluated against the standard X^2 critical values with degrees of freedom equal to 1. A complementary way of interpreting the null hypothesis is that the odds of reference group members responding 1 are the same as those of focal group members. This is referred to as the constant odds ratio hypothesis. Symbolically, the constant odds ratio is represented as α_{MH} and the null hypothesis is $\alpha_{MH} = 1$. A significant $MH_\chi 2$ indicates that the odds for the two groups vary across some or all of the 2×2 tables for the item in question. In short, the item is exhibiting DIF.

Examination of Equation 12.1 shows that if the frequency of the reference group receiving a response of 1 (i.e., A_t) is consistently greater than what we would expect or consistently less than what we would expect for each of the 2×2 tables, then we obtain a positive statistic. In the former case, one has uniform DIF in favor of the reference group, whereas in the latter case the uniform DIF favors the focal group. However, if for some of the 2×2 tables A_t is sometimes greater and for other tables it is sometimes less than what we would expect, then the $MH_\chi 2$ can approach zero, owing to cancellation occurring across the $(L-1)$ 2×2 tables. That is, for some of the 2×2 tables (e.g., for some proficiency levels) the reference group does better than expected, but this is negated by the focal group doing better than expected for other tables. When this occurs one has an interaction between group membership, item performance, and the conditioning variable, and this is evidence of nonuniform DIF. Given this possibility of cancellation, the $MH_\chi 2$ statistic is typically seen as being able to detect only uniform DIF. However, our example below shows that in some situations the $MH_\chi 2$ statistic may detect nonuniform DIF. Although this is possible, we are not suggesting the use of the $MH_\chi 2$ statistic for detecting nonuniform DIF, but rather that a significant $MH_\chi 2$ statistic does not necessarily mean the presence of only uniform DIF.

To summarize, the $MH_\chi 2$ statistic determines whether there is a relationship between performance on an item and group membership, after taking into account performance on the instrument. In other words, the statistic determines whether the odds of success for focal group members significantly differ from the odds of success for comparable reference group members across the $(L-1)$ 2×2 tables. However, the test does not give us an idea of the strength of this relationship. To obtain an indication of the degree of association we can estimate the common odds ratio across the $(L-1)$ 2×2 tables. The individual odds ratios that are summed to obtain this common odds ratio should not vary drastically from one another (Agresti, 1996). This estimate may be calculated by (Mantel & Haenszel, 1959)

$$\hat{\alpha}_{MH} = \frac{\sum_{t=1}^{(L-1)} \frac{A_t D_t}{T_t}}{\sum_{t=1}^{(L-1)} \frac{B_t C_t}{T_t}} \qquad (12.2)$$

When $\hat{\alpha}_{MH}$ equals 1, then, on average, the odds for focal group members responding 1 are the same as the odds for comparable reference group members on the studied item (i.e., no DIF on the item). A value of $\hat{\alpha}_{MH}$ greater than 1 indicates that, on average, the reference group members performed better than comparable focal group members on the item of interest (Holland & Thayer, 1988). For instance, if $\hat{\alpha}_{MH} = 2$, then reference group members, on average, have twice the odds of success as comparable focal group members. Conversely, an item with an $\hat{\alpha}_{MH}$ less than 1 indicates that, on average, the reference group members performed worse than comparable focal group members.

Although $\hat{\alpha}_{MH}$ indicates how much better or worse (on average) the focal group members performed relative to comparable reference group members, its scale is asymmetric with a lower bound of 0, an upper bound of ∞, and no DIF indicated by a value of 1. Therefore, as is typically done with odds and odds ratios, α_{MH} is transformed to a scale symmetric about 0. We can transform α_{MH} to the natural logarithmic scale to obtain a log odds ratio, $\beta = \ln(\alpha_{MH})$, where a value of 0 indicates no DIF (cf. Agresti, 1996; Camilli & Shepard, 1994). A second transformation found in the literature (e.g., Holland & Thayer, 1988) is to further transform the log odds ratio to be on the ETS difficulty delta scale (D) by $D = -2.35 \ln(\alpha_{MH})$.

The magnitude of the log odds ratio β (or the corresponding D) indicates the degree of DIF on the item. Conceptually, this may be represented by how far away the focal group IRF is from the reference group IRF. A $\beta = 0$ (or $D = 0$) indicates that the two groups performed the same on the item and the corresponding IRFs are superimposed. A positive value of β (or a negative D) indicates that, on average, reference group members tended to provide responses of 1 more often than comparable focal group members. Therefore, the reference group IRF is to the left of the focal group IRF by an amount "equal" to the magnitude of the DIF. In a proficiency testing context this means that the item is easier for reference group members than for focal group members of similar proficiency. In contrast, a negative value of β (or a positive D) indicates that, on average, focal group members tended to provide responses of 1 more often than comparable reference group members. Thus, the reference group IRF is to the right of the focal group IRF by an amount "equal" to the magnitude of the DIF. In addition to the simple point estimate of β, we can calculate a confidence interval for $\hat{\beta}$ to estimate the range within which the true logit would be expected to fall.

THE TSW LIKELIHOOD RATIO TEST

The Thissen, Steinberg, and Wainer (1988) DIF detection strategy is based on a comparison of the fit of two IRT models using the likelihood ratio test statistic introduced in Chapter 6. This comparison determines if there is a significant difference in model fit when one constrains an item to have the same location across groups versus when the item is free to have different locations across the manifest groups. Ideally, when we allow the item location to vary across the groups, the two location estimates should be identical. This would indicate that the item is performing the same in both groups. The null hypothesis tested by the likelihood ratio test (TSW-ΔG^2) is that there are no group differences in the item parameter estimates. One may also choose to include the discrimination parameter to simultaneously test whether this varies across groups.

Implementing the TSW-ΔG^2 approach is a three-step procedure. For example, assume we are investigating whether item 1 on an instrument is exhibiting DIF. In step 1 we would fit an IRT model, such as the 1PL model, to both manifest groups with the proviso that item parameter estimates for all items, except for item 1, be constrained to be equal across groups. As a result, it is possible for item 1 to have different item parameter estimates across the two groups. For step 2 we fit the same IRT model, but this time all item parameter estimates, including those of item 1, are constrained to be equal across both groups; this is the no DIF situation. Step 3 is the calculation of TSW-ΔG^2:

$$TSW\text{-}\Delta G^2 = G_2^2 - G_1^2 \qquad\qquad (12.3)$$

where G_1^2 and G_2^2 are the likelihood ratios from steps 1 and 2, respectively. TSW-ΔG^2 is distributed as a X^2 (when the sample size is large) with degrees of freedom equal to the number of item parameters allowed to differ across the groups and when the nesting model holds for the data. For example, with the 1PL model δ_j would be allowed to differ across groups and the *df* for evaluating the significance of TSW-ΔG^2 would be 1; for the 2PL model where both α and δ are simultaneously investigated, the *df* are 2, and so on. A significant TSW-ΔG^2 indicates the presence of DIF for the item under consideration. Conversely, a nonsignificant TSW-ΔG^2 indicates that the item is not exhibiting DIF. This three-step process is repeated for all the items on the instrument.

Using MULTILOG is the simplest way to perform this analysis because of the ease of specifying the equality constraints. The NEGATIVE TWICE THE LOGLIKELIHOOD value at the end of the output would be used as either G_1^2 or G_2^2, depending on which model is being fitted. To perform this analysis one would subdivide the calibration sample into the two manifest groups. The data file's structure would contain all the responses for the first group in columns 1 through L. Following these responses would be all the responses for the second group, but their responses would begin in the (L + 1)*th* column and continue to the 2L*th* column. The MULTILOG calibration would refer to the items by their ordinal positions in the data file rather than by their positions on the instrument. For instance, assuming a five-item instrument, group 1's responses to item 1 would be in column 1 and group 2's responses to item 1 would be in column 6, group 1's responses to item 2 would be in the second column and group 2's responses to item 2 would be in the seventh column, and so on. To impose the equality constraint on item 1 we would refer to items 1 and 6 (i.e., the first item on the instrument is labeled item 1 in group 1 and item 6 in group 2). Thissen et al. (1993) provide an example of implementing their procedure.

LOGISTIC REGRESSION

Logistic regression (LR) is a technique for making predictions about a binary variable from one or more variables. These predictor variables may be quantitative and/or qualitative. In the current context, the binary variable is the response to an item and the predictors might be gender and/or some measure of the construct. As such, we logistically regress the responses to item j on the construct measure and/or on gender.

In Chapter 2, Equation 2.1, we presented a general form of the LR model. By way of an example, the z in Equation 2.1 in a one predictor situation can be written as $\beta_0 + \beta_1 X$, where β_0 is the intercept (or constant), β_1 is the regression coefficient, and X is a predictor (e.g., gender). The model's p(x) may be interpreted as the conditional mean of the criterion, given x, when the logistic distribution is used (Hosmer & Lemeshow, 2000). Furthermore, we may extend z to include multiple predictors including the interaction of predictors. Therefore, the LR analysis allows us to assess the effect of one or more predictors on the observed responses for the item. Both Hosmer and Lemeshow (2000) and Agresti (1996) contain readable introductions to LR.

Conceptually, the application of LR to DIF analysis requires performing a logistic regression analysis for an item, using members of the reference group, and a second analysis for the same item with members of the focal group. The first analysis provides estimates for the constant (β_{0R}) and regression coefficient (β_{1R}) for the reference group. Similarly, the second analysis estimates the constant (β_{0F}) and regression coefficient (β_{1F}) for members of the focal group. If the intercept terms are equal (i.e., $\beta_{0R} = \beta_{0F}$) and the regression coefficients are equal (i.e., $\beta_{1R} = \beta_{1F}$), then the predicted probability curves are identical and there is no evidence of DIF. However, if the constants and/or the regression coefficients are unequal, then there is some indication of DIF. If the regression coefficients are equal (i.e., $\beta_{1R} = \beta_{1F}$), but the constants are unequal (i.e., $\beta_{0R} \neq \beta_{0F}$), then the predicted probability curves are separate and parallel to one another. This would represent uniform DIF. Conversely, if the coefficients are unequal (i.e., $\beta_{1R} \neq \beta_{1F}$), then the predicted probability curves cross and there is evidence of nonuniform DIF.

Although conceptually we may view the LR strategy for DIF analysis as two separate analyses, in practice, these two analyses are combined into a series of nesting and nested models. As a result, before we present the mechanics of the LR approach we need to supplement the terminology we have used so far.

Recall that the TSW likelihood ratio test compares a model that assumes a common *IRT-based* IRF for both the reference and focal groups (i.e., the "no DIF" model) with a second model that allows the IRFs to differ across these groups (i.e., "DIF exists" model). By imposing the equality constraints on the item parameter estimates in the "DIF exists" model, one obtains the "no DIF" model. As a result, the "no DIF" model may be seen as nested within the "DIF exists" model. Moreover, the "no DIF" model may be seen as a *reduced* version of the "DIF" model because it has fewer parameters than does the "DIF" model. Because the "DIF" model subsumes the "no DIF" model, the "DIF" model may be viewed as the *full* model. (Some individuals—for instance, Thissen et al. (1993)—prefer to call the reduced model a *compact* model and the full model the *augmented* model.) In Chapter 6 we introduced the likelihood ratio test statistic to determine whether the full model differed significantly from the reduced model:

$$\Delta G^2 = -2\ln\left[\frac{L_R}{L_F}\right] = -2\ln(L_R) - (-2\ln(L_F)) = -2[\ln(L_R) - \ln(L_F)] \qquad (12.4)$$

where L_R is the maximum of the likelihood for the reduced model and L_F is the maximum of the likelihood for the full model; we present the first form of ΔG^2 to show the "ratio" in the likelihood *ratio* test statistic.[3] The *df* for evaluating the significance of ΔG^2 are the difference in the number of parameters in the full and the reduced models.

In applying LR to DIF analysis, the full model is defined as (cf. Swaminathan & Rogers, 1990)

$$z = \tau_0 + \tau_1\Lambda + \tau_2\Gamma + \tau_3(\Lambda*\Gamma) \qquad (12.5)$$

where Λ is a measure of an individual's location on the latent variable (e.g., Λ may be θ or X), Γ is a categorical predictor variable indicating group membership for an individual (where $\Gamma = 1$ for members of the focal group and $\Gamma = 0$ for members of the reference group), and $(\Lambda*\Gamma)$ is the interaction of a person's location on the latent variable and his or her group membership.[4] Although Γ may be a manifest or latent categorical or continuous variable, in the following discussion we treat it as a categorical manifest variable to be consistent with the traditional application of LR to DIF analysis. (See Appendix E, "Should DIF Analyses Be Based on Latent Classes?" for an alternative conceptualization.) The term τ_1 indicates the relationship between the performance on the item and the person's location on the latent variable, τ_2 corresponds to the mean group difference in performance on the item (i.e., $\tau_2 = \beta_{0F} - \beta_{0R}$), and τ_3 reflects the group by person location interaction (i.e., $\tau_3 = \beta_{1F} - \beta_{1R}$).

With respect to the full model, there are two reduced models to consider. The first reduced model omits the interaction term in Equation 12.5. In this case the reduced model (1) is

$$z = \tau_0 + \tau_1\Lambda + \tau_2\Gamma \qquad (12.6)$$

A comparison of this reduced model (Equation 12.6) with the full model (Equation 12.5) tests to see whether the interaction term is necessary in order to account for response variability on the item of interest. In other words, ΔG^2 is used to determine whether we should retain or reject the null hypothesis that $\tau_3 = 0$. If we obtain a nonsignificant result (i.e., we retain the null hypothesis), then the model does not need the interaction term, given the other terms in the other model. Stated another way, we do not have evidence of nonuniform DIF for the item under consideration. Conversely, if we obtain a significant result, then there is evidence supporting the existence of nonuniform DIF and we should retain the interaction term in the model; this conclusion holds regardless of τ_2's value.

Equation 12.6 may be further compacted to create another reduced model. In this case, Equation 12.6 would be considered the "full" model and the new reduced model (2) would be

$$z = \tau_0 + \tau_1\Lambda \qquad (12.7)$$

A comparison of Equation 12.7 with Equation 12.6 would determine whether group membership is necessary to explain performance on the item, given the other terms in the model. That is, ΔG^2 is used to test the null hypothesis $\tau_2 = 0$. If we obtain a nonsignificant result, then the group membership variable may be dropped from the model because the (group) intercept terms are equal. If this is the case, then there would not be evidence of uniform DIF. However, if we obtain a significant result, then this would support the presence of uniform DIF. Implicit in this statement is that we have already determined that there is no evidence of a need for the interaction term (i.e., a comparison of Equations 12.6 and 12.5).

By appropriately formulating Λ, Swaminathan and Rogers (1990) show how the MH procedure is based on the LR model when Λ is considered to be discrete. Furthermore, the MH log odds ratio, $\beta = \ln(\alpha_{MH})$, is equal to Γ's regression coefficient in Equation 12.6 (i.e.,

τ_2). Stated another way, the magnitude of τ_2 indicates the difference between the reference and focal groups' average performance (e.g., in terms of the log odds of success) on the item; τ_2 reflects the degree of DIF on the item of interest. A complementary approach has been proposed by Zumbo (1999). Specifically, he proposed using the difference in the models' R^2s (ΔR^2) to assess the magnitude of DIF. His approach would be useful in the presence of a significant interaction.

There are at least two variants of Zumbo's (1999) approach because of the different types of R^2 statistics in logistic regression. One of these is the Nagelkerke R^2 (Nagelkerke, 1991), and a second is the weighted least squares R^2. Either of these can be used in $\Delta R^2 = R_F^2 - R_R^2$ to assess the DIF effect size in a comparison of the full model (R_F^2) with a reduced model (R_R^2). Because statistical packages like SAS and SPSS do not calculate the weighted least squares R^2, one would have to calculate it oneself. Zumbo (1999) contains an example of how to do this in SPSS. Guidelines for what constitutes a negligible, moderate, or large effect size for the weighted least squares R^2 may be found in Jodoin and Gierl (2001). In our example below we use Nagelkerke R^2.

To summarize, to perform the LR DIF procedure one implements a series of model comparisons using the ΔG^2 statistic. First, we compare the models in Equations 12.5 and 12.6 to test for nonuniform DIF (i.e., we test for an interaction term first). If there is evidence of (meaningful) nonuniform DIF, then the procedure is finished and the item is subjected to panel review to determine whether the item is biased. However, if there is no evidence of (meaningful) nonuniform DIF, then we proceed to test for uniform DIF by comparing the models in Equations 12.6 and 12.7. Again, if there is evidence of (meaningful) uniform DIF, then the item is submitted for review. These steps are analogous to not interpreting the main effects in a two-way ANOVA until after we have determined whether we have a significant interaction. Alternatively, we can directly compare the model in Equation 12.7 with the one in Equation 12.5 and perform a 2 *df* test of the presence of uniform or nonuniform. The gist of this series of model comparisons it to find the simplest model that describes the data. As is the case with other DIF methods, the LR technique is applied item by item. The null hypotheses tested are (1) $\tau_3 = 0$ (i.e., nonuniform DIF does not exist) and (2) $\tau_2 = 0$ (i.e., uniform DIF does not exist). Each statistical test is a one degree of freedom comparison. (For the 2 *df* test the null hypothesis is $\tau_2 = 0$ and $\tau_3 = 0$.) The null hypothesis of $\tau_1 = 0$ is not of particular interest because any reasonably well-constructed instrument will yield person locations that have a relationship to the odds of a response of 1. In effect, the test of $\tau_1 = 0$ is a test of a no predictor model. Although the above describes the technique's application to a binary response item, Zumbo (1999) discusses the technique's application to ordinal responses (also see French & Miller, 1996).

EXAMPLE: DIF ANALYSIS

To demonstrate the LR and MH DIF procedures we analyze data from a study by Subkoviak, Mack, Ironson, and Craig (1984). In their study, items that were expected to exhibit DIF were explicitly incorporated into an examination. Subkoviak et al. administered a 50-item four-option multiple-choice vocabulary test. The test consisted of 40 items that were drawn from the verbal section of the College Qualification Test and involved standard English vocabulary and 10 "Black slang" (B) items. Each item presented a word whose definition the examinee was to choose from one of the four options. Subkoviak et al. provided the following item as an example of a B item; its correct answer is identified by an asterisk:

Greasing   A. cleaning   *B. eating   C. arguing   D. talking

Subkoviak et al. hypothesized that the B items would exhibit DIF. Specifically, they believed that African Americans would find the B items to be easier than would Caucasian examinees. The 10 B items were randomly inserted in each block of 5 items on the test. The participants were 1008 African American and 1022 Caucasian students from two universities. The former originated from primarily urban areas and attended a predominantly African American university, whereas the latter were from the rural midwest and attended a predominantly Caucasian university.

We demonstrate a DIF analysis by using the MH and LR procedures to detect a single B item. Following traditional practice, the reference group represents the Caucasian students (i.e., the "majority" group) and the African Americans students are the focal group (i.e., the "minority" group). Therefore, given Subkoviak et al.'s hypothesis, our demonstration item should favor members of the focal group. We use the examinees' observed scores as a proxy of their locations on the vocabulary latent variable. It should be noted that, in practice, a DIF analysis would be performed using multiple combinations of reference and focal groups. That is, first the reference and focal groups would be Caucasian and African Americans, then the groups would be male and female, and so on.

MH Analysis

The SAS program for performing the MH analysis is presented in Table 12.1. The data consist of the participant's race (variable RACE, 0 = African American, 1= Caucasian) and the binary responses to items 1 through 50. These items have the variable names of i1, . . . , i50, respectively. We use the SUM statement to calculate the examinee's observed score, X. In practice, we would have a TABLES command for each item to be investigated. However, because we are examining DIF only for item 3, we have a single TABLES command. The TABLES command instructs SAS to create a three-way contingency table of observed score by examinee race by item 3's responses (i.e., tables x*race*i3). The subcommand CMH on the TABLES line indicates the calculation of the MH statistic; CMH is the acronym for the Cochran–Mantel–Haenszel statistic.

The abridged output is presented in Table 12.2. The MH value of 293.7933 (line labeled Nonzero Correlation) is significant at the 1% significance level; df =1. (The actual value of $\text{MH}_{\chi}2$ calculated according to Equation 12.1 is 295.6214, with the difference between the two reflecting the use of the "0.5" correction in Equation 12.1, but not in the SAS CMH statistic.) Using the value from the Case-Control Mantel-Haenszel line (i.e., α_{MH} = 0.1203), the magnitude of DIF for item 3 is β = ln(0.1203) = -2.118.

TABLE 12.1. SAS Program for Performing the MH Procedure on One Item

```
title 'MH DIF example analysis';
data d1;
  infile 'C:\example.dat';
  input (RACE i1-i50)(51*1.0);
  X=sum (of i1-i50);
proc freq;
  tables x*race*i3/CMH noprint;
```

The CMH analysis is done with respect to the group coded 0 (i.e., the focal group). Therefore, if α_{MH} is less than 1, then the item favors the focal group. Conversely, an α_{MH} greater than 1 indicates that the item favors the reference group and an α_{MH} of 1 indicates neutrality. For our example item, our α_{MH} of 0.1203 indicates that this item favors the focal group (i.e., African Americans). Therefore, (1) given the significant MH statistic, this item is exhibiting significant DIF across the two groups, (2) the odds of African Americans (i.e., the focal group) correctly responding to this item are more than eight times (i.e., 1/0.1203) the odds of Caucasians of similar proficiency (i.e., the reference group), and (3) on average and in terms of the log odds of success, African Americans find this item to be about twice as easy as Caucasians of comparable proficiency (i.e., $\beta = -2.118$). The significant MH would be interpreted as indicating the presence of uniform DIF on item 3. As mentioned above, this item would now be subjected to panel review to determine whether it is biased and appropriate corrective actions should be taken. (One may conjecture that the differential performance on this item is due to an opportunity to learn the relevant material.)

TABLE 12.2. Abridged MH Output

Summary Statistics for race by i1
Controlling for X

Cochran-Mantel-Haenszel Statistics (Based on Table Scores)

Statistic	Alternative Hypothesis	DF	Value	Prob
1	Nonzero Correlation	1	293.7933	<.0001
2	Row Mean Scores Differ	1	293.7933	<.0001
3	General Association	1	293.7933	<.0001

Estimates of the Common Relative Risk (Row1/Row2)

Type of Study	Method	Value	95% Confidence Limits	
Case-Control (Odds Ratio)	Mantel-Haenszel	0.1203	0.0923	0.1568
	Logit **	0.1464	0.1126	0.1904
Cohort (Col1 Risk)	Mantel-Haenszel	0.2338	0.1992	0.2844
	Logit **	0.3330	0.2837	0.3909
Cohort (Col2 Risk)	Mantel-Haenszel	1.7889	1.6638	1.9234
	Logit **	1.6850	1.5856	1.7907

** These logit estimators use a correction of 0.5 in every cell
of those tables that contain a zero. Tables with a zero
row or a zero column are not included in computing the
logit estimators.

Logistic Regression Analysis

We now analyze our data using logistic regression. For all models, X represents the observed score and RACE denotes the examinee's race. The first step is to compare the full model with the reduced model (1) to investigate the existence of nonuniform DIF. These models are

full model: $z_j = \tau_0 + \tau_1(X) + \tau_2{}^*RACE + \tau_3(X{}^*RACE)$

and

reduced model (1): $z_{j.} = \tau_0 + \tau_1(X) + \tau_2{}^*RACE$

The comparison of these two models determines whether the interaction term, (X*RACE), significantly improves model fit. If there is a significant improvement, then there is evidence of nonuniform DIF. Depending on the outcome of the first step, a second analysis is performed. This analysis determines whether the inclusion of RACE as a predictor leads to a significant improvement in model fit over simply using the observed score. The corresponding models are

"full" model: $z_j = \tau_0 + \tau_1(X) + \tau_2{}^*RACE$

and

reduced model (2): $z_j = \tau_0 + \tau_1(X)$

If there is a significant difference between these two models, then we know that the RACE predictor accounts for a significant portion of the variability in the responses to item j. Stated another way, there is evidence of uniform DIF.

Table 12.3 contains the SAS program for performing the various model comparisons. As with the MH analysis, the line X=sum (of i1-i50) creates the observed score, X. The item of interest, i3, is regressed on the predictors X, RACE, and the interaction of X and RACE in the full model (i.e., model i3=x race x*race;). The subsequent logistic regression compares the "full" model (i.e., the reduced model (1)/"full" model: model i3=x race;) and the reduced model (2) (i.e., model i3=x;). The corresponding output is presented in Table 12.4.

Convergence is achieved for all analyses. From the Model Fit Statistics section, the last entry in the Intercept and Covariates column labeled -2 Log L provides us with the models' log likelihood statistics. Specifically,

full model: $-2\ln(L_F) = 2217.517$

and

reduced model (1)/"full" model: $-2\ln(L_{R_1}) = 2258.923$

TABLE 12.3. SAS Program for Performing the LR DIF Procedure on One Item

```
title 'logistic regression DIF analysis';
data d1;
  infile 'C:\example.dat';
  input (race i1-i50)(51*1.0);
  X=sum (of i1-i50);

/* Full model */
proc logistic descending;
  model i3=x race x*race/rsquare;

/* reduce model (1)/"full" model */
proc logistic descending;
  model i3=x race/rsquare;

/* reduce model (2) */
proc logistic descending;
  model i3=x/rsquare;
run;
```

For determining the presence of nonuniform DIF, we have

$$\Delta G^2 = -2 \ln(L_{R_1}) - (2 \ln(L_F)) = 2258.923 - 2217.517 = 44.407$$

With 1 df the critical X^2 at the 5% significance level is 3.84. As a result, we have evidence of significant nonuniform DIF. To obtain a measure of the effect size we examine the difference in R^2s. SAS provides both the Cox and Snell R^2 (labeled R-Square) as well as the Nagelkerke R^2 (labeled Max-rescaled R-Square). Using the Nagelkerke R^2s for this item we have an $R_F^2 = 0.2200$ for the full model, and for the reduced model (1) $R_{R_1}^2 = 0.1958$. The magnitude of our nonuniform DIF is

$$\Delta R^2 = R_F^2 - R_{R_1}^2 = 0.2200 - 0.1958 = 0.0242$$

Therefore, although this item is exhibiting significant nonuniform DIF, the magnitude of ΔR^2 makes it questionable as to whether it should be subjected to panel review for evidence of bias.

Our estimated models are

full model: $z_3 = \hat{\tau}_0 + \hat{\tau}_1(X) + \hat{\tau}_2*\text{RACE} + \hat{\tau}_3(X*\text{RACE})$

$= 1.3330 - 0.1371(X) - 0.7714*\text{RACE} + 0.1171(X*\text{RACE})$

and

reduced model (1): $z_3 = \hat{\tau}_0 + \hat{\tau}_1 X + \hat{\tau}_2*\text{RACE}$

$= -0.5558 - 0.0481(X) + 1.9577*\text{RACE}$

TABLE 12.4. Abridged LR DIF Output for Comparison of the Full Model with the Reduced Model (1)

```
/* Full model */
                         The LOGISTIC Procedure

                          Model Fit Statistics
                                              Intercept
                                  Intercept      and
                     Criterion      Only      Covariates
                     AIC          2568.331     2225.517
                     SC           2573.947     2247.980
                     -2 Log L     2566.331     2217.517

         R-Square    0.1579   Max-rescaled R-Square   0.2200

                 Testing Global Null Hypothesis: BETA=0
         Test                  Chi-Square    DF    Pr > ChiSq

         Likelihood Ratio       348.8144      3      <.0001
         Score                  302.5715      3      <.0001
         Wald                   238.7854      3      <.0001

              Analysis of Maximum Likelihood Estimates
                                   Standard       Wald
         Parameter   DF   Estimate   Error    Chi-Square   Pr > ChiSq
         Intercept   1     1.3330    0.3626    13.5133       0.0002
         X           1    -0.1371    0.0173    63.0854       <.0001
         race        1    -0.7714    0.4484     2.9596       0.0854
         X*race      1     0.1171    0.0193    36.9106       <.0001

:
/* reduce model (1)/"full" model */
:
                          Model Fit Statistics
                                              Intercept
                                  Intercept      and
                     Criterion      Only      Covariates
                     AIC          2568.331     2264.923
                     SC           2573.947     2281.771
                     -2 Log L     2566.331     2258.923

         R-Square    0.1405   Max-rescaled R-Square   0.1958

                 Testing Global Null Hypothesis: BETA=0
         Test                  Chi-Square    DF    Pr > ChiSq
         Likelihood Ratio       307.4075      2      <.0001
         Score                  292.7168      2      <.0001
         Wald                   262.7802      2      <.0001

              Analysis of Maximum Likelihood Estimates
                                   Standard       Wald
         Parameter   DF   Estimate   Error    Chi-Square   Pr > ChiSq

         Intercept   1    -0.5558    0.1880     8.7427       0.0031
         X           1    -0.0481    0.00749   41.2621       <.0001
         race        1     1.9577    0.1211   261.3266       <.0001

                      Odds Ratio Estimates
                         Point          95% Wald
              Effect   Estimate    Confidence Limits
              X         0.953      0.939      0.967
              race      7.083      5.586      8.981
:
```

Normally, when we find significant nonuniform DIF we would not proceed to examine the item for uniform DIF.[5] This is tantamount to obtaining a significant interaction term in ANOVA and proceeding to interpret the main effects. However, because the magnitude of the nonuniform DIF is small, and for pedagogical reasons, we proceed to perform a second analysis for uniform DIF. Table 12.5 contains the results of this analysis. For the reduced model (2) we have a $-2 \ln(L_{R_2}) = 2565.709$ and from above we have a $-2 \ln(L_{\text{"f"}}) = 2258.923$ for the "full" model (i.e., reduced model (1)). Therefore, comparing the reduced model (2) with the "full" model we have

$$\Delta G^2 = -2 \ln(L_{R_2}) - (2 \ln(L_{\text{"f"}})) = 2565.709 - 2258.923 = 306.786$$

With 1 df this ΔG^2 is significant at the 5% significance level and indicates the presence of uniform DIF. (This test is similar to the MH test performed above [i.e., a test for uniform DIF].) The sign of $\hat{\tau}_2$ indicates the directionality of the DIF. Given our coding of the RACE variable, if $\hat{\tau}_2 > 0$, then the item favors the focal group. In contrast, if $\hat{\tau}_2 < 0$, then the item favors the reference group.[6] The effect size associated with this significant ΔG^2 is non-negligible:

$$\Delta R^2 = R^2_{R_1} - R^2_{R_2} = 0.1958 - 0.0004 = 0.1954$$

TABLE 12.5. Abridged LR DIF Output for the Reduced Model (2)

```
:
/* reduce model (2) */
:
                                Model Fit Statistics
                                                    Intercept
                                        Intercept       and
                    Criterion            Only       Covariates
                    AIC                 2568.331      2569.709
                    SC                  2573.947      2580.941
                    -2 Log L            2566.331      2565.709

          R-Square    0.0003    Max-rescaled R-Square    0.0004

                  Testing Global Null Hypothesis: BETA=0
          Test                 Chi-Square      DF      Pr > ChiSq
          Likelihood Ratio       0.6217        1         0.4304
          Score                  0.6223        1         0.4302
          Wald                   0.6221        1         0.4303

                  Analysis of Maximum Likelihood Estimates
                                     Standard        Wald
          Parameter    DF    Estimate   Error    Chi-Square    Pr > ChiSq

          Intercept    1     -0.8521    0.1727     24.3530      <.0001
          X            1      0.00488   0.00619     0.6221       0.4303

                        Odds Ratio Estimates
                           Point          95% Wald
                  Effect   Estimate    Confidence Limits
                  X         1.005      0.993      1.017
:
```

To summarize, the MH statistic identified item 3 as exhibiting DIF that would typically be interpreted as uniform DIF. The LR analysis indicated significant nonuniform DIF (as well as significant uniform DIF). To explain why the MH statistic is able to identify an item exhibiting nonuniform DIF, we perform the simple logistic regression of the item on the observed score separately for each racial group. The results for the reference and focal groups are presented in Table 12.6. The resulting models are

$$\text{reference group} \quad z_3 = b_{0R} + b_{1R}X = -0.5616 + 0.0199(X)$$

and

$$\text{focal group} \quad z_3 = b_{0F} + b_{1F}X = -1.3332 + 0.1371(X)$$

TABLE 12.6. Abridged Logistic Regression Output for the Reference and Focal Groups

Reference Group Results
:

```
                      Model Fit Statistics
                                          Intercept
                             Intercept       and
              Criterion        Only       Covariates
              AIC            1418.542      1415.153
              SC             1423.472      1425.012
              -2 Log L       1416.542      1411.153
```
:
```
                Analysis of Maximum Likelihood Estimates
                             Standard           Wald
   Parameter    DF   Estimate   Error    Chi-Square   Pr > ChiSq
   Intercept    1    -0.5616    0.2637     4.5353        0.0332
   X            1     0.0199    0.00860    5.3560        0.0207
```
```
                    Odds Ratio Estimates
                      Point          95% Wald
              Effect  Estimate    Confidence Limits
              X        1.020      1.003    1.037
```
:

Focal Group Results
:
```
                      Model Fit Statistics
                                          Intercept
                             Intercept       and
              Criterion        Only       Covariates
              AIC             887.445      810.364
              SC              892.361      820.195
              -2 Log L        885.445      806.364
```
:
```
                Analysis of Maximum Likelihood Estimates
                             Standard           Wald
   Parameter    DF   Estimate   Error    Chi-Square   Pr > ChiSq
   Intercept    1    -1.3332    0.3626    13.5168        0.0002
   X            1     0.1371    0.0173    63.0913       <.0001
```
```
                    Odds Ratio Estimates
                      Point          95% Wald
              Effect  Estimate    Confidence Limits
              X        1.147      1.109     1.186
```
:

A comparison of the intercepts for the two models (i.e., b_{0F} and b_{0R}) shows that they are unequal and are not within 1 standard error of one another. Similarly, comparing the two models' regression coefficient estimates (i.e., b_{1F} and b_{1R}), we see that they are unequal and differ by more than twice their standard errors. These differences reflect the DIF of the item. We can relate these differences back to the full model's estimates from Table 12.4. For instance, the difference between b_{0F} and b_{0R} equals the coefficient for the RACE variable in the full model

$$\hat{\tau}_2 = b_{0F} - b_{0R} = -1.3332 - (-0.5616) = -0.7716.$$

It is this difference in the intercepts that the MH is, in effect, capturing. With respect to the regression coefficients, the difference between b_{1F} and b_{1R} equals the coefficient for the RACE by X interaction term in the full model (Table 12.4)

$$\hat{\tau}_3 = b_{1F} - b_{1R} = 0.1371 - 0.0199 = 0.1172.$$

The magnitude of our $\hat{\tau}_2$ and $\hat{\tau}_3$ indicate the degree of uniform and nonuniform DIF, respectively.

In Figure 12.3 we plot the logit regression lines for each model; the minimum and maximum observed scores in the data are 7 and 48, respectively. As can be seen, the focal group members have an advantage over comparable reference group members throughout the observed score metric. However, we can see that this advantage varies as a function of the observed score and thereby reflects nonuniform DIF. In this case, because there is an ordinal interaction present with this item, we do not observe the cancellation that we spoke

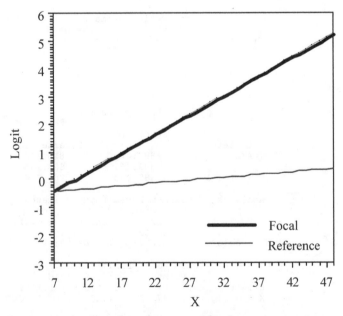

FIGURE 12.3. Logit regression lines for reference and focal groups.

about above in the "Mantel–Haenszel Chi-Square" section. Swaminathan and Rogers (1990) conjecture that in the case of nonuniform DIF the MH statistic may be able to do a better job of detecting an ordinal interaction than a disordinal interaction. (A disordinal interaction occurs when the logit regression lines cross within the observed score range.) Given the possibility of cancellation, the MH statistic is not designed for detecting nonuniform DIF. However, as this example shows, there are some cases of nonuniform DIF that the MH statistic may detect. Therefore, a significant MH statistic does not necessarily indicate uniform DIF.

SUMMARY

Differential item functioning occurs when performance on an item is a function not only of a person's location, but also of tangential factor(s). DIF may be conceptualized as occurring when an item's response function changes across different groups of respondents. The groups are typically referred to as the reference and focal groups. The focal group is the one being investigated to see if it is disadvantaged (or advantaged) by the item and, in general, is the "minority" group. The reference group is the comparison group and, in general, is the "majority" group. DIF methods not only detect the presence of DIF, but also whether the focal or reference group is favored.

There are two forms of DIF. In one form, uniform DIF, one group performs better than the other group throughout the continuum. Graphically, uniform DIF is represented as a reference group IRF that is parallel to the focal group IRF. In the other form, nonuniform DIF, the reference group performs better than the focal group for a particular portion of the continuum, whereas along a different portion of the continuum the focal group performs better than the reference group. Graphically, nonuniform DIF is represented as a reference group IRF that crosses the focal group IRF. In short, for nonuniform DIF there is an interaction between performance on the item, group membership, and location along the latent continuum, whereas for uniform DIF there is no interaction.

There are several approaches that can be used to identify whether an item is exhibiting DIF. Some of these approaches are IRT-based (e.g., TSW-ΔG^2), whereas others are not (e.g., Mantel–Haenszel Chi-Square, logistic regression). If an item is identified as exhibiting DIF, this does not automatically mean that the item is biased. For an item to be considered biased, the DIF item is subjected to review by a panel of experts to determine whether the source of an item's differential performance is relevant or irrelevant to the construct being measured by the instrument. It is the panel's conclusion that determines whether an item exhibiting DIF is also biased. As a consequence, if a researcher is developing an instrument, then he or she may simply be concerned with whether one or more items are exhibiting DIF but not whether any DIF items are also biased. If this is the case, then there would not be a need to establish a formal bias review panel. In addition, in making decisions about the removal of items exhibiting DIF, the researcher should take into account both the magnitude of the DIF and statistical significance vis-à-vis the sample size, as well as the number of different Reference/Focal group comparisons that were used in the DIF analysis (i.e., male vs. female, Racial Group 1 vs. Racial Group 2, Ethnic Group 1 vs. Ethnic Group 2, etc.). For instance, because statistical tests are influenced, in part, by the sample size, it is possible to obtain a statistically significant DIF statistic with a very large sample size even though the magnitude of the DIF is not meaningful. As a result, the researcher may wish to adopt a procedure similar to that used at ETS. For instance, only items with a significant test statistic (e.g., $\alpha = 0.05$) and $|\beta|$ of 0.64 should be culled from the instrument. (See Dorans and Holland [1993] for specific details on ETS's DIF item classification procedure.)

One potential advantage of the LR approach over the TSW-ΔG^2 approach is that LR does not require any of the assumptions underlying IRT. With respect to the MH technique, the LR approach allows an examination of both uniform and nonuniform DIF. Whether the MH$_\chi 2$ would flag an item for nonuniform DIF depends on the amount of cancellation that takes place. That is, the MH$_\chi 2$ may or may not identify nonuniform DIF. An additional potential advantage of the LR DIF method over the MH approach is that the LR approach allows the use of a nondiscrete person location predictor. In contrast, with the MH statistic the (discrete) observed scores are used for conditioning. Further, the LR technique can be used with the observed scores or with other continuous variables in lieu of the observed scores. Unlike the other approaches mentioned, the LR procedure allows for the use of covariates. Given these advantages, we prefer the LR DIF method over other DIF approaches.

NOTES

1. This chapter's presentation is concerned with changes in item parameter estimates *across groups*. However, a different form of DIF involves changes in item parameter estimates *over time*. This type of DIF is known as *item parameter drift* or *item drift* (Thissen et al., 1988). To investigate item drift one may use the Thissen et al. (1988) likelihood ratio (TSW-ΔG^2) approach discussed in this chapter.

2. The program IRTDIF (Kim & Cohen, 1992) can be used to perform the Lord's Chi-Square, Exact Signed Area, and H Statistic approaches.

3. In the context of the TSW-ΔG^2, the procedure's step 1 yields the full model (i.e., $G_1^2 = G_F^2$) and step 2 results in the reduced model (i.e., $G_2^2 = G_R^2$). Therefore,

$$\Delta G^2 = G_2^2 - G_1^2 = G_R^2 - G_F^2$$

The log likelihood statistics are

$$G_2^2 = G_R^2 = -2\ln(L_R) \quad \text{and} \quad G_1^2 = G_F^2 = -2\ln(L_F)$$

Then, by substitution, the likelihood ratio test is

$$\Delta G^2 = G_R^2 = G_F^2 = -2\ln(L_R) - (2\ln(L_F)) = -2[\ln(L_R) - \ln(L_F)]$$

4. Although DIF analyses occur in a nonexperimental setting, we refer to the product of group membership and a person's location as their *interaction* rather than as their *joint relationship* (see Pedhauzer, 1997).

5. We could compare the full model's $-2\ln L$ with that of reduced model (2) to simultaneously

test for uniform and nonuniform DIF. This would be a two *df* test with the significance level reduced to, say 0.01, to account for the multiple hypotheses being tested (Zumbo, 1999). For our example this test would be significant with a value of

$$\Delta G^2 = -2 \ln(L_{R_2}) - (2 \ln(L_F)) = 2565.709 - 2217.517 = 348{:}193$$

Furthermore, $\Delta R^2 = R_F^2 - R_{R_2}^2 = 0.2200 - 0.0004 = 0.2196$. Therefore, we have evidence of DIF and a large effect size.

6. As an example of the interpretation of the coefficient estimates in the model, assume that the reduced model (1)/"full" model is the model of interest (i.e., the interaction term in the full model did *not* lead to a significant improvement in fit). From Table 12.4 our model is

reduced model (1): $z_3 = -0.5558 - 0.0481(X) + 1.9577 * \text{RACE}$

Therefore, holding the observed score fixed and switching from the reference group to the focal group results in an increase in the log odds of obtaining a response of 1 by 1.9577. Alternatively, in terms of odds, we have that the odds that a focal group member will produce a response of 1 are exp(1.9577) = 7.0830 to 1 (note: 7.0830 is the value listed as the Point Estimate in the Odds Ratio Estimates section). In short, holding the observed score fixed, one expects the odds of focal group members to correctly respond to the item to be roughly 7 to 1 relative to comparable reference group members.

Maximum Likelihood Estimation
of Person Locations

This appendix uses the likelihood of an individual's observed response vector to estimate the person's location. We present two approaches, the first is a simplistic approach, whereas the second is a more sophisticated strategy that is commonly used. For both approaches we assume that we know the item parameters.

In general, the probability of a response vector, $\underline{x}$, is given by

$$p(\underline{x}|\theta, \underline{\vartheta}) = \prod_{j=1}^{L} p_j(\theta)^{x_j}(1 - p_j(\theta))^{1-x_j} \qquad (A.1)$$

where p_j is short for $p(x_j|\theta, \alpha, \delta_j)$, x_j is the binary response to item j, L is the number of items on the instrument, $\underline{\vartheta}$ is a matrix containing the item parameters (e.g., α and δ_js), and "$\prod$" is the product symbol. Once the responses are observed this expression becomes a likelihood function (Hambleton & Swaminathan, 1985). That is, the likelihood of person i's observed response vector, $\underline{x}_i$, is given by

$$L(\underline{x}_i|\theta_i, \underline{\vartheta}) = \prod_{j=1}^{L} p_j^{x_{ij}} (1 - p_j)^{(1-x_{ij})}$$

and

$$\ln L(\underline{x}_i|\theta_i, \underline{\vartheta}) = \sum_{j=1}^{L} (x_{ij}\ln(p_j) + (1-x_{ij})\ln(1-p_j)) \qquad (A.2)$$

where $\ln L(\underline{x}_i|\theta_i, \underline{\vartheta})$ is the log likelihood function. The location of the maximum of the likelihood function is the same as that of the maximum of the log likelihood function. In the following we use the log likelihood function and for notational convenience symbolize it as $\ln L$.

ESTIMATING AN INDIVIDUAL'S LOCATION: EMPIRICAL MAXIMUM LIKELIHOOD ESTIMATION

Empirical maximum likelihood estimation (MLE) is a comparatively crude method of determining the location of the maximum of a likelihood function. Its main advantage is that it does not require knowledge of a function's derivatives and therefore is useful for initial or exploratory work. In this approach the maximum may be determined by performing a binary search of the $\ln L$ throughout the θ

347

range of interest (this is conceptually equivalent to the bisection method used in numerical analysis). We start by setting a lower bound (LB) and an upper bound (UB) at, say –3.0 and 3.0, respectively. This range is bisected (the initial $\hat{\theta}$ is $\theta_0 = 0.0$) and we determine whether lnL is greater above or below $\hat{\theta}_0$. If lnL is less than that at $\hat{\theta}_0$, then the next iteration has a new UB set at 0 (i.e., the previous $\hat{\theta}$) and the range between this new UB and the LB is bisected. Therefore, the revised $\hat{\theta}_1$ is –1.5, the halfway point between –3.0 and 0.0. Again, we determine whether lnL is greater above or below $\hat{\theta}_1$ and the lower/upper bounds are appropriately reset. This process continues until the θ at which lnL has its maximum is determined to a desired degree of accuracy. We applied this approach to the log likelihood for the pattern 11000 (Figure A.1). The vertical line in the body of the graph shows that the location of the maximum of the log likelihood for the response pattern 11000 occurs at approximately –0.85. This value would be our $\hat{\theta}$ for this response pattern. As can be seen from Figure A.1, the $\hat{\theta}$ is the mode of the likelihood function.

ESTIMATING AN INDIVIDUAL'S LOCATION: NEWTON'S METHOD FOR MLE

The empirical MLE approach is inefficient and does not provide us with a standard error of estimate (i.e., an index of the accuracy of our estimate). Its primary advantage is that it can be applied without knowledge of the derivatives of the likelihood function. However, a more sophisticated approach provides the sample standard error of estimate and uses the derivatives of the likelihood function. The idea of a likelihood and the maximum likelihood method is presented by Fisher (1971a, 1971b). In the following we first describe the method and then apply it in the IRT context.

To understand this approach, examine the lnL function shown in Figure A.2. We have drawn a series of lines tangent to the function that vary in their respective slopes (these are the lines labeled (a), (b), and (c)). As we progress from line (a) to line (c) we see that the slope is greatest for line (a)

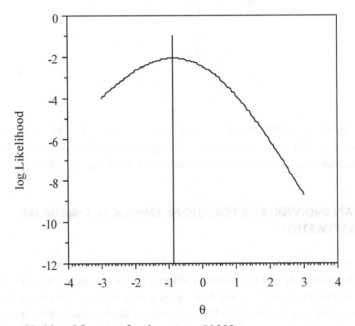

FIGURE A.1. Log likelihood function for the pattern 11000.

and decreases until for line (c) it is 0. Therefore, to find the location of the maximum of the function we simply need to determine where the slope of the tangent line is equal to zero. Symbolically,

$$\text{slope} = \frac{\text{change in Y}}{\text{change in X}} = \frac{\Delta Y}{\Delta X} = 0$$

or, alternatively, the slope is zero when

$$\Delta Y = 0$$

To find the maximum of the ln$L$ function we use an iterative process. The θ at which ln$L$ is maximized (i.e., the slope = 0) is found by iterating through a series of θs, with each iteration's $\hat{\theta}$ reflecting a refinement over the previous iteration's $\hat{\theta}$. The process continues to entertain improved θs until the difference between two successive $\hat{\theta}$s is considered to be unimportant. This approach to finding the root of an equation is called Newton's method and is a commonly used method for solving equations.[1,2]

The bisection method described above worked by bracketing a range of θ and searching the bracket for the location of the maximum of ln$L$. This location is subsequently improved or refined by halving the bracket and reperforming the search. By making the brackets progressively smaller across iterations, one could find the location of the maximum to a desired degree of accuracy. Newton's method works in a similar iterative fashion. Conceptually, Newton's method consists of a series of progressively smaller right triangles (rather than brackets). One of these triangles is shown in Figure A.3; the right triangle is inverted. The hypotenuse of the right triangle in Figure A.3 corresponds to one of the tangent lines shown in Figure A.2 (e.g., line (a)). The horizontal leg of the triangle (the "adjacent leg" to the angle ω) reflects the change in the horizontal axis, ΔX, whereas the vertical leg of the triangle (the "opposite leg" to the angle ω) reflects the change in the vertical axis, ΔY. Moreover,

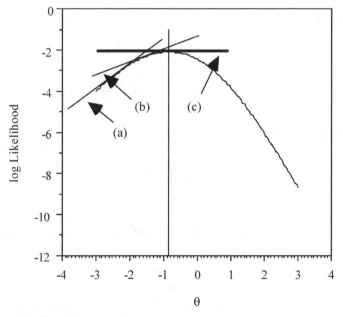

FIGURE A.2. Log likelihood function for the pattern 11000.

the "height" of the function at a point (e.g., $\hat{\theta}^{(0)}$) is the length of the opposite leg at that point and is given by $f(\hat{\theta}^{(0)})$. Stated symbolically, $\Delta Y = f(\hat{\theta}^{(0)})$.

To start Newton's method requires an initial "guesstimate" or provisional estimate $(\hat{\theta}^{(0)})$ of the maximum's location, and we stop when $\Delta Y = 0$ (i.e., when the opposite leg has zero length we have found the maximum of the function). The equality "$\Delta Y = 0$" means that $\Delta Y = 0$ is true to some desired degree of accuracy.

To improve the initial estimate, $\hat{\theta}^{(0)}$, requires knowledge of a few facts:

1. The tangent (tan) of an angle, ω, is equal to the ratio of the opposite leg over the adjacent leg. That is,

$$\tan(\omega) = \frac{\text{opposite leg}}{\text{adjacent leg}}$$

2. The first derivative of a function is the slope of a line tangent to that function and is symbolized as $f'(x)$.
3. The line that is tangent to the function in Figure A.3 is the triangle's hypotenuse.
4. The point at which the tangent line crosses the abscissa defines the length of the adjacent leg, ΔX, or $\Delta X = (\hat{\theta}^{(0)} - \hat{\theta}^{(1)})$.

Given Fact #1 and that $\Delta Y =$ "opposite leg" and $\Delta X =$ "adjacent leg," this means that

$$\tan(\omega) = \frac{\text{opposite leg}}{\text{adjacent leg}} = \frac{\Delta Y}{\Delta X}$$

Therefore, $\tan(\omega)$ is the slope of the line tangent to the function, and given Fact #3, we know that this tangent line is the right triangle's hypotenuse. Combining Facts #1–#4, recalling that $\Delta Y = f(\hat{\theta}^{(0)})$, and by substitution, one has that the

$$\tan(\omega) = \text{slope} = f'(\hat{\theta}^{(0)}) = \frac{\Delta Y}{\Delta X} = \frac{f(\hat{\theta}^{(0)})}{\hat{\theta}^{(0)} - \hat{\theta}^{(1)}} \qquad (A.3)$$

Solving for (isolating) $\hat{\theta}^{(1)}$ yields

$$\hat{\theta}^{(1)} = \hat{\theta}^{(0)} - \frac{f(\hat{\theta}^{(0)})}{f'(\hat{\theta}^{(0)})} \qquad (A.4)$$

Stated in words, Equation A.4 says that the value $\hat{\theta}^{(0)}$ may be improved upon by projecting the tangent line from the point $f(\hat{\theta}^{(0)})$ toward the abscissa (i.e., from Fact #2 we know that the tangent line is the first derivative, $f'(\hat{\theta}^{(0)})$, at $\hat{\theta}^{(0)}$). The tangent line's point of intersection with the abscissa produces a new estimate, $\hat{\theta}^{(1)}$. The change from $\hat{\theta}^{(0)}$ to the new $\hat{\theta}$ is ΔX (i.e., $\Delta X = (\hat{\theta}^{(0)} - \hat{\theta}^{(1)})$). A single application of Equation A.4 to improve $\hat{\theta}^{(0)}$ is one step or iteration. After conducting one iteration we may or may not be at the location of the maximum of the log likelihood function. How-

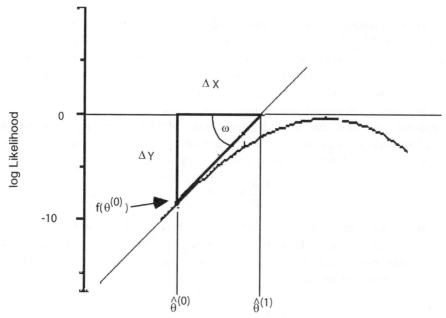

FIGURE A.3. One step in the Newton method.

ever, Equation A.4 may be reapplied to "construct" a (we hope, smaller) new right triangle using $\hat{\theta}^{(1)}$ in lieu of $\hat{\theta}^{(0)}$ (e.g., the hypotenuse of this new right triangle would be line (b) in Figure A.2). This idea of conducting multiple iterations may be symbolized by rewriting Equation A.4 as

$$\hat{\theta}^{t+1} = \hat{\theta}^t - \frac{f(\hat{\theta}^t)}{f'(\hat{\theta}^t)} \qquad (A.5)$$

where t stands for the t*th* iteration, t = 1 . . . T, and T is the maximum number of iterations. Equation A.5 says that we can improve the t*th* estimate of the location of the maximum by changing it by an amount equal to $f(\hat{\theta}^t)/f'(\hat{\theta}^t)$. As mentioned above, when $\Delta Y = 0$ (i.e., $f(\hat{\theta}^t) = 0$), then the location of the maximum has been found and we have our $\hat{\theta}$. Stated another way, we have found the maximum when the step size $f(\hat{\theta}^t)/f'(\hat{\theta}^t) = 0$ or, alternatively, $\hat{\theta}^{t+1} = \hat{\theta}^t$. Therefore, after calculating $\hat{\theta}^{t+1}$ we can check to see if $\hat{\theta}^{t+1} = \hat{\theta}^t$. If the answer is "yes," then the iterations stop because we have found the location of the maximum; the location is given by $\hat{\theta}^{t+1}$. However, if the answer is "no," then we can improve the current estimate by calculating a new step size. In effect, we refine our estimate of the location of the maximum by stepping along the log likelihood function in steps of size $f(\hat{\theta}^t)/f'(\hat{\theta}^t)$. If the function is well behaved (e.g., it is *not* flat), then the step size becomes progressively smaller as the iterations proceed. The signs of $f(\hat{\theta}^t)$ and $f'(\hat{\theta}^t)$ do not have to be the same.[3]

Because of the way decimal values are represented on a computer it is difficult to test for an equality (e.g., $\hat{\theta}^{t+1} = \hat{\theta}^t$ or $f(\hat{\theta}^t) = 0$). Therefore, the difference between successive $\hat{\theta}$s (i.e., ($\hat{\theta}^{t+1} - \hat{\theta}^t$)) is checked to see if the $\hat{\theta}$s are "indistinguishable" from one another. If they are indistinguishable, then the process is said to have *converged* and we have determined the location of the maximum. What is considered indistinguishable (i.e., what defines a zero change) is given by the *convergence criterion* (e.g., $\Xi = 0.001$). Therefore, when $(\hat{\theta}^{t+1} - \hat{\theta}^{t}) < \Xi$ is true, then we have a *converged solution*, $\hat{\theta}^{t+1}$ is the estimate of location of the maximum, and convergence is achieved in t+1 iterations. However, when $(\hat{\theta}^{t+1} - \hat{\theta}^{t}) > \Xi$, then we do not have a converged solution and another iteration is performed. How many iterations one performs depends on the maximum number of iterations, MaxIt (e.g., MaxIt = 25). As a result, there are two criteria that must be met before another iteration is performed (i.e., $(\hat{\theta}^{t+1} - \hat{\theta}^{t}) > \Xi$ and t < MaxIt). If $(\hat{\theta}^{t+1} - \hat{\theta}^{t}) > \Xi$ and if t equals MaxIt, then the estimation process stops even though it has not converged, and we have a *nonconverged* solution.

In applying Newton's method to the IRT the function of interest is the log likelihood function. That is, the function $f(\hat{\theta}^{t})$ that is set to 0 is the first derivative of the ln$L$ function, $f(\theta^{t}) = \frac{\partial}{\partial\theta}\ln L(\underline{x}|\theta)$. Therefore, the maximum of the log likelihood function is found (if it exists) when

$$\frac{\partial}{\partial\theta}\ln L(\underline{x}|\theta) = 0 \qquad (A.6)$$

If we look at the form of the step size in Equation A.5, we see that it has the form of a ratio of a function to its derivative (i.e., $f(\hat{\theta}^{t})/f'(\hat{\theta}^{t})$). In the IRT case, $f(\theta^{t})$ is the first derivative of ln$L$. As a result, the step size is equal to the first derivative over its derivative (i.e., the second derivative). Therefore, with respect to θ, the step size is

$$\frac{f(\theta^{t})}{f'(\theta^{t})} = \frac{\dfrac{\partial}{\partial\theta}\ln L(\underline{x}|\theta^{t})}{\dfrac{\partial^{2}}{\partial\theta^{2}}\ln L(\underline{x}|\theta^{t})} \qquad (A.7)$$

By substituting Equation A.7 into Equation A.5, our formula for improving our estimate of the location of the maximum of person i's log likelihood function becomes

$$\theta_{i}^{t+1} = \theta_{i}^{t} - \frac{\dfrac{\partial}{\partial\theta}\ln L(\underline{x}|\theta_{i}^{t})}{\dfrac{\partial^{2}}{\partial\theta^{2}}\ln L(\underline{x}|\theta_{i}^{t})} \qquad (A.8)$$

The equations for $\frac{\partial}{\partial\theta}\ln L(\underline{x}|\theta_{i}^{t})$ and $\frac{\partial^{2}}{\partial\theta^{2}}\ln L(\underline{x}|\theta_{i}^{t})$ vary from model to model. The simplest forms of these belong to the Rasch model. Therefore, as an example of applying Newton's method to IRT, the Rasch model is used.

For the Rasch model the t*th* iteration of the derivatives are (cf. Hambleton & Swaminathan, 1985; Wright & Stone, 1979)

$$\frac{\partial}{\partial\theta}\ln L(\underline{x}|\theta_{i}^{t}) = X_{i} - \sum_{j=1}^{L} P_{ij}(t) \qquad (A.9)$$

and

$$\frac{\partial^{2}}{\partial\theta^{2}}\ln L(\underline{x}|\theta_{i}^{t}) = -\sum_{j=1}^{L} P_{ij}(t)(1 - P_{ij}(t)) \qquad (A.10)$$

where p_{ij} is the probability of a response of 1 on the jth item by person i according to Equation 2.2. By substitution of these identities into Equation A.8 we have

$$\theta_i^{t+1} = \theta_i^t - \frac{X_i - \sum_{j=1}^{L} P_{ij}(t)}{-\sum_{j=1}^{L} P_{ij}(t)(1 - P_{ij}(t))} \tag{A.11}$$

Equation A.11 is applied until we have a converged solution or we reach the maximum number of iterations. The θ_i^{t+1} value is our estimate of person i's location, $\hat{\theta}_i$. If our solution converges, then our $\hat{\theta}$ is the location of the maximum of the log likelihood function (i.e., $\hat{\theta}$ maximizes the likelihood of obtaining the response pattern).

Focusing on the numerator of the step size,

$$X_i - \sum_{j=1}^{L} p_{ij}(t)$$

we see that it has the form of an observed score, X_i, minus the expected (trait) score

$$(\sum_{j=1}^{L} p_{ij})$$

The expected score is based on the provisional estimate of the person's location ($\hat{\theta}_i^t$), the item parameters, and the model. In effect, the estimation tries to minimize the difference between what one would expect or predict on the basis of the model and what is observed. We can also see from the numerator that there is no information about the pattern of 0s and 1s in person i's response vector. The estimation of θ is driven solely by trying to modify θ to make $\sum p_{ij}$ as close a match as possible to the observed score, X_i. The denominator of the step size is the sum of the predicted item variances. In the foregoing it is assumed that the δ_js are known. Given that our interpretation of the numerator of Equation A.11 is similar to that of the numerator of the chi-square statistic, it is not surprising that there is an alternative estimation method based on the chi-square statistic (Berkson, 1944, 1955; Baker, 1991).

As an example, assume that we are interested in estimating the θ that has the highest likelihood of producing the pattern 11000 (Table A.1). Moreover, assume that our item locations are $\delta_1 = -1.9000$, $\delta_2 = -0.6000$, $\delta_3 = -0.2500$, $\delta_4 = 0.3000$, and $\delta_5 = 0.4500$. Our convergence criterion is 0.0001. To start our estimation we need an initial guesstimate as to where the function has its maximum. There are various ways of providing this guesstimate. For example, we could assume that the individuals who produce this pattern 11000 are of average proficiency, and therefore the initial guesstimate would be $\theta^{(0)} = 0.0$. Alternatively, we can take test performance into account in making our guesstimate. For instance, we can convert X into its corresponding z-score or it may be transformed into a logit correct by $\ln(X/(L - X))$ (Wright & Stone, 1979). Using this latter approach our guesstimate for X = 2 would be $\hat{\theta}^{(0)} = \ln(\frac{2}{5-2}) = -0.40546510811$. Given this $\hat{\theta}^{(0)}$ we calculate the first and second derivatives (columns 3 and 4) as well as their ratio (column 5, labeled "Step size," Equation A.7). As indicated in Equation A.11 this step size is subtracted from $\hat{\theta}^{(0)}$ to produce an improved estimate,

$\hat{\theta}^{(t+1)}$, shown in column 6 (i.e., $\hat{\theta}^{(1)} = -0.82847618718$). In iteration 2 this $\hat{\theta}^{(1)}$ is improved upon by recalculating the values of the first and second derivatives, forming a new step size, and producing a new improved estimate, $\hat{\theta}^{(2)} = -0.83782029012$. These steps are repeated for the remaining iterations. Because iteration 3's step size of 0.00000817828 is less than our convergence criterion, we have a converged solution and the estimation process stops. The $\hat{\theta}$ after the third iteration, $\hat{\theta}^{(3)} = -0.83782846840$, would be our final estimate of the location of the maximum of $\ln L(11000)$; that is, $\hat{\theta} = -0.8378$.[4] For a pedagogical reason we perform a fourth iteration to show how little change there is from iteration 3's results.

As mentioned above, one advantage of the Newton method over the empirical MLE is the ability to obtain the sample standard error of estimate. The standard error of $\hat{\theta}$ is

$$SEE(\hat{\theta}) = \frac{1}{\sqrt{\sum_{j=1}^{L} \alpha^2 p_j (1 - p_j)}} \qquad (A.12)$$

where for the Rasch model α equals 1 and p_j is conditional on $\hat{\theta}$. To calculate p_j one uses the final $\hat{\theta}$ and the item parameters. As can be seen from Equation A.12, the magnitude of the standard error of $\hat{\theta}$ is influenced, in part, by the instrument's length. For this example the standard error for $\hat{\theta} = -0.8378$ is 0.9900. This value of almost 1 logit may be considered on the large side. Its magnitude is due, in part, to the use of five items, the items' locations, and the location of the person's estimate with respect to the items' location (i.e., this $\hat{\theta}$ falls in a gap between δ_1 and δ_2).

In general, a standard error of estimate consists of two components. The first component is the *bias* in the estimate (i.e., the signed difference between the parameter and its estimate), whereas the second component is the *mean squared error* (MSE) in the estimate (i.e., the unsigned squared difference between the parameter and its estimate); the root mean squared error (RMSE) is the square root of the MSE. The relationship between SEE, MSE, and bias is

$$SEE = \sqrt{MSE - bias^2} \qquad (A.13)$$

REVISITING ZERO VARIANCE BINARY RESPONSE PATTERNS

Figure 2.8 shows the log likelihood for a perfect response pattern, 11111. This pattern as well as the pattern 00000 have zero response variability. We can see from Chapter 2, Figure 2.8, that the func-

TABLE A.1. MLE Iteration History for Solving $\frac{\partial}{\partial \theta} \ln L(11000|\theta) = 0$

Iteration	$\hat{\theta}^t$	$\frac{\partial}{\partial \theta} \ln L(\underline{x}\|\theta^t)$	$\frac{\partial^2}{\partial \theta^2} \ln L(\underline{x}\|\theta^t)$	Step size	$\hat{\theta}^{(t+1)}$
1	−0.40546510811	−0.45534004562	−1.07642581519	0.42301107907	−0.82847618718
2	−0.82847618718	−0.00955017713	−1.02205392943	0.00934410294	−0.83782029012
3	−0.83782029012	−0.00000834401	−1.02026427006	0.00000817828	−0.83782846840
4	−0.83782846840	−0.00000000001	−1.02026269393	0.00000000001	−0.83782846841

tion's trajectory becomes asymptotic as θ increases and, for all intents, the function becomes relatively flat. Therefore, Equation A.8's step size does not decrease and the $\hat{\theta}$ will "drift off" toward infinity. Mathematically, the numerator of the step size in Equation A.11 equals 0 only when $p_{ij} = 1.0$ for all items (i.e., $X_i = \sum p_{ij}$). However, p_{ij} equals 1 only for an infinitely large $\hat{\theta}$. Therefore, the use of Newton's method for estimating θ does not provide finite estimates for zero or perfect scores. (The lnL for X = 0 would be the mirror image of the lnL presented in Figure 2.8.)

NOTES

1. Both empirical MLE and Newton's method for MLE are predicated on the assumption that the likelihood function's shape is determined by some unknown parameter, θ.

2. This method is also referred to as Newton–Raphson. Newton's method was developed about 1669 and, apparently, Raphson independently developed a simplified version of Newton's method in 1690 (Gautschi, 1997). Therefore, this method is typically referred to as Newton–Raphson, although some (e.g., Gerald & Wheatley, 1984; Gautschi, 1997) refer to it as Newton's method. However, both Newton's and Raphson's algorithms were algebraic and did not involve derivatives (Gautschi, 1997). Simpson in 1740 (cited in Gautschi, 1997) introduced the calculus description to Newton's method, and the modern version of Newton's approach seems to have appeared first in a paper by Fourier in 1831 (Gautschi, 1997).

3. The slope is equal to zero whenever a function has a maximum or a minimum. The sign of the second derivative

$$f''(\theta) = \frac{\partial^2}{\partial \theta^2} \ln L(x|\theta)$$

indicates whether a minimum or a maximum at θ has been obtained. Specifically, if $f''(\theta) < 0.0$, then it is a maximum. However, a given function may have multiple maxima/minima as well as local maxima/minima. Local and multiple maxima/minima arise when the function has multiple bends rather than a single bend as shown in Figure A.2. A local maximum (or minimum) occurs when a location is found at which the slope of the function is 0, but this location does not correspond to the highest point on the function. For example, imagine a function that is increasing, reaches a crest, bends downward into a valley, and then bends upward out of the valley to a second crest that is higher than the first crest. The first crest would be a local maximum and the second would be the function's true maximum; the floor of the valley would be a minimum. Evidence about whether the solution is at local maximum/minimum rather than at a true maximum/minimum may be obtained by using different initial starting estimates. If the various solutions produce the same estimate, then most likely a true maximum has been found.

4. If the *standard score* of X = 2 had been used as the $\theta^{(0)}$, the results would still have converged in three iterations and $\hat{\theta}^{(3)} = -0.83782846841$.

Appendix B   Maximum Likelihood Estimation of Item Locations

In Appendix A we discuss the logic and mathematics of Newton's method for locating the maximum of the lnL. We also demonstrate Newton's method for estimating a person's location. In this appendix we assume that the reader is familiar with Newton's method and show its use to estimate an item's location, δ. Analogous to what is done in the estimation of person locations in Appendix A, we assume that the persons' θs are known.

In estimating a person's location with the 1PL model, the data in Table 2.1 are reduced to six rows (X = 0, 1, . . . , 5) and only the row totals for four observed scores (X = 1, 2, 3, 4) provide information for estimating θ using MLE. Similarly, in estimating an item's location it is not the pattern of 1s and 0s on the item, but the column total or the item score, q_j, for the jth item that provides the information needed for estimating its δ (cf. Rasch, 1980). That is, the item score q_j embodies all the information for estimating the item's δ and is a sufficient statistic for estimating δ_j.

Conceptually, the likelihood function for an item specifies the likelihood of observing a particular q_j, given the various possible values of δ. For instance, how likely is it that out of 19,601 persons, 17,395 individuals got item 1 correct if the item is located at –3.0, or if it is located at –2.9, or at 3.0? As is the case with estimating person locations, if $q_j = 0$ or $q_j = N$, then the likelihood function does not have a maximum and there is no finite estimate of the item's δ. Stated another way, if $q_j = 0$, then $\delta = \infty$, and if $q_j = N$, then $\delta = -\infty$. In principle, the likelihood function for an item would be obtained in a way similar to the way it is obtained for estimating a person's location. However, a logarithmic transformation of L is typically performed to produce a log likelihood function, lnL (e.g., see Equation A.2).

The application of Newton's method in Appendix A produced an equation that allowed one to successively refine the location estimate of the maximum of the lnL (see Equation A.8). Applying Newton's method to obtain the $\hat{\delta}$ involves making the appropriate substitutions for the first and second derivatives of the log likelihood function with *respect to* δ into Equation A.8. These derivatives may be found in the literature (e.g., Baker & Kim, 2004; Hambleton & Swaminathan, 1985; Wright & Stone, 1979). Upon making these substitutions into Equation A.8 we have an equation to obtain an improved $\hat{\delta}_j$ for the jth item at the (t + 1) iteration:

$$\hat{\delta}_j^{t+1} = \hat{\delta}_j^t - \frac{f(\hat{\delta}_t)}{f'(\hat{\delta}_t)} = \delta_j^t - \frac{\dfrac{\partial}{\partial \delta} \ln L(\underline{x} \mid \delta_j^t)}{\dfrac{\partial^2}{\partial \delta^2} \ln L(\underline{x} \mid \delta_j^t)} \tag{B.1}$$

Because the derivatives in Equation B.1 are with respect to δ, they are different from those seen in Appendix A, Equations A.9 and A.10. Specifically,

$$\frac{\partial}{\partial\delta}\ln L(\underline{x}\mid\delta_j^t) = \sum_{i=1}^{N} p_{ij}(t) - q_j$$

and

$$\frac{\partial^2}{\partial\delta^2}\ln L(\underline{x}\mid\delta_j^t) = -\sum_{i=1}^{N} p_{ij}(t)\,(1-p_{ij}(t))$$

Therefore, upon substitution of these derivatives into Equation B.1 one obtains

$$\hat{\delta}_j^{t+1} = \hat{\delta}_j^t - \frac{\displaystyle\sum_{i=1}^{N} p_{ij}(t) - q_j}{-\displaystyle\sum_{i=1}^{N} p_{ij}(t)\,(1-p_{ij}(t))} \tag{B.2}$$

As is the case with estimating person location via MLE, the numerator reflects a difference between the observed item score (the number of responses of 1 on the item) and the expected/predicted score for the item based on the provisional $\hat{\delta}_j$, the known θs, and the model. We see that the numerator does not contain any information about the pattern of 0s and 1s in item j's response vector. As a result, the estimation of δ is driven solely by trying to modify δ to make $\sum^N p_{ij}$ as close a match as possible to the item score q_j. In obtaining a solution one seeks to minimize this discrepancy by iteratively improving the $\hat{\delta}_j$s until $(\delta^{t+1} - \delta^t) < \Xi$, where Ξ is the convergence criterion. In addition to Ξ, one typically has a maximum number of iterations that will be executed. Therefore, our estimation continues until either Ξ is satisfied or we reach the maximum number of iterations.

Strictly speaking, because δ is unknown it is not possible to calculate p_{ij}. However, the tth provisional estimate of δ is treated as known in order to calculate an estimate of p_{ij} in Equation B.2. In addition, for purposes of estimation, and because all persons with the same observed score have the same θ, we can approximate

$$\sum_{i=1}^{N} p_{ij} \text{ by } \sum_{X=1}^{L-1} n_X p_{Xj}$$

where n_X is the number of persons obtaining an observed score of X; because X = 0 and X = L do not produce finite estimates they are omitted from the summation and the sum runs from 1 to L − 1, not from 0 to L. Therefore, in implementations of the Newton method

$$\sum_{i=1}^{N} p_{ij} \text{ is replaced by } \sum_{X=1}^{L-1} n_X p_{Xj}$$

Newton's method converges more quickly if one starts in the neighborhood of the final solution. A starting location can be obtained by transforming the item scores to their corresponding standard scores or by using a modified logit incorrect (Wright & Stone, 1979):

$$\hat{\delta}^0 = \ln\left(\frac{N-q_j}{q_j}\right) - \sum_{}^{L}\ln\left(\frac{N-q_j}{q_j}\right)/L \tag{B.3}$$

The first term is essentially a logit incorrect (i.e., the number of responses of 0 over the number of responses of 1), whereas the second term is its average across items. Therefore, Equation B.3 provides a "centered" starting value.

We use the first item on our example's mathematics test (Chapter 2) to demonstrate the MLE of an item location. As mentioned above, the person locations are assumed to be known. For this example, for an X = 1 the persons are located at $\theta_1 = -1.9876$, for X = 2 the $\theta_2 = -0.8378$, for X = 3 the $\theta_3 = 0.1008$, and for X = 4 the $\theta_4 = 1.1800$. Table B.1 contains the MLE iteration history. The convergence criterion is set to 0.0001; $\Xi = 0.0001$. We see that convergence is achieved on the fourth iteration. Our MLE estimate of item 1's location is -2.5118; $\hat{\delta}_1 = -2.5118$. The accuracy of this estimate can be ascertained via its standard error, $\sigma_e(\hat{\delta})$:

$$\sigma_e(\hat{\delta}) = \frac{1}{\sqrt{\sum_{X=1}^{L-1} n_X p_{Xj}*(1-p_{Xj})}} \tag{B.4}$$

By using the p_{ij} obtained from the last iteration in Equation B.4, our sample standard error for $\hat{\delta}_1$, $s_e(\hat{\delta}_1)$, is 0.0246. (As is the case for estimation of person locations one can talk about the amount of information a sample provides for estimating an item's location by taking the square of the reciprocal of Equation B.4.)

Table B.2 shows the results of applying the above procedure to the remaining items on the instrument. As can be seen, our items are located throughout the continuum ranging from roughly 2.5 logits below 0 to 1.6 logits above 0. Our standard errors are on the order of two one-hundredths or less indicating reasonably accurate item location estimates. We should note that these item location estimates should not be interpreted in an absolute sense. That is, if we estimate these item locations with a different sample of examinees, we would most likely obtain a different set of estimates that, assuming model–data fit, would be highly linearly related to the estimates in Table B.2. Moreover, our $\hat{\delta}_j$s have not been centered to address the indeterminacy of the metric. This issue is discussed in Chapter 3 in the section entitled "Indeterminacy of Parameter Estimates."

TABLE B.1. MLE Iteration History for Solving $\frac{\partial}{\partial\theta}$ lnL

Iteration	$\hat{\delta}^t$	$\frac{\partial}{\partial\theta}\ln L(\underline{x}|\delta^t)$	$\frac{\partial^2}{\partial\theta^2}\ln L(\underline{x}|\delta^t)$	Step size	$\hat{\delta}^{t+1}$
1	−1.8742977754	−1232.4719284092	−2211.5954513099	0.5572772939	−2.4315750693
2	−2.4315750693	−135.2398882748	−1721.1396629280	0.0785757781	−2.5101508474
3	−2.5101508474	−2.7608102020	−1650.9197279091	0.0016722862	−2.5118231336
4	−2.5118231336	−0.0012464573	−1649.4290371237	0.0000007557	−2.5118238893

TABLE B.2. MLE $\hat{\delta}$s and Their Corresponding SEEs for the Five-Item Instrument

Item	$\hat{\delta}$	$s_e(\hat{\delta})$	Number of iterations
1	−2.5118	0.0246	4
2	−0.1592	0.0183	4
3	0.3518	0.0183	4
4	1.3203	0.0198	4
5	1.6414	0.0209	4

CONCEPTUAL DEVELOPMENT OF THE NORMAL OGIVE MODEL

Our conceptual development of the IRT normal ogive model begins with a discussion of the relationship between the observed 0/1 responses and the variable being measured. In the current context, the latent variable of interest (e.g., neuroticism, narcissism, mathematics proficiency) is measured by asking a series of questions. The responses to these questions are transformed to be a 0 or a 1. For instance, a person may be asked, "Given X = 3 + 5, what is the value of X?" In this case, the individual's response is coded as 1 if the response is 8, otherwise it is coded to 0.

One may ask, "How does the 0/1 'response' on an item relate to the latent variable being measured?" To answer this question assume that a continuous latent variable, Ω_j, determines an individual's response to an item j. Large values of this item latent variable Ω_j indicate a greater tendency to produce a response (x_j) of 1 than smaller values of Ω_j. This continuous variable is dichotomized at some point, τ_j, such that at and above this point the continuous latent variable's values are recoded as a 1, and below which they are recoded as a 0. For example, in Figure C.1 person 1 is located (μ_{1j}) beyond the cutpoint (threshold, τ_j) associated with item j. Therefore, the shaded area under the function beyond the cutpoint is the probability (π_{1j}) of a response of 1 to item j by person 1. The unshaded portion gives the probability of a response of 0 to this item by this person. This is the mechanism by which the observed 0/1 responses arise. Note that in contrast to a true dichotomy (i.e., a variable that can legitimately have only two values, such as gender), the dichotomization of this continuous variable results in an artificial dichotomy.

How does the unobserved variable Ω_j that determines the performance on item j relate to the latent variable of interest, θ? The latent variable Ω_j is a function of a common factor θ across all the items on an instrument plus an error factor that is unique to item j (Lord, 1980). Moreover, the regression of Ω_j on θ is linear (Lord & Novick, 1968). Figure C.2 depicts this regression for item j using a standard simple linear regression presentation. As can be seen the conditional distributions of Ω_j for fixed (predictor) values of θ are assumed to be normally distributed with mean $\mu_{j|\theta}$ and variance $\sigma^2_{j|\theta}$; because $\sigma^2_{j|\theta}$ is constant or homoscedastic across all conditional distributions, it is symbolized as σ^2_j. Note that although we are assuming that the latent variable Ω_j is normally distributed, we are *not* assuming that the people are normally distributed. That is, the continuous latent variable Ω_j reflects the distribution of the responses to an item j by a person who is presented the item an infinite independent number of times.

Combining the ideas behind Figure C.1 with those underlying Figure C.2 results in Figure C.3. As we see, these two conditional distributions reflect different probabilities of obtaining a response of 1 conditional on θ and item j's threshold. For a low θ value (i.e., the left conditional distribution) the item's cutpoint results in an area that is substantially less than that for a higher θ value (e.g., the

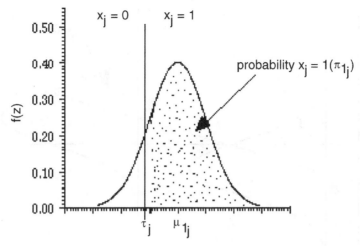

FIGURE C.1. Person 1's location relative to item j's cutpoint.

right conditional distribution). This implies that the item discriminates across the θ continuum and the degree of discrimination is related to the slope of the regression line.

To find the probability of a response of 1 (π_{1j}) for the right conditional (normal) distribution, one converts the τ_j to its corresponding z-score

$$z_{\tau_j} = \frac{\tau_j - \mu_{1j|\theta}}{\sigma_j} \qquad (C.1)$$

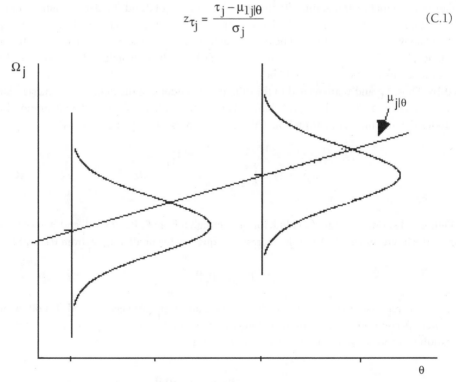

FIGURE C.2. Regression of Ω_j on θ for item j.

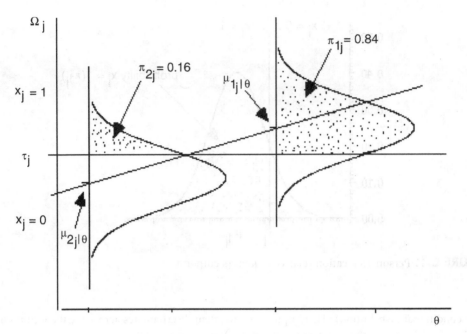

FIGURE C.3. Regression of Ω_j on θ and its relationship to item j's cutpoint.

and determines the area at and above z_{τ_j}. For convenience the metrics for Ω_j and θ are transformed (standardized) so that their marginal distributions have means of 0 and standard deviations of 1 (Lord, 1980). As such, one may use the standard unit normal curve table to determine the area (i.e., π_{1j}) that falls at and above z_{τ_j}. This area would be the probability of a response of 1 on item j conditional on θ. For instance, if $z_{\tau_j} = -1$, then $\pi_{1j} = 0.84$. In a similar fashion, the probability of a response of 1 for the left conditional distribution (π_{2j}) could be obtained. Assuming for this distribution that $z_{\tau_j} = 1$, then $\pi_{2j} = 0.16$. Thus, z_{τ_j} and τ_j are related to the difficulty of endorsing the item. Using the standard unit normal curve table to obtain these probabilities is tantamount to performing the integration from z_{τ_j} to ∞ under the unit normal distribution. This may be represented symbolically as

$$\pi(x_j = 1) = \int_{-z_{\tau_j}}^{\infty} \frac{1}{\sqrt{2\pi}} e^{-(z_{\tau_j}^2)/2} \, dz \qquad (C.2)$$

Figure C.3 shows the regression line for predicting Ω_j from θ. Because Ω_j and θ have been standardized, the intercept equals 0 and the regression equation for predicting Ω_j from θ simplifies to

$$\mu'_{ij|\theta} = \rho_j \, \theta \qquad (C.3)$$

Therefore, our regression coefficient equals the correlation, ρ_j, between Ω_j and θ. Following Lord (1980), item j's conditional standard deviation (the standard error) is $\sigma_{j \cdot \theta} = \sqrt{1 - \rho_j^2}$. By substitution of Equation C.3 and $\sigma_{j \cdot \theta}$ into Equation C.1, one obtains

$$-z_{\tau_j} = \frac{\tau_j - \mu'_{ij|\theta}}{\sigma_j} = \frac{\tau_j - \rho_j \theta}{\sqrt{1 - \rho_j^2}} \qquad (C.4)$$

Lord and Novick (1968) define item j's discrimination parameter, α_j, and its location, δ_j, in terms of the steepness of the regression line for predicting Ω_j from θ and the conditional variability about this regression:

$$\alpha_j \equiv \frac{\rho_j}{\sqrt{1-\rho_j^2}} \qquad (C.5)$$

Because τ_j is related to the difficulty of endorsing an item and

$$\frac{\tau_j}{\rho_j}$$

is the point on the continuum where the probability of a response of 1 is 0.5, item j's location, δ_j, is defined as

$$\delta_j \equiv \frac{\tau_j}{\rho_j} \qquad (C.6)$$

By substitution of Equations C.5 and C.6 into Equation C.4 one obtains, upon simplification,

$$-z_{\tau_j} = \alpha_j(\delta_j - \theta) \qquad (C.7)$$

That is, the location of item j's standardized threshold that delimits the response of 1 from that of 0 is a function of how well item j discriminates and its location on the latent variable of interest.

We can extend the idea embodied in Figure C.3 to a series of the conditional distributions of Ω_j. For each of these Equation C.2 can be used to calculate the probability of a response of 1 on item j. The graphing of these probabilities as a function of θ would produce an S-shaped curve or an ogive (Figure C.4). These probabilities may be traced by the *standard normal ogive* function:[1]

$$\pi(x_j = 1) = \int_{-\infty}^{z} \frac{1}{\sqrt{2\pi}} e^{-(z^2/2)} dz \qquad (C.8)$$

In the current context the z in Equation C.8 is replaced by z_{τ_j} (i.e., $z_{\tau_j} = -(- z_{\tau_j})$) so that by substitution of Equation C.7 into Equation C.8 one obtains the *two-parameter normal ogive model* (Lord, 1952):

$$\pi(x_j = 1 | \theta, \alpha_j, \delta_j) = \int_{-\infty}^{\alpha_j(\theta-\delta_j)} \frac{1}{\sqrt{2\pi}} e^{-(z^2/2)} dz$$

$$= \frac{1}{\sqrt{2\pi}} \int_{-\infty}^{\alpha_j(\theta-\delta_j)} e^{-(z^2/2)} dz \qquad (C.9)$$

where α_j and δ_j are the discrimination and location parameters for item j, respectively. (We use π instead of p to represent the probability from the two-parameter normal ogive.) It should be noted

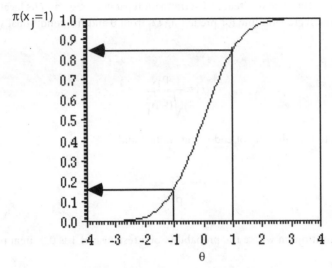

FIGURE C.4. Normal ogive with $\pi_{1j} = 0.84$ and $\pi_{2j} = 0.16$ overlaid.

that the model in Equation C.9 does *not* make "any assumption about the distribution of" θ in the total group administered the instrument (Lord, 1980, p. 32). As is the case with the 2PL model, the item is located at the point where the probability of a response is 0.5, because when $\theta = \delta_j$ the integral has the limits

$$\int_{-\infty}^{z=0}$$

and evaluates to 0.5. The term α_j is proportional to the slope of the IRF at δ_j. (Specifically, the slope is $\alpha_j/\sqrt{2\pi}$.)[2] In contrast to the use of the logit model (e.g., for the 2PL model), the model in Equation C.9 is a case of the use of the probit model.[3]

Birnbaum (1968) modified the model in Equation C.9 to include a lower nonzero asymptote parameter, χ_j, to address the observation that even "subjects of very low ability will sometimes give correct responses to multiple-choice items, just by chance" (Birnbaum, 1968, p. 404). This model is referred to as the *three-parameter normal ogive model*:

$$\pi(x_j = 1 | \theta, \alpha_j, \delta_j, \chi_j) = \chi_j + (1 - \chi_j) \int_{-\infty}^{\alpha_j(\theta - \delta_j)} \frac{1}{\sqrt{2\pi}} e^{-(z^2/2)} dz \qquad \text{(C.10)}$$

where χ_j is the pseudo-guessing (lower asymptote) parameter. Because the slope under the three-parameter normal ogive model involves the pseudo-guessing parameter, as the pseudo-guessing value increases the IRF's slope decreases. (Specifically, the slope is $\alpha_j(1 - \chi_j)/\sqrt{2\pi}$; Lord, 1975.) As is the case with the logistic models, one can obtain the *one-parameter normal ogive model* by fixing χ_j to zero and holding α_j constant across items.

THE RELATIONSHIP BETWEEN IRT STATISTICS AND TRADITIONAL ITEM ANALYSIS INDICES

In traditional item analysis the proportion of correct responses to an item is the item's measure of difficulty. This proportion is typically referred to as the item's P-value, P_j, with large values indicating easy items and small P_j values reflecting difficult items. Moreover, there are various indices for assessing an item's discrimination power. Two of these are the item's point biserial and biserial correlation coefficients.

We begin by focusing on the biserial correlation as the discrimination index. Recall that the biserial correlation coefficient is a measure of the association between a continuous normally distributed variable and another continuous normally distributed variable that has been dichotomized (e.g., a variable like Ω_j). To specify the relationship between the biserial correlation and the IRT discrimination parameter, we need to make two assumptions. First, because the biserial correlation assumes that both the dichotomized and the continuous variables are normally distributed, then we need to assume that both Ω_j and the *latent variable* θ are normally distributed. The second assumption is that there is no guessing on the item. Under these assumptions, Tucker (1946) and Lord and Novick (1968) show that the biserial correlation between the responses to an item j and the latent trait θ is related to the item's discrimination parameter by

$$\rho_{b_j} = \frac{\alpha_j}{\sqrt{1+\alpha_j^2}} \tag{C.11}$$

Therefore, as the item discrimination increases so does the correlation between the item response and the latent variable.

Because θ is unknown it is not possible to calculate the biserial correlation between the responses to an item j and the latent trait θ. However, to the extent that the observed score is a reasonable proxy or measure of θ (e.g., the instrument is of sufficient length and homogeneity; Urry, 1974), then one may calculate the biserial correlation between the responses to item j and the observed score, r_b, to estimate ρ_b. In this regard, the relationship between item j's traditional discrimination index, r_{b_j}, and the IRT discrimination parameter, α_j, may be expressed as (cf. Lord, 1980; also see Equation C.5)

$$\alpha_j \cong \frac{r_{b_j}}{\sqrt{1-r_{b_j}^2}} \tag{C.12}$$

Therefore, as the correlation between the item and the observed score increases, α_j also increases. The traditional item discrimination index can also be expressed in terms of the IRT item discrimination parameter by rearranging Equation C.12:

$$r_{b_j} \cong \frac{\alpha_j}{\sqrt{1+\alpha_j^2}} \tag{C.13}$$

As mentioned above, a second traditional discrimination index is the point biserial correlation. The point biserial correlation gives the association between a true dichotomy and a normally distributed continuous variable. We can relate the point biserial correlation between the binary responses to an item and θ to obtain the IRT discrimination parameter. To do this we need to first relate the point biserial and the biserial correlations to one another. This relationship requires knowing the height of the standard unit normal curve at the dichotomizing point. That is, to calculate the biserial correlation the continuous normally distributed variable is dichotomized at some point on the continuum. At and above this point or threshold, τ_j, the response to the item is a 1 with an area represented by the shaded region in Figure C.1, π_j. The height of the standardized normal distribution at the threshold is given by

$$Y(\tau_j) = \frac{1}{\sqrt{2\pi}} \left[\exp(\frac{-\tau_j^2}{2}) \right] \tag{C.14}$$

By using the covariance between the dichotomized item and the latent trait θ,

$$\sigma_{j\theta} = \rho_{b_j} Y(\tau_j)$$

and dividing it by the standard deviation of the dichotomized item (i.e., $\sigma_j = \sqrt{\pi_j(1-\pi_j)}$) one obtains the point biserial, ρ_{pb}, as a function of the biserial correlation

$$\rho_{pbj} = \frac{\sigma_{j\theta}}{\sigma_j} = \rho_{bj} \left[\frac{Y(\tau_j)}{\sqrt{\pi_j(1-\pi_j)}} \right] \tag{C.15}$$

As is the case with the biserial correlation, if the observed score is a reasonable proxy or measure of θ, then the point biserial correlation between the responses to item j and the observed scores, r_{pb}, serves as an estimate of ρ_{pb}; in this case the item's P-value, P_j, is used instead of π_j. By solving for ρ_b in Equation C.15 we can transform our estimated r_{pb} to its corresponding r_b and then apply Equation C.12. The point biserial is more appropriate than the biserial for situations that involve guessing.

We now turn our attention to the relationship between item j's location, δ_j, and its traditional item difficulty index, P_j. Recall that P_j is the proportion of respondents correctly responding to an item. If we assume that θ is normally distributed (specifically, $N(0,1)$), then the proportion of respondents correctly answering item j corresponds to an the area under this distribution. This area is delimited by a cutpoint, z_{t_j}, and the relationship between z_{t_j} and P_j is depicted in Figure C.5. Therefore, by using Equation C.6, assuming that there is no guessing on item j, and because we have only sample information, we can express the relationship between the traditional item difficulty index and the item's location as (cf. Lord, 1952 , 1980; Tucker, 1946)

$$\delta_j \cong \frac{z_{t_j}}{r_{b_j}} \tag{C.16}$$

where z_{t_j} is the standard unit normal deviate that delimits an area to its left equal to $1 - P_j$ and an area P_j to its right (Figure C.5). Because high values of P_j indicate the same thing as low values of δ_j (e.g., "easiness") we transform the P_j into its complement $(1 - P_j)$ so that z_{t_j} may be interpreted in a way similar to δ_j; $(1 - P_j)$ corresponds to the unshaded area in Figure C.5. The relationship between P_j

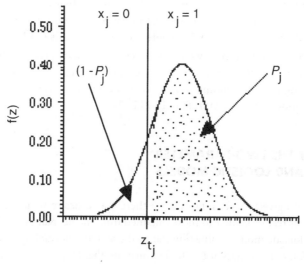

FIGURE C.5. Relationship of z_{t_j} $(1 - P_j)$, and P_j.

and δ_j is dependent on how well the item discriminates. When all items discriminate equally well, then as P_j increases δ_j decreases.

We can use Equations C.12 and C.16 to "estimate" the IRT parameters α and δ. To demonstrate this we use the traditional item statistics from our mathematics data to estimate their corresponding IRT parameters. The traditional item difficulty and discrimination indices for item 1 are $P_1 = 0.887$ and $r_{b_1} = 0.407$, respectively. Therefore, $(1 - P_j) = 1 - 0.887 = 0.113$, and from the standard unit normal table we have that $z_{t_j} = -1.2111$. Substituting these values into Equation C.16 yields an IRT location estimate of

$$\hat{\delta}_1 = \frac{-1.2111}{0.407} = -2.9757$$

and a discrimination estimate of

$$\hat{\alpha}_1 = \frac{r_{b_1}}{\sqrt{1 - r_{b_1}^2}} = \frac{0.407}{\sqrt{1 - 0.407^2}} = 0.4456$$

The relationships between P_j and δ_j, as well as between α_j and r_{b_j}, may appear to provide a convenient approach for estimating α_j and δ_j. However, there are various reasons why the JMLE (Chapter 3) and MMLE (Chapter 4) techniques are to be the preferred over using Equations C.12 and C.16. First, recall that both P_j and r_{b_j} are sample dependent, whereas α_j and δ_j are sample independent. Second, Equations C.12 and C.16 hold only when the latent variable is normally distributed and there is no guessing on the items. Third, because the observed score, X, contains error and θ does not, the X and θ are distributed differently, and these approximations using Equations C.12 and C.16 "fall short of accuracy" (Lord, 1980, p. 33). Fourth, Equations C.12 and C.16 do not provide standard errors for the α_j and δ_j estimates. As such, we do not know how accurately the parameters are being estimated. Moreover, research has shown that the approximation approaches of Equations C.12 and C.16 do not produce estimates that are as accurate as the MLE approach. For instance, Jensema (1976) compared these approximation approaches with MLE and found that the MLE estimates were more highly linearly related to their parameters than the estimates based on Equations C.12 and C.16 (for MLE we have $r_{\alpha\hat{\alpha}}$ = 0.863 and $r_{\delta\hat{\delta}}$ = 0.971; whereas using Equations C.12 and C.16 we have $r_{\alpha\hat{\alpha}}$ = 0.798 and $r_{\delta\hat{\delta}}$ = 0.963). Similar results were reported by Swaminathan and Gifford (1983). Further, the accuracy of the estimates increased as sample size and test length increased, and decreased as α increased. The foregoing notwithstanding, Equations C.12 and C.16 can be used to provide provisional estimates or starting values for MMLE and JMLE.

RELATIONSHIP OF THE TWO-PARAMETER NORMAL OGIVE AND LOGISTIC MODELS

Because of the normal ogive model's long history there was a desire with the introduction of the logistic form to make its results similar to those obtained from the normal ogive. The scaling constant $D = 1.702$ makes the logistic model's values similar to those of the normal ogive model. (See Camilli, 1994, for a presentation of the origin of D.) To demonstrate that $D = 1.702$ is optimal for minimizing the difference between the standard normal ogive function and the logistic function, we calculate the values of the standard normal ogive and logistic functions for a series of z scores from –3 to 3 for different values of D. These different D values range from 0.5 to 2.0 (inclusive). The maximum difference between the standard normal ogive and logistic functions for each D is presented in Figure C.6. As can be seen, the minimum maximum difference between the standard normal ogive and logistic functions' values occurs at 1.7. This minimum is 0.01 and agrees with that found in the literature. For example, the difference between $\pi(x_j=1|\theta, \alpha_j, \delta_j)$ and $p(x_j=1|\theta, \alpha_j, \delta_j)$ is less than 0.01 throughout the θ continuum (Haley, 1952; cited in Lord & Novick, 1968).

The introduction of the scaling constant D into Equation 5.1 results in

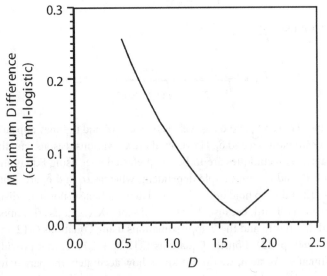

FIGURE C.6. Comparison of logistic and normal ogive for different values of D.

$$p(x_j = 1|\theta, \alpha_j, \delta_j) = \frac{e^{D\alpha_j(\theta-\delta_j)}}{1 + e^{D\alpha_j(\theta-\delta_j)}} \tag{C.17}$$

Equation C.17 produces probabilities from the logistic distribution function that are similar to those produced by Equation C.9. In effect, the use of D aligns, as closely as possible, the logistic function with the standard normal ogive function by changing the slope of logistic ogive. The standard normal ogive and the logistic functions intersect at a probability of 0.50.

The introduction of D into the model changes the formulas for both the slope and item information. With respect to the two-parameter logistic model's slope (i.e., the first derivative of the model, p_j'), the introduction of D results in the first derivative becoming

$$p_j' = D\alpha_j p_j (1 - p_j) \tag{C.18}$$

By substitution for p_j and noting that α_j is defined at $\theta = \delta$, the slope becomes

$$p_j' = D\,\alpha_j\,\frac{1}{4} = 0.425\,\alpha_j \tag{C.19}$$

Therefore, α_j is proportional to the slope of the tangent line to the IRF at δ_j.

As noted in Chapter 5, Equation 5.2, the general formulation for item information is

$$I_j(\theta) = \frac{[p_j']^2}{p_j(1-p_j)} \tag{C.20}$$

By substitution of Equation C.18 for p_j' into Equation C.20, one arrives at the item information function for the two-parameter logistic model:

$$I_j(\theta) = D^2\,\alpha_j^2\,p_j(1 - p_j) \tag{C.21}$$

Using the logistic forms offers some advantages over using the normal forms of IRT models. For instance, one advantage of using Equation C.17 is the elimination of the integral in Equations C.9 and C.10, making the mathematics simpler. A second advantage of the model shown in Equation C.17 is that, unlike with the normal ogive IRF, there are sufficient statistics for estimating person location (Lord, 1980).

When the logistic and normal ogive models provide good fit, "parameter estimates in logistic models are about 1.6–1.8 times those in probit models" (Agresti, 1990, p. 104). Therefore, the model shown in Equation C.17 may be viewed as a mathematically convenient, close approximation to the (classical form of the) two-parameter normal ogive model. However, it should be noted that D's value is not concerned with model–data fit. In this regard, and because of the indeterminacy of the metric, D may be set to any other convenient value (e.g., 1) without adversely affecting model–data fit. As a consequence, in this book the logistic model *without* the use of D (e.g., Equation 5.1) is considered to be an intrinsically useful model and we are not concerned with approximating the normal ogive form. By not using D the calibration results are on the *logistic metric*; the use of D ensures that the results are on the *normal metric*. In those situations where it is necessary to invoke D (e.g., in comparisons involving NOHARM) the reader is alerted to the use of D.

EXTENDING THE TWO-PARAMETER NORMAL OGIVE MODEL TO A MULTIDIMENSIONAL SPACE

As mentioned above, the latent variable Ω_j is a function of a common factor θ across all items on an instrument plus a term that is unique to item j. As such, the two-parameter normal ogive model may be seen as related to a unidimensional common factor analysis model (e.g., see McDonald, 1967, 1997). (It is this relationship that is used in Appendix E, "Using Principal Axis for Estimating Item Discrimination.") Moreover, this relationship may be extended to a nonunidimensional common factor model. In this respect, Ω_j is a function of multiple weighted θs:

$$\Omega_j = \rho_j'\underline{\theta} + E_j \tag{C.22}$$

where ρ_j is a vector of factor loadings (i.e., $\underline{\rho}_j = \{\rho_{j1}, \ldots, \rho_{jF}\}$), $\underline{\theta}$ is a vector of person locations (i.e., $\underline{\theta} = \{\theta_1, \ldots, \theta_F\}$), and E_j is item j's unique factor. To develop our multidimensional model we begin with the two-parameter normal ogive model. Assume that E_j and $\underline{\theta}$ are normally distributed and that Ω_j has been standardized to have a mean of 0 and a variance of 1. Therefore, Ω_j is also normally distributed; this is stated as an assumption above. Then, from above, we have that the probability of a response of 1 is (symbolically)

$$\pi(x_j = 1|\underline{\theta}) = \pi(\Omega_j > \tau_j|\underline{\theta}) = \Phi(z_{\tau_j}) \tag{C.23}$$

where $\Phi(\cdot)$ is the cumulative normal distribution function. Focusing on z_{τ_j} we have:

$$z_{\tau_j} = \alpha_j(\theta - \delta_j) = -\alpha_j\delta_j + \alpha_j\theta \tag{C.24}$$

By substitution of Equations C.5 and C.6 into Equation C.24 we can express our item's intercept in terms of the item's loading and its threshold:

$$\gamma_j = -\alpha_j\delta_j = -\left[\frac{\rho_j}{\sqrt{1-\rho_j^2}}\right]\delta_j = -\left[\frac{\rho_j}{\sqrt{1-\rho_j^2}}\right]\left[\frac{\tau_j}{\rho_j}\right] = \frac{-\tau_j}{\sqrt{1-\rho_j^2}} \tag{C.25}$$

(That is, because factor loadings are the biserial correlations of the responses with θ, Equation C.5 may be interpreted as expressing the item's discrimination in terms of its loadings.) When we substitute Equations C.25 and C.5 into Equation C.24 we arrive at

$$z_{\tau_j} = -\alpha_j\delta_j + \alpha_j\theta = \frac{-\tau_j + \rho_j\theta}{\sqrt{1-\rho_j^2}} \tag{C.26}$$

We now have a vehicle to incorporate multiple dimensions. Specifically and following McDonald (1997), we can express Equation C.26 in terms of F-dimensional vectors of factor loadings, $\underline{\rho}_j$, and person locations, $\underline{\theta}$ (also see McDonald, 1999; McDonald & Mok, 1995):

$$z_{\tau_j} = \frac{\tau_j + \rho_j'\underline{\theta}}{\sqrt{1 - \underline{\rho}_j'\Sigma\underline{\rho}_j}} \tag{C.27}$$

where $\underline{\Sigma}$ is a covariance matrix and $1 - \underline{\rho}_j'\Sigma\underline{\rho}_j$ is the item's unique variance across the F-dimensions (i.e., $1 - \Sigma \rho_f^2 = 1 - h^2$). By substitution of Equations C.5, C.25, and C.26 into Equation C.23 we arrive at a *multidimensional two-parameter normal ogive model*:

$$\pi(x_j = 1|\underline{\theta}) = \Phi(z_{\tau_j}) = \Phi\left(\frac{\tau_j + \underline{\rho}_j'\underline{\theta}}{\sqrt{1 - \underline{\rho}_j'\Sigma\underline{\rho}_j}}\right) = \Phi(\gamma_j + \underline{\alpha}_j'\underline{\theta}) \qquad (C.28)$$

In this parameterization the intercept and slopes (discriminations) are obtained by

$$\gamma_j = \frac{\tau_j}{\sqrt{1 - \underline{\rho}_j'\Sigma\underline{\rho}_j}} \qquad (C.29)$$

and

$$\alpha_j = \frac{\rho_j}{\sqrt{1 - \underline{\rho}_j'\Sigma\underline{\rho}_j}} \qquad (C.30)$$

respectively. Conversely, we have that

$$\tau_j = \frac{\gamma_j}{\sqrt{1 + \underline{\rho}_j'\Sigma\underline{\rho}_j}} \qquad (C.31)$$

and

$$\rho_j = \frac{\alpha_j}{\sqrt{1 + \underline{\rho}_j'\Sigma\underline{\rho}_j}} \qquad (C.32)$$

NOTES

1. Because the distribution is symmetric

$$\int_{-\infty}^{z} = \int_{-z}^{\infty}$$

Equation C.8 follows from Equation C.2. Moreover, below we use the symbol $\Phi(\cdot)$ to represent this *standard normal ogive* function.

2. The value of σ_j in the calculation of z_{τ_j} affects the magnitude of z_{τ_j} (Equation C.4). As σ_j increases then z_{τ_j} decreases, all other things being equal. In addition, as the z_{τ_j}s decrease the corresponding π_js decrease. Therefore, the corresponding IRF's slope decreases, all other things being held constant. Conversely, as σ_j decreases then z_{τ_j} increases and the IRF's slope increases, all other things being held fixed. As such, because α is proportional to the IRF's slope, there is an inverse relation between α and σ_j (i.e., $\alpha = 1/\sigma_j$). Because the metric is standardized to have a mean of 0 and a standard deviation of 1, the unit of measurement becomes the standard deviation unit. As a result, σ_j is referred to as a scale parameter and $1/\sigma_j$ is sometimes called *dispersion* (cf. Bock & Lieberman, 1970; Thurstone, 1925).

3. Similar models are presented by Lawley (1943, 1944), Tucker (1946), and Thurstone (1925). For example, given the cumulative normal ogive function in Equation C.8, we have that z is the unit normal deviate that delimits an area corresponding to the probability of a response of 1. Let z for person i and item j, z_{ij}, be defined as

$$z_{ij} = \frac{(\theta_i - \mu_j)}{\sigma_j} \qquad\qquad (C.33)$$

where θ_i is person i's location on the latent variable, μ_j and σ_j are the mean and standard deviation of the normal curve with respect to item j, respectively; this distribution is assumed to be normal with

$$\sigma_j = \frac{1}{\alpha_j}$$

If we take our total sample of individuals and divide it into subgroups and we redefine the standard deviation in Equation C.33 to be the standard deviation of a subgroup, σ_i, with mean μ_i, then its substitution into Equation C.2 gives Thurstone's mental age model; we're assuming that each subgroup is normally distributed. That is, Thurstone (1925; e.g., see p. 441) developed a model based on the cumulative normal distribution to determine the proportion of individuals of a specified age group correctly responding to an item.

Appendix D Computerized Adaptive Testing

"The facts are clear. From the point of view of measurement, tailored testing offers little, if any, advantage over the best that can be done with conventional testing" (Green, 1970, p. 184). Although Professor Green reached this conclusion based on the research on computerized adaptive testing (CAT) in 1970, he proceeded to present an argument against the perspective that CAT provides little advantage over conventional "paper-and-pencil" testing. In this appendix we provide a brief introduction to CAT from a proficiency assessment perspective. However, it should be noted that CAT can be applied to other psychological domains.

Computerized testing initially used the computer to simulate a paper-and-pencil test administration. This approach of administering items to an examinee without taking into account his or her responses is sometimes called a *linear test*. Therefore, the computerized linear test and the conventional paper-and-pencil testing procedure administer the same items to every examinee in a fixed fashion regardless of the examinee's responses to the items. Because the examinees most likely vary in the proficiency being measured, some items are too difficult for certain examinees, whereas others are too easy. This undermines the effectiveness of the test, but is inevitable whenever the items administered are not tailored to the individual examinee. In contrast, and in the most simplistic terms, in CAT the items administered are selected for the examinee, given the most current information about the examinee's proficiency and the items available in the pool. Although no method of administering items and scoring dichotomous responses can produce better measurement than that achieved by a "standard test" at a proficiency level equal to zero (on the theta scale), an adaptive test tries to achieve this level of accuracy *throughout* the proficiency range (Lord, 1971a). In so doing, it achieves equiprecise measurement across the continuum. Additional advantages of CAT over conventional paper-and-pencil tests are (1) a comparative (potential) test length reduction of 80% and (2) the capacity to administer questions that take advantage of the computerized administration mode and that could not be administered with a conventional paper-and-pencil test.

The concept of adapting an instrument to an individual can be traced back over a century. Throughout this time adaptive testing has had many different names, such as *tailored testing*, *response-contingent testing*, *sequential testing*, and *programmed testing*, as well as computerized adaptive testing. Regardless of what the concept has been called, it has primarily been concerned with minimizing the measurement errors associated with the estimation of an individual's location. We begin with a brief history of adaptive testing and then proceed to discussing CAT.

A BRIEF HISTORY

The first adaptive test is considered to be the individually administered Binet–Simon intelligence test developed in the early 1900s (Weiss, 1982). In this test the particular subtests administered were chosen on the basis of the examinee's current ability level as determined during the testing procedure. That is, if an examinee passes all or any of the subtests within an ability level, then a higher-ability level of subtests is administered next. Conversely, if an examinee fails all subtests at a given ability level, then the test is terminated. Therefore, the Binet test is adaptive with respect to ability level. Binet's procedure differs from present-day tailored testing in that it requires the examinee to answer all the questions associated with a particular ability level (Wood, 1973) and its administration requires a highly trained examiner rather than a computer.

In the 1940s two procedures, the staircase method and the sequential analysis system, were developed (Wood, 1973). The sequential analysis system has seen some use in mastery testing (e.g., see Reckase, 1980). The staircase method is analogous to the methods used by psychophysicists. Experimental psychologists' have used adaptive testing procedures in their psychophysical experiments for decades. Their methods, called adaptive convergence procedures, include the method of adjustment and the method of limits (Weiss, 1983).

In 1951, Hick presented all the ingredients of adaptive testing as it is now understood (Wood, 1973). In his article he stated that an intelligence test should be a branch process, with all questions having a 0.5 chance of being answered correctly. Patterson (1962; cited in Wood, 1973) took a pool of items and arranged them in such a way that an examinee, starting with an average difficulty item, would receive a harder item if he or she got the previous item correct and an easier item if he or she had answered the item incorrectly. Fixed-branching methods like those used by Patterson, and using traditional item statistics, were used during most of the 1960s.

In 1970, Lord outlined some test theory for tailored testing. On the basis of the results of various testing algorithms used in that article, he stated that better measurement could be obtained by selecting and administering, for example, the 60 most discriminating items as a conventional test rather than administering, for example, 500 items in a tailored testing procedure. It is ironic that Lord's (1970) work and its indisputably poor results marked the beginning of the integration of IRT with tailored testing procedures. In this regard, there have been a number of procedures developed.

The literature contains various taxonomies for grouping the different types of adaptive testing strategies (e.g., Hambleton & Swaminathan, 1985; Lord, 1970; Reckase, 1977; Vale, Albing, Foote-Lennox, & Foote-Lennox, 1982). These taxonomic schemes differ in their organization and terminology. For example, Reckase (1977) differentiates among methods depending on whether the adaptive testing method uses a mathematical model for determining the examinee's path through the item pool. Specifically, if the method uses a mathematical model for item selection, then the technique is classified as model-based; otherwise, the method is classified as a structure-based method. The former item selection type may be called *variable-branching* item selection, whereas the latter may be called *fixed-branching* item selection. It is this terminology that we adopt in the following discussion.

FIXED-BRANCHING TECHNIQUES

Typically, fixed-branching strategies use a predetermined or fixed routing procedure through an item pool. The arrangement of items in the pool in conjunction with the routing method define the item selection process (Patience, 1977). The item pool size is determined by the procedure used. Fixed-branching procedures may be implemented either on a computer or as a paper-and-pencil test. There are many possible fixed-branching techniques, and their number is limited only by the ingenuity of the test designer. Examples include, but are not limited to, the flexilevel test (Lord, 1971b, 1971c), the stradaptive test (Weiss, 1973), the pyramidal test (Larkin & Weiss, 1975), random-walk techniques (Lord, 1970), and the two-stage test (Cleary, Linn, & Rock, 1968; Lord, 1971d, 1980).[1] These approaches may or may not use an IRT model for person location estimation. When they do not, the proficiency estimate is a simple function of the responses to items and the items' characteristics. For instance, the estimated proficiency is the number of correct responses, a weighted composite of the items administered (e.g., the average of the difficulties of the items administered or the average of the difficulties of the items answered correctly) or the difficulty of the last item administered and the difficulty of the item that would have been administered next (Reckase, 1977; Lord, 1970).

VARIABLE-BRANCHING TECHNIQUES

Variable-branching procedures usually use an IRT model for person location estimation. (One could use a different model, such as a latent class model.) The item selection process is designed to maximize the information about an examinee's location. Two commonly used techniques are to select items that (1) produce a specified probability of a correct response for an examinee's location estimate, or (2) maximize the information function (Patience, 1977; Reckase, 1977). Because of the computations required for item selection and person location estimation, variable-branching procedures are typically implemented on a computer. (A paper-and-pencil tailored test based on the Rasch model is presented by Fischer and Pendl, 1980.) Typically, MLE, EAP, or MAP is used for estimating an individual's location. (In general, an individual's observed score is usually inappropriate as a proficiency estimate because each examinee may respond to different items and different numbers of items [Reckase, 1977].) The item pool is designed to maximize the computer program's efficiency in searching for a particular item to administer. Most of the current research in computerized adaptive testing uses variable-branching techniques.

ADVANTAGES OF VARIABLE-BRANCHING OVER FIXED-BRANCHING METHODS

Variable-branching procedures eliminate some of the problems encountered with fixed-branching methods. For instance, non-IRT-based fixed-branching tests use item characteristics that are dependent on the particular sample of examinees used in their calculation. Therefore, the item characteristics may (and probably will) vary from sample to sample and result in more error in the proficiency estimates. A second problem with these fixed-branching non-IRT techniques is that the proficiency estimates are expressed on a different metric than the item difficulty parameter estimates (Weiss, 1982). As a result, it is difficult to select items that use all the information in the examinee's response and that are of appropriate difficulty for the examinee. Third, unlike some of the fixed-branching methods, IRT-based variable-branching procedures produce proficiency estimates that are independent of the particular subset of items administered to an examinee. As a consequence, different items can be selected for administration for each examinee and the resulting proficiency estimates are on the same metric (Weiss, 1982). Further, adaptive tests can be designed to cover as wide a range of ability as desired. Lord has designed a test that places examinees from fourth grade up to graduate school on the same score scale (Lord, 1977).

A fourth problem with fixed-branching tests concerns the method of test termination. Fixed-branching tests typically terminate when a preset number of items are administered. Therefore, the degree of precision in ability estimation is not controlled by the examiner. Because with IRT-based variable-branching tests the standard error of the person estimate is directly related to the test's reliability, a test can be terminated when a predetermined level of precision is reached. In other words, a test is terminated when a particular degree of reliability is attained (Urry, 1977).

A fifth issue involves item selection. Whereas fixed-branching methods typically use a predefined item selection algorithm, the use of IRT parameters permits items to be selected on the basis of more than just their difficulty levels (Weiss, 1982). As a result, item selection can simultaneously take into account the item's difficulty, its discrimination, and the pseudo-guessing parameter. In addition, the first item to be administered can be based on considerations other than that the item happens to be of median difficulty.

A further consideration is test security. Because variable-branching methods are typically computerized, CATs are harder to compromise. For example, there are no test booklets that can be stolen, item pools that can be encrypted, and so on. Moreover, the greater flexibility in item selection of variable-branching adaptive testing methods reduces the chances of an examinee receiving the same test more than once. Of course, this consideration is valid only in comparing IRT-based variable-branching procedures with noncomputerized fixed-branching techniques.

IRT-BASED VARIABLE-BRANCHING ADAPTIVE TESTING ALGORITHM

Under certain conditions CAT leads to improved measurement as compared with conventional paper-and-pencil tests. These conditions are (1) an appropriate item response model, (2) accurate estimates of item parameters, (3) the construction of a good item pool, and (4) efficient unidimensional and multidimensional procedures for adaptive testing (Urry, 1977). Although in the following discussion we assume a unidimensional model, it is possible to use CAT with multidimensional models. The reader interested in multidimensional CAT is referred to Luecht (1996), Seagall (1996), and van der Linden (1999).

Conceptually, IRT-based variable-branching strategies consist of selecting and administering the item that is expected to most improve the current proficiency estimate. In general, these items are selected such that the examinee is expected to have about a 50% chance of correctly answering the items. The premise for this item selection strategy is that a test is most effective in measuring an examinee's proficiency "when the examinee knows the answers to only about half of the test items" (Lord, 1970, p. 140).

The CAT algorithm consists of four basic components: (1) the selection of the first item to administer to an examinee, (2) the scoring or processing of the examinee's response procedure to obtain a location estimate, (3) the selection of another item for administration (this may or may not be the same as that used for the first component), and (4) a stopping criterion/criteria for terminating an individual's test. In general, and in the context of proficiency assessment, the basic decision rule for item selection (i.e., the third component) is that if an examinee correctly answers an item, then the next item should be more difficult; otherwise, the next item should be easier.

CAT implementation requires a pool of items from which to select. Initially, this item pool can be created by administering conventional paper-and-pencil examinations, calibrating the data with the appropriate model, and linking the separate calibrations (see Chapter 11). Subsequently, items may be pretested within the CAT examinations to augment/replenish the item pool. Item pool size varies as a function of the item characteristics, test security concerns, the nature of the examination (e.g., high-stakes), breadth of content to be covered, and so on. A rule of thumb is that the number of items should be at least 8 to 12 times the average CAT length. For example, for a CAT examination that averages 25 items, this guideline would say that the item pool should have 200 to 300 items. The items' parameter estimates are treated as known when estimating an examinee's proficiency.

The computerized adaptive test typically begins with making a guesstimate as to the examinee's initial location. For example, we could assume that the examinee is of average proficiency (i.e., $\hat{\theta} = 0$), use ancillary information about the examinee to provide an initial location estimate (e.g., from a subtest), or randomly select the initial location guesstimate from within a θ range, such as -0.50 to 0.50. In general, the examinee's initial θ should be in the region corresponding to the median of the item pool difficulty distribution. This would allow movement through the pool in either direction while minimizing problems stemming from "topping-out" or "bottoming-out" of the item pool after only a few items (Patience & Reckase, 1980). (*Topping-out* refers to having an examinee location estimate that is so high that there are no items in the pool that are appropriate for administration. Conversely, *bottoming-out* occurs when the examinee's location estimate is less than the least difficult item in the item pool.) Weiss (1982) has stated that, on the basis of his personal experience, most adaptive tests are shortened by only a few items with the use of accurate initial location estimates. Stated more positively, the more accurate the initial person location estimate, the more quickly the adaptive test will converge to the individual's proficiency estimate.

Once we have an initial person location estimate we can select the first item for administration. This first item selected interacts with the approach used for obtaining the examinee's initial location estimate. As a result, there are a number of strategies that can be used for selecting this first item. For example, on the basis of the initial location estimate, the algorithm may select the most informative item in the item pool. However, if we assume that each examinee is of average proficiency, then we will always administer the same first item. In practice one needs to be concerned with overexposing items. Therefore, to avoid overexposing the first item, the algorithm may randomly select the first item from a set of items that are roughly equally informative. Some other first item selection possibilities are to simply randomly select an item of average difficulty; using the item that is most informative for a θ value corresponding to the mode of the item pool total information distribution; using the item that is most informative for a θ corresponding to the median of the item pool total information distribution; and selecting the item on the basis of external information. If we had used the randomly assigned/θ range approach, then we could simply select the most informative item for our guesstimate. If the tailored test is reasonably long (e.g., 25 items), then the choice of the initial item has almost no effect on the standard error of the final person location estimate (Lord, 1977).

After the examinee responds to the administered item, the item is scored and this information is used to estimate the examinee's θ. Any of the approaches discussed in this book, such as MLE, EAP, or MAP, can be used. The implementation of MLE and EAP for CAT is identical to that presented in Appendix A and Chapter 4, respectively. With either EAP or MAP we can estimate the person's location after scoring his or her response to the first item. However, this is not the case with MLE.

If we use MLE, then it is not possible to obtain an estimate of the person's location until he or she has provided both correct and incorrect responses; for polytomous data, see Dodd, Koch, and De Ayala (1989). Therefore, when we have either all correct or all incorrect responses we need to modify our initial θ estimate without using MLE in order to select the next item. We present three strategies that, in effect, may be considered fixed-branch approaches. One approach is to set the new $\hat{\theta}$ equal to the previous $\hat{\theta}$ plus or minus a fixed amount (e.g., step size = 0.3 logits). That is, if the examinee correctly responded to the first item, then the new $\hat{\theta}$ equals the initial estimate plus this fixed amount; otherwise the new $\hat{\theta}$ equals the initial estimate minus the fixed amount. In either case, the item administered is based on the new $\hat{\theta}$. A variant of this fixed step size approach is to use a step size after the first item and then successively divide the step size in half until we have a response vector with correct and incorrect responses. For example, if the first step size is 0.30, the second step size would be 0.15, the third step size would be 0.075, and so on. This variable step size approach seeks to minimize the possibility of topping- or bottoming-out.[2]

Once we obtain a new $\hat{\theta}$, the next item administered is the most informative item in the pool for the current proficiency estimate, the item that yields the greatest weighted information, or the one that will lead to the greatest reduction in the posterior distribution's variance.[3] The first of these three strategies is known as the maximum global information or the maximum information search and selection technique (MISS; Kingsbury & Weiss, 1983). The last two selection strategies are associated with Bayesian estimation; MISS may be used with either MAP or EAP estimation.

This process of administering items, scoring the responses, and reestimating the examinee's location continues until some termination criterion is satisfied. In this regard, there are two types of CAT examinations. In the *variable-length* CAT examination, the length of the examination may be different for each examinee. In this case, the termination criterion is either that the examinee's SEE is less than a maximum SEE criterion or that there are no more items remaining in the pool with information values greater than some minimum value; also see Jensema (1974). Typically, these criteria are used in conjunction with a maximum test length in case the minimum item information (or maximum SEE) criterion is not satisfied. The second type of CAT examination is a *fixed-length* CAT test. In this CAT the adaptive test terminates after a fixed number of items are administered. As a result, all examinees have an examination of the same length. We summarize the CAT algorithm in Figure D.1.

In Table D.1 we present the results from a variable-length CAT examination simulation. For our simulation we use MLE with a fixed step size of 0.3. Items are selected on the basis of MISS with a minimum information criterion of 0.9. The maximum test length is 30 items and the item pool size is 240 items. The table's rows represent each item administered with the item's number, α, and δ presented in the second, third, and fourth columns, respectively. For example, the first item administered is item #229 with an $\alpha = 2.580$ and a $\delta = 0.047$. To begin our CAT examination we assume that the simulee is of average proficiency (i.e., $\hat{\theta} = 0$; PREVIOUS ESTIMATE column, row 1). The most informative item in the pool for $\hat{\theta} = 0$ is item #229 with an item information of 1.658 (INFO column,

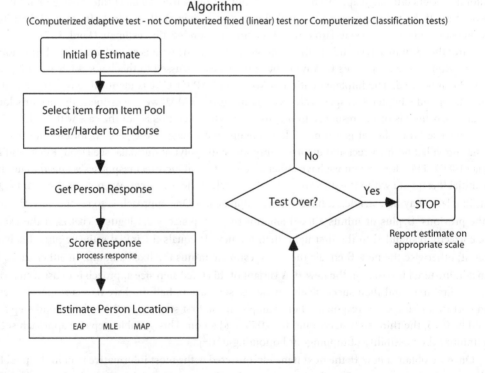

FIGURE D.1. Schematic of CAT algorithm.

TABLE D.1. CAT Examination Audit Trail for One Person

ESTIMATED THETA= 1.098
INITIAL THETA= 0.000

ORDINAL POSITION	ITEM # ADMINISTERED	A	B	PREVIOUS ESTIMATE	RESP	REVISED ESTIMATE	INFO	SEE
1	229	2.580	0.047	0.000	1	0.300	1.658	-99.90
2	181	2.954	0.560	0.300	1	0.600	1.889	-99.90
3	182	2.424	0.508	0.600	1	0.900	1.451	-99.90
4	201	2.963	1.169	0.900	1	1.200	1.880	-99.90
5	189	2.772	1.174	1.200	0	1.350	1.918	0.429
6	146	2.876	1.746	1.350	0	1.252	1.520	0.372
7	143	2.436	1.358	1.252	1	1.415	1.459	0.351
8	232	2.431	1.349	1.415	0	1.282	1.468	0.315
9	193	2.446	1.037	1.282	0	1.146	1.369	0.292
10	196	2.220	1.313	1.146	0	1.076	1.191	0.279
11	215	2.168	1.149	1.076	0	1.004	1.168	0.268
12	141	2.383	0.646	1.004	1	1.051	1.189	0.257
13	34	2.145	1.071	1.051	0	0.987	1.150	0.249
14	224	2.401	0.614	0.987	1	1.027	1.187	0.240
15	186	2.407	0.551	1.027	1	1.058	1.061	0.233
16	131	2.179	1.382	1.058	0	1.021	1.051	0.227
17	86	2.045	0.983	1.021	0	0.969	1.044	0.221
18	187	2.043	1.022	0.969	0	0.924	1.040	0.216
19	133	2.082	0.632	0.924	1	0.957	0.989	0.211
20	138	1.940	0.919	0.957	1	0.997	0.939	0.207
21	161	2.189	1.428	0.997	1	1.062	0.966	0.203
22	172	2.004	1.219	1.062	1	1.107	0.980	0.199
23	129	1.912	1.005	1.107	0	1.067	0.905	0.195
24	205	1.914	0.932	1.067	1	1.098	0.901	0.192

row 1). Because our examinee correctly responded to this item (RESP column, row 1) we add the step size of 0.3 to the initial $\hat{\theta}$ of 0 to obtain a REVISED ESTIMATE of 0.3. Based on this $\hat{\theta} = 0.3$ we select the second item to be administered. The most informative item is item #181 with an information value of 1.889 (INFO column, row 2). Again, the person correctly responds to the item and again we add the step size to our current $\hat{\theta}$.

We keep adding the step size until we administer the fifth item, at which point the examinee incorrectly responds (RESP column, row 5). Therefore, after administering five items we are able to use MLE because we now have a response vector that has at least one correct response and one incorrect response; the actual response vector is $\underline{x}$ = 11110. Our MLE $\hat{\theta}$ is 1.350 with a SEE of 0.429; the SEE = −99.900 for the first four items is used as a placeholder when we cannot use MLE. The process of item selection, reestimation of θ, and checking to see if there are any more items with information values greater than 0.9 continues until we have administered 24 items. Examining the REVISED ESTIMATE and SEE columns in conjunction with the RESP column shows the algorithm homing in on the final proficiency estimate. After the administration of the 24th item (item #205), there are no items remaining in the pool that satisfy the minimum information criterion of 0.90 and the CAT examination stops. Our person location estimate at termination is $\hat{\theta}$ = 1.098 with a SEE = 0.192. Of course, this $\hat{\theta}$ may be transformed to another metric such as the expected trait score, $\mathcal{E}T$, by Equation 4.23, or to some other target metric by Equation 4.17.

The foregoing is an oversimplification of CAT item selection. In practice, item selection involves content balancing, the pretesting of items, ensuring that items are not overused (i.e., exposure rate control), and so on. (More information on exposure rate control may be found in McBride and Martin [1983], Hetter and Sympson [1997], Stocking and Lewis [1998], Stocking and Lewis [2000], van der Linden and Veldkamp [2004], and Way [1998].) In some cases, for test security concerns the first few items may be randomly selected from item sets; these sets contain items with similar characteristics.

In general, examinees are not permitted to return to items and change answers nor to omit items. Therefore, additional implementation concerns include whether examinees should be permitted to omit items, revisit answered items, or mark items for review, or change answers to administered items; the handling of examinees who have been unable to finish; the handling of nonconvergence with MLE; and item pool characteristics (e.g., information distribution, size, etc.). There are variants of the item information approach for selecting items that may be considered for a CAT implementation. For more information on CAT, as well as a discussion of some of these issues, see Drasgow and Olson-Buchanan (1999), Parshall, Spray, Kalohn, and Davey (2002), Reckase (1989), Sands, Waters, and McBride (1997), van der Linden and Glas (2000), and Wainer et al. (2000). The reader is encouraged to visit Professor David Weiss's website (*www.psych.umn.edu/psylabs/catcentral*) for information on CAT research, software, operational CAT testing programs, and so on.

NOTES

1. A two-stage test consists of a short routing test that determines which second-stage test is most appropriate for the examinee. The second stage consists of multiple tests that vary in their difficulty, but each test is homogeneous in terms of difficulty. The examinee takes the routing test and, depending on his or her location estimate, is administered a second-stage test of appropriate difficulty. A variant of this approach uses three stages (cf. Fischer & Pendl, 1980).

The pyramidal test is sometimes called a multistage or multilevel test. Conceptually, the item pool is structured as a binary tree or Pascal's triangle. Each item in the pyramid has a lefthand branch that leads to an easier item and a righthand branch that leads to a more difficult item. The first item administered is of median difficulty and is at the apex of the pyramid. Each subsequent row (i.e., level) has its items ordered from easy to hard as one progresses across the row from left to right. As an examinee answers items, he or she progresses down through the levels of the binary tree. Which item is administered next to an examinee depends on the correctness of his or her response to the currently administered item. If the examinee correctly responds to an item, then he or she is administered a more difficult item (i.e., the item on the righthand branch); otherwise the item is an easier item (i.e., the item on the lefthand branch).

For the flexilevel test the item pool is, conceptually, an inverted V, with the item of median difficulty at the apex. The left branch of the V contains items in increasing order of easiness, whereas the right branch contains items in increasing order of difficulty. The items in each branch are numbered, beginning with 1, up to $(L - 1)/2$. The testing procedure begins with the item of median difficulty. The subsequent item selection uses a simple decision rule: If an examinee correctly responds to an item, then he or she is administered the next lowest numbered right-branch item that has not previously been answered. Conversely, if the examinee incorrectly responds to an item, then the next item administered is the next lowest numbered left-branch item that has not previously been answered. Therefore, if the examinee correctly responds to the first item, then he or she answers the first item in the right branch. Otherwise, his or her second item is the first item in the left branch. Assuming that the examinee correctly responds to the first two items, then the next item administered is the second item in the right branch, and so on. If he or she incorrectly responds to this item, then the fourth item administered is the first item in the left branch, and so on. The test terminates after $(L + 1)/2$ have been administered. For example, if we have a 71-item pool, then the test terminates after the examinee takes $(71 + 1)/2 = 36$ items. The flexilevel may be implemented as a paper-and-pencil test or on a computer (e.g., see De Ayala, Dodd, & Koch, 1990).

2. An alternative to the fixed step size strategy is to simply select an item that is midway between

the administered item's location and an item with an extreme location. In other words, if the person correctly responds to the administered item, then the next administered item would be midway between the administered item's location and the most difficult item. Conversely, if the person incorrectly responds to the administered item, then the next item would be midway between the easiest item and the administered item's location. Either of these approaches is repeated until the examinee has provided both a correct and an incorrect answer. This is also a variable step size approach.

3. Item selection for a Rasch model-based CAT involves simply choosing the item located closest to the examinee's current proficiency estimate, because all items have the same maximum item information.

Miscellanea

This appendix contains various sections that provide either background information, alternative/additional analyses, or models not covered in the chapters of this book. For instance, we briefly introduce the linear logistic test model and mixture models, as well as provide background information on odds and odds ratios and FORTRAN formats. We think that this "nether land" appendix is important, but not necessarily required to understand the material in the chapters.

LINEAR LOGISTIC TEST MODEL (LLTM)

In this book we treat the individual as a "black box." However, there are IRT models that attempt to take into account cognitive processes. One such model is Fischer's (1973) *linear logistic test model* (LLTM). The LLTM is an extension of the Rasch model that is designed to look at the cognitive operations that lead to what is observed. In the LLTM the item location parameter is a linear function of a common set of basic parameters that describe the relevant operations for the item. The LLTM is

$$P_j = \frac{e^{(\theta - \delta_j)}}{1 + e^{(\theta - \delta_j)}} \tag{E.1}$$

This model may be recognized as the Rasch model from Chapter 2. The difference between the Rasch model and the LLTM is the latter's decomposition of δ_j into a weighted linear composite of parameters that correspond to the components that describe the performance on item j. Specifically

$$\delta_j = \sum_{s=1}^{S} f_{js} \eta_s + C \tag{E.2}$$

where η_s is a basic parameter associated with elementary component s, S is the number of components, f_{js} is the weight of component s for item j, and C is a normalization constant. The constant C is

$$C = -\sum_j \sum_s \frac{f_{js} \eta_s}{L} \tag{E.3}$$

and is the mean of the location estimates prior to dealing with the indeterminacy of the metric (Baker, 1993a). The f_{js}s might be the hypothetical frequencies with which each component s influences the solution of each item j, or may simply reflect whether a component is necessary for responding to an item. When the number of components equals the number of items on the instrument, then the LLTM is equivalent to the Rasch model (Embretson, 1984).

The η_s may correspond to *cognitive operations* required to solve an item, instructional conditions (characterized by their efficacy) experienced by the individual before attempting the item, or the "difficulties" of the cognitive operations (see Embretson, 1984). In short, these components reflect the hypotheses about the psychological structure of the item. Therefore, Equation E.2 shows that the item's location is a result of the (weighted) cognitive operations that are required to respond to the item. The values of the η_ss provide information about the relative contribution of a component to the item's location (Baker, 1993a). In effect, the η_ss are like regression coefficients. The cognitive structure underlying the item set is determined prior to the calibration of the data or as part of the instrument creation process. For more information on cognitive structure/processing and how it can be used for instrument development, see Embretson (1985, 1996), Frederiksen, Mislevy, and Bejar (1993), and Irvine and Kyllonen (2002).

As an example, assume that a sample of 287 examinees is administered a 29-item mathematics test (Fischer, 1973). To answer the questions on the test the examinee must take the first derivative of a series of functions. This example is concerned with the first two questions on the 29-item test:

1. $x^3 (x^2 + 1)^5$
2. $\dfrac{x^2 - 3}{5x + 4}$

The basic rules/operations that would be used to solve the problems on the 29-item test are:

1. Differentiation of a polynomial
2. Product rule
3. Quotient rule
4. Compound functions
5. $\sin(x)$
6. $\cos(x)$
7. $\exp(x)$
8. $\ln(x)$

For the first question one needs to use rules 1, 2, and 4, whereas for the second question one uses rules 1 and 3. The operations associated with which items are indicated by the f_{js}. The f_{js} for the test may be collected into a weight matrix, $\underline{F}$. For example,

$$\underline{F} = \begin{bmatrix} 1 & 1 & 0 & 1 & 0 & 0 & 0 & 0 \\ 1 & 0 & 1 & 0 & 0 & 0 & 0 & 0 \end{bmatrix}$$

where the columns represent the eight operations and the rows reflect the two items. In this case, the interest is in the presence/absence of the operation. Therefore, the entries in $\underline{F}$ reflect whether the operation is needed (a "1") or not (a "0") for a particular item. For instance, the first column indicates that rule 1 is used for both items and the second column shows that rule 2 is used only for item 1, but not for item 2, and so on.

Fischer's calibration results showed that for the test $C = -2.092$ and

$\eta_1 = -0.199$	$\eta_5 = -0.626$
$\eta_2 = 0.061$	$\eta_6 = -0.759$
$\eta_3 = -0.290$	$\eta_7 = 0.020$
$\eta_4 = -1.750$	$\eta_8 = -0.388$

(Note that the η_ss are constant across the items.) Therefore, given that

$$\delta_j = \sum_{s=1}^{S} f_{js}\eta_s + C$$

the item location estimates for items 1 and 2 are

$$\hat{\delta}_1 = 1(-0.199) + 1(0.061) + 0(-0.290) + 1(-1.750) + 0(-0.626) + 0(-0.759) +$$
$$0(0.02) + 0(-0.388) + (-2.092) = -0.204$$

$$\hat{\delta}_2 = 1(-0.199) + 0(0.061) + 1(-0.290) + 0(-1.750) + 0(-0.626) + 0(-0.759) +$$
$$0(0.02) + 0(-0.388) + (-2.092) = -1.604$$

According to $\underline{F}$, item 1 involves more operations than item 2. As a result one may conjecture that item 1 should be more difficult than item 2. The results verify this conjecture (i.e., $\hat{\delta}_1 = -0.204$ and $\hat{\delta}_2 = -1.604$).

Although there are specialized programs for obtaining estimates for the LLTM (see Seliger & Fischer, 1994), it is possible to perform the analysis using a two-step approach that doesn't require specialized programs. This approach produces results that are similar to those of the specialized programs. The first step in this approach is the fitting of the Rasch model. The second step involves regressing the resulting $\hat{\delta}_j$s on the component variables (i.e., $\underline{F}$). The resulting regression coefficients are the estimates of the η_ss.

The usefulness of LLTM for a particular instrument depends on the accuracy of the hypothesized cognitive structure underlying the item set (i.e., the $\underline{F}$ matrix). Baker (1993a) examined the effects of the misspecification of the $\underline{F}$ matrix. He found that the parameter estimates' accuracy depended on the sparseness of the $\underline{F}$ matrix as well as the sample size. Even a small degree of misspecification had a large impact on the estimates. He concluded that "because specifying the <$\underline{F}$> matrix is a judgmental task, it must be done with great care" (p. 209). Moreover, in the LLTM the item's location is perfectly predictable by the weighted cognitive operations. However this assumption may not be tenable and it may be prudent to include a random error term in Equation E.2. Janssen, Schepers, and Peres (2004) present such a model. The reader interested in the application of an LLTM-like model would be well served by considering the Janssen et al. (2004) model.

The advantage of using a specialized program for performing an LLTM calibration is the fit information that is provided. This is particularly important when one is evaluating different cognitive structures for an item set. That is, because competing theories may lead to alternative cognitive structures for an item, the LLTM may be used for evaluating these competing theoretical explanations. For additional application examples, see Embretson (1993), Embretson and Wetzel (1987), Fischer and Formann (1982), and Spada and McGaw (1985).

USING PRINCIPAL AXIS FOR ESTIMATING ITEM DISCRIMINATION

One may use the relationship between the two-parameter normal ogive model and factor analysis (see Appendix C) to obtain item parameter estimates (Lord & Novick, 1968; Mislevy, 1986b; Takane & de Leeuw, 1987). This alternative approach for estimating the discriminations involves performing a principal axis analysis of the tetrachoric correlation matrix for the data.[1] PRELIS (Jöreskog & Sörbom, 1999) is used to obtain the tetrachoric correlation matrix, $\underline{R}_T$, shown in Table E.1. (Alternative ways to obtain the tetrachoric correlation matrix are to use an SPSS macro by Enzmann [2002], to use

TABLE E.1. Tetrachoric Correlation Matrix, $\underline{R}_T$, for the Mathematics Test Data

	Item intercorrelations			
1	2	3	4	5
1.000				
0.453	1.000			
0.368	0.502	1.000		
0.313	0.519	0.476	1.000	
0.240	0.373	0.368	0.369	1.000

TESTFACT, or, because the tetrachoric correlation is a special case of the polychoric correlation, to use SAS's `plcorr` keyword with `proc freq`.)

An exploratory principal axis analysis of $\underline{R}_T$ yields a one factor solution ($\lambda_1 = 2.1177$, $\lambda_2 = 0.1626$, $\lambda_3 = 0.0742$, $\lambda_4 = 0.0369$). If we specify the extraction of a single factor, we obtain a common factor that accounts for 42.4% of the common variance with the following factor loadings (a_js) for items 1 through 5: $a_1 = 0.5258$, $a_2 = 0.76660$, $a_3 = 0.6884$, $a_4 = 0.6748$, and $a_5 = 0.5100$. The difference between $\underline{R}_T$ and the reproduced $\underline{R}_T$ yields residuals that are all less than $|0.0005|$.

Given that the factor loadings are the biserial correlations of the responses with θ (Lord, 1980), we can use the factor loadings with Equation C.12 (Appendix C) to obtain estimates of α; $\hat{\delta}$s are obtained via Equation C.16. These $\hat{\alpha}$s are on the normal metric. Using Equation C.12 we obtain $\hat{\alpha}_1 = 0.6181$, $\hat{\alpha}_2 = 1.1938$, $\hat{\alpha}_3 = 0.9490$, $\hat{\alpha}_4 = 0.9145$, and $\hat{\alpha}_5 = 0.5928$. (As a comparison, the BILOG estimates on the normal metric are $\hat{\alpha}_1 = 0.733$, $\hat{\alpha}_2 = 1.199$, $\hat{\alpha}_3 = 0.928$, $\hat{\alpha}_4 = 0.922$, and $\hat{\alpha}_5 = 0.587$; these estimates are obtained using the command file shown in Table 5.1, but with the subcommand LOG omitted from the GLOBAL line.) If we place our $\hat{\alpha}$s on the logistic metric by multiplying them by D, we obtain $\hat{\alpha}_1 = 1.0519$, $\hat{\alpha}_2 = 2.0319$, $\hat{\alpha}_3 = 1.6151$, $\hat{\alpha}_4 = 1.5564$, and $\hat{\alpha}_5 = 1.0090$. The correlation between these $\hat{\alpha}$s with those from the Chapter 5 example, "Application of the 2PL Model to the Mathematics Data, MMLE," shows a strong linear relationship between this approach and those obtained by MMLE, r = 0.9784.

INFINITE ITEM DISCRIMINATION PARAMETER ESTIMATES

In some situations it is possible to experience difficulty in estimating an item's discrimination parameter with either JMLE or MMLE. Specifically, for some items the estimate of α may drift off to infinity. The situation where α does not have a finite estimate, is an example of a *Heywood case* (i.e., an improper solution); for example, see Bock and Aitkin (1981), Christofferson (1975), and Swaminathan and Gifford (1985). To explain why this difficulty in estimating α is related to factor analysis's Heywood case, recall that the total variance (σ^2) of each variable can be decomposed into variability that is in common across variables (*common variance*) plus variance specific to the variable (*specific variance*) and *error variance*. Specific and error variances collectively constitute *unique variance*. The complement of an item's unique variance is its communality, h_j^2; that is, $h_j^2 = 1 - \text{unique } \sigma_j^2$. A variable's communality specifies the proportion of a variable's variance that is attributable to the common factors.

Although the bounds for h_j^2 are 0.0 and 1.0, the estimate of h_j^2, $\hat{h}_j^2$, may not be within these sounds. Because h_j^2 is a measure of common variance, the estimate reflects negative common variance whenever $\hat{h}_j^2 < 0.0$. In addition, if $\hat{h}_j^2 > 1.0$, then one has a Heywood case (Heywood, 1931). In terms of variance, a Heywood case reflects negative unique variance, because for the equality in "$1 = h_j^2 +$ unique σ_j^2" to hold, the item's unique σ_j^2 must be negative.

We can estimate a communality using the triad approach (Harman, 1960):

$$\hat{h}^2 = \frac{r_{jk}r_{jl}}{r_{kl}}$$

where k and l are the two variables with the highest correlation with the variable of interest. For example, if we apply this approach to the values in Table E.1, we obtain an $\hat{h}_2^2 = 0.5473$ for the second item. However, if we change r_{34} to be 0.25 (Table E.1), then $\hat{h}_j^2 = 1.0422$ (i.e., a Heywood case) and its corresponding unique σ_j^2 is negative ($= 1 - 1.0422 = -0.0422$).

Because h_j^2 equals the sum of squared loadings across the F factors, that is

$$h_j^2 = \sum_f d_{jf}^2$$

and, with a unidimensional situation, $\sqrt{h_j^2} = a_j = r_{j\theta}$, we can use the communality for item j to estimate α_j via Equation C.12. Applying Equation C.12 to item 2 produces a nonfinite $\hat{\alpha}$. Figure E.1 shows that as a (or h^2) approaches 1.0, then α tends toward ∞. As such, if a (or h^2) ≥ 1, then α does not have a finite value.

This difficulty in estimating α does not occur in all data sets. In addition, by using a prior distribution for the estimation of α one may avoid the problem of obtaining a nonfinite $\hat{\alpha}$. An alternative strategy is to impose an upper limit on the values that the $\hat{\alpha}$s may take on (i.e., a kludge). This is the approach used in LOGIST. Unless otherwise specified by the user, BILOG imposes a prior distribution when estimating α with the 2PL and 3PL models (the 3PL model is discussed in Chapter 6); BILOG

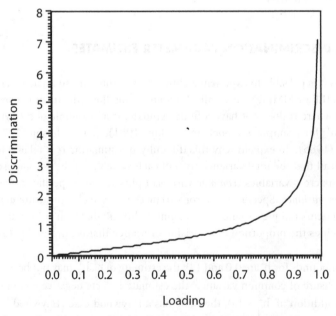

FIGURE E.1. Relationship between item loading and item discrimination.

also imposes a prior for estimating the IRF's lower asymptote, χ, for the 3PL model. The use of a prior in estimating α can be seen in the Phase 2 output in the CALIBRATION PARAMETERS section, the line PRIOR DISTRIBUTION ON SLOPES: YES. Although, in general, the use of a prior distribution (i.e., a Bayesian approach) produces estimates that may be regressed toward the prior's mean, the use of a prior with discrimination parameter estimation "has less serious implications than in the case of" (Lord, 1986, p. 161) person and item location parameters.

EXAMPLE: NOHARM UNIDIMENSIONAL CALIBRATION

In Chapter 3 we mention that NOHARM provides information about dimensionality as well as calibration results. In this section we discuss the two-parameter calibration results that were omitted from Table 3.2; NOHARM may also be used for obtaining results for the one-parameter and the three-parameter models. The input file shown in Chapter 3 (Table 3.1) produced the output shown below in Table E.2.

Chapter 10's "Estimation of the M2PL Model" section contains a brief overview of NOHARM's estimation approach. In the current context, the unidimensional two-parameter model may be seen as a special case of the M2PL. The reader interested in greater estimation detail is referred to McDonald (1967, 1997) and McDonald and Mok (1995). Our NOHARM results are on the normal metric. As such, if we wish to have the $\hat{\alpha}$s on the logistic metric we would need to multiply the $\hat{\alpha}$s by $D = 1.702$.

Our estimates are found at the end of the output in the section labeled LORD'S PARAMETER-IZATION - for the unidimensional case. The subsection Vector A : Discrimination parameters contains the item discrimination estimates. Our item discrimination estimates are $\hat{\alpha}_1 = 0.947$, $\hat{\alpha}_2 = 0.610$, $\hat{\alpha}_3 = 0.966$, $\hat{\alpha}_4 = 0.637$, and $\hat{\alpha}_5 = 1.106$. The item locations estimates are found in the subsection labeled Vector B : Difficulty parameters. As can be seen, the item location estimates are $\hat{\delta}_1 = -0.242$, $\hat{\delta}_2 = 0.550$, $\hat{\delta}_3 = 0.265$, $\hat{\delta}_4 = -2.258$, and $\hat{\delta}_5 = -0.498$. The values in these two subsections are determined from values previously presented in the output. For instance, the values labeled as Final Coefficients of Theta are the item discrimination estimates (e.g., $\hat{\alpha}_1 = 0.947$, $\hat{\alpha}_2 = 0.610$, etc.). Dividing these values into the negative of the corresponding values labeled Final Constants produces the item location estimates (i.e., $\hat{\delta}_j = -\hat{\gamma}_j / \hat{\alpha}_j$). Therefore, for item 1, we have $\hat{\delta}_1 = -0.229/0.947 = -0.242$; for item 2, $\hat{\delta}_2 = -(-0.335)/0.610 = 0.549$; and so on. The Pearson correlation coefficients between the NOHARM estimates and those from BILOG are 0.9564 for the $\hat{\alpha}$s and 0.9996 for the $\hat{\delta}$s.

The values from the Threshold Values section are estimates that correspond to the z_{t_j} shown in Figure C.5. As a result, these threshold values are related to the items' P_js and may be obtained in the way described above in Appendix C (i.e., using the inverse of the cumulative unit normal distribution for a specific P_j). NOHARM obtains these values by taking the Final Constants values and multiplying them by the square root of the values in the Unique Variances section. For example, the threshold value for item 1 would be obtained as $0.229* \sqrt{0.527} = 0.166$.

As discussed above in the "Using Principal Axis for Estimating Item Discrimination" section, item discriminations may be estimated by using factor loadings. Using the values provided in the Factor Loadings section and dividing them by the square root of the unique variances provides the item discrimination estimates. For instance, for item 1 the corresponding factor loading is 0.688 and the unique variance is 0.527. Therefore, $0.688/\sqrt{0.527} = 0.947$.

Chapter 3 shows how to interpret NOHARM's fit information to assess model–data fit. If we were interested in comparing empirical and predicted IRFs as well as obtaining item fit statistics (e.g., X^2),

TABLE E.2. One-Dimensional Output Including Item Parameter Estimates

```
                                 NOHARM
                Fitting a (multidimensional) Normal Ogive
                    by Harmonic Analysis - Robust Method
:
                                 =======
                                 Results
                                 =======
Success. The job converged to the specified criterion.

Final Constants
         1        2        3        4        5
      0.229   -0.335   -0.256    1.438    0.551

Final Coefficients of Theta
                  1
         1       0.947
         2       0.610
         3       0.966
         4       0.637
         5       1.106

:
<fit information discussed in Chapter 3>
:

Threshold Values
         1        2        3        4        5
      0.166   -0.286   -0.184    1.213    0.369

Unique Variances
         1        2        3        4        5
      0.527    0.729    0.517    0.711    0.450


Factor Loadings
                  1
         1       0.688
         2       0.521
         3       0.695
         4       0.537
         5       0.742

           LORD'S PARAMETERIZATION - for the unidimensional case
           =======================================================

Vector A : Discrimination parameters
         1        2        3        4        5
      0.947    0.610    0.966    0.637    1.106

Vector B : Difficulty parameters
         1        2        3        4        5
     -0.242    0.550    0.265   -2.258   -0.498
```

then a program like MODFIT could be used. Therefore, the combination of NOHARM and MODFIT provides a free approach to calibration and model fit assessment. The technical details of the fit calculations in MODFIT may be found in Drasgow et al. (1995).

As an example, the MODFIT plot of the empirical and predicted IRFs for item 2 is presented in Figure E.2. Because the predicted IRT (labeled IRF2) falls within the 95% error bars of the empirical IRT (labeled EMP2) there is evidence of model–data fit for this item. Although the corresponding X^2 of 15.787 is significant with 1 df (i.e., we do not have model–data fit), the sample size results in a powerful statistical test. Thus, for this item we conclude that there is model–data fit. In general, the sample sizes typically seen in IRT calibrations can result in potentially powerful statistical tests. Therefore, we suggest that significant statistical tests be interpreted in conjunction with graphical displays to see if there is a meaningful deviation between what is observed and what is predicted.

It should be noted that these MODFIT results are not directly comparable to those of BILOG because (1) MODFIT is limited to 3000 cases, whereas the BILOG results were based on all 19,601 individuals in the data, and (2) BILOG uses the calibration sample for determining the proportions, whereas MODFIT's empirical IRF is computed from a cross-validation sample. (The above use of a single program to perform both dimensionality analysis and calibration can also be accomplished through the program MPLUS for the 1PL and 2PL models.)

AN APPROXIMATE CHI-SQUARE STATISTIC FOR NOHARM

In addition to using NOHARM's RMS and GFI to determine data dimensionality, one could also use Maydeu-Olivares and Joe's (2006) M_2 statistic or Gessaroli and De Champlain's (1996) *approximate* chi-square statistic, X^2_{GD}. The former statistic is distributed as a X^2, although at present its calculation is not easily performed. The latter statistic tests the null hypothesis that the off-diagonal elements of the residual matrix are zero (i.e., the number of dimensions is correctly specified in the model). Although Maydeu-Olivares (2001) has indicated that Gessaroli and De Champlain's statistic is not distributed as a X^2, it may still be useful to provide some rough evidence to support a unidimensional or a multidimensional model of the data. For example, research has found X^2_{GD} to be useful to correctly identify dimensionality with sample sizes of 250, 500, and 1000 (e.g., De Champlain & Gessaroli, 1998; Gessaroli & De Champlain, 1996; also see Finch & Habing, 2005).

Because X^2_{GD} is based on evaluating the off-diagonal elements of the symmetric residual matrix, there are $(L^2 - L)/2$ unique off-diagonal item pairs. To calculate X^2_{GD} we use the items' observed proportion of responses of 1 (P^O) and the residual matrix's values to obtain an estimated residual correlation for each unique item pair. This estimated "residual correlation" between items j and v is

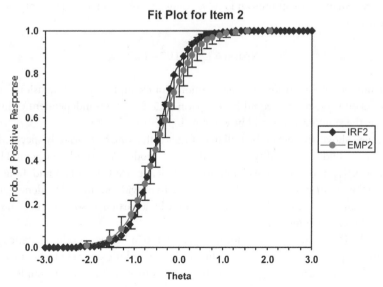

FIGURE E.2. MODFIT plot of the empirical and predicted IRFs for item 2.

$$r_{jv}^* = \frac{P_{jv}^*}{\sqrt{[P_j^o(1-P_j^o)][P_v^o(1-P_v^o)]}} \tag{E.4}$$

where P_j^o is item j's observed proportion of responses of 1, P_v^o is the observed proportion of responses of 1 for item v, and P_{jv}^* is the residual proportion of individuals who responded 1 to both items j and v (i.e., P_{jv}^* is the difference between the observed proportion of individuals who responded 1 to both items and what would be expected on the basis of the model). The P_{jv}^*s come from the NOHARM program's residual matrix and the P^os may be obtained from the main diagonal of $\underline{P}$; see Equation 3.4.

Prior to summing the estimated residual correlations across all unique item pairs, each residual correlation is transformed using the Fisher r-to-z transformation

$$z_{jv}^* = 0.5 \ln\left[\frac{1+r_{jv}^*}{1-r_{jv}^*}\right] \tag{E.5}$$

to stabilize their variances. The weighted sum of the squared Fisher zs gives an approximate chi-square for the solution

$$X_{GD}^2 = (N-3) \sum_{j=2}^{L} \sum_{v=1}^{j-1} [z_{jv}^*]^2 \tag{E.6}$$

where N is the sample size and L is the instrument length. This statistic would be calculated for each dimensional solution and its significance may be evaluated with $df = (L^2 - L)/2 - Nparm$, where Nparm is the number of estimated independent parameters in the solution's nonlinear factor analytic model. Determining Nparm's value depends on the number of dimensions, the number of items, and the number of constraints. In the exploratory case the simplest way to obtain Nparm is to count the number of unique estimates in NOHARM's Final Coefficients of Theta table. Alternatively, when there are no equality constraints and one is using NOHARM in an exploratory mode, one may determine Nparm by

$$Nparm = L*F - (L^2 - L)/2 \tag{E.7}$$

where F is the number of dimensions for the solution. For example, a two-dimensional solution with L = 5 and no equality constraints would have Nparm = (5*2 – 1) = 9 independent estimated parameters. Therefore, the solution's *df* would be equal to 1.

As mentioned above, the gist of the null hypothesis is that one has correctly specified the number of dimensions (e.g., unidimensionality) in the calibration model. As a result, one would like to obtain a nonsignificant X_{GD}^2 in order to have supporting evidence. De Champlain and Tang (1997) have suggested using the number and proportion of $|z_{jv}^*|s > 2$ to provide additional evidence supporting the result of the hypothesis test, as well as for diagnosing why a particular solution does not correspond to the specified dimensional model.

The use of the (N – 3) weighting factor in Equation E.6 indicates that this statistic's performance is influenced by sample size. The degree of influence is greater for extremely large or extremely small samples than for sample sizes of, say, 500 to 1000. For our example's large sample size we would expect its influence to lead us to falsely reject the correct dimensional solution. As a consequence, we did not use X^2_{GD} in our example. Software for calculating X^2_{GD} and obtaining its probability is available from De Champlain and Tang (1997). Alternatively, a spreadsheet program could be used to calculate the X^2_{GD} and its significance evaluated using critical values or a function like EXCEL's CHIDIST.

MIXTURE MODELS

An alternative approach for addressing the lack of model–data fit with the 1PL model is to use a *mixture models* approach. In addition, mixture models may be useful with multidimensional data. Mixture models provide a means of addressing the situation where the 1PL model may not fit the population of interest, but does fit subpopulations. For instance, it may be that one observes varying item discrimination because the (heterogeneous) population consists of a mixture of (homogeneous) subpopulations. In this case, when we apply the 1PL model to each subpopulation we obtain model–data fit. Stated another way, and as foreshadowed in the first chapter, in some cases the latent space may be conceptualized as consisting of both latent classes and latent continua. This section first presents a general introduction to latent class analysis (LCA) and then introduces the mixture of the latent class approach with IRT; LCA is briefly introduced in Chapter 1.

Our latent classes are subpopulations of individuals that are homogeneous with respect to the variable of interest. These subpopulations are not manifest groupings (e.g., high- versus low-proficiency groups), but are latent. Moreover, these latent classes may or may not be ordered.

In LCA an item is characterized in terms of the probability of a randomly drawn individual from a particular latent class providing a particular response. Extending this idea to an instrument with L items and m possible responses, one can obtain the probability of an individual's particular response pattern (or vector), $\underline{x}$, given his or her membership in latent class v by

$$p(\underline{x}|v) = \prod_{j=1}^{L} \prod_{k=1}^{m} (\delta_{k|jv})^{x_{kj}} \tag{E.8}$$

The $\delta_{k|jv}$ characterizes the item and is known as a conditional probability. That is, it reflects the conditional probability of the observed response k, given item j and the individual's membership in latent class v. If the items are binary (i.e., m = 2) and reflect proficiency items, then these conditional probabilities are, in effect, measures of item difficulty. The power x_{kj} equals 1 if and only if $x_j = k$.

The unconditional probability of the observed response vector $\underline{x}$ may be specified as the weighted average of the conditional probabilities across the G latent classes:

$$p(\underline{x}) = \sum_{v=1}^{G} \pi_v \, p(\underline{x}|v) \tag{E.9}$$

In Equation E.9 the weights, π_v, are known as the *latent class proportions* and are indices of the relative size of the latent classes in a population. The sum of the π_vs across latent classes is constrained to be 1.0:

$$\sum_{v=1}^{G} \pi_v = 1.0 \text{ with } 0 \le \pi_v \le 1.0$$

For instance, if the latent variable is, say, algebra knowledge, and the class structure consists of two classes, then π_1 might equal 0.65 and $\pi_2 = 1 - 0.65 = 0.35$. Moreover, the interpretation of the latent classes may reveal that the larger class (i.e., $\pi_1 = 0.65$) consists of persons who have mastered algebraic problems, whereas the other class consists of individuals who have not mastered the problems. In short, the latent structure consists of masters and nonmasters.

One may conceive of a situation where, with a large number of *ordered* latent classes, there would be little difference between conceptualizing the latent variable as continuous or as categorical. In point of fact, Lindsay, Clogg, and Grego (1991) have shown that a latent class model with $G \ge (L + 1)/2$ latent classes gives the same estimates of item parameters as the Rasch model; also see Masters (1985).[2] For example, for a data set with L = 4 items, a latent class model with at least three latent classes would provide item characterizations "equivalent" to those of the Rasch model that uses only item location parameters. Both Clogg (1995) and Dayton (1998) provide readable introductions to LCA.

In the current context of mixture models, assume that the data consist of a mixture of subpopulations that are different from one another in *kind*. Each of these subpopulations might be best represented as a latent class of individuals. Within each of these classes there is a latent continuum on which the individuals within the class may be placed and ordered. That is, one has a situation in which there are both qualitative *and* quantitative differences among individuals with respect to the same tasks (e.g., Rost, 1990). In effect, we have IRT model–data fit within each class, but not across the classes. Therefore, each item has parameter estimates for each class. (In the simplest case, there is only one latent class and the calibration sample contains only members from a single class.) As a result, one has model–data fit with a simple IRT model. The gist of the application of mixture models is to "unmix" the data into a set of classes, determine the classes' sizes, assign individuals to classes, and estimate the person and item parameters for each class.

A mixture model involves parameters having to do with latent classes and IRT item and person parameters. As outlined in Chapter 1, these latent classes are mutually exclusive and jointly exhaustive. The symbolic representation of the mixture model for person i and item j is similar to Equation E.9, but with the conditional response probability given by an IRT model:

$$P_{ij} = \sum_{v=1}^{G} \pi_v \, P_{ijv} \qquad\qquad (E.10)$$

The IRT model may be a dichotomous model, such as the Rasch model (Mislevy & Verhelst, 1990; Rost, 1990, 1991), or a model for ordered response categories (Rost, 1991) or unordered response categories (Bolt, Cohen, & Wollack, 2001).[3]

For example, for the mixed 1PL model p_{ijv} is

$$P_{ijv} = p(x_j = 1 \mid \theta_v, \alpha_v, \delta_{jv}) = \frac{e^{\alpha_v(\theta_v - \delta_{jv})}}{1 + e^{\alpha_v(\theta_v - \delta_{jv})}} \qquad (E.11)$$

where α_v is the common item discrimination in latent class v, δ_{jv} is item j's location in latent class v, and θ_v is the person location in latent class v. Equation E.11 specifies that the probability of a response of 1 on item j is a function of an individual's latent class membership (as indexed by v) and his or her location on the continuum within latent class v, as well as item j's parameters for the relevant latent class (α_{jv} and δ_{jv}). If $\alpha_v = 1.0$, then Equation E.10 becomes the *mixture Rasch model* or *mixed Rasch model* (Rost, 1990, 1991). The IRT assumptions discussed in Chapter 2 hold within each latent class.

Specialized software such as *MIRA* (Rost & von Davier, 1992) or *WINMIRA* (von Davier, 2001) can be used to estimate the mixture model's parameters for some of the members of the Rasch family of models. *WINBUGS* (Spiegelhalter, Thomas, Best, & Lunn, 2004) may also be used to estimate the model's parameters (see Bolt et al., 2001).

In addition to their use in addressing varying item discrimination, mixture models have been applied to the situation where the latent classes represent different problem-solving strategies (Mislevy & Verhelst, 1990). For instance, imagine that a test item consists of a three-dimensional object. Participants are then shown a second object that may be the first object, albeit from a different perspective. The participants are asked whether the second object is the same as the first. In this example, one class could consist of individuals who employ a mental rotational strategy to solve the problem, whereas a second class might consist of people employing analytical reasoning to detect feature(s) that match without performing the rotation.

As a second potential application example, assume one administers an instrument designed to measure social anxiety to a sample of individuals. This sample may consist of a mixture of three latent populations, with each latent population representing a latent class of individuals. Although the classes are unobservable, they may be interpreted or labeled in the same sense that one interprets a factor in factor analysis. Therefore, an interpretation of these classes may result in one class being labeled as persons who suffer from major depression, another class as consisting of persons who suffer from hebephrenia, and a third class that contains persons who are neither of these types of individuals. Although it may be possible to measure social anxiety on a unidimensional continuum within each class, it may not be possible to place each of these individuals on a single social anxiety unidimensional continuum.

RELATIVE EFFICIENCY, MONOTONICITY, AND INFORMATION

The effect on the information function of a monotonic transformation of θ to a new metric θ^* is that the transformed information function ($I(\theta^*,y)$) equals the untransformed information function ($I(\theta,y)$) divided by the square of the derivative of the transformation (Lord, 1974b):[4]

$$I(\theta^*,y) = \frac{I(\theta,y)}{\left[\dfrac{\partial\theta^*}{\partial\theta}\right]^2} \qquad (E.12)$$

Equation E.12 implies that the location of the maximum information may be changed by a transformation of the metric. Moreover, the shape of the information function may be changed as $\dfrac{\partial\theta^*}{\partial\theta}$ varies across the continuum (Lord, 1980).

As an example of the invariance of RE under a monotonic transformation, assume that a monotonic transformation is applied to the 1PL and 2PL model calibration results from Chapter 5. This monotonic transformation is based on the exponential function and is $\xi^* = Ke^{c\xi}$ with $\alpha_j^* = \alpha_j/c$ here ξ is either θ or δ_j, K and c are two constants that, for convenience, are set to 1, and the asterisks indicate that the parameter estimates are on the transformed metric (cf. Lord, 1980). For convenience, the item parameter estimates from Chapter 5 are presented in Table E.3.

TABLE E.3. 1PL and 2PL Models' Item Parameter Estimates for the Mathematics Data

	1PL model ($\hat{\alpha} = 1.40$)	2PL model	
Item	$\hat{\delta}_j$	$\hat{\alpha}_j$	$\hat{\delta}_j$
1	−1.950	1.226	−2.107
2	−0.586	1.992	−0.499
3	−0.264	1.551	−0.254
4	0.292	1.544	0.270
5	0.453	0.983	0.560

   The information functions on the transformed metric are given by the 1PL and 2PL models' information functions from the untransformed metric (e.g., Figure 5.5) divided by $(e^\theta)^2$ (i.e., for this transformation the denominator of Equation E.12 is $(e^\theta)^2$). These transformed 1PL and 2PL models' information functions ($I(\theta^*,2PL)$ and $I(\theta^*,1PL)$, respectively) are shown in Figure E.3; $I(\theta^*,1PL)$ is symbolized 1PL* and $I(\theta^*,2PL)$ is symbolized as 2PL* in the figure. As can be seen, the latent variable metric that use to be $-3 \leq \theta \leq 3$ becomes $0.05 \leq \theta^* \leq 20.05$. It is clear that these information functions are neither unimodal nor symmetric and do not have the same maxima as those in Figure 5.5. Moreover, both models provide their maximum information at the lower end of the transformed metric. However, the RE plot of these information functions (Figure E.4) shows the same pattern as seen in Figure 5.6. Therefore, relative efficiency is scale independent under any monotonic transformation of the metric (Lord, 1980).

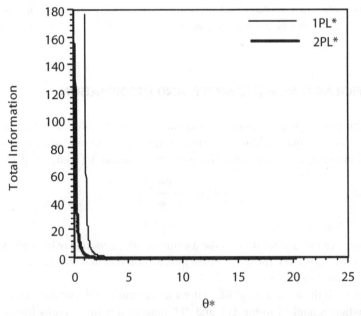

FIGURE E.3. Total information function for 1PL and 2PL model monotonically transformed metrics. 1PL information function shifted to the right by 1 unit to avoid superimposition with 2PL information function.

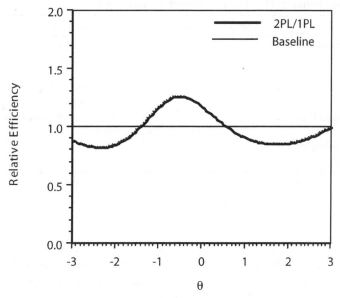

FIGURE E.4. Relative efficiency plot for monotonically transformed metric based on 1PL* and 2PL* models.

FORTRAN FORMATS

A FORTRAN format statement specifies how a FORTRAN program (e.g., MULTILOG, BILOG, EQUATE) should read and interpret the contents of a data file. A FORTRAN format begins and ends with a parenthesis. Everything within the parentheses consists of format descriptors. Some common general descriptors are presented in Table E.4; there are many more.

As an example, assume that our format statement is (10A1,T1,5(1X,1A1)). To interpret this statement the parenthesized term is decomposed into the segments defined by the commas. Therefore, our interpretation is

Format descriptor		Interpretation
"10A1"	means	read 10 alphanumeric variables that are each 1 column wide
"T1"	means	then go to column 1
"5(1X,1A1)"	means	then repeat the parenthesized terms 5 times

The parenthesized term is further broken down into two segments:

"1X"	means	skip 1 column
"1A1"	means	read 1 alphanumeric variable that is 1 column wide

That is, "5(1X,1A1)" is a shorthand way of specifying "1X,1A1,1X,1A1,1X,1A1,1X,1A1,1X,1A1."

Let us apply this (10A1,T1,5(1X,1A1)) to a line of data where the data begin with a space and successive values are separated by a space:

TABLE E.4. Some General FORTRAN Format Descriptors

Code	Meaning	Syntax	Example	Example's interpretation
A	specifies alphanumeric data	nAc	5A1	Read 5 columns as alphanumeric and each alphanumeric occupies one column
X	skip	nX	3X	Skip 3 columns
F	specifies floating point data	nFc.d	2F4.2	Read 2 real numbers that each occupy at most 4 columns and contain 2 decimal places
I	specifies integer data	nIc	1I6	Read 1 integer that occupies at most 6 columns
T	tab	Tc	T23	Go to column 23
/	skip to a new line for the current record			

Note. n = repeat factor, c = total number of columns, d = number of decimal places.

$$0\ \ 0\ \ 0\ \ 1\ \ 1$$

(i.e., the data are "ƀ0ƀ0ƀ0ƀ1ƀ1," where the ƀ indicates a blank space). Because the format (10A1,T1,5(1X,1A1)) first specifies the reading of 10 characters, each occupying one column (i.e., 10A1), the entire string " 0 0 0 1 1" is read. The next format descriptor, T1, instructs the program to return to column 1 (i.e., the first blank space). The final segment, 5(1X,1A1), specifies the rereading of the same 10 characters (i.e., " 0 0 0 1 1"). That is, skip a column and then read a column; do this five times.

Some calibration programs (e.g., BILOG and MULTILOG) allow the user to specify a case identification field. Specifically, the first format segment is associated with this identification field (e.g., 10A1 refers to the case identification field). For example, with the format (10A1,T1,5(1X,1A1)) we are using an individual's response pattern as his or her identification field and then specifying where to find the responses to be analyzed (i.e., T1, 5(1X,1A1)).

Sometimes each case has identification information, such as the person's Social Security number (SSN). For example, assume that each line of data consists of a person's SSN (with hyphens) followed by a space and then his or her response vector (e.g., 123-45-6789 00011). For this layout the, say, BILOG or MULTILOG format statement would be (11A1,1X,5A1). The 11A1 would read the SSN (including hyphens), 1X would skip the blank space following the SSN, and the 5A1 would read five consecutive columns of responses. Although the example's responses consist of the integers 0 and 1, by treating these data as alphanumerics (i.e., using the A in the format) the program allows flexibility in the data coding. For instance, our format statement could be used with a response vector that contains letters, such as "T" and "F" (e.g., 123-45-6789 FFFTT).

EXAMPLE: MIXED MODEL CALIBRATION OF THE SCIENCE TEST— NR AND 2PL MODELS, MMLE

The analysis of the ORFs for the item set in Chapter 9 (Figure 9.5) indicates that the first two items were behaving in a binary fashion. Therefore, in an attempt to improve the fit to the data the first two items are scored correct (i.e., a coded response of 1) and incorrect (i.e., a coded response of 0); we assume that there are no other reasons to keep these items' responses as polytomous data. As a result, the first two items are modeled with the 2PL model and the last two are modeled with the NR model. Although theoretically the 2PL model is subsumed by the NR model, MULTILOG's implementation does not allow the NR model calibration of items with fewer than three options; MULTILOG estimates the 2PL model as a special case of the GR model. Therefore, it is necessary to use two TEST lines to identify the items associated with the 2PL and NR models (see Table E.5 for the command file). The first TEST line specifies the use of the 2PL model with items 1 and 2, whereas the second TEST line indicates the use of the NR model with items 3 and 4. After the dichotomization of the responses for items 1 and 2 there are 64 possible patterns across the item set, all of which are observed. Table E.6 contains the abridged output.

Convergence is achieved in 26 cycles. Using the 2PL model, item 1 has an estimated item discrimination of 0.74 and a location estimate of 0.60, whereas for item 2, $\hat{\alpha}_2 = 0.81$ and $\hat{\delta}_2 = 0.36$. Because of a difference in the metrics of the NR model-only calibration and the way this mixed model calibration is implemented, we do not expect the item parameter estimates for items 3 and 4 to be the same as those resulting from NR model-only calibration. The $-2\ln L$ for this NR-2PL mixed model calibration is 51.8 with 16 free parameters (BIC = 171.7198). This $-2\ln L$ of 51.8 reflects a substantial improvement in fit over simply using the NR model for calibrating all four items. If there were no substantive reasons for treating the first two items as polytomous, then from simply a fit perspective items 1 and 2 should be treated as binary items. However, the cost of doing this is an instrument that provides less information below approximately 0.8 than when we calibrate it using solely the NR model (see Tables 9.2 and E.6's TOTAL TEST INFORMATION sections). (The similarity in the estimates for items 3 and 4 from this calibration and those from the NR model-only calibration indicates that the metrics are in close alignment to one another, so the value 0.8 would not change by very much if the metrics are linked to one another.) Therefore, the accuracy of the location estimates for individuals less than 0.8 would be less with the mixed model approach than with the single NR model item parameter estimates. This begs the question, "Is it better to use more accurate person location estimates based on a comparatively poorer-fitting model or to use less accurate $\hat{\theta}$s based on a better-fitting model?" If the purpose of the calibration is to estimate θ (in contrast to, for example, item pool

TABLE E.5. Command File for the NR and 2PL Mixed Model Calibration

```
MULTILOG for Windows 7.00.2327.2
2PL CALIBRATION OF ITEMS 1 & 2; NR FOR ITEMS 3 & 4
>PROBLEM RANDOM,
         PATTERNS,
         DATA = 'C:CompPatMix.PAT',
         NITEMS = 4,
         NGROUPS = 1,
         NPATTERNS = 64,
         NCHARS = 9;
>TEST ITEMS = (1, 2),               ⇐ Identifying items 1-2  for calibration with 2PLᵃ
      L2;
>TEST ITEMS = (3, 4),               ⇐ Identifying items 3-4  for calibration with NR
      NOMINAL,
      NC = (4, 4),
      HIGH = (4, 3);
>EST NC=500 IT=25;
>END ;
4
1234
1111
2222
0033
0044
(9A1,T1,4A1,F5.0)
```

ᵃThe text following the ⇐ is provided to help the reader understand the corresponding input.

TABLE E.6. Abridged Output for the NR and 2PL Mixed Model Calibration Example

```
           :
  NUMBER OF FREE PARAMETERS IS:    16
           :
  FIRST OBSERVATION AS READ-

  ID     2211      1
  ITEMS 2211
  NORML      0.000
  WT/CR      1.00
           :
  FINISHED CYCLE   26
     MAXIMUM INTERCYCLE PARAMETER CHANGE=    0.00077 P(   7)

     ITEM SUMMARY
           :
  ITEM    1:         2 GRADED CATEGORIES
          P(#) ESTIMATE (S.E.)
  A          1    0.74  (0.08)
  B( 1)      2    0.60  (0.10)

  @THETA:      INFORMATION:    (Theta values increase in steps of 0.2)
  -3.0 - -1.6  0.033  0.038  0.043  0.048  0.054  0.061  0.067  0.075
  -1.4 -  0.0  0.082  0.090  0.097  0.105  0.112  0.119  0.124  0.129
   0.2 -  1.6  0.133  0.135  0.136  0.135  0.133  0.129  0.125  0.119
   1.8 -  3.0  0.112  0.105  0.098  0.090  0.082  0.075  0.068

  OBSERVED AND EXPECTED COUNTS/PROPORTIONS IN
  CATEGORY(K):  1      2
  OBS. FREQ.   1076    723
  OBS. PROP.  0.5981 0.4019
  EXP. PROP.  0.5981 0.4019

  ITEM    2:         2 GRADED CATEGORIES
          P(#) ESTIMATE (S.E.)
  A          3    0.81  (0.08)
  B( 1)      4    0.36  (0.08)

  @THETA:      INFORMATION:    (Theta values increase in steps of 0.2)
           :
  OBSERVED AND EXPECTED COUNTS/PROPORTIONS IN
  CATEGORY(K):  1      2
  OBS. FREQ.   1014    785
  OBS. PROP.  0.5636 0.4364
  EXP. PROP.  0.5636 0.4364

  ITEM    3:         4 NOMINAL CATEGORIES,  4 HIGH
     CATEGORY(K): 1       2       3       4
     A(K)      -0.49   -0.54    0.29    0.74
     C(K)      -0.80   -0.41    0.51    0.70

  OBSERVED AND EXPECTED COUNTS/PROPORTIONS IN
  CATEGORY(K):  1       2       3       4
  OBS. FREQ.   192     293     564     750
  OBS. PROP.  0.1067 0.1629 0.3135 0.4169
  EXP. PROP.  0.1067 0.1628 0.3135 0.4170

  ITEM    4:         4 NOMINAL CATEGORIES,  3 HIGH
     CATEGORY(K): 1       2       3       4
     A(K)      -0.77    0.19   -0.11    0.69
     C(K)      -0.59    0.26    0.34   -0.01
           :
  TOTAL TEST INFORMATION
  @THETA:      INFORMATION:
  -3.0 - -1.6  1.328  1.368  1.409  1.453  1.497  1.541  1.584  1.625
  -1.4 -  0.0  1.661  1.692  1.717  1.735  1.745  1.747  1.742  1.730
   0.2 -  1.6  1.712  1.689  1.662  1.631  1.598  1.563  1.527  1.490
   1.8 -  3.0  1.454  1.418  1.383  1.350  1.318  1.288  1.260

  NEGATIVE TWICE THE LOGLIKELIHOOD=        51.8
           :
```

construction), then the answer to this question would hinge, at least in part, on the validity evidence for the $\hat{\theta}$s based on the mixed model and on the NR model calibration results.

EXAMPLE: MIXED MODEL CALIBRATION OF THE SCIENCE TEST— NR AND GR MODELS, MMLE

In Chapter 9 we performed a number of mixed model calibrations involving nested models. To demonstrate a mixed model calibration using non-nested models, we calibrate our science test (Chapter 9) using the GR and the NR models. The command file for performing this calibration is shown in Table E.7. As can be seen, two TEST lines are used to identify which items are associated with which model. The first TEST line specifies the use of the NR model with items 1 through 3, whereas the second TEST line indicates that the GR model should be used with item 4. The basic structure of the command file parallels that seen with the NR model (Table 9.1) and for the GR model (Table 8.3). Performing this mixed model calibration produces a $-2\ln L$ of 322.2 with 22 free parameters (BIC = 487.0897); for the NR model there are $2*(4-1) = 6$ parameters per item times 3 items, or 18 parameters, and for the GR model there are 4 parameters (i.e., one α and 3 category boundary locations), for a total number of estimated parameters of $18 + 4 = 22$. Using the GR model for item 4 we have an estimated item discrimination of 0.60 with category boundary locations of $\hat{\delta}_{41} = -2.94$, $\hat{\delta}_{42} = -0.42$, and $\hat{\delta}_{43} = 1.95$.

ODDS, ODDS RATIOS, AND LOGITS

Probabilities may be expressed in terms of the odds of an event occurring. Some treatments of IRT use the odds of an event in their discussions and we use them in Chapters 9 and 12. The *odds* of an event b occurring (i.e., a "success") is given by

TABLE E.7. Command File for the NR and GR Mixed Model Calibration

```
MULTILOG for Windows 7.00.2327.2
MIX NR & GR MODELS; ITEM 4 - 3 CATEGORIES
>PROBLEM RANDOM,
         PATTERNS,
         DATA = 'C:SCIENCE.PAT',
         NITEMS = 4,
         NGROUPS = 1,
         NPATTERNS = 256,
         NCHARS = 9;
>TEST ITEMS=(1,2,3),              ⇐ Identifying items 1-3  for calibration
      NOMINAL,                       with NR model[a]
      NC = (4,4,4),
      HIGH = (2,3,4);
>TEST ITEMS=4,                    ⇐ Identifying item 4  for calibration
      GR,                            with GR model
      NC = 4;
>EST NC=500 IT=25;
>END ;
      :
```

[a]The text following the ⇐ is provided to help the reader understand the corresponding input.

$$\text{odds}(b) = \frac{p(b)}{1 - p(b)} \tag{E.13}$$

Equation E.13 simply states that the odds of b occurring is equal to the ratio of the probability of the event b occurring to the probability that the event b does not occur. In other words, the odds of an event expresses the likelihood of the event occurring relative to its not occurring. If the event b is as likely to occur as to not occur, then the odds(b) equal 1 (i.e., $p(b) = 1 - p(b) = 0.5$). However, if the event b is less likely to occur than to not occur, then the odds(b) are less than 1. Conversely, if the event b is more likely to occur than to not occur, then the odds(b) are greater than 1.

By rearranging Equation E.13 one may obtain the probability of event b occurring expressed in terms of the odds of b by

$$p(b) = \frac{\text{odds}(b)}{1 + \text{odds}(b)} \tag{E.14}$$

Equation E.14 also shows that when an event b is as likely to occur as not (i.e., the odds$(b) = 1$), then $p(b) = 0.50$.

As an example of calculating odds, assume that the probability of b occurring (i.e., a "success") is 0.75. The corresponding odds of b occurring are 3 (i.e., 0.75/0.25) or, alternatively, the odds are 3 to 1 that b occurs as opposed to not occurring; odds are implicitly compared to 1. Conversely, the odds of b not occurring ($\overline{b}$) would be

$$\text{odds}(\overline{b}) = \frac{1 - p(b)}{p(b)} \tag{E.15}$$

In terms of our example, the odds of b not occurring is 0.25/0.75 or 1 to 3 (i.e., 0.333 to 1).

As a second example, let $p(b)$ be given by

$$p(b) = p(x = 1 | \theta, \alpha, \delta) = \frac{e^{\alpha(\theta - \delta)}}{1 + e^{\alpha(\theta - \delta)}} \tag{E.16}$$

That is, the probability of b occurring refers to a response of 1 (i.e., a "success") on an item. Therefore, we can talk about the odds of a response of 1 occurring versus a response of 0 on an item. For instance, if $\theta = -2.0$ and the item is located at -1.3 (i.e., $\delta = -1.3$), then according to Equation E.16 the probability of a response of 1 (i.e., success) is 0.3318. Expressing this probability in terms of odds we have that the odds of success on the item are roughly 1 to 2. That is, the odds are

$$\text{odds}(b) = \frac{p(b)}{1 - p(b)} = \frac{0.3318}{0.6682} = 0.4966; \text{ that is, } 0.4966 \text{ to } 1$$

(Multiplying each of these values by 2 gives us odds of 1 to 2). If this is a proficiency item, then these odds indicate that for people located at -2 we expect a correct response to this item for every two incorrect responses. Conversely, the odds of an *incorrect* response is approximately 2 to 1. That is,

$$\text{odds}(\overline{b}) = \frac{1 - \text{p}(b)}{\text{p}(b)} = \frac{0.6682}{0.3318} = 2.0138$$

Given that probabilities are always positive and sum to 1 for all the events in an event class, the odds of an event must be positive. Moreover, although probabilities fall within the range 0 to 1, their conversion to odds results in the range of odds being 0 to ∞ with a value of 1 reflecting no difference between the event occurring and not occurring. Because of this asymmetry in the odds scale (i.e., the "no difference point" occurs at 1) the odds of an event are sometimes transformed to the (natural) logarithmic scale (i.e., $\ln(\text{odds}(b))$). On the log scale a value of 0 reflects no difference between the event occurring and not occurring, positive values indicate that the odds of success are greater than of failure, and negative values reflect that the odds of failure are greater than the odds of success. This *logit transformation* gives the *log odds* or the *logit* of the event occurring. Therefore, applying this transformation to Equation E.13 one has

$$\ln(\text{odds}(b)) = \text{logit}[\text{p}(b)] = \ln\left[\frac{\text{p}(b)}{1 - \text{p}(b)}\right] \tag{E.17}$$

The transformation "$\text{logit}[\text{p}(b)]$" is sometimes called the logit link function. By substitution of Equation E.16 for $\text{p}(b)$ in $\frac{\text{p}(b)}{1 - \text{p}(b)}$ one obtains, upon simplification, that the odds for a response of 1 (i.e., event b) occurring are

$$\text{odds}(b) = \frac{\text{p}(b)}{1 - \text{p}(b)} = \frac{\dfrac{e^{\alpha(\theta-\delta)}}{1 + e^{\alpha(\theta-\delta)}}}{\dfrac{1}{1 + e^{\alpha(\theta-\delta)}}} = \left[\frac{e^{\alpha(\theta-\delta)}}{1 + e^{\alpha(\theta-\delta)}}\right]\left[\frac{1 + e^{\alpha(\theta-\delta)}}{1}\right]$$

$$= e^{\alpha(\theta - \delta)} \tag{E.18}$$

As a result, the log odds

$$\text{logit}[\text{p}(b)] = \ln\left[\frac{\text{p}(b)}{1 - \text{p}(b)}\right] = \ln[e^{\alpha(\theta - \delta)}] = \alpha(\theta - \delta) = \gamma + \alpha\theta \tag{E.19}$$

where $\gamma = -\alpha\delta$.

Equation E.19's term "$\gamma + \alpha\theta$" shows that the logit transformation has the effect of linearizing the nonlinear relationship between the continuous θ and the probability of the event of a response of 1 (i.e., $\text{p}(b) = \text{p}(x = 1|\theta, \alpha, \delta)$). As such, α reflects the slope of the logit regression line and may be interpreted as the change in the logit corresponding to a one-unit change in θ. The constant or intercept, γ, is simply the predicted logit value when $\theta = 0$. Alternatively, $\alpha\theta + \gamma$ may be interpreted as the term "$\alpha\theta$" specifying how much better in prediction one can do over the baseline odds provided by the intercept, γ. Stated another way, and for simplicity letting $\alpha = 1$, the logit $\alpha\theta + \gamma$ indicates how much knowing *only* the person's location improves our capacity to predict a response of 1 over and above just knowing the item's location (i.e., $\delta = -\gamma$ when $\alpha = 1$).

In terms of IRT, "$\alpha(\theta - \delta_j)$" (or $\gamma + \alpha\theta$) specifies the *logit success* and equals the weighted difference between the person and item locations; a logit is also known as a logistic deviate. Therefore, a person's θ in logits is his or her natural log odds for obtaining a response of 1 on items of the kind chosen to define the zero point on the scale, and an item's δ in logits is its natural log odds for a response of 0 on that item from persons with zero ability (Wright & Stone, 1979).

Just as we can obtain the probability of b from the odds of b, we can rearrange Equation E.19 to obtain the probability of b from the log odds of b (i.e., logits):

$$\ln\left[\frac{p(b)}{1 - p(b)}\right] = \alpha(\theta - \delta)$$

Applying the natural exponential function to both sides, one has

$$odds(b) = \left[\frac{p(b)}{1 - p(b)}\right] = e^{\alpha(\theta - \delta)}$$

Solving for p(b), one obtains

$$p(b) = \frac{e^{\gamma + \alpha\theta}}{1 + e^{\gamma + \alpha\theta}} = \frac{e^{\alpha(\theta - \delta)}}{1 + e^{\alpha(\theta - \delta)}} \tag{E.20}$$

Because $e^{\alpha(\theta - \delta)}$ equals the odds(b) (see Equation E.18), Equation E.20 is the conversion of the odds of a response of 1 to their corresponding probability (i.e., Equation E.14).

The reader may have recognized the "$\gamma + \alpha\theta$" term as the simple linear regression (SLR) model for predicting the criterion Y's conditional means (i.e., the means of Y's distribution for fixed values of θ). In other words, the SLR prediction equation is

$$\mathcal{E}(Y|\theta) = \beta_0 + \beta_1\theta$$

where $\beta_0 = \gamma$ and $\beta_1 = \alpha$. Analogously, because the mean of a binary variable is the proportion of 1s, the proportions shown in Figure 2.2 may be considered a series of conditional means (i.e., $\mathcal{E}(x|z) = p(z)$) and Equation E.20 may be written as

$$\mathcal{E}(x|\theta) = p(\theta) = \frac{e^{\gamma + \alpha\theta}}{1 + e^{\gamma + \alpha\theta}} \tag{E.21}$$

where x is our binary criterion (response) variable and θ is our predictor. In short, Equation E.20 may be recognized as the typical representation of a logistic regression model.

We now discuss odds ratios. A natural extension of asking about the odds of a single event is to ask about how the odds of one event relate to the odds of another event. In this regard, the above ideas about odds may be extended to describe the association between the odds of two events. This measure of association is the *odds ratio* (OR or Ω). The odds ratio is, as the name implies, the ratio of two odds (e.g., odds(b) and odds(a)). For instance, the odds ratio of b to a is

$$\Omega_{b,a} = \frac{[p(b)/(1-p(b))]}{[p(a)/(1-p(a))]} = \frac{\text{odds}(b)}{\text{odds}(a)} \qquad (E.22)$$

An odds ratio is asymmetrical about 1 with a range of 0 to ∞. An $\Omega = 1$ indicates that both events are equally likely, with a value less than 1 indicating that the odds of success for a are greater than the odds for b, and a value greater than 1 reflecting that the odds of success for b are greater than the odds for a. For instance, if $\Omega = 5$, then the odds of success for b is five times the odds of success for a. As is the case with odds, the odds ratio is sometimes transformed to a logarithmic scale ($\ln(\Omega)$) to eliminate its inherent asymmetry. The transformed odds ratio is centered at 0 (i.e., a 0 reflects no difference between the events occurring) with values greater than 0 reflecting that the log odds of success for b are greater than the log odds for a, and values less than 0 reflecting that the log odds of success for a are greater than the log odds for b. In Chapter 12 we use odds ratios in our discussion of differential item functioning.

THE PERSON RESPONSE FUNCTION

The *person response function* (PRF) provides a graphical approach to examining person–model fit; the PRF is also known as the *person characteristic curve* (Weiss, 1973). The idea of a PRF may be traced back to the works of Thorndike and Thurstone in the early part of the 20th century (Engelhard, 1990). The PRF presents the relationship of the probability of a person's response pattern and the item locations. In this regard, the PRF is the person analog to the item response function. Like the person fit statistics presented in Chapters 3 and 6, the PRF can be used for identifying misfitting individuals. In addition, the PRF may be used to identify a particular item or set of items for which person–item fit is problematic, as well as to provide diagnostic information, such as inattention, guessing, identifying copying, and so on (Trabin & Weiss, 1983; Wright, 1977b). The performance of PRF has been compared with that of the l_z index (Nering & Meijer, 1998). They found that although l_z performed well, and in some cases better than PRF, the PRF was useful in determining the reason for a misfitting response vector.

In general, the PRF is assumed to be a nonincreasing function of the item δs. Departures from this monotonicity assumption are taken as indicators of person–model misfit for all or some subset of the instrument's items. However, this assumption may be unreasonable if the items are multidimensional or the items cannot be ordered in the same way for all individuals (Sijtsma & Meijer, 2001).

To examine person fit, we compare a person's observed PRF (OPRF) with his or her expected PRF (EPRF). Trabin and Weiss (1983) argue that the shape of the OPRF provides diagnostic information concerning guessing behavior, carelessness, the precision with which the person is measured, and dimensionality information. Figure E.5 contains an example of each of these diagnoses and is adapted from Trabin and Weiss (1983). In the following, assume a proficiency assessment situation. The solid bold line is an individual's EPRF and the dotted-dashed curve reflects his or her OPRF (labeled "Good OPRF"). We would interpret the close agreement between these two curves as indicating good fit. Furthermore, the steepness of the OPRF reflects that this person is more precisely measured than he or she would have been if the OPRF had been less steep. Also shown are two additional (problematic) OPRFs labeled "B" and "C." Assume that the EPRF shown is appropriate for the persons with these OPRFs. Because the right side of person's OPRF C is greater than his or her EPRF, this person is correctly responding to items that he or she is expected to be incorrectly answering. Trabin and Weiss interpret this to indicate guessing behavior on the items located at the upper end of the continuum.

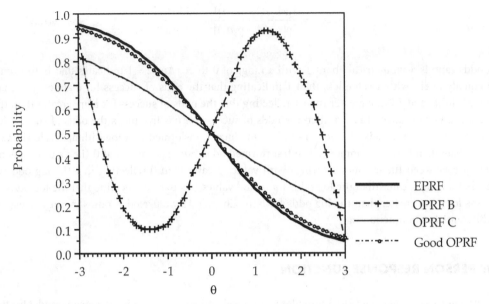

FIGURE E.5. Expected and three possible observed person response functions.

Moreover, because the observed proportion of correct responses for easy items (i.e., the left side of OPRF C) is less than would be expected according to the person's EPRF, one has evidence of careless-ness by the person. OPRF B reflects a person exhibiting inconsistent response behavior because he or she is incorrectly answering easy items and correctly answering difficult items. Because this person's OPRF reflects a deviation from a unidimensional response pattern, Trabin and Weiss (1983) suggest it reflects multidimensionality in the person.

One approach to obtaining the OPRF is to put the instrument's item into strata (s = 1 . . . S); it is preferable that all strata have the same number of items. Because each stratum consists of L_s items that are similar to one another in terms of location, the strata can be ordered on the basis of their aver-age locations.[6] Assuming dichotomous data and the strata approach, we can obtain an individual's OPRF by calculating, for each stratum, the proportion of items for which the person had a response of 1. Subsequently, these proportions are plotted as a function of stratum location level. To obtain the individual's EPRF one uses his or her $\hat{\theta}$ and the item parameter estimates to calculate the person's p_j for each item in each stratum. The average of these probabilities for the L_s items that define each stra-tum specifies the individual's expected proportion of 1s for the stratum. These averaged probabilities are then plotted as a function of the strata's locations to obtain the EPRF for the individual. To form a curve one connects the average probabilities (or in the case of the OPRF, the proportions) for each stratum. The OPRF may be overlaid on the EPRF to facilitate comparison of the two curves. In some cases it may be necessary to smooth the OPRF to reduce irregularities—for example, by using spline smoothing. Alternative approaches for PRF analysis use kernel smoothing or logistic regression to avoid the creation of strata (cf. Emmons, Sijtsma, & Meijer, 2004).

With item fit analyses we suggest that one use a combination of graphical approaches (e.g., empirical vs. predicted IRFs) and statistical indices for determining item fit. This same philosophy can be applied to assessing person fit. Specifically, a numerical index is used to identify individuals who merit further inspection and the PRF is the graphical approach for performing this inspection.

There are various indices that could be used to identify individuals for whom OPRFs and EPRFs should be created and examined. Meijer and Sijtsma (2001) present a review of some of these indices and recommend the UB statistic and Klauer and Rettig's (1990) chi-square statistic.

The UB statistic (Smith, 1985) is

$$UB = \frac{1}{S-1} \sum_{s=1}^{S} \frac{[O_s - E_s]^2}{V_s} \qquad (E.23)$$

where

$$O_s = \sum^{L_s} x_j, \ E_s = \sum^{L_s} p_j, \ V_s = \sum^{L_s} p_j(1-p_j), \text{ and } s = 1 \ldots S$$

This statistic may be standardized by a cube root transformation (Smith, 1985). As such, a standard normal table could be used to provide values that would identify individuals who warrant further scrutiny.

An alternative to the UB statistic is Klauer and Rettig's (1990) chi-square statistic. Their standardized person fit statistic is asymptotically distributed as a x^2 with the number of strata minus one as the *df*. Their statistic is

$$\chi^2_{sc} = \sum^{S} \frac{(W_s(\hat{\theta}))^2}{I_s(\hat{\theta})} \qquad (E.24)$$

where for the 3PL model the available information for estimating θ, $I_s(\hat{\theta})$, is given by

$$I_s(\hat{\theta}) = \frac{\alpha_j^2(1-p_j)}{p_j\left[(p_j-\chi_j)^2/(1-\chi_j)^2\right]} \qquad (E.25)$$

and

$$W_s = \sum^{L_s} \alpha_j \frac{\exp(\alpha_j(\hat{\theta}-\delta_j)}{1+\exp(\alpha_j(\hat{\theta}-\delta_j))p_j}(x_j - p_j) \qquad (E.26)$$

Although Equations E.25 and E.26 are written in terms of the 3PL model (Chapter 6), they are also appropriate for the 1PL and 2PL models. For example, for the 2PL model (Chapter 5) χ in Equation E.25 is set to 0. Similarly, for the 1PL model one uses Equation E.25 with the constant α and $\chi = 0$.

Klauer and Rettig (1990) have evaluated the significance of χ^2_{sc} with an α level of 0.10; a significant χ^2_{sc} indicates a misfitting person. Other indices that can be used to identify individuals for further (graphical) scrutiny may be found in Drasgow, Levine, and Williams (1985), Levine and Drasgow (1988), Meijer and Sijtsma (2001), Reise (2000), Reise and Due (1991), and van der Flier (1982).

LINKING: A TEMPERATURE ANALOGY EXAMPLE

Linking is analogous to comparing a measure of air temperature on the Celsius scale and another on the Fahrenheit scale. Because of differences in the origin and units of the two metrics, a meaningful direct comparison cannot be made between a temperature of, for example, 32 degrees on the Celsius metric, with a temperature of 32 degrees on the Fahrenheit scale without first transforming one metric to the other. This (linear) transformation (e.g., °F = 1.8°C + 32) amounts to (1) aligning the origins of the metrics to one another (i.e., the zero points) so that the "zero point" is equivalent in meaning on both scales (e.g., add 32 to the temperature on the Celsius scale so that 0°C is equivalent to 32°F), and (2) transforming the units in one metric to be the same size as the units on the other metric (e.g., 1 unit on the Celsius scale is equivalent to 1.8 units on the Fahrenheit scale). In short, the linear transformation from one metric to another involves two constants: one having to do with the units and the other having to do with the origin.

To show the parallel between this analogy and IRT metric alignment, we link the Celsius scale to the Fahrenheit scale using linear equating (Chapter 11) and the two data sets shown in Table E.8. The first data set is the annual monthly high temperature readings from Fargo, North Dakota, in both Celsius (°C) and Fahrenheit (°F), whereas the second data set consists of the annual monthly high temperature readings from Tucson, Arizona. For both data sets the Celsius scale is the initial metric and the Fahrenheit scale is the target metric; the temperature readings are analogous to item locations.

To transform the Fargo Celsius readings to Fahrenheit, we obtain the metric transformation coefficients for the Fargo data by Equation 11.5:

$$\zeta = s_{\delta *}/s_{\delta} = 24.8/13.8 = 1.80$$

and by Equation 11.6:

$$\kappa = \overline{\delta}_j{}^* - \zeta\overline{\delta}_j{}^* = 51.3 - 1.80(10.7) = 32$$

Therefore, by substitution into Equation 11.1 we have

$$\xi^* = \zeta(\xi) + \kappa = 1.80(\xi) + 32$$

where $\xi = °C$ and $\xi^* = °F$.

In Chapter 11 we stated that the transformation should be independent of the groups of indi-

TABLE E.8. Temperature Analogy for Metric Linking

Month	Fargo Daily High °F	Fargo Daily High °C	Month	Tucson Daily High °F	Tucson Daily High °C
1	15.4	−9.2	1	63.5	17.5
2	20.6	−6.3	2	67.0	19.4
3	33.5	0.8	3	71.5	21.9
4	52.6	11.4	4	80.7	27.1
5	66.8	19.3	5	89.6	32.0
6	75.9	24.4	6	97.9	36.6
7	82.6	28.1	7	98.3	36.8
8	81.6	27.6	8	95.3	35.2
9	69.6	20.9	9	93.1	33.9
10	58.4	14.7	10	83.8	28.8
11	37.2	2.9	11	72.2	22.3
12	21.9	−5.6	12	64.8	18.2
M	51.3	10.7		81.5	27.5
SD	24.8	13.8		13.3	7.4

viduals used to develop the transformation (i.e., the transformation is unique). To demonstrate this, we use our Tucson data. Our metric transformation coefficients with the Tucson data are

$$\zeta = s_{\delta^*}/s_{\delta} = 13.3/7.4 = 1.80$$

and

$$\kappa = \overline{\delta}_j{}^* - \zeta\overline{\delta}_j{}^* = 81.5 - 1.80(27.5) = 32$$

Therefore, the linking equation, $\xi^* = 1.80(\xi) + 32$, transcends the data sets and the alignment of the metrics is successful. The result of the transformation is that all the values are on a common metric. These principles for handling different temperature scales also apply for aligning IRT metrics.

SHOULD DIF ANALYSES BE BASED ON LATENT CLASSES?

In Chapter 12 we discuss traditional DIF analyses. These analyses create two subsamples with known manifest characteristics (e.g., one subsample is female, the other is male). Therefore, there is a *de facto* (perhaps innocuous) assumption that individuals within a manifest group are homogeneous. It can be argued that this assumption may not always be tenable, is not necessary to make, and that violation of the assumption may lead to false DIF conclusions. For instance, there may be a subgroup of the Focal group that is disadvantaged by one or more items, but the rest of the Focal group is not disadvantaged. In this case, the subgroup is not at all like the majority of the Focal group (i.e., the Focal group is not homogeneous). However, the relative sizes of the Focal subgroup and the majority Focal group may result in the masking of DIF for one or more items. Therefore, the items do not appear to be exhibiting DIF when, in fact, they do for the subgroup.

Consider, for example, the use of race or ethnic background for manifest grouping. This strategy treats all members of the group as equivalent and ignores intramanifest group differences. An Asian American manifest group lumps, for example, Filipino, Korean, Indonesian, Taiwanese, and Asian Indians (to name but a few) together. Similarly, a Hispanic focal group would include Cubans, Guatemalans, Mexican Americans, Peruvians, Columbians, Argentines, Puerto Ricans, and so on. These culturally distinct groups are also potentially confounded with recency of immigration. The same could be said of a Caucasian manifest group, as well as an African American manifest group. An African American manifest group would include recent immigrants from Haiti, Nigeria, Trinidad, and Ghana, as well as African Americans whose families have lived in the United States for hundreds of years. Similarly, the homogeneity of males and of females may also be questioned.

De Ayala, Kim, Stapleton, and Dayton (2003) proposed that DIF analyses should focus on latent classes (LCs), not manifest groups. By focusing on LCs one avoids the assumption that manifest groups are homogeneous. Thus, our data may reflect a mixture of multiple latent populations or classes. Within each of these latent classes there are quantitative individual differences, but the classes are qualitatively different. Within a class there is a latent continuum, and this continuum is wholly or in part different from those in other classes. Therefore, our modeling of the data involves both latent classes and latent continua; see "Mixture Models" in this appendix. There is a multidimensional aspect to this DIF conceptualization, albeit different from that seen in the multidimensional item response theory interpretation of DIF (e.g., see Ackerman, 1996; Camilli, 1992; Reckase, 1997b).

In the simplest multiclass situation the sample consists of a mixture of two latent classes. If the latent classes are functionally equivalent to the manifest groups (i.e., 100% of the Reference group members belong to one latent class and 100% of the Focal group members are in another latent class), then the manifest groups are homogeneous and the current approach to DIF analysis is appropriate. (Obviously, this would also be true if the data consisted of a one-class structure.) However, if the latent classes are not isomorphic with the manifest groups, then the latent classes contain a mixture of members from the different manifest groups. For example, one latent class may consist of 80% Reference manifest group members, whereas the other latent class may contain 80% Focal group members. According to this conceptualization, DIF analyses may be improved by determining the latent class structure first and then using this information for conducting the DIF analysis.

THE SEPARATION AND RELIABILITY INDICES

In Chapter 3 we state that the person SEPARATION index gives an indication of how well the instrument can separate or distinguish persons in terms of their latent variable locations. In this section we provide some of the technical aspects of this index and the RELIABILITY index discussed in Chapters 3 and 7. Both of these indices may be calculated for people and items. We first treat these indices for respondents and then for items.

The person SEPARATION index is the ratio of the ADJ.SD(θ) to RMSE(θ) (Wright & Masters, 1982). As such, it (1) has a lower bound of 0, (2) has no upper bound, and (3) is expressed in standard error units. According to Wright and Masters (1982), the person ADJ.SD provides an estimate of the "true" person standard deviation from which measurement error-caused bias has been removed. (Measurement error is that part of the total variability unaccounted for by the model.) The ADJ.SD(θ) is

$$\text{ADJ.SD} = \sqrt{\text{SD}_{\hat{\theta}}^2 - \text{RMSE}(\theta)^2} \qquad (E.27)$$

For example, using the analysis from Chapter 3, Table 3.4, the ADJ.SD = $\sqrt{1.39^2 - 1.34^2}$ = 0.38 and the SEPARATION = ADJ.SD/RMSE = 0.39/1.34 = 0.29; these calculated values match (within rounding) those from the table. "Large" SEPARATION values are considered better than small ones. Unfortunately, because the SEPARATION index does not have a finite upper bound, it is sometimes difficult to determine what is a good large value. However, the SEPARATION index is related to the bounded RELIABILITY index. Specifically, the SEPARATION and RELIABILITY indices are related by

$$\text{REL} = \text{SEP}^2/(1 + \text{SEP}^2) \qquad (E.28)$$

and

$$\text{SEP} = \sqrt{\text{REL}/(1 - \text{REL})} \qquad (E.29)$$

where REL is RELIABILITY and SEP is SEPARATION (Linacre & Wright, 2001).

Like coefficient alpha, the person RELIABILITY tells us about the consistency of the measures (e.g., $\hat{\theta}$s). That is, this index indicates the consistency of the $\hat{\theta}$s across instruments designed to measure the same latent variable. Its range is from 0 to 1, with values close to or at 1 considered better than values approaching or at 0. Like the SEPARATION index, the RELIABILITY index (Wright & Masters, 1982) is based on the ADJ.SD

$$\text{RELIABILITY} = \text{ADJ.SD}^2/\text{SD}_{\hat{\theta}}^2 \qquad (E.30)$$

Because RELIABILITY is bounded, it is easier to interpret than the SEPARATION index. For example, using the analysis from Chapter 3, Table 3.4, we have that the RELIABILITY for the REAL RMSE (nonextreme) line in the table is RELIABILITY = $0.39^2/1.39^2$ = 0.08. This value indicates that the mathematics instrument is not doing a good job of distinguishing people. As a result, there is little reason to believe that we would obtain the same ordering of people with a different set of items measuring mathematics proficiency (i.e., the proportion of observed sample variance that is not due to measurement error is quite low).

The item SEPARATION index gives an indication of how well the instrument can separate or distinguish items in terms of their latent variable locations. The premise of this index is that one would like items to be sufficiently well separated in terms of their locations to identify the direction and the meaning of the latent variable (Wright & Masters, 1982). In this regard, we would like to see little estimation error. This last aspect is assessed by the (item) RELIABILITY index. These two indices are calculated in a manner somewhat parallel to that used with persons. Specifically, the

$$\text{item ADJ.SD} = \sqrt{SD_{\hat{\delta}}^2 - V(\text{RMSE}(\delta)^2)} \qquad (E.31)$$

$$\text{SEPARATION} = \text{ADJ.SD/RMSE} \qquad (E.32)$$

and

$$\text{RELIABILITY} = \text{ADJ.SD}^2/SD_{\hat{\delta}}^2 \qquad (E.33)$$

V is an "overall test-to-sample fit mean square" (Wright & Masters, 1982, p. 92). An ITEM RELIABILITY of 1.00 indicates that the instrument is creating a well-defined variable.

DEPENDENCY IN TRADITIONAL ITEM STATISTICS AND OBSERVED SCORES

In Chapter 3 we discuss the concept of invariance. This property is desirable and useful because it frees the practitioner from the specific characteristics of the instrument and samples used. Below we demonstrate that this property is not present in the application of CTT, but it is exhibited in IRT.

Assume that we administer a 10-item instrument to each of two groups. Although our instrument measures mathematical reasoning (MR), the following demonstration also applies to other types of instruments, such as a delinquency scale or a survey of attitudes on global warming. The examinees' responses are scored "correct" and "incorrect." The first group consists of 1000 examinees and is high on the MR continuum, with an average number correct of 6.741 items (SD = 1.844), whereas the second group of 1000 examinees is low on this continuum (M = 1.551, SD = 1.195). We refer to the former group as the high group and the latter group as the low group.

In a traditional item analysis we calculate various indices, such as a reliability estimate, item discrimination indices, and the item difficulty index, to name just a few. One item discrimination index is the correlation between the responses on an item and the observed scores (e.g., the point biserial), and the traditional measure of an item's difficulty is the proportion of correct responses on an item (i.e., the item's P-value, P_j, or its mean). Using the high-group data, the instrument's coefficient alpha is 0.556, and for the low group the coefficient alpha is 0.404. Table E.9 contains the traditional item statistics for the two groups. As we see, the items have different characteristics across the two groups. For example, in general the items discriminate (i.e., the r_cs) better in the MR high group than in the low group. Furthermore, the item difficulties (i.e., the P_js) indicate that the items are easier in the

TABLE E.9. Traditional and IRT Item Statistics

| | Traditional | | | | IRT | |
| | High MR | | Low MR | | High MR | Low MR |
Item	P_j	r_c	P_j	r_c	$\hat{\delta}$	$\hat{\delta}$
1	0.751	0.256	0.082	0.144	-1.369	2.840
2	0.973	0.128	0.491	0.268	-4.201	0.044
3	0.365	0.278	0.011	0.090	0.691	5.052
4	0.693	0.248	0.060	0.127	-1.015	3.208
5	0.724	0.271	0.069	0.186	-1.199	3.046
6	0.494	0.306	0.022	0.125	0.030	4.319
7	0.978	0.078	0.596	0.256	-4.428	-0.476
8	0.297	0.308	0.009	0.046	1.072	5.260
9	0.856	0.240	0.169	0.197	-2.179	1.910
10	0.610	0.268	0.042	0.089	-0.560	3.612

Note. r_c is the corrected item-total correlation between an item's responses and the observed scores; P_j is the proportion of correct responses to item j.

high group than in the low group; low values of P_j indicate a difficult item and high P_j values reflect an easy item. Therefore, our interpretations of these item indices would be conditional on the sample. That is, item 1 is an "easy" item *if* it is administered to the high group, but it is a "hard" item when administered to the low group. (This is analogous to the situation in which the unit for measuring a box is the length of a string based on the shortest dimension of the box; see Chapter 1.) Moreover, this item is a poor discriminator in the low group, but a more reasonable (although not good) discriminator in the high group.

Given that the item statistics vary as a function of the sample used in their calculation, we might ask, "What is the relationship between the item statistics across the two samples?" The correlation between the item discriminations for the high and low groups is –0.852 and between the item difficulties it is 0.796. Figure E.6 shows that the *linear* relationship between the item difficulties across groups is not as strong as the correlation of 0.796 might suggest. That is, the two groups' item difficulties are nonlinearly related and are influenced to a large extent by the characteristics of the sample on which they were calculated.

We now turn to applying our 1PL model to these data. After separately calibrating the instrument for the high and low groups, we obtain two sets of $\hat{\delta}$s; see the two rightmost columns in Table E.9. As would be expected from our indeterminacy discussion (Chapter 3), the two sets of $\hat{\delta}$s are not the same. For instance, item 1 is estimated to be located at –1.369 with the high group, but the item is estimated to be located at 2.840 for the low group. However, a closer examination reveals that the relative positions among the item location estimates is essentially the same across the two. The correlation between these estimates for the high and low groups is 0.999; the scatterplot is presented in Figure E.7. Unlike the P-value scatterplot (Figure E.6), Figure E.7 shows that the near perfect correlation of 0.999 accurately reflects the linear relationship between the two sets of estimates. This very strong linear relationship shows that our IRT item characterizations transcend the sample characteristics, whereas the traditional indices do not. Moreover, although our interpretation of an item's traditional difficulty as "easy" or "hard" is conditional on the proficiency of the examinee group, with IRT we do not need this qualification after we align the metrics (Chapter 11).[7]

As is the case with most estimation problems, sample size is an important determinant of the quality of estimation. Therefore, we halve the sample size to show that the invariance of our estimates continues to exist. With half as many examinees in each sample, the correlation between the

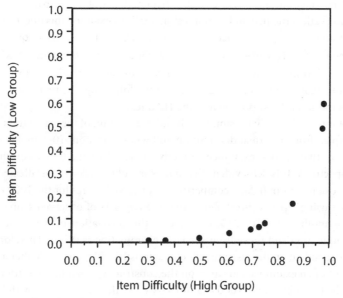

FIGURE E.6. Scatterplot of traditional item difficulties.

traditional item discriminations for the high and low groups decreases to –0.284, whereas the correlation between the traditional item difficulties becomes 0.782; the nonlinearity seen in Figure E.6 continues to exist. In contrast, the correlation between the IRT item location estimates remains strong ($r = 0.978$). As such, the effect of examinee characteristics (e.g., high vs. low proficiency) continue to affect the traditional item indices, but still do not affect our IRT item parameter estimates.

So far we have been concerned with how sample characteristics affect our item statistics. We now

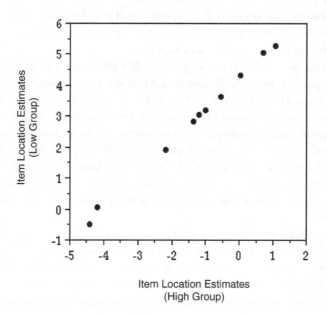

FIGURE E.7. Scatterplot of IRT item locations.

turn to the complementary question: "How do the characteristics of our instrument (e.g., the difficulty of an examination) affect the person location estimates?" To examine this question, assume that an item pool of 40 vocabulary items is divided into two tests. The first test consists of the 20 easiest items with a mean difficulty ($\overline{\delta}$) of -1.0141 with an $SD = 1.0582$ and minimum and maximum difficulties of -2.4390 and 0.5470, respectively. The second test contains the 20 hardest items ($\overline{\delta} = 1.4529$, $SD = 0.7578$, minimum $= -0.5690$, maximum $= 2.9510$). In the following, the first test is referred to as the Easy test, whereas the second test is known as the Hard test.

Through a Monte Carlo study we simulate the administration of these two tests to 1000 examinees randomly sampled from a normal distribution and whose locations (θs) are known.[8] Examining the responses, we see that the first examinee correctly answered 12 and 6 items on the Easy and Hard examinations, respectively. It is self-evident that a person's observed score is affected by the easiness or difficulty of the examination. In fact, comparing the observed scores for the 1000 examinees across the Easy/Hard tests using a paired t-test shows that the two sets of observed scores are significantly different from one another ($t = 101.215$, $p = 0.000$); the correlation between the observed scores from the Hard examination and those from the Easy examination is 0.713. Therefore, an examinee's observed score is dependent on the instrument's characteristics. Of course, whether a given score is an accurate assessment of an examinee's location on the construct is a validity question.

To estimate the locations of the 1000 examinees we use the Rasch model with EAP (Chapter 4). The estimate of the first examinee's location ($\hat{\theta}_1$) is -0.3955 according to the Easy test and 0.3790 according to the Hard test. Similar to what is seen with the observed scores, there are two different person location estimates for each person. However, if there is model–data fit these estimates should be strongly linearly related and we can linearly transform the $\hat{\theta}$s from the Easy test metric to the Hard test metric or vice versa. (How this is done is demonstrated in Chapter 4 in the discussion of metric transformation.) Whether the $\hat{\theta}$ represents an examinee's location on the construct of interest is still a validity question.

The Pearson correlation between the $\hat{\theta}$s based on the Hard test and those from the Easy test is 0.743. This correlation is similar to what we see with the observed scores. As such, we have not shown that our IRT person location estimates are not influenced by the instrument's characteristics. However, there are two primary reasons for the magnitude of this correlation. The first is that the tests provide information over a limited range of the θ continuum, and the second is the *asymptotic* nature of estimation. We discuss each of these reasons in turn.

To understand the first reason, compare the test's difficulty range with the range of person locations. Because the examinees are normally distributed we expect that approximately 99% of the examinees to be located from -3 to 3. However, the Easy test does not have items above 0.547 and the Hard examination does not have items located below -0.569. Therefore, for both examinations we need to estimate person locations that are beyond the range represented by the examination (e.g., estimating a person located above the Easy test's most difficult item, $\delta = 0.547$). At this point it appears that this argument may also be used to explain the CTT results. Therefore, it still remains to be shown that despite the Easy and Hard examinations' item location distributions we can obtain $\hat{\theta}$s that are highly linearly related—in effect, obtaining person location estimates that are not influenced by the instrument's characteristics.

The second reason, the asymptotic nature of estimation, addresses the issue of estimating person locations that are not influenced by the instrument's characteristics. In our current situation we have only 20 observations (i.e., items) for estimating the examinees' locations. In contrast, for estimating the item locations there are 1000 observations (i.e., examinees) available. It is in this discrepancy in the number of observations for estimation that we find the explanation for the magnitude of the correlation.

The $\hat{\theta}$s are *asymptotically* unbiased, which, in effect, means that one needs a large number of items to compensate for the tests' truncated item location distributions. (If the tests contained items that spanned the full range of interest, then the issue of test length would not be of as much consequence as it is in this example.) To demonstrate this issue we increase the number of items on each examination while still restricting the range of the items to be the same as the 20-item tests. Specifically, we increase the Hard and Easy test lengths to 100 items while restricting their respective difficulty ranges to match those from the corresponding 20-item tests. This means that for the 100-item Easy test there are no items more difficult than 0.547 and for the 100-item Hard examination there are no items easier than –0.569. Using these 100-item tests, the persons' locations are reestimated. The correlation between the reestimated $\hat{\theta}$s from the Easy test and those from the Hard test increases to 0.933. This is a substantial improvement over our 20-item Easy and Hard tests' results and shows that person estimation is not adversely affected by the range of item locations of the instrument. If we continue to increase the length of each test to 250, 500, and 1000 items, then the respective correlations between the Easy and Hard tests' $\hat{\theta}$s become 0.969, 0.982, and 0.987. Therefore, a test's level of difficulty does not adversely affect the person location estimation and our estimates of person location are "free" of the instrument's characteristics. Obviously, increasing the test length would not have eliminated the test dependency issue seen with CTT.

As we would expect, as the number of items increases, the corresponding standard errors, $s_e(\hat{\theta})$s, decrease. For example, the mean $s_e(\hat{\theta})$s for the 20-item tests were 0.502 for the Easy test and 0.514 for the Hard test. However, if we lengthen the tests to 100 items, then the mean $s_e(\hat{\theta})$ decreases to 0.248 for the Easy test and to 0.262 for the Hard test. Further increasing the test length to 250 and 500 items results in the mean $s_e(\hat{\theta})$s falling to 0.162 (Easy)/0.165 (Hard) and 0.109 (Easy)/0.110 (Hard), respectively. With 1000 items the mean $s_e(\hat{\theta})$ decreases to 0.063 for the Easy test and to 0.061 for the Hard test.

The preceding two observations concerning item and person location estimation may be summarized as *specific objectivity*. Loosely speaking, specific objectivity means that what one is interested in measuring does not affect the measuring instrument and the measuring instrument does not affect what is being measured.[9] When this level of objectiveness is realized then it is "possible to generalize measurement beyond the particular instrument used, to compare objects measured on similar but not identical instruments, and to combine or partition instruments to suit new measurement requirements" (Wright, 1968, p. 87). Wright (1968) has referred to the capability of obtaining item parameter estimates that are not influenced by the sample of individuals as *person-free test calibration*; this is also known as *item-parameter invariance* (Lord, 1980) and *object-free instrument calibration* (Wright, 1968). Moreover, Wright refers to the capacity to estimate a person's location "free" of the instrument's characteristics as *item-free person measurement*; this is also known as *person-parameter invariance* (Lord, 1980) and *instrument-free object measurement* (Wright, 1968). Therefore, IRT's invariance property is the realization of Thurstone's (1928) idea that "the scale must transcend the group measured" (p. 547). For an instrument to be accepted as valid, then it must not be seriously affected in its measuring function by the object of measurement, and "to the extent that its measuring function is affected, the validity of the instrument is impaired or limited" (p. 547).

NOTES

1. A tetrachoric correlation coefficient specifies the association between two variables that are continuous and assumed to be normally distributed, but that are artificially dichotomized. These

variables, X and Y, may be the dichotomization of a manifest variable(s) in a sample (e.g., X = "males 30 years and older vs. younger males" and Y = "females 30 years and older vs. females below 30") or may be a theoretical dichotomization as discussed in Appendix C (i.e., the responses of 0 and 1 are assumed to arise from dichotomizing two continuous normally distributed latent variables). As such, the coefficient is an estimate of the linear relationship between the two continuous variables if the correlation was calculated using the two continuous variables. Cross-classifying the dichotomous variables creates a 2 x 2 contingency table. This table for two variables, X and Y, is graphically repre- sented in Figure E.8 with the variables' normal distributions on the table's margins. With respect to the variables' normal distributions, the symbol z is the standard score corresponding to the p propor- tion of 1s for variable Y (i.e., p is the marginal proportion of 1s and $(1 - p)$ is the marginal proportion of 0s for variable Y). The height of the unit normal curve at z is denoted by y. In an analogous fashion, and with respect to the variable X, z' delimits the p' proportion of 1s and the ordinate value at z' is symbolized as y'. The cross-classification of the 1s and 0s for variables X and Y leads to a fourfold table with the cells' frequencies labeled by the letters A, B, C, and D.

One equation for calculating the tetrachoric correlation, r_T, involves the power series (Guilford & Fruchter, 1978)

$$r_T = r_T + r_T^2 \frac{zz'}{2} + r_T^3 \frac{(z^2 - 1)(z'^2 - 1)}{6} + \ldots = \frac{A*D - B*C}{yy'N^2} \qquad (E.34)$$

where N is the number of cases and all other terms are defined above. Equation E.34 shows that r_T contains the unknowns z and z' as well as y and y'. Therefore, obtaining r_T is a complex process and

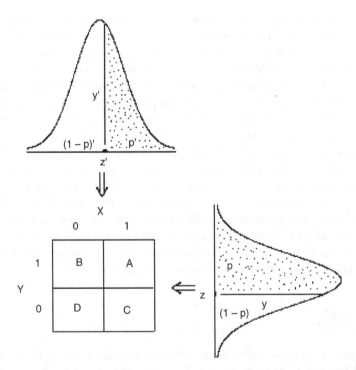

FIGURE E.8. Relationship between two continuous normally distributed variables and their dichotomization.

several approaches have been developed. For example, Divgi (1979) and Bonett and Price (2005) contain two different methods for estimating the tetrachoric correlation coefficient.

There are several situations that may lead to problems in the accuracy of the r_T estimate. For instance, if the dichotomized variable(s) has extreme proportions (e.g., p and/or p' is 0.90), guessing is present, and/or the normality assumption is not tenable, then one obtains a biased estimate of the true population relationship. As a result, the magnitude of the observed coefficients may be inappropriately large and outside the range −1 to 1. In addition, there is an increased chance of observing non-Gramian matrices (i.e., a matrix with negative eigenvalue[s]) when factor analyzing tetrachorics.

As previously mentioned, and as is the case with the analysis of phi coefficients, it is possible to observe difficulty factors with the factor analysis of a tetrachoric correlation matrix (Gourlay, 1951). In the situation where items may be correctly answered on the basis of guessing, then the tetrachoric correlation is adversely affected. However, Carroll (1945) provides an approach for correcting tetrachoric correlations for chance success; see Reckase (1981; cited in Green et al., 1984) concerning problems with overcorrecting tetrachoric correlations. An approach for testing assumptions for tetrachoric correlations is presented by Muthén and Hofacker (1988). Guilford and Fruchter (1978) suggest that "for estimating the *degree* [italics added] of correlation . . . it is recommended that N be at least 200, and preferably 300" (p. 315), as well as to avoid calculating r_T when there is a zero frequency in one cell.

2. Strictly speaking, a latent class model with $G \geq (L + 1)/2$ latent classes gives the same estimates of item parameters as the Rasch model does under conditional maximum likelihood estimation. In addition to the relationship between LCA and the Rasch model, the Rasch model is related to a log-linear model (e.g., Baker & Subkoviak, 1981; Kelderman, 1984; also see Holland, 1990a, 1990b). That is, the Rasch model may be expressed as a log-linear model for the probabilities of each unique response pattern (Cressie & Holland, 1983). In this case, it is possible to estimate the parameters via log-linear analysis (see Mellenbergh & Vijn, 1981, as well as Kelderman, 1984).

3. Yamamoto (1989) developed a HYBRID model that eliminates the constraint that the same item response model hold in each latent class. Thus, one may have different IRT models in each class or have an IRT model in one class, but not in another class. Boughton and Yamamoto (2007) show how the HYBRID model may be applied to the analysis of speededness.

4. A monotonic transformation preserves the inequalities of the untransformed values. That is, a transformation, say f(), is monotonic if for $x_0 < x_1$ one has that $f(x_0) < f(x_1)$. The graph of f() as a function of x would appear as a line that either increases or plateaus, but never decreases (i.e., a monotonically increasing function). Conversely, f() is a monotonic transformation if for $x_0 < x_1$, then $f(x_0) > f(x_1)$. In this latter case the graph of f() as a function of x would appear as a line that either decreases or plateaus, but never increases (i.e., a monotonically decreasing function). Examples of monotonic transformation are $x^* = 1/x$, $x^* = e^x$, $x^* = \ln(x)$, and sometimes $x^* = x^2$; in the case of x^2 one needs the restrictions of either $x \geq 0$ or $x \leq 0$.

5. The probability of a response of 0 for the 1PL model is

$$p(x = 0 | \theta, \alpha, \delta) = 1 - \frac{e^{\alpha(\theta-\delta)}}{1+e^{\alpha(\theta-\delta)}} = \left[\frac{1+e^{\alpha(\theta-\delta)}}{1+e^{\alpha(\theta-\delta)}}\right] - \frac{e^{\alpha(\theta-\delta)}}{1+e^{\alpha(\theta-\delta)}}$$

$$= \frac{1+e^{\alpha(\theta-\delta)} - e^{\alpha(\theta-\delta)}}{1+e^{\alpha(\theta-\delta)}} = \frac{1}{1+e^{\alpha(\theta-\delta)}} \tag{E.35}$$

Sometimes the 1PL model's exponent is written to contain the response, x. That is,

$$p(x|\theta, \alpha, \delta) = \frac{e^{x\alpha(\theta-\delta)}}{1+e^{\alpha(\theta-\delta)}} \tag{E.36}$$

Equation E.36 can be used to calculate the probability of a response of 0 and a response of 1.

6. Although the strata are ordered in terms of their average item location, this does not mean that the probability of a response of 1 will always have a direct relationship with the strata's order. In the context of proficiency assessment this ordering would be with respect to the stratum's average difficulty. Whenever we use a model that allows for item discrimination and/or the IRF's lower asymptote to vary, then it is possible to have crossing IRFs. When IRFs cross, then some individuals have a higher probability of a response of 1 on a more difficult item than on an easier item. For example, Figure E.9 contains the IRFs for two items that differ in their discriminations and difficulty. Item 1 has an $\alpha_1 = 0.75$ and a $\delta_1 = 0.75$, whereas item 2 has an $\alpha_2 = 0.45$ and a $\delta_2 = 0.80$. As can be seen, an individual with a θ above the IRFs' intersection point (e.g., $\theta = 3.0$) has a higher probability of correctly answering the easier item 1 than the more difficult item 2. This result is consistent with ordering the items according to difficulty (i.e., $\delta_2 > \delta_1$). However, for θs below the intersection point (e.g., at $\theta = -2.0$) the probability of a correct response on the more difficult item 2 is greater than on the easier item 1. Stated another way, for low-proficiency people item 2 (the hard item) is actually "easier" than item 1 because their probability of a correct response is higher for item 2 than it is for item 1. This item level observation may be extended to strata ordered by average item location. Specifically, each of our respondents may not have a probability of a response of 1 that decreases as the average stratum difficulty increases.

7. The different location estimates for the same item across groups is a reflection of the indeterminacy of metric issue discussed above. Ignoring this issue leads one to want to interpret the esti-

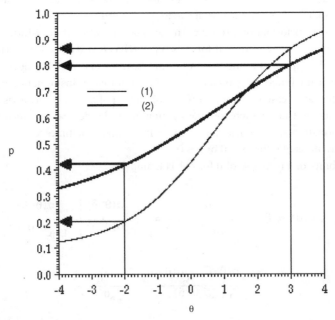

FIGURE E.9. IRFs for two items, (1) and (2), with different α_js.

mated item location of −1.369 as an "easy" item and the item estimated to be at 2.840 as a "difficult" item. However, once the low-group metric and the high-group metric are aligned with one another the interpretation of whether the item is "easy" or "difficult" is consistent across groups. One way of thinking about this is to consider the low-group metric to be analogous to the Celsius scale and the high-group metric to be analogous to the Fahrenheit scale. Whether a temperature of 30° is interpreted to be "hot" or "cold" depends on whether it is on the Celsius or Fahrenheit scale. However, once the two scales are aligned, the interpretation of 30° is the same regardless of which temperature scale one is referencing. This linking of the Celsius and Fahrenheit scales is accomplished using the (perfect) linear relationship that exists between the two scales. The linking of the different metrics is discussed in Chapter 11.

8. The best way to examine this question requires knowledge of the examinees' true locations, θs. In this way the quality of the estimated person locations may be directly assessed by comparing the estimates with their true values. An experiment in which the researcher knows parameter values (e.g., examinees' true locations) and then uses a computer to model the behavior of the construct of interest is known as a computer *simulation study*. If a simulation study uses a model (e.g., a regression model, the Rasch model) to generate the (simulated) data, then the technique is known as a *Monte Carlo* simulation study. Therefore, to address the question, "How do the characteristics of the instrument affect the person location estimates?" we conduct a *Monte Carlo* study. For this simulation 40 z-scores are randomly sampled from a unit normal distribution (i.e., a normal distribution with $M = 0.0$, $SD = 1$); this may be accomplished by using a normal distribution random number generator from a statistical package or spreadsheet program. These z-scores are considered to be the items' location parameters, δs. In addition, 1000 z-scores are randomly sampled from a unit normal distribution. These z-scores serve as the person location parameters, θs; these pseudo "people" are sometimes referred to as *simulees*.

The response data for each simulee is obtained in two phases. In the first phase the simulee's probability of a response of 1 to item j is calculated according to a model (e.g., the Rasch model) using the appropriate parameters (e.g., δ_j and the simulee's θ). In the second phase this probability is compared to a uniform random number [0, 1]. If the random number is less than or equal to the probability of the response 1, then the simulee's response to item j is coded as 1, otherwise it is coded as 0. These phases are repeated to obtain the simulee's responses to the remaining items on the instrument. The entire process is repeated for each of the remaining simulees. Harwell, Stone, Hsu, and Kirisci (1996) and Paxton, Curran, Bollen, Kirby, and Chen (2001) contain more information on conducting Monte Carlo studies.

9. Divgi (1986) argues that because of maximum likelihood bias in person locations one cannot have instrument-free estimation whenever finite instruments differ in their item locations. Moreover, it is not clear that we can *always* have a measure of a person's location that is unaffected by the items on an instrument. For instance, consider an item that would be considered to be at the synthesis level of Bloom's taxonomy of educational objectives for the cognitive domain. When an examinee encounters such an item it is possible that the process of synthesizing the relevant information leads to the person learning something that previously he or she did not know. As such, the examinee's location shifts from where it would have been if he or she had not encountered the item. Therefore, we would have one ($\hat{\theta}$) if the person is administered the synthesis item and a different ($\hat{\theta}$) if he or she had been given a different (e.g., a knowledge level) item, albeit in the synthesis item's content domain. In short, whether the item is at the synthesis or knowledge level affects our person location and its estimate. Because the item-person interaction is not immutable the measurement of individuals is not always independent of the administered items. Therefore, item-invariant measurement must be interpreted to refer to the *result* of the person—item interaction and not that the item does not affect the person.

Moreover, although we may accumulate invariance evidence across different groupings (e.g., male versus females, high versus low ability) this does not mean that we would necessarily obtain invariance evidence across other possible groupings, languages, and/or in other cultures. As such, because our invariance evidence is conditional on the specific groups, language, and culture that are used we suggest the use of the term *conditional invariance* (e.g., conditional person-parameter invariance and conditional item-parameter invariance). The best that we can do is accumulate evidence that supports our contention of invariant measurement.

References

Ackerman, T. (1992). A didactic explanation of item bias, item impact, and item validity from a multidimensional perspective. *Journal of Educational Measurement, 29*, 67–91.

Ackerman, T. (1994). Creating a test information profile for a two-dimensional latent space. *Applied Psychological Measurement, 18*, 257–275.

Ackerman, T. (1996). Developments in multidimensional item response theory. *Applied Psychological Measurement, 20*, 309–310.

Ackerman, T. A. (1986, April). *Use of the graded response IRT model to assess the reliability of direct and indirect measures of writing assessment*. Paper presented at the annual meeting of the American Educational Research Association, San Francisco.

Ackerman, T. A. (1989). Unidimensional IRT calibration of compensatory and noncompensatory multidimensional items. *Applied Psychological Measurement, 13*, 113–127.

Adams, R. J., & Khoo, S.-T. (1996). *Quest: The Interactive Test Analysis System* [Computer Program]. Melbourne: Australian Council for Educational Research.

Agresti, A. (1990). *Categorical data analysis*. New York: Wiley.

Agresti, A. (1996). *An introduction to categorical data analysis*. New York: Wiley.

Akaike, H. (1974). A new look at the statistical identification model. *IEEE Transaction Automatic Control, 19*, 716–723.

American Educational Research Association, American Psychological Association, National Council on Measurement in Education (AERA, APA, NCME). (1985). *Standards for educational and psychological testing*. Washington, DC: Author.

Anastasi, A. (1983). Traits, States, and Situations. In H. Wainer & S. Messick (Eds.), *Principals of modern psychological measurement: A festschrift for Frederic M. Lord* (pp. 345–356). Hillsdale, NJ: Erlbaum.

Andersen, E. B. (1970). Asymptotic properties of conditional maximum likelihood estimation. *Journal of the Royal Statistical Society, Series B, 32*, 283–301.

Andersen, E. B. (1972). The numerical solution of a set of conditional estimation equations. *Journal of the Royal Statistical Society, Series B, 34*, 42–50.

Andersen, E. B. (1973). A goodness of fit test for the Rasch model. *Psychometrika, 38*, 123–140.

Andersen, E. B. (1977). Sufficient statistics and latent trait models. *Psychometrika, 42*, 69–81.

Andrich, D. (1978a). Relationships between the Thurstone and Rasch approaches to item scaling. *Applied Psychological Measurement, 2*, 449–460.

Andrich, D. (1978b). A rating formulation for ordered response categories. *Psychometrika, 43*, 561–573.

Andrich, D. (1978c). Application of a psychometric rating model to ordered categories which are scored with successive integers. *Applied Psychological Measurement, 2*, 581–594.

Andrich, D. (1988). *Rasch models for measurement.* (Sage University Paper series on Quantitative Applications in the Social Sciences 07-068). Beverly Hills, CA: Sage.

Angoff, W. H. (1984). *Scales, norms, and equivalent scores.* Princeton, NJ: Educational Testing Service.

Angoff, W. H. (1993). Perspectives on differential item functioning methodology. In P. W. Holland & H. Wainer (Eds.), *Differential item functioning* (pp. 3–23). Hillsdale, NJ: Erlbaum.

Assessment Systems Corporation. (1997). XCALIBRE. St. Paul, MN: Author.

Baker, F. B. (1984). Ability metric transformations involved in vertical equating under item response theory. *Applied Psychological Measurement, 8*, 261–271.

Baker, F. B. (1990). Some observations on the metric of PC-BILOG results. *Applied Psychological Measurement, 14*, 139–150.

Baker, F. B. (1991). Comparison of minimum logit chi-square and Bayesian item parameter estimation. *British Journal of Mathematical and Statistical Psychology, 44*, 299–313.

Baker, F. B. (1992). *Item response theory: Parameter estimation techniques.* New York: Dekker.

Baker, F. B. (1993a). Sensitivity of the linear logistic test model to misspecification of the weight matrix. *Applied Psychological Measurement, 17*, 201–210.

Baker, F. B. (1993b). EQUATE 2.0: A computer program for the characteristic curve method of IRT equating. *Applied Psychological Measurement, 17*, 20.

Baker, F. B. (1996). An investigation of the sampling distributions of equating coefficients. *Applied Psychological Measurement, 20*, 45–57.

Baker, F. B. (1997). Empirical sampling distributions of equating coefficients for graded and nominal response instruments. *Applied Psychological Measurement, 21*, 157–172.

Baker, F. B., & Al-Karni, A. (1991). A comparison of two procedures for computing IRT equating coefficients. *Journal of Educational Measurement, 28*, 147–162.

Baker, F. B., Al-Karni, A., & Al-Dosary, I. M. (1991). EQUATE: A computer program for the test characteristic curve method of IRT equating. *Applied Psychological Measurement, 15*, 78.

Baker, F. B., Cohen, A. S., & Baarmish, B. R. (1988). Item characteristics of tests constructed by linear programming. *Applied Psychological Measurement, 12*, 189–199.

Baker, F. B., & Kim, S.-H. (2004). *Item response theory: Parameter estimation techniques* (2nd ed.). New York: Dekker.

Baker, F. B., & Subkoviak, M. J. (1981). Analysis of test results via log-linear models. *Applied Psychological Measurement, 4*, 503–515.

Barton, M. A., & Lord, F. M. (1981, July). *An upper asymptote for the three-parameter logistic item-response model* (Research Report No. 81-20). Princeton, NJ: Educational Testing Services.

Berkson, J. (1944). Application of the logistic function to bio-assay. *Journal of the American Statistical Association, 39*, 357–365.

Berkson, J. (1955). Maximum likelihood and minimum chi-square estimates of the logistic function. *Journal of the American Statistical Association, 50*, 120–162.

Birnbaum, A. (1968). Some latent trait models and their use in inferring an examinee's ability. In F. M. Lord & M. R. Novick, *Statistical theories of mental test scores.* Reading, MA: Addison-Wesley.

Bock, R. D. (1972). Estimating item parameters and latent ability when responses are scored in two or more nominal categories. *Psychometrika, 37*, 29–51.

Bock, R. D. (1997). The nominal categories model. In W. J. van der Linden & R. K. Hambleton (Eds.), *Handbook of modern item response theory* (pp. 33–49). New York: Springer.

Bock, R. D., & Aitkin, M. (1981). Marginal maximum likelihood estimation of item parameters: An application of an EM algorithm. *Psychometrika, 46*, 443–459.

Bock, R. D., & Lieberman, M. (1970). Fitting a response model for n dichotomously scored items. *Psychometrika, 35*, 179–198.

Bock, R. D., & Mislevy, R. J. (1982). Adaptive EAP estimation of ability in a microcomputer environment. *Applied Psychological Measurement, 6*, 431–444.

Bolt, D. M., Cohen, A. S., & Wollack, J. A. (2001). A mixture item response model for multiple-choice data. *Journal of Educational and Behavioral Statistics, 26*, 381–409.

Bonett, D. G., & Price, R. M. (2005). Inferential methods for the tetrachoric correlation coefficient. *Journal of Educational and Behavioral Statistics, 30*, 213–225.

Boughton, K. A., & Yamamoto, K. (2007). A HYBRID model for test speededness. In M. von Davier & C. H. Carstensen (Eds.), *Multivariate and mixture distribution Rasch models* (pp. 147–156). New York: Springer.

Bradlow, E. T., Wainer, H., & Wang, X. (1999). A Bayesian random effects model for testlets. *Psychometrika, 64*, 153–168.

Bridgman, P. W. (1928). *The logic of modern physics.* New York: Macmillan.

Brown, C. H. (1983). Asymptotic comparison of missing data procedures for estimating factor loadings. *Psychometrika, 48*, 269–291.

Brown, J. S., & Burton, R. R. (1978). Diagnostic models for procedural bugs in basic mathematical skills. *Cognitive Science, 2*, 155–192.

Brown, J. S., & VanLehn, K. (1980). Repair theory: A generative theory of bugs in procedural skills. *Cognitive Science, 4*, 379–426.

Brown, R. L. (1994). Efficacy of the indirect approach for estimating structural equation models with missing data: A comparison of five methods. *Structural Equation Modeling: A Multidisciplinary Journal, 1*, 287–316.

Camilli, G. (1988). Scale shrinkage and the estimation of latent distribution parameters. *Journal of Educational Statistics, 13*, 227–241.

Camilli, G. (1992). A conceptual analysis of differential item functioning in terms of a multidimensional item response model. *Applied Psychological Measurement, 16*, 129–147.

Camilli, G. (1994). Origin of the scaling constant d = 1.7 in item response theory. *Journal of Educational and Behavioral Statistics, 19*, 293–295.

Camilli, G. (1999). Measurement error, multidimensionality, and scale shrinkage: A reply to Yen and Burket. *Journal of Educational Measurement, 36*, 73–78.

Camilli, G., & Shepard, L. A. (1994). *Methods for identifying biased test items.* Thousand Oaks, CA: Sage.

Campbell, D. T., & Fiske, D. W. (1959). Convergent and discriminant validation by the multitrait–multimethod matrix. *Psychological Bulletin, 56*, 81–105.

Carlson, J. E. (1987, September). *Multidimensional item response theory estimation: A computer program* (Research Report No. ONR87-2). Iowa City, IA: American College Testing Program.

Carroll, J. B. (1945). The effect of difficulty and chance success on correlations between items or between tests. *Psychometrika, 10*, 1–19.

Center for AIDS Prevention Studies. (2003). The Voluntary HIV Counseling and Testing Efficacy Study. *www.caps.ucsf.edu/projects/c&tindex.html.*

Chen, W.-H., & Thissen, D. (1997). Local dependence indexes for item pairs using item response theory. *Journal of Educational and Behavioral Statistics, 22*, 265–289.

Choi, S. W., Cook, K. F., & Dodd, B. G. (1997). Parameter recovery for the partial credit model using MULTILOG. *Journal of Outcome Measurement, 1*, 114–142.

Christoffersson, A. (1975). Factor analysis of dichotomized variables. *Psychometrika, 40*, 5–32.

Cleary, T. A., Linn, R. L., & Rock, D. A. (1968). An exploratory study of programmed tests. *Educational and Psychological Measurement, 28*, 345–360.

Clogg, C. C. (1995). Latent class models. In G. Arminger, C. C. Clogg, & M. E. Sobel (Eds.), *Handbook of statistical modeling for the social and behavioral sciences* (pp. 311–359). New York: Plenum Press.

Coombs, C. (1950). Psychological scaling without a unit of measurement. *Psychological Review, 57*, 145–158.

Coombs, C. (1974). *A theory of psychological scaling.* In G. M. Maranell (Ed.), *Scaling: A sourcebook for behavioral scientists* (pp. 275–280). Chicago: Aldine. (Reprinted from Engineering Research Bulletin No. 34, University of Michigan, 1952.)

Cressie, N., & Holland, P. W. (1983). Characterizing the manifest probabilities of latent trait models. *Psychometrika, 48*, 129–141.

Cronbach, L. J. (1951). Coefficient alpha and the internal structure of tests. *Psychometrika, 16*, 297–334.

Davey, T., Oshima, T. C., & Lee, K. (1996). Linking multidimensional item calibrations. *Applied Psychological Measurement, 20*, 405–416.

Dayton, C. M. (1998). *Latent class scaling analysis*. Thousand Oaks, CA: Sage.

Dayton, C. M., & Scheers, N. J. (1997). Latent class analysis of survey data dealing with academic dishonesty. In J. Rost & R. L. Langeheine (Eds.), *Applications of latent trait and latent class models in the social sciences* (pp. 172–180). Munich: Waxman Verlag.

de Ayala, R. J. (1992). The nominal response model in computerized adaptive testing. *Applied Psychological Measurement, 16*, 327–343.

de Ayala, R. J. (2006). Estimating person locations from partial credit data containing missing responses. *Journal of Applied Measurement, 4*, 278–291.

de Ayala, R. J., Dodd, B. G., & Koch, W. R. (1990). A computerized simulation of a flexilevel test and its comparison with a Bayesian computerized adaptive test. *Journal of Educational Measurement, 27*, 227–239.

de Ayala, R. J. , Kim, S. H., Stapleton, L. M., & Dayton, C. M. (2003). Differential item functioning: A mixture distribution conceptualization. *International Journal of Testing, 2*, 243–276.

de Ayala, R. J., Plake, B., & Impara, J. (2001). The effect of omitted responses on ability estimation in IRT. *Journal of Educational Measurement, 38*, 213–234.

de Ayala, R. J., & Sava-Bolesta, M. (1999). Item parameter recovery for the nominal response model. *Applied Psychological Measurement, 23*, 3–19.

de Ayala, R. J., Schafer, W. D., & Sava-Bolesta, M. (1995). An investigation of the standard errors of expected a posteriori ability estimates. *British Journal of Mathematical and Statistical Psychology, 48*, 385–405.

De Boeck, P., & Wilson, M. (Eds.). (2004). *Explanatory item response models: A generalized linear and nonlinear approach*. New York: Springer-Verlag.

De Champlain, A. F., & Gessaroli, M. E. (1998). Assessing the dimensionality of item response matrices with small sample sizes and short test lengths. *Applied Measurement in Education, 11*, 231–253.

De Champlain, A. F., & Tang, K. L. (1997). CHIDIM: A FORTRAN program for assessing the dimensionality of binary item responses based on McDonald's nonlinear factor analytic model. *Educational and Psychological Measurement, 57*, 174–178.

de Gruijter, D. N. M. (1984). A comment on "Some standard errors in item response theory." *Psychometrika, 49*, 269–272.

de Gruijter, D. N. M. (1990). A note on the bias of UCON item parameter estimation in the Rasch model. *Journal of Educational Measurement, 27*, 285–288.

DeMars, C. E. (2003). Sample size and the recovery of nominal response model item parameters. *Applied Psychological Measurement, 27*, 275–288.

DeMars, C. E. (2007). "Guessing" parameter estimates for multidimensional item response theory models. *Educational and Psychological Measurement, 67*, 433–446.

Dempster, A. P., Laird, N. M., & Rubin, D. B. (1977). Maximum likelihood for incomplete data via the EM algorithm (with discussion). *Journal of the Royal Statistical Society, Series B, 39*, 1–38.

Dillman, D. A. (2000). *Mail and Internet surveys*. New York: Wiley.

Dillman, D. A., Eltinge, J. L., Groves, R. M., & Little, R. J. A. (2002). Survey nonresponse in design, data collection, and analysis. In R. M. Groves, D. A. Dillman, J. L. Eltinge, & R. J. A. Little (Eds.), *Survey nonresponse* (pp. 3–26). New York: Wiley.

Dinero, T. E., & Haertel, E. (1977). Applicability of the Rasch model with varying item discriminations. *Applied Psychological Measurement, 1*, 581–592.

Divgi, D. R. (1979). Calculation of the tetrachoric correlation coefficient. *Psychometrika, 44*, 169–172.

Divgi, D. R. (1985). A minimum chi-square method for developing a common metric in item response theory. *Applied Psychological Measurement, 9*, 413–415.

Divgi, D. R. (1986). Does the Rasch model really work for multiple choice items? Not if you look closely. *Journal of Educational Measurement, 23*, 283–298.

Dodd, B. G. (1984). *Attitude scaling: A comparison of the graded response and partial credit latent trait models* (Doctoral dissertation, University of Texas at Austin, 1984). *Dissertation Abstracts International, 45*, 2074A.

Dodd, B. G. (1987, April). *Computerized adaptive testing with the rating scale model*. Paper presented at the Fourth International Objective Measurement Workshop, Chicago.

Dodd, B. G. (1990). The effect of item selection procedure and stepsize on computerized adaptive attitude measurement using the rating scale model. *Applied Psychological Measurement, 14*, 355–366.

Dodd, B. G., & de Ayala, R. J. (1994). Item information as a function of threshold values in the rating scale model. In M. R. Wilson (Ed.), *Objective measurement: Theory into practice* (Vol. 2, pp. 301–317). Norwood, NJ: Ablex.

Dodd, B. G., & Koch, W. R. (1987). Effects of variations in item step values on item and test information in the partial credit model. *Applied Psychological Measurement, 11*, 371–384.

Dodd, B. G., Koch, W. R., & de Ayala, R. J. (1989). Operational characteristics of adaptive testing procedures using the graded response model. *Applied Psychological Measurement, 13*, 129–144.

Dorans, N. J., & Holland, P. W. (1993). DIF detection and description: Mantel–Haenszel and standardization. In P. W. Holland & H. Wainer (Eds.), *Differential item functioning* (pp. 35–66). Hillsdale, NJ: Erlbaum.

Drasgow, F. (1989). An evaluation of marginal maximum likelihood estimation for the two-parameter model. *Applied Psychological Measurement, 13*, 77–90.

Drasgow, F., Levine, M. V., & McLaughlin, M. E. (1987). Detecting inappropriate test scores with optimal and practical appropriateness indices. *Applied Psychological Measurement, 11*, 59–79.

Drasgow, F., Levine, M. V., & Williams, E. A. (1985). Appropriateness measurement with polychotomous item response models and standardized indices. *British Journal of Mathematical and Statistical Psychology, 38*, 67–86.

Drasgow, F., Levine, M. V., Tsien, S., Williams, B. A., & Mead, A. D. (1995). Fitting polytomous item response theory models to multiple-choice tests. *Applied Psychological Measurement, 19*, 143–165.

Drasgow, F., & Olson-Buchanan, J. B. (Eds.). (1999). *Innovations in computerized assessment*. Hillsdale, NJ: Erlbaum.

Dunn-Rankin, P., Knezek, G. A., Wallace, S., & Zhang, S. (2004). *Scaling methods* (2nd ed.). Hillsdale, NJ: Erlbaum.

Efron, B., & Tibshirani, R. J. (1993). An introduction to the bootstrap. *Monographs on Statistics and Applied Probability, 57*. New York: Chapman and Hall.

Embretson, S. E. (1984). A general latent trait model for response processes. *Psychometrika, 49*, 175–186.

Embretson, S. E. (1985). *Test design*. New York: Academic Press.

Embretson, S. E. (1993). Learning and cognitive processes. In N. Frederiksen, R. J. Mislevy, & I. I. Bejar (Eds.), *Test theory for a new generation of tests* (pp. 125–150). Hillsdale, NJ: Erlbaum.

Embretson, S. E. (1996). Cognitive design principles and the successful performer: A study on spatial ability. *Journal of Educational Measurement, 33*, 29–40.

Embretson, S. E. (1997). Multicomponent response models. In W. J. van der Linden & R. K. Hambleton (Eds.), *Handbook of modern item response theory* (pp. 305–321). New York: Springer.

Embretson, S. E., & Wetzel, C. D. (1987). Component latent trait models for paragraph comprehension tests. *Applied Psychological Measurement, 11*, 175–193.

Emons, W., Sijtsma, K., & Meijer, R. (2004). Testing hypotheses about the person–response function in person–fit analysis. *Multivariate Behavioral Research, 39*, 1–35.

Enders, C. K. (2001). A primer on maximum likelihood algorithms for use with missing data. *Structural Equation Modeling: A Multidisciplinary Journal, 8*, 128–141.

Enders, C. K. (2003). Using the EM algorithm to estimate coefficient alpha for scales with item level missing data. *Psychological Methods, 8*, 322–337.

Engelhard, G. (1990, April). *Thorndike, Thurstone and Rasch: A comparison of their approaches to item-invariant measurement*. Paper presented at the annual meeting of the American Educational Research Association, Boston.

Engelhard, G. (1994). Historical views of the concept of invariance in measurement theory. In M. R. Wilson (Ed.), *Objective measurement: Theory into practice* (Vol. 2, pp. 73–99). Norwood, NJ: Ablex.

Engelhard, G. (2008). Historical perspectives on invariant measurement: Guttman, Rasch, and Mokken. *Measurement: Interdisciplinary Research and Perspectives, 6*, 155–189.

Enzmann, D. (2002). *r_tetra: A SPSS-Macro* [Computer program]. Hamburg, Germany: Institut für Kriminalwissenschaften, University of Hamburg. Available at *www2.jura.uni-hamburg.de/inst-krim/kriminologie/Mitarbeiter/Enzmann/Software/ Enzmann_Software.html.*

Falmagne, J. (1989). A latent trait theory via a stochastic learning theory for a knowledge space. *Psychometrika, 54*, 283–303.

Feldt, L. S., & Brennan, R. L. (1989). Reliability. In R. L. Linn (Ed.), *Educational measurement* (3rd ed., pp. 105–146). New York: American Council in Education and Macmillan.

Ferguson, G. A. (1941). The factorial interpretation of test difficulty. *Psychometrika, 6*, 323–329.

Finch, H., & Habing, B. (2005). Comparison of NOHARM and DETECT in item cluster recovery: Counting dimensions and allocating items. *Journal of Educational Measurement, 42*, 149–169.

Fischer, G. (1973). The linear logistic test model as an instrument in educational research. *Acta Psychologica, 37*, 359–374.

Fischer, G. H. (1981). On the existence and uniqueness of maximum-likelihood estimates in the Rasch model. *Psychometrika, 46*, 59–77.

Fischer, G. H., & Formann, A. K. (1982). Some applications of logistic latent trait models with linear constraints on the parameters. *Applied Psychological Measurement, 6*, 397–416.

Fischer, G. H., & Pendl, P. (1980). Individualized testing on the basis of the dichotomous Rasch model. In L. J. T. van der Kamp, W. F. Langerak, & D. N. M. de Gruijter (Eds.), *Psychometrics for educational debates* (pp. 171–188). New York: Wiley.

Fischer, G. H., & Seliger, E. (1997). Multidimensional linear logistic models for change. In W. J. van der Linden & R. K. Hambleton (Eds.), *Handbook of modern item response theory* (pp. 323–346). New York: Springer.

Fisher, R. A. (1935). *The design of experiments.* Edinburgh: Oliver and Boyd.

Fisher, R. A. (1971a). On an absolute criterion for fitting frequency curves. In J. H. Bennett (Ed.), *The collected papers of R. A. Fisher* (Vol. 1, pp. 53–58). South Australia: University of Adelaide. (Original work published 1912)

Fisher, R. A. (1971b). On the mathematical foundations of theoretical statistics. In J. H. Bennett (Ed.), *The collected papers of R. A. Fisher* (Vol. 1, pp. 310–368). South Australia: University of Adelaide. (Original work published 1921)

Forsyth, R., Saisangjan, U., & Gilmer, J. (1981). Some empirical results related to the robustness of the Rasch model. *Applied Psychological Measurement, 5*, 175–186.

Fraser, C. (1988). *NOHARM: A computer program for fitting both unidimensional and multidimensional normal ogive models of latent trait theory* [Computer program]. Armidale, New South Wales: Centre for Behavioural Studies, University of New England.

Fraser, C., & McDonald, R. P. (1988). NOHARM: Least squares item factor analysis. *Multivariate Behavioral Research, 23*, 267–269.

Fraser, C., & McDonald, R. P. (2003). *NOHARM: A Windows program for fitting both unidimensional and multidimensional normal ogive models of latent trait theory* [Computer program]. Welland, ON: Niagara College. Available at *www.niagarac.on.ca/~cfraser/download/.*

Frederiksen, N., Mislevy, R. J., & Bejar, I. I. (1993). *Test theory for a new generation of tests.* Hillsdale, NJ: Erlbaum.

French, A. W., & Miller, T. R. (1996). Logistic regression and its use in detecting differential item functioning in polytomous items. *Journal of Educational Measurement, 33*, 315–332.

French, G. A., & Dodd, B. G. (1999). Parameter recovery for the rating scale model using PARSCALE. *Journal of Outcome Measurement, 3*, 176–199.

Gautschi, W. (1997). *Numerical analysis: An introduction.* Boston: Birkhäuser.

Gerald, C. F., & Wheatley, P. O. (1984). *Applied numerical analysis* (3rd ed.). Reading, MA: Addison-Wesley.

Gessaroli, M. E., & De Champlain, A. F. (1996). Using an approximate chi-square statistic to test the number of dimensions underlying the responses to a set of items. *Journal of Educational Measurement, 33*, 157–179.

Glas, C. A. W. (1999). Modification indices for the 2-PL and the nominal response model. *Psychometrika, 64,* 273–294.

Glas, C. A. W. (2007). Testing generalized Rasch models. In M. von Davier & C. H. Carstensen (Eds.), *Multivariate and mixture distribution Rasch models* (pp. 37–55). New York: Springer.

Glas, C. A. W., & Dagohoy, V. T. (2007). A person fit test for IRT models for polytomous items. *Psychometrika, 72,* 159–180.

Glas, C. A. W., & Falcón, J. C. S. (2003). A comparison of item-fit statistics for the three-parameter logistic model. *Applied Psychological Measurement, 27,* 87–106.

Glas, C. A. W., & Verhelst, N. D. (1995a). *Testing the Rasch model.* In G. Fischer & I. W. Molenaar (Eds.), *Rasch models: Foundations, recent developments, and applications* (pp. 69–95). New York: Springer-Verlag.

Glas, C. A. W., & Verhelst, N. D. (1995b). *Tests of fit for polytomous Rasch models.* In G. Fischer & I. W. Molenaar (Eds.), *Rasch models: Foundations, recent developments, and applications* (pp. 325–352). New York: Springer-Verlag.

Goldstein, H. (1980). Dimensionality, bias independence, and measurement. *British Journal of Mathematical and Statistical Psychology, 33,* 234–246.

Gonzalez, E. J., Smith, T. A., Sibberns, H., Adams, R., Dumais, J., Foy, P., et al. (1998). *User guide for the TIMSS international database: Final year of secondary school.* Chestnut Hill, MA: Boston College. Available at *timss.bc.edu/.*

Gourlay, N. (1951). Difficulty factors arising from the use of tetrachoric correlations in factor analysis. *British Journal of Psychology* (Statistical section), *42,* 65–76.

Green, B. (1970). Comments on tailored testing. In W. H. Holtzman (Ed.), *Computer assisted instruction, testing and guidance* (pp. 184–197). New York: Harper & Row.

Green, B. F., Bock, R. D., Humphreys, L. G., Linn, R. L., & Reckase, M. D. (1984). Technical guidelines for assessing computerized adaptive tests. *Journal of Educational Measurement, 21,* 347–360.

Guilford, J. P. (1959). *Personality.* New York: McGraw-Hill.

Guilford, J. P., & Fruchter, B. (1978). *Fundamental statistics in psychology and education.* New York: McGraw-Hill.

Gulliksen, H. (1987). *Theory of mental tests.* Hillsdale, NJ: Erlbaum. (Originally published 1950)

Gustafsson, J. E. (1980). Testing and obtaining fit of data to the Rasch model. *British Journal of Mathematical and Statistical Psychology, 33,* 205–233.

Guttman, L. (1945). A basis for analyzing test–retest reliability. *Psychometrika, 10,* 255–282.

Guttman, L. (1950). The basis of scalogram analysis. In S. A. Stouffer, L. Guttman, E. A. Suchman, P. F. Lazarsfeld, S. A. Star, & J. A. Clausen (Eds.), *Measurement and prediction* (pp. 60–90). Princeton, NJ: Princeton University Press.

Haberman, S. J. (1978). *Analysis of qualitative data: Vol. 1. Introductory topics.* New York: Academic Press.

Haebara, T. (1980). Equating logistic ability scales by a weighted least squares method. *Japanese Psychological Research, 22,* 144–149.

Hambleton, R. K., & Swaminathan, H. (1985). *Item response theory: Principles and applications.* Boston: Kluwer-Nijhoff.

Hanson, B., & Zeng, L. (2004). *ST: A computer program for IRT scale transformation* [Computer program]. Iowa City, IA: ACT. Available at *www.education.uiowa.edu/casma/IRTprograms.htm.*

Harman, H. H. (1960). *Modern factor analysis.* Chicago: University of Chicago Press.

Harwell, M., Stone, C. A., Hsu, T.-C., & Kirisci, L. (1996). Monte Carlo studies in item response theory. *Applied Psychological Measurement, 20,* 101–125.

Harwell, M. R., & Baker, F. B. (1991). The use of prior distributions in marginalized Bayesian item parameter estimation: A didactic. *Applied Psychological Measurement, 15,* 375–389.

Harwell, M. R., Baker, F. B., & Zwarts, M. (1988). Item parameter estimation via marginal maximum likelihood and an EM algorithm. *Journal of Educational Statistics, 13,* 243–271.

Harwell, M. R., Baker, F. B., & Zwarts, M. (1989). Correction: Harwell, Baker, and Zwarts, Vol. 13, No. 3. *Journal of Educational Statistics, 14,* 297.

Harwell, M. R., & Janosky, J. E. (1991). An empirical study of the effects of small datasets and varying prior variances on item parameter estimation in BILOG. *Applied Psychological Measurement, 15,* 279–291.

Hattie, J. A. (1985). Methodology review: Assessing unidimensionality of tests and items. *Applied Psychological Measurement, 9,* 139–164.

Hattie, J. A., Krokowski, K., Rogers, H. J., & Swaminathan, H. (1996). An assessment of Stout's index of essential unidimensionality. *Applied Psychological Measurement, 20,* 1–14.

Hays, W. L. (1988). *Statistics* (4th ed.). New York: Holt, Rinehart, and Winston.

Hetter, R. D., & Sympson, J. B. (1997). Item exposure in CAT-ASVAB. In W. A. Sands, B. K. Waters, & J. R. McBride (Eds.), *Computerized adaptive testing: From inquiry to operation* (pp. 141–144). Washington, DC: American Psychological Association.

Heywood, H. B. (1931). On finite sequences of real numbers. *Proceedings of the Royal Society, Series A, 134,* 486–501.

Hirsch, T. M. (1989). Multidimensional equating. *Journal of Educational Measurement, 26,* 337–349.

Holland, P. W. (1990a). The Dutch identity: A new tool for the study of item response models. *Psychometrika, 55,* 5–18.

Holland, P. W. (1990b). On the sampling theory foundations of item response theory models. *Psychometrika, 55,* 557–601.

Holland, P. W., & Rubin, D. B. (1982). *Test equating.* New York: Academic Press.

Holland, P. W., & Thayer, D. T. (1988). Differential item functioning and the Mantel–Haenszel procedure. In H. Wainer & H. I. Braun (Eds.), *Test validity* (pp. 129–145). Hillsdale, NJ: Erlbaum.

Holland, P. W., & Wainer, H. (1993). *Differential item functioning.* Hillsdale, NJ: Erlbaum.

Hosmer, D. W., & Lemeshow, S. (2000). *Applied logistic regression* (2nd ed). New York: Wiley.

Hulin, C. L., Lissak, R. I., & Drasgow, F. (1982). Recovery of two- and three-parameter logistic item characteristic curves: A Monte Carlo study. *Applied Psychological Measurement, 6,* 249–260.

Ingels, S. J., Scott, L. A., Rock, D. A., Pollack, J. M., & Rasinski, K. A. (1994). *National Education Longitudinal Study of 1988: First follow-up final technical report* (NCES 94-632). Washington, DC: U.S. Department of Education, Office of Educational Research and Improvement.

Irvine, S. H., & Kyllonen, P. C. (2002). *Item generation for test development.* Hillsdale, NJ: Erlbaum.

Jannarone, R. J., Yu, K. F., & Laughlin, J. E. (1990). Easy Bayes estimation for Rasch-type models. *Psychometrika, 55,* 449–460.

Janssen, R., Schepers, J., & Peres, D. (2004). Models with item and item group predictors. In P. De Boeck & M. Wilson (Eds.), *Explanatory item response models: A generalized linear and nonlinear approach* (pp. 189–212). New York: Springer-Verlag.

Jensema, C. J. (1974). The validity of Bayesian tailored testing. *Educational and Psychological Measurement, 34,* 757–766.

Jensema, C. J. (1976). A simple technique for estimating latent trait mental test parameters. *Educational and Psychological Measurement, 36,* 705–715.

Jensen, A. R. (1980). *Bias in mental testing.* New York: Free Press.

Jodoin, M. G., & Gierl, M. J. (2001). Evaluating Type I error and power rates using an effect size measure with the logistic regression procedure for DIF detection. *Applied Measurement in Education, 14,* 329–349.

Jöreskog, K., & Sörbom, D. (1999). *PRELIS* (Version 2.30) [Computer program]. Mooresville, IN: Scientific Software.

Kaskowitz, G., & de Ayala, R. J. (2001). The effect of error in item parameter estimates error on the test response function method of linking. *Applied Psychological Measurement, 25,* 39–52.

Kelderman, H. (1984). Loglinear Rasch model tests. *Psychometrika, 49,* 223–245.

Kendler, K. S., Karkowski, L. M., & Walsh, D. (1998). The structure of psychosis: Latent class analysis of probands from the Roscommon Family Study. *Archives of General Psychiatry, 55,* 492–499.

Kim, D., de Ayala, R. J., Ferdous, A. A., & Nering, M. L. (2007, April). *Assessing relative performance of local item dependence (LID) indexes.* Paper presented at the annual meeting of the National Council on Measurement in Education, Chicago.

Kim, S., & Kolen, M. J. (2003). *POLYST: A computer program for polytomous IRT scale transformation* [Computer software]. Iowa City, IA: University of Iowa. Program available at *www.education. uiowa.edu/casma/IRTprograms.htm.*

Kim, S.-H., & Cohen, A. S. (1992). IRTDIF: A computer program for IRT differential item functioning analysis. *Applied Psychological Measurement, 16*, 158.

Kim, S.-H., & Cohen, A. S. (1998). A comparison of linking and concurrent calibration under item response theory. *Applied Psychological Measurement, 22*, 131–143.

Kingsbury, G. G., & Weiss, D. J. (1983). A comparison of IRT-based adaptive mastery testing and a sequential mastery testing procedure. In D. J. Weiss (Ed.), *New horizons in testing: Latent trait test theory and computerized adaptive testing* (pp. 257–283). New York: Academic Press.

Klauer, K. C., & Rettig, K. (1990). An approximately standardized person test for assessing consistency with a latent trait model. *British Journal of Mathematical and Statistical Psychology, 43*, 193–206.

Klein, L. W., & Jarjoura, D. (1985). The importance of content representation for common-item equating with nonrandom groups. *Journal of Educational Measurement, 22*, 197–206.

Knol, D. L., & Berger, M. P. F. (1991). Empirical comparison between factor analysis and multidimensional item response models. *Multivariate Behavioral Research, 26*, 457–477.

Koch, W. R. (1983). Likert scaling using the graded response latent trait model. *Applied Psychological Measurement, 7*, 15–32.

Koch, W. R., & Reckase, M. D. (1979, September). *Problems in application of latent trait models to tailored testing* (Research Report No. 79-1). Columbia: University of Missouri, Tailored Testing Research Laboratory, Department of Educational Psychology.

Kok, F. (1988). Item bias and test multidimensionality. In R. Langeheine & J. Rost (Eds.), *Latent trait and latent class models* (pp. 263–275). New York: Plenum Press.

Kolen, M. J., & Brennan, R. L. (1995). *Test equating: Methods and practices*. New York: Springer-Verlag.

Kolen, M. J., & Brennan, R. L. (2004). *Test equating, scaling, and linking*. New York: Springer-Verlag.

Kolen, M. J., Hanson, B. A., & Brennan, R. L. (1992). Conditional standard errors of measurement for scale scores. *Journal of Educational Measurement, 29*, 285–307.

Kolen, M. J., Zeng, L., & Hanson, B. A. (1996). Conditional standard errors of measurement for scale scores using IRT. *Journal of Educational Measurement, 33*, 285–307.

Kubinger, K. D., & Draxler, C. (2007). A comparison of the Rasch model and constrained item response theory models for pertinent psychological test data. In M. von Davier & C. H. Carstensen (Eds.), *Multivariate and mixture distribution Rasch models* (pp. 293–309). New York: Springer.

Kuhn, T. S. (1970). *The structure of scientific revolutions* (2nd ed.). Chicago: University of Chicago Press.

Larkin, K. C., & Weiss, D. J. (1975). *An empirical investigation of two-stage and pyramidal adaptive ability testing* (Research Report 75-1). Minneapolis: University of Minnesota, Department of Psychology, Psychometric Methods Program.

Lawley, D. N. (1943). On problems connected with item selection and test construction. *Proceedings of the Royal Society of Edinburgh, 61A*, 273–287.

Lawley, D. N. (1944). The factorial analysis of multiple item tests. *Proceedings of the Royal Society of Edinburgh, Series A, 62*, 74–82.

Lazarsfeld, P. F. (1950). The logical and mathematical foundation of latent structure analysis. In S. A. Stouffer, L. Guttman, E. A. Suchman, P. F. Lazarsfeld, S. A. Star, & J. A. Clausen (Eds.), *Measurement and prediction* (pp. 362–412). Princeton, NJ: Princeton University Press.

Levine, M. V., & Drasgow, F. (1983). Appropriateness measurement: Validating studies and variable ability models. In D. J. Weiss (Ed.), *New horizons in testing: Latent trait test theory and computerized adaptive testing* (pp. 109–131). New York: Academic Press.

Levine, M. V., & Drasgow, F. (1988). Optimal appropriateness measurement. *Psychometrika, 53*, 161–176.

Levine, M. V., Drasgow, F., & Stark, S. (2001). *Program MODFIT* [Computer program]. Urbana: University of Illinois, Measurement and Evaluation Laboratory, Department of Educational Psychology. Available at *work.psych.uiuc.edu/irt/*.

Likert, R. (1932). A technique for the measurement of attitudes. *Archives of Psychology, 140*, 5–55.

Lim, R. G., & Drasgow, F. (1990). Evaluation of two methods for estimating item response theory parameters when assessing differential item functioning. *Journal of Applied Psychology, 75,* 164–174.

Linacre, J. M. (2001a). *A user's guide to WINSTEPS/MINISTEPS.* Chicago: Winsteps.com.

Linacre, J. M. (2001b). *Facets Rasch measurement software.* Chicago: Winsteps.com.

Linacre, J. M., & Wright, B. D. (2001). *A user's guide to BIGSTEPS.* Chicago: MESA Press.

Linacre, M. (2004). Rasch Model estimation: Further topics. In E. Smith & R. M. Smith (Eds.), *Introduction to Rasch measurement* (pp. 48–72). Maple Grove, MN: JAM Press.

Lindsay, B., Clogg, C. C., & Grego, J. (1991). Semiparametric estimation in the Rasch model and related exponential response models, including a simple latent class model for item analysis. *Journal of the American Statistical Association, 96*–107.

Little, R., & Rubin, D. B. (1987). *Statistical analysis with missing data.* New York: Wiley.

Livingston, S. A. (1982). Estimation of the conditional standard error of measurement for stratified tests. *Journal of Educational Measurement, 19,* 135–138.

Livingston, S. A. (2004). *Equating test scores (without IRT).* Princeton, NJ: Educational Testing Service.

Lord, F. M. (1952). A theory of test scores. *Psychometric Monograph,* No. 7.

Lord, F. M. (1968). An analysis of the Verbal Scholastic Aptitude Test using Birnbaum's three-parameter logistic model. *Educational and Psychological Measurement, 28,* 989–1020.

Lord, F. M. (1970). Some test theory for tailored testing. In W. H. Holtzman (Ed.), *Computer assisted instruction, testing and guidance* (pp. 139–183). New York: Harper & Row.

Lord, F. M. (1971a). Robbins–Monro procedures for tailored testing. *Educational and Psychological Measurement, 31,* 3–31.

Lord, F. M. (1971b). The self-scoring flexilevel test. *Journal of Educational Measurement, 8,* 227–242.

Lord, F. M. (1971c). A theoretical study of the measurement effectiveness of flexilevel tests. *Educational and Psychological Measurement, 31,* 805–813.

Lord, F. M. (1971d). A theoretical study of two-stage testing. *Psychometrika, 36,* 227–241.

Lord, F. M. (1974a). Estimation of latent ability and item parameters when there are omitted responses. *Psychometrika, 39,* 247–264.

Lord, F. M. (1974b). The relative efficiency of two tests as a function of ability level. *Psychometrika, 39,* 351–358.

Lord, F. M. (1975). The "ability" scale in item characteristic curve theory. *Psychometrika, 40,* 205–217.

Lord, F. M. (1977). A broad-range tailored test of verbal ability. *Applied Psychological Measurement, 1,* 95–100.

Lord, F. M. (1980). *Applications of item response theory to practical testing problems.* Hillsdale, NJ: Erlbaum.

Lord, F. M. (1983a). Small N justifies the Rasch model. In D. J. Weiss (Ed.), *New horizons in testing: Latent trait test theory and computerized adaptive testing* (pp. 51–62). New York: Academic Press.

Lord, F. M. (1983b). Unbiased estimators of ability parameters, of their variance, and of their parallel-forms reliability. *Psychometrika, 48,* 233–245.

Lord, F. M. (1983c). Maximum likelihood estimation of item response parameters when some responses are omitted. *Psychometrika, 48,* 477–482.

Lord, F. M. (1986). Maximum likelihood and Bayesian parameter estimation in item response theory. *Journal of Educational Measurement, 23,* 157–162.

Lord, F. M., & Novick, M. R. (1968). *Statistical theories of mental test scores.* Reading, MA: Addison-Wesley.

Luecht, R. M. (1996). Multidimensional computerized adaptive testing in a certification or licensure context. *Applied Psychological Measurement, 20,* 389–404.

Luecht, R. M. (1998). Computer-assisted test assembly using optimization heuristics. *Applied Psychological Measurement, 22,* 224–236.

Lumsden, J. (1978). Tests are perfectly reliable. *British Journal of Mathematical and Statistical Psychology, 31,* 19–26.

MacCallum, R. C., Widaman, K. F., Zhang, S., & Hong, S. (1999). Sample size in factor analysis. *Psychological Methods, 4,* 84–99.

Mantel, N., & Haenszel, W. (1959). Statistical aspects of the analysis of data from retrospective studies of disease. *Journal of the National Cancer Institute, 22,* 719–748.

Maranell, G. M. (1974). *Scaling: A sourcebook for behavioral scientists.* Chicago: Aldine.

Masters, G. N. (1982). A Rasch model for partial credit scoring. *Psychometrika, 47,* 149–174.

Masters, G. N. (1985). A comparison of latent-trait and latent-class analysis of Likert-type data. *Psychometrika, 50,* 69–82.

Masters, G. N. (1988). Measurement models for ordered response categories. In R. L. Langeheine & J. Rost (Eds.), *Latent trait and latent class models* (pp. 11–29). New York: Plenum Press.

Masters, G. N., & Wright, B. D. (1984). The essential process in a family of measurement models. *Psychometrika, 49,* 524–544.

Maydeu-Olivares, A. (2001). Multidimensional item response theory modeling of binary data: Large sample properties of NOHARM estimates. *Journal of Educational and Behavioral Statistics, 26,* 51–71.

Maydeu-Olivares, A., & Joe, H. (2006). Limited information goodness-of-fit testing in multidimensional contingency tables. *Psychometrika, 71,* 713–732.

McBride, J. R., & Martin, J. T. (1983). Reliability and validity of adaptive ability tests in a military setting. In D. J. Weiss (Ed.), *New horizons in testing: Latent trait test theory and computerized adaptive testing* (pp. 223–236). New York: Academic Press.

McDonald, R. P. (1967). Nonlinear factor analysis. *Psychometric Monographs,* No. 15.

McDonald, R. P. (1979). The structural analysis of multivariate data: A sketch of a general theory. *Multivariate Behavioral Research, 14,* 21–38.

McDonald, R. P. (1981). The dimensionality of tests and items. *British Journal of Mathematical and Statistical Psychology, 34,* 100–117.

McDonald, R. P. (1985). *Factor analysis and related methods.* Hillsdale, NJ: Erlbaum.

McDonald, R. P. (1997). Normal-ogive multidimensional model. In W. J. van der Linden & R. K. Hambleton (Eds.), *Handbook of modern item response theory* (pp. 257–269). New York: Springer.

McDonald, R. P. (1999). *Test theory: A unified treatment.* Hillsdale, NJ: Erlbaum.

McDonald, R. P., & Ahlawat, K. S. (1974). Difficulty factors in binary data. *British Journal of Mathematical and Statistical Psychology, 27,* 82–99.

McDonald, R. P., & Mok, M. (1995). Goodness of fit in item response theory models. *Multivariate Behavioral Research, 30,* 23–40.

McKinley, R. L., & Kingston, N. M. (1988, April). *Confirmatory analysis of test structure using multidimensional IRT.* Paper presented at the annual meeting of the National Council on Measurement in Education, New Orleans.

McKinley, R. L., & Mills, C. N. (1985). A comparison of several goodness-of-fit statistics. *Applied Psychological Measurement, 9,* 49–57.

McKinley, R. L., & Reckase, M. D. (1983a, August). *An extension of the two-parameter logistic model to the multidimensional latent space* (Research Report No. ONR83-2). Iowa City, IA: American College Testing Program.

McKinley, R. L., & Reckase, M. D. (1983b). MAXLOG: A computer program for the estimation of the parameters of a multidimensional logistic model. *Behavior Research Methods and Instrumentation, 15,* 389–390.

Meijer, R. R., & Sijtsma, K. (2001). Methodology review: Evaluating person fit. *Applied Psychological Measurement, 25,* 107–135.

Mellenbergh, G. J. (1982). Contingency table models for assessing item bias. *Journal of Educational Statistics, 7,* 105–118.

Mellenbergh, G. J. (1995). Conceptual notes on models for discrete polytomous item responses. *Applied Psychological Measurement, 19,* 91–100.

Mellenbergh, G. J., & Vijn, P. (1981). The Rasch model as a loglinear model. *Applied Psychological Measurement, 5,* 369–376.

Mislevy, R. J. (1986a). Bayes modal estimation in item response models. *Psychometrika, 51,* 177–195.

Mislevy, R. J. (1986b). Recent developments in the factor analysis of categorical variables. *Journal of Educational Statistics, 11*, 3–31.

Mislevy, R. J., & Bock, R. D. (1982). Biweight estimates of latent ability. *Educational and Psychological Measurement, 42*, 725–737.

Mislevy, R. J., & Bock, R. D. (1985, April). Implementation of the EM algorithm in the estimation of item parameters: The BILOG computer program. In D. J. Weiss (Ed.), *Proceedings of the 1982 Item Response Theory and Computerized Adaptive Testing Conference* (pp. 189–202). Minneapolis: University of Minnesota, Department of Psychology, Computerized Adaptive Testing Laboratory.

Mislevy, R. J., & Bock, R. D. (1997). *BILOG 3: Item analysis and test scoring with binary logistic models* [Computer program]. Mooresville, IN: Scientific Software.

Mislevy, R. J., & Stocking, M. L. (1989). A consumer's guide to LOGIST and BILOG. *Applied Psychological Measurement, 13*, 57–75.

Mislevy, R. J., & Verhelst, N. (1990). Modeling item responses when different subjects employ different solution strategies. *Psychometrika, 55*, 195–216.

Mislevy, R. J., & Wu, P. (1988). *Inferring examinee ability when some item responses are missing* (RR 88-48-ONR). Princeton, NJ: Educational Testing Service.

Mislevy, R. J., & Wu, P. (1996). *Missing responses and IRT ability estimation: Omits, choice, time limits, and adaptive testing* (RR 96-30-ONR). Princeton, NJ: Educational Testing Service.

Muraki, E. (1990). Fitting a polytomous item response model to Likert-type data. *Applied Psychological Measurement, 14*, 59–71.

Muraki, E. (1992). A generalized partial credit model: Application of an EM algorithm. *Applied Psychological Measurement, 16*, 159–176.

Muraki, E., & Bock, R. D. (2003). *PARSCALE* (Version 4.1) [Computer program]. Mooresville, IN: Scientific Software.

Muraki, E., & Engelhard, G. (1985). Full-information item factor analysis: Applications of EAP scores. *Applied Psychological Measurement, 9*, 417–430.

Muthén, B. O., & Hofacker, C. (1988). Testing the assumptions underlying tetrachoric correlations. *Psychometrika, 53*, 563–578.

Muthén, L. K., & Muthén, B. O. (1998). *Mplus user's guide*. Los Angeles: Muthén & Muthén.

Nagelkerke, N. J. D. (1991). A note on a general definition of the coefficient of determination. *Biometrika, 78*, 691–692.

Nandakumar, R. (1991). Traditional dimensionality versus essential dimensionality. *Journal of Educational Measurement, 28*, 99–117.

National Opinion Research Center. (2003). *General Social Science Survey*. Available at *www.icpsr.umich.edu:8080/GSS/homepage.htm*.

Nering, M. L., & Meijer, R. R. (1998). A comparison of the person response function and the l_z person-fit statistic. *Applied Psychological Measurement, 22*, 53–69.

Neyman, J., & Scott, E. L. (1948). Consistent estimates based on partially consistent observations. *Econometrica, 16*, 1–32.

Nunnally, J. C., & Bernstein, I. H. (1994). *Psychometric theory* (3rd ed.). New York: McGraw-Hill.

Orlando, M., & Thissen, D. (2000). Likelihood-based item-fit indices for dichotomous item response theory models. *Applied Psychological Measurement, 24*, 50–64.

Oshima, T. C. (1994). The effect of speededness on parameter estimation in item response theory. *Journal of Educational Measurement, 31*, 200–219.

Oshima, T. C., Davey, T. C., & Lee, K. (2000). Multidimensional linking: Four practical approaches. *Journal of Educational Measurement, 37*, 357–373.

Panter, A. T., Swygert, K. A., Dahlstrom, W. G., & Tanaka, J. S. (1997). Factor analytic approaches to personality item-level data. *Journal of Personality Assessment, 68*, 561–589.

Parshall, C. G., Spray, J. A., Kalohn, J. C., & Davey, T. (2002). *Practical considerations in computerized-based testing*. New York: Springer.

Patience, W. M. (1977). Description of components in tailored testing. *Behavior Research Methods and Instrumentation, 9*, 153–157.

Patience, W. M., & Reckase, M. D. (1980, April). *Effects of program parameters and item pool charac-*

teristics on the bias of a three-parameter tailored testing procedure. Paper presented at the annual meeting of the National Council on Measurement in Education, Boston.

Patz, R. J., & Junker, B. W. (1999a). A straightforward approach to Markov chain Monte Carlo methods for item response models. *Journal of Educational and Behavioral Statistics, 24,* 146–178.

Patz, R. J., & Junker, B. W. (1999b). Applications and extensions of MCMC in IRT: Multiple item types, missing data, and rated responses. *Journal of Educational and Behavioral Statistics, 24,* 342–366.

Paxton, P., Curran, P. J., Bollen, K., Kirby, J., & Chen, F. (2001). Monte Carlo experiments: Design and implementation. *Structural Equation Modeling, 8,* 287–312.

Pedhauzer, E. J. (1997). *Multiple regression in behavioral research* (3rd ed.). Fort Worth, TX: Harcourt Brace.

Petersen, N. S., Kolen, M. J., & Hoover, H. D. (1989). Scaling norming, and equating. In R. L. Linn (Ed.), *Educational measurement* (3rd ed., pp. 221–262). New York: Macmillan.

R Development Core Team. (2007). *R: A language and environment for statistical computing* [Computer software]. Vienna, Austria: R Foundation for Statistical Computing. Program available at *www.r-project.org.*

Raju, N. S. (1988). The area between two item characteristic curves. *Psychometrika, 53,* 495–502.

Raju, N. S. (1990). Determining the significance of estimated signed and unsigned areas between two item response functions. *Applied Psychological Measurement, 14,* 197–207. (A correction may be found in *Applied Psychological Measurement, 15,* 352.)

Ramsay, J. O. (1989). A comparison of three simple test theory models. *Psychometrika, 54,* 487–499.

Rasch, G. (1961). On general laws and the meaning of measurement in psychology. In *Proceedings of the Fourth Berkeley Symposium on Mathematical Statistics and Probability* (pp. 321–333). Berkeley: University of California Press.

Rasch, G. (1980). *Probabilistic models for some intelligence and attainment tests.* Chicago: University of Chicago Press. (Original work published 1960)

Reckase, M. D. (1977). Procedures for computerized testing. *Behavior Research Methods and Instrumentation, 9,* 208–212.

Reckase, M. D. (1979). Unifactor latent trait models applied to multifactor tests: Results and implications. *Journal of Educational Statistics, 4,* 207–230.

Reckase, M. D. (1980, April). *An application of tailored testing and sequential analysis to classification problems.* Paper presented at the annual meeting of the American Educational Research Association, Boston.

Reckase, M. D. (1985). The difficulty of tests that measure more than one ability. *Applied Psychological Measurement, 9,* 401–412.

Reckase, M. D. (1986, April). *The discriminating power of items that measure more than one dimension.* Paper presented at the annual meeting of the American Educational Research Association, Chicago.

Reckase, M. D. (1989, Fall). Adaptive testing: The evolution of a good idea. *Educational Measurement: Issues and Practice, 8*(3), 11–15.

Reckase, M. D. (1997a). A linear logistic multidimensional model for dichotomous item response data. In W. J. van der Linden & R. K. Hambleton (Eds.), *Handbook of modern item response theory* (pp. 271–286). New York: Springer.

Reckase, M. D. (1997b). Past and future of multidimensional item response theory. *Applied Psychological Measurement, 21,* 25–36.

Reckase, M. D., Ackerman, T. A., & Carlson, J. E. (1988). Building a unidimensional test using multidimensional items. *Journal of Educational Measurement, 25,* 193–203.

Reckase, M. D., & McKinley, R. L. (1991). The discriminating power of items that measure more than one dimension. *Applied Psychological Measurement, 15,* 361–373.

Ree, M. J., & Jensen, H. E. (1983). Effects of sample size on linear equating of item characteristic curve parameters. In D. J. Weiss (Ed.), *New horizons in testing: Latent trait test theory and computerized adaptive testing* (pp. 135–146). New York: Academic Press.

Reise, S. P. (1990). A comparison of item- and person-fit methods of assessing model–data fit in IRT. *Applied Psychological Measurement, 14,* 127–137.

Reise, S. P. (2000). Using multilevel logistic regression to evaluate person-fit in IRT models. *Multivariate Behavioral Research, 35,* 543–568.

Reise, S. P., & Due, N. G. (1991). The influence of test characteristics on the detection of aberrant response patterns. *Applied Psychological Measurement, 15,* 217–226.

Reise, S. P., & Waller, N. G. (1990). Fitting the two-parameter model to personality data. *Applied Psychological Measurement, 14,* 45–58.

Reise, S. P., & Yu, J. (1990). Parameter recovery in the graded response model using MULTILOG. *Journal of Educational Measurement, 27,* 133–144.

Rosenbaum, P. R. (1984). Testing the conditional independence and monotonicity assumptions of item response theory. *Psychometrika, 49,* 425–435.

Roskam, E. E. (1997). Models for speed and time-limit tests. In W. J. van der Linden & R. K. Hambleton (Eds.), *Handbook of modern item response theory* (pp. 187–208). New York: Springer.

Rost, J. (1990). Rasch models in latent classes: An integration of two approaches to item analysis. *Applied Psychological Measurement, 14,* 271–282.

Rost, J. (1991). A logistic mixture distribution model for polychotomous item responses. *British Journal of Mathematical and Statistical Psychology, 44,* 75–92.

Rost, J., & von Davier, M. (1992). *MIRA: A PC-program for the mixed Rasch model* [Computer program]. Kiel, Germany: Institute für die Pädagogik der Naturwissenschaften an der Universität Kiel.

Roth, R. L. (1994). Missing data: A conceptual review for applied psychologists. *Personnel Psychology, 47,* 537–560.

Rupp, A. A., & Zumbo, B. D. (2004). A note on how to quantify and report whether IRT parameyter invariance holds: When Pearson correlations are not enough. *Educational and Psychological Measurement, 64,* 588–599; Errata, *64,* 991.

Rupp, A. A., & Zumbo, B. D. (2006). Understanding parameter invariance in unidimensional IRT models. *Educational and Psychological Measurement, 66,* 63–84.

Samejima, F. (1969). Estimation of latent ability using a response pattern of graded scores. *Psychometrika Monograph Supplement,* No. 17.

Samejima, F. (1973a). A comment on Birnbaum's three-parameter logistic model in the latent trait theory. *Psychometrika, 38,* 221–233.

Samejima, F. (1973b). Homogeneous case of the continuous response model. *Psychometrika, 38,* 203–219.

Samejima, F. (1974). A normal ogive model on the continuous response level in the multidimensional latent space. *Psychometrika, 39,* 111–121.

Samejima, F. (1976). The graded response model of latent trait theory and tailored testing. In C. L. Clark (Ed.), *Proceedings of the First Conference on Computerized Adaptive Testing* (U.S. Civil Service Commission, Personnel Research and Development Center, PS-75-6) (pp. 5–15). Washington, DC: U.S. Government Printing Office.

Samejima, F. (1979). *A new family of models for the multiple choice item* (Research Report No. 79-4). Knoxville: University of Tennessee, Department of Psychology.

Samejima, F. (1990). *Predictions of reliability coefficients and standard errors of measurement using the test information function and its modifications* (ONR/RR-90-2). Knoxville: University of Tennessee, Department of Psychology.

Samejima, F. (1994). Some critical observations of the test information function as a measure of local accuracy in ability estimation. *Psychometrika, 59,* 307–329.

Samejima, F. (2001). *Non-parametric on-line item calibration* (Law School Admission Council, 1999–2001, Final Report). Knoxville: University of Tennessee, Department of Psychology.

Sands, W. A., Waters, B. K., & McBride, J. R. (Eds.). (1997). *Computerized adaptive testing: From inquiry to operation.* Washington, DC: American Psychological Association.

SAS Institute. (2002). *SAS for Windows:* Version 9.1. Carey, NC: Author.

Schaeffer, N. C. (1988). An application of item response theory to the measurement of depression. *Sociological Methodology, 18,* 271–307.

Scheffé, H. (1959). *The analysis of variance.* New York: Wiley.

Schwarz, G. (1978). Estimating the dimension of a model. *Annals of Statistics, 6,* 461–464.

Seagall, D. O. (1996). Multidimensional adaptive testing. *Psychometrika, 61*, 331–354.

Seliger, E., & Fischer, G. H. (1994). *LRSMG, LRSM, LLTM, LPCM: Program description with applications to scale analysis and measuring change* [Computer program]. Vienna, Austria: University of Vienna.

Seong, T.-J. (1990a, April). *Validity of using two numerical analysis techniques to estimate item and ability parameters via MMLE: Gauss–Hermite quadrature formula and Mislevy's histogram solution.* Paper presented at the meeting of the National Council of Measurement in Education, Boston.

Seong, T.-J. (1990b). Sensitivity of marginal maximum likelihood estimation of item and ability parameters to the characteristics of the prior ability distributions. *Applied Psychological Measurement, 14*, 299–311.

Shepard, L. A., Camilli, G., & Averill, M. (1981). Comparison of procedures for detecting test-item bias with both internal and external ability criteria. *Journal of Educational Statistics, 6*, 317–375.

Shepard, L. A., Camilli, G., & Williams, D. M. (1984). Accounting for statistical artifacts in item bias research. *Journal of Educational Statistics, 9*, 93–128.

Sijtsma, K., & Hemker, B. T. (2000). A taxonomy of IRT models for ordering persons and items using simple sum scores. *Journal of Educational Statistics, 25*, 391–415.

Sijtsma, K., & Meijer, R. R. (2001). The person response function as a tool in person fit research. *Psychometrika, 66*, 191–208.

Sinharay, S., & Holland, P. W. (2007). Is it necessary to make anchor tests mini-versions of the tests being equated or can some restrictions be relaxed? *Journal of Educational Measurement, 44*, 249–275.

Sireci, S. G. (1998). The construct of content validity. *Social Indicators Research, 45*, 83–117.

Sireci, S. G., Wainer, H., & Thissen, D. J. (1991). On the reliability of testlet-based tests. *Journal of Educational Measurement, 28*, 237–247.

Skaggs, G., & Stevenson, J. (1989). A comparison of pseudo-Bayesian and joint maximum likelihood procedures for estimating item parameters in the three-parameter IRT model. *Applied Psychological Measurement, 13*, 391–402.

Smith, R. M. (1985). A comparison of Rasch person analysis and robust estimators. *Educational and Psychological Measurement, 45*, 433–444.

Smith, R. M. (1991). The distributional properties of Rasch item fit statistics. *Educational and Psychological Measurement, 51*, 541–565.

Smith, R. M. (2004). Fit analysis in latent trait measurement models. In E. V. Smith & R. M. Smith (Eds.), *Introduction to Rasch measurement* (pp. 73–92). Maple Grove, MN: JAM Press.

Smith, R. M., Schumacker, R. E., & Bush, M. J. (1998). Using item mean squares to evaluate fit to the Rasch model. *Journal of Outcome Measurement, 2*, 66–78.

Spada, N., & McGaw, B. (1985). Learning and cognitive processes. In S. E. Embretson (Ed.), *Test design* (pp. 169–194). New York: Academic Press.

Spiegelhalter, D., Thomas, A., Best, N., & Lunn, D. (2004). WINBUGS [Computer program]. Cambridge, UK: MRC Biostatistics Unit, Institute of Public Health. Available at *www.mrc-bsu.cam.ac.uk/bugs/*.

Spray, J. A., Davey, T. C., Reckase, M. D., Ackerman, T. A., & Carlson, J. E. (1990, August). *Comparison of two logistic multidimensional item response theory models* (Research Report No. ONR90-8). Iowa City, IA: American College Testing Program.

SPSS Incorporated. (2006). *SPSS 15.0 for Windows*. Chicago: Author.

Steinberg, L. (2001). The consequences of pairing questions: Context effects in personality measurement. *Journal of Personality and Social Psychology, 81*, 332–342.

Stevens, S. S. (1946). On the theory of scales of measurement. *Science, 103*, 677–680.

Stocking, M. L., Eignor, D., & Cook, L. (1988). *Factors affecting the sample invariant properties of linear and curvilinear observed and true score equating procedures* (RR-88-41). Princeton, NJ: Educational Testing Service.

Stocking, M. L., & Lewis, C. (1998). Controlling item exposure conditional on ability in computerized adaptive testing. *Journal of Educational and Behavioral Statistics, 23*, 57–75.

Stocking, M. L., & Lewis, C. (2000). Methods of controlling the exposure of items in CAT. In W. J.

van der Linden & C. A. W. Glas (Eds.), *Computerized adaptive testing: Theory and practice* (pp. 163–182). Dordrecht, The Netherlands: Kluwer Academic Publishers.

Stocking, M. L., & Lord, F. M. (1983). Developing a common metric in item response theory. *Applied Psychological Measurement, 7,* 201–210.

Stone, C. A. (1992). Recovery of marginal maximum likelihood estimates in the two-parameter logistic response model: An evaluation of MULTILOG. *Applied Psychological Measurement, 16,* 1–16.

Stouffer, S. A. (1950). The logical and mathematical foundation of latent structure analysis. In S. A. Stouffer, L. Guttman, E. A. Suchman, P. F. Lazarsfeld, S. A. Star, & J. A. Clausen (Eds.), *Measurement and prediction* (pp. 3–45). Princeton, NJ: Princeton University Press.

Stout, W. (1987). A nonparametric approach for assessing latent trait unidimensionality. *Psychometrika, 52,* 589–617.

Stout, W. (1990). A new item response theory modeling approach with applications to unidimensionality assessment and ability estimation. *Psychometrika, 55,* 293–325.

Stroud, A. H., & Secrest, D. (1966). *Gaussian quadrature formulas.* Englewood Cliffs, NJ: Prentice-Hall.

Subkoviak, M. J., Mack, J. S., Ironson, G. H., & Craig, R. D. (1984). Empirical comparison of selected item bias detection procedures with bias manipulation. *Journal of Educational Measurement, 21,* 49–58.

Swaminathan, H., & Gifford, J. A. (1982). Bayesian estimation in the Rasch model. *Journal of Educational Statistics, 7,* 175–191.

Swaminathan, H., & Gifford, J. A. (1983). Estimation of parameters in the three-parameter model. In D. J. Weiss (Ed.), *New horizons in testing: Latent trait test theory and computerized adaptive testing* (pp. 13–30). New York: Academic Press.

Swaminathan, H., & Gifford, J. A. (1985). Bayesian estimation in the two-parameter logistic model. *Psychometrika, 50,* 349–364.

Swaminathan, H., & Gifford, J. A. (1986). Bayesian estimation in the three-parameter logistic model. *Psychometrika, 51,* 589–601.

Swaminathan, H., & Rogers, J. (1990). Detecting DIF using logistic regression procedures. *Journal of Educational Measurement, 27,* 361–370.

Swenson, W. M. , Pearson, J. S., & Osborne, D. (1973). *An MMPI source book: Basic item, scale, and pattern data on 50,000 medical patients.* Minneapolis: University of Minnesota Press.

Sympson, J. B. (1978). A model for testing with multidimensional items. In D. J. Weiss (Ed.), *Proceedings of the 1977 Computerized Adaptive Testing Conference* (pp. 82–98). Minneapolis: University of Minnesota, Department of Psychology, Psychometric Methods Program.

Takane, Y., & de Leeuw, J. (1987). On the relationship between item response theory and factor analysis of discretized variables. *Psychometrika, 52,* 393–408.

Tanaka, J. S. (1993). Multifaceted conceptions of fit in structural equation models. In K. A. Bollen & J. S. Long (Eds.), *Testing structural equation models.* Newbury Park, CA: Sage.

Tatsuoka, K. K. (1983). Rule space: An approach for dealing with misconceptions based on item response theory. *Journal of Educational Measurement, 20,* 345–354.

Theunissen, T. J. J. M. (1985). Binary programming and test design *Psychometrika, 50,* 411–420.

Thissen, D. J. (1976). Information in wrong responses to Raven's progressive matrices. *Journal of Educational Measurement, 13,* 201–214.

Thissen, D. J. (1982). Marginal maximum likelihood estimation for the one-parameter logistic model. *Psychometrika, 47,* 175–186.

Thissen, D. J., Chen, W.-H., & Bock, R. D. (2003). *MULTILOG* (Version 7.0) [Computer program]. Mooresville, IN: Scientific Software.

Thissen, D. J., & Steinberg, L. (1984). A response model for multiple choice items. *Psychometrika, 49,* 501–519.

Thissen, D. J., & Steinberg, L. (1986). A taxonomy of item response models. *Psychometrika, 51,* 567–577.

Thissen, D. J., & Steinberg, L. (1997). A response model for multiple-choice items. In W. J. van der Linden & R. K. Hambleton (Eds.), *Handbook of modern item response theory* (pp. 51–65). New York: Springer.

Thissen, D. J., Steinberg, L., & Fitzpatrick, A. R. (1989a). Multiple-choice models: The distractors are also part of the item. *Journal of Educational Measurement, 26*, 161–176.

Thissen, D. J., Steinberg, L., & Mooney, J. A. (1989b). Trace lines for testlets: A use of multiple-categorical-response models. *Journal of Educational Measurement, 26*, 247–260.

Thissen, D. J., Steinberg, L., & Wainer, H. (1988). Use of item response theory in the study of group differences in trace lines. In H. Wainer & H. I. Braun (Eds.), *Test validity* (pp. 147–169). Hillsdale, NJ: Erlbaum.

Thissen, D. J., Steinberg, L., & Wainer, H. (1993). Detection of differential item functioning using the parameters of item response models. In P. W. Holland & H. Wainer (Eds.), *Differential item functioning* (pp. 67–113). Hillsdale, NJ: Erlbaum.

Thissen, D. J., & Wainer, H. (1982). Some standard errors in item response theory. *Psychometrika, 47*, 397–412.

Thomson, William (Lord Kelvin). (1891). *Popular lectures and addresses* (Vol. 1). New York: Macmillan.

Thurstone, L. L. (1925). A method of scaling psychological and educational tests. *Journal of Educational Psychology, 16*, 433–451.

Thurstone, L. L. (1928). Attitudes can be measured. *American Journal of Sociology, 33*, 529–554.

Thurstone, L. L. (1938). Primary mental abilities. *Psychometric Monographs,* No. 1.

Thurstone, L. L. (1947). *Multiple factor analysis.* Chicago: University of Chicago Press.

Trabin, T. E., & Weiss, D. J. (1983). The person response curve: Fit of individuals to item response theory models. In D. J. Weiss (Ed.), *New horizons in testing: Latent trait test theory and computerized adaptive testing* (pp. 83–108). New York: Academic Press.

Tucker, L. R. (1946). Maximum validity of a test with equivalent items. *Psychometrika, 11*, 1–13.

Tutz, G. (1990). Sequential item response models with an ordered response. *British Journal of Mathematical and Statistical Psychology, 43*, 39–55.

Urry, V. W. (1974). Approximations to item parameters of mental test models and their uses. *Educational and Psychological Measurement, 34*, 253–269.

Urry, V. W. (1977). Tailored testing: A successful application of latent trait theory. *Journal of Educational Measurement, 14*, 181–196.

Vale, C. D., Albing, C., Foote-Lennox, L., & Foote-Lennox, T. (1982). *Specification of requirements and preliminary design* (RR ONR-ASC-82-01). St. Paul, MN: Assessment Systems.

van den Wollenberg, A. (1988). Testing a latent trait model. In R. Langeheine & J. Rost (Eds.), *Latent trait and latent class models* (pp. 31–50). New York: Plenum Press.

van der Flier, H. (1982). Deviant response patterns and comparability of test scores. *Journal of Cross-Cultural Psychology, 13*, 267–298.

van der Linden, W. J. (1998). Optimal assembly of psychological and educational tests. *Applied Psychological Measurement, 22*, 195–211.

van der Linden, W. J. (1999). Multidimensional adaptive testing with a minimum error-variance criterion. *Journal of Educational and Behavioral Statistics, 24*, 398–412.

van der Linden, W. J., & Boekkooi-Timminga, E. (1989). A maximin model for test design with practical constraints. *Psychometrika, 54*, 237–247.

van der Linden, W. J., & Glas, C. A. W. (Eds.). (2000). *Computerized adaptive testing: Theory and practice.* Dordrecht, the Netherlands: Kluwer.

van der Linden, W. J., & Veldkamp, B. P. (2004). Constraining item exposure in computerized adaptive testing with shadow tests. *Journal of Educational and Behavioral Statistics, 29*, 273–291.

Verhelst, N. D., & Glas, C. A. W. (1995). One-parameter logistic model. In G. Fischer & I. W. Molenaar (Eds.), *Rasch models: Foundations, recent developments, and applications* (pp. 215–237). New York: Springer-Verlag.

Verhelst, N. D., Glas, C. A. W., & Verstralen, H. H. F. M. (1995). One-parameter logistic model (OPLM). Arnhem, the Netherlands: CITO.

Verhelst, N. D., Verstralen, H. H. F. M., & Jansen, M. G. H. (1997). A logistic model for time-limit tests. In W. J. van der Linden & R. K. Hambleton (Eds.), *Handbook of modern item response theory* (pp. 169–185). New York: Springer.

von Davier, A. A., Holland, P. W., & Thayer, D. T. (2004). *The Kernel method of test equating.* New York: Springer.

von Davier, M. (2001). *WINMIRA 2001* [Computer program]. Kiel, Germany: Institute für die Pädagogik der Naturwissenschaften an der Universität Kiel. Available at *www.winmira.von-davier.de/.*

von Davier, M., & Carstensen, C. H. (Eds.). (2007). *Multivariate and mixture distribution Rasch models.* New York: Springer.

Wainer, H. (1983). Are we correcting for guessing in the wrong direction? In D. J. Weiss (Ed.), *New horizons in testing: Latent trait test theory and computerized adaptive testing* (pp. 63–80). Hillsdale, NJ: Erlbaum.

Wainer, H., Bradlow, E. T., & Du, Z. (2000). Testlet response theory: An analog for the 3PL model useful in testlet-based adaptive testing. In W. J. van der Linden & C. A. W. Glas (Eds.), *Computerized adaptive testing: Theory and practice* (pp. 245–269). Dordrecht, The Netherlands: Kluwer Academic Publishers.

Wainer, H., Bradlow, E. T., & Wang, X. (2007). *Testlet response theory.* New York: Cambridge University Press.

Wainer, H., Dorans, N. J., Eignor, D., Flaugher, R., Green, B. F., Mislevy, R. J., et al. (2000). *Computerized adaptive testing: A primer.* Hillsdale, NJ: Erlbaum.

Wainer, H., & Kiely, G. L. (1987). Item clusters and computerized adaptive testing. *Journal of Educational Measurement, 27,* 1–14.

Wainer, H., & Lewis, C. (1990). Toward a psychometrics for testlets. *Journal of Educational Measurement, 24,* 185–201.

Wainer, H., & Wright, B. D. (1980). Robust estimation of ability in the Rasch model. *Psychometrika, 45,* 373–391.

Walker, D. A. (1931). Answer pattern and score scatter in tests and examinations. *British Journal of Psychology, 22,* 73–86.

Walker-Barnick, L. A. (1990). *An investigation of factors affecting invariance of item parameter estimates in the partial credit model.* Unpublished doctoral dissertation, University of Maryland, College Park.

Wang, M. D. (1986, April). *Fitting a unidimensional model to multidimensional item response data.* Paper presented at the ONR Contractors Conference, Gatlinburg, TN.

Wang, M. D. (1987, April). *Estimation of ability parameters from response data to items that are precalibrated with a unidimensional model.* Paper presented at the annual meeting of the American Educational Research Association, Washington, DC.

Wang, W.-C., & Wilson, M. (2005). The Rasch testlet model. *Applied Psychological Measurement, 29,* 126–149.

Wang, X. B., Wainer, H., & Thissen, D. J. (1995). On the viability of some untestable assumptions in equating exams that allow examinee choice. *Applied Measurement in Education, 8,* 211–225.

Warm, T. A. (1989). Weighted likelihood estimation of ability in item response theory. *Psychometrika, 54,* 427–450.

Way, W. D. (1998). Protecting the integrity of computerized adaptive testing item pools. *Educational Measurement: Issues and Practice, 17*(4), 17–27.

Way, W. D., Ansley, T. N., & Forsyth, R. A. (1988). The comparative effects of compensatory and noncompensatory two-dimensional data on unidimensional IRT estimates. *Applied Psychological Measurement, 12,* 239–252.

Weiss, D. J. (1973). *The stratified adaptive computerized ability test* (Research Report 73-3). Minneapolis: University of Minnesota, Department of Psychology, Psychometric Methods Program. (NTIS No. AD 768376).

Weiss, D. J. (1982). Improving measurement quality and efficiency with adaptive testing. *Applied Psychological Measurement, 6,* 473–492.

Weiss, D. J. (1983). Introduction. In D. J. Weiss (Ed.), *New horizons in testing: Latent trait test theory and computerized adaptive testing* (pp. 1–8). New York: Academic Press.

Whitely (Embretson), S. E. (1977). Models, meanings and misunderstandings: Some issues in applying Rasch's theory. *Journal of Educational Measurement, 14,* 227–235.

Whitely (Embretson), S. E. (1980). Multicomponent latent trait models for ability tests. *Psychometrika*, 45, 479–494.

Wilson, M. (2005). *Constructing measures: An item response modeling approach*. Mahwah, NJ: Erlbaum.

Wilson, M., & Adams, R. J. (1993). Marginal maximum likelihood estimation for the partial ordered model. *Journal of Educational Statistics*, 18, 69–90.

Wilson, M., & Masters, G. N. (1993). The partial credit model and null categories. *Psychometrika*, 58, 87–99.

Wingersky, M. S., Barton, M. A., & Lord, F. M. (1982). *LOGIST user's guide* [Computer program]. Princeton, NJ: Educational Testing Service.

Wood, R., Wilson, D., Gibbons, R., Schilling, S., Muraki, E., & Bock, R. D. (2003). *TESTFACT* (Version 4.0) [Computer program]. Mooresville, IN: Scientific Software.

Wood, R. L. (1973). Response-contingent testing. *Review of Educational Research*, 43, 529–544.

Wright, B. D. (1968). Sample-free test calibration and person measurement. In *Proceedings of the 1967 Invitational Conference on Testing Problems*. Princeton, NJ: Educational Testing Service.

Wright, B. D. (1977a). Misunderstanding the Rasch model. *Journal of Educational Measurement*, 14, 219–226.

Wright, B. D. (1977b). Solving measurement problems with the Rasch model. *Journal of Educational Measurement*, 14, 97–116.

Wright, B. D. (1984). Despair and hope for educational measurement. *Contemporary Education Review*, 3, 281–288.

Wright, B. D., Congdon, R., & Shultz, M. (1988). *MSTEPS partial credit analysis* [Computer program]. Chicago: University of Chicago, MESA Psychometric Laboratory.

Wright, B. D., & Douglas, D. A. (1977). Best procedures for sample-free item analysis. *Applied Psychological Measurement*, 1, 281–295.

Wright, B. D., & Masters, G. N. (1982). *Rating scale analysis*. Chicago: MESA Press.

Wright, B. D., & Stone, M. H. (1979). *Best test design*. Chicago: MESA Press.

Wu, M. L., Adams, R. J., & Wilson, M. R. (1997). *ConQuest: Multi-aspect test software* [Computer program]. Camberwell: Australian Council for Educational Research.

Yamamoto, K. (1989). A HYBRID model of IRT and latent class models (RR-89-41). Princeton, NJ: Educational Testing Service.

Yao, L., & Schwarz, R. D. (2006). A multidimensional partial credit model with associated item and test statistics: An application to mixed-format tests. *Applied Psychological Measurement*, 30, 469–492.

Yen, W. M. (1981). Using simulation results to choose a latent trait model. *Applied Psychological Measurement*, 5, 245–262.

Yen, W. M. (1984). Effects of local item dependence on the fit and equating performance of the three-parameter logistic model. *Applied Psychological Measurement*, 8, 125–145.

Yen, W. M. (1985). Increasing item complexity: A possible cause of scale shrinkage for unidimensional item response theory. *Psychometrika*, 50, 399–410.

Yen, W. M. (1986). The choice of scale for educational measurement: An IRT perspective. *Journal of Educational Measurement*, 23, 299–326.

Yen, W. M. (1987). A comparison of the efficiency and accuracy of BILOG and LOGIST. *Psychometrika*, 52, 275–291.

Yen, W. M. (1993). Scaling performance assessments: Strategies for managing local item dependence. *Journal of Educational Measurement*, 30, 187–213.

Yen, W. M., Burket, G. R., & Sykes, R. C. (1991). Nonunique solutions to the likelihood equation for the three-parameter logistic model. *Psychometrika*, 56, 39–54.

Zeng, L., Kolen, M. J., Hanson, B. A., Cui, Z., & Chien, Y. (2004). *RAGE -RGEQUATE* [Computer program]. Iowa City: University of Iowa. Program available at *www.education.uiowa.edu/casma/EquatingLinkingPrograms.htm*.

Zieky, M. (1993). Practical questions in the use of DIF statistics in test development. In P. W. Holland & H. Wainer (Eds.), *Differential item functioning* (pp. 337–347). Hillsdale, NJ: Erlbaum.

Zimowski, M., Muraki, E., Mislevy, R. J., & Bock, R. D. (2003). *BILOG-MG* (Version 3.0) [Computer program]. Mooresville, IN: Scientific Software.

Zumbo, B. D. (1999). *A handbook on the theory and methods of differential item functioning (DIF): Logistic regression modeling as a unitary framework for binary and Likert-type (ordinal) item scores.* Ottawa, ON: Directorate of Human Resources Research and Evaluation, Department of National Defense.

Zumbo, B. D. (2007). Three generations of DIF analyses: Considering where it has been, where it is now, and where it is going. *Language Assessment Quarterly, 4*, 223–233.

Zwinderman, A. H., & van der Wollenberg, A. L. (1990). Robustness of marginal maximum likelihood estimation in the Rasch model. *Applied Psychological Measurement, 14*, 73–81.

Author Index

Subject Index

About the Author

R. J. de Ayala, PhD, is Professor of Educational Psychology at the University of Nebraska–Lincoln. His research interests include psychometrics, item response theory, computerized adaptive testing, applied statistics, and multilevel models. His work has appeared in *Applied Psychological Measurement*, *Applied Measurement in Education*, the *British Journal of Mathematical and Statistical Psychology*, *Educational and Psychological Measurement*, the *Journal of Applied Measurement*, and the *Journal of Educational Measurement*. He is a Fellow of the American Psychological Association's Division 5: Evaluation, Measurement, and Statistics, as well as of the American Educational Research Association.